Cistula Entomologica

CISTULA

ENTOMOLOGICA.

VOL. II.

WITH ELEVEN PLATES.

LONDON:

E. W. JANSON, 35, LITTLE RUSSELL STREET, W.C.

1875—1882.

FRED. T. ANDREW,

PRINTER,

ALBION PLACE, LONDON WALL, E.C.

CONTENTS.

———

A Reply to Criticisms on the "Trichopterygia Illustrata," by the Rev. A. MATTHEWS, M.A

Since the publication of the "Trichopterygia Illustrata" various criticisms on that work have appeared in the periodicals devoted to Natural History; these I have hitherto refrained from noticing, in order to make my reply more comprehensive than it could have been at any earlier period. Many of the remarks contained in these critical notices have been very complimentary, and it is gratifying to find that the faults pointed out apply entirely to errors in the letter-press, pseudo-latinisms, objections to the style of the figures, or differences of opinion as to the comparative merits of certain authors whose works I have reviewed; while the scientific and only important portions of my work have been unassailed, and by letters which I have received from many of the most distinguished Entomologists of the present time, as well as by the published remarks of others, appear to have met with universal approval.

With regard to the first of those faults which I have named, viz, errors in the letter-press, which I regret to say are far too numerous, I feel that I must take the whole blame upon myself. I foolishly consented to revise the sheets as they were struck off, a task which their author should never undertake, since his perfect knowledge of the idea intended to be expressed and his capability of repeating almost every line by heart engender a carelessness, however unintentional, to which a stranger would not be liable, and of which I now suffer the evil consequences

As to what have been termed my "pseudo-latinisms," these were in many instances perfectly intentional, and seem to me perfectly justifiable, e.g., "in Insula Hyeres," or "ad ripas fluvii Seine" must be more intelligible to most readers than resuscitating such names as "Stoechades," "Sequana," and such like,

CISTULA ENTOMOLOGICA
October 1st, 1875

B

terms for many centuries out of use, for the purpose, as it would certainly appear, of exhibiting one's superior knowledge of ancient geography.

With respect to the plates no fault has been found with those which exhibit the genera, but a little more care on the part of the engraver would have greatly improved both the appearance and utility of those devoted to the species. This may very easily be proved by comparing Plates Nos. 29 and 30 with any of those which preceed them, in many of which the superficial sculpture has been very inadequately expressed, and requires a careful comparison with the description of the species

But it is to the class of criticisms which assail my observations upon previous authors that I wish to direct attention. None of my remarks were made without careful consideration, and as they are supported by clear and obvious proofs, I trust to be able to establish the truth of all that I have written. Of criticisms of this class that published in the " Stettin Ent. Zeitung, XXXIV, p 398, from the pen of Dr Dohrn, is the most important and the most detailed. I will therefore examine his remarks seriatim. Referring to my review of Gillmeister's " Trichopterygia," Dr. Dohrn first of all quotes a notice of that same work published in the " Stettin Ent. Zeitung, T. VII, p. 59, (1846), in which Dr. Schaum says " the descriptions are splendid, short and to the point, they every where put proper stress upon the specific differences   But the most perfect in this classical work are the Plates, drawn by the author and engraved by Sturm ; the most perfect specimens which the Entomological Icononographie has to show." Dr Dohrn then quotes my own observations on Gillmeister (vid. Trichopterygia Illustrata, Introduction p. xii), and subsequently remarks " that it is more than curious that Schaum should call a work " splendid, per-fect, and classical," of which Matthews' says that he only made the confusion worse confounded, added nothing but what was known, ignored the work of other Entomologists and misused their liberality." But to say that Dr. Schaum designated Gill-meister's work as " splendid, perfect, and classical," is to affix a meaning to the learned Doctor's words which they clearly do not possess ; the terms splendid and perfect express merely Dr. Schaum's opinion of the descriptions and plates. Whether Dr.

Schaum was qualified to judge of the descriptions or diagnostic characters of a Trichopteryx may be gathered from his own words, words spoken at the time when he presented to me the collection of his American Trichopterygia. I had asked his assistance in determining their species, and in reply he said *"* I must leave them entirely to you, *for I know nothing whatever of that class."* These were the very words of my esteemed friend, and uttered on such an occasion were indelibly fixed on my mind.

But I have never found fault with Gillmeister's specific descriptions, as far as they go they are correct and good ; no amount of excellence in specific descriptions can however in any way atone for a reckless disregard of the commonest rules of nomenclature. Dr. Gillmeister was well aware that M. Allibert had already published descriptions of a great majority of the very species on which he was himself engaged, and he must also have known that M. Allibert's names had been accepted by the Entomologists of France, at all times an important part of the scientific world , if he considered M. Allibert's descriptions insufficient, he might, as I did, without difficulty have obtained an examination of the type specimens, but he adopted the readiest method of avoiding trouble, ignored the work of M. Allibert, and either substituted fresh names for his species, or quoted their names as synonyms of species to which they did not refer.

The manner in which he treated Dr Aubé was equally inexcusable. Dr Aubé with his usual kindness had forwarded type-specimens of all the species contained in his fine collection to assist Dr. Gillmeister in his work , they were subsequently returned to Dr. Aubé in a very unsatisfactory condition ; to such species as Dr. Gillmeister had recognized he had attached labels, those which he did not know he had left unnoticed It may be thought that I am making a bold assertion, but if the collection of Dr Aubé still exists, anyone who will examine it may convince himself of the fact. For in that collection he will find two examples of one of the most distinct and most striking species of the whole family, viz, *Smicrus filicornis*, labelled as having been sent to Dr. Gillmeister, and returned without remark. There may be others found in a similar condition, though, as it is a long time since I have seen the collection, I

cannot now remember their names ; but one such fact is of itself
sufficient to prove an amount of carelessness perhaps without
parallel, certainly without excuse.

But, bad as this was, his treatment of· Col. Motschulsky was
far worse In a paper published in the Bull. Mosc., 1845, V.
II., p. 504, entitled "Ueber die Ptiliens Russland," Col. Motschulsky makes the following remark, "I said in the Stettin
Zeitung that I had 33 species of Ptilium, Gillmeister wrote for
them, received them, and' returned them saying 'none new'"
By the above date it is clear that the transaction alluded to
must have taken place previously to the publication· of Dr.
Gillmeister's Monograph, it therefore both justifies my assertion
that Dr. Gillmeister had seen Col. Motschulsky's types, and
renders the publication of synonymy such as that given under
the head of " *T. depressa*," (quoted by me at length in p xii of
the Introduction to the Trichopterygia Illustrata), utterly con-
fusing and utterly inexcusable.   But that example of synonymy
is only one of many of a similar character, by means of which
the confusion becomes disseminated throughout the work.

If Dr. Gillmeister had not seen Col. Motschulsky's types and
could not comprehend his descriptions, which it is often scarcely
possible to do, he should have omitted their names altogether
from the list, or have classed them separately as " *Species
incertæ*," rather than have assigned them ad libitum to species
with which they have no connection.

In addition to all these instances of nomenclature wilfully
confused, I might reasonably have asked on what grounds did
Dr. Gillmeister ignore the *Derm. pilosellus, brunneus,* and *nitidulus* of Marsham, or the *Scaphidium punctatum* of Gyllenhal,
a name which had even then been recognized for about 40 years,
and in the place of this last substitute the far less expressive
term of *Trich. alutacea* ? But I thought that my case had been
sufficiently proved.

Dr Dohrn also complains that I assert that Dr. Gillmeister
in his Monograph did not bring forward a single fact which was
not previously known, except his observations on the Metamor-
phosis ; and to controvert my assertion cites my having adopted
four new species retaining the names which he had given them,

These Dr. Dohrn terms four new facts, he does not observe that my assertion referred to life-history and anatomy, and appears also to forget that two of these four species had been previously described by Dr. Erichson, to whom according to the strict law of priority I might therefore have assigned them. But knowing the unhandsome manner in which Dr. Erichson had abused the confidence of Gillmeister and had unkindly anticipated his work, I preferred to attach the name of *" Gill-meister"* to the species in question If I committed a fault, it arose from my desire to do justice to Gillmeister.

When to the confusion of nomenclature pervading the whole Monograph is added the great amount of erroneous anatomy, the conspicuous Labial Palpi utterly ignored, a mutilated portion of the Stipes figured as the true Mandible, and false delineations given of the Mentum and adjacent organs of the lower part of the mouth, and forms so totally diverse as the species of *Ptinella* and *Ptenidium* comprehended under one and the same generic appellation; I think that I was fully justified in saying that such work left the Trichopterygia in a state of confusion far worse than that in which it found them

In the case of Col. Motschulsky, my first impressions experienced a total revulsion. I commenced work a disciple of the common belief in his universal inaccuracy, I had imbibed the idea that his species were mere varieties, separated on untenable characters. Gradually step by step as my own knowledge of these insects increased, so pari passu did my conviction that Col Motschulsky was right in his views To assist in arriving at the truth, I determined to communicate at once with him and obtain authentic types of his species These in large numbers he immediately forwarded to me with the same ready kindness as he had formerly shown to Gillmeister, but with a very different result I found that though his descriptions were very obscure, his types were in most cases sufficient to convince any one of their specific value Indeed if an experienced Entomologist has for many years turned his attention to the study of any special class of insects, he may reasonably be supposed to know more of that class than others who have comparatively neglected them. I soon found this to be true of Col. Motschulsky, and have many times been compelled to accept his species in contradiction to my preconceived opinion

Dr. Dohrn asks whether I expect him to accept Motschulsky's " 99 *species*" on my authority? If he will refer to my work he will find that I expect nothing of the sort, I do expect that those species which I have verified by the careful examination of types will be accepted, and am fully prepared to support my position, and Dr. Dohrn must remember that their acceptation will not wholly depend upon his opinion.

But let us examine this matter more closely. The actual number of Motschulsky's *newly-named* species amounts to 85, and of these only 25 appear in my list of recognized species. Of the 43 supposed new species which I have verified by actual examination, 2 only appeared to be varieties, while 41 were good and distinct species; of these last, 16 had been previously described by other authors, and 25 were wholly new to science. Upon such facts it is only fair to conclude that a large majority of the other 42 which he has described would probably be true species The rest of his names are merely manuscript without definition.

In the year 1845 the combined efforts of all other Entomologists had resulted in the discovery of 37 species of *Trichopterygia*, while at that same period Col Motschulsky was acquainted with more than twice that number, of which above one-half were the fruits of his own persevering exertions in their pursuit and superior knowledge of their habits Well and truly then might I say that "his knowledge of the Trichopterygia exceeded that of any other Entomologist."

To contradict this assertion Dr. Dohrn brings forward the fact that Motschulsky had at one time considered the Trichopterygia to possess pentamerous tarsi. I need not again recount mistakes of a character quite as important made by professed anatomists to prove that the wisest among men are liable to error, others have committed the very same mistake, and such indeed was at one time my own impression The tarsi of a Trichopteryx are surrounded by very long diaphanous setæ, which in mounted specimens will occasionally cross the long · terminal joint of the tarsus in an oblique and so perfectly natural direction, that any one might suppose the terminal portion to be an amalgamation of three parts, nor would be convinced of the illusion without a careful examination of tarsi obtained from other specimens But be this as it may, it cannot materially affect my expressed opinion of Col. Motschulsky I never said that he was an expert anatomist, though I might have thought that his knowledge of the subject was quite equal to that of his contemporaries. I have said before that I am not qualified to express an opinion of Col. Motschulsky's proficiency in other sections of Coleoptera I have said before, and I say it again, that his knowledge of the *Trichopterygia* exceeded that of all other Entomologists

A little farther on in his Review, Dr Dohrn remarks that the name *" Dohrnii,"* given by me to the *Trich. fuscipennis* of Haldeman, cannot stand, because "by the author's own opinion *Trich. fuscipennis* is a synonym, and as there is no like-named species except the *Ptilium fuscipenne,* which dates from 1849, and is thought by the author synonymic with *Pt. Spencii.* Also Motschulsky's species *Acratrichis brunnipennis,* (Amer), Matthews remarks "An T. Dohrnii par." The facts which Dr. Dohrn has thus cited appear to me in themselves sufficient to quash the name *"fuscipennis"* altogether. It is evident that Professor Forster's *Ptilium fuscipenne* was anterior in date to *T. fuscipennis* of Haldeman, it is also certain that the same name had been applied to another species by Gillmeister, and recorded in p. 48 of his "Trichopterygia." If I had been able to recognize that species I must of course have retained its name. But though I failed, some other author may succeed in doing so, and its name may now be restored to the list without creating confusion

It appears to me that the only safe basis of nomenclature is to adhere closely to this rule, *i.e.,* that when once a name has been used to designate a certain insect, the same name cannot subsequently be applied to any other species of the same section. I say section because genera are in their very essence changeable terms, wholly subject to the will of each separate author. If therefore a specific name should merely be restricted to a genus and might again be repeated in the genus next in succession, endless changes of nomenclature would ensue, especially in a section like this, of which the whole species have already been comprised by more than one author under the name of " *Trichopteryx*," and by others under the name of " *Ptilium.*"

Taking the case before us as an example, let us suppose that the name *T. fuscipennis* is restored either to Gillmeister's or to Haldeman's species, and also that the *Ptilium fuscipenne* of Forster, and the *Ptenidium fuscipenne* of Motschulsky are both eventually discovered to be true species, the name, if not restricted to a single genus, must be repeated in all the three. Subsequently some author averse to sub-divisions re-unites the whole section under one generic term, two recognized names must then be changed for fresh appellations, but as soon as these new names had been accepted, another author arises, who determines to divide the section into various genera once more, and in consequence must again alter the names last given; and so on ad infinitum till at length the term " *fuscipennis*" would convey no possible idea either of form or species. By adhering to the rule I have mentioned, and on which I have acted, all such confusion will be avoided, while by pursuing the contrary plan endless and most harassing complications might be caused.

In the next place Dr. Dohrn mentions errors which he has observed in my account of the capture of certain species, errors so utterly frivolous that the very notice of them serves to show the difficulty of finding faults. He says "that Dr. Schaum never was in Brazil, therefore the notes on *Trich Wenkeri* and *discolor* are incorrect is certain The like is the case with the Californian *Pt. pullum*, which Dr Maklin has certainly not caught in loco " At the interview between Dr. Schaum and myself previously alluded to, he pointed out a certain group of specimens, all ticketed with his accustomed care, and said, " you must remember that this lot were taken in Brazil, all the rest were found in the United States," and, as he said nothing to the contrary, I supposed that he meant they had been taken by himself. At any rate, if *T Wenkeri* and *discolor* were actually taken in Brazil, the name of their captor must be of secondary importance in geographical relations Whether Col. Motschulsky was ever in Ceylon, or Dr. Maklin in California, must be equally unimportant I can only refer the reader to my extracts from previous authors, and add that my type of *Pten pullum* was received from M. le Comte de Mniszech, ticketed thus, " *California Maklin.*"

In the last part of his Review, Dr. Dohrn would seem to imply that I made use of Latin in order to exhibit· my superior education; the truth is that I made use of Latin, especially in the original descriptions transcribed from other authors, in order to assist persons *as ignorant as myself*, those who cannot read the languages of Germany, Sweden, or Russia. Had I used entirely my native tongue the difficulty would have been increased, as still fewer could have read English. By making use of a medium of communication universally recognized, I hoped to render my meaning intelligible to all In reference to the mistakes which I have made, I can only hope that anyone who has read the Latin in the pages devoted to the anatomy of the *Trichopterygia,* would hardly suppose that such an outrageous blunder as " in paludibus Comtis Cantabridgiensibus," (triumphantly paraded by Dr. Dohrn), could have proceeded from ignorance of the language Its true history is this, I had originally written " in paludibus Comtis Cantabridgiensis," and subsequently altered it thus, " in paludibus Cantabridgiensibus," the obliteration was overlooked by the printer, and *although corrected a second time* in the proof-sheet, the error was again with extreme carelessness reproduced in the final impression in all its deformity, a fact unnoticed by me until too late to rectify the mistake. "Tauria" is quoted from Motschulsky, and left unaltered because I did not know for certain whether he intended it for the Crimea. The transposition of the vowels in " Madiera" arose from my own carelessness in writing the word originally, and in overlooking the error in the proof. This name is spelled correctly in my extracts from Mr. Wollaston.

I think that I have now noticed all the criticisms of Dr. Dohrn. The last few lines of his Review express, I would fáin believe, the real feelings of their writer more truly than his previous remarks. I am not surprised that Dr Dohrn should have taken up arms in defence of his countryman, I respect and honour his spirit, though I doubt the expediency of eliciting more positive proofs of his friend's misdoings I have endeavoured on my own behalf to support my position, and if in so doing I have anywhere exhibited unnecessary asperity, I fear the pages of the Review must have conveyed the infection. I can never forget the kind manner in which Dr. Dohrn assisted me in my work, and however we may differ in our opinion of other men, I trust our regard for each other may remain unchanged

To Reviewers, who in a work which has carried the oral anatomy of Coleoptera to heights never before attained, and has revealed functions of certain organs previously unthought of, can find nothing more worthy of notice than errors in the letter-press and supposed defects in the plates, I need not reply, their own remarks prove the spirit by which they were inspired, and supply an answer to themselves.

As I do not intend again to revert to this subject, I will add a few words on the anatomy exhibited in the pages and plates of the "*Trichopterygia Illustrata.*" In the Appendix I have given a detailed list of the vast number of preparations which I made, in order that by comparing them with each other I might obtain a correct idea of the true outline of each separate organ. These preparations have been minutely examined and compared with my figures by Drs. Le Conte, Horn, and Sharp, and by Messrs. Crotch, Wollaston, and Janson, who all concurred in affirming the accuracy of my delineations If anyone should still feel sceptical on that point, my preparations are open to his inspection, and can be selected by the numbers affixed to them in the list. They are preserved in Canada Balsam, which up to the present moment has retained its pristine transparency.

Remarks on the synonymy of the Atlas of the Heterocera Sphingida and Noctuida, published as a portion of the results of the voyage of the "Frigate Novara," November, 1874; by R. H. STRETCH, *of San Fancisco, California*

The present paper is intended to give the result of the comparison of Plates 79 to 107 inclusive, (except figures 1–6 on Plate 82), with the collection of the British Museum, and the catalogues of the same published from 185–41866 These plates contain the groups usually classed by Entomologists between Sphinx and Noctua, and are contained in parts 1–7, 31, 32. and 35, of the Museum catalogues   The plates according to the footnotes were edited between the years 1868–1873, while the cover to the Atlas sets forth that they were published collectively in November, 1874.   It is not intended to follow the synonymy further than to indicate the identity of the species figured with the specimens existing in the British Museum, leaving for a future catalogue of these families, which I have in preparation, the question whether Mr. Walker's determinations have in all places been correct ; as well as the question of generic distribution in which the Museum catalogue is notoriously defective.

Where there can be no doubt of the priority of names, that which should have precedence is indicated in more prominent type than the synonym.

A prompt notice of this publication becomes necessary from the fact that a not inconsiderable number of species have been previously described by the late F. Walker, Esq., from types in the British Museum cabinets.   As these were all published before 1866, their names must stand except in cases of erroneous determination.   It is greatly to be regretted that there is no letter-press accompanying the Atlas   Indeed, so far as the plates alluded to are concerned, there are not even localities attached to the species figured, or any mention of the place of deposit of the types.   The latter is an important omission when we remember

that quite a large number of the species figured, were in all
probability, not collected on the Novara voyage at all! The
absolute comparison of some few species cannot be made for
want of figures of the underside, and a certain amount of uncer-
tainty sometimes arises from a knowledge of the fact that the
coloring is defective in some cases, where the peculiarity of the
markings, points out unmistakably the insect intended, as in
the case of *Holocera Smilax.*

Upwards of fifty species are enumerated which exist in the
British Museum cabinets, and were described in the catalogues
of the Museum prior to 1867, but it is not strange that some of
these should have been overlooked, from the fact of their erroneous location both in the collection and catalogue. The failure
to recognize others such as *Eterusia transversa,* Walker and
Scaptesyle bicolor, Walker is strange, for in spite of all that has
been said about the defects of Mr. Walker's descriptions, I have
been able to determine from the catalogue, a very large proportion
of the species included therein.

In the case of some few species described by Mr. Butler sub-
sequent to 1870, there may be a difference of opinion as to the
priority of names. It has been argued that because these plates
could be purchased in their uncolored condition, that their nomenclature should date from the year appended to the foot of each.
To admit this would be to introduce a troublesome element into
a nomenclature already sufficiently intricate. Whatever might
be said in favor of admitting such a claim for plates never
intended to be colored, and in which the details are consequently
carefully worked out, it cannot for a moment be admitted for
copper-plates intended to be colored, in which it is notorious
that many of the details are left to the colorist. Such plates
may be colored to represent several species, and in the absence of
letter-press who is to tell whether a certain *Lithosia* for instance
is to be white or drab, or a *Limacodes* green or brown? For
such reasons as these I should give priority to Mr. Butler's
names. In doing so I do not however ignore the right which
every Entomologist has to the adoption of his manuscript names,
where such may be known to the publisher of the species, nor
would I for a moment be understood to underrate the value of

this most important contribution to Entomological knowledge, for this is beyond question.

Among the *Noctuæ* I recognize several species described by Augustus Grote, Esq., as well as by Mr. Walker, but I leave this section to those who possess a more intimate knowledge of the group than I can pretend to.

PLATE 79.

Fig 1.   CASTNIA RUTILA, Felder, belongs to the group of which C. FONSCOLOMBEI may be considered the type, and is closely allied to that species.

Fig. 3.   *Castnia tricolor,* Felder, = CASTNIA DIVA, Butler, Lep. Exot., Pl. 17, fig. 1, (1870).

Fig. 6   SYNEMON ICARIA, Felder, = var. ? SYNEMON LÆTA, Walker. Differs as near as can be judged from the figure, only in having the black bands of the secondaries broken up into spots In the absence of letter-press it is impossible to tell whether this is a permanent form or only an accidental variation.

Fig. 7, 8.   SYNEMON PARTHENOIDES, Felder, is very near SYNEMON SOPHIA, White, sp., the maculations of the secondaries being similar, but the primaries longer, and their whitish markings more distinct. Bears about the same relation to SOPHIA that ICARIA does to LÆTA.

PLATE 80.

Fig. 1.   CHARAGIA FISCHERI, Felder, is very near C. RUBROVIRI-DANS, Walker, but the specimens in the British Museum of the latter species, are too worn to make the comparison absolute

Fig. 3.   *Pielus hydrographus,* Felder, = PIELUS LABYRINTHICUS, Cat. Lep Het. B. Mus., 1578, (1856)

PLATE 82.

Fig. 15.   *Letois similis,* Felder, = NEÆRA LATISTRIGA, Cat. Lep. Het. B. Mus., 1141, (1855).

Fig. 18.   *Zygæna subdiaphana*, Felder, is not unlikely to prove identical with Z. CONTRARIA, Walker, which has the secondaries very pale reddish.   At best it can only take rank as a variety of that species.

Fig. 19.   ZYGÆNA OCELLARIS, Felder   The specimen in the British Museum has the ground color of the ocelli white.

Fig. 21   EUCTENIA ZYGÆNYIDES, Felder, is very near to, if not identical with PROCRIS CONTRARIA, Walker, which differs in having the abdomen luteous

PLATE 83.

Fig. 7.   *Heterusia microcephala*, Felder, = ETERUSIA DIRUPTA, Cat. Lep Het B. Mus., supp., 199, (1864).

Fig 8   *Heterusia cicada*, Felder, = ETERUSIA PULCHELLA, var. ? Cat. Lep. Het. B Mus., 430, (1854)   Walker supposed his insect to be a variety of the CHALCOSIA PULCHELLA, of Kollar, but as this latter insect proves to be CHALCOSIA PHALÆNARIA, Kollar's name must sink, and Walker's be retained for this insect.

Fig. 18, 19.   *Isochroma fallax*, Felder, = SCIATHOS PUNCTIGERA, Cat. Lep. Het. B. Mus., 752, (1855).

PLATE 84.

Fig. 2.   GONOMETA POSTICA ♀, Felder, = *Pachypasa effusa*, Walker, Cat. Lep Het. B. Mus   Walker described the ♂ under the name adopted by Felder.

Fig 5.   OPSIRHINA FLEXICOSTA ♀, Felder, = O. DECORATA, ? Walker.   There is but little [if any difference between these species except that the color of the latter is reddish instead of yellowish.

Fig 9.   *Rhinogyne calligama* ♂, Felder, = *Entometa obliqua*, Cat. Lep. Het. B. Mus, 973, (1855).

Fig. 10   *Rhinogyne calligama* ♀, Felder, = PINARA CANA, Cat. Lep. Het B Mus., 761, (1855)   This latter insect is very closely allied to the *Opsirhina metaphæa* ♀, Walker, which differs in color, only in having the base of the secondaries dusky.

PLATE 88

Fig. 4, 5. HOLOCERA SMILAX, Westwood, = HENUCHA SMILAX, B. Mus cabinet.

PLATE 89.

Fig. 7. *Hyperchiria anableps*, Felder, = HYPERCHIRIA ABAS, Cat. Lep Het. B. Mus., p. 1305, (1855).   Reference being made to Cramer, Pap Exot., 1, 121, pl 77, fig A B.

PLATE 90.

Fig. 3. ORMISCODES FUMOSA, Felder, is very nearly allied to and congeneric with *Dirphia semirosea*, Walker, from Mexico.

PLATE 93.

Fig 2. *Ormiscodes trisignata*, Felder, = DIRPHIA MULTICOLOR, Cat Lep. Het., B. Mus., p. 1364, (1855).

PLATE 94.

Fig. 3 HOMOCHROA ORNATA, Felder, is very near to, if not identical with *Tagira antheræata*, B Mus cabinet

Fig 10. *Oligoclona chordigera*, Felder, = DASYCHIRA ANTICA, Cat. Lep. Het. B. Mus., p. 867, (1855)

PLATE 95.

Fig 8. OLIGOCLONA NERVOSA, Felder, = ? GAZULINA VENOSATA, Walker.

Fig. 9. *Ochrogaster ruptimacula*, Felder, = TEARA INTERRUPTA, Cat Lep Het. B Mus, p 850, (1855).

PLATE 96.

Fig 4 *Hyelora sphinx*, Felder, = HYELORA EUCALYPTUS, B Mus cab in part   Under the latter name, there are two species confounded in the B Mus. collection, but the specimens corresponding with *H sphinx*, Felder, appear to be Doubleday's' types   (see H. EUCALYPTUS, Doubleday, Proc Zool Soc., 1848)

Fig. 6. *Dicranura argentea*, Felder, = CERURA LITURATA, Cat. Lep Het. B. Mus, 988, (1855).

PLATE 98.

Fig. 17   *Chœrotricha nobilis,* Felder, = ORGYIA JOSIATA, Cat. Lep Het B Mus., 326, (1865)   Felder's genus, = GOGANA, Walker, of which the type is ATROSQUAMA, Walker.

PLATE 99.

Fig 1.   DARALA ZONATA, Felder, is very near D. FERVENS, Walker.

Fig 9.   *Xenosoma nigricosta,* Felder, = ELORIA FLAVICEPS, Cat. Lep Het B Mus, supp, 339, (1865)

Fig. 10.   *Xenosoma Erycinoides,* Felder, = ELORIA DISCALIS, Cat. Lep. Het. B Mus, p. 1726, (1856).

PLATE 100

Fig 19   ZERENOPSIS LEOPARDINA, Felder, is very nearly allied to and congeneric with DEIOPEIA LEPIDA, Walker.

Fig 26   *Isochrya eburneigutta,* Felder, = ENDYRA PHEDONIA, Cat Lep Het B Mus., p. 1685, (1856).

PLATE 101

Fig. 1.   *Panthea Chavannesi,* Felder, = BATHYRA SAGATA, Cat. Lep Het. B Mus, supp., 403, (1865).

PLATE 102.

Fig 3   *Eucyrta subulifera,* Felder, = RHIPHA STRIGOSA, Cat. Lep. Het B Mus., p 273, (1854).

Fig 9   *Euplesia vittigera,* Felder, = AUTOMOLIS SPHINGIDEA, Perty. sp   The specimen of *E. vittigera,* Felder, in the Museum cabinet, does not differ appreciably from those labelled A. SPHINGIDEA, Perty.

Fig 10   *Euplesia ochrophila,* Felder, = APICONOMA OPPOSITA, Cat. Lep. Het B Mus, p. 260, (1854).

Fig. 18   *Eurerea thalassica,* Felder, = ACRIDOPSIS MARICA, Cat. Lep. Het. B Mus., p. 269, variety of same.

PLATE 103.

Fig. 2. *Leptosoma maculosum*, Felder, = Nyctemera bijunc-
tella, Walker, Cat Lep. Het B Mus., supp., p. 1880,
(1866)

Fig. 3. *Leptosoma tricolor*, Felder, = Nyctemera apicalis, var.,
Cat Lep. Het B Mus., p. 395, (1854). The band on
the primaries of this species not unfrequently assumes a
tendency to yellow.

Fig. 9. *Esthema confluens*, Felder, = Esthema confluens,
Butler, Trans. Ent. Soc, pt 1, (April, 1872).

Fig. 10 *Esthema venosa*, Felder, = Esthema speciosa, Cat
Lep Het. B. Mus., supp., p 1873, (1866).

Fig 11. *Esthema calida*, Felder, = Eucyane Hytaspes, Butler,
P Z S, p 82, (January, 1871), Lep. Exot., pl. 61, fig.
6, (April, 1874).

Fig 12 *Esthema jucunda*, Felder, = Eucyane temperata, Cat.
Lep Het. B Mus, pt. 7, p 1656, (1856)

Fig. 16. *Hyalurga irregularis*, Felder, = Hyalurga albovitrea,
Cat Lep Het B Mus., supp, p 159, (1864).

PLATE 104.

Fig. 4. *Stenele Aletis*, Felder, = Chrysauge repanda, Cat. Lep
Het B Mus, p 375, (1854)

Fig. 7 Polyptychia fasciculosa, Felder, = ? Josia Erynnis,
Cat Lep. Het B Mus, p 315.

Fig. 12 *Josiomorpha longivitta*, Felder, = Josia penetrata,
Coll B. Mus, being but a large form of that insect

PLATE 105.

Fig. 2. *Terna major*, Felder, = Phæochlæna brevilinea, Cat.
Lep Het B Mus, p 469, (1854).

Fig. 3. *Terna minuta*, Felder, = Virbia mentiens, Cat. Lep
Het. B. Mus., p. 471, (1854).

Fig. 4. *Dioptis Erycinoides*, Felder, = Dioptis ithomeina,
Butler, Cist Ent., iv, p. 87, (January, 1872). Lep Exot,
pl 61, fig 8, (April, 1874).

c

Fig. 5   *Dioptis Salvini*, Felder, = DIOPTIS NOCTILUCES, Butler, Cist. Ent , iv, p. 88, (January, 1872).   Lep. Exot., pl. 61, fig 7, (April, 1874).

Fig. 8.   *Gnatholophia longinervis*, Felder, = EUCONTHA SUBLACTI-GERA, Cat. Lep. Het. B. Mus., supp., p 383, (1864).

Fig. 22.   *Josia lugens*, Felder, = *Josia hyperia*, Cat Lep Het. B. Mus., p. 306, which = JOSIA PILARGE, loc. cit. p. 305, (1854).

Fig. 27.   *Antiotricha verata*, Felder, = MENNIS INTEGRA, Cat. Lep Het. B. Mus , supp , p. 181, (1864).

Fig. 31.   *Adelphoneura nerias*, Felder, = GLISSA BIFASCIES, Cat. Lep Het. B. Mus., supp , p. 186, (1864).

PLATE 106.

Fig. 2.   AGANAIS RENIGERA, Felder, is very near if not identical with HYPSA MEMBLIARIA, Cramer, sp., which varies greatly in the amount of yellow on the wings.

Fig 3.   *Aganais albifera*, Felder, = HYPSA PLANA, Cat Lep. Het. B. Mus., p. 450, (1854).

Fig. 4   *Agape cyanopyga*, Felder, = HYPSA CHLOROPYGA, Cat. Lep. Het. B. Mus., p. 455, (1854).   *Hypsa analis*, is a snyonym, being described from a specimen in which the spots are very pale

Fig. 5.   *Termessa hamula*, Felder, = TERMESSA DISCREPENS, Cat. Lep. Het. B. Mus , supp.; p. 265, (1864).   The specimen in the Museum cabinet has lost the fringes to the wings, and hence shows the black round the emargination faintly.

Fig. 8   *Cratosia parallela*, Felder, = CISSURA DECORA, Cat Lep. Het B Mus., p. 489, (1854)

Fig. 11.   *Lithosia bifasciata*, Felder, = CYLLENE TRANSVERSA, Cat. Lep. Het B Mus , p 544 (1854).

Fig 18.   *Teinopyga reticularis*, Felder, = DEIOPEIA EXTREMA, Cat. Lep. Het. B. Mus., p. 573, (1854).

Fig 23.   PYRALIDIA DESERTA, Felder, = ? *Lithosia nexa*, Boisduval, Lép. de Californie, (1868–9).

Fig 25.   *Dichromia Nietneri*, Felder, = SCAPTESYLE BICOLOR, Cat Lep Het B Mus , supp., p 182, (1864)

Fig. 26. PTYCHOGLENE ERYTHROPHORA, Felder, = *Lithosia mini-ata*, B. Mus. cabinet, *nec.* Cat Lep. Het. B Mus, p 512, (1854), which = HYPOPREPIA FUCOSA, p. 487, (1854).

PLATE 107

Fig. 5. *Agarista Moorei*, Felder, = EUSEMIA MOOREI, Boisduval Mon. des Agaristides

Fig. 6 AGARISTA LINDIGII, Felder, belongs to the genus *Phasis*, Walker, and is near JOSIA SEPARATA, Walker, 1645, (1856).

Fig. 8. *Agarista Batesii*, Felder, = PHASIS NOCTILUX, Walker, Cat Lep. Het. B. Mus, p. 312, (1854)

Fig 10. *Agarista ægoceroides*, Felder, = EUSEMIA TRANSIENS, Walker, .sp., Cat. Lep Het. B Mus., p. 1588, (1854) This insect with several others included in the same genus, must be separated from METAGARISTA, Walker, as they differ in the form of the antennæ from those organs in the generic type M. TRIPHÆNOIDES, Walker. The latter insect is near PAIS, Hubner, while the others with simple antennæ are related to EUDRYAS, Boisduval, from North America. For the species thus separated I would propose the name SEUDYRA, with the EUSEMIA TRANSIENS, of Walker, as the type. Cat Lep Het. B. Mus, p 1588, (1856)

Fig. 14. ÆGOCERA RUBIDA, Felder, judging by the figure, appears to differ little from Walker's Æ MAGNA, if it be not identical, and the types of this in the cabinet are scarcely distinguishable from those labelled *Æ. Latreillii*, H.S.

Fig 17 *Charilina intercis*, Felder, = CHARILINA AMABILIS, Cat Lep Het B. Mus., p. 516, (= *Aegocera ?amabilis*, p 58, loc. cit)

Fig. 18, 19, 20. *Tyndaris lætifica*, Felder, = CALLIDULA ERYCI-NATA, of the British Museum cabinet and catalogue

Fig. 28 *Callidula erycinoides*, Felder, = CALLIDULA EVANDRUS, of the British Museum cabinet and catalogue

Revision of the genus Spilosoma *and the allied groups of the Family* Arctiidæ; *by* ARTHUR G. BUTLER, F.L.S., F.Z.S., &c.

The genera of *Arctudæ* into which *Spilosoma* has been divided are closely allied , their structural differences are such as would not be recognized in many families as of generic value , still, as sub-divisions of a large group of insects, they are useful, and on that account I adopt them.

The following species do not belong to this group of genera.— *Spilosoma marmorata*, which is a *Digama* (a genus probably allied to *Deiopeia*); *S. rubescens*, which is congeneric with *Arctia strigatula*, *S. submacula, obscurum*, and *Aloa rhodophæa*, which will together form a genus not far from *Alope*, *S. fulvia* which seems to me to be a mutilated *Hypsa*; *S. costata*, something like the latter and of doubtful location; *Aloa tripartita, dentata*, and *erosa*, and *Creatonotos ? vuteria*.

Spilosoma dilecta, Boisd. may be anything, it cannot, I think, belong to the group

Genus AREAS. *Walker.*

Areas imperialis.

Euprepia imperialis, Kollar, Hugel's Kaschmir, p. 466, pl. 21, fig. 1, (1848).
Himalayas. B M

Walker refers this species to *Hypercompa*, but I am satisfied that its true position is in *Areas*, notwithstanding the startling differences in the pattern of the primaries.

Areas orientalis.

Areas orientalis, Walker, Lep Het. 3, p. 658, n. 1, (1855).
Sarawak (*Wallace*), Java (*Horsfield*).
N. India, Silhet. B M.

Arcas melanopsis.

Arctia melanopsis, Walker, Lep. Het. supp. 1, p. 280, (1864).
Ceylon   B.M.

Areas delineata.

Aloa delineata, Walker, Lep. Het., p 700, n. 3, (1855).
Natal, S. Africa.   B.M.

Areas lutescens. ·

♂, ♀.   *Spilosoma lutescens*, Walker, Lep. Het. 3, p. 672, n.
16, (1855).
♂.   *Halesidota nivulata*, Walker, Lep Het. supp. 1, p. 309,
(1864).
Sierra Leone, Natal, S Africa.   B.M.

Areas luctinea.

Phalæna luctinea, Cramer, Pap. Exot. II, pl. 131, fig. D,
(1779).
Bombyx sanguinolenta, Fabricius, Ent. Syst. III, 1, p. 473, n.
206, (1793)
N. India, Moulmein, Ceylon, Java.   B.M.

Areas cardinalis, n sp.

♀.   Snow-white, crest, margin of collar, abdomen and costa of
primaries scarlet ; antennæ black ; pterygodes with a central
black spot ; abdomen with dorsal and lateral series of black spots ;
primaries with two black spots at end of cell, one at the upper
and the other (smaller) at the lower extremity , secondaries with
end of cell, a large trifid marginal anal patch, and a subquadrate
smaller patch at centre of outer margin, all black ; palpi scarlet
with black tips, coxæ and upper surface of femora scarlet, tarsi
blackish ; venter sordid white with lateral black spots ; primaries with only one black spot at end of cell, otherwise as above ;
secondaries with the base red, a sub-basal costal black spot, otherwise as above   expanse of wings 3 inches, 1 line.
Phillipine Islands, (*Cuming*).   B.M.

Easily distinguished from *A. luctinea* by its scarlet abdomen,
and the large black marginal patches of secondaries.

Areas roseicostis, n. sp.

♂   Snow-white; crest, a few scales on margin of collar, abdomen, costa of primaries, and a diffused costal nebula on secondaries, scarlet; antennæ black, abdomen with a dorsal series of transverse black bars, and lateral series of spots; primaries with a minute black litura on median nervure at origin of second and third branches, a second upon the lower radial, a third on the first median, and a fourth near the end of the submedian nervure, secondaries with a black spot at end of cell, a second smaller one at apex, and three (larger) along the outer margin; palpi scarlet with black tips, coxæ and upper surface of femora scarlet; knees, tibiæ above, and tarsi black; venter white with lateral black dots; primaries with two black spots at end of cell; secondaries with the base rosy, a black sub-basal costal spot; costal rosy nebula only visible through the wing, otherwise as above. expanse of wings 1 inch, 11 lines.

Rockingham Bay, Australia, (*Macgillivray*).   B.M

Areas Moorei, n. sp

♂.   Snow-white, scape of antennæ, front margin of collar, abdomen, and costa of primaries, scarlet; antennæ black, abdomen with a dorsal series of transverse black bars, and lateral series of black dots; primaries with two minute black points at end of cell; secondaries with a black spot at end of cell, a second at apex, and a third, submarginal, on discoidal interspace; palpi scarlet, fringed with white, with black tips, coxæ and femora above reddish, knees and middle tibiæ above black, tarsi black spotted with whitish; wings below red at base with a black costal spot, otherwise as above. expanse of wings 1 inch, 6 lines.

Almorah, N. India, (*Boys*).   B.M

This species, like the two preceding is at once separated from *A. lactinea* by its scarlet abdomen, it also has much less scarlet about the collar, and no black spots on the tegulæ. I have named it after Mr. F. Moore of the E India Museum

Areas costalis.

Alpi costalis, Walker, Lep. Het. supp. 1, p 301, (1864).
N. Australia.

Areas marginata.

Bombyx marginata, Donovan, Ins. New Holland, pl. 34, fig. 2, (1805).

Tasmania, (*Doubleday*)   B.M.

If the species which we possess is that represented by Donovan, his figure must be very bad.

Genus ALOA.   *Walker.*

Aloa punctistriga.

♀. *Spilosoma punctistriga*, Walker, Lep. Het. 3, p. 676, n. 28, (1855)

N. India. B M.

Aloa candidula.

♂   *Aloa candidula*, Walker, Lep. Het. 3, p. 704, n. 7, (1855).

Nepaul, (*Hardwicke*).   B.M.

Possibly the male of the preceding species.

Aloa diminuta.

♂   *Aloa diminuta*, Walker, Lep. Het 3, p 705, n. 8, (1855).
♀. *Creatonotos emittens* ♀, Walker, Lep. Het. 3, p. 639, n. 2, (1855).

Spilosoma strigata, Walker, Charact. Lep. Het, p. 10, n. 15, (1869).

N. India, (*Hamilton and James*).   B.M.

Aloa rubricosta.

Creatonotos rubricosta, Moore, Proc Zool. Soc., p. 573, (1872).

Manpuri, N.W. India, (*Horne*), Bombay.   Coll. F. Moore.

This species seems to be nearly allied to *A. punctistriga.*

Aloa emittens.

♂, ♀. *Creatonotos emittens*, Walker, Lep. Het. 3, p. 638, n. 2, (1855)
♂. *Aloa candidula, var.* Walker, l. c., p. 704, n. 7, (1855)

Ceylon, (*Templeton and Wenham*).   B.M

♂, ♀ *variety* Altogether more rosy in colour with a prominent black spot at end of discoidal cell of secondaries

S. India. B M.

Aloa punctivitta.

Spilosoma ? *punctivitta,* Walker, Lep. Het. 3, p. 673, n. 18, (1855)

Port, Natal, (*Gueinzius*) B M.

Creatonotos interruptus being congeneric with *Aloa integra, bivittata,* &c , the name *Creatonotos* must be referred to them , and thus *Aloa candidula* will become the type of *Aloa* Walker. In *Aloa* thus restricted the antennæ of the sexes differ, in *C. interruptus* they are alike, it will not come into the *Spilosoma* group

Genus SEIRARCTIA *Packard.*

Seirarctia innotata

Spilosoma innotata, Walker, Lep. Het. 3, p. 674, n. 20, (1855). Egypt, (*Burton*). B.M.

Seirarctia scita.

Aloa scita, Walker, Lep Het supp. 1, p 302, (1864). Sierra Leone, (*Foxcroft*). B.M.

Seirarctia echo

Phalæna echo, Smith and Abbot, Ins. Georg , p. 135, pl. 68, (1797).
Hyphantria echo, Clemens, Proc. Acad. Nat Sci Phil., p 531, (1860).
Spilosoma echo, Morris, Syn. Lep N. Am App , p 342, (1860).
Georgia.

Seirarctia clio

Seirarctia clio, Packard, Proc. Ent. Soc Phil. 3, p. 120, (1864) ; Stretch, Ill. Zyg, and Bomb. N. Am. 1, p. 82, pl 3, fig. 1, (1872)
California Coll. Dr. Behr.

Seirarctia trivitta.

Spilosoma ? trivitta, Walker, Lep Het. 3, p. 673, n. 19, (1855).
Port Natal, (*Gueinzius*).   B.M.

Seirarctia quadriramosa.

Euprepia quadriramosa, Kollar, Hugel's Kaschmir, p. 468, n.
VI, (1848).
N. India.   B.M.

Genus LACYDES.   *Walker.*

Lacydes spectabilis

Chelonia spectabilis, Tauscher, Mém Mosc., p. 212, T. 13, 6,
(1806), Ménétries, Enum corp anim. III, pl. 18, fig 3, a and
b, (*larva*), (1863).
Bombyx intercisa, Freyer, Neuere Beitr Schmett. IV, p. 118,
pl. 356.
Europe   B M

African sub-genus, with shorter palpi.

Lacydes vocula.

Bombyx vocula, Stoll. supp. Cramer, pl. 31, fig. 5
S Africa, (*Shepherd*), Knysna, (*Trimen*).   B.M.

Lacydes ramivitta, (? vocula var.)

♂   *Spilosoma ramivitta*, Walker, Tr. N. H. Soc. Glasgow, 1,
p. 337, (1873).
Congo.

Lacydes arborifera, n. sp

♂   Snow-white, back of head and collar, and base of abdomen
testaceous, abdomen ochreous, a brown longitudinal streak on
pterygodes, and another on centre of thorax ; abdomen with
dorsal and lateral series of black dots ; antennæ whitish testaceous, primaries with an irregular apical-costal olivaceous-brown
streak, a central longitudinal streak of the same colour, forking
from below at first median branch and trifurcate from origin of
second and third median branches to outer margin ; a third streak

along the sub-median nervure, secondaries with a black dot at end of cell; venter testaceous, costa of primaries below testaceous; otherwise as above: expanse of wings 1 inch, 1 to 2 lines.

Loanda, August, 1872; Ambriz, October, 1872; (*Monteiro*) B.M.

Allied to *L vocula*, but much less marked with brown than in any examples of that species, also smaller and paler in colouring.

*Lacydes lineata.**

♀. *Spilosoma linea*, Walker, Lep. Het. 3, p 671, n. 12, (1855)

♂. *Spilosoma dorsalis*, Walker, l. c. n 13, (1855).

♂. *Spilosoma strigatum*, Wallengren, Wien Ent Monatschr. 4, p. 161, n. 5, (1860); Kongl. Svensk. Akad Handl. 5, p 49, n. 2, (1865)

Var. ♀ ? *Spilosoma truncatum*, Walker, Lep Het. 7, p. 1781, (1856)

S Africa, (*Argent and Smith*), Natal, (*Gueinzius*), Cape, (*Drege*). B.M.

The example mentioned as coming from West Africa is generically distinct

Genus EPILACYDES, *n gen.*

Differs from the preceding genus in its altogether less woolly thorax, and from the African section in its much longer palpi Type *E simulans*.

Epilacydes simulans, n sp

♂. In appearance very like *Lacydes lineata* ♀, but altogether paler in colour, with no bifurcate termination to the median streak of primaries; thorax narrower.

Head pale stramineous, brownish in front, antennæ black; palpi black above, whity-brown below, collar and thorax stramineous, the latter with a dorsal black streak, abdomen golden orange with dorsal black spots and lateral black points, primaries silky stramineous with a black streak, slightly widening from

---

* This is evidently more correct than *linea*, but if preferred the name *dorsalis* may be adopted.

base, along median nervure, to near centre of lower discoidal
interspace, secondaries creamy whitish, wings below creamy
white, yellowish along costa, pectus and venter stramineous:
expanse of wings 1 inch, 5 lines

West Africa   B.M

Genus ALPHÆA. *Walker.*

Alphæa fulvohirta.

Alphæa fulvohirta, Walker, Lep. Het. 3, p 684, n. 1, (1855).
Darjeeling   B M

Alphæa varia of Walker appears to me to be referable to the
genus *Ardices*

Genus ARDICES. *Walker.*

Ardices fulvohirta

♂, ♀   *Ardices fulvohirta* ♂, Walker, Lep Het. 3, p. 710, n.
1, (1855).
♀   *Spilosoma conferta,* Walker, l. c. supp. 1, p 295, (1864).
Tasmania   B.M.

Ardices subocellata.

♀.   *Spilosoma subocellatum,* Walker, Lep. Het. 7, p. 1697,
(1856)
♂, ♀. *Ardices fulvohirta,* ♀, Walker, Lep. Het 3, p. 710,
n. 1, (1855)
Tasmania, S. Australia, W. Australia, Kangaroo Island.   B.M

The typical form of this species is less heavily marked than the
bulk of the examples formerly placed as females of *A. fulvohirta,*
but it is clearly only a case of variation: as indicated by Walker,
this species chiefly differs from the preceding in its scarlet abdomen, femora, and lateral margin of collar.

Ardices divisa.

Arctia divisa, Walker, Lep. Het. 3, p. 614, n. 39, (1855)
Himalayas.   B M.

This species was retained in *Arctia,* by Mr. Moore, probably
on account of a tendency which it exhibits to follow the pattern

of *A imbuta*, Walker, next to which species both authors place it; the latter however seems to me to be better located in *Pericallia* A. *divisa* is without question the Indian representative of *Ardices fulvohirta*, and differs considerably from *Arctia* in the character of its palpi.

Ardices liturata

Ardices liturata, Walker, Charact. Lep. Het., p 12, n. 19, (1869)

Had it not been for the mention of blackish hindwings, I should have supposed this to be a faded example of *A. subocellata*.

Ardices canescens, n sp

White ; front margin of thorax scarlet ; antennæ black ; abdomen scarlet with dorsal and lateral series of black dots , primaries with a small spot on interno-basal area, a short oblique band across the middle of the cell, a sub-costal spot at end of cell, a band upon disc from costa to inner margin, (trifurcate at costa and bifurcate towards inner margin), and three or four bifid submarginal spots, olivaceous brown , all the markings intersected by white nervures , base of costal margin blackish , secondaries with a spot at end of cell, a second near apex, and a streak at anal angle, olive brown , palpi scarlet with black tips, a fringe of scarlet scales round the eyes ; side of coxæ, tibiæ, and tarsi, blackish , venter creamy whitish expanse of wings 1 inch, 10 lines.

Australia, (*Brenchley*). B. M.

Possibly an extreme variety of *A subocellata*, but with the wings much less heavily marked, and without any black streaks on the pterygodes and thorax.

Ardices? varia

Alphæa varia, Walker, Lep Het supp 1, p. 297, (1864). Massuri, (*Hearsey*) B M

Genus ICAMBOSIDA. *Walker.*

Icambosida nigrifrons.

Icambosida nigrifrons, Walker, Lep. Het supp. 2, p 401, (1865).
Darjeeling, (*Atkinson*) B M.

I do not consider this to be congeneric with *Spilosoma*, as suggested by Mr Moore in 1875 ; as these genera go, it is sufficiently distinct to be kept separate.

Genus SPILOSOMA   *Stephens.*

Spilosoma menthastri.

Bombyx menthastri, Esper, Eur. Schmett., pl 66, figs. 6–10, (1786)
Phalæna lubricipeda, Linnæus, Syst Nat. II, p. 829, n 69, (1766).
Phalæna erminea, Marsham, Linn. Trans 1, p 70, pl. 1, fig. 1.
Bombyx mendica, Rossi, Faun Etr. II, p. 174, n 1093.
var. *Spilosoma Walkerii,* Curtis, Brit Ent. II, pl. 92.
var. *Chelonia Luxeri,* Godart, Hist Nat Lep Fr. IV, p 37, n. 4.
Europe, (*Becker*)   B M.

Spilosoma puncturium.

Phalæna Bombyx. puncturia, Cramer, Pap Exot. IV, p 233, pl. 398, fig D, (1782)
Hakodadi, (*Whitely*).   B.M.

Spilosoma sanguica.

Spilosoma sanguica, Walker, Lep. Het. supp. 1, p. 294, (1864)
Shanghai.   B.M

Spilosoma punctulatum.

Spilosoma punctulatum, Wallengren, Wien Ent. Monatschr. 4, p. 161, n 5, (1860), Kongl. Svenska, Vetensk Akad Handl. 5, p 49, n 1, (1865)
Interior of Caffraria

Allied to *S menthastri*

Spilosoma urticæ

Bombyx urticæ, Esper, Eur. Schmett. III, p 20, pl. 83, fig. 2, (1789).
Phalæna papyratia, Marsham, Linn Trans. 1, p. 72, pl. 1, fig. 4, (1791)
Europe, (*Becker*).   B M.

Spilosoma ? mutans.

Spilosoma mutans, Walker, Lep Het. 7, p. 1697, (1856)
Hab. ? Coll. Hope, Oxford.

Spilosoma ? melanostigma.

Spilosoma melanostigma, Erschoff, Horæ Soc. Ent Ross. VIII,
p. 316, (1872)
Turan.

Unfortunately the work in which this species is described is
not in the Museum Library, so that I have been unable to
identify it : if Erschoff follows Staudinger, it may be *Phragma-*
tobia, or, any other genus of *Arctiidæ.*

Spilosoma virginica

Bombyx virginica, Fabricius, Ent Syst. supp , p 437, (1798)
Spilosoma virginica, Walker, Lep Het 3, p. 668, n 6,
(1855) , Riley, 3rd. Rep. Ins. Mo , p. 68, figs 28, a–c, (1871) ;
Stretch, Ill. Zyg , and Bomb N. Am 1, p. 131, pl. 6, fig 6,
(1872)
Trenton Falls, Hudson's Bay, Nova Scotia, Georgia, Massachusetts B M

Spilosoma latipennis.

♀. *Spilosoma latipennis,* Stretch, Ill Zyg , and Bomb N
Am. 1, p 133, pl. 6, fig. 5, (1872)
Atlantic States, (*Angus*) Coll Stretch

Spilosoma vestalis.

Spilosoma vestalis, Packard, Proc. Ent Soc Phil. 3, p. 125,
(1864) ; Stretch, Ill. Zyg., and Bomb N. Am 1, p. 133 , pl. 6,
figs. 7, 8, (1872).
California, (Presented by Mr Stretch, 1875) B M

Section DIONYCHOPUS, (*Hubner*), *Schrenck*

Dionychopus albus

Chelonia alba, Bremer, Beitr. Schmett Fauna Nordl. China's,
p. 15, n. 71, (1853).
N. China.

Dionychopus niveus.

Dionychopus niveus, Ménétriés, Bull de l'Acad. St Petersb. XVII, p 218, n. 23, Schrenck's, Amur-Lande, p. 52, pl. IV, fig 6, (1859).

♀ Japan, (*Pryer and Whately*). B M

The published figure of this species is very poor, but the description puts its correct identification beyond question.

Dionychopus? erythrozona.

Euprepia erythrozona, Kollar, Hugel's Kaschmir, p 468, n. VII, (1848)

Massuri.

Genus SÆNURA. *Wallengren.*

Sænura lineata.

Spilosoma lineata, Walker, Lep Het 3, p 672, n 17, (1855).
Aloa simplex, Walker, l c, p. 699, n. 1, (1855).
Sænura alba, Wallengren, Wien. Ent. Monatschr 4, p 162, n. 8, (1860), Kongl Svenska Veten Akad. Handl. 5, p 49, n 1, (1865)

Natal. B M.

Sænura flava.

Sænura flava, Wallengren, Wien Ent Monatschr. 4, p. 162, n. 9, (1860) ; Kongl Svensk. Akad. Handl 5, p. 49, n 2, (1865).

Caffraria

Genus HYPHANTRIA. *Harris*

This genus is very close to *Spilosoma.*

Hyphantria cunea

Bombyx cunea, Drury, Ill Ex Ent 1, p. 36, pl. 18, fig. 4, (1770).
Hyphantria cunea, Fitch, 3rd. Rep Ins N York, p 384, (1856) ; Stretch, Ill Zyg. and Bomb N Am. 1, p. 205, pl. 8, figs. 18–20, (1874).
Phalæna punctatissima, Smith and Abbot, Lep. Ins. Georg., p. 139, pl. 77, (1797)
Hyphantria punctatissima, Harris, Ins Inj Veg., 3rd. ed, p. 358, (1862).

United States. Georgia. B.M.

Hyphantria congrua.

Spilosoma congrua, Walker, Lep Het. 3, p. 669, n. 8, (1855). Georgia, (*Milne*). B.M.

The only examples now representing this species in the collection are what I believe to be a male variety of *H. cunea,* and a female ? *Spilosoma virginica,* without abdomen; what Mr. Walker may have done with the species since Mr. Grote described it, it is impossible to say.

Hyphantria textor.

Arctia textor, Harris, Cat Ins Mass, (Hitchcock's Rt., p 591), (1833).
Hyphantria textor, Harris, Ins. Inj Veg., p. 255, (1841); Riley, 3rd. Rep. Ins. Missouri, p 130, figs. 55, a–c, (1871); Stretch, Ill. Zyg., and Bomb. N. Am. 1, p 206. pl. 8, fig. 21, (1874).
Georgia, (*Abbot*), Sp. ead. ? Texas. B.M.

Hyphantria candida, (? præc. var.).

Spilosoma candida, Walker, Lep. Het. supp. 1, p 291, (1864)
Hyphantria textor, Grote, Trans. Am Ent Soc., p. 18, (1867). N. America. B.M.

If Mr Walker has rightly identified *H. textor,* (as Mr. Stretch tacitly admits); the *S. candida* of the supplement is a decidedly larger and more woolly insect: still Mr. Grote may be correct in considering the two forms con-specific

Hyphantria punctata.

Hyphantria punctata, Fitch, 3rd. Rep. Ins. N. York, p. 387, (1856); Stretch, Ill. Zyg,, and Bomb. N Am. 1, p. 204, (1874). United States. B.M.

I believe this to be only a variety of *H. cunea,* with which all the white examples (♂ and ♀) must be associated; it differs from the typical form in only possessing one series of black spots on primaries, there is however an intermediate form with only the two central series prominent, whilst the typical form has four series on primaries and one on secondaries.

Genus ALPENUS   *Walker.*

Alpenus maculosus.

Phalæno-Bombyx maculosa, Cramer, Pap Exot IV, p. 156,
pl. 370, fig. D, (1782).

Spilosoma ? maculosum, Walker, Lep. Het. 7, p 1696, (1856).

Ecpantheria assimilis, Hubner, Verz. Bek. Schmett, p. 183,
n. 1890, (1816).

Sierra Leone, (*Foxcroft*).   ♂, ♀.   B.M.

Alpenus æqualis.

♀. *Alpenus æqualis,* Walker, Lep. Het. 3, p. 686, n. 1,
(1855).

♀.   *Ecpantheria indeterminata,* Walker, l. c , p. 697, (1855).

Halesidota ? maculaia, Walker, Lep. Het. supp. 1, p. 314,
(1864)

W. Africa, Ashanti, Congo. ♀, B M.

Clearly a local form of the preceding species, it chiefly differs
in having several large black sub-marginal spots in secondaries.

Alpenus marginalis.

♀. *Aloa marginalis* Walker, Lep Het. 3, p. 701, n 4, (1855).
Sierra Leone, (*Morgan*).   B M

Alpenus multiguttatus.

Hypercompa multiguttata, Walker, Lep. Het. 3, p. 657, n.
20, (1855).

Nepal, (*Hardwicke*).   B.M

Alpenus spilosomoides.

Deiopeia spilosomoides, Walker, Lep. Het. supp. 1, p. 263,
(1864).

N. India (*Strachey*)   B M

Probably this will turn out to be merely a dwarfed form of
the preceding species.

Alpenus maculifascia.

♀. *Spilosoma maculifascia,* Walker, Lep. Het. 3, p. 676, n.
29, (1855)

♂. *Spilosoma canspnrcatum*, Walker, 1 c. 7, p 1698, (1856). Java, (*Horsfield*). B.M.

Alpenus bifurca.

Aloa bifurca, Walker, Lep. Het. 3, p 700, n. 2, (1855) Sierra Leone, (*Morgan*). B M.

Genus EYRALPENUS, *n. gen.*

Allied to *Alpenus* and *Spilarctia*, but differing from the former in its broad and short wings, more prominent thorax and stouter legs, and from the latter in its less pointed primaries, with less oblique outer margin and its shorter antennæ. Type *E testaceus*.

Eyralpenus testaceus

Spilosoma testacea, Walker, Lep Het. 3, p. 670, n 11, (1855). *Spilosoma subflavescens*, Walker, l. c supp 1, p. 293, (1864). Natal, (*Gueinzius*). Zoolu, (*Angas*). B.M

Genus LEUCARCTIA. *Packard.*

Leucarctia acrea

♀. *Bombyx acreá*, Drury, Ill. Ex. Ent. 1, pl. III, fig. 2, (1770).

♂. *Bombyx caprotina*, Drury, l. c., fig. 3, (1770); Cramer, Pap. Exot. III, pl CCLXXXVII, fig C, (1782)

♂, ♀. *Phalæna acria*, (sic), Smith and Abbot, Lep Ins. Georg., p. 133, pl LXVII, (1797).

Arctia pseudermuiea, Harris, Mass Ag Rep, p 332, pl. 1, (1823).

Leucarctia acrea, Packard, Proc. Ent. Soc Phil 3, p. 124, (1864), Stretch, Ill. Zyg., and Bomb. N. Am 1, p 99, pl. 4, fig 1–3 , pl. 10, fig 6, (1872).

New York, Georgia, British Columbia, Canada, Mexico   B M.

Leucarctia mexicana.

Spilosoma mexicana, Walker, Lep Het supp. 1, p 291, (1864). Oaxaca, (*Sallé*)   B.M.

Leucarctia californica.

Leucarctia californica, 'Packard, Proc. Ent. Soc. Phil. 3, p. 125, (1864)

San Francisco

Leucarctia albida

♂ . *Leucarctia albida*, Stretch, Ill Zyg , and Bomb. N. Am. 1, p. 203, pl 8, fig. 22, (1874).

California. Coll Stretch

Judging from the figure alone, I am at a loss to know how this species differs from *Spilosoma virginica,* however, I have little doubt that Mr. Stretch has found it structurally different; the head seems rather prominent and too broad for that species.

Leucarctia permaculata.

Leucarctia permaculata, Packard, Rep. Peab. Acad. IV, p. 86, (1872).

S. California.

Genus PHISSAMA. *Moore.*

Phissama albistriga.

Aloa albistriga, Walker, Lep. Het. supp. 1, p. 303, (1864).

S. India, (*Walhouse*). B.M.

Phissama transiens

Spilosoma transiens, Walker, Lep. Het III, p 675, n. 22, (1855).

Aloa isabellina, Walker, Lep. Het. III, p. 705, n. 10, (1855).

Silhet, Moulmein, Sarawak, Celebes. B.M .

Phissama vacillans.

Amphissa vacillans, Walker, Lep. Het 3, p. 685, n 1, (1855).

Aloa vacillans, Walker, l c 7, p. 1702, (1856).

Borneo, Philippines, Hong-Kong. B.M.

Genus EUCHÆTES. , *Harris.*

Euchaetes egle.

Bombyx egle, Drury, Ill. Ex. Ent. II, p. 36, pl. 20, fig. 3, (1773)

Spilosoma egle, Westwood, Ed. Drury, (1837); Stretch, Ill. Zyg, and Bomb. N Am. 1, p. 185, pl. 8, fig 4, ♀, (1874).
Euchœtes egle, Harris, Ins. Inj Veg., p 257, (1841).
var? *Euchœtes eglenensis*, Clemens, Proc. Acad. Nat. Soc. Phil., p. 533, (1860)
United States. B.M.

Euchœtes bipunctata.

Halesidota bipunctata, Walker, Lep Het. 3, p 738, n. 9, (1855).
Pará, (*J. P. G. Smith*). B.M.

Euchœtes oregonensis.

♂. *Euchœtes oregonensis*, Stretch Ill Zyg., and Bomb. N. Am. 1, p. 187, pl 8, fig. 7, (1874).
Oregon. Coll. Stretch.

Euchœtes collaris.

Hyphantria collaris, Fitch, 3rd. Rep. Ins. N. York, p. 265, (1856).
♂. *Euchœtes collaris*, Stretch, Ill. Zyg, and Bomb. N Am. 1, p. 188, pl. 8, fig 5, (1874)
Tanada antica, Walker, Lep. Het. 7, p. 1745, n. 1, (1856).
Arctia sciurus, Boisduval, Ann. Soc. Ent. Belg. 12, p 79, (1868).
Georgia, (*Abbot*). B.M.

Walker's specimen is a small one, and not much like Mr. Stretch's figure, I have no doubt however that it is con-specific.

Tanada conscita of Walker being a *Callimorpha*, I suppose the generic name must be transferred (if adopted) to *Tanada ? amplificata.*

Euchœtes elegans

♂. *Euchœtes elegans*, Stretch, Ill. Zyg., and Bomb. N. Am. 1, p. 189, pl. 8, fig. 6, (1874).
California. Coll. Stretch.

This species has a scarlet abdomen.

Euchœtes aurata, n. sp.

Chiefly differs from *E. insulata* of Walker in its deep golden colour, which covers the wings and body uniformly : expanse of wings 1 inch, 6 lines.

Espiritu Santo, (*Higgins*).   B.M.

This is so much deeper in colour than any of the varieties of *E. insulata*, that I have considered it necessary to name it.

Euchœtes insulata

Halesidota insulata, Walker, Lep. Het. 3, p. 734, n. 5, (1855).

Jamaica, Haiti, Venezuela, Sta Martha, Santarem.   B.M.

Specimens from the last three localities are paler in colour than those from Jamaica and Haiti

Euchœtes ? jussuew.

Arctia jussuew, Poey, Centurie de Lép. Cuba, (1832).

Cuba

The figure of the moth is so poor, that I feel very uncertain as to its systematic position; the palpi are represented as prominent, which is not a character of this genus, but this may be an error in drawing

Genus PAREUCHÆTES.   *Grote.*

Pareuchœtes cadaverosa

Pareuchœtes cadaverosa, Grote, Proc. Ent. Soc. Phil. V, p. 245, (1865).

Cuba.

Pareuchœtes affinis.

Pareuchœtes affinis, Grote, Proc Ent. Soc. Phil V, p. 245, (1865).

Cuba

Genus VANESSODES.   *Grote and Robinson.*

Vanessodes clarus.

Vanessodes clarus, Grote and Robinson, Trans. Am. Ent. Soc. III, p. 176, (1871)

Texas

Genus PYRRHARCTIA *Packard*

Pyrrharctia isabella.

Phalæna isabella, Smith and Abbot, Lep. Ins Georg., p 131, pl. 66, (1864)

Pyrrharctia isabella, Packard, Proc. Ent. Soc. Phil., p 121, (1864).

var. *Pyrrharctia californica,* Packard, l. c., (1864).

Trenton Falls, Massachusetts, California? B.M.

I cannot see sufficient reason, in Mr Packard's comparative description, for separating *P. californica* as a species; it is well known that the *Arctiadæ* are more subject to variation than most groups of Lepidoptera, and may be lighter or darker in colour, or differ slightly in contour, from the same batch of eggs · we have two or three examples labelled with a dark green ticket, (which generally indicates species received by us from California, if not from Europe), one of these is darker and more heavily marked than usual, but I should not hesitate for a moment to place it with *P. isabella.*

Genus SPILARCTIA, *n. gen.*

Chelonia, *Godart,* (restricted)

Spilarctia lubricipeda

Phalæna-Bombyx lubricipeda, Linnæus, Syst. Nat II, p 839, (1766)

Chelonia lubricipeda, Godart, Pap de France IV, p. 358, pl. 37, fig. 3.

Bombyx lubricipedatus, Haworth, Lep Brit., p. 110.

Phalæna lepus, Retz. Gen., p. 37, n. 47.

var. *Bombyx radiatus,* Haworth, Ent. Trans 1, p 336.

var. *Bombyx Luxerii,* Godart, Pap de France IV, p 360, pl. 37, fig. 4.

Europe, (*Becker*). B.M.

Spilarctia fluvalis.

Spilosoma fluvalis, Moore, Proc Zool. Soc, p. 809, (1865).

Darjeeling, (*A. E Russell*). Coll. F. Moore.

Spilarctia punctata.

Spilosoma punctata, Moore, Cat. Lep. Mus, E. I. C. II, p. 355, n. 854, (1858–9).
Java, (*Horsfield*).   B.M.

Spilarctia indica

Arctia indica, Guérin, Voy. Delessert, Hist Nat, p. 93, (1843).
Neilgherries

Apparently allied to *S. lubricipeda,* but much more spotted.

Spilarctia sub-fascia.

Spilosoma sub-fascia, Walker, Lep Het. 3, p. 678, n. 33, (1855).
Ceylon, (*Templeton*).   B.M.

Spilarctia stigmata

Spilosoma stigmata, Moore, Proc. Zool. Soc, p 809, (1865).
Darjeeling, (*Atkinson*).   B.M.

Spilarctia multivittata.

Spilosoma multivittata, Moore, Proc. Zool Soc., p. 808, (1865).
Darjeeling, (*Atkinson*).   B M.

Spilarctia rhodophila.

Spilosoma rhodophila, Walker, Lep. Het. supp. 1, p. 294, (1864).
? *Spilosoma rubidorsa,* Moore, Proc Zool. Soc., p. 808, (1865).
Darjeeling, (*Atkinson*).   B.M.

Spilarctia lativitta.

Spilosoma lativitta, Moore, Proc. Zool. Soc., p. 809, (1865).
Darjeeling, (*Atkinson*).   B M.

This species appears to be nearly allied to *S. rhodophila* of Walker, but the thorax is more woolly, and the primaries are narrower than in any other species of this genus

Spilarctia ? cognata.

Spilosoma cognata, Walker, Charact Lep Het., p. 11, (1869) Hab ?

Mr. Walker could hardly have chosen a less appropriate name for this species: in publishing descriptions of so many Lepidoptera from Norris' and other collections, nearly all without localities, this author unnecessarily burdened the synonymy with scores of names, the species referable to which will most of them probably never be cognate.

Spilarctia obliqua.

Spilosoma obliqua, Walker, Lep Het. 3, p. 679, n. 34, (1855) ♀, Sydney, ♂, ♀, New South Wales. B.M.

Spilarctia nydia, n. sp.

Cream coloured, abdomen crimson, with dorsal and lateral series of black spots, primaries with a black spot near base of submedian nervure, and two or three in an oblique series from the internal margin beyond the middle of the wing ; secondaries with a black spot at end of cell, three large black spots placed obliquely towards anal angle, and two smaller apical submarginal spots ; upper surface of palpi and femora, coxæ and anterior margin of thorax, carmine, frons, tips of palpi, tibiæ, and tarsi, dark brown, venter with lateral series of black spots, primaries with a large black spot at end of cell, and an oblique streak from inner margin to near apex ; secondaries as above. expanse of wings 2 inches, 5 lines.
Nepal. B.M.

Spilarctia ione, n sp.

♀. Creamy-white, abdomen rosy, with dorsal and lateral blackish dots, anal segments ochraceous; antennæ black; secondaries with a small black spot at end of cell, a second smaller, on discoidal interspace towards outer margin, and two near anal angle ; frons, tips of palpi, tibiæ and tarsi black-brown ; anterior lateral margin of pectus and femora, carmine, venter with a few lateral blackish points ; primaries below with a blackish spot at end of cell, a few dots near apex, an oblique streak from interno-median to discoidal interspace, and a nebulous longitudinal interno-median patch, greyish brown : secondaries with the blackish spots less distinct than above : expanse of wings 1 inch, 10 lines.
Hakodadi, Japan, (*Whitely*) B.M

This and the preceding species are allied to *C. subcarnea*, they were placed by Mr. Walker with his *S. suffusa.*

Spilarctia subcarnea.

Spilosoma subcarnea, Walker, Lep. Het. 3, p. 675, n. 25, (1855).

Hong-Kong, (*Bowring*).   B M.

Spilarctia abdominalis.

Spilosoma abdominalis, Moore, Cat. Lep., E. I. C. 2, p. 356, n 857, (1858–9).

N. India, (*Buckley*).

Appears to be allied to the preceding species.

Spilarctia sordida.

Spilosoma sordida, Moore, Proc. Zool. Soc., p. 808, (1865).

Darjeeling.   Coll. A. E. Russell

Spilarctia ? brunnea.

Spilosoma brunnea, Moore, Proc. Zool. Soc , p. 574, (1872).

Bombay.   Coll. F Moore.

Spilarctia ? todara.

Spilosoma todara, Moore, Proc. Zool. Soc., p. 574, (1872).

Coonoor, Nilghiris, (*Day*).   Coll. F Moore

Spilarctia dentilinea.

Spilosoma dentilinea, Moore, Proc. Zool. Soc., p. 573, (1872)

Sikkim.   Coll F. Moore

Seems allied to *C. bifrons.*

Spilarctia confusa, n. sp.

♂, ♀. Whity-brown, or dull cream coloured, abdomen crimson, with dorsal and lateral series of black dots ; antennæ black , primaries with a curved oblique series of black dots from inner margin to beyond end of cell , several submarginal discal black dots, (sometimes forming a zigzag series to apex) ; secondaries deeper coloured than primaries, tinted with rose colour, especially towards inner margin, a black spot at end of cell ; a black submarginal spot on discoidal interspace, and two or three towards anal angle, zoned with creamy whitish ; primaries below, especially of the male suffused with rose-red, a black spot at end of cell ; apex pale , secondaries paler than above, very slightly tinted with pink; a black spot at end of cell; female with other black spots as above · palpi red with brown tips, coxæ and upper surface of femora carmine, tibiæ and tarsi partially brown ; venter creamy with a few lateral black dots   expanse of wings, ♂ 1 inch, 7 to 10 lines ; ♀ 2 inches, to 2 inches 2 lines.

N. India, N Bengal, &c.   B.M

Spilarctia rubitincta

Spilosoma rubitincta, Moore, Proc. Zool Soc., p. 809, (1865).
Spilosoma subtincta, Walker, Lep Het supp 5, p 1907, (1866).
Darjeeling, (*A. E. Russell*)   Coll F. Moore.

The description of this species is incomplete, but it appears to be allied to *S suffusa* of Walker · we have a species nearly agreeing with the description from Japan.

Spilarctia bifrons.

Aloa bifrons, Walker, Lep Het 3, p. 705, n. 9, (1855).
N. China, (*Cuming and Fortune*)   B M.

Spilarctia suffusa.

Spilosoma suffusa, Walker, Lep. Het. 3, p. 677, n. 32, (1855).
Punjaub, (*Hearsay*)   B M

Spilarctia casigneta.

Spilosoma casigneta, Kollar, Hugel's Kaschmir, p. 469, n 8, (1844)
Spilosoma sanguinalis, Moore, Proc Zool Soc , p. 810, (1865).
Darjeeling, (*Atkinson*).   B.M.

Spilarctia discinigra

Spilosoma discinigra, Moore, Proc. Zool. Soc., p 810, (1865).
Darjeeling.   Coll. A. E. Russell.

Spilarctia rubilinea.

Spilosoma rubilinea, Moore, Proc Zool. Soc., p. 810, (1865).
Darjeeling, *(Atkinson).*   B M.

Genus LEUCALOA, *n. gen.*

Allied to *Spilarctia,* more robust, head and tegulæ more smoothly scaled, not so fluffy, antennæ thicker, palpi thicker; front pair of legs much less hairy, all the legs stouter and smoother; wings below fluffy towards the base; discocellulars of all the wings strongly and regularly angulated; markings of primaries transverse, linear.   Type *Spilosoma eugraphica* of Walker.

Leucaloa eugraphica.

Spilosoma eugraphica, Walker, Lep. Het. supp. 1, p. 292,
Aloa undistriga, Felder, Reise der Nov. Lep. 4, pl. C, fig. 21,
(1874).
Cape of Good Hope.   B.M.

Leucaloa curvilinea.

Spilosoma curvilinea, Walker, Lep. Het. 3, p 671, n. 14,
(1855).
Congo, *(Richardson)*   B M.

I feel doubtful whether the following genus really belongs to this group, although Dr. Wallengren has placed it here.

Genus TÆNIOPYGA. *Wallengren.*

Tæniopyga eumela.

Phalæna eumela, Cramer, Pap Exot. IV, pl. 347, fig. G,
(1782).
Tæniopyya eumela, Wallengren, Kongl. Svenska. Vetensk.
Akad. Handl., 5, p. 50, n 1, (1865).
S. Caffraria.

Ovios sylvina appears to me to be allied to this species.

Descriptions of hitherto uncharacterized Australian Phytophaga, *by* JOSEPH S. BALY, F.L.S., &c

The present paper contains the descriptions of some interesting Australian Insects recently added to my collection, the greater number of which were collected in Western Australia by Mr. Duboulay.

Duboulaia flavipennis, mihi.

Since the publication of my description of this insect, I have obtained a specimen of the ♂ sex; it is only one third the size of the ♀, (Long. 5 lin.), the thorax is slightly broader, the last segment of the abdomen has its apical margin produced into a short obtuse lobe, the surface of which is depressed and concave, and the hinder thighs are more incrassate, in all other respects it agrees with the other sex.

Duboulaia fulva, n sp

Elongata, subcylindrica, fulva, nitida, subtus pube adpressâ dense vestita, supra glabra; thorace subcordato, sub-crebre punctato, medio vittâ obsoletâ instructo, elytris parallelis, sub-crebre punctatis, utrisque vittis quatuor impunctatis instructis Long 6½ lin

Hab Western Australia; a single specimen collected by Mr. Duboulay.

Head coarsely punctured, sparingly clothed with adpressed hairs; clypeus depressed, wedge-shaped, distinctly separated from the face. Thorax slightly longer than broad, sub-cordate, somewhat closely punctured, on the middle of the disk is an impunctate, ill defined vitta, most distinct, and slightly raised on the basal half. Scutellum semi-ovate, pale piceous. Elytra broader than the thorax, their surface more finely and less closely punctured than the latter, each with four impunctate vittæ, abbreviated near the apex and not raised above the general surface of the disk, running parallel and close to the suture is a single sulcate stria Hinder thighs thickened, armed beneath near the apex with a short tooth.

Duboulaia rugosa, n. sp.

Oblonga, convexa, nigra, tibiis elytrisque castaneis; his ruguloso-punctatis, pube adpressâ sub-squamiformi sparse obtectis,
suturâ, margine exteriori, ante medium dilatatâ, vittulisque nonnullis nigris, thorace sub-cordiformi, rugoso, foveolato-punctato,
pube sub-squamiformi vestito.   Long 5 lin

Hab. Western Australia; a single specimen in my cabinet
from Mr. Duboulay's collection.

Head coarsely rugose, closely foveolate-punctate, sparingly
clothed with adpressed whitish hairs; eyes sub-cuneiform, their
inner margin nearly straight; antennæ about two fifths the
length of the body.   Thorax longer than broad, sub-cordiform,
flattened on the disk, rugose, foveolate-punctate, in each puncture is inserted a single adpressed, sub-squamiform white hair,
Elytra much broader than the thorax, truncate at the base,
oblong-ovate, convex, coarsely punctured, the punctures, which
have each a single adpressed hair similar to those of the thorax,
arranged in striæ near the suture, placed irregularly on the disk;
interspaces between the striæ smooth, those on the outer disk
coarsely elevate-reticulate; humeral callus thickened, prominent,
bounded within by a double row of punctures, the interspace
between which is raised and sub-costate.   Body beneath clothed
with adpressed whitish hairs, pleuræ, tibiæ and tarsi castaneous.
Hinder thighs thickened, armed on the lower edge near the apex
with a row of small teeth

This remarkable insect, of which I know but a single specimen (probably a ♀), differs from the typical species, *D. flavi-*
pennis, in having the spine on the lower edge of the hinder
femora replaced by a row of small teeth

Polyoptilus Lacordairei.   Germ.

Fœmina.   Thorax subcordiformis, pube adpressâ sparse vestitus, elytris abbreviatis, apice divaricatis, femoribus posticis
inermibus.   Long 3–4 lin

The male of this species was alone known to Germar; the
female, although long existing in our collections, has hitherto
remained uncharacterized.

Polyoptilus Waterhousii, n sp.

Mas.   Elongatus, sub-cylindricus, piceus, nitidus, supra
(antennis exceptis) nigropiceus; thorace sub-cordato, distincte

punctato ; elytris punctato-striatis, ad marginem exteriorem et ad apicem confuse punctatis, obscure fulvis, sutura marginequc exteriori piceis, fascia lata basali, vitta brevi humerali punctoque prope suturam fulvis ornata, maculisque duabus, una prope medium, altera apicem versus positis, nigro-piceis ; clypeo 5-angulo, latitudine longiori; antennis modice robustis, articulis 4 to et 5 to. inter se æqualibus, utrisque 3 tio fere duplo longioribus. Long 5 lin.

Hab. Western Australia ; two males in my own collection brought over by Mr. Duboulay.

Very nearly allied to *P. Erichsonii*, Lac., both in coloration and in sculpture, it may however be at once known by the following distinctive characters The clypeus, which in *P. Erichsonii* is as broad as, or even slightly broader than long, is in the present species distinctly elongate ; the antennæ are more robust, the third and following joints being distinctly flattened, the third is scarcely more than half the length of the fourth and fifth, these joints being of nearly equal length—in *P. Erichsonii* the third joint is longer, and the third, fourth, and fifth gradually increase in length ; the thorax in the present species is shorter, its broadest portion being nearer the apex than in the older insect.

Polyoptilus pachytoides, n. sp

Elongatus, sub-cylindricus, nigro-piceus, nitidus, femoribus basi tibiisque (his apice exceptis) pallide rufo-piceis ; elytris fulvis, utrisque limbo maculisque duabus, prope marginem lateralem positis, nigris. Long. 4½ lin.

Hab Western Australia ; collected by Mr. Duboulay.

Head rugose, sparingly clothed with adpressed whitish hairs ; clypeus elongate, pentagonal, its apex wedge-shaped, extending upwards between the encarpæ ; labrum, anterior edge of clypeus, apex of jaws and the palpi piceous ; antennæ nearly equal to the body in length, second joint very short, third and fourth each three times the length of the second, equal, second, third, and fourth joint stained with piceous. Thorax about a third longer than broad, cylindrical, slightly depressed on either side the disk, sides constricted just behind the middle, surface rugose, coarsely punctured, sparingly clothed with adpressed whitish hairs Elytra much broader at the base than the thorax, gradually attenuated to the apex, coarsely punctured, shining, rugose

Polyoptilus Pascoei, n. sp,

Mas. Elongatus, angustatus, sub-cylindricus, piceus, nitidus, thorace sub-cordato, ante basin paullo constricto, distincte punctato; elytris parallelis, punctato-striatis, interspatiis convexis, sub-costatis. Long 4½ lin.

Hab. Western Australia; a single specimen collected by Mr. Duboulay.

Clypeus longer than broad, pentagonal, its apex very acute; upper portion of face and vertex closely punctured, clothed with adpressed hairs; eyes very large and prominent, shining black; antennæ equal to the body in length, second joint very short, third one half longer than the second, fourth more than twice as long as the third, fourth and following joints slightly compressed. Thorax longer than broad, sub-cylindrical, constricted in front of the base; surface glabrous, strongly but not very closely punctured. Elytra broader than the thorax, parallel, strongly punctate-striate, interspaces convex, sub-costate, extreme apex of elytra irregularly punctured. Hinder thighs armed beneath near the apex with a single tooth

Lamprolina Jansoni, n sp.

Elongata, convexa, subtus metallico-violacea, nitida, thoracis apice et lateribus, abdominis apice pedibusque rufo-fulvis, tarsis nigris, supra rufo-fulva, antennis (articulo basali excepto) læte cæruleis, scutello obscure æneo, elytris coeruleo-viridibus, tenuiter punctatis, punctis ad suturam et ad marginem exteriorem striatim dispositis, thorace transverso, utrinque intra marginem foveolato, disco lævi. Long. 3½–4 lin.

Hab. Rockhampton, Australia.

Head smooth, clypeus separated from the face by a semi-circular groove, from the upper edge of which run three grooved lines, the middle one short and perpendicular, the lateral ones oblique and extending upwards and outwards towards the upper angle of the eye, antennæ rather more than half the length of the body, the basal joint, and occasionally the basal half of the second, rufo-fulvous, the rest dark metallic blue Thorax twice as broad as long, sides parallel, converging in front, anterior angles acute, scarcely produced; disk slightly convex, smooth, impunctate, or only impressed in some specimens with a few fine punctures, sides thickened, separated from the disk by a row of deep, strongly punctured fovea Elytra slightly broader than thorax, elongate-ovate, narrowly rounded at the apex; convex, finely but distinctly punctured, punctures arranged in longitudinal rows on the inner disk and near the outer margin, irregularly placed on the remainder of their surface. Abdomen shining violaceous, last two segments violaceous.

Lamprolina impressicollis, n. sp.

Elongata, convexa, nitida, subtus æneo-violacea aut obscure metallico-purpurea; thoracis apice et lateribus, abdominis apice extremo, pedibusque rufo-fulvis, tarsis nigris, supra rufo-fulva, capite piceo, antennis (basi exceptâ) nigris, thorace rude punctato, utrinque intra marginem excavato-foveolato; elytris metallico-viridibus aut metallico-cœruleis, distincte punctatis, punctis ad suturam et ad marginem exteriorem striatim dispositis. Long. 4 lin.

Hab. Champion Bay; Rockhampton.

Clypeus transverse semi-ovate, smooth, finely punctured, separated from the face by a semi-circular groove, above which is a coarsely punctured depressed space; antennæ half the length of the body, robust, slightly increasing in thickness towards the apex, bluish black, two lower joints rufous. Thorax twice as broad as long, sides diverging from base towards the apex, suddenly converging at the apex itself, anterior angles acute; above coarsely and irregularly punctured, rufo-fulvous, basal and anterior borders narrowly edged with piceous, lateral margin thickened (more especially towards the anterior angle) and separated from the disk by a row of coarse irregular foveæ. Scutellum obscure rufous, more or less tinged with æneous. Elytra broader than the thorax, parallel, convex, distinctly punctured, the punctures arranged in striæ on the inner disk and near the lateral margin, irregularly placed over the rest of the surface. Abdomen with the lateral margin of the penultimate and the entire margin of the ultimate segments narrowly edged with rufous.

Stethomela fraternàlis, n. sp.

Oblonga, convexa, rufo-fulva, nitida, antennis (basi apiceque exceptis) nigris, pectore abdomineque plus minusve æneo-tinctis, supra viridi-metallica, thorace fortiter punctato, punctis æneo-micantibus, hic · illic irregulariter congregatis; elytris infra humeros foveis nonnullis irregulariter impressis, distincte punctatis, punctis in striis gemmellatis dispositis. Long. 5 lin.

Hab. Port Bowen, Queensland, (*Simson*)

Mouth rufo-fulvous; clypeus very short, transverse, separated from the face by a deep groove, above which is a closely punctured triangular space; antennæ slender, about half the length of the body, four or five joints at the base and the apical half of the terminal one rufo-fulvous, the rest black. Thorax twice as broad again as long, sides straight and parallel, rounded and converging in front, anterior angles acute; upper surface coarsely punctured, the punctures collected in irregular patches on the

E

disk, more crowded and larger on the sides. Elytra slightly broader than the thorax, sides parallel, apex broadly rounded; above convex, sides impressed below the shoulders with three or four irregular foveæ; strongly but not coarsely punctured, the punctures irregularly placed in eight double rows on each elytron; interspaces smooth, impunctate. Prosternum, metasternum and abdomen almost entirely æneous, hinder thighs also with an æneous tinge.

Stethomela limbata, n. sp.

Oblongo-ovata, convexa, nitida, subtus picea, thorace, metas-terno, femoribusque rufis; supra rufo-testacea, verticis maculâ, thoracis maculis tribus, transversim positis, scutelloque nigro-piceis, antennis, nigris, elytris viridi-æneis, regulariter punctato-striatis, utrisque flavo-limbatis.   Long. 3⅔ lin.

Hab. Australia.

Clypeus very short, bounded above by a slightly angular trans-verse groove, apex of jaws black; front with a transverse nigro-piceous patch, the anterior margin of which is tri-lobate. Thorax nearly three times as broad as long, sides straight and slightly converging to the apex, anterior angles obtuse; surface finely punctured, disk impressed on either side towards the outer margin with a large fovea; a large ill-defined patch covering the middle of the disk and a small one on either side, sub-rotundate, nigro-piceous.

Stethomela cornuta, n. sp.

Ovata ♂, oblongo-ovata ♀, subtus obscure cuprea, supra rufo-cuprea, aureo-micans, thorace sparse hic illic punctato; elytris regulariter punctato-striatis, interstitiis lævibus.

Mas.   Mandibulis porrectis, forcipatis, apice acutis.   Long. ♂ 4 lin.; ♀ 4½ lin.

Hab. Port Bowen, Queensland, (*A. Simson*).

This species is remarkable not only in the genus but also in the whole family for the peculiar form of the mandibles in the ♂, in that sex these organs are large, forcipate and strongly pro-duced directly forwards, their apices being acute and their inner surfaces deeply grooved, in the ♀ on the contrary they are of the normal size and form; antennæ slender, one third the length of the body. Thorax twice as broad as long, sides rounded and converging from base to apex, disk sparingly punc-tate. Elytra broader than the thorax, broadly ovate, moderately convex, regularly punctate-striate, the interspaces between the striæ smooth, impunctate; below the humeral callus are several large indistinct foveæ.

Description of a new species of the Lucanoid genus Cantharolethrus, *Thomson; by* Major F. J. SIDNEY PARRY, F.L.S.

C. Steinheili, Parry, n. sp. (♂ var. med.).

C.·niger, nitidissimus, glaberrimus *Mandibulæ* elytris paulò
breviores, robustæ, arcuatæ, supra leviter canaliculatæ, intus
prope basin binodoso-dentatæ, ad apicem fortiter bifurcatæ, et
dente.acuto·subarmatæ *Caput* fere quadratum, antice emarginatum, disco triangulariter excavato, sub lente sparsim irregulariter punctulatum, clypeo parvo, nodoso, vix conspicuo. *Antennæ*
elongatæ, articulis cylindricis, clava grisco-velutinosa. *Prothorax*
transversus, sparsim punctutatus, in medio longitudinaliter canaliculatus, postice impressionibus duabus sat profunde notatus,
lateribus antice dilatatis, marginibus minute serrulatis, angulis
posticis obliquis, emarginatis. *Elytra* glabra, linea marginali
reflexa, punctata, humeris prominulis spina minima nodosa
instructis. *Scutellum* sparsim punctulatum *Pedes* punctati,
tibiis anticis apicem versus tuberculis ·minutis irregulariter
armatis. *Subtus* pectore, capiteque lateribus varioloso-punctatis.
Long. corp unc. 1, mandib. lin. 5.

Hab. Columbia; sp. un Mus. Steinheil.

. For the opportunity of describing this new and interesting
species I am indebted to Mr. Edward Steinheil, of Munich, who
has kindly entrusted it to me with other interesting Lucanoid
Coleoptera found by him in his recent travels in Central America.

Mr. Steinheil informs me that he found two specimens only,
♂ and ♀ (dead), in the month of March, near Santa Rosa, in the
central Cordilleras, between Cartago and Mauizales; the same
traveller also discovered examples, ♂ and ♀, of *C. Luxeri*, but
in a different locality, (East Columbia) ⁻ The female of the latter
is evidently identical with the insect recently described as *C
Luxeri* ♀, from a specimen in the British Museum, by Mr.
Charles O. Waterhouse, (Cist. Ent. I, p 364), and will probably
prove identical with *Pholidotus Reichei*, Hope, the type specimen of which is now in Mr. Thomson's collection, and has been
noted by him (Ann. Soc. Ent. Fr. 4e. Ser. II) as being possibly

the ♀ of *Cantharolethrus Luxeri.*   *C. Steinheili* is closely allied
to *C Buckleyi*, (Trans. Ent Soc , 1872, p. 77, Tab. 1, figs. 1
and 2), but is at once distinguished by its more conspicuously
dilated thorax, by its head being almost quadrate instead of narrowed at the base as in *C. Buckleyi*, and further by its mandibles being opaque and slightly concave on their upper surface
instead of shining and convex, moreover their apical bifurcation
is much stronger and the sub-apical tooth more acute and situate
closer to the apex : judging from the extraordinary difference in
the size of the female, the *var. max.* of the male must prove to
be of very considerable magnitude.

C. Steinheili, Parry, n. sp. (♀. var max).

C. niger, capite prothoraceque nitidis, valde varioloso-punctatis, elytris subvelutinoso-opacis.

Mandibulæ depressæ, granulosæ, apicibus acutis.   *Caput* magnum, quadratum, angulis anticis rotundatis, in medio ad basin
sat profunde foveatum   *Antennæ* nigræ, capite mandibulisque
paulo longiores, articulis cylindricis, clava griseo-velutinosa.
Prothorax transversus, valde varioloso-punctatus, in medio
late canaliculatus, disco irregulariter rugoso-lineato ; lateribus
semicirculariter arcuatis, regulariter minute nodoso serratis; angulis posticis emarginatis, vix dentatis   *Elytra* paulo depressa,
sub lente crebre regulariter punctata , humeris prominulis, tuberculo minuto nodoso instructis, linea utrinque erosa sinuata, ab
angulo humerali fere ad medium discendente, notata   *Scutellum*
nitidum, grosse et profunde punctatum, linea laterali glabra.
Corpus subtus nitidum, grosse et profunde punctatum; abdomen
minute punctulatum   *Tibiæ* omnino muticæ.   Long. cers.
(mandib incl.) unc. 1, lin. 3.
   Hab. Columbia   Mus. Steinheil.

Both from the description and figure of *C Reichei* it is impossible, I think, as has been suggested to me, to affiliate thereto
the insect now described.   The very remarkable difference in the
form of the thorax is alone sufficient to separate the two species ;
in *C. Steinheili* this segment is considerably wider, with the
sides evidently more arcuate and much less serrated, and finally
the strong spine, so prominent in the posterior angle of *C. Reichei*,
is totally absent, and I reiterate my opinion that *C. Reichei* will
in all probability prove to be the ♀ of *C. Luxeri.*

Descriptions of new species of Heteromerous Coleoptera, *with synonymical notes*, *by* CHAS. O. WATERHOUSE.

Ceropria madagascariensis, Dej. MS

In the British Museum there are specimens with this name attached They agree well with Fairmaire's description of *C. Coquerelii*, (Ann. Soc. Fr., 158), except that the interstices of the striæ of the elytra are said to be "fere planis," and the fourth interstice "reliquis paulo angustiore."

In the Museum specimens the interstices are distinctly convex, (the striæ being very strong), and I can perceive no difference in the width of the interstices. Should there prove to be two species, it may be convenient to adopt Dejean's name.

Hab Madagascar, (*Crossley*). B.M.

Meloe compressipes, n. sp

Cæruleus, subtus nigro-cæruleus, capite crebre fortiter punctato, vertice canaliculato. Antennis articulis tribus apicalibus atris Thorace longitudine haud latiori, supra plano, crebre fortiter punctato, antice omnino rotundato, postice paulo angustato, lateribus rectis ; basi leviter emarginato, disco fortiter canaliculato. Elytris thorace paulo latioribus, at $2\frac{1}{4}$ longioribus, postice paulo ampliatis, fortiter longitudinaliter rugatus, margine interno regulariter arcuato. Abdomine confertim minus fortiter punctato, segmento ultimo et penultimo supra medio fere impunctato. Pedibus compressis.

Long. (sine abdom.), 9 lin.

Resembles *M. Chevrolati*, Fairm., but differs in having the thorax rounded in front ; in having the antennæ thickened towards the apex, the apical joint being large and a little longer than the two preceding joints taken together. The head is very strongly and thickly punctured ; the thorax is more strongly but rather less thickly punctured The elytra are covered with strong rugæ which are longitudinally confluent, the internal border is gently arcuate, (and not angulate as represented in the figure of *M. Chevrolati*).

Hab, Madagascar. B.M.

Zonitis nigripes, n. sp.

Obscure-testaceus; ore, antennis, pectore, pedibus elytrorum-que apice nigris. Capite nitido, subtiliter, punctulato   Thorace nitido, obsolete punctulato, longitudine vix latiori, ante medium rotundato angustato, postice vix angustato.   Elytris thorace duplo latioribus, breviter pubescentibus, confertim subtiliter punctatis, singulis costis tribus vix perspicuis ornatis.

Long. 7¾ lin , lat 2½ lin.

Head a little narrower than the thorax, rounded behind the eyes   Antennæ long, reaching to the middle of the elytra. Thorax gently convex, with a slight impression in the middle near the posterior margin   Elytra with the shoulders rounded, with the apical fifth black ; each with three obsolete costæ, the first and third abbreviated

Hab. Madagascar.   B.M.

Zonitis purpureipennis, n. sp.

Viridi-aureus, violaceo-micans   Elytris purpureis, parce forti-ter punctatis   Abdomine cupreo-micanti.   Long. 6½–8 lin.

Golden-green, with deep blue reflections.   Head irregularly punctured.   Antennæ long, blue, with the apex dull black. Thorax scarcely longer than broad, much narrowed in front of the middle, flattened above, shining-blue, sparingly and obscurely punctured in front, with a central channel and three punctures on each side of it strongly impressed   Scutellum golden-green   Elytra broad, slightly convex, bright purple, shining, with large punctures scattered over the surface   Coxæ black , legs blue.

Hab. Australia, Victoria.   B.M.

Zonitis violaceipennis, n. sp.

Niger, nitida ; elytris violaceo-purpureis.   Long. 6 lin.

Head very long and narrow, nearly impunctate, scarcely nar-rower behind the eyes.   Thorax a little longer than broad, very slightly convex, not punctured but with a strong central channel and a round fovea on each side of it behind the middle ; sides nearly parallel behind, gradually narrowed in front.   Elytra broad, with deep punctures irregularly scattered over the surface.

Hab. Swan River.   B.M.

This and the preceding species are very closely allied. They both have purple elytra, but the colouration in other respects is different; the punctuation of the elytra in the present species although still sparse is less so than in the preceding species. The head in *Z. purpureipennis* is broadest across the eyes, and obliquely narrowed behind, whereas in the present species the sides are nearly parallel The thorax in the former is flattened above, suddenly narrowed in front, but in this it is gently convex, and gradually narrowed in front.

The males of both species have the penultimate segment of the abdomen deeply triangularly emarginate, and the last segment excavated.

Zonitis tricolor, Le Guillou, (1844)

This is a common species which has the elytra æneous with the base yellow. I am convinced, however, that the *Z. æneiventris* of Redt., (Reis. Novara), is only a variety having the elytra entirely yellow. Both forms are received from Melbourne, Moreton Bay, &c.

Zonitis flaviceps, n. sp.

Nigrescens, sat nitidus ; capite flavo ; clytrorum basi margini-busque anguste flavo-piceis. Long. 4½ lin

Head triangular, yellow, broadest at the posterior angles, not very thickly punctured, with a longitudinal impressed line in front Thorax black, shining, gently convex, narrowed slightly behind, more so in front, as broad as the head, not visibly punctured, with a longitudinal impressed line behind. Scutellum rounded at the apex Elytra one-third broader than the thorax, parallel, pitchy-black, very thickly and somewhat strongly punctured, the extreme base and the lateral margins dirty-yellow. Underside of the body and legs pitchy-black , claws pitchy.

Hab. Swan River. B.M.

Note.—I have just had occasion to refer to Blanchard's figure and description of *Bolitophagus angulifer* from New Zealand It appears to me to be without doubt the insect described by Fabricius as *Dermestes scaber*, (the type of which is in the British Museum), and known in our catalogues as *Pristoderus scaber.*

Opatrum serricollis, Walker, belongs to the genus *Bradymerus*, (Bolitophaginæ).

Rygmodus pedinoides, White, as figured and described by Blanchard, (Voy. Pol. Sud.), has little in common with White's insect which I have already recorded as belonging to the *Hydrophilidæ*; Blanchard's insect appears from the figure to belong to the *Helopidæ*.

Tanychilus metallicus, White, as figured and described by Blanchard is an *Amarosoma*, (*Helopidæ*). *Tanychilus* of Newman belongs to the family *Cistelidæ*, and as the genus was well known to White, (Newman's types being in the Museum), it would seem highly probable that Blanchard's insect is quite distinct from White's, especially as we possess a species of *Tanychilus* from New Zealand, which agrees very nearly with White's description.

Notes on the Coleopterous Family Cleridæ, *with descriptions of New Genera and Species ;* by the Rev. H. S. Gorham.

In preparing the present paper on the Cleridæ, I have found myself obliged to deviate in some measure from my original plan.

I had intended at the first to attempt a complete revision of the family,—a work that a very slight acquaintance with the catalogued species would soon make it apparent to any one was needed. But as I went on I found it impossible to gain acquaintance (excepting in certain genera) with more than half the described species ; and this from the very reason that former authors have found themselves situated as myself. Attractive as a family from their varied patterns and colouring, nearly every author of note has added his quota to the list of species, the types of which are scattered or lost , while few possessed any general knowledge of the family as such, and hence referred their species to genera with which they often have no affinity. In revising the family it will be necessary, then, to commence with the genera, which under such treatment have often become mere collections of heterogeneous species.

I have kept before myself in this work the necessity of (I.)—Indicating the true type of every genus, or at least of selecting the type from the original constitution, where none was fixed by the founder. II.—Eliminating from the genus such species as could not be associated with the type without rendering any definition useless. III —Creating new genera for such of these species as could not be brought into any existing ones.

Cistula Entomologica,
August 7th, 1876.

F

In the first place then I have given as I hope in a succinct form an analytical "Table of Genera" compiled from the characters given by Spinola, Lacordaire, and others, using, however, only such as I have been able to verify; this is followed by observations on such genera as appear generally misconstrued; concluded by critical remarks on the species and a list of synonyms

The collections which are the basis of this paper are firstly, the collection of Mr. W. W. Saunders, containing a great many of Mr. Wallace's species from the Malay Islands, as well as a fine series of South American and Australian insects; this collection has passed into my own hands. Secondly, the Cleridæ of M. Guérin Méneville containing several old and scarce species. Thirdly, those obtained in the Philippine Isles by Dr. Semper. And lastly, several Cleridæ being my own collection from various sources chiefly obtained through Mr Janson I have had the advantage of consulting Mr. White's and Newman's types in the British Museum collection, access to which has freely been given me by the authorities there

With Mr Chevrolat I have been in correspondence frequently, and have to acknowledge his goodness in communicating to me types of a few of his species, as well as in examining several species sent by me to him, nearly all which were returned as new to him. The result is that in the present paper 66 species are described as new in the two first sub-families, and 5 new genera established. This appears to me as a mere instalment of what requires to be done before a systematic arrangement can be settled, or any general conclusion drawn from the distribution of the Cleridæ Of North American species I have seen but few, though they must be numerous

The system followed is in general that of Lacordaire, very nearly corresponding as well with the order of the genera in the catalogue of MM Gemminger and Harold, to which constant reference will be made, as being the only complete list of published species up to 1869 Since that date M. Chevrolat has described 112 species, Revue et Mag. de Zool 1874, and I have just received a second Memoir from the same author, ("Memoire sur la famille des Clerites," par A. Chevrolat Paris 15 Mars, 1876,) containing the addition of three new genera *Poecilochroa, Tarandocerus, Dereutes,* reference to which will be found in their proper place here, and of 118 new species, of which I am at present unable to speak, being unacquainted with them except by the descriptions there offered. I shall only here allude to those species concerning which I have had communications with M. Chevrolat.

CLERIDÆ.

Synopsis of Sub-families.

		All the joints of tarsi visible above	Tillides.
five jointed, pro-thorax without parapleuræ.	four joints only visible above.	Eyes cut out in front . . .	Clerides.
		Eyes cut out on internal sides	Phyllobenides.
		Eyes entire	Hydnocerides.
four jointed, pro-thorax with p.		Antennæ pectinate or at least with some joints serrate . .	Enoplides.
		Antennæ terminate by a club .	Corynetides.

(Tarsi.)

I. TILLIDES.

Synopsis of Genera.

A. Antennæ at least serrate.
    a. Body glabrous,—labrum not visible .   Cylidrus.
           do.   do   distinct . Denops.
    a a. Body more or less pubescent.

F 2

b.   Claws bifid,—with tooth   .   .   .   Tillus.
     do.   without tooth   .   .   Perilypus.
b b. Claws simply toothed.
c.   Antennæ gradually enlarged   .   .   Philocalus.
d.   Antennæ of ♂ with apical joint very long   Macrotelus.
e.   Antennæ flabellate or serrate   ·   .   Cladiscus.
f.   Antennæ almost filiform   .   .   . Cymatodera.
b b b Claws cut out   .   .   .   .   .   Pallenis.
AA.   Antennæ with 3· or 4-jointed club.
a.   Claws bifid, without tooth   .   .   Gastrocentrum.
a a. Claws toothed.
b.   Antennæ with 3 jointed club abrupt   .   Callimerus.
c.   do.   do.   laxly articulate   Stenocylidrus.
a a a. Claws simple ·   .   .   .   .   . Dupontiella.

Cylidrus, Lat. 1825.

Type C cyaneus, Fab.

Cylidrus alcyoneus, Pascoe, *Cylidrus pallipes*, Chev, Rev. et Mag de Zool. 1874, p 29., *Cylidrus Vescoi*, Fairmaire, *Cylidrus cyaneus*, Fab

These all appear to pertain to one species   It is widely spread from Madagascar to the Islands of the Pacific, the only continental locality given being India ; C. *pallipes* Chev. was originally referred to Taiti and Java (White Cat. B. M p. 1.)   The smaller and narrower specimens are probably males, and it varies in colour from purplish to blue-green

Cylidrus Wallacei, Thomson

Readily known by its black legs, and wider and brighter elytra. Borneo. I have a specimen from Penang, differing a little in the punctuation of the thorax, but I doubt if it is distinct

Epiteles contumax, Newm. Ent. p. 403, G and H. Cat. Col p. 1786. Certainly a *Cylidrus*, very nearly allied to if not the same as *C. nigrinus* White.

Cylidrus balteatus, Klug.

Chiefly differs from *fasciatus* by the black abdomen.
Cylidrus abdominalis Klug. Given as = *fasciatus* in Gemm. and Har. Cat. Col. but without the locality Brazil. There is, however, most clearly a *Cylidrus* closely allied to *fasciatus*, differing in the form of the fascia, from Brazil   I think it may be a transported species which has obtained a settlement and become modified. The name must stand as specific

DENOPS, Steven

Type D. albofasciata, Charp.

Differs only from *Cylidrus* in the porrected labrum and developement of the tarsal lamellæ.

PHILOCALUS, Klug.

Type P. succinctus, Kl.

Judging by the figure and locality, *Tillus compressicornis*, Klug. ought to be referred to this genus rather than to *Macrotelus*.

MACROTELUS, Klug.

Type M. terminatus, Say.

Macrotelus subnotatus, Wwd., G. and H. Cat. 1723.
Macrotelus uniformis, Wwd , G. and H. Cat. l. c.

These African species cannot be retained here.

Macrotelus sanguineus and *Mniszechii*, Thoms., [Chev. Mem. 1876 p. 44] must be eliminated ; they are probably *Philocali*.

CLADISCUS, Chev

Type C. strangulatus, Chev.

Cladiscus gracilis, White, *C Prinseppi*, Wh
C longipennis, Wwd., as well probably as the rest described
differ from the type in having the antennæ pectinate   I do not,
however, think they can be separated generically.

TILLUS, Oliv. 1790.

Type T. elongatus, Lin.

Tillus bipartitus, Blanch , G. and H. Cat. p 1724. = " *Tillus
bifasciatus ?*, Humb " Chev Mem 1876. p. 4. *Tillus
(Clerus) carus*, Newm., G and H. Cat 1 c. These species
do not pertain to the *Tillides*   The former most resembles a
Thanasimus but has the palpi all securiform ; while the second
forms the type of a new genus, *Paratillus*.

Tillus hilaris, Westwood is congeneric with *bipartitus* which it
much resembles

Tillus Semperanus, n sp

Niger, antennarum basi, palpis, femorum basi, tibiis, tarsis,
elytrisque basi rufis, his fasciâ fere rectâ, maculâque sub-apicali
albidis. Long. lin. 2½.

A very distinct little *Tillus* ; compared with *unifasciatus* the
following differences will be observed, the base of the antennae,
i.e., the first three or simple joints are pale, as are also the tibiæ
and tarsi ; the thorax is very much narrowed behind, the base
of the elytra is only narrowly red, and they are also adorned
with a pale spot before the apex.
Hab. Bohol Philippines (Semper.)

Obs. I have a specimen referred to *notatus*, Klug from India
which closely agrees with the species described above, *notatus*
Kl. should have the breast red, as well as the disc of the thorax
only black.

GASTROCENTRUM, Genus novum.

Caput prothoracis latitudine, oculi modice granulati antice excavati.

Palpi max. articulo ultimo oblongo , lab eodem securiformi

Pronotum æquale antice transversim impressum postice constrictum.

Antennæ 11-articulatæ, capite et thorace breviores, articulis 2–7 perbrevibus, haud intus acuminatis, 8–11 his latiores.

Mesosternum inter coxas intermedias carinatum et productum carinâ post coxas profunde fossulatum.

Abdominis segmentum primum inter coxas posteriores mucionatum, metasterno receptum.

Tarsi 5-articulati, articulis 4 primis valde lamellatis.

Corporis forma elongata.

Type G. pauper, sp n

Gastrocentrum pauper, n. sp

Nigro-piceus nitidus pube brevissima griseo-flava vestitus, ore, palpis, antennis, pedibus, abdominisque apice rufopiceis Long. lin. 6

Head shining, irregularly and obsoletely punctate, pitchy, epistoma and mouth yellow, jaws blackish, eyes not very coarsely facetted, cut out, a carina runs from the incision. Pronotum very obsoletely and confluently punctured, a curved impression in front, and narrowed and rather constricted at the base, nearly twice as long as wide, of about the same width as the head at the widest part. Elytra half as wide again as thorax, sides parallel, with rows of oblong punctures at uneven distances, and vanishing near the suture and in the apical third ; they are clothed with a fine, grey, silkly pubescence. Leg pitchy-red, underside pitchy. The metasternum is produced into a process between the intermediate coxæ, which is deeply sulcate, the abdominal process is also sulcate, and both are pointed.

Hab. Luzon, Philippines (Semper.)

PERILYPUS, Spin.

Type P. carbonarius, Spin.

PALLENIS, Cast.

Type P. tricolor, Cast.

If *acutipennis* be taken as the type, the name *Jodamus* must be retained for the genus.

STENOCYLIDRUS, Spin.

Type S. azureus, Klug.

CYMATODERA, Gray.

Type C. Hopei, Gray.

It seems probable that the smaller species associated with this type will eventually have to be separated.

Cymatodera pulchella Wh , G. and H. Cat. Col. p. 1727, does not pertain to the *Tillides.* It is, I think, a *Pelonium.*

[BOSTRICHOIDES, Montrouzier.]

(*Type B. angustatus,* Mont.)

Not admissible among the *Cleridæ* without confirmation. The characters given are discordant with the group, without any evidence being offered of its affinity.

DUPONTIELLA, Spin. -

Type D. ichneumonoides, Spin.

Dupontiella fasciatella, Spin. Mon II. p. 172. pl. 8. fig. 5 = *Tarsostenus univittatus* Rossi.

Remarkable as not having lamellæ to the tarsi, yet apparently not to be placed in any other family.

CALLIMERUS, Genus novum.

Caput latum, oculi subtiliter granulati, prominuli, antice profunde sed anguste excavati, hirtuli. Antennæ art. tribus vel quatuor ultimis clavam compressam formantibus. Palpi max. art, ult. subulato, lab his multo longiores, art. ult. valde securiformi

Pronotum oblongum, medio latissimum

Elytra elongata apice interdum truncato (type), interdum etiam mucronato, (*C. mirandus*), vel integro, (*C. amabilis, C. gratiosus*) Tarsi 5-articulati articulo basali facile observato.

Type [*Clerus.*] *dulcis* Westwood, Proc. Zool. Soc 1852 p. 50. Gemm. et Harold Cat. Col. p. 1736. Hab. E. India, Siam, Ins. Philippines.

= *Xylobius*, White, Cleridæ p. 50 (*X albovarius*) nec. Lac Genera des Col. IV. page 119.

There are two types of insects which I think should be associated in this genus, some which like the type have the body and elytra of a steel blue colour elegantly spotted and marked with spots of ashy or white scales, while the others are of an uniform testaceous hue, or spotted with that colour, the elytra and parts of the body more or less thickly clothed with scales

It is one of the most peculiar genera among the *Cleridæ*, while its 5-jointed tarsi bring it into close connection with the *Tillides*, the finely granulated eyes, widely separated antennæ with a simple 3-jointed club composed of joints closely applied to each other, and sometimes truncate elytra are characters not hitherto recorded in that section. The species which I conceive to belong to the genus as yet known to me are ·

Sec. 1.　Elytra blue with spots or lines of scales.

Callimerus dulcis Westw. loc. cit Java, Siam.
C. *albovarius* Westw. loc cit. E. India.
Gem. et Har., p. 1735 (*Clerus.*) White Cleridæ, p. 50 (*Xylobius.*)

Callimerus mirandus, n. sp.

Cœruleus, squamis albidis variegatus, ore, antennis, pedibusque flavis. Elytris lunulis tribus, prima humerum cingente, secunda et tertia hac conjunctis, apicibus in marginem desinentibus, apice oblique truncato angulo externo mucronato.　Long, lin. 5, ♂ ♀ Hab. Penang.　[Coll. Saunders]　Parry.

Face thickly covered with white scales, (especially the ocular excavation) Prothorax oblong, sides widened in the middle. Elytra conspicuously punctured, the punctures often coalescing, their apex obliquely truncate, the internal angle having a very small mucro, the external a larger one Legs antennæ, and part of the mouth pale yellow, exterior of the tibiæ darker The margin of the thorax, base of elytra, three spots near to their margin (connected by an angulated line) scutellum, breast and sides of abdomen are clothed with white scales. Underneath the fifth segment is deeply emarginate, and ciliated.

Callimerus amabilis, n sp

Ater, ore, antennis, pedibusque flavis, prothoracis marginibus lineâque mediana, pectore, abdomine, elytrorum basi, maculisque tribus albo-squamosis Long. lin. 4½.

Head covered with scales between the eyes, less thickly on the crown Thorax more narrowed behind than in front, black, granulose, rather shining near front margin and with a blue tinge there. Elytra black granulate-punctate, the patches of scales consist of the base, an oblique mark from the scutellum to near the outer margin, a central spot on the suture, a fascia one third from apex, and the suture narrowly from thence to apex. Exterior of femora and tibiæ dark, mandibles black.

Hab. Laos. A single specimen [Mouhot.]

Callimerus gratiosus, n. sp.

Ater, capite atro-cœruleo plus minusve squamis albidis ; prothorace (medio excepto), scutello, elytrorum macula basali, fasciis tribus suturâ interruptis, guttisque duabus suturæ approximatis, metasterni, abdominisque limbo albo-squamosis ; ore antennis, pedibusque flavis Long lin 4.

The elytra of this species are more parallel than in the preceding species. The prothorax is equally narrowed before and behind, and not much enlarged in the middle ; the elytra are opaque, deeply and coarsely punctured, but not granulose, the markings are more or less connected in different specimens, the apical fascia returns up the suture till it almost unites with the preceeding one, the legs are very hairy slightly darker at the knees and exterior of femora and tibiæ.

Hab. Philippines. East Mindanao [Semper.]

Callimerus pulchellus, n. sp

Albo-squamosus, prothorace guttis quinque, elytris guttis sex, limbo tenuiter, atris, denudatis ; ore, antennis, pedibusque flavis. Long. lin. vix 4.

In the denuded spots on the elytra their sparse deep puncturing is visible, the thorax is little narrower than the head, the sides somewhat angularly widened, the legs are hairy but with no darker marks

Hab Philippines [Semper.]

Sec. 2. Species of an uniform ochreous colour

Callimerus insolutus, Pascoe [*Lemidia.*]

Pallide ferrugineus, capite et thorace subnitidis, elytris pube brevi et squamis griseis undique vestitis, apice truncato. Long lin. 4–5.

Head obsoletely punctured, shining, thorax with a few large punctures, a linear constriction in front and an impression on each side about the widest part, it is considerably constricted behind ; the elytra are widest near the base, gradually narrowed to near the apex, obsoletely punctured, the punctures tending to form series. In some specimens the elytra are dark at the humeral angle, and at the sides The abdomen has the apex darker, legs hairy, tarsi and apex of tibiæ of the hinder pair dark.

Hab. Siam [Mouhot] ; Luzon, E. Mindanao [Semper] , Celebes [Wallace.]

Sec 3. Elytra fasciated, without scales, club of antennæ 4-jointed.

Callimerus latifrons, n. sp.

Nigro-piceus, nitidus, labro superne, palpis labialibus, antennarum clavâ, pedibus totis, elytrorum fasciâ basali, maculâque pone medium reniformi pallide testaceis. Long lin 4.-

Head wider than thorax, in front clothed with grey scales,
antennæ basal joint and four at apex testaceous, the rest pitchy,
club not so abrupt as in preceeding species and of four joints,
maxillary palpi pitchy, pale at tip   Thorax constricted in front,
much narrowed behind, punctured. Elytra coarsely and thickly
punctured, a basal fascia (widest in centre) and two kidney-
shaped spots, almost touching suture, yellow ; apex truncate.

Hab. Philippines [Semper.]

II. CLERIDES.

Synopsis of Genera.

A. Antennæ serrate
a. Palpi all securiform ; tarsi 5 joints visible,   Axina.
b   do.   tarsi 4 joints only visible, Serriger.
a a max: palpi, last joint cylindric,—
c. eyes coarsely facetted   .   .   .   Priocera.
c c. do. finely   do.   .   .   .   Tillicera.
A A   Antennæ forming a flat club   .   Placocerus
A A A. Antennæ with 3 or 4 jointed club.
B. Claws simple
C. Palpi all securiform.
d. Antennæ with apical joint long   .   Phloeocopus.
d d.   do.   not long, club laxly articulate,—
e. form depressed, eyes coarse   .   Thaneroclerus.
          do   eyes fine .   .   .   Platyclerus.
f. form subcylindric, eyes coarse .   .   Opilo.
f f.   do.   eyes fine.
g. hind femora longer than body .   .   Olesterus.
h. do. not longer, elytra rugose at base Trogodendron.
h h. do. do. elytra evenly punctured   .   .   Sallea.
d d d. Antennæ with club connate
i. form narrow, cylindric   ˙   .   .   Tarsostenus.
j. form depressed   .   .   .   .   Aulicus.
k. form broad, bulky   .   .   . · .   Zenithicola.
C C   Labial palpi only securiform
l. eyes coarse, elytra sub-parallel .   .   Natalis
          do.   elytra contracted at base .   Cormodes.

l l   eyes fine, elytra contracted at base   .   Pezoporus.

m.   do.   elytra not contracted
         club of antennæ lax   ,   .   .   Cleronomus.

n.   do. not lax, tarsi with lamellæ of
         ordinary size   .   .   .   .   Epiclines.
         —of very small size   .   . ,   .   Calendyma.

B B. Claws toothed.   .

o.   Antennæ almost filiform   .   .   .   Derestenus.

o o.   do.   with club lax and long.

p.   terminal joint falciform, eyes fine,
         widely separated   .   .   .   .   Clerus.

q.   separated by a narrow band   .   .   Stigmatium.

1.   —approximate   .   .   .   .   Omadius.

p p. terminal joint simply acuminate   Cleromorpha

o o o. Antennæ with club lax but not long,
         eyes coarse, scarcely cut out   .   Orthrius

         do.   do,   well cut out

s   Palpi same shape at apex   .   Eburifera.

t.   Palpi different, max only securiform   Thanasimus.

o o o o. Antennæ with club abrupt.

u.   terminal joint excavate   .   .   Scrobiger, Eleale.

u u.   do.   not excavate   .   .   Trichodes.

v.   Antennæ with club securiform   .   .   Erymanthus

The following genera placed among the *Clerides*, I have not
seen characterised, and am unable to tabulate, *Apteroclerus* Woll.,
Microclerus, Woll , *Micropterus*, Chev , *Dereutes*, Chev.

PRIOCERA, Kirby.

Type P. variegata, Kirby.

AXINA, Kirby.

Type A. analis, Kirby

Chiefly differs from *Priocera* in having both pairs of palpi
securiform.

It is surprising M Chevrolat should have referred *Thanasimus marmoratus*, Kl (*Chinensis*, F.) to this genus, to which both it and his *Axina retrocincta* [Rev. et. Mag. de Zool. 1874 pp. 32, 33.] have merely a superficial, and not a very strong likeness   They have the antennæ with a lax 3-jointed club, and the labial palpi only securiform.

PHLOEOCOPUS, Guérin.

Type P. tricolor, Guérin.

Sexual characters are noticeable here, the males have the longer apical joint of antennæ, and fifth abdominal segment cut out

Phloeocopus Buqueti, Spin. Mon. I. p. 340, plate 18, f. 3. appears ill placed in this genus, and would be more naturally referred to *Thanasimus*   It is unknown to me except from description.

OPILO, Latreille.

Type O. mollis, L. ?

The distribution of this genus is remarkable, it being found in apparently every part of the world excepting North America, but only represented in South America by a single Chilian species, *punctipennis* Chevr.

I have seen specimens of the type from the Philippines, and Mr. Lewis found it in Japan.

Opilo apicalis White, Cleridæ p. 19, App. p 56. (*Notoxus*) *O. apicalis*, Chev, Rev. et Mag. de Zool 1840 p 296, *pinustus* Ch. Rev. et Mag. 1874 p. 285 has the priority.   I would, therefore, propose the name of *Whitei* for the former.

Opilo sinensis, n sp.

Rufus, subnitidus, tenue pilosus, capite et pectore nigro piceis, elytris piceis vel nigro piceis, maculâ humerali obliquâ, alterâque apicali, et fasciâ medianâ a suturâ interruptâ aurantiacis   Long lin. 4½—5½

Antennæ, mouth, palpi, prothorax, legs and abdomen red, thorax with a constricted line in front and near hind margin, a little wrinkled transversely on the disc, but not channelled. The markings on the elytra in one of my specimens are of a beautiful orange red

Hab   Foochow, China [G. Lewis.]

Opilo Pascoii, n sp.

Niger, nitidus, antennis, palpis, pedibus, elytrorum basi, pectoreque rufis, thorace glabro, antice transversim, medio fortiter sulcato, margine basali constricto albido , elytris pone medium fasciâ communi apiceque summâ albâ, usque ad fasciam fortiter seriatim punctatis, inde ad apicem glabris.   Long lin 4½

In colour singularly like *Paratillus bipartitus*, but in addition to its larger size it is not likely long to be confounded with that species, the thorax being smooth and shining and the legs longer with much less compressed femora   The Elytra have 7 or 8 rows of very large square punctures, a little confused at the shoulder and continued into the white fascia, *but not beyond it.* The sixth ventral plate is red.

Hab   New South Wales. [Pascoe.]

NATALIS, Castelnau

Type N cribricollis, Spin.

Notwithstanding that Castelnau's characters may have been erroneous, the fact remains that *cribricollis* was the species to which he applied the generic name   Chevrolat's note [Mem sur la famille des Clerites p 4] is founded on a confusion, there is no " *O cribricollis*, Spin , du Chili "   *N. Laplacei* was referred to Chili in error

CORMODES, Pascoe

Type C. Darwini, Pascoe

Tillicera, Spin.

Type T javana, Spin.

Tillicera mutillæcolor, White, is a *Stigmatium* described by the author from a specimen without antennæ; the naming mutilated and unique specimens is scarcely an excuse for such an oversight. It has been redescribed by Chevrolat as *Stigmatium dimidiatum*, Rev. et Mag 1874, p 63.

Serriger, Spin.

Type S. Reichei, Spin.

Serriger Coffini, White, Cler App p. 53 has no affinity here, the antennæ have a 3-jointed club It falls in Chevrolat's genus *Salleu*

Placocerus, Klug.

Type P. dimidiatus, Kl.

Apteroclerus, Woll

Type A. fusiformis, Woll.

Pezoporus, Klug.

Type P. coarctatus, Kl.

Derestexus, Chev.

Type D quadrilineatus, Chev.

Microclerus, Woll.

Type M. Dohrnii, Woll.

Micropterus, Chev.

Type M. brevipennis, Chev.

Cleronomus. Klug.

Type C bimaculatus, Kl.

M. Chevrolat (Mem. 1876, p 5) points out that the 11 species standing under the name in G. and H Cat. p 1732, 1733 really belong to five distinct genera, viz —

1. *Cleronomus*, K. 2. *Phonius*, Chv., *Type sanguinipennis*, Chv.
3. *Systenoderes*, Spin. *Type amœnus* Sp
4. *Colyphus*, Spin *Type C. signaticollis*, Sp , other species. *C. cinctipennis*, Sp , *interceptus*, Sp., *rufipennis*, Sp. and
5 *Poecilochroa*, Chev *Type cyanipennis* Kl , which he says equals *dasytoides*, White, Cler. p 50 (*Systenoderes*), this latter genus being characterised briefly (loco supra cit) and including *thoracicus* Ol (*Clerus*, Spin.) and a new species, *Haagi*, Chv.

I have not seen *Colyphus* or *Phonius* ; *Poecilochroa* is most like *Cleronomus* , and *Systenoderes* is certainly a distinct genus

THANASIMUS, Lat.

Type T formicarius, L.

If the rigorous rule were observed this generic name could not stand, Fabricius having been the first to indicate a type for *Clerus* in *formicarius*, L. But in this case a fresh term would be needed for the species of the *ichneumoneus* type, and nothing but confusion can arise from disturbing the present accepted arrangement.

Thanasimus accinctus, Newm forms the type of a new genus *Metabasis*.

Thanasimus anthicoides, Wwd , G and H. Cat. p. 1733 repeated sub *Clerus*, loc. cit. p 1735 It is better placed here.

Thanasimus apicalis Chev = *Opilo id* , Mem 1876 p 4

Thanasimus chinensis, F. = *marmoratus*, Kl. This species cannot rest here, yet, unless a new genus be made for it, it can scarcely be placed elsewhere It has no affinity with *Axina* to which Chevrolat refers it. The antennæ have 3-jointed club, and max. palpi are cylindric

Thanasimus marmoratus, Chevr , G and H. Cat p 1734 = *marmoratus* Kl., *chinensis*, F. loc cit p. 1733

G

Thanasimus rufimanus, n. sp

Niger, nitidus, pilosus, antennis, palpis tibiis anticis, tarsisque quatuor primis rufis, elytris apice fulvo pubescenti.   Long lin. 4.

Head rather narrower than thorax, eyes finely granulate, labium, palpi, and antennæ clear red, latter with the three last joints widened, terminal joint acuminate and a little curved. Thorax much as in T. *formicarius* clothed with long greyish pubescence. Elytra longer than those of *T. formicarius*, the series of large close punctures do not commence for one quarter the length and terminate a little beyond the middle ; a well pronounced humeral callus, the space between it and the scutellum tumid , the apex is densely clothed with a golden yellow shining pile. Legs blue-black, anterior tibiæ, and anterior and middle tarsi red

Hab   New South Wales, (Saunders).

ORTHRIUS, Genus novum

Type O. cylindricus.

Caput declivum, thoracis latitudine, oculi fortiter granulati, haud vel vix excavati.   Labium emarginatum, antennæ 11 art., articulis tribus ultimis clavam formantibus, laxe articulatam, ultimo apice acuminato   Palpi max. art. ult subulato ; lab. eodem fortiter securiformi.

Pronotum oblongum, antice transversim impressum postice constrictum.

Tarsi 4 antici, art. quinque supra prebentes , postici, 4 tantum visibiles

Corpus elongatum, sub-cylindricum.

Allied to *Thanasimus*, and also, in the structure of its tarsi, to *Clerus*.   It is more elongate and cylindric in form than either. The eyes scarcely if at all cut out, are very remarkable in this section.

Orthrius cylindricus, n. sp.

Rufo-ferrugineus, nitidus, antennis, pedibus, elytrisque piceis, his humero, fasciâ medianâ (suturâ interruptâ,) maculâque juxta apicem pallide flavis, Long lin. 4—4$\frac{1}{4}$.

Var fasciâ medianâ integrâ ad suturam ampliatâ, maculâque communi rotundatâ juxta apicem aurantiacis.

Head thickly and coarsely punctured, labium deeply excavated, pale yellow, thorax thickly punctured and somewhat granulose, transversely impressed in front as in *Thanasimus*, (channelled in the middle in the variety) contracted below the middle, and with a constriction just below the base   Elytra of the width of the thorax, sides parallel, covered with small punctures irregularly disposed, but having a tendency to form striæ, in the variety the interstices are slightly raised   In the type the humeral callus, a fascia near the middle (widening into a round spot near the suture) and a small spot near the apex are pale yellowish.   The variety is of a brighter rufous colour, and has the central fascia wider and expanded towards the base common to both elytra, as well as a largish spot in the place of the two near the apex.   Antennæ as long as head and thorax, joints 2-8 rather longer than wide, 9-10 a little widened, 11 oval, acuminate, and with the point re-curved.

Two specimens New South Wales, [Saunders] and two, *var.*, Coll. Parry.

METABASIS, Genus novum

Type Thanasimus accinctus, Newman, Ent p. 364.

Caput prothoracis latitudine, oculi subtiliter granulati vix excavati. Antennæ apicem versus paulo incrassatæ. Palpi max. art. ultimo fusiformi; lab eodem fortiter securiformi, tarsi 5 articulati, art 4 tantum visibiles supra

Considerable confusion exists about the species described by Mr Newman.

M Chevrolat has attempted to revive the genus *Chalciclerus*, Spin by associating it with another of Newman's species, *pulcher*. The latter is an *Eleale*, and the two species have nothing in common   Chev also gives *Zenithuola fulgens*, Chv as a synonym of C. *pulcher* Newm. [Mem 1876 p 5], C *bimaculatus*, Spin. is in my opinion quite distinct.

The present species is also (see Chevr, MS) *Lemidia inanis*, Germ. [Gem. et Har. Cat. Col. 1748.]

The ♂ is *Clerus medianus* Westw. White Cleridæ p 17 sub. *Thaneroclerus*.

Newman's original assignment of it to *Thanasimus* is nearest the truth. From that genus it differs in the structure of the antennæ, from *Clerus* in that of its tarsi which have four joints only visible above in the anterior and middle pairs (*Clerus* shewing 5.) From both, however, it diverges in the form and sculpture of the thorax, and in most minor details.

CLERUS, [Geoffroy], Fab.

Type *C ʼichneumoneus*, Fab.

It is clear that if we follow Fab., Spinola, and Lacordaire in adopting this name for the present genus, it must be on the hypothesis that it had to Geoffroy a family signification, and that he would probably have placed any insect belonging to the group under the term , any how, as he did not indicate a type there can be no reason why the first of his three species should be taken rather than either of the others.

I have seen no species from other parts of the world than America, which can properly be referred to this genus. It is, broadly speaking, peculiar to Tropical America, the species from the United States are abnormal.

Clerus albovarius, Wwd , G. and H. Cat. p. 1735. = *Callimerus id.* (*Tillides*) *vide ante*

Clerus anthicoides, Wwd , G. and H. Cat p. 1735. = *Thanasimus id.*, loc. cit. p. 1733.

Clerus dulcis. Wwd , G and H Cat. p 1736 = *Callimerus id.* (*Tillides* ante)

Clerus guttulus, White. G and H Cat p 1736 is congeneric with *Tillus bipartitus* (Ante p. 62). These Australian species are grouped under *Paratillus*

Clerus longulus, Spin G. and H Cat. p. 1736, evidently an *Epiclines* belonging to the section for which M Chevr has made the genus *Dereutes*, Mem. 1876 p. 29.

Clerus nodicollis, Bohem., Ins. Caff I. 2. p. 495 ; is an *Opilo*, and = *Opilo tuberculicollis*, Chev. Rev et Mag 1874 p 7, 33.

Clerus novemguttatus, Wwd., Proc. Zool. Soc. 1852 p. 49. G. and H. Cat. p. 1737 v. *Cleromorpha*, Gorh.

Clerus Paivæ, Woll., G. and H. Cat. p 1737 should probably form a new genus, it is certainly not a *Clerus*.

Clerus sobrius, Walker, G. and H Cat. p. 1738.
= *Clerus sphegeus*, Fab., G. and H loc. cit
Clerus thoracicus, Oliv. Spin , Lec., G. and H , loc cit
= *Poecilochroa id* , Chev., Mem. 1876 p 5 (v. *Cleronomus*)
Clerus zebratus Wwd , Proc. zool. soc. p. 43 is an *Omadius*.
Clerus annulatus, Eschsch , G. and H Cat p 1735. Gem and Har., Chevr., White, all give *C. variegatus*, Spin. as a synonym of this species, but incorrectly if the species generally known as *annulatus* is correctly determined.

Clerus femoralis, n. sp.

Niger, thorace piloso, elytris dimidio basali flavo, lineâ humerali alterâque ante medium curvatâ plus minusve distinctis nigris, apice griseo sericeo, femoribus rufis. Long lin. 4—4½.

Head sparingly punctured shining, antennæ black, basal joint red, spotted above with black , thorax densely clothed with black pile   The femora alone are red   Breast with a golden yellow depressed pile

Hab.   Parana, (Saunders).

Clerus sigma, n. sp.

Niger, nitidus, pube erectâ tenuiter vestitus, elytris maculâ basali (prope fasciam medianam curvatum angulose productâ) flavâ, apice griseo hispido   Long lin. 3½.

Entirely black with the exception of a spot at the base of the elytra continued along the suture till it nearly meets a curved middle fascia, which are yellow, this fascia starts from the margin, but does not quite touch the suture   The antennæ are short and stout   Head punctured clothed with ashy hair. Thorax with short, not close, black hairs   Legs with grey pubescence.

Hab.   Brazil, (Saunders.)

Clerus binodulus, n. sp.

Rufo-testaceus, prothorace, (margine antico pallido excepto) capite antennis pedibusque nigris, his femoribus basi, illis articulis duobus primis rufis, elytris basi rufis, tuberculis duobus humeroque elevatis, pone medium fasciâ curvatâ apiceque albidis, inter fasciam et apicem nigris, in apice pallido, strigâ nigrâ. Long. lin. 4½.

Elongate, parallel, head rather shining, thorax with the extreme front margin pale yellow Elytra finely rugose at the base, and with a few elevated lines but not striate, the first of these elevated lines terminates in a raised long tubercule half-way between the suture and the humeral callus, which is rather prominent About the middle of the margin, a narrow pale fascia commences which curves backwards to the suture, this is margined with black on the basal side, the apical third is pale and contains an oblique blackish fascia. The last segment of the abdomen is black Base of the antennæ, and of the femora red

Hab. Peru, Amazon, (Saunders).

This species is apparently allied to C. *mutabilis*, Chev. (Rev. et Mag. de Zool 1874 p 40) and in the pattern of the elytra resembles *versicolor*, Lap.

Clerus festivus, n. sp.

Rufus, antennarum clava, prothoracis disco tibiisque fuscis, elytris basi binodulosis, medio flavo-fasciatis, pone fasciam nigris, apica maculâ rotundâ croceâ, angulo apicali albido Long lin. 4.

Head pitchy-red, pubescent, mouth pale, mandibles black, thorax densely clothed with pile varying in colour as the portions do, front margin and sides and base red, disc pitchy. Elytra roughly punctured at the base, the shoulder raised, and each with a tubercule covered with erect black setæ, about the middle a curved whitish yellow fascia commencing on the margin but scarcely reaching the suture, margined with black on the basal side, beyond this the elytra are pitchy-black, with their apical angle white, and with an orange yellow round spot (similar to that in *annulatus* Kl but smaller) near the apex, this spot is rather shining Underside and legs red, posterior femora touched with pitchy on their underside, apex of abdomen and tibiæ darker

Hab. Amazon, (Saunders)

Clerus Salvini, n. sp.

Niger, pilosus, elytris nigris, basi rubris, rugose sub-seriatim punctatis fasciâ medianâ curvatâ basin versus nigro-marginatâ, alterâque apicali interrruptâ albidis, vel rubis Long. lin. 3½.

Head and thorax a little shining, sub-coriaceous ; basal joint of the antennæ, terminal joint of the labial, and maxillary palpi excepting the tip pitchy-red. Epimera of the meso- and meta-sterna red. Legs entirely black

Hab. Guatemala

Obs Differs only from *decussatus*, Kl. by the colour of the thorax, legs, parts of the mouth, and underside. I have one specimen (Salvin) taken at an altitude of 5000 feet, also another from the same locality (Saunders).

Clerus gaudens, n. sp

Niger, nitidus, punctatus, elytris maculâ basali oblongâ, alterâque apicali transversâ, fasciis duabus in medio, primâ arcuatâ augustâ, secundâ latâ ad suturam attenuatâ, albidis ; hac extus miniatâ. Long lin 3—3$\frac{1}{2}$

Head and thorax punctured, latter with a transverse arcuate impression disappearing in the side, base constricted, length greater than width . Elytra most distinctly punctured in the middle, on the sides, punctures having a tendency to form lines The first spot is elongate oval, then a fascia, beginning about one third below the shoulder on the margin, not reaching the suture, then a broad sub-quadrate spot on the margin of a fine vermillion red terminating in a yellow point near the suture, a yellow transverse spot near apex. The rest of the insect is entirely black.

Hab. Parana, (Saunders).

Obs. Somewhat resembles *miniatus* and its allies.

Clerus hieroglyphicus, n. sp.

Elongatus, niger, nitidus, prothorace margine antico griseo pubescente, elytris macula triangulari prope suturam, fasciâ medianâ a sutura interruptâ, apiceque summo albido-testaceis, ante apicem fasciâ pubescente indutis. Long lin. 4$\frac{3}{4}$.

Unlike any species of this genus known to me.

The two wedge-shaped spots immediately before the fascia form together an equilateral triangle narrowly divided (as well as the fascia itself) by the suture, with its point towards the apex of the elytra, the fascia commences on the margin, its edge towards the base is rounded and almost meets the other side, near the suture, which side is straight, the extreme apex is yellowish (the suture however and margin narrowly black) and is preceeded by a band of grey pubescence narrowest near the margin.

Hab. Amazon, (Saunders).

Clerus felix, n. sp

Niger, nitidus, antennis, palpis, pedibusque rufis, elytris fasciâ medianâ ad suturam interruptâ albidâ, apice cinereo-pubescente. Long. lin. $2\frac{3}{4}$—$3\frac{1}{2}$.

Somewhat resembling *fluvosignatus* but narrower and with the legs and antennæ and palpi clear red, last 6 joints of antennæ fuscous, mandibles pitchy, fascia of the elytra narrower than in *fluvosignatus*, contracted to a point before reaching the suture, elytra obsoletely punctured (in one of the two individuals I possess there is a tendency to become striate) a distinct sutural stria commences one third from the base

Hab. Parana, (Saunders).

Clerus Badeni, n. sp.

Fuscus, sub-opacus, crebre subtiliter punctatus, elytris thoracis latitudine, nigro-fuscis, basi et suturâ anguste rufo-piceis fasciâ medianâ latâ alterâque ante apicem pallide flavis, apice piceâ, antennarum basi articuloque apicali rufis, pedibus fuscis, femorum basi, tarsis et corpore rufis.   Long. lin. $5\frac{1}{4}$.

Head clothed with ashy hairs.   Thorax less thickly pubescent, very closely and irregularly punctured, with a curved transverse obsolete impression in front   Elytra little wider than the thorax, parallel, very thickly but obsoletely punctured, each with two fine raised lines, indistinct but visible with a common glass ; their base is rufous with a spot of red hairs on each side of the scutellum, a transverse and rather irregular yellow band at the middle, and a narrow oblique one before the apex

Hab Mexico, (Dr. Baden).

Apparently allied to *C. crabronarius*, Spin

Clerus errans, n sp.

Rufus, elytris thorace latioribus, fasciis duabus, anteriore integrâ, posteriore a suturâ interruptâ, pectore, pedibusque nigris. Long. lin. $3\frac{1}{2}$.

Rather shining, clothed with a fine erect pile. Head with a deep double fovea between the eyes, antennæ pale red at the base, the basal two or three joints pitchy above, the club fuscous. Thorax with a few scattered punctures, not much narrowed behind, base margined. Elytra half as wide again as thorax, rather convex, sides parallel, apical half of suture with a stria, disc with indistinct and irregular series of punctures The narrow black fasciæ do not touch the margin, and the posterior one is indented on its front margin. Breast black, rest of underside red Hab.—? (Dr. Baden).

Resembles *C. bicinctus* Klug. The black legs and breast will distinguish it.

Clerus vulpinus, n. sp

Niger, supra dense tomentosus, capite, prothorace disco nigro excepto, elytrorum basi apiceque, rufo-villosis, elytris fasciis duabus (anteriore interruptâ) nigris, a fasciâ medianâ flavâ, fere nuda, separatis, sutura antice cinereo pilosâ Long. lin. 4¾.

Var. ? a. Minor, elytrorum basi nigro, pilis rufis fasciato, fasciâ medianâ flavâ ad suturam interruptâ. Long. lin. 4.

Thorax very globular, nearly as wide as elytra, densely clothed with rufous pile, black in the centre, anterior constriction scarcely visible. Elytra cylindric, base narrowly and apex widely rufo-villous, two black nearly straight fasciæ (the anterior interrupted) and a median pale yellow one, the latter nearly denuded and showing distinct punctures Legs black with grey pubescence Antennæ with two joints at the base red.
Hab.—? (Dr. Baden). *Var.* Mexico, (Saunders)

Clerus cupriascens, n. sp

Capite et thorace nigro-æneis elytris sub-violaceis his multo latioribus, antennarum basi, ore, pedibus, abdomineque læte rufis, tarsis fuscis. Long. lin. 5½

Head and thorax very obsoletely and closely punctured, scarcely shining, finely pubescent, the latter with the base margined, and transversely impressed in front Elytra impunctate but with several rows of small tubercules, only distinct near the suture, and three raised costæ or lines on each, the first of which (or the one nearest the suture) coincides with a row of raised points, shoulders very prominent, beyond the middle a denuded curved fascia and a similarly denuded spot near the apex, round these the grey pubescence is thicker.

Hab -- ? (Dr. Baden).

Allied to *holosericeus*, White.

Clerus deliciolus, n sp.

Niger, nitidus, capite et thorace rufis, elytris maculâ basali, fasciisque tribus suturâ interruptis flavis, antennarum basi apiceque, palpis, femoribus (ex parte) tarsisque pallide testaceis, Long lin. 3.

Head and thorax glabrous, rusty red (in one example clouded with pitchy on the disc) clothed with a few dark coloured setæ, shining; antennæ with two or three joints at the base, and the club pale, the apical joint especially so, the rest pitchy.   Elytra blue black with a few scattered punctures, spots, 1 basal, nearly round, then a short broad fascia not touching margin, only a little oblique, then a fascia of same width starting from margin nearly straight, the apical fascia starts from margin, but leaves the apex and suture narrowly black.   Femora and tarsi pale, the former with their half next the tibiæ pitchy above, rufous beneath.

Hab   Amazon, (Saunders).

Clerus atriceps, n. sp

Rufo-testaceus, punctatus, nitidus, capite elytrisque nigris, his basi, fasciâ medianâ et apice flavis   Long. lin. 3½.

Head black, shining, sparsely and deeply punctured.   Thorax clear rusty red, the extreme front margin black, disc very sparingly, front more thickly, but less deeply punctured   Elytra with the basal half thickly and roughly punctured, almost striate, the large punctures irregular in shape and frequently united, yet on the whole arranged in rows, as far as the commencement of the apical yellow; their base (narrowly at the shoulder, more widely round the scutellum), a middle fascia (entire in some, interrupted by a fine line at the suture in others), and the apex for about a quarter the length of the elytron are pale yellow, the body, legs, antennæ and palpi pale red.

Hab. Guatemala, (Saunders), also from Aceytuna in the same district, at an elevation of 5,100 feet.   (O. Salvin).

Clerus melanocephalus, n sp.

Rufo-testaceus, nitidus, capite, thoracisque margine antico nigris, elytris violaceis fasciâ latâ in medio, punctisque duabus parvis prope apicem testaceis Long. lin. 3¼

Somewhat resembing the preceeding, the head is narrower, and almost glabrous, thorax clear testaceous red, except the front margin which is black as far as the anterior constriction, smooth Elytra violet with a wide band a little behind the middle, and two small round spots before the apex testaceous, shoulders more raised than in *atriceps,* elytra as far as the middle with a few scattered small punctures, not arranged, and only visible under a strong lens.

Hab. Para.

CLEROMORPHA, Genus novum.

Type Clerus novem guttatus, Westw. (G. and H. Cat. p. 1737)
Hab. Australia, Brisbane, &c.

Differs from *Clerus* in many particulars. Antennæ with 4-jointed club, terminal joint not falciform Tarsi with 4 joints visible only above ?

This genus is proposed for the little insect described by Mr. Westwood from Australia, although it somewhat resembles a *Clerus* in outline, it has little in common with any American species A careful dissection would, I have no doubt, reveal further discrepancies I think it sufficient here to indicate the type of my genus, it being a well known species.

THANEROCLERUS, Spin

Type T Buquetii, Lefebr.

PLATYCLERUS, Spin

Type P. planatus, Cast.

AULICUS, Spin.

Type A. Nero, Spin. ?

Lacordaire takes *instabilis* Newm as the type, but in his Monograph Spinola seems to consider *Nero* to be so, and *instabilis* is figured [pl. 28, fig 1.] without antennæ. I think there is no doubt the American species must be separated from the Australian, and would suggest the name *Phlogistus* for the latter genus. I have not, however, ventured on the alteration at present, not having had an opportunity of examining any American species referred to this genus Chevr. [Rev. et Mag. de Zool 1874 p 48] describes three species from Cuba, *basicollis*, *albo-guttulatus*, and *bilineatus*.

Aulicus bilæniatus, Spin. II p 148, G. and H. Cat. p. 1739 forms the type of his genus *Musca*, and notwithstanding Lacordaire's note, Gen. des Col p 452, it seems that this species must be dissociated from the remainder The club of the antennæ is serrate.

AULICUS, Spinola

Aulicus imperialis, n. sp.

Cæruleus, nitidus, thorace violaceo, disco fossulato, lateribus fortius ampliatis, - elytris fortiter striato-punctatis, lateribus purpureis. Long lin. $3\frac{1}{2}$–4

Head blue, distinctly rather coarsely punctured, a small shallow fovea between the eyes Antennæ and palpi yellow. Thorax with its sides very much widened below the anterior constriction, and equally narrowed before and behind, disc much depressed, bluish violet above, blue beneath Elytra with rows of closely packed large square punctures, ceasing before the apex, those nearest the suture and margin terminating first, of a beautiful blue at the suture as far as the first row of punctures and to the second near the scutellum, the remainder of a fine coppery violet or purple Legs blue, purple above

Hab. Queensland, (Saunders).

Aulicus sculptus, Mc Leay, Tr. E S N.S.W., 1875 (*Thanasimus.*)

Subtus cæruleus, capite thoraceque æneo-piceis, elytris fortiter striato-punctatis, fasciâ medianâ purpureâ, vel violaceâ, basi, apiceque purpureo, æneo, viridique variegatis. Long lin $3\frac{1}{2}$–4.

Head punctured, eyes not prominent, thorax a little wider than head, rather thickly and distinctly punctured, disc even, anterior constricted line deep, sides not much widened but evenly rounded. Elytra at their base fully twice the width of thorax, a little narrowed below the shoulder, with rows of transverse rather obsolete punctures, which reach neither the base nor the apex, the base itself is smooth, a little tumid near the scutellum, this portion is bluish encircled by crimson copper shading off into brilliant golden and finally blue, the same colours being repeated in inverse order beyond a median purple fascia, which is much widened at the margin and suture. Underside blue, abdomen black. Antennæ and palpi testaceous, legs blue, tarsi pitchy, anterior pair fuscous red

Hab Rockhampton, Queensland In most collections

Obs. This species is sometimes wrongly referred to *Necrobia eximia*, White, *Aulicus splendidus*, Chev, Rev et Mag. de Zool 1874 p. 15 seems to me to be the same. It differs a little in facies from typical species of the genus, especially in the prothorax less widened, and with a rectilinear constriction in front.

Aulicus albo-fasciatus, n. sp.

Niger, subtus viridi-cæruleus, capite et thorace crebre punctatis, elytris fortiter punctato-striatis, ante medium albo-fasciatis, apice ferrugineo, lævi, antennis, palpis, tarsisque anticis testaceis. Long. lin vix 4

Above black, scarcely shining, body beneath and legs bluish green, anterior tarsi testaceous, middle and hind pairs pitchy above. Thorax with the sides rounded, widest in the middle, moderately depressed on the disc. Elytra widest at the base, thence narrowed gradually to near the apex. with about 10 series of large square punctures vanishing just before the rusty yellow apex, a little before the middle is a nearly straight white fascia, interrupted by the sutural stria which is pitchy throughout.

Hab. Rockhampton, Queensland.

Aulicus smaragdinus, n sp

Viridis, nitidus, capite thoraceque sparsim punctulatis, elytris fortiter punctato-striatis, punctis transverso-quadratis, ante apicem evanescentibus, antennis, palpis, pedibusque rufis, genubus intermediis et posticis piceis. Long. lin. 2¾.

The head and thorax in this neat little species are rather brassy, and very shining. The elytra are of a clear emerald green, brassy near their margin.

Hab. Queensland

Aulicus affinis, n sp.

Longior, viridis, nitidus, capite thoraceque parce leviter punctatis, elytris punctato-striatis, basi sublævibus, palpis antennis, pedibusque anticis testaceis, posticis subtus rufis. Long. lin. 3

Possibly only a variety of the preceeding, from which it differs in being longer and less depressed, of a deeper and bluer green, the head and thorax being finely punctured, the punctures on the elytra more closely packed, being almost crenate striate. the middle and hind legs having the femora dark, only red in part beneath, the tibiæ and tarsi of these almost entirely dark,

Tarsostenus, Spinola

Type T. univittatus, Rossi.

Sallea, Chevrolat.

Type S. necrobioides, Chev.

This genus has been erected by M. Chevrolat, Rev. et Mag. de Zool. 1874 p. 35, for two insects which are, he says, congeneric with the insect known to us as *Serriger Coffini*, White, if so it cannot be placed, as he suggests, near *Chariessa* among the *Enoplides*. I have not seen either of M Chevrolat's species, and base my observations on *S. Coffini*, the latter is certainly not a *Serriger*, but belongs to the *Clerides* and should, I think, be placed not far from *Trogodendron*, though departing widely from it in form.

Trogodendron, Guèrin.

Type T. fasciculatum, Schreib.

Trogodendron monstrosum, n. sp.

Nigrum, sub-opacum, elongatum, sub-cylindricum, capite cum thorace sparsim nigro-villosum, creberrime punctatum. Elytris thoracis latitudine, lunulâ medianâ, et guttâ obliquâ ante apicem, sutura approximatâ, eburneis, parum elevatis, inter his nigro-velutinis, a basi usque ad lunulam grosse seriatim punctatis. Antennis testaceis, articulo ultimo in ramis duobus longis obducto, pedibus nigris, tarsis rufis. Long lin. 5. ♂ ?

This very remarkable species is the only instance I have seen in this family of a bifid termination of the antennæ I have indeed heard that a species of *Scrobiger* has similar antennæ in the ♂, and it is to be presumed that the present is a sexual difference, rather than a mere monstrosity of which it has all the appearance , the four of five joints preceeding the last are strongly transverse, and the singular bifurcation springs from each side of the penultimate, each ramus is curved and compressed

Hab Queensland, (Saunders).

Scrobiger, Spinola.

Type S splendidus, Newm

Olesterus, Spinola.

Type O australis, Spin.

Olesterus gracilis, n sp

Niger, subnitidus, pilosus, capite et thorace subtiliter punctatis, elytris dimidio basali striato-punctatis, apice sub-lævi, cinereo pubescente, medio albo fasciato, antennis articulis tribus basalibus rufo-testaceis, pedibus longis, tibiis curvatis. Long lin. 3¾.

Head opaque, very closely and confluently punctured, thorax rather more shining, sides straight for half the length, then strongly narrowed to their base, a well impressed constricted line in front. Elytra sub-parallel, cylindric, the second interstice and humerus raised at the base , the punctured striæ produced to beyond the white fascia, terminating at the apical grey portion, below the fascia the punctuation is crenate   Legs hairy, black, all the tibiæ moderately curved.

Hab. Australia, (Pascoe).

Obs. I have not seen *Olesterus australis*, Spin   There is a species in the British Museum allied to it, and the present species I have little doubt is congeneric

EBURIFERA, Spinola.

Type E callosa, Klug.

It seems hardly likely that the two species added to this genus, *patricia*, Klug, G. and H cat. p. 1741, and *violacea*, Fab., G. and H cat loc. cit , can really belong to it

ZENITHICOLA, Spinola

Type Z. australis, Spin.

The vertical front of the mesosternum is remarkable, and makes this one of the best defined genera among the *Cleridæ* The added species differ somewhat in form from the type *Zenithicola fulgens*, Chevr., G. and H. cat p. 1741, = *Eleale (Chalciclerus) pulcher*, Newm., sec., Chev. Mem. 1876 p. 5

ERYMANTHUS, Klug.

Type E. gemmatus, Klug

TRICHODES, Herbst.

Type T. octopunctatus, Fab.

M. Chevrolat reinstates, and I think with reason, the following species which appear only as synonyms in G. and H. Cat *T. zebra*, Fald , *T. affinis*, Chv., *T. viridifasciatus*, Chv , and *T. carceli*, Chv.

In the case of *T. gulo*, Parreys, he has, however been misled by a merely sexual character,—the truncation of the elytra, which is only found in the female of *crabroniformis*

T. Olivieri, Klug, G. and H. Cat. p 1744 = *T. syriacus*, Spin Mon. pl. 20, f. 6, which name must stand. *T. Olivieri*, Chev. is quite distinct and has the priority.

CALENDYMA, Lac.

Type C. chilensis, Cast

Remarkable for the almost absent lamelle of the tarsi.

ELEALE, Newman

Type E. viridis, Guérin.

Lacordaire has pointed out that Spinola was in error in assigning simple claws to the tarsi, his character of their being heteromerous is also quite misleading, (Mon. I. p. 279, *Chalciclerus*)

Perhaps the best character is the excavation of the terminal joint of the antennæ, termed by Lac (Genera p. 462) "un faux article peu distinct" *Eleale* is a synthetic type, the same structure of the *antennæ* being seen in *Scrobiger*; while certain species show affinity to *Tricholes* (e g *lepida*), the pronotum is quite that of *Calendyma*

Eleale aspera, Newm. = I suspect, *viridis,* Guérin.

Eleale pulcher, Newm   I have shewn above [*Metabasis et Zenithicola*] that M. Chevrolat is confused with regard to this species. His notes, Rev et Mag 1874 p. 20 —Mem. 1876 p 5., cannot apply to Newman's insect which is a typical *Eleale.*

Eleale bimaculata, Spinola is, in my opinion, notwithstanding Chev. note, Mem p. 5, quite distinct from *pulcher,* Newm

Eleale scrobilatus, Spin Mon. I p 156 (*scrobiculata,* G. and H. Cat. 1745) is probably an *Aulicus*; Spinola, as not unusual, gives a wrong reference to pl 15 fig. 6   Fig 4 is given as *foveolatus* Newm., and this is no doubt the insect described, and is not an *Eleale.*

Eleale simulans, Pascoe, G and H. loc cit, is a variety of *lepida,* Pascoe without doubt.

Eleale opiloides, Pascoe, Ann and Mag N. H 1876 Vol xvii. p. 51, the genus is, as Mr Pascoe observes, doubtful, but it has no affinities here. It is, in fact, as I suspect most New Zealand *Cleridæ* will prove to be, a new genus

Eleale lanata, Chev. Rev et Mag 1874 p. 20 = *simplex,* Newm. ♂., Chev Mem 1876 p 22.

H.

Eleale Aulicodes, n. sp.

Viridis, subnitidus, crebre sub-rugulose punctatus, antennis fuscis, viridi-micantibus, femoribus apice, tibiis tarsisque extus cupreis. Long. lin. 4.

Short, brilliant emerald green, closely, deeply, and somewhat rugosely punctured Elytra a little more coarsely punctured in the basal half than near the apex. Legs green at the base, the extreme tip of femora, and tibiæ externally, bright coppery ; two last joints of antennæ strongly transverse, the apex emarginate, truncate

Hab, N.W Australia, (Saunders).

Eleale brevis, n. sp.

Brevis, sub-depressus, obscure viridis, sub-nitidus elytris crebre punctatis, apice fere glabris, antennis flavis, pedibus obscure cupreis. Long. lin. 3¼.

Head greenish, shining, not very closely punctured, front impressed between the eyes. Thorax with the sides evenly rounded, more closely and coarsely punctured, punctures confluent. Elytra rather flat on the disc, humeral angles prominent, forming right angles, and a little polished, the sides shewing a slight tendency to purplish copper, extreme apex smooth, yet with a few scattered punctures Antennæ yellow, terminal joint quadrate, compressed at its apex. Legs black with a coppery reflection. Underside clothed with ashy grey hairs

Hab. Freemantle, Australia.

Eleale latefasciata, n. sp.

Nigro-æneus, sub-opacus, subtus nigro-cæruleus, elytris fasciâ mediânâ latâ fulvescente, apice nigro-cæruleâ, crebre confuse punctatis, antennis palpisque testaceis. Long. lin 3½.

Head and thorax thickly and confusedly punctured, brassy black, a little shining between the punctures, eyes deeply cut out, antennæ and mouth yellow, apical joint of former though excavated, yet but narrowly so at its apex, and not on its side. Elytra brassy black at their base, the shoulders rather prominent and shining, a wide fulvous fascia, widest on the margin where it is nearly equal to half the length of the elytron, the apical third or rather more bluish black ; the extreme apex smoother, shining, legs brassy black, the four anterior tibiæ and the tarsi fuscous. The breast, a spot in front and one at the base on each side of the thorax, scutellum and extreme tip of the elytra are clothed with white depressed hairs.

Hab. Rockhampton, Queensland.

Synopsis of Species.

A —Apex of elytra not smoother than the rest.
  unicolor, Spin. — *viridis*, Guérin — *Reichii*, Spin. — *aulicodes*, Gorh

B —Apex of elytra smooth and brilliant.
a —Elytra unicolorous.
  excavata, Westwd.—*brevis*, Gorham.—*obscura*, Newman. —*simplex*, Newman.—*intricata*, Klug, Spin

b — Elytra with a fulvous spot or fascia
  bimaculata, Spin —*latefasciata*, Gorh —*pulcher*, Newm.

b. b.—Elytra with a fascia and fulvous apex
  lepida, Pascoe —*var simulans*, Pascoe.

c.—Elytra yellow, apex black
  sellata, Pascoe.

EPICLINES, Chev.

Type E. Gayi, Chev.

It is not easy to follow M. Chevrolat's views on this genus It is given twice in his catalogue (Rev et Mag. pp. 21, 23,) followed by certain species detached under the name *Eurymetopum*, Blanch. The latter name is inadmissible, vide Lac. Genera p. 463 note (1) ; it is in fact a synonym of the Chilian genus

Chevrolat has more lately, Memoire sur la Fam. &c. 1876 p 29, described a number of species under the generic title *Dereutes* It is not clear what are the characters which distinguish this genus from *Epiclines*, or that M Chevrolat is acquainted with the type of Blanchard's genus [*maculatus*, Bld.], or what species he regards as the type of *Dereutes* It would seem to be Chevrolat's view that only two species (*Gayi* and *Basalis*) are to be retained under *Epiclines*. Nor can the genus be included among the *Hydnocerides*. The eyes being (though slightly) emarginate, I see no reason to depart from the position assigned it by Lacordaire, Chevrolat and others.

Epiclines costicollis, Spin. Two specimens of this from Mr. Lewis were found, as he assures me, at Hakodate, Japan.

HEMITRACHYS, Genus novum

Type H bizonatus, Gorh.

Caput prothoracis latitudine, oculi excavati, subtiliter granulati, mandibulæ fortiter dentatæ; palp. max. art. ult. filiformi, lab eodem elongati, securiformi; antennæ articulis 5–11 compressis, subquadratis Pronotum granulosum, antice in tertiâ parte constrictum. Elytra ad basin pronoto latiora, inde gradatim angustata Tarsi articulo 2do duobus sequentibus longiores.

This genus is apparently most nearly allied to *Stigmatium*, the wide flat antennæ, (not serrate however), and granulose pronotum, are unlike anything to be found in that genus.

Hemitrachys bizonatus, sp. n.

Rufo-ferrugineus, capite, antennis, elytris, abdomineque nigris Elytris basi summo ferrugineo, fasciis duabus albidis, rectis, usque ad fasciam primam crenato-rugosis, inde ad apicem nitidis, fere glabris Long lin 4–4½

Head shining, front punctured. Thorax longer than wide, but much swollen below the front constriction, this part is strongly granulose on the disc; on each side is a rather large impressed point round which the granulations are absent, the base is strongly constricted but very close to the hind margin Elytra rugosely crenate-striate as far as the first pale fascia, the extreme base brick red, this colour continued a little down the suture, scutellum red, the second fascia is sub-apical, both are testaceous and clothed with bright yellow hairs Legs stout, rather short, femora red excepting the posterior pair, which with the tibæ and tarsi are black

Hab Singapore Borneo (Wallace)

STIGMATIUM, G. R Gray.

Type S cicindeloides, Gray.

The character (so constantly repeated) of the very short first joint of the tarsi is illusory, the basal or abortive joint is at least as easily visible in the majority of species as in *Omadius*; indeed apart from general facies (which form no guide in several abnormal species) the width of the head between the eyes, which here forms a band is the only constant character I can find, and in this it is approached by some *Omadii* The present addition brings the number described to about 60, and some revision with a comparison of types is needed

Stigmatium is more widely diffused than *Omadius*, extending to the African continent Both occur in Australia, *Stigmatium* predominating.

Stigmatium Philippinarum, n. sp.

Nigro-piceus, nitidus, palpis, pectore, abdomine pedibusque rufis, his femoribus intermediis atque posticis exparte, tarsisque nigro-piceis ; elytris basi granulosis, striato-punctatis, pube griseâ sericeo-micante variegatis Long. lin 5-7½ ♂ ♀ Femina segmento quinto abdominali apice exciso.

The principal characteristics which separate this species from the larger *Stigmatia* already described are the presence of a depressed sutural region extending for half the length of the elytra, expanding into a square patch of a lighter red than the rest of the elytra, this depression or flattened space being clothed with griseous hairs, (shining when viewed sideways, especially with the head of the insect towards one), and the *commencement* of a fascia of these hairs on the margin about a third from the apex, but no trace of the fascia towards the suture as in *rufiventre* &c , the apex itself is also densely clothed with them, with the exception of four minute spots which are nude The series of granules resolve themselves into punctures before the middle, the third and fourth being carried on a puncture or two further than the succeeding four striæ The granules 'in all these larger species appear to be the spaces between the punctures, which are raised, giving the idea of a rasp. Underneath the metasternum and abdomen are entirely red ; the middle and posterior femora are more or less pitchy at their apices, their tibiæ and tarsi pitchy. Antennæ pitchy black.

Hab Luzon (Semper.)

Stigmatium encaustum, n. sp

Nigro-piceus, nitidus, pectore, abdomine, coxis et femoribus rufis, elytris regione suturali antice, apiceque pube micante tenuiter vestitis. Long lin 6-7¾.

Almost nude, dark pitchy black, with a slight bluish tint on the elytra, the flattened portion of the elytra even more distinctly depressed than in the preceding species, of a pitchy red colour clothed with very fine yellowish hairs, the apex is also sparingly clothed, but there is scarcely any other trace of pile upon the elytra. The front of the head, sides of the thorax and breast, and legs with fine grey silky down. Antennæ nearly black. Labial palpi red, maxillary pitchy with paler apex

Hab. Bohol, Philippine Isles (Semper).

Stigmatium sub-fuscum, n. sp.

Fusco piceus, sub-nitidus, antennarum basi palpisque testaceis, abdomine rufo, elytris pilis flavis variegatis, fasciâ pone medium fere nudâ. Long. lin. 4–6

Distinguished by its generally dull pitchy colour, and antennæ with testaceous basal joint, femora and coxæ paler than the general ground colour, and red abdomen. The elytra have the usual rasp formed granulations but not more than eight series on each elytra, nor do they end in distinct punctures. The chief pattern to be discerned in the pile is a broad fascia about the middle, widest on the margin, and a reniform lunule beyond the nude band which separates these two markings; both, however, are very indistinct, and have only their edges clearly visible.

Hab. East Mindanao, Philippine Isles (Semper).

Stigmatium centrale, n. sp

Fuscus, abdomine et pedibus pallidioribus, his genubus atquo annulo in femoribus, tibiisque fuscis, elytris fasciâ latâ in medie pallidâ sericeo micante, humeris rufo-piceis. Long. lin. 3¾–4¼.

Head pale, spotted with fuscous, antennæ pale at base and apex, fine, hairy, thorax carinate at the base, two indistinct tubercules on each side of the disc below the anterior constriction, sides little wider than the base. Elytra distinctly punctate-striate, the striæ continued to near the apex, which is pale and sub-mucronate. Underside pale, the sides of the breast fuscous, but the meta-thoracic parapleuræ entirely red

Hab. East Mindanao; N.E Luzon (Semper).

Obs. This species has somewhat the facies of an *Omadius,* but the width of the head between the eyes, and the antennæ are related rather to *Stigmatium.*

Stigmatium tapetum, n. sp.

Fusco-piceum, striato-punctatum, elytris pone medium fasciâ tenui nigro-piceâ, femoribus quatuor posticis apice fuscis. Long. lin. 3–4.

Depressed, pitchy, varied with fuscous, and with patches of silky grey pile; the legs and antennæ, head and sides of the thorax are thickly set with fine setæ. Antennæ and palpi red, mandibles black. Width of the thorax in the middle about equal to the length. Elytra with series of distinct punctures as far as the narrow dark fascia, the latter nearly straight, produced up the margin towards the base; behind the fascia the grey pile is denser but exhibits small denuded spots, which are formed by little tubercules on the interstices of the striæ, which are continued without punctures to the apex, the latter more denuded and marked with fuscous. Breast pitchy, abdomen red.

Hab Mindanao (Semper). Sarawak (Wallace). Siam (Mouhot).

Stigmatium ? *iodinum*, n. sp.

Nigro-cyaneum vel violaceum, prothorace brevi transverso, antennis basi, palpis, pedibusque flavis, his tibiis nigris, abdomine testaceo. Long lin. 3.

Head and thorax very short, the latter with the disc rather depressed and the sides much rounded and very suddenly contracted to the base. Antennæ longer than head and thorax, thin, joint 2 short, 3 and 4 elongate, 5 to apex shorter, triangularly serrate, fuscous. Elytra with the sides nearly parallel, deeply punctate striate to the apex, dark steel blue or violet, mouth testaceous. Legs bright yellow, tibiæ obscure green. Underside steel blue, abdomen yellow

Hab —Mysol, Aru., (Wallace).

Stigmatium violaceum, n. sp.

Violaceum vel cæruleum, tenuiter pubescens, ore antennis (clavâ exceptâ), pedibus, abdomineque flavis. Long. lin. 3½.

Longer than the preceding, and more pubescent, head and thorax short, the latter sub-quadrate, sides moderately rounded, obsoletely punctured with a thin pubescence. Elytra punctate-striate, the striæ little distinct and almost-vanishing before the apex Antennæ shorter and stouter than in *iodinum* joints 8, 9, 10 alone serrate, club fuscous. Legs entirely pale yellow.

Hab —Mysol, Dorey, (Wallace).

Stigmatium scapulare, n sp.

Nigrum, ore testaceo, antennis, palpis, pedibus, abdomineque
rufis, elytris testaceis, sub-pubescentibus, basi, angulo humerali,
et fasciâ pone medium tenuiter interruptâ nigris, striato-punctatis. Long lin. 5¼

Head sub-opaque, eyes prominent, wider than prothorax, the
latter moderately widened, base and front nearly equal in width,
rather shining; elytra at the base of the width of the eyes,
narrowed to the apex, ten striæ on each with large but rather
shallow punctures, deeper at the base   The entire humeral
angle is black, as is an irregular fascia behind the middle, widest
a little before the margin, reduced to half the width near the
suture, there are two indentations on the apical side.   Antennæ
only with very short setæ , legs finely pubescent, abdomen clear
red.

Hab. Menado, Moluccas, (Wallace)

Stigmatium inscriptum, n sp.

Nigro-piceum sub-parallelum, fronte, antennis, palpis, pedibusque testaceis, his femoribus posticis basi et annulo fuscis ,
elytris fuscis, basi late, fasciâque medianâ (ramum basin versus
emittente) rufis, apice pilis griseis litteram x formantibus.   Long
lin. 4½.

Var. ? Rufo-testaceum, prothorace, elytris fasciis duabus,
margine laterali et apice piceis

Head with the eyes wider than thorax, thorax longer than
wide, with a constriction in front and near base, an indistinct
carina in the middle of the disc.   Elytra rather deeply punctate-
striate, striæ continued to near apex, sides parallel.   Antennæ
short, joints 9 and 10 strongly transverse, 11 compressed, as
long as 5 preceding.

Most nearly allied to *S. Omaliodes*, smaller and differently
marked.

Hab. *Type* New Guinea.   *Var. ?* Ceram, (Wallace).

Stigmatium Omaliodes, n. sp.

Fuscum, sub-opacum, capite testaceo, fusco variegato, antennarum basi pedibusque testaceis, his femoribus tibiisque fusco-
annulatis, elytris dimidio basali obscure ferrugineis, post medium
fuscis, sericeo variegatis   Long. lin 6–7.

The pattern of the elytra of this species it is almost impossible to describe ; the basal half or rather more is of a dirty reddish colour, beyond which is an irregular dark fascia more or less intersected by the sericeous pile which clothes the apical third, which is, however, relieved by fuscous spots Of the two specimens which I refer to this species, one has the femora and tibiæ all ringed with fuscous, while the other has the front and hind pair only spotted, the middle ones quite clear, the tibiæ with a ring only shewing above distinctly. The antennæ are shorter than the head and thorax, and are not setose, they have joint 11 equal to joints 8, 9, 10, which are triangular acuminate internally.

Hab. Aru and Dorey, (Wallace).

Obs. I have a third specimen, from New Guinea, which I refer with doubt to the same species, it is smaller than either, and has the legs entirely yellow.

Stigmatium obscuripenne, n. sp.

Elongatum, sub-parallelum, griseo-fuscum, thorace oblongo, fortiter biconstricto, elytris fasciis tribus obscuris, fuscis, ore pedibusque testaceis, tibiis quatuor primis basi, posticis basi apiceque nigris. Long. lin 5–5½.

Eyes having the excavation clothed with shining pile. Thorax oblong, sides moderately rounded below the anterior constriction, obscurely carinate. Elytra striate, punctures indistinct, somewhat rasp-formed at the base, three indistinct denuded fascia may be traced, the surface generally being covered with obscure grey pubescence Legs pale greenish testaceous, tibiæ all with their bases narrowly black, the hinder pair more widely so at the apex

Hab. Dorey, Mysol, (Wallace).

Stigmatium pallidiventre, (Chev), n. sp.

Sub-nitidum, pallide testaceum, vel obscure brunneum, elytris piceis fortiter punctato-striatis, striis integris, tibiis pallide viridibus. Long. lin 2½–2¾.

Head and thorax shining, pale yellow or brown, mandibles pitchy at the tip, antennæ fine and setose, longer than head and thorax, the latter with a constricted line, curved, on the disc in

front. Elytra pitchy with a greenish brassy reflection, with
series of deep, distinct punctures, which are generally continued
to the apex, legs pale with light greenish tibiæ

Hab Mysol

Obs   This is the first of a series of little species, which are
not nearly allied to any that are described, so far as I am aware,
they are perhaps most easily compared to *S. ambulator*, Westw.

The present species was returned to me by M. Chevrolat, to
whom I sent it, as unknown to him with the name attached
which I have adopted.

Stigmatium tergo-cinctum, (Chev), n. sp

Sub-nitidum, pallide testaceum, elytris piceis subæneis, fortiter
punctato-striatis, apice albidis, thoracis disco infuscato.   Long.
lin 2–2¼.

Differs from the preceding in its smaller size and pale apex
of the elytra, as well as in the tibiæ not being greenish , the
thorax is not tumid below the anterior constriction as in *pallidi-
ventre*. . The antennæ are very fine and hairy, longer than the
head and thorax.

Hab Mysol, Aru

Also returned by M. Chevrolat as unknown to him.   Two
specimens, which I cannot separate from those described above,
have the head and thorax pitchy, and the femora and even the
apex of the elytra more or less infuscate ; they are from Dorey
and New Guinea

Stigmatium pusillum, n. sp

Piceo-testaceum, elytris piceis, cinereo-pubescentibus fasciis
tribus paulo distinctis didrnatis, antennis pedibusque pallide
testaceis, his femoribus posticis apice infuscatis   Long lin. 2.

Allied to the two preceding, but more pubescent than either ;
the head is rather more obscure in colour than the prothorax
the antennæ hairy, passing the base of the thorax   Elytra
punctate-striate, striæ entire, clothed with erect setæ, and also
with a thin depressed pubescence, the coloration is very obscure,
but three bands or interrupted spots which are darker than the
ground colour can be distinguished.

Hab. Sarawak and Celebes, (Wallace).

Stigmatium lineare, n sp

Sub-parallelum, testaceum, elytris nigro-piceis, punctato-striatis, striis ante apicem obliteratis, basi, suturâ, fasciis duabus arcuatis, apiceque 'cinereis, pedibus fere albidis, genubus brunneis   Long. lin. 2¼

Distinguished by the longer and more linear elytra , the prothorax is small, as long as wide, sides rounded, with a few setæ ; the elytra are pale at the shoulder with very few setæ, but depressed brown pubescence, the markings are shining cinereous scales   Antennæ long, nearly twice as long as head and thorax
Hab Sarawak, (Wallace)

Stigmatium ignobile, n. sp.

Piceum, sub-opacum, elytris punctato-striatis, striis fere integris, pedibus pallidis, femorum apice tibiarumque annulo nigris Long. lin. 2¼–3.

Very similar to *pusillum* in form and marking, but much larger, two fasciæ and some spots near the base and apex of the elytra are discernable of shining scales, the marking of the legs will also help to distinguish this species.
Hab. Menado, (Wallace).

Stigmatium inconspicuum, n. sp.

Rufo-piceum, sub-nitidum, parcius pubescens, elytris striatis, striis fere integris, antice punctatis, margine laterali ad medium, fasciisque tribus discoidalibus obliquis nigro-fuscis.   Long lin 2½.

Similar to *S. lineare* in form, elongate parallel   Antennæ fine, hairy, passing the base of the thorax, the latter transverse, impressed on each side of the disc   Elytra fully three times as long as thorax, brownish red, with indistinct oblique markings running from the margin to the suture, directed towards the apex.   Legs pale, varied with pitchy
Hab. Batchian and Kaioa, Ternate? (Wallace)

Stigmatium divisum, n. sp.

Rufum, elytris apicem versus angustatis, fortiter punctato-striatis, striis integris, humeris dimidioque apicali nigris, thoracis disco breviter auropiloso, femoribus albidis, genubus fuscis. Long. lin 3¼.

Rather broad, head pitchy red, antennæ fine, setose, rather long Thorax obsoletely carinate, as wide as the eyes, and scarcely less so than the elytra at their base ; the latter red for the basal half excepting the shoulders, with series of large distinct squarish punctures indistinct near the apex, the apical half is black, bordered with a few shining scales, and having a narrow fascia of the same, not distinct, before the apex.　　Legs, very pale, almost white, femora pitchy at the apex, tibiæ red, narrowly pitchy at the knees, tarsi a little darker.

Hab. Sarawak, (Wallace).

Stigmatium egenum, n. sp.

Elongatum, semiopacum, piceum, capite thorace vix latiore, elytris punctato-striatis, striis apicem versus obsoletioribus, fasciâ ante medium interruptâ rufâ, pedibus pallidis femorum apice et tibiis piceis   Long. lin. $2\frac{1}{4}$–$2\frac{3}{4}$.

Parallel, head and thorax pitchy black, the latter with the constricted line deeply marked before and behind, antennæ not setose, long, rigid.　Elytra punctate-striate, striæ almost vanishing one third from apex, varied with ashy scales, and with a pale spot, or interrupted fascia one third from base   Underside pale brown, femora white to near apex which is brown, tibiæ darker.

Hab. Type, Sarawak　　*Var. ?* Singapore, (Wallace)

Stigmatium vitreum, n. sp.

Vitreo-viride, corpore infra rufo-ferrugineum, antennis, pedibusque testaceis, his femoribus basi albidis.　Long lin. 3–$3\frac{1}{4}$

Antennæ long, setose, head shining, the whole upper surface of a beautiful shagreen or vitreous hue, here and there clothed with shining yellow scales, elytra with series of punctures continued to apex.　Legs rusty red, base of femora and coxæ almost white.

Hab. Sarawak, (Wallace).

Stigmatium audax, n. sp.

Nigrum, sub-nitidum, obsolete creberrime punctatum, elytris rubris, fasciâ latâ pone medium apiceque nigris, basi rugose granulato, pectore rubro. Long. lin $4\frac{1}{2}$.

Allied to *S mutillæcolor*, White *(Tillicera)* but smaller, and to be distinguished by the red fascia near the apex of the elytra. In the single specimen I have the elytra are entirely free from scales, this, however, may be owing to abrasion, their base is rugulose with rasp-formed punctures, beyond the red portion these granulations are visible as small tubercules to very near the apex.´ Breast red, abdomen black.

Hab. Timor, (Wallace).

Stigmatium versipelle, n, sp.

Oblongum, parallelum, flavo-villosum, fuscum, elytris basi granuloso-punctatis, versus apicem densius flavo-pubescens, fasciâ irregulari apicali quasi denudatâ, pedibus fuscis, femoribus basi albidis, tarsis dilutioribus. Long lin. $5\frac{1}{2}$–6.

Rather depressed, head and eyes brownish, villose, antennæ hairy, scarcely longer than head and thorax, the latter pitchy with shining yellow irregularly disposed pile. Elytra with the basal portion rasp-punctured or granulose, the granules little elevated, below the middle a large patch of bright yellowish pubescence, extending to the apex, widest near the suture, with small denuded tubercules, a dark irregular fascia, partially denuded, before the apex. Legs brown, base of the femora and palpi pale yellow. Underside pitchy.

Hab. Queensland, [Rockhampton].

OMADIUS, Lap.

Type O indicus, Cast.

Divergent as the typical forms of this genus are from *Stigmatium*, the genera nevertheless shade off insensibly into each other. The comparative width between the eyes being the most constant character I can discover. In *Omadius* these organs are usually almost contiguous, while in *Stigmatium* they are always separated by a narrow band.

Omadius nigropunctatus, Chev (Rev. et Mag. de Zool. 1874 pp. 22, 67) = *O. mediofasciatus*, Westwood (Proc. Zool. Soc. 1852 p 44, pl. 26, fig. 1)

Omadius nebulosus, Klug, G. and H. Cat. p. 1746, is a *Stigmatium* very near *S. tapetum*, supra

M. Chevrolat describes several species from New Guinea and New Caledonia.

Omadius aurifasciatus, n. sp.

Elongatus, piceus, thorace elongato, disco inæquali, postice obsolete carinato, antice punctato, elytris piceis, basi rugosis, fasciis duabus, unâ in medio sitâ, apud suturam latissimâ, alterâ inter medium et apicem obliquâ, suturam non attingente, apiceque ipso testaceis, auro-pilosis, micantibus, pectore rufo-brunneo, abdomine pedibusque rufis.   Long. lin. 6–7

Head pitchy, labrum pale, somewhat wrinkled on the crown, roughly punctured between the eyes   Thorax very long, nearly twice as long as wide, the disc rough and uneven, clothed with a few golden green hairs behind.   Elytra with the shoulders rather raised, ferruginous at the base, with rough, irregular, and confused punctures and granulations as far as the middle fascia, this, commencing in a point on the margin, is widest at or shortly before the suture, it is (with the second fascia and the apex) distinctly pale, but is densely clothed with a brilliant golden green pile ; the second fascia commences narrow on the margin, and is directed obliquely backwards towards the base, terminating in a round spot *before the suture*, the apex is less densely clothed but is shining   Legs, antennæ and palpi rich rusty red, posterior femora a little darker in the middle

Hab. East Mindanao, Philippines, (Semper).

Obs.   Of four specimens, two have the elytra apparently less acuminate, and the fifth segment of the abdomen emarginate, and a sixth ventral plate conspicuous, these are, I think, females, but I am not able satisfactorily to ascertain their sex.

Omadius nimbifer, n. sp.

Piceus, pube olivaceo vestitus, capite testaceo, thorace nitido, obsolete carinato, utrinque tuberculis tribus, elytris fasciis tribus piceis, primâ sub-basali irregulari, secundâ pone medium latâ, tertiâ sub-apicali nec marginem nec suturam attingente, pedibus testaceis, tibiis et femoribus piceo-annulatis.   Long lin $6\frac{1}{2}$–$7\frac{1}{2}$.

Allied to *O. semicarinatus*, Chev from which it differs as follows . the thorax is longer and less widened on the sides, the carina at the base is less distinct, but three tubercules on each side are very distinct ; the elytra are not so confusedly marked, and the pile is a brighter olive-green, the striæ are continued obsoletely for nearly the whole length, but raised costæ are not to be seen as in *semicarinatus* , the legs are rusty-red, with their knees and a ring on the femora and tibiæ pitchy, the anterior pair being less distinctly marked   Antennæ testaceous, joints 3, 4, 5 pitchy

Hab. East Mindanao and Luzon, Philippines, (Semper).

Omadius vespiformis, n sp.

Ferrugineus, thorace piceo, nitido, tuberculis nonnullis discoid-alibus instructo, elytris lateribus sub-parallelis, testaceis, fasciis tribus. piceis, unâ sub-basilari, alterâ paulo pone medium ad marginem latiore, tertiâ sub-apicali, a suturâ tenuissime inter-ruptis   Long lin $5\frac{1}{2}$–$6\frac{1}{2}$.

Head wide, front between the eyes wider than usual in this genus, very finely clothed with a golden pile, thorax almost glabrous, with no trace of a carina, but with two tubercules in the centre, and about two on each side of the disc.   Elytra rather wider than the head, the yellow portion clothed with golden yellow, and the pitchy with black pubescence, but sparingly so; the central fascia usually the widest, and all are occasionally narrowed near the suture, which is itself very narrowly yellow.   Legs, antennæ, palpi, entirely red, mandibles pitchy

Hab. East Mindanao, Philippines, (Semper)

Omadius notatus, n sp

Piceo-olivaceus, pube tenui grisea vestitus, thorace fere plano, antice et postice subliliter constricto, elytris punctato-striatis, fasciis tribus, duobus anterioribus e maculis duabus formatis, tertiâ obliquâ piceis denudatis; abdomine pedibusque rufis, his femoribus maculatis et tibiis nigro-annulatis.   Long. lin 5

Head little wider than the thorax, front of the usual width between the eyes, epistoma thickly clothed with silvery shining hairs   Thorax almost cylindric, opaque, the constrictions not deep, clothed with shining pile of an olive-green colour   Elytra at the base about as wide as the head, thence widened to the middle, from which again they gradually narrow to near their apex; the first fascia is formed of two spots often united, the second is irregular, deeply indented, but not consisting of separate spots, the third touches neither the suture nor margin, but is a single rather large spot, the interspaces are olive-green, with denuded spots.   Antennæ pitchy with pale basal joint.

Hab. East Mindanao, Philippines, (Semper)

Obs. This species is certainly very near to *O. fasciipes*, Wwd , but is usually larger and has the middle fascia deeply indented on both sides.

Var. Ternate, (Wallace).   Siam, (Mouhot).

Omadius filifrons, n. sp.

Piceo-testaceus, pube tenui argenteâ vestitus, front inter oculos lineari, elytris sub-costatis, obsolete punctato-striatis, fasciis tribus e maculis obscurioribus formatis, pedibus testaceis, piceo-notatis, pectore abdomineque piceis.   Long. lin 5–5½

Allied to the preceeding, but readily distinguished by the exceedingly narrow space between the eyes, which indeed approach nearer than in any other *Omadius* known to me.

Hab. Dorey and Batchian (Wallace).

Omadius radulifer, n sp.

Piceo-olivaceus, pube tenui griseâ vestitus, thorace cylindrico, disco transversim strigoso ; elytris olivaceis, basi tenuiter testaceo, fasciis tribus undulatis e maculis piceis formatis, abdomine pedibusque piceis, his femorum basi testaceis.   Long lin. 4½–5.

Very nearly allied to *O notatus*, but more robustly built, the front between the eyes is rather wider, the thorax *transversely wrinkled on its disc*, the elytra with granulations (formed by the raised edges of the punctures) at the base ; (in *notatus* the punctures are simple), the abdomen and tibiae *pitchy black*.   The colour is not so bright as in *notatus*, and the fasciæ are more obscure   .

Hab. Celebes and Menado (Wallace)

Omadius femoralis, n sp

Elongatus, postice attenuatus, piceo-olivaceus, capite et thorace viridi-olivaceis, hoc medio carinato, utrinque oblique impresso, elytris basi sub-granulatis, fasciis tribus nigro-piceis, unâ sub-basilari vix conspicuâ, ad marginem latiore ; alterâ infra medium, latâ, margine apicali indentatâ ; tertiâ sub-apicali maculiforme paululum distinctâ   Antennis rufo-piceis, articulo primo et ultimo albidis, pedibus testaceis, tibiis nigro-annulatis, femoribus basi exceptâ viridibus, abdomine rufo.   Long lin. 5½–6.

Resembling a small specimen of *O. mediofasciatus*, Wwd., but easily distinguished by the characters given above
Hab. Menado, (Wallace).

Omalius posticalis, n sp

Brevior, niger, prothorace transversim subtiliter rugoso, elytris piceis cinereo pubescentibus, basi seriatim punctatis, striis fere integris, fasciâ latâ pone medium nigrâ, pedibus nigris, tibiarum atque femorum basi, tarsisque testaceis, pectore et abdomine rufis Long lin 4½

A little like *O. femoralis*, but the fascia is placed further behind, the antennæ are much shorter, the two basal joints pale, but the short club entirely black, the thorax transversly wrinkled especially in front, and shorter than in *femoralis*, legs nearly black, only the base of thighs and tibiæ and underside of anterior thighs pale, breast red, &c.
Hab Philippines, (Semper).

Omalius cylindricus, n. sp.

Elongatus parallelus, nigro-fuscus, capite testaceo, prothorace medio carinato, elytris nigro-violaceis, basi, fasciis duabus obliquis, unâque in medio curvatâ, cum suturâ, flavo micantibus sericeis, apice sub-truncato, fulvo pedibus fuscis, femoribus posticis supra, anticis infra, tarsisque testaceis Long lin. 5–6½

Femina ? Abdomine segmento quinto ventrali in valvulis duobus lateralibus producto, dorsali his obtegente, quarto emarginato

Very cylindric, head with the eyes about the width of the elytra, thorax finely carinate in the middle of the disc, and somewhat transversely wrinkled in front, with an oblique sulcus on each side of the base Elytra parallel, their apex sinuate truncate, sutural angle a little acuminate and produced, punctate- striate at the base, striæ produced, but obsolete near apex The first oblique fascia of shining hairs starts from the humerus towards the suture, near which it sometimes meets the median curved band, the third fascia is only conspicuous in one of the two examples before me, it runs from the margin near the apex towards the middle fascia, but does not nearly reach it The antennæ have the fifth to tenth joints acuminate internally, the last long, pointed at apex, they are fuscous excepting the basal joint which is pale yellow beneath. The organisation of the fifth ventral plate is very extraordinary in the female, unlike any

K

thing I am acquainted with, it appears to be cleft and developed
into two lateral plates, these are completely covered by the
dorsal plate which is convex and sulcate externally.

Hab Sarawak, (Saunders).

Omalius augusticeps, n sp.

Elongatus, sub-parallelus, nigro-piceus, antennarum articulis
duobus basalibus et ultimo, tarsisque pallidis ; elytris fasciis
duabus arcuatis, apiceque albidâ, griseo sericeis.   Long. lin. 5.

Allied to the preceding, head with the eyes of the width of
the thorax, the latter twice as long as wide, opaque, obsoletely
constricted before and behind, elytra having the sides parallel,
apex simply rounded, pale, the rest pitchy or fuscous, obsoletely
punctate-striate, striæ entire.   Underside, legs, and antennæ of
the colour of the body, with the exception of the tarsi, and two
basal and the apical joint of the antennæ.   The latter are
simple as far as the sixth joint, from whence they are widened
and compressed   Legs very long.

Hab Sarawak, Borneo, (Wallace).

Obs   It will be seen from the above description that this
species, though resembling *cylindricus,* differs from it in many
particulars, notably in the width of the head, and structure of
the antennæ, which are not strongly serrate.   In the single
specimen I have the abdomen is simple.

Omalius abscissus. n. sp.

Elongatus, ferrugineus, nitidus, capite, prothorace, elytrisque
nigris, his basi, apice fasciâque abbreviatâ medianâ tenui rufis.
Long lin.

Allied to *O. prioceroïdes,* Thoms, but smaller, and the elytra
with series of punctures, of which those near the base are large
and irregular, while the remainder, extending from the red basal
portion to the middle, are very fine and obsolete   Near the
middle of the elytra is a very narrow arcuate fascia reaching
neither the margin nor the suture, the apex is obscurely red, but
the black of the elytra shades off into this colour.   The labrum
is yellow, and the epistoma clothed with yellow hairs as in
prioceroïdes ; front of the usual width between the eyes, *i.e*,
they are only separated by a narrow band, thorax oblong shining   Legs, with the coxæ, red.

Hab. Batchian, (Wallace)

[To be concluded in our next part.]

On the Lepidoptera referred by Walker to the genus Dioptis *of Hubner , by* AUTHUR G BUTLER, F.L S ,F.Z.S.

In the second volume of his Catalogue of Lepidoptera Heterocera, Walker quotes 32 species as belonging to the genus *Dioptis*, these species he groups under 13 sub-generic headings ; he begins with a new form which he calls *D discreta*

Genus EROCHA   *Walker*

Group 1.   EROCHA.   *Walker*

Erocha discreta

Dioptis (Erocha) discreta, Walker, Cat. Lep Het 2, p. 319 (1854). Ega (*Bates*)   Type B M

This genus is referable to the *Pyralites* and is allied to Walker's Genus *Erilusa*, it will form a group with that genus, with *Vitessa* and other Old World genera.

Genus ERBESSA   *Walker.*

Group 2.   ERBESSA   *Walker.*

Erbessa sobria

Dioptis (Erbessa) sobria, Walker, Cat Lep. Het 2, p 319, n 2 (1854). Pará (*Bates*)   Type B.M.

This genus and the following are allied to *Rhosus* of Walker, Lep Het 2, p. 359 ; the latter genus should be extended to include *Melanchroia clavigera* and *M. æruginosa*

Genus PSEUDERBESSA   *Butler*

Easily distinguished from the preceding by the neuration of secondaries, the second and third subcostal branches being emitted from a long footstalk, and the second and third median branches from a short footstalk   In *Erbessa*, the subcostals are emitted from a very short footstalk, the medians from the end of the cell, at its junction with the lower discocellalar.   Type *D. umbrifera.*

Pseuderbessa umbrifera.

Dioptis (Euagra) umbrifera, Walker, Cat Lep Het. 2, p. 326, n 12 (1854).
Parà, (*Bates*).   S. America (*Warwick*).   Type B M.

Psuederbessa decorata.

Phelloe decorata, Walker, Cat. Lep. Het. Suppl 1, p. 146 (1864).
Ega (*Bates*).   Type B.M

Genus PHELLOE.   *Walker.*

Group 3.   PHELLOE.   *Walker.*

Phelloe glaucaspis.

Dioptis (Phelloe) glaucaspis, Walker, Cat Lep. Het. 2, p. 320, n. 3 (1854).
Parà, (*Bates*)

Phelloe munda.

Phelloe munda, Walker, Cat. Lep. Het. Suppl 1, p 146 (1864),
Parà, (*Bates*).

The genus *Phelloe* belongs to the *Melameridæ,* and is allied to *Scotura, Getta, Phintia, Inonda, Myonia,* &c. &c.

Genus LEUCOPSUMIS.   *Hubner.*

The following species is referable to this genus of the *Zygænoid Arctiidæ;* the neuration being exactly similar.

Group 4.   ERCHIA.   *Walker* (part)

Leucopsumis semistria.

Dioptis (Erchia) semistria, Walker, Cat Lep. Het 2, p. 321, n. 4 (1854).
Amazons, (*Bates*).

Leucopsumis is nearly allied to *Ctenucha.*

Genus ERCHIA. *Walker*

Group 4.   ERCHIA, Walker (part).

Erchia porphyria

Sphinx porphyria, Cramer, Pap. Exot IV. p. 227 , pl. 397, fig. E (1782).

Centronia porphyria, Hubner, Verz. bek Schmett p 122, n. ·1325 (1816).

Dioptis (Erchia) porphyria, Walker, Cat. Lep. Het. 2, p. 321, n. 5 (1854).

Surinam.

Walker originally described the *Læmocharis machilis* of Herrich Schaffer as this species (compare Cat Lep. Het 1, p 157, and VII. p. 1604)

Erchia glaucopoides.

Dioptis (Euagra) glaucopoides, Walker, Cat. Lep Het. 1, p. 325, n 11 (1854).

Parà, (*Bates*)

The genus *Erchia,* as thus constituted, is only distinguished from my new genus *Metriophyla* by its shorter and broader wings , it belongs to the *Zygænoid Arctiidæ.*

Genus PHARA   Walker.

Phara trivittata

Dioptis (Phara) trivittata, Walker, Cat. Lep. Het. 2, p. 322, n. 6 (1854)

Hab —? Type B.M.

Phara nyctemeroides

Olina nyctemeroides, Walker, Char. Het Lep p. 6 (1869).

Hab.—? Type B.M.

The genus *Phara* is closely allied to *Leucopsumis,* but has the abdominal lines of *Erchia*; *P. nyctemeroides* is very near to *P. trivittata*; but is, I think, distinct

Genus DRYMŒA   *Walker*

Drymœa hesperoides

Dioptis (Drymœa) hesperoides, Walker, Cat. Lep. Het. 2, p. 323, n 7 (1854).

New Grenada   Type B.M

Drymœa unimaculata, n sp

Wings above black, with a blue shot, primaries with a large hyaline white spot immediately beyond the end of the cell; secondaries with the costa brown; body greenish black; head, and sides of abdomen spotted with whitish, primaries below with a cuneiform interno-median white streak, internal area greyish brown, apical area streaked between the veins with silver, secondaries silver with the veins (excepting the discocellullars) black, body below sordid white, legs black expanse of wings 1 inch, 7 lines

E Peru, (*Degand*)   Type B M

The genus *Drymœa* is clearly allied to *Phelloe*

Genus EUAGRA   *Walker.*

Euagra cælestina.

Phalœna cælestina, Cramer, Pap. Exot. IV. p. 107, pl. 345, fig. G (1782).

Dioptis (Euagra) cælestina, Walker, Cat Lep. Het. 2, p. 324, n 8 (1854)

Dioptis (Agyrta) interclusa, Walker, l. c. p. 328, n. 14 (1854).

Parà, (*Bates*).   B.M.

Euagra angelica, n. sp.

Nearly allied to *E cælestina*, but the hyaline spot of primaries larger, not cut by the second median branch, but almost filling the interspace between the first and second branches; expanse of wings, 1 inch, 4 lines.

New Granada, Pacho, Province of Cundinamarca (*Janson*). Type B.M.

Euagre hæmanthus.

Dioptis (Euagra) hæmanthus, Walker, Cat Lep. Het 2, p 324, n. 9 (1854).

Mexico, (*Argent*)   Type B.M

In this species the hyaline patch of primaries only fills the upper half of the interspace between the first and second median branches

Section NEPE.   *Walker*

Median branches of primaries rather closer together.

Euagra intercisa, n sp.

Differs from the preceding in having a hyaline white streak cut by the median nervure of primaries and running from the base to the hyaline discal patch, with which it is continuous   expanse of wings 1 inch. 5 lines.

Venezuela, (*Dyson*).   Type B M

We have two examples of this species, on one of which I found a label, in Mr Walker's handwriting, bearing the above name; it is the *Dioptis (Agyrta) auro* of Walker (nec Hubner).

Euagra fenestra

Dioptis (Nepe) fenestra, Walker, Cat. Lep Het 2, p. 337, n. 31 (1854)

Hab —? Type B.M.

I cannot conceive Mr. Walker's object in separating this species generically from *Euagra,* there being very little structural difference   *Euagra,* and the following three genera are *Zygænoid Arctiidæ,* allied to *Leucopsumis*

CALLAGRA, n. gen.

Closely allied to *Euagra,* but the first median branch of secondaries emitted at a greater distance from the second, and the lower radial emitted from the third median (with which it forms a fork) considerably nearer to its origin, thus shortening the footstalk

Type *C. azurea.*

Callagra azurea.

Dioptis (Euagra) azurea, Walker, Cat. Lep Het. 2, p 325, n. 10 (1854)

Brazil.

This species most nearly resembles *Euagra hæmanthus*, but is smaller, shorter in the wing, and has a smaller hyaline spot in primaries, the collar also, instead of being carmine, has a yellow spot on each side.

Callagra splendida, n sp.

Like a small example of *Agyrta dux* wings black with a blue shot, primaries with a large hyaline triangular white patch, crossed by the median nervure and its first branch, from the middle of the wing to the base, a subapical oblique hyaline white spot, secondaries with a broad central hyaline white streak, from the base to near the outer margin, interrupted by the median nervure and its branches; head black margined with white, palpi carmine at base, otherwise black, antennæ black, collar carmine; thorax metallic blue-green, with a central longitudinal white line, tegulæ blue-green, white externally, with a white central line; abdomen blue-green with a central white streak, sides pale brown, front trochanters white, other trochanters cream-colour, remainder of legs brown streaked with white, venter cream-colour, the anus and a line on each sides brown. expanse of wings 1 inch, 7 lines

Brazil.   Type B.M

MYDROMERA, n. gen

Readily distinguished from *Euagra* by the extreme shortness of the footstalk from which the third median and lower radial branches are emitted, and from the fact that the second median is emitted some distance before the end of the cell Type *M. isthmia.*

Mydromera isthmia.

Euagra isthmia, Felder, Reise der Nov Lep. 4, pl. CV. fig. 24 (1874)

New Granada   B.M.

Genus AGYRTA. *Hubner.*
Group 8. AGYRTA *Walker.*

Agyrta dux.

Dioptis (Agyrta) dux, Walker, Cat. Lep Het. 2, p 327, n 12 (1854)
Venezuela, (*Dyson*)   Type B M.

The insect from Honduras is distinct.

Agyrta æstiva, n sp

Differs from the preceding in the much more restricted longitudinal hyaline white streak, and the straighter and broader postmedian oblique band of primaries: expanse of wings 2 inches, 1 line
Honduras, (*Dyson*).   Type B.M.

Agyrta micilia

Phalæna micilia, Cramer, Pap. Exot III., p. 62 , pl. 228, fig. G (1779).
Limacodes micilia, Duncan, Nat Libr XXXVII , Exot. Moths. p 179 ; pl 22, figs 1, 2.
Tropical America, (*Becker*)   B M

Agyrta auxo.

Hipocrita linciformis Auxo, Hubner, Samml Exot. Schmett, 1.
Agyrta auxo, Hubner, Verz bek. Schmett p 177, n 1829.
Dioptis (Agyrta) micilia, Walker, Cat. Lep. Het 2, p 329, n. 16 (1854).
Venezuela, (*Dyson*)   B M.

Agyrta ? lucida.

Agyrta lucida, Walker, Cat. Lep. Het. Suppl 1, p 147 (1864)
Bogota.

Not having seen this species, I am unable to decide its true position ; I feel almost certain from its peculiar coloration that it is not an *Agyrta.*

MICRAGYRTA, n. gen.

Resembles *Agyrta*, excepting in its small size, but the arrangement of the veins in secondaries is almost exactly that of *Empyreuma*, the principal difference being, that the radial passes through the centre of the discocellulars, and, as a recurrent nervure, divides the cell into two parts.

Type *M. gavisa*.

This genus must be placed between *Histiœa* and *Empyreuma* in the *Zygœnidœ*.

Micragyrta gavisa.

Agyrta gavisa, Walker, Cat. Lep. Het. Suppl. 1, p, 147 (1864)
Ega, (*Bates*).

Micragyrta diminuta.

Dioptis (Agyrta) diminuta, Walker, Cat. Lep. Het. 2, p. 328, n. 15 (1854).
Parà, (*Bates*)

Genus ISOSTOLA.   *Felder*.

This genus belongs to the *Pericopiinœ*, and is allied to *Eucyane*.

Isostola rhodobroncha.

Isostola rhodobroncha, Felder, Reise der Nov. Lep 4, pl. CIII, fig 15 (1874).
Hab.—?

Isostola divisa

Dioptis (Agyrta) divisa, Walker, Cat Lep. Het. 2, p 329, n. 17 (1854).
Parà, (*Bates*).   Type B.M.

Isostola cyanomelas.

Phanoptis cyanomelas, Felder, Reise der Nov Lep. pl. CIV. fig. 10 (1874).
Hab.—?

Isostola vicina, n. sp.

Nearly allied to *I. divisa*, but differing in its smaller size ; the hyaline cuneiform patch, upon median areâ of primaries, extending nearly to the base and divided throughout its length by the median nervure ; the postmedian hyaline band, tapering to a point at its upper end ; the subapical fasciole reduced to a narrow bifid litura , central hyaline streak of secondaries much narrower , expanse of wings 1 inch, 8 lines

S. America, (*Warwick*).   Type B.M

METASTATIA, n gen.

Only differs from *Hyaleuceria*, in neuration, in the fact that the radial, instead of forming a fourth median branch, is continuous with the recurrent nervure.   Type *M pyrrhorhœa*.

The body of *Metastatia* is much less robust than in *Hyaleuceria*

Metastatia pyrrhorhœa.

Hyelosia pyrrhorhœa, Hubner, Samml Exot. Schmett Zutr p. 12, n 22, figs. 43, 44 (1806)

Dioptis (Agyrta) pyrrhorhœa, Walker, Cat. Lep Het 2, p 330, n. 18 (1854).

Parà, (*Smith and Bates*)

This genus of course belongs to the *Zygænoid Arctiidæ*, and represents one of the few instances in this group in which the median nervure of secondaries is not four-branched

Genus GNOPHÆLA. *Walker.*

Group 9.   GNOPHÆLA. *Walker.*

This is a well-marked genus of the *Charideinæ* including *G. vermiculata, G. hopfferi*, and other species   Walker only quotes the following :

Gnophœla œquinoctialis.

Dioptis (Gnophœla) œquinoctialis, Walker, Cat. Lep. Het. 2. p. 331, n. 19 (1854), Boisduval, Lep. Guat. p 87 (1870).

Venezuela (*Becker*).   Type B.M.

Genus HYRMINA.   *Walker.*

Group 10.   HYRMINA.   *Walker.*

This and the following genera will come after *Erbessa*, being succeeded by *Gonora, Scaptia Aletis, Curuba, Bythuria, Secusio, Nyctemera,* and allies, all of which may be referred to the *Nyctemeridæ.*

Hyrmina areolata.

Dioptis (Hyrmina) areolata, Walker, Cat. Lep. Het. 2, p. 332, n 20 (1854)

Epilais melda, Boisduval, Lep. Guat. p. 78.

Brazil, (*Argent*).   Type B M.

Mr Walker confounded several species under this name, but it would be useless to describe them without figures, as they differ in points which can scarcely be made clearly intelligible by description alone.

Mr. Boisduval gives Nicaragua and Quito as the localities of this species.

Hyrmina onega.

Dioptis onega, Bates, Trans Linn Soc. XXIII, pl. LV, fig. 12 (1862).

Laurona onegia, Walker, Cat. Lep. Het. Suppl. 1, p 149 (1864)

Ega, (*Bates*).   Type B.M.

Hyrmina noctiluces.

Dioptis noctiluces, Butler, Cist Ent. 1, p. 88 (Jan 1872), Lep Exot. p. 176, n 2, pl. LXI, fig. 7 (1874).

Var. *Dioptis erycinoides,* Felder, Reise der Nov. Lep. 4. Tab. CV, fig. 4 (1874).

Cartago, Costa Rica, (*Van Patten*).   Type B M.

Hyrmina ithomeina.

Dioptis ithomeina, Butler, Cist. Ent 1, p 87 (Jan. 1872), Lep. Exot p 175, n 1 ; pl. LXI, fig. 8 (1874)

Dioptis Salvini, Felder Reise der Nov. Lep. 4, Tab. CV, fig. 5 (1874).

Cartago, Costa Rica, (*Van Patten*).   Type B.M.

Hyrmina phelina.

Dioptis phelina, Felder, Reise der Nov. Lep. 4, Tab CV, fig. 6 (1874)

S. America.   B M.

This species was mixed up with *H. areolata* by Mr Walker.

Hyrmina cyma.

Dioptis cyma, Hubner, Samml. Exot Schmett. Zutr. figs 17, 18 (1806) ; Verz bek Schmett. p 174, n 1792 (1816).

Dioptis (Hyrmina) cyma, Walker, Cat. Lep. Het. 2, p 332, n. 21 (1854)

Parà, (*Smith and Bates*).   B.M

The species from Demerara is distinct, this species is figured by Bates (Trans. Linn. Soc. XXIII, pl. LV, fig. 13, 1862)

Hyrmina leucothyris, n. sp.

Allied to the preceding species, but has the primaries coloured exactly as in *H. aeliana ;* the postmedian band being broken up into two spots, and the subapical streak reduced to a quadrifid spot, expanse of wings 1 inch 6 lines

Ega, (*Bates*),   Type B M.

Hyrmina aeliana.

Dioptis aeliana, Bates, Trans. Linn. Soc. XXIII, pl. LV, fig. 10 (1862)

Laurona aeliana, Walker, Cat. Lep. Het. Suppl. 1, p. 150 (1864).

Ega, (*Bates*).   B.M

Genus DIOPTIS, *Hubner*.

Dioptis Ilerdina.

Dioptis Ilerdina, Bates, Trans. Linn Soc. XXIII, pl LV. fig. 11 (1862)

Laurona Herdina (sic), Walker, Cat Lep Het Suppl. 1. p. 149 (1864).

Ega, (*Bates*).   B.M.

Dioptis meon.

Phalæna meon, Cramer, Pap Exot. 1, p. 118, pl LXXI, fig. F (1779)

Dioptis meon, Hubner, Verz. bek. Schmett. p. 174, n 1793 (1816).

Laurona meon, Walker, Cat Lep. Het. 7, p. 1653 (1856).

Surinam.

Dioptis pheloides.

Monocreagna pheloides, Felder, Reise der Nov. Lep. 4, Tab. CV, fig. 7 (1874).

Hab —?

Genus LAURONA. *Walker.*

Group 10 (part) HYRMINA, and 11 LAURON, *Walker*

In this genus the median branches of secondaries are all separate; the sexes are also dissimilar.

Laurona vinosa.

Sphinx vinosa, Drury, Ill. Exot. Ent. p. 47; pl. 23. fig 4

Callimorpha ? vinosa, Westwood, ed. Drury, l c.

Dioptis (Hyrmina) vinosa, Walker, Cat Lep. Het 2, p. 332, n. 22 (1854)

"Antigua" *Drury*. Hab.—? B.M.

Laurona rica.

Dioptis rica, Hubner, Samml Exot. Schmett. Zutr. figs. 531, 532 (1806).

Dioptis (Lauron) rica, Walker, Cat. Lep. Het. 2, p. 333, n. 23 (1854).

♂ Sta Martha (*Bouchard*), ♀ Venezuela (*Dyson*) B.M.

Several species were confounded under this name by Mr. Walker.

Laurona panamensis, n. sp

♀ Intermediate in character between *L. rica* and *L. syma.*

Wings greyish hyaline, veins black; primaries with the apical half black, crossed through its centre by an oblique regular white band ; costal and internal areoles black, intersected by a narrow orange streak, secondaries with a narrow black outer border; body brown, head blackish, white-spotted, tegulæ orange ; abdomen greyish on its dorsal region, with a central dark brown longitudinal line; body below whitish, legs black and white, sides of pectus orange, venter white with a dark brown central stripe; expanse of wings 1 inch, 11 lines.

Veragua, (*Salvin*)   5 examples   B M.

Laurona syma

Dioptis (Lauron) syma, Walker, Cat. Lep. Het 2, p. 334, n. 24 (1854).
Laurona subafflicta, Walker, l c. Suppl. p 148 (1864).
Epilais Zetila, Boisduval, Lep. Guat. p. 78 (1874)
" Bogota " *Boisduval*. Hab.—? B.M.

Laurona leucophœa.

Dioptis (Lauron) leucophœa, Walker, Cat Lep. Het. 2, p. 334, n. 25 (1854)
Venezuela, (*Dyson*) Para (*Grahame*).   Type B M

Laurona rufilinea.

♀ *Laurona rufilinea*, Walker, Cat. Lep. Het. Suppl. 1, p. 148 (1864).
♂, ♀ Ega, (*Bates*).   Type B.M.

The male is very similar to that of the preceding species.

Laurona partita.

Dioptis (Lauron) partita, Walker, Cat. Lep. Het. 2, p. 335, n. 27 (1854)
Parà, (*Bates*).   Type B M

Laurona ergolis

Dioptis (Lauron) ergolis, Walker, Cat. Lep Het 2, p 335, n. 28 (1854).
Jamaica, (*Gosse*).   Type B.M.

Laurona Domingonis, n. sp

♀ Nearly allied to *L. ergolis*, but smaller, shorter in the wing; the white band of primaries shorter; the orange streaks shorter, ill-defined; the streak across the median branches obsolete, expanse of wings 1 inch, 9 lines.

St. Domingo, (*Tweedie*).   Type B M

This species agrees with Boisduval's description of his *Dituxis sona* * ; but I cannot think it the same as a Guatemala form.

Genus Locha, *Walker.*

Group 12   locha, *Walker.*

Locha hyalina.

♀ *Dioptis (Locha) hyalina*, Walker, Cat Lep Het 2, p 336, n. 29 (1854)

♂ *Erycinopsis diaphana*, Felder, Reise der Nov. Lep 4, pl ˙CV, fig. 9 (1874).

S. America, (*Johnson*).   Type B M.

Locha diaphana.

˜ *Phalæna (Noctua) diaphana*, Drury, Ill Exot Ent. III, p 30, pl 22, fig 4.

Callimorpha ? diaphana, Westwood, ed. Drury, l.c.

Dioptis (Locha) diaphana, Walker, Cat. Lep Het 2, p. 336, n. 30 (1854).

Brazil.

Locha perspicua, n sp

♂ General aspect of *L. hyalina* ♂, but smaller, with broader borders. Wings hyaline white, the veins and borders black; primaries with a rather broad black band from costa, above end of cell, to outer margin on first median interspace, head and thorax black, with central interrupted white line; abdomen above dark gray, below sordid white; legs brown expanse of wings 1 inch, 5 lines

Chontales, Nicaragua (*Janson*).   Type B.M.

* Lep Guat, p 79

Genus GONORA, *Walker*.

I am doubtful whether Walker intended to include this genus in his *Dioptidæ*, but it immediately follows *Laurona* in his Supplement.

Gonora heliconiata

Gonora heliconiata, Walker, Lep Het. Suppl. 1, p. 151 (1864)

Phelodes æquatorialis, Felder, Reise der Nov. Lep. 4, Tab CIV, fig 9 (1874).

Epilais æquatorialis, Boisduval, Lep. Guat. p 78.

Bogota (*Stevens*).   Type B M

The genus *Scaptia*, which follows, will contain *Chrysauge lutescens, repanda, calida* n. sp., *aletis*, and *translata*.

Walker has referred his *Dioptis hyelosioides* to his genus *Gerra*, which, he says, is allied to *Josia* not having seen either genus or species I will not attempt to question the correctness of this act.

Descriptions of New Species of Phytophagous Coleoptera ; *by* JOSEPH S. BALY, F.L.S , &c.

Mastostethus picticollis, mihi.

Subelongatus, postice vix attenuatus, depressus, pallide fulvus, antennis capitis et thoracis maculis, scutello pleuris pedibusque nigris, femoribus anticis quatuor subtus, posticisque fere totis, fulvis ; elytris flavis, fasciâ basali ad marginem abbreviatâ, alterâ prope medium integrâ, lineâ pone medium, apiceque nigris Long 5½ lin

Hab Columbia.

Head irregularly but not very closely punctured, the extreme vertex, a frontal vitta, the inner orbits of the eyes, a spot at the base of each antenna, a transverse stripe across the clypeus, together with the base of the labrum, black ; apices of jaws nigro-piceous, antennæ (with the exception of the extreme base of the first joint) entirely black.   Thorax rather more than twice as broad as long at the base ; basal margin sinuate on either side ; apical border transversely truncate , sides straight, quickly converging from base to apex, anterior and posterior angles distinctly produced, acute ; upper surface finely and irregularly but not closely punctured, on each side, near the hinder angle, is a large shallow fovea, just in front of this, near the outer margin, are several irregular faintly impressed excavations , a transverse spot on the centre of the disk, its anterior margin deeply emarginate, together with an irregular longitudinal patch on either side near the lateral border, black ; this patch is connected at its upper extremity by a shorter one with the lateral margin of the thorax, which is itself broadly edged, more especially on its under surface, with black   Scutellum broader than long, trigonate, its surface distinctly punctured   Elytra broader than the thorax, scarcely narrowed towards their apex, surface depressed, rather closely punctured, pale flavous, a basal fascia which is gradually dilated from the suture to the outer margin, and extends across the humeral callus but is abruptly arrested on the outer side of the latter, black, a common transverse band which extends directly across the middle of the disk, together with the apical sixth of the elytra also black ; between the medial fascia and the apical patch, the suture and outer margin are both narrowly edged with black.

Mastostethus speciosus, mihi.

Sub-elongatus, sub-depressus, niger, nitidus, femoribus anticis quatuor abdomineque obscure piceis, thorace tenuiter et remote punctato, maculis quatuor rufis ornato; elytris fere parallelis, distincte et sub-crebre punctatis, pallide flavis, marginibus basali et laterali, vittâ humerali arcuatâ, fasciâ prope medium erosâ apiceque nigris   Long. 5 lin

Hab Ecuador, collected by Mr Buckley.

Vertex finely and remotely punctured, space between the eyes closely punctured, medial line smooth, impunctate, impressed at its lower extremely with a deep longitudinal fovea, which terminates in the deep transverse groove separating the face from the clypeus, anterior border of the latter together with the edge of the labrum rufous   Thorax twice as broad as long at the base, basal margin obsoletely bisinuate on either side, the medial portion obtusely truncate, middle of anterior border distinctly sinuate, sides straight, converging from base to apex, anterior and posterior angles produced laterally, acute; upper surface nitidous, very finely but remotely punctured, on either side, placed perpendicularly near the lateral border, are two irregular rufous spots   Scutellum broader than long, trigonate, its apex broadly rounded. Elytra broader than the thorax, parallel, the apex regularly rounded; surface sub-depressed, distinctly and rather closely punctured, pale fulvous, the basal margin, a narrow line along the lateral border, a curved vitta on the humeral callus, attached at its base to the basal margin, together with the apex black, in addition, placed somewhat obliquely about the middle of the disk, is a deeply crenulate black fascia, which forms with its fellow a broad, slightly arched, transverse band, stretching entirely across the two elytra, the apical patch, which occupies more than a fourth of the surface, has its anterior edge irregular.

Mastostethus Buckleyi, mihi.

Sub-elongatus, postice attenuatus, sub-depressus, rufo-piceus, ore, antennis, capitis et thoracis maculis, tibiis tarsisque nigris; elytris nigris, tenuiter punctatis, fasciâ latâ ante medium alterâque augustiori ante apicem positis, flavis   Long. 5½ lin.

Hab. Ecuador

Head finely and distinctly punctured, the punctures distant on the vertex, crowded along the inner orbit of the eye; the mouth, the palpi excepted, a longitudinal vitta on the front, a small spot on the extreme vertex and another on either side at the base of

the antennæ, black.   Thorax twice as broad as long at the base,
basal margin obsoletely bisinuate on either side, its medial
portion transversely truncate ; middle of anterior border slightly
sinuate, sides straight, feebly bisinuate, anterior and posterior
angles acute, surface finely but not closely punctured, impressed
on each side close to the hinder angle with a deep fovea , the ·
disk is ornamented with five black spots placed as follows, one
medial, transverse and bilobate larger than the rest, the others
arranged in a quadrangular form one near each anterior and
posterior angle.   Scutellum broader than long, trigonate, its
apex broadly rounded and stained with black   Elytra broader
than the thorax, tapering from the base towards the apex, finely
but distinctly punctured   Body beneath clothed with coarse
fulvous hairs, hinder thighs moderately incrassate.

Mastostethus pictus, mihi.

Anguste oblongus, depressus, pallide fulvus, nitidus, capitis
maculis sex, thoracis maculis decem, scutello, unguiculis, tarsis
posticis, tibiis dorso antennisque nigris ; elytris tenuiter punctatis, nigris, utrisque maculis quinque fulvis , pleuris picco-
maculatis ; femoribus nigro-lineatis, posticis valde incrassatis,
subtus spinâ validâ armatis   Long 5 lin

Hab Columbia.

Head distinctly punctured, the punctures remote on the vertex,
crowded on either side along the inner orbit of the eye, in the
medial line is an oblong fovea , a triangular spot on the extreme
vertex, a frontal vitta, a small spot on either side just
within the insertion of the antenna, a transverse spot on the
clypeus, together with a spot at the base of the labrum, black ,
apices of jaws likewise black.   Thorax more than twice as broad
as long ; basal margin faintly tri-sinuate , sides rounded and converging from base to apex, hinder angles laterally produced,
acute, anterior angles slightly produced, sub-acute ; surface
finely but remotely punctured, ornamented with ten black spots,
placed as follows, one on the middle of the apical border, four
transversely across the middle, and five transversely at the
base, of these latter the three inner are attached to the basal
margin, and the two lateral ones are free   Elytra broad, parallel,
rather broadly rounded at the apex , above depressed, rather
strongly punctured, black, each nearly covered with five large
fulvous patches, arranged as follows, one attached to the middle
of the base, within the humeral callus, two obliquely below the
base, the inner one obliquely oblong, attached to the scutellum,

the outer one quadrangular placed just below the basal spot, two across the middle, the inner close to the suture, the outer not far from the lateral margin and sending from its antero-external angle a narrow sub-marginal vitta to the basal margin, the fourth larger than any of the preceding, and subquadrangular is situated below the middle near the outer margin, and lastly a large trigonate patch which occupies the whole of the apical surface of each elytron and is only separated from the apex itself by a narrow marginal line, the anterior border of this patch is very irregular.

Mastostethus Jansoni, mihi.

Elongatus, postice vix attenuatus, subdepressus, flavus, capite thoraceque fulvis, pleuris, capite inter oculos et macula verticali, antennis brevioribus (apice pallido excepto), thoracis plagâ magnâ basali, tarsis, femoribus et tibiis anticis quatuor dorso, posticisque totis nigris, elytris distincte punctatis, nigris, utrisque lineâ marginali ante medium abbreviatâ, vitta obliquâ curvatâ basi, fasciâque communi pone medium pallide flavo-albidis Long 4 lin

Hab Banks of the river Amazon, a single specimen in my collection.

Head smooth, vertex impunctate, face between the eyes punctured on either side, the intermediate space impunctate ; antennæ considerably less than half the length of the body, slender, six lower joints black, the others yellowish white, the 7th—10th stained above with black Thorax twice as broad at the base as long, sides converging from base to apex, very slightly rounded, angles acute, surface smooth, impunctate, impressed at the base on either side with a large deep fovea, a large transverse quadrangular patch at the base, together with a narrow line in the middle of the apical border black, the basal margin between the quadrangular patch and the lateral angle also narrowly edged with the same colour Scutellum trigonate, rounded on the sides, the apex acute Elytra broader than the thorax, slightly attenuated from the base towards the apex ; above depressed, finely punctured, black, each with a narrow vitta, commencing at the shoulder and terminating before the middle of the lateral border, a broad slightly curved vitta which runs obliquely outwards from the scutellum towards the outer disk, terminating just before the middle of the latter, together with a common transverse band placed below the middle, nearly halfway between the latter and the apex, yellowish white.

Mastostethus basalis, mihi.

Elongatus, postice attenuatus, depressus, rufo-fulvus, nitidus, antennis, facie inter oculos, tibiis posticis apice, tarsis ejusdum paris elytrisque nigris, his fasciâ basali rufo-fulvis   Long 4½ lin

Hab Brazil, Minas Geraes.

Vertex smooth, nearly impunctate, face punctured on either side along the inner orbit of the eye, antennæ equal in length to the head and thorax, a broad transverse band between the eyes black .Thorax twice as broad at the base as long, basal margin sinuate on either side, its medial portion obtusely truncate ; sides straight, converging from base to apex, hinder and anterior angles produced, acute , surface impressed on either side, close to the hinder angle, with a deep fovea, just in front of the latter but rather nearer to the centre of the disk is a small shallow oblong impression ; disk finely but not closely punctured Scutellum broader than long, trigonate, its apex acute, surface finely but remotely punctured, impressed in the middle with a faint fovea Elytra gradually attenuated from base to apex, distinctly punctured, black, a transverse basal band, emarginate on the humeral callus, rufo-fulvous

Mastostethus placidus, mihi

Elongatus, parallelus, modice convexus, pallide flavo-fulvus, antennis, tibiis dorso tarsisque nigris, femoribus dorso piceo lineatis, thorace flavo, fulvo maculato , elytris sat crebre punctatis, pallide flavis. Long 4½ lin

Hab Mexico

Vertex smooth, nearly impunctate, space between the eyes stained with pale rufo-fulvous, coarsely punctured on either side, medial line together with the clypeus nearly free from punctures ; on the centre of the clypeus is an indistinct piceous spot , labrum nigro-piceous , antennæ rather longer than the head and thorax, seven outer joints moderately dilated   Thorax twice as broad as long, base narrowly margined, sides rounded and converging from base to apex, hinder and anterior angles produced, acute , above moderately convex, impressed on each side close to the hinder angle with a distinct fovea, finely and remotely punctured , disk stained with a bilobate patch on either side and with a short vitta in front of the base pale rufo-fulvous Scutellum broader than long, trigonate, its apex rounded, surface

smooth, impressed with a few fine punctures. Elytra broader
than the thorax, sides parallel, rather broadly margined ; above
moderately convex, coarsely punctured, interspaces on the outer
disk transversely wrinkled. Hinder thighs moderately thickened ;
metasternum elevated, its apex obtuse

Mastostethus fraternus, mihi.

Anguste oblongus, postice paullo attenuatus, dorso depressus,
fulvus, nitidus, capite, facie inferiori exceptâ, tarsis, tibiis
posticis apice elytrorumque dimidio postico nigris, elytris
tenuiter punctatis, punctis apicem versus minus distinctis.
Long 5 lin.   ·

Hab Brazil.

Head smooth, nearly impunctate, with the exception of the
impressed punctured space on either side bordering the inner
orbit of the eye, lower portion of face and the mouth (the
apices of the jaws excepted) fulvous   Thorax twice as broad
at the base as long, basal margin bisinuate on either side, the
medial portion transversely truncate ; sides nearly straight, converging from base to apex, hinder angles laterally produced,
very acute ; upper surface smooth, impunctate   Scutellum trigonate, its apex obtuse. Elytra broader than the thorax, slightly
narrowed towards the apex, surface finely punctured, the punctures becoming still finer behind the middle , the base to just
before the middle fulvous, the rest of the surface to the apex
black. Hinder thighs strongly thickened, apex of last abdominal
segment impressed with a small deep fovea; metasternum
strongly impressed   This species is very nearly allied to *M.
bicolor*, it differs in having the whole of the head (the lower
part of the face excepted) and all the tarsi black , it is also a
larger insect and the elytra are much more finely punctured
I only know a single specimen, formerly in the collection of Mr
W. W. Saunders

Megalopus elongatus, mihi.

Angustatus, parallelus, subtus nigro- flavoque variegatus,
supra nigro-hirsutus, pedibus flavis, femoribus dorso, tibiisque
anticis quatuor antice infuscatis , scutello, capite thoraceque
nigris, hoc limbo maculisque quatuor transversis positis, flavis ;
elytris sordide flavis, apice argenteo-sericeis, basi margine tenui
apiceque piceis, utrisque apicem versus prope suturam puncto
pallide flavo ornatis   Long. 4½ lin.

Hab Bogota

Head coarsely, front finely punctured, face between the eyes
variolose punctate on either side, intermediate space thickened,
nearly free from punctures Thorax cylindrical, deeply constricted at the apex, less deeply so at the base, rather strongly
but not very closely punctured, shining black, the entire limb
with the exception of a short space in the middle of the apical
and basal margins, pale yellow, in addition are four small concolorous spots placed transversely across the lower portion of
the disk, the two lateral ones confluent with the limb. Elytra
parallel, elongate, depressed along the suture, basilar space
elevated, bounded on either side by an oblique groove, surface
coarsely but not closely punctured, clothed with suberect black
hairs, at the apex is a distinct patch of silvery sericeous
pubescence, on each elytron, placed close to the suture, is a
small yellow spot.

Megalopus vittaticollis, mihi.

Elongatus, parallelus, flavus, nitidus, supra pube nigro
vestitus, capite (facie inferiori exceptâ), thoracis maculâ apicali
et utrinque vittulâ, tibiis tarsisque posticis nigris, thorace
transverso, apice valde, basi modice constricto ; elytris parallelis,
basi elevatis, dorso depressis, lineâ laterali, lineâ submarginali,
suturâ apiceque fuscis, vittâ basali, callo humerali positâ nigrâ.

Mas Trochanteribus posticis obtuse spinosis, femoribus ejusdem paris valde incrassatis, subtus ad basin tuberculo obtuso
armatis, tibiis posticis robustis, curvatis, basi attenuatis, intus
ante apicem sinuatis. Long 5 lin

Hab. Nauta, Upper Amazons.

Head coarsely punctured, face between the upper part of the
eyes impressed with a deep ill defined oblong fovea, below which
is a raised triangular impunctate space, extending downwards
to the upper margin of the clypeus, lower half of the latter,
together with the mouth fulvous, clothed with concolorous hairs ;
apices of jaws piceous Thorax transverse, subcylindrical,
strongly constricted in front, moderately so at the base, sides
just in front of the hinder angle armed with a large acute
tubercule ; surface coarsely punctured, a longitudinal space on
the middle of the disk free from punctures ; a transverse medial
patch on the anterior border, together with a short vitta on
either side just in front of the basal margin, black. Scutellum
trigonate. Elytra broader than the thorax, depressed, longitudinally and irregularly excavated along the inner disk, basilar
space slightly elevated, the apex, a marginal line, a faint

N

sutural stripe, together with a very narrow and indistinct vitta extending downwards from the humeral callus, and abbreviated before reaching the apex, fuscous, on the humeral callus is a black bifurcate patch, the inner ramus of which is connected with the medial longitudinal vitta, and the outer one with the lateral border.

Description of a New Genus and Species of Lucanoid Coleoptera *from the interior of Tasmania ·* by Major F. J. SIDNEY PARRY, F.L.S.

HOPLOGONUS*, Gen. nov.

Habitu fere generis *Lissotes*, at caput depressum, nec convexum ; mandibulæ porrectæ, nec falcatæ ; in utroque sexu prothorace angulis posticis elytrisque angulis humeralibus spino sub-erecto armatis ; oculi minuti.

Hoplogonus Simsoni, n. sp. ♂, ♀ (var. max).

Plate I. figs. 1, 2, 3.

H. niger, nitidus, mandibulis elongatis, robustis, intus edentatis, capite prothoraceque fere longitudine, in medio dente forti armatis ; capite transverso, sub- depresso, antice porrecto, lineâ marginali sinuatâ, augulis ante oculos acutis, lateribus in medio obtuse productis , clypeo parvo, conico , clava antennarum ut in gen *Lissotes*, oculi vix cantho incisi ; pronoto capite elytrisque latiori, sub-convexo, prope angulis anticis profunde foveato, medio leviter canaliculato, angulis anticis productis, rotundatis, posticis fortiter obliquis, spino minuto, suberecto armatis, elytris brevibus, subconvexis, late costatis, augulis humeralibus spino acuto, suberecto instructis , scutello parvo ; tibiis anticis extus 3- vel 4- dentatis, quatuor posticis in utroque sexu spino acuto armatis

Long. mandibulæ 4 lin , capitis 1½ lin., prothoracis 2½ lin , elytrorum 5 lin.

Hab Tasmania.   Coll. Parry & Fry.

♀ with the body broader, the prothorax narrower, its posterior angles less oblique, the suberect spine considerably more prominent, with but a faint indication of a median line, and the foveæ near the anterior angles shallower. The head is small, quadrate, slightly inflated at the sides. The mandibles short, slightly curved towards the apex, internally edentate, emarginate at the base, with a small shining tubercular process in the centre. The elytra exhibit no trace of the smooth elevated ridges

* 'οπλον arma et γωνος angulus

conspicuous in the male; in both sexes the punctuation of the head and thorax is less diffuse, being considerably deeper on the head, and in the centre of the prothorax is a small cluster of punctate impressions, more conspicuous in the female than in the male.

This remarkable and interesting new insect has been recently discovered in the interior of Tasmania by Augustus Simson, Esq, who, in a letter addressed to Mr. E. W. Janson, expresses the opinion that it is subterraneous in its habits, having been found whilst digging a trench in some mining operations   As the insect has not been dissected I am not in a position to state, whether, as occurs in the genera *Lissapterus* and *Lissotes*, its condition is apterous or not   Five specimens have been received exhibiting a slight variation in the size of the prothoracic spines

Notices of new or little known CETONIIDÆ. by OLIVER E. JANSON No. 1.

Cotinis polita, n. sp.

C nigra, nitida, convexa; clypeo crebre rudeque punctato, apice rotundato, parum producto ; thorace vage profunde punctato , elytris parce subtilissimeque subseriatim punctatis Long ♂ 20, ♀ 23 mm , lat. ♂ 11, ♀ 13½ mm.

Black, shining , head convex and smooth at the base, clypeus thickly, deeply and coarsely punctate, with an elevated longitudinal ridge extending from the crown nearly to the apex, margin reflexed, apex slightly produced, rounded.

Thorax finely and sparsely punctate on the disc, the punctures coarser and denser at the sides, especially near the anterior angles, where they become confluent, basal lobe large, depressed, nearly covering the scutellum, a central impressed longitudinal line, effaced on the disc, but distinct behind

Scutellum very narrow and acute.

Elytra sparsely and very finely punctate, the punctures arranged in indistinct rows on the disc and sides, larger and confused at the apex, suture depressed near the scutellum, elevated posteriorly ; epimera thickly and coarsely punctate.

Pygidium convex, transversely strigose, with a large shallow depression on each side.

Beneath sparsely arcuate-punctate at the sides, abdomen with a few shallow punctures arranged in an irregular transverse row on segments 2–4, confused on 5–6 , mesosternal process rather short, flat, rounded at the apex; femora and hinder pairs of tibiæ fringed with black hairs, anterior tibiæ obtusely tridentate

Female larger, with the clypeus broader and more strongly punctate, the thorax also is more densely punctate, and the anterior tibiæ are stouter, with the teeth acute.

The only specimens of this well marked species which I have seen, were captured by my brother, Mr. E. M. Janson, in the province of Chontales, Nicaragua , its nearest ally appears to me to be *C. subviolacea,* G. & P. Coll. Janson.

Stenotarsia Scotti, n. sp. Plate I. fig. 7.

S. nigra, supra opaca, capite nitido, thorace, scutello, elytris- que obscure croceis, thorace plaga magna discoidali, scutello marginibus elytrisque maculis quatuor nigris. Long 14 mm , lat 7 mm.

Black, above (with the exception of the head) opaque, thorax, scutellum and elytra of a dirty saffron yellow, the first with a large discoidal patch, the second with its margins, and the last with four (two on each) spots black.

Head black, shining in front, dull behind, finely and rather sparsely punctate ; clypeus dilated anteriorly, its apex rounded and distinctly emarginate, margins reflexed , lamellæ of antennæ rufous at their tips.

Thorax nearly circular, truncate in front, impunctate, of a sordid saffron yellow, with a large subquadrate black patch (widest at the base, sinuate at the sides and apex) covering nearly the entire disc, sides fringed with coarse yellowish grey hairs.

Scutellum impunctate, of the colour of the thorax, its base broadly its margins narrowly pitchy.

Elytra coarsely but shallowly and very sparsely punctate, with a slightly raised longitudinal ridge on the disc, separately rounded at the apex, the sutural angle slightly produced, of the colour of the thorax, each with two black spots, one, small, nearly round, near the apex of the scutellum, the other trans- verse quadrate, at about one third from the apex and nearly equidistant from the suture and lateral margin ; epimera black.

Pygidium large, nearly vertical, pitchy red, transversely stri- gose.

Beneath black, abdomen tinged posteriorly with red, shining, sparsely arcuate-punctate, clothed with a sparse, yellowish grey pubescence, of which a patch is particularly conspicuous at the side of each segment · mesosternum scarcely produced, its apex truncate , legs black, shining, punctate and pubescent, anterior tibiæ tridentate, the upper tooth obsolete, posterior tarsi very long and slender, the three basal joints taken together distinctly longer than the tibiæ.

Hab. Madagascar

For the only specimen I have seen of this charming species I am indebted to Mr. Scott, to whom I have dedicated it.

This species is most nearly allied to *S crocata*, G. and P , and bears even a closer resemblance to the *Trichiides* than does that species. The intermediate legs and anterior tarsi are unfortunately wanting in my specimen.

I may here mention that the four species described by Gory and Percheron (Silb. Rev. Ent. III. pp. 128–129) must, as conjectured by Prof. Burmeister (Handb. f. Entom. III. p. 591) thirty-five years since from an examination of the actual types, be reduced to two, *coccinea* being the ♀ of *crocata*. and *velutina* the ♂ of *vermiculata*, a position of affairs ignored by Mess. Gemminger and v. Harold in their Catalogus Coleopterorum IV (1869).

Pygora ornata, n. sp.

P. nigra nitida, elytris striatis, plaga disci rubra, albo-quadri-maculatis, pygidio convexo. Long 15–17 mm. lat. $6\frac{1}{4}$–$7\frac{1}{2}$ mm

Head closely and rather coarsely punctate, clypeus slightly narrowed anteriorly, its sides straight, its apex rounded and shallowly emarginate, its margins reflexed, its central portion convex, impressed in front.

Thorax with a few scattered punctures at the sides, lateral margins elevated and angularly produced in the middle, base shallowly emarginate in front of the scutellum, posterior angles nearly rectangular their extreme apices rounded

Scutellum very acute, convex, impunctate.

Elytra abruptly narrowed behind the humeral angles, thence slightly widened towards the apex, where each is separately and strongly rounded, suture depressed, the disc of each with three deep longitudinal striæ, of which the inner two are curved and extend from about one fourth from the base to the apex, the outer one short, reaching from near the base to about the middle, there are a few punctures at the commencement of each of the striæ, and a short sinuous row of them between the outer stria and the lateral margin and reaching the base ; on the disc of each elytron is a large, nearly semicircular red patch of which the convex side is turned towards the suture, and two silvery white spots, one small, oval, situate near the lateral margin about one fourth from the apex, the other, larger, transverse, trilobed, at the inner side of the apex, epimera with a white spot above.

Pygidium large, convex, smooth in the centre, strigose and with an oblong transverse spot at each side, apex pubescent.

Beneath black, shining, with large white patches on each side ; mesosternal process broad, apex obtusely pointed ; abdomen spotted with white on each side and in the central depression ; tibiæ fringed with black hairs, intermediate femora with an elongate white spot near the base ; anterior tibiæ tridentate, the upper tooth small, posterior tibiæ with an angular projection within near the base, and a small tooth in the middle without ; four posterior tarsi long and furnished internally with stout bristles, claws very large and acute.

The female has the thorax broader, with the lateral margins less angular, the pygidium is narrower, the abdomen is not impressed nor spotted with white in the centre, the anterior tibiæ are more acutely dentate, the posterior are destitute of the angular projection on the inner side near the base, the tarsi are much shorter and the claws conspicuously smaller.

Hab. Madagascar   Coll. Janson

Closely resembles *P. conjuncta*, G. & P (Westwood, Trans. Ent. Soc. Lond. 1874 p 478 Tab. VIII. fig. 5) in general appearance, but is more convex and shining, the head much narrower, the elytra have only two white spots on each, the red marking is brighter and of a different form, and the pygidium of the female is not tuberculate, it is also less punctured above, and the sculpture of the elytra is different.

The only specimens I have seen of this elegant species I obtained, with many other fine *Cetoniidæ*, from the rich collection recently made by Mr. Crossley.

Eupœcila Miskini, n. sp. Plate I. fig. 5. ♀.

E nigra, nitida, flavosignata, elytrorum lateribus rufis, pedibus nigris, femoribus posticis flavo-maculatis.   Long 18 mm.

Head shining black, a transverse band between the antennæ continued anteriorly along the sides, and a small spot in front of it, yellow, sparsely punctate between the eyes; clypeus finely punctate, sides rounded and moderately reflexed, apex acutely emarginate, antennæ and palpi reddish brown.

Thorax shining black, a longitudinal line in the centre terminating in a short transverse mark just above the scutellum, and a marginal band on each side almost united in front, not quite reaching the posterior angles and partly interrupted near the anterior angles by a waved- black spot, yellow, impunctate, anterior margin slightly produced in the centre, basal margin strongly trisinuate

Scutellum shining black, acute, with a broad central longitudinal yellow stripe, finely punctate on each side at the base.

Elytra shining black, reddish at the sides, a longitudinal curved stripe on the basal half of the disc dilated internally at its apex almost to the suture, and containing a small black spot, two transverse spots placed obliquely behind the middle, and a curved spot at the apex, yellow, a sutural row of shallow punctures and a few very faint points on the disc; each elytron separately rounded at the apex, the sutural angle produced into a minute spine

Pygidium shining black, with a curved mark on each side, and a subquadrate spot at the apex, yellow, convex, finely transverse strigose.

Beneath shining black, with yellow markings at the sides, abdomen with transverse yellow stripes, mesosternal process long, pointed and slightly incurved at its apex; legs black, posterior femora with a yellow stripe on the outer side, anterior tibiæ acutely tridendate.

Hab. Cape York (N.E. Australia)   Coll. Janson.

Closely allied to *E. Australasiæ*, but presenting abundant distinguishing characters.

The only specimen I have seen of this interesting species has been recently received from W. H. Miskin, Esq, of Brisbane, to whom I have much pleasure in dedicating it.

Protætia niveoguttata, (Chevr.) n. sp.   Plate I fig. 4

P. olivacea, supra opaca, capite nitido, corpore albo maculato, capitis guttis 6, thoracis 16, scutelli 2, elytrorum circa 27 albis Long 22 mm, lat. 12 mm.

o

Head shining, green, with two spots on the clypeus, two between the eyes, and two, very small, at the base white and slightly impressed, sparsely punctate ; clypeus rounded at the sides, apex truncate and reflexed , antennæ pitchy

Thorax olive-green, opaque, with sixteen white spots, one at each of the anterior angles, an arcuate transverse row of six in front, a row of four across the centre, one at each of the posterior angles, and two near the hinder margin just above the scutellum ; sparsely punctate at the sides, posterior angles rounded, base deeply trisinuate.

Scutellum olive-green, opaque, basal angles white, elongate, apex obtuse, impunctate

Elytra olive-green, opaque each with eighteen (and one common) white spots, arranged thus, six along the outer margin, one at the base midway between the scutellum and the shoulder, two transversely and slightly obliquely on the disc at one sixth from the base, one common to both elytra at apex of scutellum, one in centre of disc about one fourth from base, one near the suture nearly midway from the base, one midway within the third and fourth marginal spots, three in a transverse row about one third from apex, one close to the suture at one sixth from apex, one opposite the sixth marginal spot, and one just within the sutural apical margin ; with a central longitudinal costa, obsolete at the base, coarsely and shallowly punctate, the punctures arranged in regular rows within the costa, more numerous and confused outside it ; suture shining, elevated posteriorly and terminating in an acute spine at the apex , epimera shining, green, with an elongate white spot above.

Pygidium transversely strigose, green, slightly shining, with two basal and four marginal white spots

Beneath green, shining, spotted with white, coarsely and sparsely punctate at the sides , mesosternal process dilated and rounded at the apex, abdomen nearly impunctate, a white spot on the antero-lateral angle of segments 1–4, segment 5 with two white spots at the base, one on each side at one fourth from the lateral margin ; legs green, shining, punctate, a small white spot on the knees, and one at the apex of each of the four posterior femora ; anterior tibiæ tridentate, posterior femora and tibiæ very robust, the latter curved, the inner apical spine very large.

Female broader, slightly shining and distinctly punctate above, without white spots on the head, and with only two marginal spots on the pygidium ; the elytra are not spined at the apex, the two apical segments of the abdomen are thickly and coarsely punctate throughout, and the posterior tibiæ are nearly straight with the apical spine smaller

Hab. Cambodia. Coll. Janson.

This species has been long known, I have seen it labelled " *Gouloti*," and Major Parry informs me 'that in the Paris collections it is called " *niveoguttata*, Chev.," but as I have been unable to find a description of it, I thought it would be useful to describe and figure it, and as the first of the names above mentioned is preoccupied, I have adopted the specific appellation bestowed upon it by Mons Chevrolat.

Diaphonia notabilis ?, White, ♀ Plate I. fig. 6.

Diaphonia notabilis, White in Stokes' Voy I p. 506. Pl. I. fig. 5 ♂ (1146).

It is not without considerable hesitation that I refer the insect here figured to the *D notabilis*, White; compared with the type, in the Collection of the British Museum, and which is the only exponent I have yet seen, the insect now under consideration presents the following differences it is much broader, the posterior angles of the thorax are rounded, the head is black, with the sides of the clypeus and a transverse curved band at the base yellow, the thoracic discoidal black patch has a longitudinal yellow line in the centre at the base, the pygidium is entirely yellow, the penultimate and apical segments of the abdomen are yellow, margined with black, the remaining segments are black with a yellow spot on each side, and the posterior femora are reddish yellow with the extreme apex and base only black

. Hab. Cape York. Coll. Janson.

A single specimen communicated by W. H. Miskin, Esq., of Brisbane.

Explanation of Plate I.

Figs, 1, 2 & 3—*Hoplogonus Simsoni*, Parry, ♂, ♀

   ,,   4—*Protaetia niveoguttata*, (Chev), O. E. Janson, ♂.

   ,,   5—*Eupœcila Mishini*; O. E Janson, ♀.

   ,,   6—*Diaphonia notabilis*?, White ♀.

   ,,   7—*Stenotarsia Scotti*, O. E Janson.

Notices of new or little known CETONIIDÆ; by OLIVER E. JANSON. No. 2.

Ceratorrhina loricata, n. sp.

C. rufo-flava, nitida, opalizans, thorace scutelloque viridi-olivacco tinctis, elytris viridi-ochraceis, macula humerali apicalique nigris ; capite elongato, profunde longitudinaliter excavato, marginibus lateralibus oblique reflexis, vertice processu bidentato instructo, clypeo utrinque producto, in medio cornu porrecto, apice bifido, armato, ♂. Long. 28 mm.

Reddish testaceous, shining, base of head green, thorax and scutellum with an olive green tint, elytra yellow with a green reflection, the suture green, a small spot at the shoulder, and one on the apical callus black ; beneath red, segments margined with olive green, legs red with a greenish tinge, knees pitchy ; the entire upper surface when examined with a lens presents an extremely minute and dense puncturation

Head sparsely and shallowly punctured, deeply excavated, the sides obliquely elevated, basal margin produced into a short bifid protuberance, clypeus acutely produced on each side, and armed in the centre with a rather short stout porrect horn, which is dilated and slightly emarginate at its apex.

Thorax rather deeply punctured at the sides, sparsely on the disc, a narrow median space smooth, anterior angles slightly produced, posterior angles rounded, basal margin rather strongly tri-sinuate

Scutellum with a few scattered punctures, apex obtuse.

Elytra finely punctured, with several irregular rows of larger punctures on the disc, suture slightly elevated and acutely produced at the apex.

Pygidium finely transversely strigose.

P

Beneath coarsely punctured, abdomen almost impunctate, feebly longitudinally impressed; mesosternal process broad, apex obtusely pointed, and bent inwards; legs punctured, anterior femora densely hirsute on their inner margin.

Hab. Angola

About a dozen specimens of this very distinct species were taken in a cluster on a flower by the late Dr. Welwitsch, who gave me the specimen above described, together with several other new and interesting *Cetoniidæ*; it is evidently nearly allied to *C. quadrimaculatus*, F, differing, however, considerably in the structure of the head and in coloration

Glycyphana scutellata. n. sp.

G. atra, supra opaca, capite nitido, thorace lateribus posticeque late sanguineo-marginato, scutello magno, apice obtuso, elytris nigro-piceis gutta marginali aurantiaca, pygidio utrinque albo maculato, subtus piceo-nigra, nitida, pectoris et abdominis lateribus late albo-squamosis, ♂. Long. 11 mm.

Head shining black, base opaque, with a small white spot on each side, somewhat coarsely but not very closely punctured, centre longitudinally elevated, apex of clypeus impressed and slightly emarginate

Thorax transverse, slightly emarginate above the scutellum, velvety black, margined at the sides and base with dull red, faintly and sparingly punctured ·

Scutellum short, very broad, and obtusely rounded at the apex, velvety black, impunctate.

Elytra rich brown-black, velvety, with a kidney shaped orange marginal spot just behind the middle, faintly punctured in rows, those next the suture assuming striæ towards the apex.

Pygidium velvety brown, hirsute, with a white spot on each side.

Beneath pitchy-black, shining, broadly crusted with white at the sides, sparingly punctured and hirsute; mesosternal process short, very broad, dilated and almost truncate at the apex; legs punctured and hirsute, femora and hinder pairs of tibiæ fringed with golden hairs, anterior tibiæ bidentate.

Hab. Borneo.

Allied to *G. celebensis*, Wall., and *G. torquata*, Fab., but differs from all the species with which I am acquainted in its broad obtusely rounded scutellum, form of mesosternal process and coloration.

Glycyphana andamanensis, n. sp.

G. supra viridis, opaca, capite thorace elytrisque ochraceo maculatis, subtus pedibusque rufo-viridis   Long. 13–14 mm

Above green or black, opaque, finely hirsute, clypeus, underside and legs greenish red or greenish black, shining.

Head coarsely punctured, a narrow band on each side ochreous; apex of clypeus slightly emarginate, the angles rounded, margins not elevated ; antennæ pitchy, apex of lamellæ reddish.

Thorax sparingly punctured on the disc, more coarsely so at the sides, a narrow lateral border and two spots on each side of the disc ochreous

Scutellum impunctate, obtuse at the apex, with ochreous scales on each side at the base

Elytra with five rows of punctures on the disc, the three next the suture continued from the middle to near the apex by three deep straight simple striæ, sides with numerous elongate punctures becoming confluent and forming irregular transverse striæ towards the apex, suture elevated posteriorly, forming a ridge and terminating in an acute spine at the apex : there are usually ten ochreous spots on each, five discal and five marginal, of the former one is placed near the base, one just below it nearer the suture (this spot is often absent), one at the origin of the three simple sutural striæ, and two at their apex, of the latter (the marginal spots), the first is near the humeral angle, the next two placed transversely just behind the middle, the fourth at the outer apical angle and the fifth at the apex; the epimera are margined with ochreous scales above.

Pygidium strigose, red, margined and spotted with ochreous scales.

Beneath punctured, crusted with ochreous at the sides; mesosternal process short, broad and rounded at the apex, with a transverse impressed line ; femora and hinder pairs of tibiæ fringed with brownish hairs, anterior tibiæ with an acute subapical tooth, in the female acutely angulated about the middle

Hab. Andaman Islands.

A very variable species apparently most nearly allied to *G. moluccarum*, Wall., which it resembles in its elongate form; in a long series of specimens before me some have the spots very large and conspicuous whilst in others they are scarcely preceptible.

Glycyphana nicobarica, n. sp.

G. supra laete viridis, opaca, capite nigro albo bimaculato, thorace marginibus maculisque quatuor albis, elytris maculis septem albis ornatis, subtus nitida, lateribus albis Long 12 mm.

Head black, slightly shining, with two small white spots at the base, closely punctured, the punctures coarser and confluent at the sides and base, margins of clypeus depressed, apex slightly emarginate and impressed.

Thorax transverse, strongly rounded behind, slightly emarginate above the scutellum, opaque green, a large spot at the anterior angles continued narrowly along the lateral margins, and four small spots on the disc white, sides coarsely punctured and hirsute

Scutellum obtuse at the apex, opaque green, impunctate.

Elytra with numerous shallow, elongate punctures arranged in rows on the disc, irregular and setiferous at the sides and apex, opaque green, with seven white spots on each, one on the disc near the base, one just below it at the margin, three in a row along the suture (the third being at the apex), and two larger, transverse, on the margin behind the middle, the epimera are also white

Pygidium strigose with a smooth, elevated longitudinal line, red with a white angular mark on each side.

Beneath brownish-green, shining, punctured and hirsute, with large white patches at the sides, apex of abdomen reddish; mesosternal process short, broad, slightly rounded and transversely grooved at the apex; legs shining black, punctured and hirsute, trochanters reddish, anterior tibiae with three acute lateral teeth

Hab. Nicobar Islands

Allied to *G. glauca,* Blanch , and *G. aromatica.* Wall., two specimens now before me (apparently females), and several others which I have seen exhibit no marked variation.

Protaetia andamanarum, n. sp.

P. atra, supra opaca, subtus nitida, elytris aurantiaco-variega-tis, apice spinosis, ♂. Long. 21–23 mm

Head short, clypeus quadrate, shining black, punctured, centre convex, apical margin slightly elevated and sinuous; antennæ brownish-red.

Thorax black, opaque, convex, basal margin strongly trisinu-ous, lateral margins slightly raised.

Scutellum black, opaque, elongate, apex obtuse.

Elytra black, opaque, several small spots close to the lateral margin before the middle and one larger and angular behind the middle rich orange, sides and apical portions faintly punctured, apical margin strigose, suture elevated posteriorly and acutely produced at the apical angle.

Pygidium convex, deep brown, opaque, faintly and sparsely punctured, apical margin fringed with short brownish hairs.

Beneath shining black, punctured at the sides; mesosternal process short, much dilated and rounded at the apex; legs shining black, punctured and strigose, anterior tibiæ with three lateral teeth, the upper one almost obsolete, anterior femora and hinder pairs of tibiæ fringed with brown hairs, tarsi short and stout.

Female larger and more robust, with some small orange spots at the sides of the thorax, the elytra slightly costate behind, not produced at the apical angle, the orange markings larger and supplemented by an elongate spot near the base, some small ones near those on the lateral margin, a group of irregular spots just behind the middle and close to the suture, and a similar group nearer the apex, pygidium shining black, transversely strigose, the underside more closely punctured.

Hab Andaman Islands. Coll. Janson.

A very variable species not obviously allied to any other of the genus, several specimens now before me from Mr. Higgins's collection differ considerably in the extent of the orange mark-ings, the most conspicuous being a male which is entirely black, with the exception of a minute spot on each side of the elytra, also a female with the basal spot almost obsolete, only two small spots on the disc, about the middle, and the apical group entirely absent ; I have seen no males presenting any indication of the discal spots, which appear to be always more or less present in the opposite sex.

Diplognatha viridula, n. sp.

D. aneo-viridis, nitidissima, subtus cupreo tincta, clypeo subtiliter punctato, thorace lateribus confertissime punctato-rugoso, elytris subtiliter striato-punctatis, ♂   Long. 20 mm

Entirely dark green, very shining, above with a brassy reflection, underside tinged with coppery.

Head finely and sparsely punctured, more coarsely so at the base, forehead slightly convex ; clypeus short, slightly convex in the centre, apex and sides elevated, especially at the angles.

Thorax strongly lobed behind, slightly emarginate above the scutellum, posterior angles rounded, disc impunctate, sides very finely punctured and strigose.

Scutellum narrow, convex, impunctate.

Elytra with a sutural and several indistinct discal rows of extremely fine punctures, the sides and apex finely strigose, suture elevated at the apex, the angle rounded and slightly produced, the apical callus very prominent.

Pygidium finely transversely strigose, with a small round depression on each side.

Beneath coarsely punctured and strigose at the sides ; mesosternal process broad, obtusely rounded at the apex ; abdomen longitudinally impressed ; legs coarsely punctured, anterior tibiæ acutely tridentate externally, intermediate and posterior tibiæ with one acute tooth, about one-third from the apex.

Hab. West Africa (Cape Coast).   Coll Janson.

The specimen now before me, and one in Major Parry's collection, are all I have seen of this fine species ; it is evidently allied to *D. gagates*, Fab. which it resembles in size and form.

Synonymia.

Allorhina hypoglauca, Westw , Trans Ent. Soc Lond. 1874, p. 475,=*Lansbergei*, Sallé, (1857).

The locality given (Nicaragua), is probably erroneous, Mr. Higgins's specimen is from Bogota.

Euryomia quadrimaculata, Westw., l. c., p. 477, (1874),= *stella,* G.P., (1835).

Burmeister locates it in the genus *Epixanthis,* but it is undoubtedly a *Euryomia.*

Clinteria tricolorata, Westw., l. c., p. 477, (1874),=*suavis,* Burm. (1847).

The locality given (India), is evidently a mistake, its habitat is S. Africa, I possess a specimen from N'Gami.

Anochilia marginicollis, Westw, l c., p 479, (1874),= *laevigata,* G.P., (1835). (quite distinct from and totally unlike *A. cingulata*).

A long series of this species collected by Crossley exhibit great variation as regards colour.

Euphoria Belti, Sharp, Journ Linn Soc. Zool. xiii, p 137, (1877),=*Candezei,* O. Janson (1875).

On some Heliconoid Danainæ *and* Heliconidæ *in the Collection of the British Museum ;* by Arthur G Butler, F.L.S., &c.

In his great paper on the Lepidoptera of the Amazon Valley, Mr. Bates has regarded the genus *Mechanitis* (typical) as consisting of but one extremely variable species ; among the varieties he ʻdescribes, two are named, as being better marked forms than the others ; but to my mind the differences are no greater than between the typical species *M. polymnia* and the other forms in the genus.

In the case of *M. olivencia,* Mr. Bates says, " It is a variety of *M. polymnia* which varies in an important part of structure ; but this remark would be equally applicable to " var. 2," of which we read " hind wings of the ♂ more angular than in *M. polymnia,* the apex being as if truncated."

As I desire to see consistency in our nomenclature, and moreover find it extremely awkward not to have names for the supposed forms of *M. polymnia,* I shall follow Mr Bates's example both in the above-mentioned paper, and in the Entomologist's Monthly Magazine I , p. 33, and name them.

Egaensis group.

1 *Mechanitis obscura.*

M. egaensis var. 1, Bates, Trans. Linn. Soc. xxiii., p. 532, (1862.)

♂, ♀ Ega, (*Bates*) B.M.

Also found at Pupunha, Rio Jurua.

The above form may very possibly be a race of *M egaensis* with which it occurs , but it is very common, and differs constantly in the much deeper tint of the wings and wider black bands.

2. *Mechanitis truncata.*

M. egaensis var. 2.   Bates, l.c.
Ega.   B.M.

This is a very small species, I do not think it a variety.

3 *Mechanitis pannifera,* n. sp

Differs from *M. egaensis* in having the postcellular spot of primaries divided in the centre and edged internally by a sulphur yellow expansion of the postmedian band ; the tawny subapical area replaced by an irregular sulphur yellow spot; secondaries with the median and marginal bands united into a large brown patch which occupies the greater part of the wing.

Obydos and Ega   B M.

4 *Mechanitis plagigera,* n sp

Differs from *M. egaensis* in its much narrower black bands and smaller black spots, also in having only a small diffused yellowish subapical spot instead of the curved tawny and yellow streak.

Prainha, on the Amazons.   B.M.

Polymnia group.

5 *Mechanitis visenda,* n. sp.

Differs from *M. polymnia* in the much broader internal black streak, absence of yellow patch across the end of the cell, and presence of an ill-defined subapical yellow spot in primaries; secondaries with the central transverse black band double the width, and the marginal black border narrower

Pará and Tapajos   B M.

Genus Heliconius, *Fabricius*

6. *Heliconius lativitta,* n. sp.

Allied to *H. vesta,* but with a broad oblique sulphur yellow patch just beyond the cell of primaries, instead of the curved yellow band and large discal spot of that species , a small spot in the end of the cell.

Ega, Rio Jurua, Purus and Madeira, and Guayaquil.   B M.

I believe that Bates has wrongly identified *H. aglaope*, of Felder, and that it is a species much resembling the above.

7. *Heliconius mutabilis*.

H. thelxiope, var. 4, Bates, Trans. Linn. Soc. xxiii, p. 558.

The yellow spot in the cell is sometimes wanting, and the spots which border the inner edge of the red band are three in number and well-defined.

Serpa. B.M.

This may be an extreme variety of *H. lucia* which occurs also at Serpa.

8. *Heliconius coralii*, n. sp

Like *H. callicopis*, of Cramer (the male figure) but larger, and with the basal area of the primaries broadly red.

Common at Serpa. B.M.

This is most like *H. elimæa*, but the scarlet patch is not broken through, but simply has a black spot in the centre.

Notes on Japanese RHOPALOCERA, *with descriptions of new species*, by OLIVER E JANSON

The species here described or recorded as Japanese are chiefly from a very fine and extensive collection made by F. M Jonas, Esq, during four years sojourn in the Island of Niphon, the first set, including the uniques, is now 'n the possession of Messrs. Salvin and Godman, the Heterocerous portion of the collection will probably soon occupy Mr. Butler's attention.

Erebia niphonica, n sp

Above dark brown, body and base of wings blackish; primaries with a large ochreous patch beyond the middle extending from the sub-costal nervure almost to the inner margin, subovate, slightly narrowed in the middle and dentate externally. containing a double black spot in front, and a smaller round one behind; secondaries with an ill defined reddish-brown transverse band beyond the middle, containing three small round black spots near its outer edge, the one nearest the anal angle with a white pupil; beneath brown, primaries marked as above; secondaries with the band slightly indicated by dusky brown, the white pupil alone distinct In the female the black spots on both wings have conspicuous white pupils above and below, the spots on the upper side of secondaries are only partly surrounded with reddish-ochreous in place of the band in the male, beneath they have a large dusky white basal patch and a conspicuous silvery white sinuous band. Expanse of wings 1 inch 10 lines

This interesting species (the first of the genus discovered in Japan) was taken by Mr. Jonas on Assamayama, at an elevation of about 7,000 feet, and to whose liberality I am indebted for the specimens described above, it appears to me to be most nearly allied to *E. stygne*, Fisch, Ent Russ. I, t. 1, f. 2.

Argynnis lysippe, n. sp

Allied to *A laodice*, Pall, and *A japonica*, Ménét, but considerably larger, and with the primaries much more produced at the apex. Above it differs from *japonica* in being of a darker and slightly greenish tint, with the fringes dirty brown; the primaries have the second and third transverse marks in the cell angular, closer together and united at their lower ends, the black spots are larger, the second and fifth of the inner series narrower, more curved, and continued inwardly along the nervures; the secondaries have the inner series of spots united and forming an irregular zigzag band, and the marginal line is greenish-brown; beneath, the primaries have a large greenish apical patch extending further inwardly and along the outer margin than the brown one of *japonica*, the sub-marginal black spots are very indistinct, and the transverse row of white spots is entirely absent; the basal half of secondaries is greener, and the reddish transverse basal line is not waved, the silvery spots are better defined, the apical half is darker, with two rows of ill defined lunular spots, and a marginal band metallic green. Expanse of wings $3\frac{1}{2}$ inches

This species, although closely allied to *laodice*, var. *japonica*, Ménét., is evidently quite distinct, the male now before me was taken with several other specimens, by Mr Jonas, on Assam-ayama; I have examined a considerable number of *A. japonica*, recently received from Japan, but find none offering indications of an intermediate form between it and *A. lysippe*.

Argynnis fortuna, n. sp.

Allied to *A aglaia*, the black markings on upper side of primaries somewhat similar, but the posterior spot of the inner transverse series much nearer the outer margin, being in a line with the discal row, the corresponding spot of which is small and also nearer the outer margin, the submarginal row of spots are smaller, and the marginal band much narrower; the secondaries differ in having the inner zigzag band produced into a rather long point on the centre of the wing, which replaces the third spot of the discal series; beneath, the primaries have a greenish apical patch with three inner and four marginal silvery spots; the secondaries are greenish, speckled with black, two small spots just beyond the cell and a short submarginal fascia ochreous, the silvery spots are disposed as in *aglaia*, except the fourth and seventh of the discal series, which are very small and nearer the outer margin, and the marginal spots are larger. Expanse of wings 2 inches 10 lines.

This is probably the species erroneously referred to *aglaia*, by Mr. Murray, the above mentioned characters will serve to separate it at once from that species, as well as from *jamadeva*, Moore.

Neptis Pryeri, Butl.

Neptis Pryeri, Butler, Trans Ent. Soc. Lond. 1871, p. 403 ; Lep Ex. p. 184, t. 63, f. 4.

Limenitis arboretorum, Oberthur, Etudes Ent. 2, p 24, t 3, f. 3 (1876).

Several specimens taken by Mr Jonas at the foot of Oyama agree perfectly with the descriptions and figures quoted, thus leaving no doubt of the identity of M. Oberthur's species with *N. Pryeri*.

Neptis alwina, Brem

I am indebted to Mr Fenton for a specimen of this fine species, Mr. Jonas has also taken several at the foot of Oyama.

Dichorragia nesimachus, Boisd

Two specimens taken by Mr Jonas in a mountain pass about 100 miles N W of Yedo must be referred to this species, which appears hitherto to have only been received from North India

Lycæna bætica, Linn.

Several specimens of this common and widely distributed species have been taken by Mr. Pryer at Yamato ; I have not found it recorded before from Japan

Niphanda fusca, Brem.

Thecla fusca, Brem Beitr. Schmett, N. China's, p. 9, Ménét Cat. Mus Petrop Lep. 1., t. 4, f. 5 ♀
Amblypodia dispar, Brem Lep Ost. Sib., p. 24, t. 3, f 4. ♂
Polyommatus fuscus, Oberth Etudes Ent 2, p. 20, t. 4, f 5. ♀

A pair of this species received from Mr. Fenton agree well with the figures above quoted, and are the only specimens I have seen from Japan.   Mr. Moore considers it should be placed in his genus *Niphanda*.

Thecla japonica, Murr.

Dipsas japonica, Murray, Ent. Mo. Mag. xi, p. 169.
Dipsas taxila, Hew, Ill. Diur. Lep. supp , p 16, t 6, f 16, 17, (nec Brem)

Mr. Murray, in his last list of Japanese Rhopalocera, considers this species to be possibly identical with *smaragdina*, Brem.; but, as Mr. Butler has already stated, it is perfectly distinct from that species and far more closely allied to *taxila*, Brem., with which Mr. Hewitson has apparently confounded it, since his figures above quoted are evidently intended for this species. His description of the underside, however, does not agree with the figure, but applies much better to the true *taxila*, which also occurs in Japan. How Mr. Murray overlooked the fact that this insect had been figured two years prior by Mr. Hewitson in his great work on the Lycaenidæ, to which family he (Mr. Murray) devotes his special attention, I am utterly at a loss to comprehend

Thecla orientalis, Murr.

Dipsas orientalis, Murray, Ent Mo Mag. xi, p 169

Although Mr Murray states his description is of the male of this species, it is evident he had never seen that sex, as several individuals recently received from Japan exhibit a similar sexual dissimilarity to that extant in *T. japonica*, being of a brilliant green above, paler than in that species, and without the black external margin to primaries, the underside agrees perfectly with the female.

This is a much rarer species than *japonica*, and the male was not discovered until last year, when Messrs Pryer and Jonas took several in company with the females near Yokohama

Thecla mera, n. sp

Above dark brown, secondaries produced at the anal angle and with a short outer tail, the inner one long, its apex white; beneath pale brown, both wings crossed beyond the middle by a fine waved white line, margined with dusky brown on its inner side, divided by the nervures, bent inwards posteriorly, and ending at the abdominal margin, anal region of secondaries pale orange, with a large black spot between the tails, and a row of four smaller ones just above it, anal angle black, speckled with pale blue, a fine white marginal line, and a row of obscure dusky brown sub-marginal spots near the apex Expanse of wings 1½ inch

Several specimens of this species were taken by Mr Jonas at Matzabaro, about 200 miles N.W. of Yedo ; it is allied to *T. micans*, Brem , and *T cærulescens*, Motsch.

In referring to Bremer's descriptions of *micans* and *cærulea* in his Beitr zur Schmetterlings-Fauna d Nœrd-China's, and the figures of those species given by Ménétriés in the Cat Lep. de l'Acad. Imp., I find the latter author has transposed the names, tab. iv, fig. 4 is Bremer's *micans*, and fig. 3 *cærulea*.

Thecla enthea, n sp.

Above dark brown, disc of primaries lighter ; secondaries .with one long tail, white at its apex ; beneath white, primaries with seventeen conspicuous black spots, arranged thus, two near the base, the upper one large, one at the end of the cell, three in an oblique row on the costal margin beyond the middle, and an irregular transverse row of five, followed by a submarginal row of six, apical margin rather broadly brown ; secondaries with three spots in a row at the base, a small one in the cell, an elongate one at its end, a similar shaped one between it and the anal angle, three along the abdominal margin, a curved transverse row of six beyond the middle, and a submarginal row of five, those at the base and near the costal margin black, but towards the apex the wings become dusky and the spots pale brown, margined with white, anal region pale orange, with two small black spots at the base of the tail, and one at the anal angle. Expanse of wings 1⅓ inch.

Two specimens taken by Mr Jonas, near the River Yokawa, about 140 miles N.W. of Yedo, are all I have seen of this distinct species.

Thecla Jonasi, n. sp.

♀ Above orange, slightly golden, base of wings blackish, primaries with an apical black border, wide in front but narrowed towards the inner angle ; secondaries somewhat produced

at the apical angle, tails black, tipped with white, margin
between the tail and anal angle slightly emarginate and edged
with black ; beneath brownish-ochreous ; primaries with a
narrow brown streak at the end of the cell, and a transverse
brown band (almost divided into spots by the nervures) midway
between it and the apex, extending from the costa almost to the
inner margin, where it becomes narrow and of a darker brown ;
secondaries with a brown streak at the end of the cell, and a
fine transverse white line beyond the middle, divided by the
nervures, and edged with black on its inner side, commencing
at the costa, turned inwards posteriorly, and ending just above
the anal angle, which is orange-red and the lobe black. Expanse of wings 16–22 lines.

Allied to *T. lutea*, Hew., but it is of a darker orange above,
without the black spots on secondaries, has more elongate wings,
and is very differently marked on the underside.

A few specimens of this very distinct and interesting species
were found by Mr. Jonas flying about a chesnut tree near the
River Yokawa, at the foot of Assamayama.

Papilio macilentus, n. sp.

Allied to *P. demetrius*, Cram , but with all the wings narrower
and much more elongated ; primaries above dusky black, the
black streaks between the nervures very narrow ; secondaries
with the outer margin strongly notched, the tails long and narrow, black, costa pale yellow, four small indistinct spots along
the outer margin, and a broad ring on the abdominal margin
dull red ; beneath the primaries are paler than *demetrius* and
somewhat shining , secondaries with four lunular spots along
the outer margin, an interrupted ring on the abdominal margin,
and a spot near the anal angle pale red. Expanse of wings $3\frac{3}{4}$—
$4\frac{1}{4}$ inches.

The very long slender wings are sufficient to distinguish this
species at once from *P. demetrius*, Cram , the only species which
resemble it in other respects , it appears to be confined to the
mountains, and has been taken by Messrs. Pryer and Jonas on
Oyama.

Papilio alcinous, Klug.

Mr. Murray has erroneously referred the female of this species
to *P. mencius*, Feld., both sexes of which are figured by Gray
as a variety of *alcinous*, but I have not seen it from Japan.

Pamphila ochiacea, Brem.

The specimens which I refer to this species differ from Bremer's figure in having the secondaries slightly produced at the anal angle, the figure is probably incorrect in that respect, as it otherwise agrees precisely.

Pamphila subhyalina, Brem.

Japanese specimens before me differ from Ménétriés' figure in having the secondaries produced at the anal angle, in being of a brighter yellow above and of a much paler colour beneath. The female is rather larger, of a 'paler yellow above, with the spots on the primaries more distinct, and without the black discal streak

Pamphila venata, Brem.

There are several specimens in Mr. Jonas's collection of what I consider to be only a variety of this species, they differ from Menétriés' figure in having a broader black margin and a much narrower black discal streak on primaries.

Pyrgus inachus, Ménét.

I am indebted to Mr. Fenton for a specimen of this species, it has also been taken by Mr. Jonas.

Pyrgus sinicus, Butl.

P. sinicus, Butler, Ann. Nat. Hist., 1877, p. 96.

Japanese specimens which I have, agree precisely with the type in the National collection.

Cyclopides ornatus, Brem.

A single specimen of this species was taken by Mr Jonas near Yokohama Kirby locates it in the genus *Astictopterus*, Feld., but the typical species of that genus are apparently very different insects.

Isoteinon lamprospilus, Feld.

I. lamprospilus, Felder, Wien Ent. Mon. vi, p. 30 (1862),
Reis Nov. Lep. iii, t 74, f. 20

Pamphila vitrea, Murray, Ent Mo. Mag. xi, p. 171 (1875)

This well marked species has been re-described by Mr. Murray
as a *Pamphila* Japanese specimens sent home by Messrs.
Pryer and Jonas agree exactly with Felder's description and
figure.

Description of a New Species of ATTACUS : by ARTHUR G. BUTLER, F.L.S., &c.

Attacus Atbarinus, n. sp.

♂ Allied to *A. bauhiniæ* from Senegal, but much larger, the wings much less falcate and broader; the ocellated spots more rounded, not touching the discal white band; the submarginal chain-band uniform in colour; the white patch on internal area of primaries restricted, and forming a sub-basal quadrate patch, wings above plum-colour irrorated with white, especially over the basal two-thirds, the latter bounded by a white band, bordered within with chocolate brown, strongly arched on each wing, and widening from the costal to the inner margins; a large central rounded hyaline patch on each wing, bordered with white, sordid sulphur yellow and black: discal area rather brighter than the remainder of the ground-colour, excepting near apex of primaries where it becomes pearly grey; an irregular submarginal clay-coloured apical patch bordered internally by a carmine and white undulated line, the latter terminating in a large oval black spot irrorated at its internal or smaller end with white; outer border broadly testaceous, interrupted internally by ten or eleven brown-edged sordid testaceous elliptical spots in couples; secondaries with the outer border undulated internally, intersected by a lunulate brown line, above the sinuations of which is a series of elliptical blackish spots; basal area (corresponding with a quadrate patch on internal area of primaries) snow white; head and thorax plum-colour, varied with greyish hairs; palpi, antennæ and legs olive brown, sides of meso- and meta-thorax below white; abdomen above and below snow-white, banded with red-brown; wings below much more densely irrorated with white; interno-basal area of primaries, and base of costal area of secondaries snow-white, otherwise as above; expanse of wings 5 inches, 1 line.

Atbara, Abyssinia.

Descriptions of new species of CRYPTOLECHIA *from the Amazons ;*
by ARTHUR G. BUTLER, F.L.S.

1. *Cryptolechia anceps*, n. sp.

Primaries pinky-whitish, a spot in the cell, a second at the
end of the cell, a third at the origin of the first median branch
and a sigmoidal discal series, brown ; a marginal series of black
spots ; fringe white ; secondaries shining creamy-whitish ; body
corresponding in colour with the wings ; primaries below stramineous ; a marginal series of black dots ; fringe silvery-white,
secondaries whitish stramineous ; body below creamy-whitish.
Expanse of wings 25 mm

Lower Amazons ; 6th April

Allied to *C ignobilis* of Zeller, but larger and without the
costal black spots on primaries.

2. *Cryptolechia sericata*, n. sp.

Primaries pale shining silky flesh-colour ; costal margin
yellow ; a dot at the end of the cell, and an arched discal series,
dark brown ; a marginal series of black dots ; two pale brown
costal spots, one above the end of the cell, the other larger and
near to apex ; secondaries pale stramineous ; body-corresponding
in colour with the wings ; wings below pale stramineous ; body
below silvery whitish. Expanse of wings 25 mm.

South bank of Rio Negro and Rio Madeira ; June

3 *Cryptolechia oblita*, n. sp.

Primaries pale pinky brownish ; a blackish dot on the lower
discocellular, a wavy transverse line beyond the cell, followed by
a 3 shaped line (its concavities towards the base), from costal to
inner margin, both pale brown ; a marginal series of blackish
dots terminating the nervures ; internervular folds strongly
pronounced ; secondaries creamy whitish ; body corresponding
in colour with the wings ; wings below creamy whitish, primaries
slightly tinted with testaceous. Expanse of wings 22 mm.

West bank of Rio Negro ; June.

Somewhat allied to the preceding, but at once distinguishable, irrespectively of the markings, by the rounded apex of primaries.

4. *Cryptolechia fallax,* n sp.

Primaries pale shining greyish brown ; an abbreviated oblique darker line from the base of the costa, and a second line (not abbreviated), crossing the centre of the cell, angulated upon the median vein, whence it runs very obliquely ,to near external angle , discocellulars, and a subapical costal spot, dark brown ; external area rather paler than the rest of the wing , a series of marginal blackish dots ; secondaries testaceous ; body corresponding in colour with the wings ; under surface stramineous Expanse of wings 22 mm

South bank of Rio Negro ; June.

5 *Cryptolechia stabilis,* n. sp

Primaries pale brown, with three dark brown triangular costal spots, the central one being largest , a blackish dot on interno-median fold, a second on lower discocellular, a curved discal series, and a marginal series . secondaries whity-brown ; body corresponding in colour with the wings ; under surface whity-brown, excepting the body, the internal area of primaries, the discoidal cell and internal area of secondaries, which are white Expanse of wings 26 mm.

Rio Jurua, 12th January ; Gepatiny, Rio Purus, 29th September.

6. *Cryptolechia tabida,* n. sp

Silvery whity-brown : primaries with three brown costal spots at equal distances increasing in size and in definition towards the apex ; a brown white-centred rounded spot on basal third of margin ; a dot on lower discocellular, a transverse falciform inner discal series, and a marginal series, dark brown , indications of transverse 3 shaped brownish line beyond the cell, secondaries with apical half slightly greyish, under surface creamy-whitish Expanse of wings 28 mm.

Lages ; 5th January

Allied to *C. Burmanniana* of Cramer

(To be continued)

Notes on the Trichopterygia *found in America by the late*
G. R. Crotch, Esq., with descriptions of the new species.

By the Rev. A. Matthews, M.A

While my lamented friend, Mr Crotch, was so actively and so
successfully engaged in collecting insects in America, he did not
forget the friends whom he had left behind   The sight of a
Trichopteryx would no doubt recall to his mind the many hours
of interesting study we had spent in each others company, and
many an anxious search through the pages of antiquated
Entomological works made with unwearied patience for my
special benefit.   Thus it happened that whatever part of the
world might chance to be the scene of his explorations, the
Trichopterygia were ever in his mind, and the number of these
atoms which he possessed at the time of his death proves with
what zeal they had been collected.   Dr. Le Conte. in whose
hands the collections of Mr Crotch were placed, has with great
care grouped the various species and transmitted a large selection
of them to me; by his kind permission, I am now able to
publish the result of my examination.   These collections did
not, however, comprise the whole of Mr Crotch's discoveries in
the Trichopterygia ; he had not been very long in America
before he sent to me a few species which he had found in the
Eastern States, though I regret to add that the package did not
reach me when he was alive.   In this lot, among many of the
forms usual in that region, there were two very interesting new
species ; of these one was a *Trichopteryx*, presenting the very
peculiar form of *T. variolosa* but much smaller, and of an
intensely deep black colour with a shining and almost impunctate
surface ; the other was a very small species of *Nossidium*
Both these have been already described in " Cistula Entomologica," vol. I. p 298, under the names of *T. morrens* and *Nossidium
posthumum.*

Q

The labours of Mr. Crotch were latterly confined to the Western side of the Continent, and more especially to the parts bordering on the Pacific Coast, on this account the species which he met with differ much from those which inhabit the Eastern or Atlantic States. Species such as *T. Haldemanni* or *T. aspera*, abundant in the Eastern States, seem to be entirely absent from those on the other side, where their places are supplied by forms of a different and more European type. Some genera, as *Ptenidium* and *Ptinella*, are wholly unrepresented in Mr Crotch's collections; this is the more surprising as Mr Crotch was a most expert and successful collector of *Ptinella*. With his previous knowledge, therefore, of their habits it is not probable that he would have overlooked situations in which they were likely to occur. Again, genera rarely met with in other parts of the world, appear more abundant in this region. Of the nineteen species which I have examined two belong to the scarce genus *Actidium*, and three to *Ptilium*, a form almost exclusively European.

It must always happen when a collection of *Trichopterygia* arrives from any fresh locality, that a large number of the species will prove to be distinct from any previously described; indeed, I believe the genus *Trichopteryx* alone to be one of the most extensive in the whole of the Coleoptera. Nevertheless, Col Motschulsky met with much unmerited vituperation, for, as his critics are pleased to term it, making so many new species, and I shall probably be considered guilty of the same crime. But it will be found impossible to describe or conscientiously distinguish animals belonging to this group on any other plan; individuals, which when examined by an ordinary lens appear sufficiently similar to belong to the same species, will, if placed under a compound power high enough to exhibit their superficial sculpture, be found to bear the same affinity to each other as *Carabus monilis* bears to its congener *C. nemoralis*.

In distinguishing the species of *Trichopterygia* the superficial sculpture, especially of the thorax, is a most important diagnostic; so much so that the difference between allied species may be more easily recognized by this than any other means, and individuals grouped according to sculpture will generally be found to agree in every other character.   It sometimes, but very rarely, happens that similar sculpture exists in totally dissimilar species, but in all these cases the size, form, or the length of limbs contradicts the possibility of their identity.   Among the species described in the following pages, *T. vicina* and *T. cognata* respectively approach the European *T. picicornis* and *T. fascicularis*, but after the most careful comparison, I feel convinced that they cannot be associated with those species.

The most interesting among the captures of Mr. Crotch, are *Hydroscapha natans*, and *Motschulskium sinuatocolle*, of these the former is one of those synthetic forms whose true position it is so difficult to determine, and the latter a remarkable insect previously known only by a much mutilated and unique example in the collection of Dr. Le Conte.

List of *Trichopterygia* found by Mr. Crotch in America.

The species marked W, were found on the Western side, those marked E, on the Eastern side of the Continent.

Hydroscapha natans, Le Conte.   W.
Nossidium posthumum, Matth.   E.
Motschulskium sinuatocolle, Matth.   W.
Actidium Crotchianum, n. sp.   W.
    ,,   politum, n. sp   W
Ptilium Columbianum, n sp.   W.
    ,,   humile, n. sp.   W.
    ,,   obscurum, n. sp.   W.
Nephanes læviusculus, Matth.   E
Trichopteryx mœrens, Matth.   E.   allied to *T. variolosa.*
    .,   aspera, Hald.   E.
    ,,   parallela, Motsch   W.
    ,,   vicina, n. sp.   W.   allied to *T picicornis*
    ,,   castanea, n. sp.   W.   ,,   *T. Edithæ.*
    ,,   Californica, n sp.   W.   ,.   *T Letherryi.*
    . ,,   xanthocera, n sp.   W.   ,,   *T. Hornii.*
    ,,   parallelopipeda, n sp.   W.   ,,   *T Hornii.*
    ,,   diffinis, Motsch.   W.
    ,,   cognata. n. sp   W.   ,,   *T. fascicularis*

Trichopteryx abrupta, Hald.   W.

,,   Henrici, Matth   W.

,,   Sitkaensis, Motsch.   W.

,,   Crotchii, Matth.   W

Actinopteryx fucicola, Allib.   E

Actidium Crotchianum, n sp

L.c $\frac{3}{16}$ l = 0·062 m   Ovale valde convexum nigrum haud
nitidum, pilis brevissimis albidis vestitum ; capite magno oculis
modicis prominulis , pronoto brevi transverso, capite haud
longiori parum latiori, sat nitido, profundius et confertissime
punctato, fere tuberculato, depressione magnâ transversâ prope
basim notato, margine basali fere rectâ , elytris ovatis fere ad
media latissimis, ordinibus rectis confertissime asperatis, apicibus
rotundatis , pedibus atque antennis sat longis nigris

Caput sat magnum, antice productum, valde convexum, confertim tuberculatum, sat nitidum.   Oculi modici prominuli.
Antennæ sat longæ piceo-nigræ articulo nono vix incrassato

Pronotum breve transversum, capite vix longius parum latius,
sat nitidum, confertissime tuberculatum, depressione transversâ
ad basim notatum, lateribus rotundatis, angulis posticis rotundatis, margine basali fere rectâ humeris elytrorum incumbenti.

Scutellum modicum triangulare confertim asperatum

Elytra ovata valde convexa, sat inflata, ad media latissima,
capite atque pronoto plus quam sesqui longiora, parum latiora,
ordinibus transversis leviter sed confertissime asperata, apicibus
attenuatis et rotundatis, aliquantum dilutioribus

Pedes sat longi graciles piceo-nigri

Subtus totum piceum

Differt ab *Act Boudieru,* cui affine est, staturâ majori, formâ
latiori inflatâ, sculpturâ leviori, atque antennis crassioribus.

Habitat Americam septentrionalem in Columbiâ Britannicâ a
Dᵒ Crotch lectum.

Actidium politum, n. sp.

L c $\frac{4}{16}$ l = 0 050 m.   Ovale convexum nigrum nitidissimum,
pilis brevissimis sparsissime indutum ; capite sat magno ; pronoto
brevi sat parvo, capite vix latiori, nitidissimo punctis remotis

valde indistinctis notato, postice latissimo, lateribus leviter rotundatis, margine basali valde rotundatâ ; elytris ovalibus ante
media latissimis nitidissimis, ordinibus distinctis sinuatis levissime
asperatis, apicibus valde rotundatis; pedibus atque antennis
piceo-nigris

Caput magnum antice longius productum et valde rotundatum
nitidissimum, punctis valde indistinctis atque foveâ indistinctâ
ad frontem utrinque impressum.   Oculi sat parvi prominuli
Antennæ articulis basalibus piceis *reliquis* exemplo viso *effractis*.

Pronotum breve sat parvum, capite haud longius parum latius,
nitidissimum, punctis remotis valde indistinctis notatum, ad
basim latissimum lateribus leviter rotundatis et leviter marginatis,
basi valde rotundatâ humeris elytrorum incumbenti

Scutellum modicum triangulare punctis sat magnis impressum.

Elytra ovalia capite atque pronoto parum longiora et latiora,
ante media latissima, nitidissima, ordinibus distinctis sinuatis
levissime asperata, striatim punctata, apicibus latis valde rotundatis sat dilutioribus, suturâ postice elevatâ.

Pedes sat longi nigro-picei

Subtus piceum ore atque metasterno dilutioribus.

Differt staturâ minutâ, superficie glabrâ nitidissimâ et sculpturâ.

Habitat Americam septentrionalem in Californiâ apud San
Diego a D° Crotch lectum.

Ptilium Columbianum, n. sp.

L c $\frac{7}{16}$ l = 0·087 m   Elongato-ovale convexum ferrugineum
vel castaneum pilis flavescentibus sat dense vestitum, capite
magno oculis magnis prominentibus ; pronoto modico, capite
parum latiori, tuberculis distinctis sat irregulariter dispositis
interstitiisque nitidis vix reticulatis ornato, margine basali rotundatâ parum reflexâ nitidâ ; elytris longis, capite atque pronoto
fere duplo longioribus, sat profunde asperatis, apicibus parum
rotundatis, pedibus atque antennis longis gracilibus læte flavis

Caput modicum antice triangulariter-elongatum, tuberculis
ordinibus transversis dispositis ornatum.   Oculi magni prominentes.   Antennæ prælongæ graciles læte flavæ.   Palpi maxillares
magni flavi.

Pronotum sat paivum, capite parum bievius et latius, convexum, feie ad basim latissimum lateiibus valde iotundatis et marginatis, tubeiculis sat magnis distinctis sat irregulaiiter dispositis, inteistitiisque nitidis vix reticulatis oinatum, maigine basali rotundatâ levitei ieflexâ nitidâ angulis rotundatis.

Scutellum modicum triangulaie elongato-acuminatum confeitim et profunde asperatum

Elytia longa elongato-ovalia, capite atque pionoto feie duplo longioia pone media latissima lateiibus levitei maiginatis ordinibus distinctis fortiter sinuatis aspeiata, apicibus latis paium rotundatis.

Abdomen pygidio solo exserto

Pedes longi lœte flavi

Subtus totum testaceum.

Diffeit a *Pt Spencei* staturâ magnâ, formâ pionoti, atque antennis prœlongis ; a *Pt. Sharpi* pionoto majoii et latioii feie ad basim latissimo, atque sculpturâ multo levioii.

Habitat Ameiicam septentrionalem in Columbiâ Biitannicâ atque in Californiâ a D° Crotch frequenter lecta.

Obs.—Exemplis nonnullis hujusce speciei elytia aliis multo latioia sunt sed utpote *Ptilium Spencei* modo eodem vaiiat, distinctionem tantum sexualem habeii censeo.

Ptilium humile, n. sp.

L c. $\frac{5 \cdot 6}{16}$ l. $= 0\ 062—0\ 075$ m.   Elongatum modice convexum feiiugineum pilis flavis sat dense vestitum, capite sat magno oculis magnis piominulis ; pionoto parvo, capite bieviori vix latiori, tubeiculis sat magnis confeitissime ornato, lateribus rotundatis, margine basali levitei sinuatâ nitidâ reflexâ angulis obtusis, elytiis elongato-ovalibus, ordinibus sinuatis sat remotis modice asperatis ; apicibus ovalibus , pedibus atque antennis lœte flavis

Caput sat magnum antice elongatum tuberculis parvis confertissime obtectum.   Oculi magni prominuli nigiescentes. Antennæ bieves sat iobustæ lœte flavæ.

Pronotum parvum breve, capite bievius vix latius feie ad medium latissimum lateribus valde iotundatis fortiter maiginatis atque setis duabus brevibus pone media instructis, tuberculis sat magnis confertissime obtectum, margine basali leviter sinuatâ reflexâ nitidâ angulis obtusis.

Scutellum modicum triangulare elongato-acuminatum confertim asperatim.

Elytra elongato-ovalia, capite atque pronoto plusquam duplo longiora vix latiora, ad media latissima, ordinibus sinuatis sat remotis modice asperata, apicibus ovalibus angulis suturalibus fere rectis

Abdomen pygidio solo exserto.

Pedes breves robusti læte flavi

Subtus totum ferrugineum.

Differt a *Pt. Columbiano* staturâ multo minori, formâ angustiori, antennis brevibus robustis, et sculpturâ pronoti

Habitat Americam septentrionalem rarum in Californiâ apud San Diego a Dᵒ Crotch lectum.

Ptilium obscurum, n sp.

L c. ¡ᵣ̅ 1 = 0 075 m   Ovale convexum piceum pilis sat longis densius vestitum, capite magno obtuso oculis haud prominentibus; pronoto modico, capite longiori et latiori, tuberculis magnis ordinibus fortiter sinuatis dispositis interstitiisque nitidis leviter reticulatis ornato, lateribus leviter rotundatis, margine basali leviter rotundatâ angulis obtusis ; elytris sat brevibus ad apices latissimis, ordinibus sinuatis profunde asperatis ; pedibus atque antennis flavis.

Caput magnum antice obtusum, tuberculis parvis ordinibus rectis dispositis interstitiisque nitidissime leviter reticulatis ornatum.   Oculi sat magni haud prominentes.   Antennæ modicæ flavæ articulo secundo incrassato

Pronotum magnum convexum, capite longius et latius, · ad basim latissimum lateribus leviter rotundatis, tuberculis magnis ordinibus fortiter sinuatis dispositis interstitiisque nitidissimis leviter reticulatis ornatum, margine basali leviter rotundatâ angulis obtusis

Scutellum breve triangulare haud acuminatum modice asperatum.

Elytra sat brevia, capite atque pronoto haud longiora vix latiora, ad humeros pronoto angustiora, ordinibus sinuatis profunde asperata, apicibus validissime rotundatis late dilutioribus

Abdomen pygidio solo exserto

Pedes modici lætre flavi.

Subtus piceo-castaneum ore coxis apice metasterni atque segmentis ultimis ventris flavis

Differt a *Pt. Columbiano* statura minori, formâ latiori, capite et pronoto majoribus, elytris latioribus et multo brevioribus, scutello breviori obtuso, et colore piceo

Habitat Americam septentrionalem in Columbiâ Britannicâ in fungo quodam a Dᵒ Crotch lectum.

Trichopteryx cicma, n. sp.

L c. [frac] 1 = 0·075 in Oblonga parum convexa nigerrima pilis brevibus flavis parce vestita, capite permagno lato oculis vix prominentibus; pronoto magno convexo ad basim latissimo, tuberculis parvis indistinctis ordinibus remotis sinuatis dispositis, interstitiisque nitidissimis profunde reticulatis ornato, angulis posterioribus latis longe productis; elytris fere quadratis lateribus parallelis, pronoto parum angustioribus, ordinibus remotis sinuatis modice asperatis, apicibus latis minime rotundatis; pedibus lætre flavis; antennis nigris.

Caput permagnum latum nitidissimum, tuberculis indistinctis ornatum. Oculi magni haud prominentes. Antennæ modicæ nigræ

Pronotum magnum convexum, capite longius et latius, ad basim latissimum lateribus leviter rotundatis, late marginatis margine dilutiori, tuberculis parvis ordinibus remotis sinuatis dispositis, interstitiisque nitidissimis profunde reticulatis ornatum, margine posteriori fere rectâ angulis latis productis dilutioribus.

Scutellum magnum triangulare confertim asperatum.

Elytra brevia quadrata lateribus parallelis, capite atque pronoto haud longiora, parum angustiora, ordinibus remotis sinuatis modice asperata, interstitiis reticulatis, suturâ postice elevatâ, apicibus vix rotundatis anguste dilutioribus

Abdomen parum exsertum segmento apicali tridentato.

Subtus nigra ore atque coxis dilutioribus.

Differt a *T' picicorni* staturâ majori, sculpturâ pronoti multo leviori atque diversâ, antennisque longioribus, alioque valde consimilis.

Habitat Americam septentrionalem in Columbiâ Britannicâ a Dᵒ Crotch lecta.

Trichopterygia castanea, n sp

L c $\frac{7}{10}$ l. = 0 087 m.   Oblonga convexa rufocastanea sat nitida pilis aureis dense vestita ; capite modico oculis haud prominentibus ; pronoto modico ante basim latissimo augulis longe productis, tuberculis parvis ordinibus sinuatis regulariter dispositis, interstitusque nitidis profunde reticulatis ornato ; elytris oblongis lateribus fere parallelis, ordinibus sinuatis irregulariter asperatis, interstitus reticulatis, apicibus latis rotundatis ; abdomine sat longius exserto ; pedibus atque antennis pallide flavis

Caput modicum antice productum tuberculis minutis interstitiis reticulatis ornatum   Oculi sat magni haud prominentes Antennæ longæ crassiores, articulis duobus basalibus permagnis, læte flavæ.

Pronotum modicum capite longius et latius, ante basim latissimum lateribus rotundatis et marginatis, tuberculis parvis ordinibus sinuatis dispositis, interstitiisque nitidis profunde reticulatis ornatum, margine basali depressâ sinuatâ angulis acutis longe productis late flavis.

Scutellum magnum triangulare elongatum confertim asperatum.

Elytra oblonga convexa translucida, lateribus marginatis fere parallelis, capite atque pronoto longiora haud latiora, ordinibus sinuatis sat profunde asperata interstitus reticulatis, apicibus latis rotundatis.

Abdomen sat longius exsertum obtusum segmento apicali minute bidentato

Pedes robusti læte flavi

Subtus castanea ore coxis margine posteriori metasterni atque apice ventris flavescentibus

Differt a *T. Edithæ* staturâ majori, formâ parallelâ pedibus atque antennis crassioribus, atque pronoto ad basim latissimo.

Habitat Americam septentrionalem in Columbiâ Britannicâ a Dᵒ Crotch lecta.

Trichopteryx Californica, n. sp

L c $\frac{7\cdot8}{16}$ l. = 0·087—0·100   Oblonga sat convexa castanea
nitida, pilis brevibus aureis vestita; capite magno lato, oculis
modicis haud prominentibus ; pronoto magno lato angulis posterioribus valde productis, tuberculis minutis ordinibus irregularibus dispositis, interstitiisque nitidis profunde reticulatis
ornato , elytris oblongis lateribus fere rectis, ordinibus sinuatis
confertim sat leviter asperatis; abdomine sat exserto ; pedibus
atque antennis læte flavis.

Caput magnum latum nitidum, tuberculis minutis interstitiisque nitidis ornatum.   Oculi modici haud prominentes   Antennæ
longæ sat graciles læte flavæ.

Pronotum magnum convexum, capite paulum longius multum
latius, ad basim latissimum lateribus rotundatis et marginatis,
piceo-castaneum angulis late atque lateribus flavescentibus,
tuberculis minutis ordinibus irregularibus dispositis, interstitiisque nitidis confertim reticulatis ornatum, margine posteriori
fortiter sinuatâ angulis acutissimis longe productis.

Scutellum magnum triangulare confertim asperatum.

Elytra oblonga rufo-castanea suturâ dilutiori, capite atque
pronoto aliquantum et longiora et angustiora lateribus rectis fere
parallelis, ordinibus sinuatis confertim asperata interstitiis nitidis,
apicibus latis parum rotundatis, suturâ postice elevatâ.

Abdomen sat exsertum obtusum segmento apicali tridentato.

Pedes modici sat graciles læte flavi.

Subtus picea ore coxis et margine posticâ metasterni flavis,
metasterno profunde reticulato.

Differt a *T. Lethierryi,* cui affinis est, staturâ multo minori,
elytris longioribus, pedibus brevioribus, sculpturâ leviori et pube
brevissimâ.

Habitat Americam septentrionalem apud Lacum Tahoe in
Californiâ a Dº Crotch lecta.

Trichopteryx xanthocera, n. sp.

L c. $\frac{8}{16}$ l. = 0·100 m.   Oblonga sat lata convexa, piceo-nigra
elytris rufescentioribus, pilis modicis pallidis vestita, capite
magno oculis haud prominentibus ; pronoto magno convexo
postice dilatato, tuberculis minutis irregulariter dispositis inter-

stitusque nitidis reticulatis ornato, angulis posticis longe productis flavis; elytris quadratis haud attenuatis, ordinibus distinctis sinuatis asperatis, suturâ rufescenti, apicibus latis parum rotundatis; abdomine parum exserto, pedibus atque antennis lætissime flavis.

Caput magnum latum nitidum, tuberculis exiguis interstitiisque glabris ornatum   Oculi modici haud prominentes.   Antennæ longiores sat graciles lætissime flavæ.

Pronotum magnum convexum postice dilatatum capite longius et multo latius, ad basim latissimum, tuberculis minutis ordinibus transversis fere rectis dispositis, interstitiisque nitidis indistincte reticulatis ornatum, lateribus parum rotundatis flavo-marginatis, margine posteriori depressâ sinuatâ angulis longe productis flavescentibus.

Scutellum magnum triangulare confertim asperatum.

Elytra quadrata brevia, capite atque pronoto haud longiora aut latiora, ordinibus distinctis sinuatis sat profunde asperata, lateribus fere rectis, suturâ rufescenti, apicibus latis parum rotundatis dilutioribus.

Abdomen sat exsertum obtusum rufo-piceum segmento apicali minute tridentato.

Pedes sat robusti læte flavi.

Subtus toto rufo-picea metasterno obscurato.

Differt a *T. Hornii* staturâ majori, formâ quadratâ et latiori; elytris rufo-piceis, sculpturâ leviori atque antennis læte flavis.

Habitat Americam septentrionalem in Columbiâ Britannicâ a D° Crotch lecta

Trichopteryx parallelopipeda, n. sp

L e $\frac{1}{16}$ l. $= 0$ 100 m.   Oblonga convexa sat nitida nigra pilis, sat longis flavis vestita, capite modico oculis haud prominentibus, pronoto modico valde convexo, ad basim latissimo angulis posticis longius productis, tuberculis modicis ordinibus irregularibus confertim dispositis interstitiisque nitidis profunde reticulatis ornato, elytris oblongis haud attenuatis, ordinibus sinuatis asperatis, interstitiis profunde reticulatis; antennis sat brevibus piceo-nigris, articulo octavo parvo ; pedibus læte flavis.

Caput modicum latum, tuberculis parvis interstitiisque nitidis reticulatis ornatum Oculi modici haud prominentes. Antennæ sat breves piceo-nigræ articulo octavo parvo.

Pronotum modicum valde convexum, capite longius et latius, ad basim latissimum lateribus parum rotundatis leviter marginatis, tuberculis modicis ordinibus irregularibus confertim dispositis interstitiisque nitidis profunde reticulatis ornatum, margine basali depressâ leviter sinuatâ angulis productis dilutioribus.

Scutellum magnum triangulare profunde et confertim asperatum et reticulatum

Elytra oblonga haud attenuata, capite atque pronoto longiora haud latiora lateribus fere rectis leviter marginatis, ordinibus sinuatis confertim asperata, interstitiis profunde reticulatis, apicibus latis rotundatis anguste dilutioribus.

Abdomen paulum exsertum.

Pedes modici læte flavi

Subtus nigra ore coxis et margine posteriori metasterni piceis, metasterno profunde asperato.

Differt a *T. Hornii* formâ oblongâ parallelâ, pronoto ad basim lasissimo, atque antennis multo brevioribus piceo-nigris.

Habitat Americam Septentrionalem in Columbiâ Britannicâ a Dᵘ Crotch lecta.

Trichopteryx cognata, n. sp

L c $\frac{1}{10}$ l. = 0·112 m   Ovalis sat angusta convexa nigra pilis brevissimis pallidis vestita, capite sat parvo oculis prominulis ; pronoto modico, ad basim latissimo angulis acutissimis longe productis, tuberculis parvis ordinibus sat irregularibus dispositis confertim ornato, interstitiis nitidis reticulatis ; elytris oblongis parum attenuatis angustis valde convexis, ordinibus transversis confertissime asperatis, interstitiis profunde reticulatis, apicibus parum rotundatis anguste dilutioribus ; abdomine longe exserto ; pedibus flavis , antennis piceis.

Caput sat parvum, sat nitidum tuberculis exiguis confertim ornatum. Oculi modici prominuli Antennæ modicæ graciles piceo-testaceæ.

Pronotum parvum valde convexum, capite parum longius et latius, ad basim latissimum lateribus leviter rotundatis, tuber-

culis minutis ordinibus irregulaiibus confertim dispositis, interstitiisque dense reticulatis ornatum, margine basali depiessa
leviter trisinuatâ angulis longe productis extremis dilutioribus

Scutellum magnum triangulare acuminatum, confertim aspeia-
atum.

Elytra oblonga attenuata, capite atque pronoto nec longioia
nec latioia lateribus leviter rotundatis, ordinibus densis leviter
sinuatis confertim asperata, apicibus attenuatis valde rotundatis
dilutioribus extiemis albidis.

Abdomen longe exsertum obtusum segmento apicali minute
tridentato.

Pedes robusti femoribus infuscatis tibiis læte flavis.

Subtus nigra oie biunneo metasterno profunde reticulato.

Dijlert a *T fasciculari* staturâ minoii, formâ angustioii, capite
atque pronoto minoribus, atque antennis piceis.

Habitat Americam septentrionalem in Columbiâ Britannicâ a
Dᵒ Crotch lecta, exemplo unico viso.

Descriptions of *New Species* of Phytophagous Colropirra : by Joseph S Baly, F.L S, &c., *(continued from page* 130*).*

Dinophthalma fasciata, mihi.

Anguste ovata, postice attenuata, nigra, nitida, subtus argenteo-sericea, thorace elytrisque fulvis, illo minute sed distincte punctato, plagâ male definitâ ad marginem apicalem adfixâ, nigro-'piceâ ; his punctato-striatis, striis ad apicem confusis, fasciâ latâ curvatâ communi extrorsum abbreviatâ nigrâ instructis. Long. 3 lin.

Hab. Amazons, Rio Tapajos.

Head smooth and shining, finely and remotely punctured, impressed between the eyes with a distinct fovea ; inner border of eye coarsely strigose ; three lower joints of antenna· pale piceous beneath Thorax two and a half times as broad as long, sides rounded, converging from the middle to the apex, anterior and posterior angles obsolete; basal margin rather deeply sinuate just within the outer angle ; surface smooth and shining, (seen under a lens) distinctly punctulate. Scutellum distinctly punctured. shining, trigonate, its apex broadly rounded. Elytra with the sides distinctly lobed at the base, attenuated towards the apex ; surface distinctly punctate-striate, the punctures irregularly placed in the striæ, the striæ themselves confused and entirely lost on the hinder disk , just below the middle is a broad common sublunate transverse patch, abbreviated and produced anteriorly on the outer margin. Body beneath densely clothed with silvery hairs; apex of the last abdominal segment broadly concave-emarginate

Dinophthalma nigriceps, mihi.

Anguste ovata, postice attenuata, fulva, nitida, capite, scutello, pectore, genubus, tibiis quatuor anticis dorso, posticis totis, tarsisque nigris Long 2¼ lin.

Hab. Para

Head smooth and shining, impressed with a few fine punctures, visible only under a lens ; mandibles with a rufous line ; palpi pale fulvous. Thorax nearly three times as broad as long, sides rounded, slightly converging towards the apex, anterior and

posterior angles obsolete ; above transversely convex, smooth and
shining, the middle of the anterior margin stained with black.
Scutellum large, trigonate, shining black, its apex piceous.
Elytra distinctly lobed at the base, finely but distinctly punctate-
striate, interspaces smooth and shining, impressed here and there
with distinct punctures   Body beneath sparingly clothed with
adpressed hairs, apical segment of abdomen trilobate

Dinophthalma consimilis. mihi.

Anguste ovata, postice attenuata, fulva, nitida, antennis (basi
exceptâ), tibiis apice tarsisque nigris   Long 1¾–2 lin.

Hab Para, Rio Tapajos, Ega

Head smooth, impunctate, eyes bordered within by a deep
groove, four lower joints of antennæ pale piceous, the rest black
Thorax more than twice as broad as long ; sides rounded at the
base, converging from the middle to the apex, anterior angles
distinct, hinder angles obsolete ; surface under a lens minutely
but distinctly punctured. Scutellum large, trigonate, sides
sinuate near the apex, the latter rounded   Elytra finely
punctate-striate, the interspaces impressed with fine punctures,
which render the striæ indistinct   Body beneath clothed with
adpressed hairs ; apex of the last abdominal segment trilobate,
the middle lobe indistinct

Protophana Amazona, mihi.

Subtus obscure rufa, dense albido tomentosa, abdominis lateribus pygidioque cupreis ; supra cuprea, glabra, thoracis lateribus
capiteque inter oculos albido-pilosis , elytris obscure cupreis,
fortiter et irregulariter punctato-striatis, utrisque maculâ humerali, antice emarginatâ, fulvâ ornatis ; antennis nigris. Long.
2½ lin.

Hab. Borders of the river Amazon.

Similar in form and coloration to *P. tomentosa*, Lac., it is,
however, very distinct from that species, and may at once be
known by its entirely glabrous elytra, and also by the punctures
on their surface being arranged in irregular striæ   Face concave
between the eyes, the latter distinctly notched, surface finely but
distinctly punctured, vertex granulose ; clypeus not separated
from the face by a sutural line, its surface obliquely deflexed,
smooth, impunctate, the anterior border deeply angulate-
emarginate. Thorax twice as broad as long at the base, basal
lobe reflexed, obtusely truncate ; sides rounded and narrowed
from base to apex, more quickly converging towards the latter,

hinder angles acute, anterior obtuse; surface finely but distinctly punctured, transversely sulcate in front of the basal lobe; disk glabrous, sides and extreme base clothed with adpressed coarse white hairs. Scutellum trigonate, cupreo-aeneous, its surface finely punctured. Elytra deeply and coarsely punctured, the punctures irregularly arranged in longitudinal striæ, interspaces on the middle disk transversely wrinkled.

Themesia grandis, mihi.

Late oblonga, læte viridi-ænea, nitida, supra glabra, subtus dense albido-tomentosa, antennis nigris, labro fulvo.   Long. 5½ lin

Hab. Brazil, a single specimen, formerly in the collection of the late A. Deyrolle

Body above entirely glabrous, with the exception of some adpressed hairs on the head, and a very few others near the anterior angles of the thorax.   Head closely punctured, strigose-punctate on the vertex; face concave between the eyes; labrum subquadrate, transverse, not distinctly separated from the face, fulvous, its sides thickened, its anterior edge emarginate ; jaws prominent; antennæ black   Thorax nearly twice as broad as long; sides broadly rounded at the base, then obliquely converging to the apex, anterior angles broadly truncate, hinder angles obsolete ; above transversely convex at the base, sub-cylindrical at the apex, obliquely and broadly excavated towards the sides, the latter reflexed , surface finely and closely punctured, the punctures stronger and sparser on the disk, entirely glabrous, with the exception of a very few coarse adpressed whitish hairs just behind the anterior angles   Scutellum pentangular, its apex acute, its surface smooth, remotely punctured   Elytra much broader than the thorax, the humeral callus prominent; sides obliquely converging from base to apex, the latter rounded: above convex, slightly depressed transversely below the humeral callus, finely and somewhat closely punctured.

Similar in form to *T. auricapilla*, but twice its size and easily separated by the absence of the dense pubescence clothing the base and sides of the thorax.

Megalostomis generosa, mihi.

Oblonga, sub-cylindrica ♂, magis ovata ♀, supra tenuiter, subtus cum thoracis lateribus dense flavo pubescens, picea, pedibus pallide rufo-piceis, genubus, tarsis antennisque nigris ; elytris laete testaceis, fascia prope medium et utrisque plagâ

N

transversâ male definitâ, ante apicem positâ, nigris.   Long. 4 lin
    Hab. Ega, Upper Amazons.

Head sparingly clothed with adpressed yellowish hairs, vertex
and upper part of front smooth and shining, nearly impunctate ;
face between the eyes excavated on either side, the excavated
spaces divided by a distinct longitudinal ridge which runs
upwards from the clypeus, surface of excavations closely punctured, inner orbit of eye strigose-punctate ; clypeus transverse,
its upper border concave-emarginate on either side, the middle
produced, acute ; anterior margin obliquely truncate on either
side, slightly angulate-emarginate in the middle, surface rather
closely punctate, jaws normal ; antennæ longer than the head
and thorax, black, the under surface of the first, together with
the whole of the second and third joints piceous.   Thorax twice
as broad as long, sides slightly diverging and rounded at the
extreme base, thence obliquely converging to the apex, anterior
angles slightly produced laterally, acute ; upper surface finely
punctured, disc clothed with very fine silky hairs, only visible
under a lens, sides densely covered with yellowish hairs.   Elytra
bright testaceous, irregularly punctured, sparingly clothed with
short fulvous hairs ; a broad band at the base, another across the
middle and an ill defined transverse patch just before the apex
of each elytron, black.

Megalostomis interrupto-fasciata, mihi.

Oblonga, sub-cylindrica, supra tenuissime, subtus dense pubescens, rufo-picea, pedibus pallide rufis, genubus, tarsis, scutello,
orbitis antice antennisque nigris, thorace tenuiter punctato ad
latera pube adpressâ vestito, disco fere glabro, elytris rufo-
testaceis, sparse pubescentibus, sub-seriatim punctatis, basi, fasciâ
interruptâ prope medium et utrisque maculâ sub-apicali ad
marginem adfixâ nigris   Long. 4 lin.

Mas. capite magno, pone oculos lobato, thorace elytris equilato,
lateribus rectis
    Hab. Ega.

Vertex nearly impunctate, minutely granulose; front impressed
with a deep oblong fovea; space between the eyes finely but not
very closely punctured, excavated on either side, the excavations
being divided by a central longitudinal ridge ; clypeus not
distinctly separated from the face, transverse, its anterior border
obliquely truncate on either side, transversely truncate and
obsoletely emarginate in the middle, surface finely punctured,
irregularly excavated, antennæ equal in length to the head and

thorax, entirely black, jaws and labrum also black, the anterior edge of the latter emarginate. Thorax more than twice as broad as long; sides rounded at the extreme base, thence straight and parallel to the apex, anterior angles acute, slightly produced laterally; surface very finely punctured, disc nearly glabrous, sides sparingly clothed with fine whitish pubescence Scutellum closely covered with adpressed hairs Elytra parallel, slightly attenuated near the apex, sparingly clothed with fulvous hairs. which are more crowded towards the apex, distinctly punctured, the punctures arranged in ill defined longitudinal rows; rufo-testaceous, a narrow band at the base, an interrupted fascia across the middle, together with an ill defined sub-apical patch attached to the outer margin black Body beneath densely clothed with adpressed cream coloured hairs.

Megalostomis coerulea, mihi.

Oblonga ♂, oblong-ovata ♀, supra metallico-coerulea, tenuiter pubescens, antennis nigris; subtus nigro-coerulea. dense albido-tomentosa, abdomine pallide piceo. Long 3½ lin

Hab. Amazons.

Head near similar in both sexes; vertex tumid; face excavated between the eyes, and furnished with three longitudinal ridges, one on the medial line, the others, one on either side, just within the inner orbit; the lateral ridges are less regular than the medial, and are rendered still less distinct by a number of irregular, raised vittæ; anterior edge of clypeus slightly angulate-emarginate, whole surface of head sparingly punctured; antennæ black. Thorax with its basal lobe transversely truncate; sides abruptly diverging at the extreme base, thence converging and very slightly rounded to the apex, anterior and posterior angles acute; above transversely convex, sub-cylindrical at the apex, distinctly punctured, on either side just in front of the middle is a deep obliquely transverse depression, surface clothed throughout with fine sub-depressed griseous hairs, which are more crowded on either side, and form an ill-defined lateral patch. Scutellum trigonate, its apex rounded, surface finely but distinctly punctured, covered with adpressed hairs. Elytra more closely punctured than the thorax, clothed with similar hairs. Body beneath densely clothed with adpressed whitish pubescence, which entirely conceals the colour of the surface.

Doryphora bilunata, mihi.

Oblonga, convexa, piceo-fulva, supra prasina, antennis piceis; elytris regulariter punctato-striatis, utrisque vittâ brevi suturali

basi positâ et vix pone scutellum productâ, lunulâque longitudinali a basi fere ad medium extensâ, basi cum vittulâ connexâ
nigris. Long. 6½ lin

Hab. Pebas, Upper Amazons

Head finely punctured, antennæ slender, much less than
half the length of the body, piceous, two basal and two upper
joints, together with the mouth, piceo-fulvous Thorax more
than twice as broad as long ; sides straight and parallel, rounded
and converging before the middle, anterior angles slightly produced, sub-acute ; upper surface finely punctured, extreme
lateral margin pale greenish yellow. Scutellum piceo-fulvous,
edged with nigro-piceous. Elytra slightly broader than the
thorax ; sides nearly parallel, broadly rounded at the apex,
regularly punctate-striate, interspaces plane, very minutely
granulose, each elytron with a very short black sutural vitta,
commencing at the base and scarcely extending beyond the
scutellum, together with a longitudinal concolorous curved line
joined at the base with the sutural stripe, and extending from
the middle of the basal margin for one-third the length of the
elytra, its concavity looking inwards, inflexed limb together
with the extreme lateral border pale yellowish-green

Doryphora Jansoni, mihi

Oblongo-ovata, convexa, nigra, subtus nitida, supra opaca,
thorace disco obscure rufo, ad latera aeneo-nigro ; elytris rufo-
testaceis, tenuiter bifariam punctatis; spino valido. Long. 5 lin.

Hab. Brazil, a single specimen formerly in the collection of
Mr W. W. Saunders.

Head obscure greenish-black, opaque, marked on the vertex
with an indistinct bifid rufous spot ; antennæ scarcely exceeding
half the length of the body Thorax more than twice as broad
as long ; sides sub-parallel, rounded and converging in front,
anterior angles ; acute surface opaque, impunctate, obscure
rufous on the disc, obscure greenish-black on the sides ; extreme
lateral and apical margins nitidous Elytra broader than the
thorax broadly rounded at the apex, very finely punctate-
striate, the striæ arranged in double rows, irregular near the
outer margin

Stenispa vespertina, mihi

Filiformis, sub-cylindrica, subtus cum antennis nigra, nitida,
supra coeruleo-metallica, thorace longitudine vix latiori, tenuiter,
remote punctato, elytris parallelis, prope apicem angustatis,

tenuiter punctato-striatis, striis integris, interspatiis minute granulosis, tenuiter ruguloso-strigosis. Long. 2¾ lin.

Hab. Brazil, New Friburg

Thorax scarcely broader than long, sides narrowly margined, straight and parallel, rounded and converging at the apex ; apical margin sinuate on either side, its middle portion produced, basal margin deeply concave on either side, the medial lobe obtusely rounded , above finely and distantly punctured, general surface, seen under a deep lens, very minutely granulose. Scutellum pentangular, the lateral angles rounded, the apical one moderately produced, acute Elytra rather broader than the thorax; sides parallel, faintly sinuate in the middle, rounded and converging from the termination of their middle third to the apex, the extreme apices conjointly emarginate , apical margin finely serrulate ; above finely punctate-striate, the striæ distinct to the apex, interspaces granulose, finely and irregularly strigose.

Stenispa attenuata, mihi.

Filiformis, postice attenuata, sub-cylindrica, obscure cuprea, nitida, antennis nigris; thorace tenuiter, sub-remote punctato, elytris ante medium ad apicem attenuatis, tenuiter punctato-striatis, striis apicem versus deletis Long. 2¾ lin.

Hab. Panama.

Head finely punctured, front and upper portion of face impressed with a fine grooved line, which terminates on the vertex in a small fovea , antennæ slender, rather more than a third the length of the body, entirely black. Thorax slightly longer than broad, sides straight, narrowly margined, anterior angles produced, sub-acute ; apical margin slightly sinuate on either side, its middle portion slightly produced ; basal margin deeply concave-emarginate on either side, the medial lobe obtusely rounded ; upper surface sub-remotely punctured, the interspaces (seen under a deep lens) very finely granulose-strigose ; on the basal margin on either side the medial lobe, is a small fovea Scutellum large, pentagonal, the lateral angles acute Elytra rather broader at the base than the thorax, sides parallel in front, attenuated from before the middle to the apex, the latter conjointly emarginate, apical margin finely serrulate, the sutural angle armed with a minute tooth ; above convex, the humeral callus slightly thickened, finely punctate-striate, the puncturing entirely obsolete near the apex, interspaces minutely granulose, here and there faintly reticulate-strigose. Apical segment of abdomen concave-emarginate.

Descriptions of new species of Cryptolechia *from the Amazons,*
by Arthur G. Butler, F L.S.

(Continued from page 164.)

7 *Cryptolechia inflata,* n. sp

Primaries with angular apex; shining pinky-whitish, sparsely
irrorated with black , a black dot in the cell and a second at the
end of the cell, but both inconspicuous owing to the black scales
scattered around ; a brownish squamose streak across the cell
and costal area near the base ; an ill-defined red-brown spot on
the centre of the costa, and a second near to apex, from each
of which an arched squamose line runs outwards and, nearly
parallel to the margin, across the disc ; a marginal series of
black dots, followed by a series of white dots on the fringe ;
secondaries pale stramineous, slightly deeper in colour at the
apex , body corresponding in colour with the wings ; under
surface pale stramineous   Expanse of wings 30 mm

Lages, 5th January ; Mabidiry, Rio Purus, 30th September.

8. *Cryptolechia vaga,* n. sp.

Primaries with rounded apex, pale stramineous , a sub-costal
dot near the base, a second just before the middle, a zigzag
oblique line crossing the wing just beyond the cell, a spot on
inner margin, and a sigmoidal sub-marginal series of dots, all
pale brown ; a marginal series of minute blackish dots; fringe
silvery-white ; secondaries silky-white, with the veins, basal
area, and a marginal line pale silky stramineous , body above
testaceous ; below sordid white, legs snow-white : wings below
creamy white.   Expanse of wings 24 mm

Prainha, 17th December.

9. *Cryptolechia tinctipennis,* n. sp.

Primaries clay-coloured, with a shining pinky gloss, fringe
incurved so as to look grey in certain lights; a spot in the cell,
a second at the end of the cell, and a waved discal series of

about six, all black ; three brown ill-defined costal spots, the two first emitting an oblique streak to just in front of the two black discoidal spots; the third much larger, close to apex, emitting no streak ; secondaries bronzy brown, costal area pale ; thorax clay-coloured, abdomen pale greyish brown ; body below whitish ; wings below pale shining brown. Expanse of wings 22 mm.

Rio Negro, 4th July.

10. *Cryptolechia capada*, n. sp.

Wings above sordid pinky-whitish ; primaries with a dot in the cell, a second on first median branch, and a third on the discocellulars, blackish-brown ; an obliquely arched interrupted series of dots from the costal nervure (a little in advance of the first blackish dot) to near the inner margin, a dentated arched discal line parallel to the outer margin, and a series of marginal dots, brown ; body sordid whitish above, white below , primaries below pale brown, the veins slightly darker, the costal and internal borders whitish, fringe white ; secondaries whitish, costal margin brown , discocellular black. Expanse of wings 21 mm.

San Antonio, Rio Negro, 6th December.

11. *Cryptolechia salutaris*, n. sp.

Primaries above shining whity-brown ; crossed obliquely from the internal to the costal margin by a broad band of reddish bronze, limited on either side by a slightly irregular darker line, and interrupted internally at its lower extremity by a spot of the ground colour, enclosing a crescent of brown (its concavity towards the base); a spot of blackish on the discocellulars , a dark brown lunule below the base of the first median branch, and a second crossing the first median interspace, their concavities towards one another , a wavy brown dotted discal transverse line ; margin and fringe golden bronze colour ; secondaries pale shining brown, costal area whitish , body pale brown ; under surface uniform whity-brown. Expanse of wings 22 mm.

Ayrao, Rio Negro, 3rd July

12. *Cryptolechia nitens*, n. sp

Primaries above shining pinky-brown , costal margin white, interrupted by brown spots; costal area greyish ; three dark brown costal spots, the first small. before the middle, the second large, oblong, just beyond the middle, the third longer and

narrower than the second near apex, the two last connected
below by an arched bracket of the same colour; a semi-circular
black and grey spot before the middle of the inner margin; an
oblique litura across the sub-costal area, and an Σ shaped zigzag
transverse line beyond the cell, brown, indistinct; a 7 shaped
series of six dots crossing the lower two-thirds of the disc;
margin and fringe bronzy; secondaries shining pale brown,
thorax pinky-brown; the palpi, head and collar spotted with
white; abomen pale brown, white below; wings below shining
pale brown. Expanse of wings 23 mm.

Teffé, 18th October.

This and the three succeeding species have the apex of
primaries angular.

13. *Cryptolechia annosa,* n sp

Primaries shining slaty-grey, fringe and costal margin rust-
red, the former intersected by a greyish line; a dot at the end
of the cell, and a marginal series, blackish, an indistinct arched
discal streak from sub-costal area to external angle, secondaries
silky-brown, fringe as in primaries; body corresponding in
colour with the wings, below whitish; wings below pale brown.
especially the secondaries, costal margins and fringes tinted with
rust-red   Expanse of wings 25 mm.

Near Santa Cruz, Rio Solimoes, 9th December.

14 *Cryptolechia evanescens,* n sp.

Above shining pale greyish brown or dove colour, the primaries slightly paler than the secondaries, with a blackish dot at
the end of the cell, and a second below it; body below whitish;
wings below shining whity-brown   Expanse of wings 25 mm.

Gepatiny, Rio Purus, 29th September.

15 *Cryptolechia curtipennis,* n sp

Wings above pale brown, especially the primaries which are
shining and have a pinky gloss, inner margin and a dot at end
of cell, black; an oblique line crossing the cell from the costa,
and two crossing the upper half of the disc, convergent and
uniting near the middle of the outer margin, smoky-brown;
fringe much depressed; vertex of head, collar and thorax,
greyish-brown; frons and palpi whitish; abdomen testaceous;
under surface whitish. Expanse of wings 22 mm.

Mabidiry, Rio Purus, 30th September.

16. *Cryptolechia ærinotata*, n. sp.

Primaries with rounded apex, greyish-brown, the external half of the cell, the area beyond it, and a transverse patch placed at right angles to it and parallel to the inferior extremity of the outer margin, pale brassy-green ; a blackish dot at the end of cell ; secondaries shining brown : body above brown, below whitish ; wings below whity-brown   Expanse of wings 24 mm.

Forest at San Vicenzio, Rio Purus.

17. *Cryptolechia marcida*, n. sp.

Primaries sericeous ; basal two-thirds pale strammeous, with a pink tinge, and the base and costal area greyish, crossed in the centre from costa to median nervure, by an oblique brown line, and limited externally by an in-arched squamose brown edge; end of cell terminating in an irregular annular reddish-brown marking, its inner edge ⋜ shaped ; disc pale strammeous ; outer border greyish-brown, widest at apex ; secondaries pale strammeous; head whitish, thorax greyish, abdomen brownish testaceous ; under surface creamy whitish   Expanse of wings 25 mm.

Rio Jurua, 6th November.

18. *Cryptolechia strigivenata*, n. sp

Primaries shining whity-brown, all the veins from just beyond the middle of the wings rather broadly darker brown ; two parallel oblique series, of three or four dots each, crossing the centre of the wing, and an arched dotted line angulated near the costa, crossing the disc, dark brown ; a marginal series of black dots, secondaries shining creamy-white ; head and thorax whity-brown, abdomen pale testaceous, under surface creamy-white.   Expanse of wings 17 mm.

Near Santa Cruz, Rio Solimoes, 9th December

19 *Cryptolechia urbana*, n. sp.

Pale silvery-grey, with faint brownish tint ; primaries rather darker than the secondaries; the markings as in the preceding species, excepting that they are less strongly defined, and that the discal line is very feebly angulated near the costa ; palpi and body below white; wings below rather paler than above and without markings   Expanse of wings 18 mm.

Rio Jutahi, 5th February

20. *Cryptolechia alligans*, n, sp.

Primaries above rather pale brown, with a lilac gloss; costal and outer margins narrowly golden-bronze colour; inner margin dark brown; a blackish dot at the end of the cell; secondaries shining testaceous, greyish towards the base; body grey, the head and prothorax sordid testaceous, below creamy-whitish, anal segments reddish; wings below pale shining fawn colour, costa of primaries ochreous   Expanse of wings 16 mm.

West bank of Rio Negro, 14th and 16th June, 4th of July; Gaviao, Rio Jurua, 6th and 10th November.

A common little species, with much depressed fringes to the wings, so that in some lights they appear almost black.

21 *Cryptolechia peccans*, n sp.

Primaries above pale reddish-brown, with a lilac gloss; the triangular costal spots at equal distances, the innermost smallest, and two unequal spots, one above the other, across the cell, black; an oblique line uniting the innermost costal spot, the discoidal spots and the centre of inner margin, brown; a slightly curved brown transverse discal line; a dot on discocellular and a marginal series, blackish; secondaries pale stramineous, becoming reddish at apex; body rosy-brownish, palpi whitish-black at the base, abdomen whitish; body below white; wings below pale stramineous, tinted externally with rose-red. Expanse of wings 18 mm.

Santarem, Rio Jutahi, 1st February, 1875

22 *Cryptolechia Traili*, n. sp.

Primaries greyish-brown, shining; the basal two-thirds almost covered by large irregular pale yellow carmine-bordered spots, two of which cross the cell, and three of which form a triangle below it; disc pale yellow, bounded on each side and intersected through the centre by crenulated carmine lines; costal margin, fringe and inner margin, carmine; secondaries creamy white, fringe rose-red, becoming yellowish towards anal angle; primaries below rosy, the costa whitish; secondaries creamy-white, tinted externally with rose colour. Expanse of wings 20 mm.

Forest before Arimanahy, 3rd January.

Allied to *C. incensatella* and to *C. fervida* of Zeller.

23. *Cryptolechia virginalis*, n. sp.

Above silvery white ; primaries with the apex angular ; three or four marginal black dots towards apex ; wings below with the margins and veins yellowish , body below white, tarsi of legs testaceous. Expanse of wings 17 mm.

Boaventura, Rio Jutahi, 24th January, 1875.

24. *Cryptolechia Javanica*, n. sp.

Above shining snow-white ; primaries with three oblong sub-basal spots followed at basal third by an irregularly zigzag transverse line, two parallel discal lines widening and zigzag towards the costa, and the fringe, brown ; a dark brown spot closing the cell ; a marginal series of black dots ; secondaries brownish towards apex and outer margin, the fringe depressed ; body white ; primaries below sordid white, the veins and margin brownish, costal and internal border snow white ; secondaries white, slightly sordid towards apex ; a marginal brown line. Expanse of wings 22 mm.

Rio Javary, 5th December.

Near to *C. cretifera* of Felder.

25. *Cryptolechia rosacea*, n. sp.

Primaries above clay-coloured with a rosy gloss ; a distinct brown streak, externally diffused, running from basal fourth of costa to external third of inner margin ; a diffused sub-quadrate costal patch near apex, bounded externally by a slightly arched line which crosses the disc, both brown ; a marginal series of black dots ; fringe grey externally ; secondaries whitish, the external half tinted with rose-red ; body corresponding in colour with the wings ; body below white, the palpi, upper surface of anterior tibiæ, and under surface of hind tarsi, rosy ; wings below rose-red, the bases and internal areas whitish. Expanse of wings 29 mm.

Rio Tanimá, Rio Negro, 31st July.

Allied to *C. lumerella*.

26. *Cryptolechia trilineata*, n. sp.

Primaries above silver grey, base brownish ; basal third of inner margin dark brown ; three oblique irregular dark brown lines, externally diffused, crossing the wing at equal distances, the outermost one deeply and broadly excavated and macular ; a marginal series of black spots ; fringe white ; secondaries shining smoky-brown, costal area silver ; a white marginal line ; fringe silver grey ; body dark silky grey, head white in front ; body below white ; wings below silver grey.   Expanse of wings 29 mm.

Rio Javary, 3rd December.

The coloration and marking of this species approaches that of some species of *Antæotricha.*

The species above described were all collected by Mr. Trail on the Amazons.

Monograph of the Coleopterous genus CALOCHROMUS *of the family* LYCIDÆ; by CHAS. O. WATERHOUSE.

CALOCHROMUS, Guérin, 1833.

The species of this genus differ from all the other *Lycidæ* (except *Homalisus*) in having the elytra without distinct carinæ separated by rows of punctures ; the whole surface of the elytra is finely and densely punctured and pubescent, and there are generally two or three obscure raised lines on each elytron. The species of the genus will probably be found to be numerous ; some of them very much resemble *Telephorus* in their appearance. The males have the antennæ much longer, and less compressed, than in the females, and the penultimate segment of the abdomen is notched or emarginate at the apex Before attempting to determine any species it is quite necessary to ascertain the sex of the specimen for which a name is sought.

I. Maxillary palpi very short, thick and compact, the apical joint nearly globular

C. glaucopterus, Guérin.

Cyaneo-niger, sub-nitidus. thorace elytrorumque basi flavis. Long 5½–7 lin.
Hab. Dorey and Waigiou. Brit Mus.

C. scutellaris, Erichs (Pl. II, f. 1).

Niger, nitidus, elytris ferrugineo-flavis, pubescentibus Long. 4–5½ lin.

Thorax with a deep mesial channel, deepest behind, with a fine line running through the middle of it, from the anterior to posterior margin , the lateral impressions very deep, the anterior one not separated from the posterior. The elytra are subparallel, rusty-yellow, sometimes with the scutellar region black.
Hab. N.W. Australia. Brit. Mus.

C. *basalis*, n. sp. (Pl. II, f. 2).

Niger, nitidus; elytris dimidio basali ferrugineo, quadri-costatis, apicem versus paulo angustatis. ♀. Long 5 iin.

Closely allied to *C. scutellaris*, but relatively broader; thorax broader, with a deep mesial impression, broader in the middle; there is a deep round fovea at the anterior angle, and a deep impression within the posterior angle, the part between the anterior fovea and the posterior impression raised, so that the impressions are not confluent as in the preceding species. The antennæ are broader than in *scutellaris*, in which the fourth joint is twice as long as broad, whereas in *basalis* it is not more than $\frac{1}{3}$ longer than broad.

Hab. Swan River.   Brit. Mus.

C. *Guerinii*, W. MacLeay.

Cyaneo-niger; thorace elytrisque ochraceis pubescentibus, his apice cyaneo-nigris.   Long. 5½–6 lin.

Hab. Cape York; Rockhampton.   Brit. Mus

One example in the Museum collection has the sutural line of the thorax black, and the apex of the elytra very slightly tipped with blue-black.

II.   Maxillary palpi less compactly jointed, apical joint not globular.

* Head visible from above; forehead tuberose; a narrow space between the eye and the antennal pit.

C. *melanurus*, n. sp (Pl. II, f. 3)

Cyaneo-niger, nitidulus; brevissime pubescens; thorace medio canaliculato, ad angulos anticos impresso, intra angulis posticis foveâ rotundatâ impresso, basi marginato; elytris ferrugineo-flavis, dense pubescentibus, prope suturam striatis, interstitiis convexiusculis, apice nigro.   Long. 4½–7¼ lin.

Forehead between the eyes very prominent   Antennæ as long as the elytra, the two basal joints shining, the rest finely punctulate   Thorax very delicately and closely punctured, scarcely pubescent; disc with a fine mesial line, more deeply impressed behind, there is a deep impression at each anterior angle, the posterior angles are rather inflated, and within them

there is a deep impression ; the base is margined. The elytra
are rusty yellow, dull and pubescent, bluish-black at the apex,
striated near the suture, the interstices rather convex.

Hab. Penang, Java, Sumatra. Brit. Mus.

C. orbatus, n. sp. (Pl. II, f. 4).

Statura omnino praecedentis, differt tamen antennarum articulo
tertio longiori ; elytris totis ferrugineis   Long. 5–6½ lin.

This species differs only from *C. melanurus* in having the
elytra uniform rusty yellow, and in having the third joint of
the antennae nearly three times as long as its greatest width,
whereas in *C melanurus* it is at most twice as long as broad.

Hab. Philippine Islands, and Darjeeling. Brit. Mus.

** Forehead gently convex ; head generally not visible from
above : margin of the antennal pit contiguous to the eye.

C. apicalis, Hope* (Pl. II, f. 5).

Omalysus apicalis, Hope, Gray, Zool. Miscel. 1831, p. 26.

Niger ; elytris rufis, plagà magnà basali nigrà ; thorace
transverso, medio canaliculato, utrinque bumpresso, angulis
rotundatis ; elytris thorace paulo latioribus, postice parum
ampliatis, apice rotundatis, pubescentibus, singulis dorsim lineis
quinque impressis, interstitiis angustis convexiusculis ♂. Long.
6 lin., lat. 2⅙ lin.

Rather a broad species   Antennae rather stout, half the length
of the body, fourth joint as long as the two previous joints
taken together, the fifth a little shorter, the sixth and ninth
slightly increasing in length, very little compressed, truncate at
their apex   Thorax a quarter broader than long, moderately
shining, all the angles rounded, especially the anterior, the
central impressed line reaching from the posterior to the
anterior margins, well defined and of equal depth ; on each side
are two large deep impressions separated from each other by an
oblique ridge. The elytra are at the base a little broader than
the thorax, a little wider posteriorly, red, with a black patch
extending from the base to the posterior two-thirds, leaving
the margins and the apex red ; each elytron has five impressed

---

* *O maculicollis* and *O lineatocollis*, Hope. 1 c, are *Telephoridæ*
O lineatus, Hope, is at present unknown to me

lines, the interstices narrow and slightly convex. The penultimate segment of the abdomen has a trapezoidal emargination at the apex.

Hab. Nepal.   Brit. Mus.

The above description is taken from Hope's original specimen.

C. *æmulus*, n. sp. (Pl. II, f. 6.)

Niger, sub-opacus; thorace medio canaliculato, utrinque biimpresso; elytris dimidio basali ferrugineo-flavo, singulis tricostatis. Long. $3\frac{1}{2}$–$4\frac{3}{4}$ lin

Head convex, shining, rather closely and excessively finely punctured, rostrum* very short, strongly transverse, at the base of each antenna there is a slight round tumour; mandibles pitchy.   Thorax shining, clothed with very delicate grey pubescence only visible in some lights.   Elytra densely pubescent, with the basal half rusty-yellow, each with three distinct rooflike costæ, and with an indication of a fourth.

♂ Antennæ nearly as long as the elytra, third joint a little elongate, very obliquely truncate at the apex, fourth joint as long as the two preceding taken together, compressed, broader than the third, the 5th to 10th the same length as the third, the eighth, ninth and tenth diminishing in width, the fifth to eighth with the lower anterior angle a little produced, the eleventh joint a little longer and much narrower than the preceding   Thorax sub-quadrate, rather straight at the sides, arched in front, with a deep mesial longitudinal channel, and on each side two deep foveæ, the raised portion dividing the foveæ oblique. Penultimate segment of abdomen triangularly emarginate at the apex, and with a deep longitudinal mesial channel.

♀ Antennæ $\frac{2}{3}$ the length of the elytra, third joint as broad at its apex as long, fourth to ninth scarcely longer than broad, the tenth a little narrower, eleventh narrowed at the apex Thorax a little broader than long, rather narrowed in front; the rest as in the male

Hab. Sarawak (Wallace)   Brit Mus.

---

* The portion of the head which is in front of the insertion of the antennæ, not strictly a rostrum in this genus, but I use the word as a convenient one

C rugatus, n. sp. (Pl. II, f. 7)

Elongatus, niger ; elytiis piceo-testaceis, dense rubio-sericeis, stiis impiessis, interstitiis convexiusculis, 2° et 4° sub-costatis ♂. Long 5½ lin

Head gently convex, impressed on the forehead ; iostium extremely short, space between the antennal pit and base of the mandible about half the diameter of the antennal pit   Antennæ about ⅔ the length of the elytia and (foi the genus) iather slender, the sixth to tenth joints slightly diminishing in length, and a trifle more slender, eleventh joint a little longei, parallel, scaicely acuminate at the apex   Thorax black, margined, delicately pubescent, disc transversely impressed behind the middle, deeply impiessed in front of and behind the oblique lateral ridge. Penultimate segment of abdomen with a deep incision.

Hab Allahabad (J. C. Bowring, Esq).   Brit. Mus.

C. ruber, n. sp. (Pl. II, f. 8).

Elongatus, niger supra, piceo-testaceus dense rubro-seiiceus ; thoiace medio longitudinalitei canaliculato, lateribus bifoveatis ; elytris minus elongatis unicoloribus, obsolete bicostatis ♀. Long. 5¾ lin.

Antennæ compressed, thiid joint as long as the two piecedng togethei, fourth a little longer, truncate at the apex, fifth to ninth neaily the same form, but gradually more obliquely truncate at the apex, so that the lower anterior angle becomes more acute but is not produced, the tenth joint is rathei smaller, very obliquely truncate, the eleventh narrow, parallel, acuminate at the apex.

Hab. Allahabad (J. C. Bowring, Esq.).   Brit. Mus.

This species is veiy close to *C. rugatus*, and I thought that it might, peihaps, be the female of that insect, but the lateral oblique iidge of the thorax is placed moie posteriorly (see fig), and the lateral impressions aie not so well defined ; the space between the antennal pit and the base of the mandible is also much greater.

C. velutinus, n. sp. (Pl. II, f. 9).

Elongatus, piceo-niger, supra piceo-testaceus, dense flavo-rufo-sericeus ; thoiace sat tiansverso, medio canaliculato, utrinque fortiter impresso ; elytris obsolete bicostatis ; abdomine cyaneo-nigro.   Long. 5½ lin.

Rather shorter and broader than the preceding, thorax more transverse, and with the ridge which divides the lateral impression much more directed forwards, rostrum almost none, *i.e.*, the space between the antennal pit and the base of the mandible is less than half the diameter of the pit, whilst in *C. ruber* this space is quite equal to the diameter of the antennal pit. Third joint of the antennæ as long as the first, as long as its greatest width, obliquely truncate at the apex, the fourth joint as long as the two preceding together, a little longer than broad, very little narrowed at the base, straight at the apex, the fifth to tenth about the same length as the fourth, but gradually diminishing in width, scarcely oblique at the apex, their lower anterior angle a little less than a right angle, eleventh joint much narrower, longer, parallel, acuminate at the apex. Thorax $\frac{1}{6}$ broader than long, a little narrowed in front, disc convex, with a rather fine mesial channel, the sides deeply impressed, the usual oblique ridge very much directed forwards, almost parallel with the lateral margin. Elytra very gradually and very little enlarged posteriorly, each with two narrow little raised costæ, with an indication of a third.

Hab. Burmah (J. C. Bowring, Esq.) Brit. Mus.

C. restitus, n. sp. (Pl. II, f. 10).

Elongatus, postice paulo ampliatus, niger; vix cyanescens; thorace nigro (vel rubro), tenuissime rubro-sericeo, elytris rufo-testaceis, dense rufo-sericeis, bicostatis, apice nigro. ♂ Long. 3–4 lin.   ♀ Long. 5–6 lin.

♂ Antennæ about $\frac{2}{3}$ the length of the elytra, moderately broad in the middle, tapering to the apex. Rostrum extremely short, the space between the antennal pit and the base of the mandible about $\frac{1}{3}$ the diameter of the antennal pit. Thorax black, delicately clothed with very fine silky-red pubescence, only visible in certain lights, discoidal channel rather deep, lateral impressions deep and well defined. Scutellum black. Elytra clothed with bright red pubescence; each elytron with two not very prominent costæ; the apex black. Under side and legs black, scarcely tinged with blue. Penultimate segment of abdomen emarginate.

♀ Antennæ rather shorter and broader than in the male. Rostrum a little more prominent, the space between the antennal pit and the base of the mandible about $\frac{1}{2}$ the diameter of the pit. Thorax reddish-yellow, with the sides and mesial line black. Each elytron with three distinct costæ, the apex broadly black.

Var. ♀. Thorax entirely red, pubescence more dense. Elytra bicostate, the costæ narrower.

Hab. Penang (J. C. Bowring, Esq)   Brit. Mus

C. *lepidus*, n. sp. (Pl II, f 11).

Cæruleus, nitidus ; thorace vix brevissimo pubescenti ; disco longitudinaliter fortiter impresso, lateribus bimpressis ; elytris piceo-testaceis, dense fulvo-rufo-pubescentibus, striis vix perspicue impressis, apice anguste nigro ; antennis pedibusque violaceis. Long. $3\frac{1}{2}$–$4\frac{1}{2}$ lin

A more slender species than any of the preceding, and distinct by the beautiful shining blue thorax and violet antennæ   The anterior angles of the thorax are much deflexed and, consequently, do not show the margin so distinctly ; the disc has not a fine mesial line, but a deep longitudinal impression ; the lateral fossæ are deep, but the oblique ridge which divides them is not so well defined as in most of the species

♂ Antennæ rather slender. Elytra with scarcely any trace of costæ. Penultimate segment of abdomen with a deep incision.

♀ Antennæ very slightly dilated   Thorax more narrowed in front   Elytra bicostate

Hab. Java (♂), Penang (♀), (J. C. Bowring, Esq.). Brit. Mus.

The two examples are from different localities, but as they agree so well in general character, I have ventured to associate them as sexes.

C. *longipennis*, n sp. (Pl. II, f. 12).

Elongatus, sub-parallelus, niger ; thorace supra piceo, dense rufo-pubescente, medio foveolâ lanceolatâ impresso, lateribus bimpressis ; scutello piceo, rufo-pubescente ; elytris longissimis, dense rufo-pubescentibus, apice nigris, singulis 2- vel 3-costatis, costis angustioribus ♀. Long $6\frac{1}{4}$ lin., lat. $1\frac{1}{3}$ lin

Forehead evenly convex, black, very finely pubescent, rostrum about three times as broad as long; maxillary palpi very stout. Antennæ $\frac{3}{4}$ the length of the elytra, compressed, third joint about twice as long as broad, emarginate at the apex, the fourth to ninth joints about equal in length, the lower anterior angle obliquely and much produced, increasingly so as they approach the apex, the tenth joint very oblique, a little smaller than the ninth, the eleventh compressed fusiform. Thorax a little broader than long, somewhat narrowed in front, all the angles distinct but obtuse, densely clothed with bright red pubescence, disc convex, with a deep lanceolate fovea nearly reaching from the anterior to the posterior margins. Elytra very long, densely clothed with bright red pubescence, the apex black; each with three not very distinct narrow costæ, the outer one very obsolete.

Hab. Sumatra (E C. Buxton, Esq)   Brit. Mus

*** Intermediate coxæ (in the male) with a strong spine; base of femur with a strong tooth; tibiæ curved.

C. *dispar*, n sp. (Pl. II, f. 13).

Cyaneo-niger, sat nitidus; elongatus, parum convexus; thorace marginato, medio canaliculato, utrinque biimpresso; elytris rufis, dense pubescentibus, postice paulo ampliatis.   Long. 6 lin.

This species has somewhat the appearance of *C. orbatus*, but has the elytra more ample behind, less bluntly rounded at the apex, and the thorax is margined all round   The antennæ are nearly as long as the elytra, not very approximate at their base. Clypeus gently emarginate. Intermediate coxæ with a strong acute spine; the femur with a strong tooth near their base; the intermediate and posterior tibiæ strongly curved. The penultimate segment of the abdomen is deeply notched in the middle.

Hab. Borneo. Brit. Mus.

Notes on the Lepidopterous Genera CARAMA *and* TRICHETRA, *with descriptions of new species; by* ARTHUR G. BUTLER, F.L S.

The genus *Trichetra* was originally described by Westwood for the reception of a new and singular *Liparide* from Tasmania; subsequently a second species of the same genus was described and figured by Curtis, under the new generic and specific names of *Arcturus Sparshalli*.

In the fourth part of his Lepidoptera Heterocera Mr Walker incorrectly identified the species named by Curtis, and, finding generic differences between his (Walker's) *A Sparshalli*, and the *T. mesomelas* of Westwood, and also discovering the fact that *Arcturus* was preoccupied in the Crustacea, he named the genus *Carama*.

The type of Walker's *C. Sparshalli* is from Para, that of Curtis's *A. Sparshalli* is probably of Australian origin.

CARAMA, *Walker.*

1 *Carama Walkeri*, n sp.

Carama Sparshalli, Walker (nec Curtis), Lep. Het 4, p. 844.
♂ Para. Sp. ead. ? ♀ Mexico. Brit Mus

Walker confounded no less than four species under this name in the cabinet. It would create confusion to retain it for his type.

2. *Carama virgo*, n. sp.

Smaller than the preceding, the primaries shorter and broader in comparison, less glossy, antennae comparatively longer, with the scape more woolly; the radiating hairs on the tegulae of only about half the length; the abdomen less woolly : all the tarsi below black. Expanse of wings 1 inch 6 lines.
♂ Vera Cruz; ♀ New Granada Brit. Mus.

3 *Carama orina* ? (Sepp. Surin Vlnd.)

About the same average size as the preceding , it differs from *C Walkeri* in its smaller size, the shorter, broader, and less glossy primaries ; the abdomen above white, banded with yellow in the female ; the pectus and anterior coxae barely tinted with black , tarsi below testaceous Expanse of wings, ♂ 1 inch. 2 lines; ♀ 1 inch, 3–7 lines.

♂ Bolivia; ♀ Venezuela. Brit. Mus.

The radiating hairs on the tegulæ are well-developed in this species

4. *Carama plumosa*, n. sp.

Nearly allied to the preceding, but (excepting in its smaller size, and the black upper surface of the anterior pair of legs) agreeing with *C. Walkeri*. Expanse of wings ♂ 1 inch, 2 lines: ♀ 1 inch, 5 lines.

♂, ♀ Santarem   Brit. Mus.

5 *Carama ? nivea* (Cramer, Pap. Exot.).

Surinam

This appears to belong to the genus.

Trichetra, *Westwood* *

1   *Trichetra sparshalli* (Curtis, Brit Ent. vii, pl 336). Australia ?

2. *Trichetra fraterna*, n. sp.

Differs from *T. sparshalli* only in having the anterior legs white, not black above   Expanse of wings ♂ 1 inch. 9 lines; ♀ 2 inches, 2 lines

Moreton Bay. Brit. Mus

The female has all the wings white, the thorax black, the tegulæ testaceous internally ; a large sandy-brown anal woolly mass

3 *Trichetra stibosoma*, n. sp

♀ Differs from *T. mesomelas*, in having the abdomen snow-white as in the preceding species, and with the anus tufted with brown above. Expanse of wings 2 inches 2 lines.

N. S Wales   Brit. Mus

4. *Trichetra mesomelas* (Walker, Lep. Het. 4, p. 845).

♂, ♀ Tasmania   Brit Mus.

The two genera are easily distinguished, *Carama* having a radiating brush of white hair on each tegula in the males, and *Trichetra* a crest of projecting hair on the front of the head. there are, moreover, other less evident characters

---

* Agassiz gives this as White's genus, but he nowhere diagnoses it, and the species figured in Grey's Australia are not congeneric

On various genera of the Homopterous family MEMBRACIDÆ, *with descriptions of new species ;* by ARTHUR GARDINER BUTLER, F.L.S., F.Z.S., &c.

In the present paper I propose to give a list of the species which appear to me to be referable to the following six genera of *Smiliinæ*—*Hille, Polyglypta, Entylia, Cyphonia, Ceresa* and *Telamona,* giving the synonymy wherever a species has been more than once described, and descriptions of the new species in the Collection of the British Museum.

In some points of synonymy I differ from Dr. Stal, but then it must be borne in mind, thât since his examination of Walker's types, he has not fully revised the synonymy which he formerly proposed for *Entylia* and some other genera.

Family MEMBRACIDÆ.

Sub-Family SMILIINÆ (Smiliida, *Stal*).

HILLE, *Stal.*

1. *Hille maculicornis.*

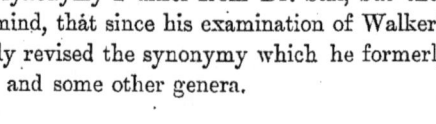

Oxygonia maculicornis, Fairm., Ann. Ent. Sér. 2, iv, p. 303, 6, pl. 5, fig. 20 (1846).
Bogota.

2. *Hille notata.*

Hille notata, Stal. Ofv. Vetensk. Akad. Förh. 1869, p. 235.
Bogota.

Only differs from the preceding in the shorter and basally broader dorsal process, which is in the same position ; and also in the lateral spot of the hind process of the thorax.

3. *Hille conspersa.*

Hille conspersa, Stal, Ofv. Vetensk. Akad. Förh. 1869, p. 236.
Bogota.

T

Most nearly allied to *H. notata*; the colours excepted, it differs only in the slightly more depressed dorsal process of the thorax, in front gradually slanting, instead of almost perpendicular.

4. *Hille conica.*

Oxygonia conica, Fairm., Ann. Ent. Sér. 2, iv, p. 302, 3 (1846).
Triquetra reticulata, Walker, List. Homopt. ii, p, 524 (1851).
Colombia. Brit. Mus.

5. *Hille perfecta.*

Thelia perfecta, Walker, List. Homopt. Suppl., p. 138 (1858).
Rio Napo. Type Brit. Mus.

This species differs from *H. conica* in the much less prominent anterior process, and its much more oblique anterior margin; also in its tawny colouring with black longitudinal dorsal stripe.

6. *Hille nutans.*

Hille nutans, Stal, Ofv. Vetensk. Akad. Förh. 1869, p. 236.
Bogota.

Seems allied to the preceding, but the black dorsal carina is not indicated in Dr. Stal's description, so that it is probably distinct.

7. *Hille sulphurea*, n. sp. Pl. III, f. 1.

Sulphur-yellow; pronotum covered with rather close brown punctures, five lateral polished longitudinal lines on each side, the third and fourth from the central carina abbreviated; dorsal keel black, its highest point less prominent and not so acute as in *H. conica*, its front margin oblique and hardly perceptible, sub-sinuate; the front of the thorax (excepting in its less-prominent keel), much as in *H. dorsalis*; the width at the humeral angles about equal to the height in the centre; humeral angles and a small λ like marking over each eye, black; head about twice as broad as long, spotted with black; tegmina testaceous, paler along the anterior margin, veins reddish; corium yellowish; tarsi of legs slightly brownish. Length 9 mm.

Bogota. Type Brit. Mus.

General coloration of *H. dorsalis*; but, viewed laterally, more like *H. perfecta* in form.

8. *Hille dorsalis*

Oxygonia dorsalis, Fairm., Ann. Ent. Sér. 2, iv, p. 303, 5 (1846).
Triquetra venosa, Walker, List Homopt ii, p. 523, 14 (1851). Colombia.

9. *Hille sobria.*

Triquetra sobria, Walker, List. Homopt. ii, p. 523, 13 (1851)· Quito.

10. *Hille pacifica.*

Oxygonia pacifica, Fairm , Ann. Ent. Sér. 2, iv, p. 302, 4 (1846).
Brazil.

11. *Hille sobrina.*

Oxygonia sobrina; Stal, Kongl Vctensk. Akad. Handl 1862, p. 28.
Rio Janeiro.

Nearly allied to *H. pacifica*, the elevated dorsal portion of the thorax less slanting in front and moreover not so high. Thorax with the elevated dorsal part, seen from the side, rounded in front , running off gradually behind into a central longitudinal carina It also differs in coloration.

POLYGLYPTA, *Burmeister.*

1. *Polyglypta reflexa*, n. sp. Pl. III, f 2.

Piceous ; pronotum long, slender, rugose rather than coarsely punctured, with the internal carinæ behind the head yellow, and two spots on the first and third carinæ at the terminal third, five lateral carinæ the second of which is abbreviated and extends only a short distance behind the humeral angles; anterior process of about one fourth the length of the insect, slightly depressed, posterior extremity tapering. slender and reflexed; tegmina smoky brown, the corium piceous ; body and legs testaceous. Length 14 mm.
Guatemala. Type Brit. Mus.

The most strongly marked species in the genus, in form quite unlike anything hitherto described.

2. *Polyglypta costata.*

♀ *Polyglypta costata*, Burmeister, Handb. Ent ii, 1, p. 142, 1; Silb Revue Ent iv, p. 177, 1, pl. 36, figs 5–7 (1836).

♂ *Polyglypta pilosa*, Fairm. Ann. Ent. Sér. 2, iv, p. 296, 2 (1846).

0 *Polyglypta strigata*, Walker, List. Homopt. Suppl. p. 136 (1858).

· ♂, ♀ Mexico. Brit. Mus.

3. *Polyglypta dorsalis.*

Polyglypta dorsalis, Burmeister, Silb. Revue Ent. iv, p. 178, 2 (1836).

var. *Polyglypta maculata*, Burmeister, l c , n. 3 (1836).

var. *Polyglypta pallipes*, Burmeister, l.c , n 4 (1836)

Polyglypta nigella, Fairm., Ann. Ent. Sér. 2, iv, p. 298, 10 (1846).

Mexico, Chiapas. Brit. Mus.

I have associated the above on the authority of Dr. Stal, but the three forms are readily separated ; *P pallipes*, not only by its black colouring, but the distinctly shorter, though variable, anterior thoracic horn.

4. *Polyglypta lineata.*

Polyglypta lineata, Burmeister, Silb. Revue Ent. iv, p. 179, 4 (1836).

0 *Polyglypta abbreviata*, Walker, List Homopt. Suppl p. 136 (1858).

Mexico (Oaxaca). Brit Mus

5. *Polyglypta tridecim-costata.*

Polyglypta tridecim-costata, Fairm., Ann. Ent. Sér. 2, iv, p. 299, 11 (1846).

Mexico.

Greenish, with short anterior horn, thirteen carinæ.

6. *Polyglypta fusca*, n. sp. Pl. III, f. 3.

Chocolate-brown, coarsely punctured ; pronotum with four lateral carinæ , anterior process (from the humeral angles) about one-third the length of the entire insect, laterally compressed,

with the usual marginal and central carinæ, broad at the base
and very slightly ascending at the apex ; tegmina hyaline testaceous ; legs testaceous. Length 11 mm.

Mexico. Type Brit. Mus.

Allied to *P. pallipes*, but differing in colour and in the
anterior process being more robust and much wider at its base.

7 *Polyglypta hordeacea*, n sp. Pl. III, f. 4.

Straw-yellow, coarsely punctured with chocolate-brown,
sparsely setose ; the dorsal region, an oblique interrupted band
beyond the middle and the terminal two-sevenths of the pronotum chocolate-brown ; four lateral longitudinal carinæ ;
anterior process straight, rather narrow, more than a third the
length of the entire insect, with marginal, two abbreviated basal,
and two continuous central longitudinal carinæ ; its under
surface brown with one central carina ; body, legs, and tegmina
testaceous. Length 13 mm

Pará. Type Brit. Mus.

Allied to *P. dorsalis*, but with the pronotum and especially
the anterior process considerably straighter, the latter not
ascending at the tip, and with two central continuous longitudinal carinæ.

8. *Polyglypta tricolor*, n. sp. Pl. III, f. 5.

Blackish brown, the dorsal region tawny or ochraceous ; a
short litura at the base of the anterior process confluent with a
broad arched band on the anterior part of the inner margin, and
an oblique band a short distance behind it, sulphur yellow edged
with black ; five lateral carinæ, the anterior process rather long,
more or less obliquely ascending, with two strongly marked
longitudinal carinæ. Length 12 mm

(Oaxaca), Mexico, and Peru. Type Brit Mus.

Allied to *P. maculata*, but at once distinguished by its greater
length, much less width at the humeral angles, longer anterior
process with more prominent carinæ, and different coloration.

9. *Polyglypta bogotensis*.

♀ *Polyglypta bogotensis*, Fairm., Ann. Ent. Sér. 2, iv, p. 297,
4 (1846)

Polyglypta nigriventris, Fairm , l.c , n. 6 (1846).

Ɔ *Polyglypta straminea*, Walker, List. Homopt. ii, p 544, (1851).
0 ♂ *Polyglypta viridimaculata*, Fanm. Ann. Ent. Sér. 2, iv,
p. 298, 7 (1846).
Ɔ *Polyglypta interrupta*, Walker, List. Homopt. ii, p. 545,
(1851).

     ♂, ♀ Colombia. Brit. Mus.

10. *Polyglypta brevivitta.*

Polyglypta brevivitta, Walker, List. Homopt. ii, p. 545, n. 13
(1851)
     Venezuela.   Type Brit. Mus

ENTYLIA, *German.*

1. *Entylia sinuata*

Membracis sinuata, Fabr., Ent. Syst. Suppl. p. 513, 4 (1798).
Membracis emarginata, Fabr., l.c, n. 5.
Entylia impedita, Walker, List Homopt. Suppl. p. 137.
     Canada ; United States   Brit Mus

I differ entirely from Dr. Stal in the synonymy which he
gives to the species of this genus   In his sectional, or perhaps
specific diagnoses, he gives the height of the thoracic processes,
their width and angulation at the apex, and the depth of the
sinus between them, as distinctive characters : so far so good—
but *M. sinuata* and the type of *E. impedita* agree not only in
these very characters but in coloration, whilst *E. bactrina* differs
chiefly in the stronger angulation and expansion of the anterior
process (at least in our example), *E. concisa* in the greater
length and almost falcated inner edge of the anterior process,
E. decisa in the falcated opposed inner edges of both processes
and its black coloration, *E. accisa* in its shorter processes and
consequently much shallower sinus and its blackish and yellow
coloration, *E. indecisa* in similar structural characters to the
last and its brown and yellow coloration, *E. reducta* in its still
shorter processes and shallower sinus. I should have no objec-
tion to considering the whole of the above mentioned forms as
varieties of one inconstant species ; but if we are to admit two,
we must of necessity accept several others.

2. *Entylia bactriana*

Entylia bactriana, Germar, Silb. Revue Ent: iii, p. 248, 3.
North America? Brit. Mus.

3. *Entylia accisa.*

Entylia accisa, Walker, List Homopt. ii, p. 548 (1851).
var. *Entylia indecisa*, Walker, l.c., p 549 (1851)
North America, Trenton Falls. Types Brit Mus.

4. *Entylia concisa.*

Entylia concisa, Walker, List. Homopt. ii, p. 547 (1851).
var. melan *Entylia decisa*, Walker, l c., p 548 (1851)
E. Florida. Types Brit. Mus.

5. *Entylia reducta.*

Entylia reducta, Walker, List. Homopt. ii, p. 549 (1851).
United States Type Brit. Mus.

6. *Entylia inæqualis*, n. sp. Pl. III, f 7

Sordid testaceous or whity-brown, the pronotum crossed
obliquely by two whitish lines, the anterior one, running from
the infero-posterior angle of the anterior process, edged externally with black, the posterior one, running from the infero-
posterior angle of the hinder process, edged on both sides with
black, the anterior process formed as in *E. sinuata*, but the
posterior process much shorter and rounded in front, so as to
approach the form of *E. gemmata*, a hyaline spot behind it.
Length 5 mm.
Guatemala. Type Brit Mus

7. *Entylia mira*, n. sp. Pl III, f. 8.

Whity-brown, the dorsal region from the hind margin of the
anterior process to behind the posterior process reddish-brown;
a band of the ground colour running obliquely from behind the
posterior process, the dorsal region beyond this band mottled
with reddish-brown; head and legs pale reddish-brown; pronotum with the anterior dorsal process projecting slightly
forward, the postero-superior angle being its highest point,
posterior process rounded, its hind margin very oblique. Length
5½ mm.
Mexico. Type Brit. Mus.

8. *Entylia turrita*, n. sp. Pl. III, f. 9.

Reddish-brown, a whitish spot near the centre of the inner
or inferior margin of the pronotum, and a whitish oblique band
from the back of the posterior process, both very ill-defined;
anterior process small, rounded in front, with two lateral longitudinal carinæ; posterior process barely indicated by a slight
convexity of the dorsal line; body blackish, legs testaceous.
Length 4 mm.

Rio Janeiro. Type Brit. Mus.

Allied to *E. gemmata*.

9. *Entylia gemmata*.

Entylia gemmata, Germar, Silb. Revue Ent. iii, p. 248, 1.
Entylia corniculata, Fairm. Ann. Ent. Sér. 2, iv, p. 300, 2,
pl. 5, fig. 31 (1846).
var. *Entylia incisa*, Walker, List Homopt. ii, p 548 (1851).
Colombia, Brazil. Brit. Mus.

10. *Entylia fallax*.

Entylia fallax, Stal, Kongl. Vetensk. Akad. Handl. 1862,
p. 28.
Constancia. Brit Mus.

CYPHONIA, *Lap*

1. *Cyphonia trifida*.

Membracis trifida, Fabr. , Ent Syst. iv, p. 12, 19.
Cyphonia ornata, Lap., Ann. Ent. 1, p. 230, pl. 6, fig. 4.
Brazil. Brit. Mus

2. *Cyphonia proxima*.

Cyphonia proxima, Fairm. , Ann. Ent. Sér 2, iv, p. 502, 2
(1846).
Mexico. Sp. ead? Ega and Pará Brit. Mus.

3. *Cyphonia flavo-vittata*.

Cyphonia flavo-vittata, Stal, Ofv. Vetensk Akad. Forh. 1869,
p. 242.
Bogota.

Apparently nearly allied to the preceding species.

4. *Cyphonia clavata.*

Membracis clavatus, Fabr. Ent Syst iv, p. 13, 20.
Membracis bulbifera, Germar, Mag Ent. iv, p. 30, 40.
Brazil. Brit. Mus.

5. *Cyphonia nasalis*

Cyphonia nasalis, Stal, Kongl. Vetensk. Akad. Handl. 1862,
p. 34.
Rio Janeiro.

Apparently nearly allied to the preceding, but with the
central lobe of the head, a spot on each side of the thorax just
behind the spines, another on each side beyond it, and the legs
pale yellowish, the tibiæ with sub-basal and apical dark brown
bands.

6. *Cyphonia furcata*

Combophora furcata, Burmeister, Silb. Revue Ent 1, p. 231,
10 (1833).
Brazil Sp. ead? Brit. Mus.

I think it doubtful whether this is distinct from *C. clavata.*

7. *Cyphonia hispida.*

Cyphonia hispida, Walker, List. Homopt. Suppl. p. 156
(1858).
Tejuca, Rio. Type Brit. Mus

8. *Cyphonia hirta.*

Heteronota hirta, Germar, Silb. Revue Ent. iii, p. 255, 2.
Brazil. Sp. ead? Mexico. Brit. Mus.

9. *Cyphonia clavigera.*

Centrotus claviger, Fabr., Syst. Rhyn. p 17, 5.
Brazil. Brit Mus.

10. *Cyphonia flava.*

Combophora flava, Burmeister, Silb. Revue Ent. 1, p. 231, 11.
Brazil. Brit. Mus

11. *Cyphonia capra.*

Combophora capra, Burmeister, Silb. Revue Ent. 1, p. 231,
22.

Brazil   Brit. Mus.

Our example does not perfectly agree in colouring with
Burmeister's description.

12. *Cyphonia braccata.*

Heteronota braccata, Germar, Silb. Revue Ent. iii, p. 254, 1.
Brazil.

The species referred to this by Walker is quite distinct, and
agrees in structure with *C. flava.*

13. *Cyphonia rectispina*

Cyphonia rectispina, Fairm., Ann. Ent. Sér. 2, iv, p. 502, 6.
Mexico.   Brit. Mus.

14. *Cyphonia formosa,* n sp.   Pl. III, f. 6

Ochraceous, sparsely setose ; horns black with a broad tawny
band, occupying nearly the whole of the apical half ; hemelytra
testaceous hyaline, with the corium and veins ochraceous, base
and a sub-basal annular marking black ; legs ochraceous, with
the proximal extremities of the joints black , form similar to .
C. rectispina, but the anterior horns shorter and more slender
and both pairs of horns more divergent and curved. Length,
including the closed tegmina, 8 mm.

Mexico.   Type Brit. Mus

A very beautiful little species.

15. *Cyphonia fasciata,* n sp.

Cyphonia capra ? Walker (nec Burmeister).

Structure of *C. flava,* excepting that the posterior spines are
slightly more divergent ; ochraceous, the frons, tarsal claws
and pronotum black, the horns rugose at the base ; the three
terminal spines ochraceous, banded with black , tegmina testaceous hyaline, veins ochraceous dotted with black on the front
margin ; body longitudinally banded with grey. Length, including tegmina, 5 mm.

Brazil.   Type Brit Mus

CERESA, *Amyot and Serville.*

1. *Ceresa diceros.*

Membracis diceros, Say, Narr. Exp. App. Jour. Acad. Nat. Soc. Phil. p. 299

United States. Brit. Mus.

2. *Ceresa bubalus*

Membracis bubalus, Fabr., Ent. Syst. iv, p. 14, 23
Ceresa borealis, Fairm, Ann. Ent Sér. 2, iv, p. 284, 5.
Nova Scotia, Lake Huron, Canada. Brit. Mus.

3. *Ceresa taurina.*

Ceresa taurina, Walker, List. Homopt Suppl. p. 131 (1858).
New York. Type Brit. Mus.

Nearly allied to the preceding species.

4. *Ceresa constans*

Thelia constans, Walker, List. Homopt. ii, p. 563 (1851).
United States. Type Brit. Mus.

5. *Ceresa basalis.*

Ceresa basalis, Walker, List Homopt. ii, p. 527 (1851).
Nova Scotia. Type Brit Mus.

6. *Ceresa albidosparsa.*

Ceresa albidosparsa, Stal, Eugenies Resa, p. 283, 186.
California? Brit. Mus.

Is not this a slight variety of *C. alta* of Walker?

7. *Ceresa unguicularis.*

Ceresa unguicularis, Stal, Kongl. Vetensk, Akad. Handl. 1862, p. 26.
Rio Janeiro.

8. *Ceresa alta.*

Ceresa alta, Walker, List. Homopt. ii, p 529 (1851).
—? Type Brit. Mus

Like large examples of *C. taurina,* and still more like *C. constans.*

9. *Ceresa bifasciata.*

Ceresa bifasciata, Fairm. Ann. Ent. Sér. 2, iv, p. 286, 13 (1846).
Brazil

Seems allied to *C. taurina*, but the extremity of the prothorax with a dark oblique band and two or three black dots.

10. *Ceresa terminata.*

Ceresa terminata Fairm., Ann. Ent. Sér. 2, iv. p. 287, 16 (1846)
Colombia.

11. *Ceresa ustulata.*

Ceresa ustulata, Fairm, Ann. Ent. Sér. 2, iv, p. 285, 7 (1846).
Ceresa plana. Walker, List Homopt. 2, p. 529 (1851).
Brazil. Brit. Mus.

12. *Ceresa axillaris.*

Smilia axillaris, Germar, Silb. Revue Ent. iii, p 235, 8 (1835).
Ceresa terminalis, Walker, List Homopt. 2, p. 528 (1851).
Constancia and Lower Amazons. Brit. Mus.

13. *Ceresa malina*

Smilia malina, Germar, Silb. Revue Ent. iii, p. 236, 9 (1835).
Brazil. Brit. Mus.

14. *Ceresa suffusa.*

Ceresa suffusa, Walker, List Homopt. ii, p. 530 (1851).
—? Type Brit. Mus.

15. *Ceresa robusta,* n. sp. Pl. III, f. 10.

Somewhat allied to *C. malina*, but much higher, with the pronotum concave between the humeral horns, the latter compressed at the tips; pronotum olivaceous, rather finely but densely punctured, with a shining central longitudinal line in front, convex behind the humeral horns and laterally slightly compressed, terminating abruptly in a sharply acuminated spine-like process ; horns castaneous, black at the tips ; terminal spine black ; body reddish-tawny ; tegmina testaceous hyaline, the base and the veins towards the anterior margin mahogany-red ; a black dot at external angle, and a large black spot at apex. Length 10 mm.

Brazil   Type Brit. Mus.

This insect has the same angular thoracic projections at the base of the tegmina as in *C. malina*, but the form of the pronotum differs considerably from all described species.

16 *Ceresa Sallé.*

Ceresa Sallé, Stal, Stett. Ent. Zeit. 1864, p. 70
Mexico.

17. *Ceresa Stalii*, n. sp. Pl. III, f. 11.

Allied to *C. cavicornis*, but the pronotum higher, highest in the centre, slightly bisinuate between the anterior horns, the latter curving a little more upwards ; altogether paler in colour, the tegmina with a black spot on the inner margin. Length, including tegmina, 11 mm.

Mexico.   Type Brit. Mus.

18 *Ceresa testacea.*

Ceresa testacea, Fairm., Ann. Ent. Sér. 2, iv, p 284, 4 (1846).
Mexico   Brit. Mus.

Allied to *C suffusa* of Walker, but larger.

19 *Ceresa patruelis.*

Ceresa patruelis, Stal, Stett. Ent. Zeit 1864, p. 69.
Vera Cruz.   Brit Mus

20. *Ceresa affinis*

Ceresa affinis, Fairm., Ann. Ent. Sér. 2, iv, p. 284, pl. 5, fig 21 (1846).
Brazil.   Brit. Mus.

21. *Ceresa brevis.*

Ceresa brevis, Walker, List. Homopt. ii, p. 528 (1851).
New York   Type Brit. Mus.

Allied to *C. brunnicornis*; it has the front of the prothorax distinctly convex.

Ceresa fortis of Walker belongs to *Nassunia* of Stål.

22. *Ceresa extensa.*

Ceresa extensa, Walker, Insecta Saund. Hom. p. 68 (1858).
Colombia.   Type Brit. Mus.

23. *Ceresa integra.*

Ceresa integra, Walker, Insecta Saund. Hom p. 67 (1858).
—? Type Brit. Mus.

24. *Ceresa recta.*

Ceresa recta, Walker, Insecta Saund. Hom. p. 68 (1858).
—? Type Brit Mus

Ceresa? obliqua of Walker is *Hyphinoe camelus*

25. *Ceresa distans*, n sp.

Nearly allied to *C. vitulus*, but of a deeper colour, more coarsely punctured, the front of the pronotum seen from above sub-angulated instead of regularly convex, the horns rather shorter and less recurved, the terminal spine-like process shorter, the lateral white streak barely perceptible; dull testaceous, with the horns and margins of the pronotum and the legs somewhat reddish. Length, including closed tegmina, $8\frac{1}{2}$ mm.
Brazil.   Type Brit. Mus.

26. *Ceresa rufescens*, n. sp.

Also near to *C. vitulus*, but larger, of a reddish colour, the front of the pronotum distinctly sub-angulated, the horns being in an oblique line from the centre on each side and longer, terminal process considerably longer, a lateral yellow streak above the semicircular impression; tegmina with brown veins, yellowish-brown at the outer margin.   Length $6\frac{1}{2}$ mm.
Brazil.   Type Brit. Mus.

27. *Ceresa vitulus.*

Membracis vitulus, Fabr. Ent. Syst Rhyn p 20, n. 21.
Smilia pallens, Germar. Silb. Revue Ent. iii, p. 235, 6 (1835).
Ceresa spinifera, Fairm., Ann. Ent. Sér. 2, iv, p. 214, 6 (1846).
Ceresa curvilinea, Walker, List Homopt. Suppl. p. 132 (1858)
Ceresa excisa, Walker, Insecta Saund. Hom p. 68 (1858)
Brazil. Brit. Mus.

28. *Ceresa brunnicornis.*

Smilia brunnicornis, Germar, Silb. Revue Ent. iii, p. 235, 7 (1835)
Buenos Ayres —? Brit. Mus

29 *Ceresa cavicornis*

Ceresa cavicornis, Stal, Eugenies Resa, p. 284, Stal, Ofv Vetensk. Akad. Forh. 1869, p. 246
Monte Video, (*Stal*), Colombia Brit. Mus

30. *Ceresa? fastidiosa*

Triquetra fastidiosa, Fairm, Ann. Ent Sér. 2, iv, p. 281 (1846).
Colombia. Brit Mus.

It is impossible from Fairmaire's description to know whether his species has a conical horn on each side of the prothorax or one in the centre . if on both sides, as in our example, I see no reason for separating it generically from *Ceresa affinis* or *C. cavicornis* ; if however, the horn is in the centre (a conical prominence on the anterior part of the prothorax), the species might be an abnormal form of *Hille* or a *Potnia*

31. *Ceresa discolor.*

Ceresa discolor, Fairm., Ann Ent. Sér. 2, iv, p. 286, 12 (1846).
Brazil.

The humeral horns are extremely short in this species.

32. *Ceresa femorata.*

Ceresa femorata, Fairm., Ann. Ent. Sér. 2, ix, p 289, 24 (1846).
Ceresa uniformis, Fairm , l.c., n. 25 (1846).
Mexico.   Brit. Mus.

33. *Ceresa chlorotica.*

Ceresa chlorotica, Fairm. Ann. Ent Sér. 2, iv, p. 289, 23 (1846)
South America.

34. *Ceresa puncticeps*

Ceresa puncticeps, Stal, Stett. Ent Zeit. 1864, p. 70.
Mexico.

TELAMONA, *Fitch.*

1. *Telamona unicolor.*

Telamona unicolor, Fitch, Cat. Ins. State Cab. Nat. Hist. p 50 (1851).
New York.   Brit. Mus.
Confounded with *T. collina* by Walker.

2. *Telamona collina.*

Thelia collina, Walker, List Homopt ii, p. 565, 35 (1851).
New York   Type Brit. Mus.

Much more coarsely punctured than the preceding species, and with the humeral processes longer and more acuminate.

3. *Telamona fasciata.*

Telamona fasciata, Fitch, Cat Ins. State Cab Nat. Hist. p. 50 (1851)
Thelia cyrtops (part), Fairm., Ann. Ent. Sér. 2, iv, pl. 5, fig. 13 (1846).
Hemiptycha diffusa, Walker, List. Homopt. Suppl. p. 143 (1858).
Orilla, Canada W.   Brit. Mus.

4. *Telamona projecta*, n. sp. Pl. III, f. 11.

Allied to *T. monticola*, but much more slender in build, the humeral ear-like processes more acute, the dorsal process projecting noticeably forwards, more oblique at the top; and the colouring dull clay-brown mottled with sepia. Length 10 mm.

Hab. —? Type Brit. Mus.

This species was obtained at the sale of the Entomological Society's Collection, and formerly belonged to Kirby, it bears no indication of a locality excepting the letter *T'*

5. *Telamona monticola.*

Membracis monticola, Fabr., Ent. Syst. Rhyn. p. 7, 4.
United States, E. Florida. Brit. Mus.

One example of this species was included by Walker under *T. collina.*

6. *Telamona coryli.*

Telamona coryli, Fitch, Cat. Ins. State Cab. Nat. Hist p. 51 (1851).
New York.

7. *Telamona ampelopsidis.*

Membracis ampelopsidis, Harris, Ins Mass. p. 181 (1841); Entom Corresp. p. 334 (1869)
United States. Brit. Mus.

Differs from *T. monticola* in the squarer form of the thoracic crest and the three reddish bands on the prothorax. .

8. *Telamona concava*

Telamona concava, Fitch, Cat. Ins. State Cab. Nat. Hist. p. 50 (1851).
New York.

9. *Telamona tristis.*

Telamona tristis, Fitch, Cat. Ins. State Cab. Nat. Hist. p. 51 (1851)
Thelia scalaris, Walker (nec Fairm), in Coll. Brit. Mus.
North America. Brit. Mus.

10. *Telamona quercûs.*

Telamona querci, Fitch, Cat. Ins State Cab Nat Hist. p 51 (1851).

New York.

11. *Telamona cyrtops.*

Thelia cyrtops, Fairm., Ann. Ent. Sér 2, iv, p. 310, 17 (1851)

Telamona reclivata, Fitch, Cat. Ins State Cab. Nat. Hist. p 51 (1851).

Nova Scotia.   Brit. Mus

12 *Telamona molaris*, n. sp   Pl III, f 13.

Brown, irregularly variegated with black; allied to *T. cyrtops*, but differently coloured, the pronotum much shallower, the dorsal process distinctly bifid, with a lateral compressed vertical sulcus; the tegmina hyaline, with blackish veins and broad external border   Length 10 mm.

Saskatchewan, N America   Type Brit Mus

Presented to the Collection by Dr Hooker, and collected by M. Bourgeau

13 *Telamona mexicana*

Telamona mexicana, Stal, Ofv Vetensk Akad Forh. 1869, p. 249, 1

Mexico

14. *Telamona ? gibbosa.*

Hemiptycha gibbosa, Walker, List. Homopt Suppl p 142 (1858).

Ega.   Type Brit. Mus.

T. acuminata has as much right in my opinion, to be made the type of a new genus, as *T' scalaris* and *T. cristata* have; I cannot, therefore, include it in *Telamona*, but would propose the name *Glossonotus* for it on account of the tongue-like form of the dorsal process of the pronotum

Descriptions of new or little known species of COLEOPTERA *from various localities; by* CHAS. O. WATERHOUSE.

MELOLONTHIDÆ.

Apogonia nigrescens. Hope

Gray's Zool Miscell., 1831, p 23

Oblongo-ovata, convexa, nitida, nigra, elytris ænescentibus; clypeo crebre fortiter punctato; fronte crebre minus fortiter punctata, thorace creberrime evidenter punctato, augulis anticis prominulis, paulo depressis, scutello basi discrete punctato; elytris crebre fortiter punctatis, dorsim costis duabus angustis lævibus; abdomine lateribus, pygidioque crebre fortissime punctatis; metasterno lateribus confertim evidenter punctato Long. 5 lin

The punctures on the clypeus are rather close together and very strong, those on the forehead are less strong. The anterior angles of the thorax are unusually prominent and flattened, the punctuation is very even and distinct, the spaces between the punctures are not greater than the diameter of the punctures, the sides (viewed laterally) are much rounded behind the middle, and the posterior angles are very obtuse. The elytra are covered with large deep punctures, the spaces between the punctures a little greater than the diameter of the punctures: the usual two smooth costæ are well defined, and along the sides are five rows of strong punctures. Pygidium with a smooth raised mesial line.

Hab. Nepal (Hardwicke). Brit Mus.

Apogonia proxima, n sp

Nigro-ænea, convexa, nitida; thorace creberrime fortiter punctato, angulis anticis acutiusculis, haud depressis, scutello subtilius haud crebre punctato; elytris crebre fortiter punctatis, dorsim costis duabus angustis lævibus; abdomine lateribus pygidioque crebre fortissime punctatis, metasterno lateribus regulariter crebre fortiter punctatis Long 5 lin

This species is closely allied to the preceding, but differs as follows ·—Clypeus very short, very strongly and densely punctured, the punctures touching one another Forehead rather more deeply punctured. Thorax (viewed from above) gradually narrowed in front, the sides gently arcuate, the punctuation is rather stronger than in *A. nigrescens*, very close, the intervals between the punctures equal to the diameter of the punctures, the sides (viewed laterally) are less rounded posteriorly, the anterior angles (although slightly acute) are not prominent and are not flattened. The punctuation of the scutellum is not very close, finer than in *A. nigrescens*, and equally distributed over the surface. The punctuation of the elytra is the same, but of the five lateral rows of strong punctures, the pair proceeding from the shoulder are separated by a small space from the other three, and this space is punctured as the rest of the elytra. The punctuation of the sides of the metasternum is strong, and the spaces between the punctures are rather less than the diameter of the punctures, whereas in *A. nigrescens* the punctures are smaller and almost contiguous to each other. Pygidium with a short raised mesial line.

Hab. Andaman Island (R. Meldola, Esq.).   Brit Mus

In the Museum collection is a specimen named *ærea*, Bl., which differs from both the preceding in having the thorax (when viewed from above) rounded at the sides, and when viewed laterally very much rounded (almost from the anterior angle), the posterior angle not defined, and the scutellum is almost smooth, &c.

Apogonia rauca, Fabr.

The following notes from the type specimen of this species in the Banksian collection may be useful. Clypeus deeply punctured, the interspaces a little less than the diameter of the punctures; forehead rather less deeply punctured and the distances between the punctures average about $1\frac{1}{2}$ times the diameter of the punctures, the sides are very much rounded. The scutellum has two lines of punctures on each side The punctuation of the elytra is very deep and coarse, the intervals about half the diameter of the punctures, the second dorsal costa is very narrow and somewhat obsolete posteriorly, the frequently found third costa is not discernible, as the punctures on this part of the elytra are in lines, between the extreme margin and the most lateral line of punctures there are a few large punctures below the shoulders. The sides of the metasternum are very strongly punctured, the interspaces about equal to the diameter of the punctures. The sides of the abdomen are thickly and deeply punctured ; the pygidium has some large punctures placed not very closely along the sides, the middle with a few stray punctures, and no trace of a raised line. The general colour is æneous.

Anomala punctatissima, Walker (Ann. Mag. Nat. Hist. 1859, iii, p. 56), agrees admirably with the type *Apogonia rauca*, except that it has the scutellum almost smooth   I believe it to be a mere variety

Apogonia polita, n. sp.

Oblongo-ovata, convexa, nigra (vix purpurascens), nitidissima; clypeo sat crebre evidenter punctato; fronte minus crebre distincte punctata ; thorace convexo, haud crebre subtiliter punctulato; scutello lœvi ; elytris haud crebre, evidenter punctatis, bigeminato-striato-punctatis   Long 5 lin.

A highly polished robust species. Clypeus rather closely and very distinctly punctured ; forehead rather less strongly punctured, the intervals between the punctures about $1\frac{1}{2}$ times the diameter of the punctures   The thorax is highly polished, the punctures are rather obsolete on the disk, more distinct at the sides, distant from each other from 2 to 3 times the diameters of the punctures, on the disk the punctures are more scattered. The punctures on the elytra are distinct (but not very large), distant from each other about 3 times the diameter of the punctures; finer on the sides ; of the usual pairs of rows of punctures, the first pair are parallel and the space between them is rather broad, and with a few punctures scattered over the surface ; the second pair are rather closer together and include a row of small punctures , the third pair are very similar to the second ; at the sides are three rows of punctures (including the marginal line), the intervals between them almost destitute of punctures   The sides of the metasternum and abdomen are very strongly and rather thickly punctured, less thickly on the abdomen (which is pitchy); the punctures on the pygidium are not very close

Hab Siam (J. C Bowring, Esq)   Brit Mus

Apogonia coriacea, n. sp

Oblonga, parum convexa, nitida. supra nigro-ænca, subtus æneo-picca , clypeo brevi, fortiter sat crebre punctato, fronte

haud crebre subtiliter punctulata ; thorace brevi, parce subtilissime punctulato; scutello lævi , elytris oblongis, creberrime. subtiliter coriaceo-punctulatis punctis majoribus sat crebre inter-
spersis , propygidio opaco, parce subtiliter punctulato ; pygidio
æneo, basi punctis nonnullis adsperso.   Long. 6⅔ lin , lat. 3⅔ lin.

This fine species is conspicuous by its large size, smooth
thorax, and fine punctuation on the elytra, besides the more
usual coarse punctures   The dorsal costæ are very narrow and
inconspicuous

Hab. Ceylon   Brit. Mus

Apogonia nana, Walker.

Trigonostoma nana, Walker, Ann Mag Nat. Hist 1859, iii,
p. 55

Piceo-testacea, nitida , clypeo brevi, fronte haud crebre
punctulata ; thorace haud crebre subtilius punctulato, lateribus
evidenter punctatis , elytris fortiter sat crebe punctatis, lineis
duabus vix convexis instructis.   Long 2½ lin

The punctuation of the head is not very close and is rather
obscure, especially in the middle of the forehead.   The disc of
the thorax is finely and sparingly punctured, the sides more
distinctly and more closely punctured.   The punctuation of the
elytra is rather strong and close , the usual two dorsal smooth
lines are not very well defined, especially the second ; there is
a line of strong punctures along the margin, the space between
this row of punctures and the margin is smooth and convex.
Metasternum smooth   Sides of the abdomen rather thickly and
strongly punctured.   Pygidium not very thickly and moderately
strongly punctured.

Hab Ceylon. Brit. Mus.

There can be no doubt that this species is an *Apogonia*
although it is a little narrower than the majority of the species.

Apogonia ænescens, Hope.

Gray's Zool. Miscell., 1831, p. 23.

Clypeus not separated from the head by any distinct suture.
closely and moderately strongly punctured; head moderately,
closely and strongly punctured.   Apical joints of the maxillary
palpi unusually inflated in the middle, acuminate at the apex.
Thorax thickly punctured with rather strong (but not large)

punctures, the spaces between them a little less than the diameter of the punctures, a little less close on the disc and front margin; the sides (viewed laterally) gently rounded behind the middle Scutellum distinctly but not thickly punctured at the sides. Elytra thickly and strongly punctured, the punctures irregular and the intervals between them about equal to the diameters of the punctures; of the usual dorsal costæ, the first is rather broad (especially posteriorly), and is punctured rather less strongly than the rest of the elytra, the third costa is rather indistinct, and does not reach the shoulder; on the sides are three rows (including the marginal one) of strong punctures   Legs pitchy, anterior tibiæ with two small teeth   Abdomen thickly and strongly punctured at the sides.   Pygidium with large strong round punctures, leaving only narrow intervals between them.

Hab Nepal (Hardwicke).   Brit Mus.

Apogonia brunnea, Hope, is only a paler form of this species The description given by Blanchard (Cat. Coll Ent. p. 228), of "*brunnea,* Hope," can scarcely refer to this species   "*capite parce subtiliterque punctato,*" and "*scutello lævi,*" do not apply to Hope's insect.

Apogonia pallescens, n. sp

Ovata, convexa, antice angustior piceo-ænea, nitida; capite haud crebre, subtilius punctulato; thorace elytris angustiori, sat crebre evidenter punctato; scutello lateribus punctulatis; elytris æneo-testaceis, convexis, paulo ampliatis, fortiter punctatis, parum distincte bigeminato striatis; tibiis anticis angustis, apice haud dentatis, basi solum denticulis tribus acutis extus armatis. Long $3\frac{3}{4}$ lin

The linear anterior tibiæ at once distinguish this from the majority of the species of the genus, there are three small sharp teeth near the base on the outer edge   The clypeus pitchy-cupreous, very distinctly and rather closely punctured.   The punctures on the head are small, not very close together, the intervals between them averaging three times the diameter of the punctures   Thorax very shining, æneous, rather narrowed in front, the punctures are very distinct, but not very large, moderately close, the intervals between them averaging $1\frac{1}{2}$ times the diameter of the punctures.   The elytra are rather ample and convex, rounded at the sides, the punctuation is strong, and moderately close, the intervals between the punctures scarcely more than the diameter of the punctures, towards the sides the punctures are smaller and less close; the usual costæ arc only indicated by double lines of punctures, the space between the first pair is rather broad and punctures nearly as the rest of the elytra, the second pair arc not so distinct and become obsolete posteriorly, the third costa is only indicated by a line of punctures below the shoulder ; at the sides arc three lines of punctures (including the marginal line). The sides of the abdomen arc very strongly and thickly punctured ; the punctures on the pygidium are not numerous, but arc very strong.

Hab. Penang (J. C. Bowring, Esq.).   Brit. Mus.

TRICHIIDÆ.

Inca Davisii, n. sp.

Elliptica, convexa, obscure cuprea; thorace evidenter punctato, disco foveolis tribus bene impresso; scutello sat crebre fortiter punctato, apice lævi ; elytris obscure purpureo-nigris, opacis, velutinis, ad latera suturamque maculis sæpe confluentibus fasciâque dentatâ obliquâ sordide-albidis ornatis , corpore subtus cupreo, nitido, punctato, ♀ .   Long. 21 lin , lat 11 lin.

Closely allied to *I. bifrons,* F., but broader, of a coppery colour. and with the scutellum rather thickly and strongly punctured.   Head finely frosted, forehead a little raised in the middle ; clypeus transversely impressed behind, convex in front, the front obliquely emarginate on each side   Thorax $\frac{1}{6}$ broader than long, moderately shining, moderately, thickly and distinctly punctured, a little more narrowed in front than behind ; disk with strong horse-shoe shaped impression in front of the middle and a deep round fovea on each side.   Scutellum strongly and rather thickly punctured, smooth at the apex only.   Elytra dull brownish-black , the marking are nearly as in *I bifrons,* but the spots are rather larger, and the oblique band rather broader and with its angulations less sharp

Hab. Peru.   Brit. Mus.

A single specimen of this species was presented to the Museum by Mr. William Davis, after whom I have named it.

ŒDEMERIDÆ.

Sessinia Atkinsoni, n. sp.

Elongata, angusta, nigra ; thorace rufo, lævi; elytris olivaceis, confertim ruguloso-punctatis, ante apicem fasciâ angustâ albidâ , abdomine flavo nitido, apice nigro.   Long. $3\frac{1}{3}$ lin.

Head black, rather short and broad, rather thickly and very finely punctured, the vertex sparingly punctured, clypeus deeply and transversely impressed   Thorax scarcely broader than the head, about as long as broad, widest in front of the middle, much rounded at the sides narrowed behind, sparingly and scarcely visibly punctured, with a shallow impression on each side of the disk   Elytra bluish-green, one-quarter broader than the thorax, very closely finely but distinctly punctured, with a transverse narrow whitish band near the apex   Abdomen shining, yellow, with the apex black, very delicately and not very closely punctured, or rather scratched.

Hab. Tasmania (E D Atkinson, Esq.)   Brit Mus.

Sessinia sublineata, n. sp

Elongata, angusta, cyaneo-nigra, grisco-pubescens, capite crebre fortiter punctato; thorace capite paulo latiori, latitudine vix longiori, confertim fortiter punctato, dorsim utrinque impresso, postice angustato, lateribus antice rotundatis; elytris thorace $\frac{2}{5}$ latioribus, subtilius ruguloso-punctatis.   Long 3 lin

Rather a long, narrow species, bluish-black.   Head rather narrow, very thickly and distinctly punctured, with a smooth spot on the forehead   Thorax in front a little broader than the head, broadest in front of the middle, moderately narrowed behind, the punctuation rather strong and very crowded, the punctures not large, there is a well marked impression on each side, and the punctuation here is finer.   Scutellum thickly punctured.   Elytra rather finely and very thickly rugulose, each elytron with two fine costæ, the pubescence near the suture forms two greyish stripes, that on the sides is nearly black.

Hab. Tasmania (E. D. Atkinson, Esq), S Australia (Bakewell).   Brit Mus.

CASSIDIDÆ.

Epistictia inornata, n. sp.

Oblongo-ovata, piceo-testacea, sub-nitida; fronte crebre punctulata, nigro-variegata : thorace crebre subtiliter punctulato, disco parcius punctulato, utrinque punctis duobus nigris lævibus; elytris crebre fortiter punctatis, marginibus lævioribus, parum reflexis; humeris puncto nigro notatis, ore, genubus tarsisque nigris.   Long. $3\frac{1}{2}$–$4\frac{3}{4}$ lin.

A little longer than *E viridimaculata*, and rather straighter at the sides. Thorax with the sides less reflexed, very finely punctured, the base very slightly lobed in the middle. Elytra strongly and rather thickly punctured, but much less strongly than in *viridimaculata*, the punctures are pitchy and each is furnished with one or two short fine hairs, the surface is more even, and there are no raised lines, the margins are rather more incrassate. Each elytron has a single black spot on the shoulder.

Hab Lake Nyassa (Thelwall), Zambesi (Simons)   Brit. Mus.

Descriptions of new species of LEPIDOPTERA *from North China;* by W B PRYER.

Neptis intermedia, n sp   Pl. IV, f. 1

Thorax iridescent green, upper side ground colour brown-black. F w. in costal half a longitudinal white streak from base two-thirds across wing, interrupted towards the end by a band of the ground colour ; in outer half six large white spots form a sort of bow-shaped band across the wing, bending inwards towards the inner margin ; a submarginal line of irregularly shaped white spots . h.w a transverse straight white band from inner half of abdominal margin to outer half of costa ; from just above anal angle a thinner white band or streak, interrupted by the ground coloured nervures, crosses the wing nearly to the anterior angle.   Under side dark chocolate, shading into lead colour on inner margin of f w., markings much the same as on upper side, the submarginal row of spots on f w. being more distinctly marked, and there are generally some additional white marks on the margin itself , h w. in addition to the upper side markings, there is a thin submarginal white line, a some-what indistinct white line between the two central bands, and from the base there are two short white streaks, one a little way along the costa and the other below it.   Expanse of wings $2\frac{1}{3}$ inches to $2\frac{1}{2}$ inches

Inhabits the greater part of North China, common ; it also occurs in Japan.

Lampides filicaudis, n. sp.

Upper side ground colour smoky brown-black, alike in both sexes, the only markings being a just discernible submarginal row of spots on the h w faintly edged with slaty-blue.   Under side slaty-grey, the usual *Lycaena* like spots large, black, well marked, and narrowly edged with white   The tail is very diminutive, and hardly distinguishable except in newly emerged specimens , the space between the two anal spots of the marginal and submarginal rows is more or less orange.   Expanse of wings 10 lines to 1 inch.

Abundant everywhere in hilly districts in North China.   Has a curious habit of settling on the sides of bare rocks.   This species has probably been overlooked from its similarity to the females of some of the common *Lycaenidæ*.

Euchloris procumbaria, n. sp   Pl. IV, f. 2.

Light green.   F w three indistinct whitish lines from costa to inner margin, just within posterior angle a white blotch encircled by a brown-red line· h.w. anterior angle with two somewhat diamond shaped white blotches, surrounded by a brown-red line, which runs for a short distance along the outer margin, and again becomes apparent at the anal angle, fringe spotted with same colour.   Expanse of wings 1 inch.

Shanghai, rather rare.

Cataclysta Sabrina, n. sp   Pl. IV, f. 3.

Prevailing colour light brownish-yellow.   F w. with white markings from base to centre, a large white somewhat V-shaped mark in the outer half of wing, the tips of the V being broadest and the apex pointing towards the posterior angle of f w., the inside of the outer half of the V margined with grey, from close to anterior angle, nearly across the wing, a transverse white streak with very narrow edging of black on the outer side, and an equally narrow black marginal line : h w. base white, on inner half of centre a broad white transverse streak edged on both sides with grey, and a fainter white streak down abdominal margin, turning off above anal angle across the wing nearly to anterior angle, where there is another faint whitish streak just within it ; on outer margin four largish silver centred black spots   Expanse of wings 1 inch 3 lines.

About streams at the Snowy Valley (Chekiang Province), not common.

Cataclysta bifurcalis, n. sp.   Pl. IV, f. 4.

Prevailing colour brownish-yellow   F.w. with a broad white horizontal streak from base to centre of wing, a somewhat conspicuous dark spot on costa, which forms the left hand top of an irregular lead coloured V-shaped mark, on outer half of costa a white wedged-shaped mark, with a small yellow streak on the centre, a white streak narrowly edged with black on the outside, just within the outer margin; on the edge of wing an interrupted black line or row of spots: h.w. with a broad conspicuous white streak edged with black from abdominal margin to costa, a very narrow double line along outer margin, with three small black spots on the outer half of the marginal line, and a minute white or silvery spot above the last black one, anterior angle considerably indented. Expanse of wings 11 lines.

About streams at the Snowy Valley (Chekiang Province), not common.

Hydrocampa interruptalis, n. sp.   Pl. IV, f. 5.

Prevailing colour ochraceous-yellow. F.w. with a well marked black ring, with white pupil, side by side above it are two more white spots nearly surrounded with black, on outer margin is an irregular black streak, very slightly divided by the ground colour in the middle. H.w. on inner half a black line starts from costa, proceeds nearly to anal angle, and returns to costa, on the outer half more or less elbowed in the middle of its upward course; from the apex of the elbow to the costa a short brown mark margined with black; a broad white transverse streak on the inner half of wing towards the middle, and a second broad white mark from costa half across the wing on outer half; a marginal irregular white streak interrupted about the middle.

This species is subject to much variation, in one specimen the black line described above as starting from and returning to the costa of h.w. merely crosses the wing to the abdominal margin, and the elbowed line instead of being an unbroken and distinct continuation of it, starts considerably nearer the anal angle; and in another specimen the entire marginal white streak both in upper and lower wing is not interrupted at all. Expanse of wings 11 lines.

Common on some ponds about Shanghai.

Hydrocampa nigrolinealis, n. sp.   Pl. IV, f. 6.

Ground colour brown, markings much the same as in *H. interruptalis*, the white spots and black lines being boldly and distinctly marked : h.w. including the very narrow fringe line, with seven black transverse lines, and a black edged large white mark just below the costa in the centre; an uninterrupted white line, elbowed in the middle, and black edged on both sides, extends from the costa, outside the white mark, to the abdominal angle. Expanse of wings 1 inch.

Occasionally taken on ponds round Shanghai.

Oligostigma insectalis, n. sp.　Pl. IV, f. 7

F.w. prevailing colour greyish-brown . several longitudinal whitish streaks from base to beyond middle, the largest of them just above the inner margin, turned upwards and terminating at the costa , a transverse white streak just within the outer margin · h.w. upper half streaked with greyish-white and black three-quarters of the way across the wing, rest of wing brown-yellow ; a central longitudinal interrupted black edged white streak ; narrow marginal black line with a row of small black dots just within the margin, notched at its tip.　Expanse of wings 8 lines

On the clear water canals about Shanghai, not common.

Oligostigma regularis, n sp.　Pl IV, f 8

Basal half of both f. and h w. streaked with white and greyish-black ; outer halves pale brown, with a white streak more or less edged with greyish-black.　Interior angle entire Expanse of wings 6 lines.

Common amongst water-weeds round Shanghai.

Pyrausta Minnehaha, n sp.　Pl IV, f. 9

Body grey.　F w. a delicate rose tint ; on outer half, a line of slightly darker colour, elbowed in the middle, and terminating on the inner margin : h w. grey, two transverse lines nearly across the wing, one commencing above the middle and one below　Expanse of wings 11 lines.

I took three specimens of this pretty little insect close beside a cascade at the Snowy Valley (Chekiang Province) ; it also occurs in Japan.

Lepyrodes bistigmalis, n sp.　Pl IV, f. 10.

Dull grey-brown, with whitish markings.　F.w. the elbowed line with about half-a-dozen faintly indicated spots, forming a transverse line on the outside, and three, rather more conspicuous, on the inside , about the centre of the wing is a somewhat larger spot, intersected by the elbowed line ; nearer the base are two small white spots, one obliquely below the other . h w. with several irregular white markings about the centre, through part of which runs a continuation of the elbowed line of the former ; near the base are two distinct spots, one nearest the abdominal margin rotundate, the other linear and reaching the margin Expanse of wings 9 lines.

Common at the Feng Whan Shan (hills) near Shanghai

Lepyrodes Fengwhanalis, n. sp. Pl IV. f. 11.

F.w rather light brown, a transverse straight line near the base, several irregular whitish markings in the centre, and a well defined row of triangular spots, edged on the outside with dark brown, within the outer margin h w. with the basal line continued, but not quite so straight, a white elbowed line across centre of wing, the space between it and the continuation of the straight line somewhat darker, with two white spots, an irregular interrupted white line within outer margin, and a rather large triangular white spot on the costa, within the elbowed line. Expanse of wings 10 lines

Feng Whan Shan (hills) not common

Hemerosia aurantiana, n. sp Pl. IV, f. 12.

F.w. inner two-thirds orange-brown, outer third black, with numerous minute red markings : h.w. dark grey. Expanse of wings 6 lines.

Shanghai, one specimen

LEPIDOTARPHIUS, n. gen

Head obtuse; palpi small, drooping, divergent; wings elongate; body elongate, flattened; scales of thorax and base of wings very dense and closely packed.

This genus is apparently intermediate between *Butalis* and *Pancalia*, and the characteristics of the body indicate a close relationship to *Staintonia*

Lepidotarphius splendens, n. sp Pl. IV, f. 13.

Thorax and head burnished metallic-green, second abdominal segment deep black, rest of abdomen rich yellow, anal tuft plum colour f.w. basal half burnished metallic-green, outer half rich yellow, with 7 apparently raised bright golden spots· h w dark grey. Expanse of wings 8 lines.

Occasionally taken amongst reeds; not uncommon at ponds on the Shanghai race-course.

Remarks on certain species of the Lepidopterous genus Ophideres, *and their capacity for piercing the epicarp of fruits; by* George L. Pilcher.

Having seen that the Moths, *Ophideres fullonia, materna, imperator,* and *salaminia,* have been exciting attention, both in England and France, on account of their supposed power of piercing through the rind of oranges, in order to suck the juices of the fruit, I may, I hope, be pardoned for presenting the results of my own observations as regards the conclusions which have been arrived at.

M. A. Thozet, of Rockhampton, was the author of the letter in the "Rockhampton Bulletin," May, 1875, which is quoted both by Mr F Darwin in his paper in the "Journal Microscopical Science," on the Structure of the Proboscis of *O. fullonia,* and also by M Kunckel in his paper, read by M. Emile Blanchard before the French Academy of Sciences, and copied into the "Gardener's Chronicle," though it appears that M. Thozet had written to M. Kunckel on the subject before.

M. Thozet states "that *O. fullonia* punctures the rind of the orange, extracts the juice in the corresponding division of the orange, leaving free access to the air, and withdrawing the support to the rind, which, of course, sinks as soon as decomposition begins," and the fruit falls.

Mr. Darwin's and M Kunckel's remarks are on the structure of the proboscis of the moth, and its adaptation to the facts mentioned in M Thozet's letter.

X

M. Thozet's letter was replied to by Mr Miskin, of Brisbane, a well-known entomologist, who utterly repudiated the idea of *O. fullonia* puncturing the oranges, and said, "*O fullonia* is really only following the well-known habits of its tribe—that of extracting the juice of fruit, which has already been penetrated by the action of other agents, the interior parts being thus exposed to the operations of the moth fraternity, which otherwise, would not be attracted by the fruit." This statement of Mr. Miskin's is in entire accordance with my own observations Not only do the *Ophiderida* attack the oranges, but also the ripe guava, peach, and especially the banana ; so much so, that Queensland Lepidopterists take advantage of their well-known tastes to effect their capture The *modus operandi* is to hang up fully ripe bananas, with *incisions made in the skin*, to which the different species of *Ophideres* (as well as other moths), resort in numbers. Such is the preference of *Ophideres* for the banana, that Mr. Miskin tells me that he has hung up oranges, cut in halves, in close proximity to the bananas, and that the former have not attracted a single specimen, and that those bananas which are ripest, almost fermenting, draw most insects.

M. Kunckel describes the proboscis as "a veritable auger," a perfect model of design as a perforating instrument ; whilst, Mr. Darwin says "that the insect must employ a thrusting motion, and not any kind of revolving movement, and the proboscis must accordingly be considered as a saw;" so that these two observers do not agree at all as to the mode in which the proboscis is used.

Mr Darwin's theory of a "thrusting motion" seems to me the only motion which is possible, but I cannot myself imagine a more unfitting tool than a saw to perform the operation of making a hole. Would any carpenter attempt to pierce a plank, even with the finest key-hole saw, without first boring a hole right through the wood with a gimlet?

It was from the examination of the proboscis of the moth some eight years ago, that I first began to doubt the statements about the capability of an insect, fitted with such an instrument, to perforate the tough rind of an orange, though the apparatus appeared adapted for enlarging a hole already existing.

I then made enquiries, and ascertained that the oranges fell off in other colonies in Australia, where the *Ophideridæ* were unknown, and being thus strengthened in my supposition that the moth was, at all events, not the primary enemy of the orange, I endeavoured to find out what was.

I accordingly obtained a number of newly fallen oranges for examination. On squeezing these with the hand, a small drop of juice was seen to exude from the orange, and on opening the corresponding quarter of the orange, two or three maggots were visible, varying in size, according to the stage of growth at which they had arrived, only the division in which the larvæ were was effected; the remaining quarters appeared to be sound and eatable I then enclosed a number of the oranges in boxes with a little sand, and at the end of a fortnight, the fly (of which I have sent two specimens to Mr. Janson)* appeared; and I thought I could now see how it was that superficial observers had been led to think that the moth was the destroyer of the orange; whereas it was only an accomplice after the fact Now also, I could admire the wonderful perfection of the mechanism of the proboscis of the moth, and see how well it was adapted for enlarging a hole already made by some other insect, though totally unfitted for commencing one, and that to this hole it was attracted by the drop of juice exuding from it.

---

* These specimens, doubtless referable to the genus *Trypeta*, Meig, I have deposited in the national collection at the British Museum the species is evidently distinct from any therein extant, its nearest ally appears to be *T. serratulæ*, Linn (Loew europ Bohrfliegen, p 62, T. x f. 1) —*Ed,*

The frill of bristles on the dorsal part of the proboscis, would seem to assist in pressing the under rasping surface down upon the object to be operated on   The spines on the lower surfaces are, I think to prevent the insertion of the proboscis to too great an extent, as the moth might not otherwise be able to withdraw it easily, when occasion might require.

When the moth is engaged in sucking, the upper wings are partially opened, and then margins together with those of the lower wings, and the hinder part of the abdomen, seem to be pressed against the fruit ; the forelegs raise the head and the fore part of the body, so that there is a considerable interval between the head and the orange or banana, and consequently it is evident that the proboscis is only buried in the fruit to a certain depth.

Rockhampton, Queensland,
    28th March, 1877.

On new species of CATOCALA and SYPNA from Japan; by ARTHUR
G. BUTLER, F.L.S.

CATOCALIDÆ

1. Catocala Zalmunna, n sp

Closely allied to C. electa, but much larger, the primaries of
a more silver-grey tint; the reniform spot large and yellowish,
the black markings finer; secondaries above more distinctly shot
with lilacine, the angular belt with its inferior half narrower,
outer border rather more narrowly white, primaries below with
the white discal band narrower and more angular, the white
border confined to the apex and fringe; secondaries with the
black band more constricted in the centre. Expanse 3 inches
5 lines.

Yokohama (Jonas); Hakodaté (Whitely). Brit Mus

2. Catocala nivea, n sp.

Primaries grey, striated with greyish-brown, three angulated
transverse brownish belts, the outer and inner ones interrupted
at both extremities by irregular black lines bordered with
greenish-white, the central one also interrupted by the reniform
spot which is cream colour bordered with greenish-white, veins
spotted with black and white; an undulated brownish discal
belt, a marginal series of black edged quadrate white spots, the
third of which is connected with the black line on the outer
transverse angulated belt by a longitudinal jet-black stripe;
secondaries white, with an abbreviated angulated band just
beyond the end of the cell, an irregularly arched discal band
a series of convex submarginal lituræ, and a ⋀ shaped marking
near the apical margin, black head white; collar brown, white
in front, crossed by two dark brown lines, thorax white speckled
with grey and black, abdomen grey · wings below white, with
irregular central black belt; base grey; a broad blackish discal
band, outer border of primaries greyish-brown, fringe white;
secondaries with a grey spot at the end of the cell, outer border
sparsely speckled with brown, more densely on the upper discoidal interspace : body below whity-brown. Expanse 4 inches
3 lines.

Yokohama (Jonas)   Brit. Mus.

A marvellously distinct species.

3. *Catocala ella*, n. sp.

Allied to *C conversa*, from which it differs in its superior size, the greenish-grey colouring of the primaries with much more sharply defined markings; the brighter ochreous secondaries, with the central black band widest towards the costa and gradually tapering to the abdominal margin; the wider and more regular black border, notched near the anal angle; the broader and brighter ochreous belts below (not partly white); the angular black band of secondaries below regular and widest towards the costa Expanse 2 inches 7 lines.

Yokohama (Jonas) Brit. Mus.

4. *Catocala bella*, n. sp.

Allied to *C neogama*, primaries slightly narrower, of a more slaty-grey tint, with the outer border dusky and reddish tinted; secondaries with a broader black central band, a broader black outer border, and with the apex and fringe white instead of ochreous; primaries below with the bands white instead of ochreous, the outer border whitish; secondaries with the anterior half of the bands, the apex, and fringe white instead of ochreous: body below white. Expanse 2 inches 6 lines

Yokohama (Jonas). Brit. Mus

5. *Catocala Jonasu*, n. sp.

Primaries silver-grey, whitish in and beyond the discoidal cell, crossed by two black lines as in *C. neogama*, white edged; reniform spot and a rounded spot below it black edged; a transverse row of black spots just beyond the cell; a partly black edged dentated discal white streak (diffused internally) from the costa to the external angle; a submarginal series of black dots; fringe white; secondaries ochraceous with brownish internal streaks from the base to the central band, the latter angulated, almost divided in the centre; outer border black, very broad near apex, abruptly and deeply excavated on lower radial and median interspaces, less deeply bisinuated beyond; apex and fringe pale ochraceous: body grey, abdomen brownish; wings below white, yellowish towards the inner margins, primaries crossed by three and secondaries by two black bands; body below white, abdomen with the anal segments and sides yellowish. Expanse 3 inches.

Yokohama (Jonas). Brit. Mus.

6. *Catocala mirifica,* n sp.

Allied to *C. paranympha,* but the primaries pale silver grey, almost white, with a broad dark brown costal patch occupying the apical quarter of the wing, and upon which alone the black markings are distinctly visible, traces of discal and marginal brownish belts below the brown patch; two apical greyish nebulæ; secondaries of a brighter tint, the central band slightly narrower, and the abbreviated black outer border wider and a little shorter; thorax whitish like the primaries, abdomen testaceous; head and collar brown speckled; under surface paler than in *C. paranympha,* the yellow belts broader; primaries with the pale outer border scarcely distinguishable excepting at apex, fringe yellow; secondaries with the black belts more regular and not obliterated towards the costa; body below white. Expanse 2 inches 3 lines.

Yokohama (Jonas). Brit. Mus

7. *Catocala xarippe,* n. sp

Allied to *C. Polygama,* but considerably larger; the secondaries with the central black belt broader, not so sharply defined; the costal as well as the abdominal area broadly brown; the outer black border, broader more regular, not interrupted, but with a notch in it near the anal angle; under surface altogether whiter and with the basal area more dusky. Expanse 2 inches 4 lines.

Hakodaté (Whitely). Brit. Mus.

8. *Catocala esther,* n. sp.

Allied to *C. consors,* but the primaries blackish, the central band with straight inner edge, whitish irrorated with grey and testaceous; outer border broadly grey, its inner edge undulated, and crossed by an undulated black stripe; secondaries of a clearer orange colour, with the central band blacker and narrower and the outer border blacker and more angular; thorax blackish, whitish in the centre and behind, abdomen clothed with sordid ochraceous scales; under surface altogether more defined, the borders blacker. Expanse 2 inches 4 lines.

Yokohama (Jonas). Brit. Mus.

Also allied to *C. prolifica.*

9. *Catocala vulcanica*, n. sp.

Allied to *C. consors*; considerably larger, but with almost similar black markings on the primaries; primaries above slaty-grey densely irrorated with sulphur yellow scales; a diffused oblique broad band near the base, the costal area at the base, the reniform spot, some scales above it, the centre of internal area, some streaks partly bordering the discal zigzag black lines and a sparse sprinkling of scales over the whole wing, ferruginous; secondaries bright ochreous, with central and interno-median confluent bands somewhat resembling a large black **u**; outer border very broad and black, abruptly constricted to a mere connecting line near the anal angle and joining the central band just before the constriction, interrupted externally by two convex ochreous spots, between which are four dots; fringe spotted with blackish; thorax grey, collar and tegulæ reddish, abdomen testaceous; wings below ochreous, primaries crossed by three black belts, outer border brownish, fringe whitish; secondaries crossed by two black bands, the inner one L shaped, the outer one tapering, excavated near the anal angle; an abbreviated grey internal dash; pectus whitish, legs speckled with black, tarsi black banded with creamy-whitish; venter yellowish. Expanse 3 inches 2 lines.

Yokohama (Jonas); Hakodaté (Whitely). Brit. Mus.

EREBIDÆ.

1. *Sypna picta*, n. sp.

Above fuliginous brown, primaries darker than the secondaries; central area paler brown, crossed by a broad white band spotted with brown traversed by blue lines, and (owing to the presence of a large central costal brown patch) forking from the middle of the cell to the costa; reniform spot divided by the outer branch of the band, and with a central ochreous spot, outlined in black, beyond it; a large pale brown apical patch, bounded internally by a large 3 shaped black character, which in some examples is continued as a dentated line to the inner margin; a submarginal series of black edged white spots; a pale undulated marginal line, and a second less distinct similar line on the fringe; secondaries slightly paler at the base and across the inner half of the disc, the latter pale area being partly bounded internally by an abbreviated dusky streak or line: outer border broadly dusky; an abbreviated dentated black edged whitish subanal line, and a submarginal series of black edged white spots; fringe whity-brown, traversed by a broad dusky band ; under surface pale brown, crossed by two whitish discal streaks separated by a greyish-brown centre streak ; disc beyond fuliginous, the apical and inferior or external angles whitish speckled with brown, a whitish spot at the end of each discoidal cell ; a submarginal series of black dots ; antennæ below furruginous. Expanse 2 inches 1–5 lines

♂, ♀ Hakodaté (Whitely), ♂ Yokohama (Jonas) Brit· Mus.

A common but beautiful species ; in some examples the whole outer border on the under surface of secondaries is pale.

2. *Sypna achatina*, n. sp

Allied to the preceding, but with the pale areas of the primaries and the whole of the secondaries paler, with the dark lines well marked ; primaries crossed in the centre by an irregular H like character, formed of two white edged blue speckled bands, united by a slender blue line just below the middle ; the anterior band interrupted by the reniform spot, which is yellowish ; a white dot in the cell ; secondaries with two subcentral lines, the outer one angulated and distinct, outer border separated into alternately dusky and pale streaks ; otherwise much like *S picta*. Expanse ♂ 2 inches, ♀ 2 inches 5–7 lines.

♂, ♀ Hakodaté (Whitely) ; ♀ Yokohama (Jonas) Brit. Mus.

Also allied to *S. albilinea*.

3. *Sypna fumosa*, n sp

Like the preceding, excepting in the absence of the H shaped band, the yellowish inner border of the reniform spot well marked, the white spot in the cell more or less distinct ; a small costal U· shaped marking bluish in the male, whity-brown in the female ; a well marked broad irregular transverse discal band, and the apical area paler than the ground colour ; secondaries with the apical fringe creamy yellowish Expanse ♂ 2 inches 1 line ; ♀ 2 inches 3–7 lines

♂ Yokohama (Jonas) ; ♀ Hakodaté (Whitely). Brit. Mus.

4 *Sypna fuliginosa*.

Fuliginous brown, traversed by darker and paler lines ; primaries (especially in the male) shot with violet ; a broad partly black edged tolerably regular brown belt, slightly paler than the ground colour just beyond the cell; a white dot in the cell; reniform spot streaked with testaceous internally, blackish edged externally; external area slightly paler than the ground colour, black edged internally, border as in the three preceding species; secondaries (excepting in the apical fringe) almost as in *S. picta*; under surface similar Expanse ♂ 2 inches; ♀ 2 inches 5 lines.

♂ Yokohama (Pryer), ♀ Hakodaté (Whitely).　Brit Mus.

Allied to the preceding but much darker, the transverse band of primaries less irregular, the male distinctly shot with violet; it approaches *S. cœlisparsa*.

Notices of new or little known CETONIIDᴇ, by OLIVER E JANSON. No. 3.

Gymnetis Goryi, n. sp.

Gymnetis rufilateris, G. P. Mon. p 350, t 70, f. 3 (nec Illiger)

G. breviter sub-quadrata, supra viridi-cinerea, opaca, nigro-variegata, elytris lateribus sanguineis nigro-interruptis ; subtus nigra, cinereo-variegata, parce punctata et nigro-villosa, processu mesosterni conico, leviter deflexo. Long. 18–20 mm.

This species differs from *G. rufilateris*, Illiger, in its short quadrate form (the elytra being nearly as broad behind as at the base), in the greater extent of the black markings, in having the red lateral bands of the elytra interrupted by four black spots, in the colour of the underside and the form of the mesosternal process, which in this species is only slightly bent, whereas in *rufilateris* it is very large and almost vertical.

Bolivia (Buckley).

Clinteria cariosa, n. sp.

C nigra, sub-nitida, confertim punctata, thorace albo bi-punctato ; elytris leviter bi-costatis, 14-albo-guttatis. Long. 14–15 mm

Var elytris lateribus late rufis.

Head finely punctured, the punctures very close and confluent, a small space at the base convex and smooth ; clypeus slightly depressed on each side, the sides almost straight, the anterior angles rounded, apical margin slightly elevated on each side, emarginate and impressed in the centre ; black slightly shining ; antennæ pitchy-black.

Thorax only slightly narrowed at the sides from the base to the middle, thence abruptly narrowed, posterior angles rounded, the posterior lobe small ; very coarsely and closely punctured, the punctures very close and confluent at the sides and in front, a narrow median line and the basal margin smooth, three rather shallow depressions placed obliquely on each side of the disc ; black, slightly shining, the two basal depressions (and sometimes the central two) with a small white spot

Scutellum much produced and very acute at the apex, longitudinally impressed ; black

Elytra with the suture and two carinæ on each moderately elevated, the interstices with irregularly coarsely punctate striæ and scattered fine punctures, the sides and apex with confluent punctures, a large shallow depression behind the scutellum and a smaller deeper one on the shoulders ; pitchy-black, shining, fourteen small white spots on each, arranged thus, one on the basal margin, one in the humeral depression, four along the suture, two between the carinæ, two outside the outer carina and four along the lateral margin.

Pygidium closely and irregularly strigose, sparsely pubescent , pitchy-black, several small spots at the base and a larger one on each side, close to the margin, white.

Beneath and legs strigose, shining black with sparse golden pubescence , abdomen with transverse rows of coarse punctures, a small white spot at the sides of the four basal segments ; mesosternal process short, finely punctured, rounded at the apex , anterior tibiæ with three obtuse lateral teeth, the upper one almost obsolete, the apical one long

Lake Nyassa

Allied to *C. permutans*, Burm., but very distinct. A few specimens taken by Mr. F A Simons near Livingstonia, are the only ones I have seen.

Lomaptera yorkiana (Thoms), n. sp

L lacte viridis, nitida, thorace lateribus medio sub-explanatis, tenuiter parce punctatis ; pygidio medio transversim acute carinato Long. 25–27 mm.

Bright green very shining.

Head sparsely punctured at the base, the punctures finer and very dense at the apex : sides of the clypeus straight scarcely elevated, obliquely narrowed in front, the apical points acute, the emargination deep and triangular ; antennæ black tinged with green, the apex reddish

Thorax convex, broad, the sides almost straight for about two thirds from the base, thence abruptly narrowed, anterior margin slightly produced over the head, posterior lobe large, nearly covering the scutellum, slightly emarginate at its apex, the disc very finely and remotely punctured, the sides with coarser punctures

Elytra very finely and remotely punctured, the sides with distinct transverse impressions along the lateral emargination, and transversely strigose posteriorly ; the shoulders with a distinct tubercle, usually black, the apex of each separately rounded.

Pygidium coarsely strigose, the centre produced into an acute transverse ridge

Beneath finely strigose here and there, penultimate segment of the abdomen deeply punctured, the apical segment transversely strigose , mesosternal process long, slightly curved ; legs strigose and punctured, anterior tibiæ with three long acute lateral teeth, intermediate and posterior tibiæ unarmed.

Cape York, N.E. Australia.

Closely allied to *L. wallisiana*, Thoms , but differs in its much broader form, darker colour, and in the shape of the thorax, which, in *wallisiana* is regularly rounded at the sides from the base.

I have adopted the name proposed for it by Mr. Thomson, who has kindly compared it with his type of *wallisiana*, and pointed out to me the characters which separate it from that species.

Lomaptera nicobarica, n. sp.

L late ovata, convexa, nigra, nitidissima ; elytris lateribus punctatis, apice acuminatis. Long. 25–27, lat 14–15 mm.

Deep black, very shining, elytra slightly metallic.

Head longitudinally depressed and coarsely punctured on each side, the centre and margins finely punctured, base smooth ; anterior points of the clypeus produced and somewhat acute, the emargination deep and triangular

Thorax convex, anterior margin slightly produced over the head, posterior lobe broad, nearly covering the scutellum, sides somewhat prominent in the middle, disc smooth, coarsely but sparsely punctured at the sides, the lateral margins slightly elevated.

Scutellum impressed at the apex and acute.

Elytra convex, here and there slightly depressed, the disc smooth and very shining, the sides with scattered punctures at the base but towards the apex they become closer and confluent, forming irregular striæ; suture with an almost obsolete row of punctures, slightly elevated and terminating in an acute point at the apex.

Pygidium transversely convex, slightly impressed in the middle, very finely and closely strigose.

Beneath very coarsely but sparsely punctured, prothorax and anterior coxæ strigose; abdomen slightly strigose at the sides with a faintly marked central line, penultimate segment with a transverse row of punctures and a few at the sides of the preceding one; mesosternal process long, almost cylindrical, incurved and obtuse at the apex, legs punctured and strigose, with short stout black setæ, anterior tibiæ with three acute lateral teeth.

The female has the abdomen more convex, without the central line, and with numerous punctures at the sides and on the penultimate segment, the anterior tibiæ are also much broader.

Nicobar Islands.

Allied to *L. pulla*, Bilb, but differing greatly in its broad convex form, sparse punctuation, etc. A considerable series of this species recently received exhibit scarcely any variation. *L. pulla* appears not to occur in the Nicobars although it is common in the Andaman Islands.

Gnathocera rufipes, n. sp

G. sub-quadrata, capite atro, nitido, vitta utrinque maculisque duabus basalibus albis; thorace fortiter punctato, rufo-fulvo, linea media longitudinali interrupta, maculis duabus antice et duabus utrinque albis; elytris fulvis, pygidio albo-bimaculato; pedibus rufis. Long 14–16 mm.

Head closely strigose, the base punctured, with a smooth, elevated longitudinal line in the centre, sides of clypeus elevated and sinuous, the apical points sharp and convergent at their tips, anterior margin straight; shining black, a longitudinal stripe on each side between the eyes and two small round spots at the base, white

Thorax convex, closely and coarsely punctured, anterior angles prominent, basal margin deeply emarginate above the scutellum; reddish fulvous, the margins paler, a narrow impressed, longitudinal central line interrupted in the middle, two small spots on the anterior margin near the angles, a very small one on each side about the middle close to the lateral margins and two at the base near the posterior angles, white.

Scutellum faintly punctured, fulvous with a fine impressed white line.

Elytra with the suture and two longitudinal carinæ on each, strongly elevated and smooth, the disc with rows of coarse, shallow, and numerous smaller punctures, the sides and apex coarsely strigose ; fulvous, the suture narrowly black.

Pygidium finely transversely strigose, reddish fulvous, sides piceous, with a large round spot on each side at the base, white.

Beneath blackish-green, shining, with large white patches at the sides ; mesosternal process long, narrow and curved ; abdomen with a central row of white spots in the longitudinal depression, and a white stripe at the sides of each segment ; legs slender, pale red, tarsi pitchy-black, the femora with a longitudinal white stripe on their outer side

The female is rather broader and more strongly punctured with the central line of the thorax only slightly indicated, and the spots smaller, the pygidium is shorter and the abdomen is convex without the central row of spots.

Angola

Closely allied to *G. angolensis*, Westw., but differs in its broader and more quadrate form, stronger punctuation, colour of legs, the markings on its thorax, and in not having the anterior margin of its clypeus produced into a point in the centre.

Gnathocera lurida, n. sp

G. pallide fulva, nitida ; capite viridi, utrinque maculis tribus albis ; thorace plaga media magna viridi, linea media longitudinali, macula utrinque antice, vittaque brevi postice albis ; scutello viridi, linea media alba.   Long. 11–12 mm.

Head coarsely and irregularly strigose, the base closely punctured, sides of clypeus sharply elevated, the apical points acute and convergent at their tips, anterior margin semi-circularly emarginate ; dark green, shining, a small spot on each side at the base, two elongate spots on the forehead, and two at the base of the clypeus white ; antennæ pitchy.

Thorax somewhat abruptly narrowed from the middle, the disc rather finely punctured, the punctures coarser at the sides , pale fulvous, shining, a large oval discal patch green, a central impressed longitudinal stripe, a spot on each side close to the anterior angles and a short stripe near the lateral margins for about half their length from the posterior angles, white.

Scutellum with scattered punctures at the sides; shining green, an impressed central longitudinal line, white.

Elytra somewhat dilated about the middle, the suture and two longitudinal carinæ on each strongly raised and with scattered fine punctures, the interstices and sides very coarsely and shallowly punctured, the apex strigose; pale fulvous, shining.

Pygidium convex, transversely strigose, pitchy-black, with a sub-ovate white spot on each side.

Beneath greenish-black, shining, with large patches of white at the sides, mesosternal process narrow, apex acute, fulvous; abdomen with a transverse white stripe at the sides of each segment and a row of spots in the central depression; legs fulvous, the femora with a longitudinal white stripe on their outer side.

The female is rather broader than the male, with the teeth on the anterior tibiæ obtuse, and the abdomen convex without the central spots.

Angola.

Several specimens of this distinct little species were given to me by the late Dr. Welwitsch who found it in considerable numbers; it is most nearly allied to *G. gracilis*, O. Janson

Gnathocera gracilis, n. sp.

G. pallide fulva, nitida, capite viridi, vitta utrinque, maculisque duabus basalibus albis, thorace antice viridi, vittis tribus albis, scutello lævi   Long. $12\frac{1}{2}$–14 mm.

Head finely and closely strigose, the base with scattered punctures, sides of clypeus elevated and sinuous, the apical points acute and nearly straight, anterior margin slightly prominent in the centre; dark green, a spot on each side at the base close to the eyes, and a longitudinal stripe on each side of the clypeus white, antennæ pitchy.

Thorax gradually narrowed from the base, the disc finely punctured, the punctures coarser and confluent at the sides; fulvous, shining, the disc and apex green, a central impressed longitudinal stripe and one on each side close to the lateral margins, extending from the base to the apex, white.

Scutellum impunctate; fulvous slightly tinged with green, shining.

Elytra parallel-sided, the suture and two longitudinal carinæ on each strongly raised and with scattered fine punctures, the interstices rather coarsely and very closely punctured, the punctures confluent and forming irregular striæ at the sides and apex; pale fulvous, shining.

Pygidium flat, finely irregularly strigose; greenish-black with a large triangular white patch on each side

Beneath greenish-black, shining, the sides broadly white; mesosternal process rather broad, apex obtuse, pale yellow, abdomen broadly white at the sides, with a row of small white spots in the central depression; legs pale red, the femora with a longitudinal white stripe on their outer side.

Angola

Allied to *G. trivittata*, Swed, the specimen from which I have taken the above description was given to me by the late Dr. Welwitsch, there are also specimens in Mr. Higgins's collection found by Monteiro, at Bembe.

Gnathocera cruda, n. sp.

G. viridis, nitida, elytris scutelloque viridi-fulvis; capite vitta utrinque maculisque duabus basalibus albis; thorace albo-trivittato; elytris linea marginali alba postice dilatata, pygidio utrinque albo-biplagiato. Long. 17 mm.

Head coarsely strigose, base coarsely but sparingly punctured, with the centre slightly longitudinally raised and smooth, sides of clypeus sharply elevated, the apical points slightly curved and acute, the anterior margin slightly prominent in the centre; shining green, a small spot on each side at the base, close to the eyes, and a broad longitudinal stripe on each side of the clypeus white; antennæ black, the club and palpi red.

Thorax rather sparingly and finely punctured on the disc, the punctures coarser and confluent at the sides, lateral margins strongly raised in the middle, basal margin deeply emarginate above the scutellum, shining green, sides and base slightly fulvous, a central impressed narrow longitudinal stripe and one on each side near the lateral margins (almost interrupted in the middle), white.

Scutellum large with the apex acute, impunctate; fulvous green, shining.

Y

Elytra deeply emarginate at the sides just behind the humeral angles, somewhat dilated behind the middle and thence obliquely narrowed, the suture and two longitudinal carinæ on each strongly elevated, the interstices coarsely punctured in rows, with scattered fine punctures, the sides and apex with the punctures closer and confluent; fulvous green, shining, with a narrow impressed white line along the outer margin terminating in a triangular spot at the apical sutural angle.

Pygidium irregularly transversely strigose; sparsely pubescent, greenish black, with a large elongate oblique patch of white on each side

Beneath shining green, broadly white at the sides, mesosternal process long and curved, apex obtuse, fulvous green; abdomen with large transverse patches at the sides, and a row of large spots in the central depression, white, legs pale fulvous, femora fringed with golden hairs, and with a longitudinal white stripe on their outer side

The female is broader than the male, has the abdomen convex in the centre, without spots, and the anterior tibiæ broader with the three external teeth stronger

Livingstonia, Lake Nyassa

A very distinct and pretty species, most nearly allied to *G. trivittata*, Swed. The only specimens I have seen are the ♂ and ♀ now before me, recently brought home by Mr F. A. A Simons

Gnathocera villosa, n sp

G viridis, sub-nitida, fortiter punctata, pilosa; thorace vitta marginali alba; elytris fulvo-viridis, linea marginali punctoque suturali postice ochraceis. Long. $13\frac{1}{2}$–$15\frac{1}{2}$ mm

Head closely and coarsely punctured, the base sparingly punctured, sides of clypeus sharply elevated, the apical points somewhat obtuse, anterior margin slightly elevated in the middle, shining green with long golden-brown pubescence, the lateral excavations of the clypeus white'

Thorax closely and coarsely punctured, basal margin tri-sinuous, shallowly emarginate above the scutellum, posterior angles strongly rounded; shining green with long golden-brown pubescence, a stripe on each side from the anterior angles to about one-third from the base, white.

Scutellum broad, triangular, coarsely punctured and pubescent, sides smooth; shining green.

Elytra widest behind the middle, the suture and two feebly raised narrow longitudinal carinæ on each smooth, the outer one rather indistinct, the interstices very closely and coarsely punctured, especially at the sides and apex ; greenish fulvous, pubescent and shining, a small round spot between the suture and inner carina about one-third from the apex and a broad marginal stripe, slightly turned inwards at the apex, ochreous-white.

Pygidium finely irregularly strigose, dark green with an ovate ochreous-white spot on each side.

Beneath shining green, pubescent, with large patches of white at the sides; mesosternal process short, apex obtuse and glabrous, abdomen with large transverse white stripes at the sides and a row of large quadrate spots in the central depression, legs coarsely punctured, pubescent, shining green, anterior and intermediate femora narrowly edged with white, posterior femora white on their outer sides except at the base and apex.

Angola

Allied to *G. hirta*, Burm., but very distinct, a female specimen I have before me has the pubescence very short and sparse

The following tabulation of all the species of the genus *Gnathocera* will assist in their determination.

1 Mesosternal process long and curved apex more or
   less bent inwards
   A Upper side shining
      a. Anterior margin of clypeus with an acute point in
         the centre, legs black
         * Thorax and underside without markings - - - *Afzeli*
         ** Thorax and underside with white markings
         † Thorax with a central impressed white stripe *elata.*
         †† Thorax without a central stripe - - - - - *angolensis*
      b Anterior margin of clypeus without a central
         point, legs red
         * Elytra fulvous without markings
         † Thorax fulvous, with a fine white interrupted
            central line - - - - - - - - - - - *rufipes.*
         †† Thorax green on the disc, central line broad
            and entire
            ‡ White marginal lines of thorax interrupted,
               scutellum green with a white central
               line - - - - - - - - - - - - - - *lurida*
            ‡‡ White marginal lines of thorax entire,
               scutellum fulvous without a central line - *gracilis.*
         ** Elytra with white marginal markings

\ 2

† Elytra fulvous with marginal spots - - - - *trivittata.*
†† Elytra greenish with a marginal line - - - *cruda*
B Upper side dull, velvety - - - - - - - - - - - *varians.*
2 Mesosternal process short, apex bent outwards
A Upper side dull, velvety, thorax with white central
      stripe - - - - - - - - - - - - - - - - *impressa.*
B Upper side shining, pubescent, thorax without
      central stripe - - - - - - - - - - - - - - *villosa.*
3 Mesosternal process scarcely produced, tuberculiform - *hirta.*

G. elata, Fab., has been considered synonymous with *trivittata,* but it is quite distinct, I have only seen specimens from Sierra Leone ; *trivittata* comes rather commonly from Angola.

G. angolensis, Westw., has been referred by Messrs. Gemminger and v Harold in their Catalogus Coleopterorum, to the genus *Heterorhina* ¹

G. impressa, Oliv , appears to be very rare, the only specimen I have seen is in my collection, and comes from Damara Land·

Elaphinis levis, n sp.

E atra, opaca, capite nitido ; thorace lateribus testaceis, albo-niculatis ; elytris macula transversa punctisque plurimis prope apicem rufo-testaceis ; pygidio albo maculato ; subtus nigra nitida, abdomine utrinque albo-guttato   Long 11–12 mm.

Var. elytris testaceis, regione scutellari apiceque nigris.

Head longitudinally convex in the centre, slightly impressed on each side between the eyes, finely and closely punctured, the punctures coarser and sparse on the base but confluent and forming striæ at the sides ; clypeus rather deeply emarginate in front, the apical points obtuse and elevated, the sides depressed ; black, very shining at the base : antennæ black.

Thorax convex, transverse, the posterior angles strongly rounded, basal margin slightly sinuous, anterior margin slightly elevated and shining in the centre, very sparingly and finely punctured , dull black, the lateral margins narrowly testaceous, with five or six small white spots

Scutellum short and broad, rounded at the apex, impunctate ; dull black.

Elytra sub-quadrate, slightly dilated behind the middle, the sutural angles a little produced and elevated, the suture and two carinæ on each slightly elevated and smooth, the interstices with two punctate striæ and several lateral rows of punctures ; dull black, an irregular, sinuous, transverse mark close to the apex and some small obscure spots just before it reddish testaceous ; the epimera black with a testaceous spot above.

Pygidium strigose at the sides, the centre with coarse, shallow, semi-circular · punctures ; dull black with some small chalky-white spots.

Beneath and legs strigose and punctured, shining black, sparsely pubescent ; mesosternal process prominent, short, the apex obtuse; abdomen with two rows of white spots on each side, a transverse row of punctures on each segment , anterior tibiæ with two long, curved and acute lateral teeth

Livingstonia, Lake Nyassa.

Allied to *E. nigritula,* Bohm.

Mr. Simons found this species plentifully on flowers The variety given above looks very different, but intermediate forms occur in which the elytra are more or less variegated with black, the white spots at the sides of the thorax are sometimes absent.

Anoplochilus indutus, n. sp.

A. ovatus, convexus, rufo-brunneus, nitidus, viridi micans, pilosus, confertim punctatus; elytris 4-carinatis, maculis 8-albis Long. 14 mm.

Reddish-brown with a metallic green tint.

Head very closely and finely punctured, a small round space at the base smooth, rather densely covered with fine silvery pubescence ; clypeus quadrate, the sides acutely elevated, anterior margin straight and strongly turned up

Thorax very convex, widest just behind the middle, anterior angles produced and acute, posterior angles strongly rounded, the basal margin strongly emarginate above the scutellum, an impressed median line on the anterior half, closely and finely punctured, with a very fine and rather dense silvery pubescence

Scutellum strongly depressed at the sides, sparsely but rather coarsely punctured.

Elytra convex, slightly depressed round the scutellum, the sides only slightly sinuous behind the shoulders, the suture and four carinæ on each rather strongly elevated, the second most pronounced, the interstices with rows of coarse irregular confluent punctures, the sides and apex coarsely and irregularly punctured and strigose, the disc rather sparsely pubescent, more densely so at the sides ; each with eight impressed white spots, arranged thus, two close together on the third carina before the middle, one close to the suture just behind the middle, one, also sutural, about one-fifth from the apex, three along the lateral margin and one close to the apical sutural angle

Pygidium very finely strigose with rather dense short pubescence.

Beneath closely strigose, and with dense pubescence at the sides ; mesosternal process broad and flat, rounded at the apex, punctured, and with an impressed longitudinal line ; abdomen with scattered punctures in the centre, the penultimate segment closely punctured ; legs punctured and pubescent, anterior tibiæ with three lateral teeth, the first somewhat obsolete, the second large and prominent, the apical one very long and curved, posterior tibiæ with the inner apical spine large, broad and concave on its outer side, the two basal joints of the tarsi acutely produced on each side

Livingstonia, Lake Nyassa.

A very peculiar species resembling *A variabilis*, G P. (*Macromimus spinitarsis*, M. Ly.), in the armature of its legs.

Oxythyrea lucens, n. sp.

O. nigra, nitida, thorace lateribus late rufis, vitta marginali maculisque tribus utrinque albis ; elytris læte viridibus, nitidissimis, linea marginali interrupta maculisque plurimis albis ; pygidio rufo   Long. 10 mm

Head rather closely and finely punctured, the clypeus very finely punctured in front, impressed on each side, the sides slightly rounded, the apex elevated on each side, the centre slightly impressed , shining black ; antennæ black with the apex reddish.

Thorax very finely and sparsely punctured, the punctures coarser and much closer in front, the sides rather prominent in the middle, posterior margin strongly rounded ; bright red, the centre broadly black, shining, a broad, irregular stripe on each side close to the margin, and a longitudinal row of three spots on each side of the disc, impressed and white.

Scutellum acute at the apex, impunctate ; shining black.

Elytra abruptly narrowed behind the shoulders, slightly dilated behind the middle, sulcate on the disc and along the suture behind, apical sutural angles produced and acute, six discal and three marginal rows of irregular punctures on each, those next the suture assuming striæ towards the apex; light green, very shining, a narrow interrupted marginal line, two spots at the side placed transversely just behind the middle, a small one on the shoulder, four or five along the centre of the disc, two or three elongate spots next the suture on the apical half and a large one at the apex, white, epimera black with a white spot above.

Pygidium with numerous variolose punctures; red with an irregular white mark on each side.

Beneath and legs strigose and sparsely hirsute; shining black with several white spots at the sides, the margins of the prothorax and the abdomen red, mesosternal process broad with a transverse impressed line.

Livingstonia, Lake Nyassa

Allied to *O. vitticollis*, Bhn.

Found abundantly by Mr Simons on flowers; some specimens have the white spots on the elytra larger and more or less confluent, and the thorax is sometimes only narrowly margined with red at the sides.

Tephrœa rufo-ornata, n. sp

T. ovata, depressa, atra, sub-opaca, subtiliter punctulata ; thorace marginibus (ante scutellum interruptis), vittaque abbreviata antice rufis; elytris vitta lata obliqua longitudinali rufa ornatis ; subtus nigra, nitida ; pygidio rufo. Long 15, lat. 8 mm.

Head flat, very closely and finely punctured, the base more coarsely so, with a small smooth space in the centre; clypeus slightly rounded at the sides, apical margin slightly elevated and emarginate; black, slightly shining ; antennæ black, the apex reddish.

Thorax rather convex, the sides slightly prominent in the middle, basal margin strongly rounded and deeply emarginate above the scutellum, posterior angles slightly prominent but obtuse, deeply but rather sparsely punctured, dull black with a broad marginal band, interrupted before the scutellum, and a central longitudinal stripe from the anterior margin to just behind the middle, dull red.

Scutellum broad, rounded at the sides, the apex obtuse, with scattered punctures on each side ; dull black

Elytra obliquely narrowed from the shoulders, depressed round the scutellum, the suture elevated posteriorly, with rows of coarse semicircular punctures, those near the suture assuming striæ towards the apex, the punctures at the sides smaller and irregular, the apex coarsely strigose ; dull black, a broad longitudinal stripe on the disc of each from the shoulder to apical callus, dull red ; epimera black coarsely punctured above.

Pygidium longitudinally elevated in the centre, very coarsely and irregularly strigose ; dull red.

Beneath and legs strigose, shining black, sides of the prothorax and apex of the abdomen red ; mesosternal process short, strongly dilated and truncate at the apex ; anterior tibiæ with two rather obtuse lateral teeth

Livingstonia, Lake Nyassa

Only two or three specimens of this very distinct species were taken by Mr. Simons ; it is allied to *T Napaea*, Bhn.

Protaetia advena, n sp.

P. olivaceo-ferruginea, opaca ; capite cupreo, nitido ; thorace lateribus maculisque quatuor ochraceis, elytris punctis lineolisque plurimis ochraceis ; subtus cuprea ochraceo-varia. Long. 15 mm

Head finely punctured, the punctures rather close at the base and on the forehead, but sparse on the clypeus, the centre slightly longitudinally elevated, clypeus slightly narrowed in front, the sides elevated, apical margin strongly turned up, rounded at the angles ; greenish cupreous, shining, the base slightly opaque

Thorax obliquely narrowed from the base, the posterior angles strongly rounded, basal margin trisinuous ; finely, sparsely and indistinctly punctured, the punctures closer and more distinct at the sides ; opaque olive-green, the centre and margins slightly ferrugineous, two small spots placed obliquely on each side of the disc behind the middle, a narrow lateral border and some irregular contiguous. spots near the posterior angles ochreous-white

Scutellum broad, strongly rounded at the apex, finely punctured on each side at the base ; opaque olive-green.

Elytra with very indistinct rows of punctures on the disc, a slightly elevated longitudinal ridge in the centre behind the middle, the suture also elevated posteriorly and terminating in a short acute point at the apex, ferrugineous tinged with olivaceous, with numerous small spots and irregular, wavy lines ochreous-white.

Pygidium strigose ochreous-white, an ill-defined spot in the centre and a smaller one on each side ferrugineous.

Beneath shining cupreous, the sides coarsely punctured, hirsute and variegated with ochreous ; mesosternal process strongly dilated and rounded at the apex, with a transverse impressed line and fringe of whitish hairs ; abdomen closely punctured in the centre, the sides with somewhat triangular white spots, the basal, penultimate and apical segments with transverse spots ; legs cupreous, punctured and hirsute, anterior tibiæ with three lateral teeth, the upper two almost obsolete

Cape York, N.E. Australia

This species is somewhat similar to *P mandarinea*, Weber, in colour and markings but is otherwise very distinct ; it is the only one of the genus yet discovered in Australia.

Protaetia conspersa, n. sp.

.P. angustata, cupreo-fusca, opaca, capite cupreo-nitido ; thorace punctis 16 ochraceis ornato ; elytris guttis pluribus (20–22) ochraceis notatis, subtus cupreo micans. Long. 17 mm

Head convex in the centre between the eyes, finely and sparsely punctured, the sides with coarser punctures ; anterior margin of clypeus slightly elevated and impressed in the centre, the sides depressed ; cupreous red, shining, the base dull ; antennæ pitchy.

Thorax obliquely narrowed from the base, finely and sparingly punctured, the sides coarsely strigose, basal margin shallowly emarginate above the scutellum, the posterior angles rounded ; cupreous brown opaque, with sixteen very small ochreous spots arranged thus, two on the anterior margin, six in a curved transverse row in front, a transverse row of four just behind the middle, two at the base and one on each of the posterior angles.

Scutellum large, the apex obtuse, impunctate ; dull cupreous

Elytra strongly rounded at the apex, the sutural angles obtuse, with four rows of confluent semi-circular punctures behind the middle, the disc and sides with rows of rather coarse punctures, the region of the scutellum smooth; cupreous brown with about twenty irregularly disposed small ochreous spots on each.

Pygidium transversely strigose; cupreous, slightly shining, with brownish pubescence.

Beneath and legs cupreous red, shining, very coarsely and closely strigose, sparsely pubescent; mesosternal process short, strongly dilated and rounded at the apex; abdomen coarsely punctured, the four basal segments smooth in the centre and with a transverse ochreous spot on each side; anterior tibiæ with three acute lateral teeth, all the knees with a small white spot.

Borneo.

Pachnoda Simonsi, n. sp.

P rufo-flava, opaca; capite nigro, nitido; thorace trivittato; elytris postice plaga nigra albo-pupillata maculisque 7–8 albis; subtus rufo-brunnea, nitida, albo-varia. Long. 16–17 mm

Head closely punctured, the punctures confluent on the clypeus, the base with dense long yellow pubescence; clypeus short, the sides strongly and acutely elevated, the apical margin raised and slightly sinuous; pitchy black, shining; antennæ reddish

Thorax regularly rounded at the sides, basal margin broadly emarginate above the scutellum, posterior angles rounded, rather finely and indistinctly punctured, sparsely pubescent at the sides; reddish-yellow, opaque, a broad oblique, rather ill-defined stripe on each side of the disc, narrowed anteriorly, and a short narrow central one at the base, reddish-brown.

Scutellum large, impunctate, reddish-yellow, opaque, narrowly margined with reddish-brown.

Elytra as broad in the middle as at the base, somewhat truncate at the apex, with indistinct rows of rather coarse punctures; reddish-yellow, opaque, five or six small spots on the margin, one in the centre near the base, and one close to the suture about one fourth from the apex, white, a conspicuous round black spot with a small white pupil, about the middle near the suture.

Pygidium finely strigose and pubescent; reddish-brown, opaque, with a large angular mark on each side, white.

Beneath reddish-brown, shining, broadly variegated with white at the sides, strigose and with long golden pubescence; abdomen with a double series of large transverse white spots on each side, the centre slightly impressed in the male; mesosternal process short, the apex dilated and rounded ; legs reddish-brown, intermediate femora with a white stripe on the outside, the posterior femora with a similar stripe on each side, anterior tibiæ with three lateral teeth, the upper one obtuse the others acute, hinder pairs of tibiæ with one acute tooth about the middle.

Lake Nyassa.

A few specimens of this species were taken by Mr. Simons at Monkey Bay, near Livingstonia ; it somewhat resembles *P. leucomelana*, G. & P., in coloration, but is otherwise very different.

Diplognatha striata, n. sp

D. nigra nitida, subtus fusco-testacea ; clypeo antice, thorace marginibus lateralibus anguste, pygidioque maculis duabus flavis, elytris profunde punctato-striatis.   Long. 19–21 mm.

Var. a. tota nigra.

Var b. supra rufo-brunnea ; capite punctis duabus, thorace vittis duabus maculisque lateralibus nigris.

Head short and broad, finely rugose, the base smooth, sides of clypeus strongly elevated and sinuous, anterior margin broadly emarginate, concave beneath, the angles produced, obtuse and turned up ; shining black, the clypeus yellow.

Thorax very coarsely and shallowly punctured at the sides, the punctures very close and confluent in front, but much finer and sparse on the disc, the posterior angles strongly rounded, the basal margin slightly produced and feebly emarginate above the scutellum ; shining black, the sides narrowly margined with yellow.

Scutellum long and narrow, the apex acute, impunctate, the sides strongly impressed ; shining black.

Elytra depressed behind the scutellum, each with six deep punctate striæ, the outer one abbreviated, the interstices slightly convex and smooth, the sides and apex very finely strigose and punctured, the shoulders with a shallow punctured fovea, and a deep elongate depression near the margin , pitchy-black, shining.

Pygidium slightly convex in the centre, very finely strigose , black, slightly shining, with a large yellow marginal spot on each side.

Beneath sparsely strigose at the sides, reddish-yellow, shining, blackish in parts ; mesosternal process slightly swollen and rounded at the apex ; abdomen with a central depression, the segments margined with black ; legs reddish-yellow, a stripe on the posterior femora, the knees, the outer edge of the tibiæ, and the tarsi pitchy-black, anterior tibiæ with three lateral teeth, the lower two large and acute.

The female is rather broader, more strongly punctured and strigose, has the apical angles of the clypeus less produced, the legs much stouter and the abdomen sparsely punctured and convex in the centre

Livingstonia (Simons).

A very distinct species, probably most nearly allied to *D. Blanchardi*, Schaum ; I have also specimens from the Zambesi.

Characters of new or little known species of the Coleopterous genus HOPLIA ; by CHAS O. WATERHOUSE.

MELOLONTHIDÆ

Hoplia aurantiaca, n. sp.

Oblonga, parum convexa, rufo-picea, squamis aurantiacis et ochraceis fulgidis dense vestita. Long. 3 lin , lat 1½ lin.

A pitchy red species densely clothed (even on the legs and tarsi) with bright golden and ochraceous round scales, the ochraceous scales form on the thorax a patch above each anterior angle and a line on each side of the middle, on the elytra a small spot on the side (about the middle), and a larger oblique sub-apical patch which does not reach the suture, these ochraceous scales appear also golden when viewed obliquely; beneath each shoulder is a round brownish spot. The scales on the abdomen and pygidium are more silvery. Clypeus with the margins strongly reflexed and the angles much rounded. Thorax a little narrower than the elytra, ¼ broader than long, distinctly narrowed in front and behind, angular at the sides, regularly convex Elytra ¼ longer than broad, moderately depressed above (but not flat), the sides sub-parallel, scarcely arcuate, the sub-apical callosity very little prominent In some lights the golden scales on the elytra present a mark like an *x*, embracing the more ochreous scales. Anterior tibiæ with three teeth

Varieties (1) The ochraceous markings replaced by more fuscous scales, the markings more extended. (2) Scales dusky brown, an ɷ shaped mark on the thorax, and an r on the elytra obscure golden.

Hab. Java (Dr. Ploem).

Hoplia Bowringii, n. sp

Oblonga, picea, squamis argenteo-aureis densissime vestita ; elytris dorsum leviter quadri-impressis Long. 3 lin , lat. 1⅔ lin.

Very close to the preceding, but relatively shorter and broader, and the scales are brighter, whiter and uniform in colour. The thorax is rather broader. Elytra relatively shorter, a little more convex (especially at the suture), rather more arcuate at the sides, and on the dorsal region four very shallow impressions may be traced. Legs and tarsi clothed with scales; the anterior tibiæ with two teeth.

Hab Penang (J. C Bowring, Esq.). Brit Mus.

Hoplia fulgida, n. sp

Breviter oblonga, picea, squamis læte aureis densissime vestita. Long. 3 lin., lat. 1⅔ lin

Very close to the preceding, but clothed with bright golden scales, which on the elytra and pygidium are flattened as if rolled together, those on the head and thorax are more yellow-golden than those on the rest of the body. The thorax is narrower than in either of the preceding species, and is more narrowed in front and behind, and is more angular at the sides. The elytra are only ⅕ longer than broad, and have a fuscous spot under each shoulder; on the disc of each elytron there is a round dark spot, but this may be the result of accident, or merely a sexual mark, as one specimen of *H Bowringii* has a similar spot. The tarsi are distinctly longer than in the preceding species, and the scales which clothe the posterior pair are narrower.

Hab. Malacca (Captain W. S. Pinwell). Brit. Mus.

Hoplia aurata, n. sp

Oblonga, dorsin depressa, picea, squamis aureis densissime vestita; elytris litterâ *x* e squamis albis ornatis. Long 3⅙ lin, lat. 1⅔ lin.

Very like *H aurantiaca,* but flatter on the back of the elytra, and the scales which clothe the elytra and pygidium are flattened as if rolled together. Thorax very convex in the middle with three very slight impressions, one in the front in the middle and two near the scutellum, the sides are evenly arcuate; on each side of the disc there is a fuscous spot. Elytra ¼ longer than broad, very flat on the back, distinctly impressed on each side about the middle, a little constricted behind the shoulders, which are angularly prominent; on each elytron there is a crescent of white scales which together form an *x*, the spaces embraced by these crescents appearing a little darker than the rest of the elytron ; below each shoulder there is a very small fuscous spot. The anterior tibiæ are tridentate. The legs and posterior are clothed with scales.

Hab. Sarawak.   Brit. Mus.

Hoplia squamacea, White.

Ann. and Mag Nat. Hist., xiv. 1844, p. 424.

" Head, thorax, elytra and podex covered with pale yellow shining scales, underside of body covered with similar but somewhat paler scales, those on the side with a pinkish hue.   Legs ferruginous, with several hoary scales and hairs."   Length $3\frac{1}{2}$ lin.

Pitchy, densely clothed with pale greenish-golden not very bright round scales, the scales not so densely packed as in the preceding species, regularly and evenly convex.   Thorax a little narrower than the elytra, gently rounded at the sides, the base with a slight mesial lobe   Elytra $\frac{1}{4}$ longer than broad, evenly convex, nearly straight at the sides, shoulders blunt and not at all prominent, the sub-apical callosity very slightly visible.   Legs rather long, sparingly clothed with small narrow whitish scales ; anterior tibiæ tridentate ; tarsi without scales.

Variety.   Scales more silvery, tinged with pink.

Distinct from all the preceding by its more evenly convex form, and by the absence of scales on the tarsi

Hab. Hong Kong (J. C. Bowring, Esq.)   Brit Mus.

Hoplia squamigera, Hope.

Gray's Zool Miscell., 1830, p. 24.

" Squamosa, corpore supra flavo-virescente, subtusque subaurato, tibiis anticis bidentalis "   Long. $3\frac{1}{2}$ lin.

This species has more the form of an *Ectinohoplia*, with angular sides to the thorax, and flat elytra.   Thorax at the widest part $\frac{3}{4}$ the width of the elytra, a little broader than long, convex, much narrowed in front and behind, the anterior angles very acute and prominent, the sides strongly angular in the middle, and gently sinuate behind the middle, the base regularly arcuate, the disc longitudinally impressed.   Elytra very flat, a trifle longer than broad, the shoulders nearly rectangular, blunt, the sides scarcely arcuate, no distinct sub-apical callosity   Legs long, tibiæ and tarsi sparingly clothed with small narrow pale greenish scales.   All the upper surface of the insect is densely clothed with dull pale yellow-green scales ; the pygidium bright pale silvery-green.

Variety.   Scales above rather bright golden-green.
Hab. Nepal.   Brit. Mus.

Hoplia scutellaris, n sp.

Oblonga, supra depressa, opaca, supra squamis viridi-albis, subtus squamis fere albidis dense vestita ; scutello, tibiis tarsis-que squamis viridi-argenteis micantibus tectis.   Long. 3½ lin., lat. 2 lin

Forehead, thorax and elytra densely clothed with small round dull greenish-white scales, the sides of the thorax and the whole underside of the insect densely clothed with nearly white (or extremely pale green) scales.   The scales on the scutellum, tibiæ and tarsi are narrower, closer, and pale silvery-green   Thorax evenly convex, the sides distinctly but not very strongly angular in the middle, the base with a rather broad mesial lobe.   Scutellum rather large, triangular, a trifle longer than the width at the base.   Elytra a little broader than the thorax, ¼ longer than broad, even and flat on the back, parallel at the sides, the shoulders distinct but blunt, the sub-apical callosity not conspicuous , there are some lines of minute black dots, from which proceed short black hairs   Anterior tibiæ with three teeth, but the uppermost very obsolete; anterior tarsi almost without scales Antennæ and parts of the mouth black

Hab. N. China (Fortune).   Brit Mus

Allied to *H Paivæ,* Woll., but smaller and less broad, a little less depressed, thorax gently sinuate on each side at the base, scutellum larger, elytra relatively a little longer, &c

Remarks on Japanese RHOPALOCERA and descriptions of five apparently new species; by OLIVER E. JANSON.

Erebia niphonica, O. Jans., Pl. V, f. 5.

Erebia niphonica, O. Janson, Cist. Ent. II, p. 153 (1877).

Vanessa Pryeri. n. sp., Pl. V, f. 2.

Allied to V. angelica, Cram., but smaller and with the external dentations of the wings much stronger and more acute ; above bright fulvous red, the black spots smaller than in angelica and clearly defined, the apical margins rather broadly ochreous, speckled with brown and bordered inwardly with brown lunular marks ; beneath ochreous-brown or chocolate suffused with pinkish towards the apex, a central band and numerous fine irregular transverse lines on both wings, and several marks in the cell of the primaries similar to angelica, but darker and more clearly defined, the L shaped silvery mark on the secondaries large and conspicuous. Expanse of wings 2–2¼ inches.

Yokohama

I have much pleasure in dedicating this species to my friend, Mr. H. Pryer, who has taken both it and angelica in large numbers, and has expressed the improbability of their being varieties of one species. I have examined a large series of both sexes and find the characters given above are always constant; the colour of the underside of Pryeri varies slightly, but is always very distinct from the pale yellow of angelica.

I adopt Cramer's name of angelica, as I cannot see any reason for considering that species identical with the c-aureum, Lin.

Linneus's description, although almost useless for the purpose of identification, agrees quite well with the species figured by Cramer as c-aureum, Lin., and Fabricius's description of the Linnean species applies without doubt to the same, although he erroneously described the female as another species under the name of interrogationis The figures of both sexes given by

z

Hubner again represent the same species, I cannot, therefore, see that anything but confusion can arise by adopting the views of Godart in considering the *c-aureum*, Linn., a distinct species from the *c-aureum* of all other authors, the only evidence in favour of which is that Linneus states his species is from Asia instead of North America, and we know the old writers are so frequently wrong in the localities they give that no dependance can be placed on them

Mr. W. H. Edwards, in an elaborate paper extending to nine pages in the Trans Amer. Ent. Soc., has further complicated matters by fancying he had identified the *c-aureum*, Cram, Fab. (*nec* Lin.), and the *interrogationis*, Godt (*nec* Fab), with a third species which he re-names *Fabricii*; he even calls this species the red-winged *Grapta*, in contradistinction to the allied species which has the posterior wings black, how came he then to reconcile the figure of Cramer which has distinctly black wings, and the description of Fabricius, which is evidently taken from Cramer's figures, with his red winged species?

Mr. Kirby, in his Catalogue of Diurnal Lepidoptera, follows the views of Mr. Edwards, but still further adds to the confusion, and at the same time displays his ability in the identification of species, by adding to *c-aureum*, Lin, the reference to Hubner's figures, and then quoting *angelica*, Cram., as a synonym , if he has really compared the figures of these two authors, and recognised them as representing one and the same species, the numerous similar anomalies in his work can be easily accounted for.

The synonymy of the four species to which I have referred is as follows :—

1. *c-aureum*, L (*nec* Godt , *nec* Edw., *nec* Kby.) North America.
       c-aureum, Cram. ♂
       c-aureum, Fab. ♂ .
       interrogationis, Fab. ♀ .
       interrogationis, Godt. ♂ , ♀ .
       c-aureum, Hubn. ♂ , ♀ .
       interrogationis, Edwards.
       interrogationis, Kirby.

2. *Fabricii*, Edwards ....North America.
    c-aureum, Cram. (*sec.* Edwards).
    c-aureum, Fab. (*see.* Edwards).
    interrogationis, Godt. (*sec.* Edwards).

3. *angelica*, Cram. ....China, Japan
    c-aureum, Godt (*nec* Lin.)
    c-aureum, Edwards (*nec* Lin.)
    c-aureum, Kirby (*nec* Lin.)
    c-aureum. Hubn. (*sec* Kirby !)

4. *Pryeri*, O. Jans. . ...Japan.

Araschnia fallax, n. sp Pl. V, f. 3.

Above brownish-black; the thorax with greenish iridescent
pubescence; apical margins of the abdominal segments narrowly
bordered with white; antennæ black, the underside spotted with
ochreous, apex of the club red; primaries with a γ shaped mark
near the base, and two short transverse lines in the cell pale
brown, a transverse band on the' disc strongly interrupted near
the middle, five small spots in a curved row near the apex, and
a small linear spot about the middle and close to the margin
pale ochreous, five irregular sub-marginal spots brick-red,
secondaries with a transverse pale ochreous band before the
middle and two fine undulating brick-red lines on the apical
half, united anteriorly and interrupted by the nervures, the
fringes of both wings spotted with white; beneath pale ochreous,
the base of the wings with several irregular red-brown and
black marks, the former margined with dark brown, the centre
of both wings without markings, leaving a broad transverse
band of the ground colour, the apical third occupied by a broad
red-brown band, bordered on either side by sub-quadrate blackish spots, the centre with several small white spots, the apical
margin with two fine black lines, the anal angle of secondaries
with a small blue spot Expanse of wings 2 inches 2 lines.

Yokohama (Pryer, Fenton).

Although resembling *A. prorsa*, Lin., in reality more nearly
allied to *A. burejana*, Brem.; the differences existing between
them being similar to those which obtain between *A. levana* and
prorsa, it might be inferred that they are only permanent
dimorphic conditions of one species but the assertion of
Mr. F. Jonas that they appear at the same season and in
different localities is opposed to this inference.

*Thecla fasciata,*n. sp , Pl. V, f. 4.

Above brownish-black, the wings deep black towards the apex, a fine line round the eyes and small spots on the underside of the antennæ white ; primaries with a broad purple stripe between the third median and sub-median nervures, commencing close to the base and extending about two-thirds along the wing, there are also some scattered purple scales in the cell, the fringes of both wings and the apex of the tails white ; beneath fuscous-brown, the markings very similar to *T. japonica*, Murr., and *taxila*, Brem. Expanse of wings 1 inch 8 lines.

Yokohama (Pryer, Jonas).

Closely allied to *T. japonica*, but differing from the female of that species in its shorter, broader and less rounded wings, in its darker colour, and in having the purple markings described above. I have only seen three specimens which are females.

Leucophasia vibilia, n. sp.

Above creamy-white, the body black, dusted with white ; primaries with the basal half of the costa and four short ill-defined longitudinal stripes at the apex dusky-black , beneath cream coloured, the posterior part of the primaries white, the costa broadly dusted with black ; secondaries strongly dusted black on the anal half and on the costa, leaving a narrow longitudinal stripe of the ground colour, the dusky-black scales become rather sparse on the apical margin, but are very close and form an obscure transverse band about one-third from the apex. Expanse of wings $1\frac{1}{2}$–$1\frac{3}{4}$ inches.

Nambu, North Japan (Pryer).

Differs from *L. amurensis*, Mén., besides the colour and markings, in have the primaries more acutely pointed at the apex. It is also allied to *L. Duponchelli*, Staud.

*Terias beth[*ese*]ba, n. sp.*

♂ Above lemon-yellow, the primaries narrowly margined with black on the costa, the apical black band commencing on the costa about one-third from the apex, thence obliquely narrowed to about one-third across the wing, and then gradually narrowed to the anal angle, the posterior two-thirds having three well marked semi-circular emarginations on its inner edge ; secondaries with a very narrow black marginal line slightly dilated anteriorly; beneath rather paler yellow than above, with fine sparingly scattered black scales, which form two indistinct transverse bands on the secondaries, the extremity of all the nervures marked with a very small black spot; the body black above, with pale yellow pubescence on the thorax, the sides of the abdomen yellow with a fine black longitudinal line, the underside and legs pinkish-white.

The female is smaller and of a paler yellow than the male, with the wings rather thickly speckled with black, the apical band on the primaries ends abruptly just before the anal angle, and the secondaries have a narrower black margin and a large rather ill-defined black spot at the anterior angle. Expanse of wings 1 inch 4 lines–1 inch 8 lines

Yokohama (Pryer).

Allied to *T. laeta*, Bdv., but differs in having the primaries more rounded at the apex, and in its paler colour and in the form of its markings.

Terias Jaegeri, Ménét.

This species is allied to the Indian *T. laeta*. Boisduval mentions a Japanese variety of it, but I think there is no doubt it is distinct from that species, I have examined nearly a hundred specimens and find they differ in several constant characters from their Indian ally, the sexes present scarcely any difference in size or coloration; the locality given by Ménétriés (Hayti) is of course erroneous.

Papilio macilentus, O. Janson, Pl. V, f. 1.

Papilio macilentus, O. Jans, Cist Ent. II, p. 158 (1877).

Pamphila mathias, Fabr.

Eparyyreus mathias, Butl., Cat. Fabr. Diurnal Lepidop. p. 275, t. iii, f. 8

I am indebted to Mr. H. Pryer for specimens of the male of this widely distributed species, which have enabled me to identify it with the description and figure above quoted; as I had previously only seen female specimens from Japan, I was not able to satisfactorily determine to what species they pertained.

On the genus AMBLYOPINUS, and description of a new species from Tasmania; by the Rev. A. MATTHEWS, M A.

The genus *Amblyopinus* was instituted by M Solsky in 1875*, to receive two species of *Brachelytra*, which had been found in South America, in the condition of pseudo-parasites upon certain species of Field Mice. In form as well as in their habits these animals were somewhat anomalous, and it was not without hesitation, that M. Solsky placed them among the *Tachyporidæ*.

In the summer of 1877, Mr. Janson received a collection of Coleoptera from Mr. Simson, of Gould's County, Tasmania, among which he noticed two specimens of a strange looking *Brachelytron*, and on reference to the list of localities found that they had been taken from the fur of a living Rat. This unusual habitat brought M. Solsky's Memoir to his recollection, and he very kindly forwarded the insects to me for dissection, sending at the same time the whole of M. Solsky's descriptions, transcribed verbatim from the original publication.

Since then I have dissected one of these insects, with great care, and have made complete preparations of every part of their external anatomy I have also carefully compared each part with fresh dissections of the analagous organs of the *Tachyporidæ* and the *Staphylinidæ*, and will now proceed to detail the result of my observations

It is first of all necessary to presume that the insect which I am about to describe is a true species of *Amblyopinus*, but on this point, although I have never seen any of the specimens found by M Solsky, I have very little doubt, his figures and descriptions are so full and clear, that I think their generic identity is obvious.

But if this is the fact, I cannot coincide with M. Solsky in placing *Amblyopinus* among the *Tachyporidæ*; the only.

---

* *Horæ Societatis Entomologicæ Rossicæ*, T. xi, p. 10.

character in which *Amblyopinus* agrees exclusively with the *Tachyporidæ* consists in the laminate extension of the frontal covering of the head, or what might have been termed the clypeus, if that part had been defined.   I do not think that this one point of resemblance is sufficient to counterbalance the discrepancies which exist in many characters of much greater differential importance   In the *Tachyporidæ* the intermediate coxæ are comparatively small and rather deeply and abruptly imbedded in the meso-sternum, which is not in any way depressed for their accommodation.   In *Amblyopinus* the meso- and meta-sterna are of a totally different type, and the former of these parts is deeply depressed for nearly the whole of its length and breadth to receive the very large intermediate coxæ, which are entirely free; a form precisely similar to that exhibited by *Philonthus* and *Quedius*   The mandibles, though of a very peculiar shape, are long, much curved, and armed with long and very strong teeth, as in many *Philonthi*; while on the other hand the mandibles of the *Tachyporidæ* are for the most part short, robust and simple.   From *Quedius*, to which in many respects it bears a strong resemblance, *Amblyopinus* differs materially in the *Episterna* of the prothorax; in the former these parts are excessively enlarged and produced triangularly until they almost meet behind the anterior coxæ, covering, as pointed out by Dr. Erichson, the prothoracic stigmata; in the latter the *Episterna* are small and linear, indeed, scarcely observable, and the prothoracic stigmata are open and uncovered, and large as in *Philonthus*; this important character, together with the general diversity of form, will be sufficient to separate *Amblyopinus* from *Quedius*, although in many anatomical details these genera are almost identical.

It will be observed that in the preceding paragraph I have called the triangular plates, which in *Quedius* and some other genera extend over the prothoracic stigmata, *the Episterna*, and I think that I am justified in using that term, by dissections which I have made of the prothorax; these immersed in Canada Balsam exhibit, as in diagram 8, a suture proceeding from the anterior extremity of the prosternum, in a line somewhat sub-parallel with the margin of the pronotum to within a short distance from its base.   A faint suture is also visible at the base

Rev. A. MATTHEWS *on the genus* Amblyopinus. 277

of the triangular portion, which may therefore constitute the true *Epimeron*. And if these processes were produced until they met behind the anterior coxæ, which in some species they very nearly do, they would then completely enclose the coxæ, and present a form entirely analagous to the prothoracic episterna and epimera of *Trichopteryx*. This anatomical definition is also more likely to be correct on account of the high development of the *Brachelytra* as a class, which will hardly permit the universal disappearance of any important portion of the anatomical structure of the true Coleopterous type.

It appears to me that *Amblyopinus* is much more closely allied to *Philonthus* than to any other genus; indeed, the only anatomical difference between them consists in the prolongation of the frontal plate, and in the peculiarly placed and almost rudimentary eye of the former, I might also add, in the deflexed angles of the pronotum. But for these differences I should at once have concluded that at least the present species had been a true *Philonthus*. All this, however, may not affect the species described by M. Solsky.

It the insect which I have examined be a true *Amblyopinus*, I should place that genus among the " *Staphylini genuini*," of Dr Erichson, and in close proximity to *Philonthus*. When we consider the intimate anatomical affinity between *Philonthus* and *Quedius*, it seems unnatural to separate those genera by the interval occupied in some lists by *Staphylinus* and its immediate allies, and that the arrangement would be improved by placing *Amblyopinus* as the connecting link between them In the present species we find the form and outline of a true *Philonthus*, combined with the distinctive characters of *Amblyopinus*.

I have thus noticed the principal points in which *Amblyopinus* either differs from or agrees with the various genera to which it seems to bear any affinity; and having done this, will not enter upon a detailed description of each separate part.

By the figures and diagrams in the accompanying plate it will be seen that the organs of the mouth are almost identical with the corresponding parts of both *Quedius* and *Philonthus*; the same similarity also prevails throughout the whole anatomy, except those points which I have already noticed, and all these parts have been described with great accuracy by Dr Erichson in his "*Genera et Species Staphylinorum.*" But I think it would be better to consider the parts, which in his description of the complex organ termed "the labium," Dr Erichson distinguishes by the names "segmentum primum" and "segmentum innominatum," as together forming the true mentum, in fact a mentum duplex, a very common form throughout the whole class; a strictly analogous formation also exists in the labrum of *Amblyopinus*, vid f. 2, and other genera of *Brachelytra*.

The discrepancies which exist between my figures of some of the organs of the mouth, and those given by M. Solsky, I do not consider of material importance, for it is utterly impossible to discern the true outline of any of these parts unless the preparation is immersed in Canada Balsam

AMBLYOPINUS, *Solsky.*

Amblyopinus Jansoni, n sp , Pl. VI.

L c. $2\frac{1}{2}$–3 lin $=$ 5–6 mm   Rufo-testaceus longe setosus, capite atque pronoto magnis nitidissimis; elytris perbrevibus rugose punctatis ; abdomine sat longo medium versus latiori rugose punctato; pedibus atque antennis modicis, illis robustis

Caput magnum nitidissimum, rugis perlevibus sinuatis confertissime dispositis per totum eleganter notatum, punctis duobus magnis et profundis supra oculum, duobus minoribus ad angulum posteriorem, quatuor exiguis curvatim dispositis in disco utrinque, atque quatuor equidistantibus, exterioribus permagnis, ad basim impressum,   Oculi minuti ovales glabri lenticulis nullis instructi in recessu profundo sub laminæ frontalis margine laterali siti.   Antennæ modicæ articulo tertio secundo longiori.

Pronotum sat magnum sub-ovale capite fere pariter longum et latum nitidissimum, rugis perlevibus sinuatis confertissime dispositis per totum eleganter notatum, levissime et remote punctatum, punctis duobus parvis ad mediam marginem anteriorem, tribus ad angulum utrumque anteriorem deflexum, atque singulo ad angulum utrumque posteriorem impressum, marginibus laterlaibus atque basali leviter reflexis   E punctis hisce omnibus et capitis et pronoti setæ erectæ plerumque longæ et validæ exoriuntur.

Scutellum sat magnum, sat deplanatum ad apicem rotundatum, rugis transversis impressum.

Alæ nullæ.

Elytra perbrevia, pronoto et breviora et angustiora rugose punctata nitida pilis sat longis átque validis vestita, setâ longâ validâ erectâ ad humerum utrumque instructa, apicibus oblique truncatis atque setis validis fimbriatis.

Abdomen elongatum pone medium latissimum, segmentis septem compositum, sex primis rugose punctatis atque pilis longis robustis, extremis multo longioribus, dense vestitis, segmentis 2-6 setis erectis longis validis aut duabus aut tribus equidistantibus utrinque instructis, lateribus profunde marginatis, segmento apicali sat obtuso simplici, levius punctato et pilis brevioribus vestito ; segmentis ventralibus sex profunde punctatis atque pilis densis vestitis, margine posteriori segmentorum 4 et 5 setis quatuor erectis instructâ, stylis analibus quatuor sat magnis setis longis instructis.

Pedes modici robusti, tibiis quatuor posterioribus calcaribus longis et validis armatis, tarsis anticis dilatatis, intermediis articulo basali valde elongato et incrassato sub-cylindrico, subtus sulco longitudinali profundo impresso margine exteriori fortiter pectinatâ, interiori setis instructâ, articulis 2-3-4 profunde bilobatis atque setis longis marginatis

Differt a speciebus adhuc descriptis formâ *Philonthoidea*, et corpore setoso punctis multis foveolatis impresso

Habitat Tasmaniam sub pelle Muris Ratti detectus.

EXPLANATION OF PLATE VI.

Fig. 1. *Amblyopinus Jansoni.*

„ 2. Labrum.

„ 3. Mentum, Labium, Lingua and Labial Palpi.

„ 4. Mandibles.

„ 5 Maxilla and Maxillary Palpi

„ 6. Head in profile to shew the eye.

„ 7. Intermediate Leg.

„ 8. Longitudinal section of the Pronotum of *Quedius* shewing the probable Episternon and Epimeron, (*a a*).

On some BUTTERFLIFS *recently sent home from Japan by Mr. Montague Fenton* , by ARTHUR G. BUTLER, F.L.S., F Z.S., &c.

Mr. Fenton's letter, accompanying the present consignment, is directed from Daigaku Yobimon, Tokei Japan ; the species are as follows :—

1. *Vanessa Fentoni,* n. sp. (No. 60).

Wings bright tawny ; primaries with black markings as in *V. satyrus* of the United States, excepting that the two spots upon the median interspaces are of twice the size ; secondaries with the black spots across the middle arranged as in *C-album* ; outer border broadly and irregularly black, intersected by six broad sub-confluent lunated tawny spots ; outer margin irrorated with tawny ; bases of the wings, abdominal border of secondaries and body as in the allied species ; wings below extremely like *V. satyrus,* but paler and with the bands less strongly defined ; the silver *C* shorter, and, therefore, less like a *G*   Expanse of wings 2 inches 3 lines.

This species belongs to the *V. egea* group rather than to that of *C-album,* the pattern of the under surface being far more like the former than the latter ; in form it scarcely differs from *V. 1-album,* excepting that the apical portion of the primaries is slightly narrower ; in the pattern and coloration of the upper-side it is very like *V. satyrus,* to which it is evidently more nearly allied than to any other known species.

2. *Argynnis rabdia,* Butler (No. 79).

The example sent is the largest that I have yet seen.

3. *Melitæa niphona,* n. sp. (No. 84).

♀ Allied to *M. athalia* of Europe, but considerably larger ; the discal line placed farther from the submarginal one, and almost divided into spots in the primaries : wings below altogether paler than in *M. athalia,* the secondaries being creamy white, with the markings sharply defined and similar to those of *M. athalia.* Expanse of wings 1 inch 11 lines.

This is like a gigantic race of *M. athalia.*

4. *Melitæa scotosia,* n. sp. (No. 83)

♀ Allied to *M. ætheria* of Europe, but dull tawny, with all the veins black, the black spots of double the width, and the disc of the primaries (as well as the submarginal lunules) pale , below altogether duller in colour than *M. ætheria,* the veins upon the apical area of primaries strongly defined ; the black spots of primaries of double the width, and the black lines of secondaries distinctly wider. Expanse of wings 2 inches 4 lines.

One of the most dingy looking species I have hitherto seen.

Mr. Fenton forwards an excellent drawing of a *Neptis,* allied to *N. alwina,* which, as it is certainly new, I describe as follows :—

5 *Neptis excellens,* n. sp. (No 58).

♀ Wings above black-brown; sinuations of the fringes white; primaries with a narrower white streak from the base (widening beyond the middle, notched at the end of the cell and then tapering to a point), just above the median vein , an irregular interrupted discal series of white spots, the first of which is an oblique sub-costal dash or abbreviated line, the second, third and fifth are large, more or less pyriform spots, the fourth and sixth are smaller, and the seventh is a bifid oblique internal dash ; two white sub-marginal dots, one opposite to the third, and one to the sixth of the discal series ; secondaries with a rather wide straight white belt across the basal third, and running from near the middle of the sub-costal vein to the inner margin near the base ; a discal series of white spots slightly diverging from the white belt towards the inner margin, where they are only separated by the veins ; wings below red-brown ; the white markings of the upper surface much widened ; the discal spots of primaries almost forming a continuous belt ; a complete sub-marginal series of whitish spots, but only the third, sixth and seventh large and white , internal area dark, sub-costal vein and base of cell whitish , secondaries with a white sub-basal patch silvery-bluish internally ; the white belt continued upwards at an angle to the costal vein, a lilacine streak between it and the discal series of spots ; a sub-marginal series of lilacine lunules. Expanse of wings 3 inches 2 lines

The next description I also take from an admirable drawing.—

6. *Pararge achinoides*, n. sp. (No. 39).

Extremely close to *P achne* of Europe, but the ocelli of the primaries of nearly equal size throughout, and the pale streak beyond the cell more strongly defined, secondaries with the ocelli larger, an additional indistinct one near anal angle ; a pale streak across the median branches behind the ocelli ; wings below with all the ocelli decidedly larger and white-pupilled, the white streak of secondaries becoming obsolete towards the front of the disc, and therefore not enclosing the ocelli. Expanse of wings 2 inches 3 lines

The wings are of the brown colour common to *Lethe Sicelis*

7. *Lycæna argia*, Ménétriés (No 103*a*)

From the Akutsu river bed.

8. *Lycæna microargus*, n. sp (No. 104*a*).

Above very like *L. argia* and *L. orgon*; lilac, with dentated blackish outer border and snow-white fringes ; below with the ground-colour of *L. pylaon* (*triton ?* Fabr); the markings exactly as in *L. argus*, excepting that the sub-marginal black spots of the secondaries have no trace of metallic colouring about them, and the orange belt connecting the two series of black spots is paler Expanse of wings 1 inch 1 line.

As is the case with several of the Japanese Moths, this species unites the characters of several European forms.

9. *Chrysophanus phlœas*, Linn. (No 99).

This may possibly be *C chinensis*, but I cannot at present see how it differs from typical *C. phlœas*, the example was sent to Mr. Fenton, was it taken in Japan ?

10. *Thecla orientalis*, ♀, Murray (No. 98*b*).

Mr. Fenton adds the word "*Bandai*" to the name of this species, but does not state whether it is the native name of the species or of the locality where it was captured; I cannot find it in Keith Johnston's Atlas,

11. *Terias Betheseba*, O. Jans. (No. 25).

12. *Gonepteryx Rhamni*, Linn. (No. 12).

The specimen sent was not taken at Tokei, but was forwarded
to Mr. Fenton; it differs markedly from *G aspasia*, both in
form and coloration, and agrees in all respects with the European type   Was it also captured in Japan ?

- 13. *Synchloë crucivora*, ♂, Boisduval (No. 17).

Mr. Fenton regards this as *C. rapæ*, of which it doubtless is
the Japanese representative, but its considerably greater size,
broad apical patch and more dusky basi-costal area to the
primaries readily distinguish it; the average expanse of the
wings is about a quarter of an inch in excess of the European
species.

14. *Pamphila Jansonis*, n. sp. (No. 125).

♂ Bronzy olive-brown, with sordid white fringes to the
wings; primaries with two small spots placed obliquely towards
the end of the cell; five dots between the sub-costal branches
(the first two very small and wide apart) and an oblique series
of five discal spots (the upper four in a decreasing series, pointing towards the apex, the first small and linear, just above the
middle of the sub-median vein), hyaline white; a slender
oblique brand connecting the first and second spots; secondaries
with four small spots, the first and last punctiform, in a zigzag
series not far from the apex; body normal, palpi sordid white;
primaries below with the costal third, excepting at apex, densely
covered with sordid ochraceous scales; hyaline spots as above,
an additional white spot between the first and second of the
oblique discal series, secondaries sordid ochraceous, with a broad
greyish-brown pyramidal area on the interno-median interspace;
a silvery-white spot in the cell and four towards apex, the
second of which is reniform; body below sordid greyish.
Expanse of wings 1 inch 8 lines

Most nearly allied to *P. pellucida* of Murray, but widely
distinct; it occurs, according to Mr. Fenton, "on the Koshiu-
kaido in Shimodzuke", although the form of the body in this
species with its somewhat short thorax reminds one of *Isoteinon*,
the antennæ are identical with those of *Pamphila*.   I have

named this species after Mr. Oliver Janson, whose interest in Japanese Butterflies is well known, and has produced most satisfactory results.

15. *Pamphila rikuchina*, n. sp.

Deep purplish-brown, the basal area of the wings clothed with tawny scales, fringes ochreous, especially at the anal angle; primaries with two ochreous spots at the end of the cell (the upper one punctiform); a rather broad irregular angulated discal ochreous belt, not reaching the inner margin, and divided into nine spots by the veins, which are black; secondaries with an arched series of five ochreous spots on the disc; body olivaceous, abdomen clothed with ochraceous hair scales; palpi pale greenish-yellow; wings below paler than above, more broadly and densely sprinkled with ochraceous scales; the secondaries with the abdominal area, particularly at anal angle, broadly ochraceous; body below greenish-grey. Expanse of wings 1 inch 4 lines.

A very distinct species occurring at " Rikuchin."

16. *Pamphila ochracea*, (Bremer No. 120).

17. *Pamphila florinda*, n. sp. (No. 113a).

♂, ♀ Above like *P. comma*, but deeper in colour; below altogether redder in tint, with scarcely a trace of pale spots, only two or three being indistinctly traceable in the secondaries; the veins also not tipped with black. Expanse of wings ♂ 1 inch 6 lines, ♀ 1 inch 5 lines.

There is the same difference between the sexes as in the European insect, the male being tawny with purplish-brown borders and grey-streaked oblique black brand, the female purplish-brown with the usual straw-yellow or ochreous spots; the position of the species will be between *P. comma* and the *P. sylvanus* of Japan

18. *Pamphila sylvanus var.* Esper (No. 113).

This form is barely distinguishable from *P. sylvanus*, unless we conclude that the Hakodaté form is the latter species and the Yokohama form is distinct; the latter may then be distinguished by its greater size and deeper coloration. The *P. venata* of

A A

Ménétriés is widely distinct from the insect usually called *P. venata* in collections; I have seen a specimen from N. China in Dr. Staudinger's Collection.

19. *Pamphila sylvatica*, Bremer (No. 119*a*).

20. *Pamphila leonina*, n. sp. (No. 119).

Bright fulvous, with black veins and moderately broad purplish-brown outer borders (narrower than in the preceding species); primaries with a slender oblique linear black brand; secondaries with the basal area and abdominal border dusky; wings below clearer than above, with black veins and linear black margin; primaries with the base (excepting upon the costa and the brand) as above black; legs and front of palpi yellow, hinder part of palpi and venter white. Expanse of wings 1 inch 3 lines

This species is allied to *P. sylvatica*, but markedly distinct; it is frequently mistaken for the *P. venata* of Bremer, but (as I believe) simply because it has black veins; in the form of its wings it is totally dissimilar.

Descriptions of new COLEOPTERA from Madagascar, recently added to the British Museum Collection; by CHAS. O. WATERHOUSE.

A small collection of insects has recently been received at the British Museum from Madagascar. They were collected by Mr. Robert Toy in the forests in the neighbourhood of Antananarivo. Among the Coleoptera are some very interesting new forms, particularly among the Lamellicorns and Longicorns.

The following are the new species :—

RUTELIDÆ.

Adoretus strigatus, n. sp.

Oblongo-ovalis, piceo-flavus, sat crebre fortiter punctatus, punctis setiferis; thorace utrinque strigâ nigrâ notato; pectore abdomine pedibusque nigrescentibus pilosis. Long. $6\frac{1}{4}$–$8\frac{1}{2}$ lin., lat. 4–$4\frac{1}{2}$ lin.

Of rather a broad, depressed form. Head, thorax and elytra moderately thickly and very strongly punctured; clypeus semicircular, densely and strongly punctured, with the margin reflexed. Thorax strongly transverse, the sides gently arcuate; on each side, at a little distance from the margin, is a longitudinal black stripe. Scutellum sparingly punctured at the sides. Each elytron has the usual three costæ indicated by lines of punctures. The punctures on the upper surface of the insect are furnished with short, stiff (but decumbent), pale hairs. On the underside the pubescence is finer and longer.

Adoretus vittatus, n. sp.

Oblongo-ovalis, convexus, nitidus, piceo-niger; thorace medio obscure castaneo; elytris vittis duabus flavo-piceis. Long. 9–10 lin., lat. 5–$5\frac{1}{4}$ lin.

This species is remarkable for its coloration, which somewhat resembles that of *Antichira cincta*. It is almost entirely destitute of pubescence on the upperside. Thorax moderately convex, shining, the disc generally castaneous and smooth, there are a few punctures scattered over the sides, and there is an irregular triangular patch of rather strong punctures on each side of the base. Scutellum with three or four punctures on each side. Elytra with the three usual costæ ill-defined, the interstices sparingly, finely and irregularly punctured ; each elytron has a pale pitchy stripe commencing in the middle of the base and reaching nearly to the apex (leaving a quadrangular scutellar patch and the suture black) ; a second stripe commences below the shoulder and does not quite reach the sub-apical callosity, this stripe is frequently interrupted in the middle, apex with minute tubercles. Antennæ pitchy.

♂ Head smooth, clypeus with a few distinct punctures ; fifth abdominal segment smooth.

♀ Head with moderately close distinct punctures behind, near the eyes, and some fine punctuation along the front margin; clypeus finely and rather closely punctured ; fifth abdominal segment densely and finely rugulose below.

Adoretus albosetosus, n. sp.

Niger, æneo-purpurascens, nitidus, lævis ; thorace fortiter transverso, margine basali utrinque parce punctato ; elytris oblongis, subtiliter punctulatis, haud costulatis, infra scutellum et utrinque leviter impressis, ad apicem declivis, setis nonnullis albidis ornatis ; antennis femoribusque anticis pallide piceis ; femoribus posticis maximis, subtus ad apicem fortiter calcaratis ; tibiis posticis crassis, curvatis. Long. 8½ lin., lat. 5 lin.

This species is so remarkable that I at first thought it would be necessary to propose a new genus for its reception. I think, however, that as the peculiarity rests mainly in the structure of the posterior legs which may be only a sexual character, it will be better to wait until the sexes are known. Its robust convex form, the entire absence of costæ on the elytra (which appear smooth unless examined with a lens), and the white stiff bristles (which are pointed at their apex) on the elytra give the species a marked character in the genus *Adoretus*. The posterior coxæ are produced posteriorly into a spur. The apex of the posterior tibiæ is produced below to about the middle of the fifth tarsal joint.

PRIONIDÆ.

Hoplideres rugicollis, n. sp.

Elongatus, parallelus, piceo-niger ; capite thoraceque crebre fortiter rugosis, his lateribus acute quadrispinosis ; scutello subtilius ruguloso-punctato ; elytris parum nitidis, fere parallelis, circa scutellum nitidis parcius punctatis, humeris acute spinosis, ♀ . Long. 21 lin., lat. 8 lin.

Very close to *H. spinicollis,* from which it differs in having the elytra more parallel, not expanded at the sides, and the head (especially round the eyes) and thorax are decidedly more rugose ; the spines also on the sides of the thorax are more slender.

CERAMBYCIDÆ.

Arrhythmus, n. gen.

General form somewhat that of *Eligmoderma.* Head very similar to that of that genus, but with the antennal tubercles more flattened and not divided in the middle, with only a very slight spine at the vertex. Antennæ about $\frac{1}{3}$ longer than the whole insect, slender, particularly towards the apex, slightly pubescent below. Thorax sub-cylindrical. Elytra rather flat above, at their base twice as broad as the base of the thorax, distinctly constricted a little before the apex, which, in consequence, appears somewhat expanded. Femora very much enlarged at the apex, compressed ; tibiæ compressed. Abdomen narrowed towards the apex.

The position of this rather singular insect is somewhat doubtful, but after a careful examination I am of opinion that it should be placed at the end of the *Eligmoderminæ.* The antennal tubercles are not, however, divided as they are in that group, and in this respect it approaches more to the *Callidiopsinæ,* but in all other characters it accords better with the former.

Arrhythmus rugosipennis, n. sp.

Elongatus, nitidus, niger, antennis articulis 4–11 pluminusve flavescentibus ; capite thoraceque tenuissime griseos pubescentibus ; elytris crebre fortiter punctatis, dimidio apicali anguste flavo-marginato, disco maculis duabus rotundatis flavis ; pedibus flavis, femoribus apice nigris, ♂ . Long. 9 lin.

The antennæ are dull yellow, with the first three joints and the apices of the fourth to tenth joints black, the black scarcely visible on the eighth to tenth joints. The thorax at its widest part about as wide as the head, a little narrowed in front and behind, thickly and strongly punctured, with indications of transverse rugæ, the disc with a very small tubercle on each side. The elytra are very strongly and closely punctured, with the margin just at the sinuation and the apex, as well as two dorsal spots, yellow.

Logisticus, n. gen.

General build of *Toxotus meridianus,* but more elongate, and with totally different head. Head long and rather narrow, the portion in front of the eyes a little longer than broad, depressed, a little broader at the apex than in front of the eyes ; maxillary palpi long ; eyes moderately prominent, coarsely granular, nearly contiguous below, narrowly divided above, not much emarginate in front ; antennæ as long as the body, slender, inserted on the rostrum in front of the eyes. Thorax nearly as in *Toxotus* but quadrinodose above Elytra very long, truncate at the base, narrowed to the apex, each elytron terminating in two short spines. Abdomen narrow, acuminate Legs very long, rather slender, femora not incrassate, tarsi rather broad and very hairy, the claw joint comparatively short, very slender at the base, suddenly widened at the apex, claws strong and suddenly bent from the base.

After a very careful examination, I am of opinion that this genus should be placed next to *Artelida* in the *Toxotinæ.* The produced rostrum, spined apices to the elytra and especially the coarsely granular eyes suggest affinity with the *Uracanthinæ,* but the antennæ are not inserted in the emargination of the eye as in that group, and the general build of the thorax elytra and legs is decidedly more that of the *Toxotinæ.* The tarsi are very like those of *Artelida,* but the spatulate claw joint is unlike that of any genus that I can remember, and the suddenly bent claws are also peculiar. With regard to the coarse granulation of the eyes, it must be borne in mind that an approach to this is already seen in *Artelida,* and that great difference exists in the closely allied genera of this group The granulation in *Sagridola* is extremely fine, in *Mastododera* and *Artelida sericeus* the granulation is much less fine, and in *Artelida crinipes* it is almost coarse.

Logisticus rostratus, n. sp.

Pallide fusco-griseus, sericeus ; antennjs pedibusque brunneis, femoribus obscurioribus, ♂ . Long. 12 lin

Pale brownish-grey, the antennæ, elytra, tibiæ and tarsi paler and yellowish-grey. Head a little longer than the thorax and not quite as broad, with a distinct longitudinal impressed line between the eyes Thorax constricted in front, strongly angular in the middle of each side, the disc not very strongly quadrino-dose, with a transverse impression at the base. Elytra very long, at their base not quite twice as broad as the base of the thorax, gradually narrowed to the apex, finely and moderately thickly punctulate in the humeral region. Legs very long, but the posterior femora do not nearly reach to the apex of the elytra.

LAMIIDÆ.

Tragocephala jucunda, Gory.

Two specimens of this species have been received, which differ from those already in the British Museum, in the following manner : Antennæ a trifle longer and stouter. The yellow markings clear sulphur-yellow not bordered with white ; the bands on the elytra less flexuous; the yellow on the occiput very narrow. Thorax without any spot on the hind margin.

These differences are probably sexual, as the two examples above noticed are males, those already in the Museum Collection are females.

The following species were collected by the late Mr. Crossley in Madagascar, but we have no indication of the precise locality in which they were found .—

CETONIIDÆ.

Euchilia puncticollis, n. sp.

Æneo-viridis, rubro-varia ; capite thoraceque fortiter sat crebre punctatis; elytris fortiter striatis, interstitiis convexis parce sat distincte punctulatis, marginibus punctis nonnullis majoribus aspersis , femoribus piceis. Long. 7½ lin.

Relatively shorter than *E. sulcata,* with the thorax more convex. Clypeus not quite so deeply notched, finely but dis-tinctly punctured ; forehead more strongly punctured, coppery-red on the vertex. Thorax deep coppery-red with a mesial line and the middle of the base green. Scutellum green. **Elytra** not quite so flat as in *E. sulcata*, coppery-red, the region of the shoulders, the subapical callosity, and the extreme apex, green, the shoulders themselves dark blue ; each elytron has six very strong dorsal striæ, the interstices convex, the sides with two striæ, of which the first is composed of strong close punctures. Legs obscure pitchy, the femora dull red.

Anochilia fascicularis, n. sp.

Nigra, nitida, punctulata ; elytris striato-punctatis ; pedibus ferrugineo-flavis ; corpore subtus femoribusque longe ferrugineo-pubescentibus, ♀. Long. 11 lin.

Clypeus thickly and rather strongly punctured, triangularly notched at the apex, very slightly longitudinally impressed on each side. Antennæ and palpi ferrugineous. Thorax $\frac{1}{4}$ broader than long, obliquely narrowed in front of the middle, distinctly and moderately punctured, the base straight at the scutellum, obliquely emarginate on each side Scutellum elongate triangular, nearly smooth. Elytra at the base about $\frac{1}{4}$ broader than the thorax, a little narrowed posteriorly, the sides rather straight , each with four or five lines of fine punctures which are not very close together, there are also a few other fine punctures scattered over the surface, the apex is striolate. · Pygidium with a few semicircular punctiform impressions, with two ferrugineous spots Legs rusty-yellow, femora hirsute, tibiæ with long ferrugineous fringe on the inner side, tarsi scarcely longer than the tibiæ. Sides of the sterna and abdomen with long rusty hair, that on the abdomen forming tufts at the sides visible from above. Prosternum short broad triangular.

Madagascar (Crossley).

Pygora costifer, n. sp.

Oblonga, depressa, nigra, subnitida ; capite thoraceque crebre fortiter punctatis ; elytris sat brevibus subopacis, fortiter striolato-punctatis, dimidio basali piceo, lateribus a costa superantibus ; abdomine medio cæruleo. Long 6 lin.

Head thickly and strongly punctured ; clypeus with the sides straight, a little narrowed at the apex, which is triangularly notched, impressed on each side, raised in the middle, impressed above the notch. Thorax moderately convex, rather thickly and strongly punctured, broadest behind, gradually narrowed anteriorly, the sides gently arcuate, margins incrassate, the base nearly straight, a little emarginate above the scutellum. Scutellum elongate triangular, with a line of fine punctures on each side. Elytra rather short, a little narrowed posteriorly, with an oblong impression near the side extending from below the shoulder to a little beyond the middle, bounded on the inner side by an obtuse costa, and on the outer side by a strong costa which surmounts the deflexed portion of the side ; the suture itself is deeply impressed, the margins of the impressions sub-costiform ; the punctuation is rather irregular, but the larger horse-shoe punctures are arranged in lines (crowded in the lateral impression). The second, third and fourth segments of the abdomen are a beautiful deep sky-blue Anterior tibiæ with three small teeth at the apex. Tarsi rather short.

Pantolia polita, n. sp

Elongata, deplanata, lævis, nigra ; singulo elytro pone medium striis brevissimis punctorum ; pedibus piceis. Long. 7 lin.

Resembles *Dirrhina iris*, but with the head differently formed. Clypeus nearly parallel sided, gently emarginate at the apex, which is finely and closely punctured, with a longitudinal deep channel on each side, this channel is longitudinally finely strigose. Thorax as in *D. iris*, but not quite so flat, and with the lateral channel deeper posteriorly and extending to the posterior angles. Elytra with a narrow transverse shallow impression, a little behind the middle composed of very short lines of strong punctures; the suture from the middle to the apex is somewhat raised and marked on each side by an impressed line ; the extreme lateral margins and apex are rather strongly striolate-punctate. Pygidium very closely and finely striolate.

CALANDRIDÆ.

Dichthorrhinus, n. gen.

Allied to *Eugnoristus*, but of a broader form and much depressed. Rostrum as long as the thorax, slender, straight, a little narrower at the apex, deeply channelled above, thick at the extreme base, and with two short, stout, acuminate, flexuous horns, projecting over the insertion of the antennæ ; antennal scrobes deep, nearly reaching the base of the rostrum, continued anteriorly by a slight channel. Antennæ as long as the rostrum, stout, the scape very thick, narrowed at the base, funiculus as long as the scape, with six nearly equal cylindrical joints, the club compressed, shining, not visibly jointed, a little spongy at the apex. Head very small, eyes contiguous below, a little separated above. Thorax broad, depressed, much rounded at the sides Scutellum very small. Elytra not broader than the thorax and $\frac{1}{3}$ longer, flat on the back, a little narrowed posteriorly, obtuse at the apex, striated. All the coxæ very widely separated, the sterna nearly flat. Abdomen with the first segment as long as the two following take together, the first and second segments not separated in the middle by any distinct suture, flattened. Legs very long and slender. The first and second joints of the tarsi narrow, the third very large, broad, sub-trapeziform, not bilobed, claw joint rather small and slender, inserted in the middle of the upper surface of the third joint.

Very close to *Eugnoristus*, but with the rostrum channelled above ; antennæ with only six joints to the funiculus, and not inserted quite at the base of the rostrum, &c.

Dichthorrhinus bicornis, n. sp

Niger, albo-squamosus, rugosus, depressus ; rostro supra basin cornubus duobus divaricatis, thorace lato, depresso, crebre fortiter punctato, lateribus bene rotundatis, elytris depressis, thorace vix angustioribus, fortiter punctato-striatis, interstitiis planiusculis, crebre fortiter punctatis Long. (sine rostro) 8 lin, lat. 3 lin.

The white scales are scattered over the upper surface of the thorax, but are close together and form a patch under each side ; they are also scattered over the surface of the elytra, but form a fascia a little before the apex ; there are also white spots on the sides of the sterna and abdomen, and the base of the femora are clothed with white scales.

CERAMBYCIDÆ.

Enthymius, n. gen.

General characters of *Torotus* but differing as follows · Head short and broad, rather convex, neck thick, with the sides parallel; muzzle very short ; eyes not very finely granular, rather large and moderately prominent, with a small but deep emargination in front ; antennæ ♀ moderately slender, inserted immediately outside the emargination of the eye, compressed, not quite as long as the body, the third and fourth joints subparallel, the fifth to tenth much narrowed towards their base, the internal apical angle of the sixth to tenth joints rather produced; thorax as broad as long, constricted in front, with a moderately prominent tubercle on each side, a little before the middle, disc with a round swelling on each side near the base; elytra ♀ not much narrowed towards the apex, gently convex.

The specimen on which I found this genus has been in the British Museum for some years, but was not described on account of the difficulty of determining its position. I feel sure, however, that the place that I assigned to it near *Toxotus* is the correct one. The very short muzzle is foreign to this group, but the insertion of the antennæ outside the emargination of the eye accords better with the *Toxotinæ* than elsewhere. The granulation of the eyes is much less fine than in the true *Toxotus*, agreeing, however, in this respect with the Californian *Toxotus cervinus,* Walker (which is said to be a synonym of *T. spurcus,* Lec.). The head having a thick neck with parallel sides is uncommon in this group, but something similar is seen in *Mastododera.*

Enthymius dubius, n. sp.

Crassus, rufo-piceus, dense cervino-pubescens; capite sat magno, fronte linea longitudinali tenui impressâ; thorace capite paulo latiori, disco paulo depresso; elytris parum convexis, apicem versus vix angustatis; antennis pedibusque obscurioribus. Long. 13 lin.

Hab. Madagascar (Crossley). Brit. Mus.

LAMIIDÆ.

Leucographus, n. gen.

Closely allied to *Eummetes,* but with the prosternum between the coxæ very broad, gently concave anteriorly, the upper part slightly leaning over posteriorly. Mesosternum very broad, trapezoidal and horizontal between the coxæ, perpendicular in front. Antennæ a little longer than the body, the fifth joint much shorter than the preceding and more slender, the sixth to eleventh gradually diminishing in length, compressed, fringed on the inner side (especially the apical joints), the eighth, ninth and tenth joints with a slight angle at the base on the inner side. Elytra with the shoulders not advanced anteriorly.

Leucographus albovarius, n. sp.

Ater, opacus, velutinus; thoracc lato, lateraliter angulato, albo-variegato; scutello lato, medio albo-lineato; elytris latitudine ¼ longioribus, basi ferc truncatis, apicem versus angustatis, depressis, circa scutellum convexioribus, guttis numerosis strigaque obliqua albidis.   Long. 10 lin

Head very broad, with a white stripe between the antennæ. Antennæ with the first joint and the base of the other joints grey.   Thorax broad, strongly but obtusely angular at the sides, with numerous whitish spots which are more close towards the sides, and nearly form a cioss on the disc   Elytra broader at the base than the broadest part of the thorax, narrowed towards the apex, with the sides straight, the apex obtuse, the shoulders are slightly sloping, obtuse; there are numerous small white spots scattered about the base, a line of spots on each side of the suture, an oblique stripe a little before the middle, and six spots which on the two elytra are arranged in the form of a wide W behind the middle.   Tibiæ grey, except at the extreme apex.

There is a striking similarity of coloration between this and *Tophoderes frenatus* its compatriot in the *Anthribidæ*.

Descriptions of a new genus and three new species of LEPIDOPTERA *from Madagascar*; by ARTHUR G. BUTLER, F.L.S., F.Z.S.

The three following species have been received in a small collection made by Mr. Robert Toy in a forest near Antananarivo :—

Eusemia hypopyrrha, n. sp.

Upper surface velvety-black ; head and collar spotted with sulphur-yellow, a white spot on each tegula close to the humeral angles of the thorax ; abdomen with the lateral margins of the segments and the sides orange ; primaries with two spots near the base, and a broad slightly curved and rounded central belt, which does not reach the costal margin, sulphur-yellow ; secondaries with the fringe white at apex ; body below orange ; head black, spotted with yellow ; primaries paler than above, orange at the base ; a basi-subcostal streak of sulphur-yellow uniting with the broad central belt ; disc of the wings chocolate-brown ; secondaries bright carmine, with the base of the costal margin orange ; outer half of the costal margin black ; a broad external black border tapering to the anal angle ; a subapical whitish spot. Expanse of wings 3 inches 4 lines.

This is the most robust species that I have yet seen, it is most nearly allied to *E agrius* of Herrich-Schäffer, but is considerably larger, has a broader and sulphur-yellow belt across the primaries, and no belt upon the secondaries ; whether *E. agrius* has the hind wings carmine below like *E. zea* of the same plate I cannot tell, but I suspect it has

Anchirithra, n gen.

Dréatæ affine ; alæ anticæ angustæ dense squamosæ, cellula brevi, vena subcostali sex-ramosa. ramis secundo et tertio ramisque quinto et sexto e pediculo emissis ; nervula discocellulari angulata et recedente ; vena radialli vera absente ; vena mediana quadriramosa ; posticæ vena costali ramulo subbasali costam versus currente, vena subcostali pone cellulam furcata, ramo

superiore cum vena costali confluente; vena radiali cum subcostali continua; nervula discocellulari perobliqua, vena mediana
quadriramosa, ramis tertio quartoque a pediculo pone cellulam
emissis; corpus robustum, lanare, antennis longis late_pectinatis;
palpis brevibus, dense pilosis. Gen. typ. *A. insignis.*

Anchirithra insignis, n. sp.

Body silky whity-brown, the antennæ and prothorax pale
ferruginous; primaries sericeous whity-brown, with slightly
yellowish costal margin and reddish external border continuing
to the middle of the inner margin; two parallel longitudinal
ferruginous stripes dividing the wing into three nearly equal
areas; secondaries pale ferruginous, under surface uniformly
pale ferruginous without markings. Expanse of wings 1 inch
8 lines.

A peculiar looking species with rather strange neuration.

Parasa singularis, n. sp.

Thorax bright gas-green; abdomen pale stramineous; pri-
.maries bright green; the base pale ferruginous, bounded externally
by a darker line of the same colour and followed by two unequal
triangular patches of silvery-white; median vein silvery-white;
fringes ferruginous; a basi-subcostal streak and the outer border
white; secondaries pale stramineous with testaceous fringe;
body below ferruginous; wings pale stramineous with the costal
area broadly pale ferruginous, the discoidal area of primaries and
basi-costal area of secondaries being deeper in colour. Expanse
of wings 1 inch 9 lines.

Quite unlike any species known to me.

Notices of new or little known CETONIIDÆ; by OLIVER E. JANSON. No. 4.

Ischnostoma rostrata, n. sp.

I. nigro-picea, opaca, sparse nigro-setosa, capite postice maculis duabus, clypeo vitta utrinque, thorace basi et marginibus lateralibus, elytris marginibus externis suturaque postice anguste margaritaceo-albis ; clypeo elongato, antice utrinque profunde exciso, angulis acutis, medio in processu clavato producto, ♂. Long 21, lat. 10 mm.

Head coarsely punctured and sparsely pubescent; clypeus twice as long as broad, anterior angles strongly produced into acute and slightly convergent points, sides almost straight, anterior margin with a central narrow porrect horn transversely produced at the apex, the centre with an elevated longitudinal ridge; dull black, two spots between the eyes and a stripe on each side of the clypeus pearly white; antennæ black, club not very long, yellow beneath.

Thorax almost hexagonal, obliquely widened from the base to the middle, thence narrowed to the front, basal margin slightly rounded, anterior margin slightly emarginate, sides and apex with coarse scattered punctures and sparse black setæ; dull brownish black, the sides and base narrowly margined with pearly white.

Scutellum large, triangular, the sides with an impressed marginal line, impunctate; dull brownish black.

Elytra half as long again as the thorax, strongly rounded behind, the disc with two faintly elevated longitudinal ridges, impunctate; dull piceous-black, the shoulders slightly shining, with a narrow pearly white marginal line commencing just behind the humeral angle, extending to the apical angle and continued more narrowly along the suture for about half its length.

Pygidium large and vertical, slightly swollen, smooth, dull silky black, with a small white spot on each side.

Beneath pitchy black, slightly shining, finely striolate, and with long black hairs; mesosternum punctured and impressed in the centre, the process very small, abdomen compressed, the centre of each segment with a row of setiferous punctures; legs long, shining black, with coarse punctures and long pubescence, anterior tibiæ with two large obtuse lateral teeth.

Caffraria.

Allied to *I. cuspidata*, Fab. (*pica*, M. Ly.), and *I. nasuta*, Schm; but at once distinguished from the former by the form of the frontal horn, and by not having the clypeus constricted at the base, and from the latter by its longer and differently armed clypeus, shorter antennæ and different colour. The only specimen I have seen is a male in my own collection, which was recently brought home by Mr. Mansel Weale.

Heteroclita? scitula, n. sp.

H. elongata, villosa, supra nigra, opaca, thorace lateribus et punctis minutis antice albis, elytris rufo-testaceis, albo-punctatis, sutura nigra, pygidio utrinque albo-maculato; subtus nigra, nitida; tibiis anticis extus acute bidentatis, ♂. Long 9½, lat. 5 mm

Head rather coarsely but shallowly punctured, the base with long ashy-white pubescence; clypeus large, dilated at the sides, strongly rounded in front, the margins acutely elevated, the apex shallowly emarginate, slightly convex in the centre, the sides strigose, shining black with a white spot on each side at the base of the clypeus; antennæ pitchy black, the club long and reddish.

Thorax rather broader than long, the sides straight from the base to the middle, anterior margin with a small elevated ridge in the middle, posterior angles strongly rounded, basal margin nearly straight, dull black, rather coarsely punctured and covered with a dense ashy-white pubescence, a marginal band on each side branched inwardly in the middle, and several small spots on the anterior half white

Scutellum obtuse at the apex, dull black with several small white spots, the base punctured and pubescent.

Elytra with prominent humeral angles, faintly punctured at the sides and apex, the disc with two slightly elevated indistinct longitudinal ridges; pale yellowish-red, opaque, sparsely pubescent, suture black, a sutural and two discal rows of small spots and irregular confluent marks and spots at the sides and apex white; epimera, black, densely pubescent and with a white spot above,

Pygidium large, the margin acute, black, slightly shining, strigose, and pubescent, with a large mark on each side united at the base and several small spots in the centre white.

Beneath shining black, strigose and with dense long ashy pubescence at the sides; mesosternal process very short, dilated and truncate at the apex; abdomen deeply longitudinally impressed in the centre, the sides with broad white stripes; legs shining black, punctured and pubescent, tarsi reddish, anterior tibiæ broad with two large acute lateral teeth.

. Natal.

Although this pretty little species resembles *Heterochta Raeuperi*, Schm., in several respects, its narrower form, bidentate anterior tibiæ and differently formed thorax cause me to refer it to that genus with considerable doubt, and as I have seen but a single male specimen, and know *Raeuperi* by description only, I have not considered it advisable to establish a new genus until an opportunity occurs of examining more material.

Gymnetis alboscripta, n sp.

G. nigra, nitida, elytris nigro-piceis fascia angulata impressa alba ornatis, thorace lateribus albo-marginatis, pygidio et corpore subtus albo-maculatis, ♀. Long. 22, lat 11 mm.

Head closely punctured, an impression on each side between the eyes, the centre convex and smooth; clypeus short, quadrate, its sides slightly elevated, its apical margin acutely elevated and rounded; shining black; antennæ pitchy black

Thorax with large variolose punctures at the sides and finer scattered punctures towards the middle, the posterior lobe and centre smooth, anterior margin slightly elevated in the middle; shining black; lateral margins white.

. *Scutellum* almost concealed, the apex produced and very acute.

Elytra depressed and almost impunctate in the region of the scutellum, rather coarsely punctured on the disc and behind the middle, the punctures rather finer and forming several indistinct rows at the base but confused and confluent at the sides, apex strigose, sutural angles slightly produced and acute; pitchy black, shining, with an irregular, angulated and interrupted, impressed, transverse, white band just behind the middle; the epimera punctured and clothed with white scales above

Pygidium finely and rather deeply strigose; black, slightly shining, an elongate mark on each side white.

. B B

Beneath coarsely punctured and strigose, shining black, with several small white marks at the sides; mesosternal process broad, rounded at the apex, finely punctured; abdomen with coarse elongate punctures at the sides, apical segment very closely punctured, a double series of four transverse linear white marks on each side; legs shining black, coarsely punctured with black hairs, anterior tibiæ with three acute lateral teeth.

Oaxaca, Mexico.

Allied to *G. 10-guttata*, C. Waterh.

Desicasta Thomsoni, n. sp.

D. lata, sub-depressa, nigra, nitida, elytris limbo postice rufo-piceo, pedibus sanguineis, tarsis nigris; elytris seriatim lateribus vage obsolete punctatis, ♂. Long. 28, lat 15 mm.

Head very sparsely and finely punctured, clypeus longitudinally convex in the centre, sides acutely elevated and nearly straight, apex deeply emarginate and impressed in the centre, the apical points obtuse and elevated; antennæ reddish.

Thorax very sparsely and finely punctured on the disc, the sides coarsely but not very closely punctured, posterior lobe obtuse and depressed at the apex.

Elytra broad, rather flat, the sides almost straight, and abruptly rounded at the apex, suture depressed at the base but elevated posteriorly and terminating in a small acute point at the apex, the disc slightly wrinkled and with rows of rather coarse unequal punctures, sides finely and obsoletely punctured; shining black at the base but pitchy towards the sides and apex, and becoming bright red at the margin from the middle to the sutural angle.

Pygidium very finely transversely strigose, pitchy-red.

Beneath shining black, abdomen reddish towards the apex, coarsely punctured at the sides; mesosternal process long, broad and flat, the apex rounded; abdomen deeply longitudinally impressed in the centre, apical segment slightly strigose; legs very sparsely punctured, bright red, knees and apex of tibiæ pitchy, tarsi black, tibiæ and anterior femora fringed with black hairs, the anterior tibiæ with two very acute lateral teeth.

Panama.

Allied to *D. haematopus*, Schm., but differs in colour, in its finer and sparser punctuation, and in its broader, depressed and posteriorly truncate form; in the latter respect it more nearly resembles *Reichei*, Thoms., but the form of the mesosternal process will at once separate it from that species.

I have named this species after Mr. James Thomson who has recently established the genus *Desicasta* for the reception of the American species which were formerly included in the African genus *Stethodesma*.

Euphoria Steinheili, n. sp.

E nigro-picea, purpureo tincta, supra opaca, elytris obscure purpureis, sparse albo signatis ; subtus nitida, flavo pilosa, Long 15–17, lat. $7\frac{1}{2}$–$8\frac{1}{2}$ mm.

Var. nigro-olivacea.

Head with a slight longitudinal impression on each side, and a feeble transverse ridge at the base of the clypeus, very closely and coarsely punctured, the punctures confluent at the base, apex of the clypeus strongly elevated, rounded and very slightly notched in the centre; shining black ; antennæ pitchy black, the lamellæ rather large and red at the apex.

Thorax regularly rounded at the sides, the base somewhat produced and emarginate above the scutellum, rather finely and sparsely punctured, the punctures coarser at the sides and furnished with fine setæ ; dull purple brown.

Scutellum impunctate, apex acute, dull purple-brown.

Elytra with two slightly elevated smooth longitudinal carinæ, united at the apical callosity, the disc with several rows of irregular shallow semicircular impressions, the sides sparsely punctured and strigose towards the apex, the suture elevated posteriorly, the apical angles acute and slightly prominent ; dull purple red with small white spots near the suture about one fourth from the apex, at the sides and near the apical angles ; epimera shining brown, strigose and pubescent above.

Pygidium finely strigose, shining red-brown, with sparse grey setæ.

Beneath purple brown, shining, strigose and with pale yellow pubescence; mesosternal process dilated and rounded at the apex ; abdomen coarsely punctured and with three large foveæ on each side, the centre deeply impressed , legs dark brown, shining, coarsely strigose and sparsely pubescent, tarsi black, anterior tibiæ with three strong lateral teeth.

Panama.

Allied to *E. Lesueuri*, G. P. A second specimen that I have is olivaceous black, the elytra being reddish towards the margins and with several additional white spots about the middle of the disc.

Euphoria abreona, n. sp.

E. fulvo-testacea, subopaca, flavo pilosa, capite viridi-aeneo, elytris nigro-brunneo variegatis, pygidio nigro, utrinque albo maculato, subtus nigro-acnea nitida ; clypeo apice valde reflexo, ♂. Long. 15, lat 8 mm.

Head coarsely and very closely punctured, a slightly elevated longitudinal ridge at the base; clypeus slightly constricted at the base and narrowed in front, the apex strongly reflexed; greenish cupreous, shining, the base with dense long yellow pubescence ; antennæ pitchy black, the lamellæ nearly as long as the head.

Thorax rather finely and sparingly punctured on the disc, the punctures at the sides, coarser and confluent, the base slightly produced and emarginate above the scutellum, the anterior margin slightly elevated and shining ; reddish fulvous, opaque, with short yellow pubescence.

Scutellum acute at the apex, impunctate; fulvous.

Elytra with two feeble longitudinal carinæ, the suture elevated and produced into a short point at the apex, the disc and sides with rows of indistinct punctures, apex strigose; dull reddish fulvous with sparse yellow pubescence, two rows of small spots on the disc, a spot on the shoulder and several irregular, somewhat confluent marks at the sides and apex brownish-black ; the epimera cupreous, strigose and pubescent above.

Pygidium finely and closely strigose and pubescent; pitchy black, brownish in the middle, an ochreous white spot on each side.

Beneath brassy-black, shining, with long pale yellow pubescence, closely strigose at the sides ; mesosternal process short, dilated and rounded at the apex ; legs strigose, punctured and pubescent, brassy-black, anterior tibiæ with three lateral teeth, the upper one almost obsolete, the others very acute.

Bogota (Chesterton).

Allied to *E. iridescens,* Schm , but more like *E. inda,* Lin., in colour and markings.

Descriptions of some uncharacterized species of Crioceridæ; by
Joseph S. Baly, F.L.S , &c.

Lema Kirbyi.

Oblonga, fulva, nitida, antennis infuscatis, thorace maculis
irregularibus quatuor, mesosterno maculâ utrinque, metasterno
medio femorumque posticorum quatuor maculâ antica nigro-piceis ;
thorace sub-cylindrico, dorso convexo, longitudine vix latiori ;
lateribus prope medium profunde constrictis, disco basi late
transversim depresso, antice convexo, minute punctato ; elytris
thorace latioribus, sat profunde punctato-striatis, punctis apicem
versus minus fortiter impressis, interspatiis planis, ad apicem
convexiusculis ; plagâ magnâ discoidali et utrimque unâ pone
medium sub-trigonatâ, nigro-piceis.   Long. 3 lin.

Hab. Sierra Leone ; a single specimen formerly in the collection of the Rev W. Kirby.

Neck deeply constricted, face trigonate, front impressed with
a small fovea, immediately in front of which is a small shallow
transverse impression; antennæ filiform, nearly three-fourths
the length of the body, obscure flavous at the base, stained
outwardly with fuscous.   Thorax slightly broader than long ;
sides strongly constricted, the apex of the constriction obtuse ;
above convex, broadly and abruptly depressed at the base, the
depression extending from side to side, entirely across the thorax,
disc finely punctured, stained on either side with two irregular
nigro-piceous spots   Scutellum sub-quadrangular, its apex
slightly emarginate.   Elytra much broader than the thorax,
convex, not distinctly excavated below the basilar space, strongly
and deeply punctate-striate, the ninth stria entire, the puncturing
finer and less deeply impressed towards the apex; interspaces
plane, slightly convex at the apex, where the striæ themselves
are distinctly sulcate.

Lema Livingstoni.

Anguste oblonga, sub-cylindrica, picea, nitida, subtus dense
aureo-sericea ; capite pedibusque nigro-piceis, femoribus, apice
exceptis, obscure fulvis ; antennis nigris, articulo basali sordide

fulvo; thorace transverso, sub-cylindrico, lateribus medio sat
profunde angulato-constrictis, disco impunctato, ante basin
profunde transversim sulcato, medio utrinque leviter transversim
impresso; elytris oblongis, utrisque sordide fulvo limbatis,
fortiter punctato-striatis, interstitiis planis, ad apicem leviter
convexiusculis. Long. 2¼ lin.

Var. A   Thorace pedibusque sordide fulvis.

Hab. Banks of the Niger, my collection; *Var.* A. Senegal,
collection of Mr. M. Jacoby.

Lower portion of head clothed with golden-sericeous hairs;
eyes deeply emarginate; antennæ rather more than half the
length of the body, black, the basal joint obscure fulvous, the
following three piceous   Thorax about one-fifth broader than
long; sides broadly and deeply constricted, the constriction
extending the whole length of the sides, its angulate apex being
placed exactly in the centre of the latter; disc impressed
immediately behind the middle, with a deep transverse sulcation,
and on either side in front of the latter with a faintly impressed
transverse groove.   Elytra much broader than the thorax,
oblong, parallel; convex, slightly excavated below the basilar
space, strongly punctate-striate, the interspaces plane, faintly
convex at the apex.

Lema ornatula.

Anguste oblonga, sub-cylindrica, nigra, nitida, capite thoraceque piceo-testaceis, antennis extrorsum nigris, pedibus thoracisque basi flavis; thorace sub-globoso, ante basin constricto, disci
medio et ad latera fortiter punctato; elytris fortiter punctato-
striatis, interspatiis convexis; nigro-piceis, utrisque vitta latâ
irregulari, a basi fere ad apicem extensâ, flavâ ornatis. Long.
1¼ lin.

Hab. West Coast of Africa.

Head trigonate, vertex shining, impunctate; antennæ rather
more than half the length of the body, distinctly thickened from
the fifth to the eighth joints, thence very slightly attenuated
to the apex, seven lower joints pale piceous, the rest black.
Thorax scarcely longer than broad, deeply. constricted at the
base, a broad longitudinal space on the middle disc together
with the sides coarsely and deeply punctured   Elytra much
broader than the thorax, slightly attenuated towards the apex,
convex, slightly excavated transversely below the basilar space,
deeply punctate-striate, the interspaces thickened, sub-costate,

those on the middle disc less strongly thickened than the others ; .
obscure piceous, each elytron with a broad irregular obscure
fulvous vitta, extending from the base nearly to the apex.

Lema Bouchardi.

Anguste oblonga, rufo-fulva, nitida, antennis (articulo basali
excepto) tibiis tarsisque nigris ; thorace sub-cylindrico, sub-
quadrato, lateribus minus profunde constrictis, disco ante basin
transversim sulcato, antice lœvi, impunctato ; elytris thorace
multo latioribus, oblongis, convexis, infra basin transversim
excavatis, basi distincte, ad apicem minute punctato-striatis ;
interspatiis planis, apice obsolete convexiusculis. Long. 3¾ lin.

Hab. Guatemala.

Neck constricted, front faintly impressed with a longitudinal
groove ; labrum and antennæ (the basal joint of the latter
excepted) black ; antennæ filiform, about two-thirds the length
of the body. Thorax as broad as long, sub-cylindrical ; sides
deeply constricted in the middle, the apex of the constriction
sub-angulate ; disc smooth, impunctate, rather deeply impressed
in front of the base with a transverse sulcation, on the middle
of which is a small distinct fovea. Elytra much broader than
the thorax, transversely excavated below the basilar space,
regularly punctate-striate, the ninth stria entire, the punctures
finely but deeply impressed, much finer towards the apex ;
interspaces very faintly convex at the apex, the outer interspace
thickened.

Lema pulcherrima.

Elongata, sub-cylindrica, nigra, nitida, antennarum apice
flavo-albidis ; femoribus thoraceque flavis, hoc transverso, lateribus valde constrictis, dorso lœvi, vix pone medium leviter
transversim sulcato ; elytris parallelis, evidenter punctato-striatis,
flavis, fasciâ basali postice utrinque emarginatâ, maculâ sub-
apicali transversim ovali suturâque apice cyaneis. Long. 4 lin.

Hab. Brazil, Minas Geraes.

Head shining black, front minutely strigose, impressed with
a very fine longitudinal groove ; antennæ filiform, four-fifths
the length of the body, three upper joints yellowish-white.
Thorax nearly one-fourth broader than long ; sides deeply
constricted in the middle ; disc nearly impunctate, transversely
sulcate behind the middle, the sulcation broad but not deeply
impressed. Elytra broader than the thorax, narrowly oblong,

parallel, not distinctly excavated below the basilar space, regularly punctulate-striate, the ninth stria from the suture entire, the tenth stria sulcate; the punctures rather strongly impressed at the base, finer and shallower towards the apex; interspaces plane, faintly thickened at the apex, outer interspace thickened and sub-costate for its whole length.

Lema mutabilis.

Sub-elongata, sub-cylindrica, fronte foveâ elongatâ impresso, antennis sat gracilibus, filiformibus; thorace latitudini fere æquilongo, lateribus vix ante apicem tuberculo acuto instructis, medio sat profunde angulatim constrictis, disco lævi, impunctato, ante basin profunde transversim sulcato; elytris thorace latioribus, parallelis, convexis, infra basin sat fortiter sub-oblique transversim excavatis, spatio basilari distincte elevato, leviter convexo, regulariter punctato-striatis, punctis super sulcum sub-basalem magis fortiter impressis; interspatiis planis, ad apicem convexiusculis. Long. 2⅔ lin.

A. Corpus rufo-testaceum, elytris metallico-cæruleis.

B.   „   „   antennis (basi exceptâ) pectore pedibusque nigris, antennis infuscatis.

C.   „   totum fulvum.

Hab. West Coast of Africa, Old Calabar, Camaroons.

Head smooth, impunctate, front impressed with a narrow elongate fovea; lower portion of face clothed with aureo-sericeous hairs, apex of clypeus and labrum nigro-piceous; antennæ slender, filiform, two-thirds the length of the body. Thorax scarcely broader than long; sides armed just behind the apex with an acute tubercle, deeply constricted, the apex of the constriction angulate; disc shining, impunctate, very deeply impressed in front of the base with a transverse sulcation. Elytra broader than the thorax, parallel, convex, longitudinally excavated within the humeral callus, transversely and somewhat obliquely excavated below the basilar space, the basilar space itself distinctly thickened; convex, regularly punctate-striate, the ninth stria entire, the punctures distinct but not large, of equal size and depth to the apex of the elytra, those on the sub-basilar excavation coarser and more strongly impressed than the rest; interspaces plane, slightly convex at the apex.

Lema Murrayi.

Sub-cylindrica, rufo-testacea, nitida, pectore, abdominis disco tibiisque apice obscure piceis, tarsis antennisque nigris, his apice

piceis, thorace longitudine vix latiori, ante basin profunde constricto, antice convexo, lævissimo, minutissime punctato, utrinque
lineâ transveisâ impresso ; scutello obscure rufo ; elytris parallelis, thorace latioribus, sat fortiter punctato-striatis, interstitiis
minute granulosis, planis, apice leviter convexiusculis ; metallico-
cæruleis aut nigris, apice extremo rufo-testaceis. Long. 2½ lin.

Var. A. Pectore abdominisque disco . rufo-testaceis.

Hab. Guinea, Gabon ; *Var.* A. Old Calabar.

Head trigonate, vertex and front finely punctured, the latter
impressed with a small oblong fovea ; lower portion of face
clothed with golden pubescence ; labrum nigro-piceous ; antennæ
more than three-fouiths the length of the body, filiform, black,
the two lower joints rufo-piceous, the intermediate ones black,
the three or four upper ones obscure nigro-piceous, third and
fourth joints equal, each twice the length of the second.
Thorax scarcely broader than long, sub-cylindrical, deeply
constricted in front of the base, the sulcation extending downwards on the constricted sides ; disc in front convex, veiy
minutely punctured, impressed on either side with a transveise
gioove Scutellum rather longer than broad, sides slightly
converging from base to apex, the latter truncate. Elytra
broader than the thorax, parallel, slightly flattened along the
. sutuie, excavated transversely on the inner disc below the base ;
rather strongly punctate-striate, the interspaces minutely granulose, plane, sometimes irregularly wrinkled on the transverse
depression, convex at the extreme apex. Body beneath clothed
with adpressed sericeous hairs

This species must stand close to *L. apicipennis*, Lac.

Lema Stevensi.

Oblonga, convexa, læte rufo-testacea, nitida, subtus aureo-
sericea ; thorace sub-cylindrico, longitudini fere æquilato, lateribus medio constrictis, disco lævi, minute punctato, ante basin
piofunde transversim sulcato ; elytiis thorace multo latioribus,
convexis, dorso leviter deplanatis, infra basin leviter transversim
excavatis, regulariter punctato-striatis, punctis ante medium
magnis, profunde impressis ; interspatiis planis, ad apicem convexiusculis ; metallico-cæruleis, violaceo tinctis, apice extremo
rufo-testaceo Long. 3 lin.

Hab. Burmah.

Head constricted behind the eyes, vertex and fiont shining,
impunctate, the latter thickened, impiessed with a distinct fovea ;
antennæ four-fifths the length of the body, filiform, more iobust

than in *L. Mouhoti*; lower edge of clypeus and the labrum black. Thorax not broader than long, sub-cylindrical; sides strongly constricted in the middle, the fundus of the constriction broad and forming at its upper end a distinct angle with the disc ; upper surface deeply impressed at some distance behind its middle with a broad transverse sulcation, surface minutely punctured, the puncturing on a longitudinal space on the middle disc, and on either side near the anterior angle, more distinct than on the rest of the surface. Scutellum similar in form and coloration to *L. Mouhoti*. Elytra much broader than the thorax, broadly oblong, convex, somewhat depressed along the suture, distinctly excavated below the basilar space, regularly punctate-striate, the interspaces plane, impressed here and there with very minute punctures, moderately convex at the apex, the punctures on the striæ on the anterior disc very large and deeply impressed, those on the hinder disc much smaller and shallower.

I have named this species after my friend Mr. S. Stevens, through whom I formerly received it.

Lema subapicalis.

Anguste oblonga, læte rufo-testacea, nitida, femoribus apice extremo, tibiis, tarsis, antennisque (harum articulo primo prætermisso) nigris; thorace longitudine vix latiori, lateribus medio sat profunde constrictis, disco lævi, medio lineatim punctato, ante basin transversim sulcato ; elytris oblongis, infra basin transversim excavatis, fortiter punctato-striatis, interstitiis planis, ad apicem vix convexiusculis; metallico-cæruleis, utrisque puncto marginali, ante apicem posito, rufo-testaceo ornatis. Long. 3½ lin.

Hab. Guatemala.

Head trigonate, shining, impunctate ; neck constricted ; antennæ filiform, nearly three-fourths the length of the body, black, the basal joint rufo-testaceous. Thorax slightly broader than long, sides constricted in the middle, the apex of the constriction obtuse ; above smooth and shining, impressed before the base with a broad, deep, transverse sulcation, middle disc with a broad vitta of minute punctures scarcely visible without a lens. Scutellum wedge-shaped, obscure rufous, its apex piceous, obtusely truncate. Elytra much broader than the thorax, oblong, convex, slightly flattened along the suture, transversely excavated below the basilar space, regularly punctate-striate, the ninth stria from the suture entire ; the punctures on the basilar space and on the transverse depression large and deeply impressed, those on the rest of the surface finer ; interspaces impressed here and there with minute punctures, plane, faintly convex at the apex.

Lema Mouhoti.

Sub-elongata, sub-cylindrica, pallide rufo-testacea, nitida ; antennis corpori fere æquilongis, filiformibus ; thorace latitudine vix longiori, lateribus medio sat profunde constrictis ; disco lævi, medio et ad latera tenuiter punctato, pone medium transversim sulcato ; elytris 'anguste oblongis, parallelis, metallico-cærulcis, infra basin vix depressis, ante medium profunde, pone medium minus fortiter punctato-striatis, interspatiis planis, apice leviter convexiusculis Long. 3 lin.

Hab. Siam ; Mountains of Laos, Pachybouri, collected by the late M. Mouhot.

Head deeply constricted behind the eyes, vertex smooth, impunctate ; front impressed with a faint fovea, lower face sparingly clothed with aureo-sericeous hairs ; lower edge of the clypeus and jaws piceous ; labrum black ; antennæ rather slender, filiform, about equal to the body in length. Thorax scarcely longer than broad ; sides deeply constricted, the fundus of the constriction broad and forming at its upper end an abrupt angle with the disc of the thorax ; disc nitidous, deeply sulcate transversely behind the middle, a broad medial vitta together with a space on either side near the anterior angle, finely punctured. Scutellum narrowed from base to apex, the latter truncate, faintly emarginate, piceous. Elytra broader than the thorax, parallel, convex, obsoletely excavated below the basilar space, regularly punctate-striate, the ninth stria from the suture entire ; the punctures on the anterior disc large, foveolate and deeply impressed, those on the hinder disc finer and less strongly impressed ; interspaces plane, obsoletely convex at the apex. Body beneath clothed with very short golden sericeous hairs.

Lema amazona.

Sub-elongata, subtus flava, nitida, supra nigra, antennis apice albidis, thorace fere quadrato, prope medium' sat profunde constricto, lævi, nitido, margine basali flavo, elytris thorace latioribus, distincte punctato-striatis, interstitiis apicem versus leviter convexiusculis, margine laterali, apice dilatato, fasciâque communi prope medium, ad suturam antrorsum paullo producto flavis Long 3¼ lin.

Hab. Pebas, Upper Amazons.

Vertex and front shining, impunctate, the latter faintly impressed with an oblong fovea ; antennæ four-fifths the length of

the body, three upper joints fuscous-white. Thorax subquadrate, rather broadly constricted across the middle, shining
black, the basal margin fulvous. Elytra much broader than
the thorax, broadly oblong, convex, transversely excavated
below the basilar space, distinctly punctate-striate, the ninth
stria from the suture entire, interspaces plane, slightly thickened
at the apex; the outer half of the basal limb, the lateral margin,
dilated at the apex, and .a transverse band across the middle,
dilated slightly upwards on the suture, fulvous.

Lema Steinheili.

Anguste oblonga, nigra, nitida, pedibus (tibiarum apice extremo tarsisque exceptis), thoracoque fulvis, antennis apice
albidis , thorace transverso, vix pone medium profunde constricto, lævi, impunctato; elytris late oblongis, convexis, infra
basin leviter depressis, regulariter punctato-striatis, punctis
magnis, sat profunde impressis; interstitiis apicem versus
leviter convexis; nigris, purpureo vix micantibus, limbi basalis
dimidio externo, limbo laterali, apice dilatato, fasciâque communi prope medium fulvis. Long. 3¼ lin.

Hab. Columbia.

Head elongate-trigonate, vertex smooth, impunctate; front
impressed with a deep oblong fovea; antennæ nearly equal to
the body in length, filiform, the four lower joints fulvous, the
apices of the second to the fourth black, the under surface of
the seventh, together with the whole of the succeeding four
joints, yellowish-white. Thorax about one-fifth broader than
long, very deeply constricted just behind the middle, shining,
impunctate. Elytra much broader than the thorax, slightly
flattened along the suture, faintly excavated below the basilar
space; regularly punctate-striate, the punctures large, foveolate,
deeply impressed, the ninth stria from the suture entire; interspaces smooth, slightly thickened towards the apex, irregularly
wrinkled on the anterior disc below the basilar space.

Lema fraternalis.   .

Anguste oblonga, pallide rufo-picea, nitida, fronte femorumque dimidio externo (apice extremo excepto), nigro-piceis;
thorace sub-quadrato, rufo-fulvo, lateribus medio sat profunde
constrictis, disco pone medium leviter transversim sulcato, medio
lineatim et ad angulos anticos confuse tenuiter punctato; elytris
oblongo-ovatis, dorso leviter deplanatis, basi vix elevatis, infra
basin obsolete transversim excavatis, regulariter punctato-striatis,
punctis ante medium magis fortiter impressis, interstitiis planis;
nigris, purpureo tinctis, limbo exteriori, apice lato, fasciâque

communi prope medium flavis, limbo apiceque extremo roseo tinctis. Long. $3\frac{1}{4}$ lin.

Hab. Nauta, Upper Amazons.

Face trigonate, front, face between the eyes, together with the upper orbit of the latter, nigro-piceous, basal joint of antennæ and clypeus piceo-fulvous; antennæ filiform, about three-fourths the length of the body. Thorax nearly sub-quadrate, sub-cylindrical, sides deeply constricted in the middle, disc impressed behind the latter with a broad shallow transverse groove, in the centre of which is a single fovea; a longitudinal space on the middle disc, together with the sides near the anterior angles very finely punctured. Elytra much broader than the thorax, oblong-ovate, convex, slightly flattened along the suture, faintly excavated transversely below the basilar space, the latter indistinctly thickened; regularly punctate-striate, the ninth stria entire, the punctures at the base rather large and deeply impressed, those on the hinder disc very fine and shallow; interspaces plane, the outer one thickened and sub-costate.

Nearly allied to *L. Dia,* the antennæ shorter and the thorax narrower than in that species.

Lema Salvini.

Sub-elongata, pallide fulva, nitida, pectore, tibiis, tarsis, scutello capiteque nigris, antennis filiformibus, piceis, basi et apice sordide fulvis, articulo basali nigro; thorace sub-cylindrico, longitudine vix latiori, lateribus profunde constrictis, disco ante basin modice transversim sulcato, utrinque pone apicem leviter impresso, medio lineatim et ad latera confuse tenuiter punctato; scutello trigonato; elytris anguste oblongis, parallelis, regulariter punctato-striatis, flavis, lineâ suturali et utrinque vittis angustis duabus, a basi ad longe pone medium extensis, basi confluentis, nigris Long 3 lin.

Hab. Guatemala.

Vertex smooth, impunctate, front impressed with a distinct fovea, on either side of which are several fine punctures; orbit of eyes coarsely punctured; antennæ filiform, about four-fifths the length of the body, pale piceous, the second and third joints together with the three upper ones obscure fulvous, the basal joint (its apex excepted) shining black. Thorax slightly broader than long, sides deeply constricted near the middle, the apex of the constriction obtuse, disc transversely sulcate before the base, and impressed in the middle just before the sulcation with a single fovea, a broad longitudinal space on the middle disc, together with either side near the anterior angle finely punctured; on either side the middle disc, just behind the apical margin, is a faint depression. Scutellum trigonate, longer than broad, its apex obtuse. Elytra much broader than the thorax, narrowly oblong, parallel, convex, not excavated below the basilar space; rather deeply punctate-striate, the punctures much finer at the apex, the ninth stria entire; interspaces plane, slightly convex at the apex, the outer one thickened and sub-costate for its whole length; each elytron with a narrow sutural line and two linear vittæ, black, these vittæ (one sub-marginal and the other discoidal) extend from the base to more than half-way between the middle and the apex, they are confluent at the base and form on the humeral callus a trigonate patch.

Lema lineatipennis.

Anguste oblonga, rufo-fulva, nitida, antennis (articulo basali excepto) tarsis, tibiis anticis apice posticisque quatuor totis, nigris; thorace longitudine latiori, lateribus sat modice constric-tis, disco lævi, ante basin leviter transversim sulcato; elytris oblongis, fortiter punctato-striatis, striâ nonâ late interruptâ, medio costiformi, interspatus transversim rugulosis, ad apicem longitudinaliter elevatis; flavis, lineâ suturali, et utrinque vittâ a basi fere ad apicem extensâ, ante apicem extrorsum dilatatâ, nigris. Long. 2½ lin.

Hab. Brazil.

Face subelongate-trigonate, front impressed with an oblong fovea; antennæ nearly two-thirds the length of the body, filiform, black, the basal joint fulvous, its extreme apex piceous, the second piceous beneath. Thorax rather broader than long; sides moderately constricted in the middle, disc very faintly depressed transversely in front of the base, the middle of the depression impressed with a single fovea; a longitudinal space in the middle, and the sides near the anterior angles finely punctured. Elytra broader than the thorax, oblong, convex, somewhat flattened along the suture, the basilar space very slightly thick-ened, strongly punctate-striate, the ninth stria from the suture only visible at base and apex, its intermediate portion costiform, interspaces irregularly wrinkled transversely on the inner disc, longitudinally thickened at the apex, the outer interspace thick-ened for its whole length; the suture, abruptly dilated just before its apex into a common elongate patch, together with a discoidal vitta on each elytron black; the latter commences on the humeral callus immediately below the base, and extends nearly to the apex of the elytron, just before its termination it is dilated outwardly into an oblong spot, which extends to the inner edge of the thickened lateral interspace.

Lema nitidiceps.

Anguste oblonga, sub-cylindrica, rufo-testacea, nitida, capite nitidissimo, nigro, antennarum articulis ultimis tribus pallide flavis; thorace transverso, dorso vix pone medium late transversim sulcato, lateribus medio profunde constrictis; elytris oblongis, nigris, evidenter punctato-striatis, interstitiis fere planis, ad apicem paullo elevatis, tenuissime, irregulariter, strigosis. Long. 3⅓ lin.

Hab. Upper Amazons; collected by Mr. Bartlett.

Head shining black, glabrous, vertex very minutely punctured, the puncturing only visible under a lens; front impressed with a small oblong fovea, antennæ filiform, four-fifths the length of the body, black, the three upper joints pale yellowish-white Thorax nearly one-fourth broader than long; sides deeply constricted in the middle, the apex of the constriction obtuse, disc sub-cylindrical, broadly and deeply excavated transversely just behind the middle, shining, impunctate. Elytra broader than the thorax, oblong, convex, very faintly depressed below the basilar space; distinctly punctate-striate, the ninth stria from the suture broadly interrupted; interspaces nearly plane, very finely strigose, slightly thickened at the apex, the second and eighth from the suture more elevated than the rest. Outer edges of tibiæ and the tarsi stained with piceous.

Lema vittatipennis.

Anguste oblonga, nigro-picea, nitida, capite inferiori antennisque (harum basi obscure fulvâ exceptâ) nigris; abdomine thoraceque piceo-fulvis, hoc longitudine paullo latiori, lateribus profunde constrictis, sub-cylindrico, ante basin sat profunde transversim sulcato, et sulci medio foveâ unâ impresso, basi obsolete transversim strigoso, disco lævi, medio lineatim, et lateribus anticis tenuissime punctato; elytris oblongis, thorace multo latioribus, infra basin vix transversim depressis, basi sub-fortiter, pone medium tenuiter punctato-striatis; interspatiis planis, ad apicem obsolete convexiusculis, ante medium hic illic obsolete rugulosis; nigris, utrisque limbo marginali vittâque latâ discoidali, basi et apice connexis, fulvis Long 2¾ lin.

Var. A Abdominis segmentis piceo marginatis

,, B Corpore subtus cum capite pallide piceo, abdomine fulvo, antennis nigris.

Hab. Amazons, Para, Nauta.

Very closely allied in form, sculpturing and in the coloration of the elytra to *L. virgata*, Lac.; at once separated from that insect by its paler under surface, unicolorous and much more finely punctured thorax (the transverse sulcation being at the same time much more deeply impressed) and by the different relative lengths of the third and fourth joints of the antennæ; .in *L. virgata* the third joint is nearly equal in length to the fourth, in the present species it is distinctly shorter.

Crioceris discrepens.

Elongata, sub-cylindrica, picea, nitida, subtus aureo-sericea, thorace sat elongato, cylindrico, lateribus leviter constrictis, disci medio et lateribus anticis tenuiter punctato; scutello aureo-sericeo; elytris thorace multo latioribus, anguste oblongis et ad apicem paullo attenuatis, basi obsolete elevatis, infra basin transversim depressis, foveolato-striatis, striis ad latera valde interruptis, pone medium deletis

Mas. Antennis sat robustis, corpore longitudini paullo brevioribus, articulis cylindricis, intermedis paullo compressis. Long. 4½ lin.

Hab. Siam, Mountains of Laos.

Face elongate, neck deeply constricted, vertex and front nitidous, impunctate, the latter impressed with a longitudinal groove; orbit of eyes and lower face closely punctured; antennæ robust, nearly equal to the body in length, the joints cylindrical, the fifth to the ninth very slightly compressed and laterally dilated. Thorax about a fifth longer than broad, cylindrical, constricted at the extreme apex, sides armed behind the latter with a small obtuse tubercle; broadly but not deeply constricted in the middle, upper edge of the constriction bounded by a distinct longitudinal ridge, immediately above which is a longitudinal groove; surface nitidous, very minutely punctured, a longitudinal space on the middle disc, together with the sides near the anterior angles more distinctly punctured; at the base are several faint ill-defined transverse grooves   Scutellum narrowly oblong, aureo-sericeous. Elytra much broader than the thorax, narrowly oblong, slightly attenuated towards the apex, very slightly thickened at the base, transversely excavated below the basilar space, foveolate-punctate, the punctures arranged in longitudinal rows, the rows on the sides are much interrupted and all below the middle entirely obsolete Thighs thickened, the hinder pair nearly reaching to the apex of the elytra, abdomen with four longitudinal rows of patches of aureo-sericeous hairs.

From *C semipunctata*, the only species with which it can be confounded, it is known by its narrower form, by its larger thorax, longer and more slender antennæ, and by the golden colour of the pubescence on the scutellum and under surface of the body.

New genera and species of CARABIDÆ *from Tasmania* ; by
H. W. BATES, F.L.S.

The following descriptions are founded upon the collections
recently received in England from Mr. Simson and Mr. Atkinson,
who have made large additions to the knowledge of the Coleopterous Fauna of Tasmania, the former in the Southern and Central
districts of the Island, and the latter in the North. Mr. Alexander
Fry lent me for the occasion, a fine series of species sent by Mr.
Simson, and kindly presented me with examples of most of them.

Percosoma sulcipenne

Niger, nitidus; occipite transversim grosse punctato · thorace
cordato, antice minus rotundato-dilatato, angulis posticis subrectis · elytris oblongo-ovatis, humeris distinctis ibique et lateribus
margine explanato-incrassato, post medium leviter ampliatis,
apicem versim gradatim attenuatis ; supra striatis, striis versus
marginem et apicem latis, granulato-opacis. Long. 26–30
mm. ♂, ♀.

Similar in general form to *P. carenoides* (White), but thorax
much narrower, being less dilated immediately after the anterior
angles , the base is depressed in the same way, and the sides
parallel for a short distance preceding the nearly rectangular
hind angles; the depressed part is rugulose, and the sides have a
row of punctures bearing long setæ. The elytra are striated
throughout, the three striæ nearest the suture being finely impressed, the others deeper and broader, and towards the apex all
greatly widened and minutely granulate-opaque. The fifth stria,
near the base, has three large setiferous punctures. The head is
similar in form to that of *P. carenoides*, but the occiput bears a
transverse row of three large setiferous punctures on each side,
and the sulcus near the eyes is deeper ; the orbit behind the eyes
forms a tumour nearly as large as the eye itself.

Northern Tasmania (Atkinson). Coll. H. W. Bates.

Lychnus strangulatus.

Elongato-ovatus, supra sub-planatus, nigerrimus politus :
capite mox pone oculos sulco profundo lævi impresso ; foveis

C C

frontalibus extus curvatis, intus ramum brevem emittentibus : thorace cordato, antice vix rotundato-dilatato, post medium usque ad angulos posticos valde angustato, his rotundatis : elytris dorso planatis, striis vix conspicuis, interstitiis planissimis.

Femora antica ♂ subtus prope medium fortiter dilatata fere dentata ; ♀ ovata modice incrassata.　Long. 19–21 mm. ♂, ♀.

Agrees with Mr. Putzeys' description of his genus *Lychnus*; which, however, contains no mention of the remarkable constriction of the head behind the eyes.　The present species must nevertheless, be closely allied to *L. ater*.　In five examples ♂, I fail to detect any trace of punctuation in the striæ, and the latter are extremely faint, except near the apex, where they are more pronounced, owing to the elevation of the interstices. In one of the examples ♀, however, the striæ are distinctly punctured.

Central districts (Simson); North Tasmania (Atkinson).　Coll. A. Fry and H. W. Bates.

Lychnus striatulus.

L. strangulato simillimo, differt tantum statura minori elytrisque distinctius striatis interstitiis convexis.　Niger, minus nitidus ; elytris oblongo-ovatis, paullo angustioribus et supra minus planatis.　Long. 17 mm. ♂.

Differs from *L strangulatus* only in being smaller, proportionately narrower, and in the elytra being more distinctly striated, or rather the feebly or not at all incised striæ are separated by convex interstices　The striæ have no traces of punctuation.　In its narrower, more oblong and convex form it resembles the ♀ of *L strangulatus* more than the ♂ ; but both the specimens before me are clearly males, having the broad, sub-dentiform dilatation of the undersurface of the anterior tibiæ.

Central Tasmania (Simson)　Coll. A. Fry and H. W. Bates. Mr. Janson has a third example.

A third species of *Lychnus*, taken by Mr. Atkinson in Northern Tasmania, is convex and punctate-striate in both sexes.　This may possibly be the *L. ater* of Putzeys, if we may suppose that author to have overlooked the occipital strangulation.

MIROSARUS, n. gen.

(Sub-Fam. Anisodactylinæ)

G. '*Selenophoro* similis. Corpus oblongo-ovatum. Caput
antice obtusum ; foveis frontalibus parvis. Mentum fere eden-
tatum Ligula angusta, apice bisetosa, paraglossis eam superantibus, latis, auriculatis, ad ligulæ angulos superiores intus
conjunctis. Palpi apice modice attenuati, truncati. Elytra
interstitio tertio pluripunctato. Tarsi ♂, quatuor anteriores
articulis 4 dilatatis (2–4 late cordatis), plantis. squami-setis
erectis dense vestitis, scopam planam simulantibus.

Recent describers of Australian *Harpali*, following the example
of Dejean, have paid no attention to the shape and clothing of the
dilated tarsal joints of the males, and have consequently mingled
together in one genus the most diverse generic forms, belonging
even to distinct sub-families. The present very distinct genus
is common in all the temperate parts of the country, and many
closely allied species, races or varieties, have been described by
Castelnau and W. Macleay, Jun. They may be known at once
by their exact resemblance to the common American species of
Selenophorus. The emargination of the mentum has a scarcely
perceptible angular prominence in the middle and is sometimes
quite edentate.

Mirosarus insularis.

Nigro-cupreus, antennis basi, palpis (partim) tibiis et tarsis
fulvo-testaceis ; elytris ♂ nitidis, ♀ sub-opacis thorace transversim quadrato, lateribus arcuatis antice paullo magis quam
postice angustato, angulis posticis rotundatis, margine postico
medio late sinuato, basi utrinque coriaceo-punctato, foveis latis ;
margine laterali reflexo, rufescenti · elytris ante apicem sinuatis,
supra acute striatis, striolaque scutellari elongata, interstitiis
planis, 3, 5 et 7 versus apicem cæteris latioribus, tertio punctis
umbilicatis sex conspicuis Long. 9 mm.

The amount of pale colouring on the basal joints of the
antennæ and on the palpi is very variable, but the scape is
generally of a clearer red. The thorax is much broader than
long, and its sides are more arcuated than in allied species from
Continental Australia, the widest part being a little anterior to
the middle. The punctures of the third interstice are all
situated in the middle of the interstice, and not near the striæ
. South or Central Tasmania (Simson).

The species must be closely allied to the *Harpalus margini-collis*, of Castelnau, from Melbourne, but he gives only three lines as the size.

Hypharpax puncticauda.

Oblongus, fusco-cupreus ; antennis basi, palpis, tibiis et tarsis piceo-rufis, tibiis apice obscurioribus : thorace transverso, angulis obtusis fere rotundatis, lateribus leniter arcuatis, fovea basali utrinque oblongo, subfortiter impressa · elytris apice obtusis, ante apicem sinuatis, striatis, interstitiis usque ad apicem planis, tertii puncto supra declivitatem posteriorem sito.   ♂ Femora postica incrassata subtus haud dentata, tibiis flexuosis.   Long. 8 mm.

Allied to *H. æreus* (Dej.), but larger. Apparently also very near *H. Novæhollandiæ* (Castl), which is described as having the "tibiæ very strongly arched," but the author does not describe the form of the femora. He says the species is common near Melbourne, and a Melbourne *Hypharpax* common in collections has the femora distinctly dentate beneath. The tibiæ in that species would be correctly described as "strongly arched" ; but in *H. puncticauda* they are not arched, but flexuous, especially towards the apex   The colour of the present species is dull coppery, often with an æneous tinge. With regard to surface polish there appear to be two forms of ♂, in one of which the elytra are sericeous opaque (as usual in ♀ *Harpali*), and in the other more shining. The thorax is about equal in width at base and extremity, although the gentle arcuation of the sides seems to narrow the hind a·little more than the fore part. There is a very short scutellar striole. The situation of the elytral puncture near the apex is not an uncommon character in *Hypharpax*.

South or Central Tasmania (Simson).

THENAROTES, n. gen.

(Sub-Fam. ANISODACTYLINÆ.)

Gen. *Acupalpus* et *Bradycellus* forma et coloribus similis ; at tarsorum 4 anteriorum plantis 2–4 æqualiter, dense squamipilosis ut in *Anisodactylo*. Corpus elongatum subdepressum. Capite antice obtusum, sulcis frontalibus extus ad oculum curvatis. Palpi acuminati. Menti sinus medio dentatus.   ♂ Tarsi antici articulo primo lineari, vix dilatato, subtus nudo, 2–4 late cordatis (in tarsis intermediis angustioribus), plautis dense squami-pilosis.

Closely allied to *Lecanomerus* (Chaud.) from which it differs only in the lesser dilatation of the four anterior ♂ tarsi, and in the more elongate and flatter body, which gives the species quite a different facies. In *Lecanomerus* the first joint of the dilated male tarsi is not expanded like the 2–4th; but it is much shorter and less linear than in *Thenarotes* The *Lecanomeri* are shorter, more ovate and convex. Both genera are numerous in species in Australia, *Lecanomerus* extending also to New Zealand. *Lecanomerus marginatus* (Reed) of Chili, belongs to *Thenarotes* rather than to *Lecanomerus*.

Thenarotes Tasmanicus.

Bradycello Verbasci (Dufts) similis ; at paullo magis elongatus et depressus Rufo-testaccus, nitidus, antennis, palpis et pedibus pallidioribus ; elytris utrinque plaga elongata post medium nigra subiridescenti · thoracc cordato-quadrato, antice longe rotundato, postice paullo ante basin subsinuatim angustato, angulis posticis obtusis, margine basali utrinque obliquo, foveis basalibus latis grosse punctatis : elytris oblongis, fortiter striatis, absque striola scutellari, interstiitis convexis, tertio pone medium unipunctato. Long. 4½–5 mm.

South or Central Tasmania (Simson). In Mr. Janson's collection and my own.

Oopterus Tasmanicus.

Drimostoma ? Tasmanica, Castelnau, Notes on Austr. Col., Tr. Roy. Soc. Vict. ii, vol. 8, p. 199.

A small glossy insect, taken by Mr. Simson, with ovate, almost gibbous elytra, obsoletely striated, agrees very well with Castelnau's description. It has a pubescent third antennal joint and acuminate palpi, agreeing in these and in others respects with the genus *Oopterus*. The mandibles are long and slender, the forehead has two long straight furrows, and the thorax is deeply and broadly impressed on each side of the base, with a carina near the hind angle. The elytra at the apex have a strongly raised carina in the position of the seventh interstice, on the inner side of which is the trace of a recurved striole connected along the apex with the sutural stria. The second antennal joint is nearly as long as the third.

Trechus Diemenensis.

Sub-elongatus, depressus, thorace relative parvo, quadrato ; subtus piceo-rufo, ventro rufo-testaceo ; capite thoraceque rufocastaneis, elytris nigro-piceis, palpis et pedibus flavis, antennis rufo-testaceis ; thorace quadrato, antice leviter rotundato, postice paullulum sinuato-angustato, angulis posticis rectis, ibique margine explanato-reflexo, margine basali utrinque obliquo, foveis basalibus magnis, lævibus . elytris oblongo-ovatis, humeros versus haud angustatis, punctulato-striatis, disco utrinque bipunctato. Long. 5 mm.

South or Central Tasmania (Simson).

Similar in general shape to such species as *Tr. palpalis;* but the thorax is relatively smaller, and the explanated and reflexed lateral margins, especially towards the hind angles, amply distinguish it.

Rhabdotus floridus.

Elongato-oblongus, capite thoraceque supra viridi-æneis, elytris læte purpureis sericeo-nitentibus ; palpis rufis, gracilibus, articulis ultimis apice paullo attenuatis ; capite ovato, oculis haud prominulis : thorace quadrato, postice quam antice latiori, angulis posticis acutis : elytris oblongis, fere parallelis, apice valde obtuse rotundatis, supra striatis, interstitiis paullo convexis tertio post medium 2-4 punctato . corpore subtus, antennis pedibusque nigris, tibiis et tarsis rufescentibus. Long. 17–21 mm. ♂, ♀ .

Distinguished from *Rhabdotus reflexus* (Chaud.) by the rich uniform purple colour of the elytra ; similar in shape and in the striated upper surface of the tarsi and the form of the palpi. The eyes are encased behind by an orbit longer than themselves; the frontal furrows are broad, but not deeply incised. The thorax is nearly as long as broad, narrowed to the front and very gradually and slightly narrowed behind, with the hind angles acute ; the lateral rims are thick and the margins reflexed and explanated towards the hind angles ; the base is transversely depressed. Head and thorax are glossy, brassy-green. The elytra are very obtusely rounded at the apex (most so in the ♀) and the margin is but slightly sinuate before the apex ; the striæ are moderately sharply impressed. In certain lights the rich purple colour changes into golden.

(Atkinson).

Notonomus tubericauda.

N. politulo (Chaud), affinis, elongatus, niger politus; thorace fere quadrato, angulis posticis subrectis; elytris apice distincte sinuatis, humeris haud dentatis, supra foititer,. simpliciter striatis, interstitiis prope apicem angustioribus, tertio excepto dilatato et in ♀ valde tuberoso Long. 16 mm.

Glossy-black, without iridescence ; palpi, terminal joint of the antennæ and tarsi pitchy-red. Head oval, eyes scarcely prominent and encased behind in an orbit one half their size ; frontal sulci shallow, rest of head smooth. Thorax nearly quadrate, rather broader than long, sides slightly rounded near the middle, thence nearly straight to the hind angles which are obtuse though distinct ; surface polished, smooth, basal fovea on each side long and moderately deep, Elytra oblong in ♂ with sides slightly rounded, more ovate in ♀ with sides strongly rounded , distinctly sinuate near the apex, humeral fold arcuated and not projecting at the shoulder ; striæ deep and interstices nearly plane, but becoming much deeper, with interstices narrower towards the apex ; the third interstice has two large punctures, the posterior of which (near the apex), is the centre of a dilatation, slightly elevated in the ♂ , but raised into a prominent tubercle in the ♀ .

South or Central Tasmania (Simson).

Mr. Simson had ticketed the males and females as separate species.

Lestignathus Simsoni.

L. cursori (Erichs.) multo minor. Elongato-ovatus, gracilis, antennis palpis pedibusque plus minusve rufo-piceis ; capite angusto, oculis prominulis : thorace quadrato, antice modice rotundato, post medium leviter angustato ; angulis posticis rotundatis : elytris oblongo-ovatis, mox pone humeros leviter rotundato-dilatatis, medio iterum paullulum contractis, apicem versus longe sinuatim-angustatis, apice productis juxta suturam rotundatis; supra acute striatis, interstitiis planis, tertio 3-punctato. Long. 11 mm

Differs from *L. cursor*, besides its very much smaller size, by the shape of its head, due to the greater roundness and prominence of the eyes. The mandibles also are longer and more slender, and the inner dentiform prominence before the apex is smaller and sharper. The thorax is of the same shape, but rather shorter; as in *L. cursor*, it is quadrate, gently rounded, the greatest width being a little before the middle, and posteriorly slightly sinuate and narrowed to the rounded hind angles. The elytra are conspicuously sinuated towards the apex, and the latter is produced (although rounded near the sutural angle); in *L. cursor*, there is no trace of this peculiar formation.

South or Central Tasmania (Mr. Simson)　Coll. A. Fry and H. W. Bates.

The genus *Zargus*, Wollaston, Insecta Maderensia, p. 31 (1854) is closely allied to, if not identical with, *Lestignathus*, Er. (1842).

Scopodes Tasmanicus.

Oblongus, omnino niger, elytris fortissime sericeo-micantibus ; labro antice triangulariter valde producto, apice obtuso, convexo, laevi : capite supra minus recte striolato : thorace valde transverso, quadrato, angulis anticis rotundatis, posticis obtusis, marginibus anticis et posticis medio paullo rotundatis, lateralibus medio sinuatis ; supra subtiliter transversim striolato · elytris oblongis, humeris distincte sed obtuse angulatis, apice leviter sinuatim truncatis, supra laete undulato-sericeis utrinque 3 foveolatis, striis latis vage impressis. Long. 6 mm.

A large, oblong, rather parallel-sided species, distinguished from all others known to me by the broad and short, quadrate thorax. The eyes are very large and protuberant ; the labrum strongly advanced in the middle, the obtuse point reaching beyond the mandibles when closed. The thorax equals in width the head (with the eyes), and is but slightly narrowed behind. The anterior margin (like the posterior) is a little arcuated forward in the middle ; the anterior angles are rounded, the lateral margin before the middle gradually and very slightly sinuated, the hind angles being distinct but obtuse and reflexed. The whole insect is deep black, brightly shining beneath, and extremely lustrous or satiny on the elytra.

Generally distributed (Simson, Atkinson).

Mr. Simson has sent also a single example of the apparently rare *Scopodes boops* (Erichson).

DIABATICUS, n. gen.

Gen. *Pinacoderae* similis et affinis, sed tarsis Gen. *Plochioni* et capite Gen. *Xanthophaeae*. Corpus glabrum. Caput elonga-

tum, orbitu post-oculari rotundato-angustato, collo distincto.
Ligula bisetosa Palpı labiales ♂ securiformes, modice dilatatı.
Mentum sinu maxime dentato. Antennæ articulo 3io glabio.
Thorax margine postico late sed breviter lobato Elytra elongata
apice valde obtusa, vix truncata, interstitiis sparsim punctulatis, tertio bipunctato. Tarsi supra glabri, depressi, articulo
4to breviter emarginato, 5to basin versus haud gradatim atten-
uato ; ungues fortiter denticulatæ; ♂ anterioıes articulis tribus,
intermedii articulis duobus, subtus biseriatim squamulatis.

A genus formed for the reception of *Plochionus australis*
(Erichson) ; which Baıon Chaudon, apparently not having seen
in naturâ, placed doubtfully as a synonym to his *Xanthophœa
picipennis ;* but which has none of the distinctive characters of
the group to which *Xanthophœa* belongs ; the ligula being
bisetose, and the tarsi glabrous above &c. The position of the
genus seems to be near the American group *Pinacodera*, and
Eıichson's species has, in fact, gıeat ıesemblance to *P. punctigera.* The tarsi are, however, flattened and broadened as
in *Plochionus pallens*, and the form. of the head is that of
Xanthophœa.

Diabaticus australis.

Plochionus id., Erichson, Beitr., Insectenfauna v. Vandiem.,
p. 124.
South or Central Tasmania (Simson). Coll. A. Fry and
H. W. Bates.

In addition to the above, the following previously described
species have been sent to England by Messrs. Simson and
Atkinson :—

Scaraphites Macleayi, Westw.
Clivina ——— a species closely allied to *Cl. Austı alasıœ*
(Boh), probably a small form of ıt.
Promecoderus brunnicornis, Dej.
      ,,   *modestus*, Casteln.
      ,,   *ovicollis*, Casteln.
      ,,   *gibbosus*, Gray.
Percosoma carenoides, White.
Notonomus politulus, Chaud.
      ,,   *chalybeus*, Dej.
Cenctus coracinus, Erichs.

Hormochilus monochrous, Chaud.
Leptopodus sollicitus, Erichs.
Rhabdotus reflexus, Chaud.
Rhytisternus cyathoderus, Chaud.
Drimostoma ? *alpestris,* Castelu.
Simodontus elongatus, Chaud.
Dicrochile punctipennis, Castelu.
Lestignathus cursor, Erichs.
Cyclothorax ambiguus, Erichs.
Dyscolus dilatatus, Erichs.
Amblytelus curtus, Fab.
Homethes sericeus, Erichs.
Philophlœus australis, Dej.
Agonochila corticalis, Chaud.
    „   *binotata,* Chaud.
    „   *biguttata,* Chaud.
Sarothrocreps corticalis, F.
Xanthophœa infuscata, Chaud.
Sphallomorpha decipiens, Westw.
Adelotopus hæmorrhoidalis, Erichs.
Scopodes boops, Erichs.

Description of a new species of PTILIUM, *discovered by Mr. Aug. Simson, in Tasmania;* by the Rev. A. MATTHEWS, M.A.

The beautiful insects described in this paper were found by Mr. Aug. Simson, of Brighton, Tasmania, already known as the discoverer of *Amblyopinus Jansoni.* They belong to the first section of the genus *Ptilium,* which has hitherto only contained the rare and elegant species, *Pt. angulicolle* and *Pt. Halidaii;* from both of these the present species may be known by the extraordinary sculpture of the thorax, which is traversed in nearly straight lines by distinct. rows of minute rings, touching each other at their sides, so as to present the appearance of chains. Two specimens only were found by Mr. Simson, and forwarded to Mr. Janson, who very kindly presented them to me.

Ptilium Simsoni, n. sp.

L.c. $\frac{5-6}{16}$ lin. = ·63–·75 mm. Oblongo-ovale, læte castaneum nitidum pilis aureis vestitum; capite magno oculis magnis haud prominentibus; pronoto sat magno postice constricto, annulis impressis, ordinibus transversis sat remotis catenulatim dispositis elegantissime exsculpto, depressione magnâ ovali divergente basim versus utrinque in disco notato; elytris modicis ovalibus profunde asperatis, apice valde rotundato; pygidio sat longe exserto; pedibus atque antennis flavis.

Caput sat magnum triangulare antice rotundatum, foveis magnis umbilicatis interstitiisque nitidis ornatum. Oculi magni haud prominentes. Antennæ sat longæ robustæ læte flavæ.

Pronotum modicum, capite paulum longius vix latius, ad medium latissimum, lateribus antice rotundatis postice leviter constrictis, foveis magnis profundis umbilicatis, sive annulis parvis, ordinibus transversis sat remotis catenulatim dispositis, interstitiisque glabris nitidis ornatum, impressione longitudinali latâ profundâ antice divergente, e basi usque ad medium extensâ, utrinque in disco notatum, margine basali leviter rotundatâ leviter reflexâ, angulis fere rectis.

Scutellum modicum triangulare profunde punctatum.

Elytra integra translucida ovata ad media latissima, capite atque pronoto longiora et paulum latiora, ordinibus distinctis sinuatis tranversis modice asperata, apice lato rotundato dilutiori.

Alæ amplæ sub elytris visæ

Abdomen pygidio solo exserto.

Pedes robusti læte flavi.

Subtus castaneum ventris segmentis ultimis dilutioribus.

Differt hæc species pulcherrima ab omnibus sculpturâ eximiâ.

Habitat Tasmaniam exemplis duobus a D° Simson captis.

Description of Twenty-five new species of Cicindelidæ ; by H. W. Bates, F.L.S.

Cicindela Millingeni.

C. quadrilineatæ (F.), proxime affinis ; magis elongata, lateribus parallelis. Aurato viridis, epistomate et fronte læte violaceis, elytris albis, sutura et vitta angusta discoidali olivaceis, vitta basin longe haud attingenti, ante apicem cum sutura linea angusta interrupta connexa · labro brevissimo, verticaliter arcuato, medio haud abrupte convexo, margine recto, tridentato . thorace recte quadrato, pleuris dense albopilosis. antennis basi, pedibus corporeque subtus læte viridibus, hoc lateribus dense albopilosis Long. 8 lin. ♀.

Bushire, Persian Gulf. Dr. C. Millingen.

Cicindela phosphora.

Elongata, convexa, lateribus parallelis ; elytris purpureis velutino-opacis, vitta intra-marginali (paulo post medium terminata), guttaque marginali ante apicem albis · capite et thorace olivaceo-æneis alutaceo-opacis, hoc lateribus medio fere rectis, juxta basin et apicem rotundato-angustato ; fronte omnino subtiliter strigoso, collo crasso, oculis modice prominulis labro (♂) medio rotundato-producto obtuse tridentato ; palpis maxillaribus piceis . corpore subtus cyaneo, nudo ; pedibus cupreis, tarsis cyaneis. Long. 6 lin. ♂.

Mexico. From M. J. Thomson's coll., ticketed with the M.S. name here adopted.

Cicindela Rutherfordi.

C. nitidulæ, Dej., formâ simillima, at differt colore obscuro, elytrisque ♀ nigris signaturis obsoletis Elongata, angusta, capite thoraceque obscure viridi-æneis · elytris ♂ olivaceo-nigris, margine toto, macula subscutellari, linea elongata obliqua e lunula humerali, altera ascendenti curvata e lunula apicali (apice libera) fasciaque valde flexuosa mediana albis ; ♀ fere nigris marginibus cyaneis, signaturis indistinctis vel nullis, macula. humerali et apicali exceptis corpore subtus pedibusque auratis,

lateribus dense albotomentosis, trochanteribus viridi-æneis.
Long. 4½–5 lin. ♂, ♀.

Cameroons. Collected by Mr. D. G. Rutherford.

Cicindela graphica.

C. *interstinctæ* (Schonh.) valde affinis vel ejusdem var. geographica; colore obscuriori, signaturis albis nec fulvis; elytrorum
lunulâ apicali distinctius formata, interrupta, parte superiori
majori triangulari haud fasciam cum guttula suturali efficienti.
Purpureo-fusca interdum fere nigra, subtus cyanea lateribus
cupreis, pedibusque violaceis: elytris lunula angusta humerali,
altera latiori interrupta apicali, guttulis utrinque quatuor et fascia
angusta (utrinque hamata) mediana albis   Long. ♂ ♀ 8 lin.

Angola. Collected by Mr. Rogers.

Cincindela gabonica.

C. *interstinctæ* (Schonh.) affinis.   Capite et thorace rubro-
cupreis; elytris viridi-fuscis, signaturis omnibus fulvis latis,
scilicet.—lunula breviori lata humerali, fasciis duabus macu-
laribus, altera mediana altera subapicali, maculaque apicali
fulvis: corpore subtus aurato-viridi, lateribus femoribus purpureo-cupreis, tibiis et tarsis cyaneis.   Labro medio apice
abrupte producto ♀ valde ♂ brevius tridentato. Long. 10 lin.
♂, ♀.

R. Ogowé, Gaboon.   Collected by Mr. R. B. N. Walker
Very distinct from C. *interstincta* by the form of the labrum.

Cicindela olivia.

C. *opigraphæ*, Dej, forma similis at elytris magis parallelis,
guttulisque discoidalibus albis.   Elongata, thorace angusta,
elytris passim granulosis, obscure olivaceis, lunulis basi et apice
maculisque duabus marginalibus ut in C. *opigrapha*, sed guttulis
duabus discoidalibus, prima ante secunda post medium · capite
thoraceque nigro-viridibus opacis, hoc griseo piloso; labro ♂
albo, margine antico flexuosa, medio producto unidentato; palpis
gracilibus viridi-æneis, labialium articulo penultimo flavo:
corpore subtus pedibusque cyaneis, illo lateribus longe albo-
piloso, femoribus auratis.   Long. 5½ lin. ♂.

Chamusuri and Moradabad, India.   Three examples from
Judge Benson's collection.

Cicindela Monteiroi.

C. catenæ (F.) affinis. Capite et thorace cupreis, hoc toto et illo postice albo-incumbenti-piloso, labro albo, antice producto acute spinoso: elytris fere nigris, margine (basali incluso), vittula subscutellari, fasciaque obliqua mediana vix flexuosa albis: corpore subtus medio cyaneo, genibus (sub oculos) nudis striatis, prothoracis episternis violaceis, nudis, cæteris albo-tomentosis: pedibus viridi-æneis, femoribus subtus violaceis. Variat elytris guttula alba subsuturali ante medium. Long. 5½ lin. ♂, ♀.

Delagoa Bay. Sent home in some numbers by the late Mr. J. J. Monteiro.

Cicindela cabinda.

C. leucopteræ (Dej.) formâ similis, sed major, et signaturæ fere ut in *C. nitidula* (Dej.) Viridi-ænea, fronte, antennarum-que basi plus minusve rufo-auratis, corpore subtus pedibusque læte viridi-æneis, elytris punctatis viridi-sericeis, margine, sutura, macula subscutellari, linea elongata obliqua e lunula humerali, altera ascendenti curvata e lunula apicali, fasciaque mediana valde flexuosa albis. ♂ Thorace quadrato, elytris versus apicem angustatis. ♀ Thorace trapezoidali, angulis posticis paulo lobatis; elytris ante medium rotundato-dilatatis, ibique margine anguste explanatis, versus apicem valde recte oblique angustatis. Long. 4½ lin. ♂, ♀.

Landana (Loango). From Dr. Uhson More; many examples mixed with *C. nitidula* (Dej.)

The curved line in prolongation of the apical lunule does not (except in rare albino examples) reach the white margin, as it does in *C. nitidula, nilotica,* and others

Cicindela ovas.

C cabindæ (v. supra) formâ utriusque sexus eâdem; differt solum elytrorum signaturis albis latioribus, linea curvata e lunula apicali cum margine connexa. Long. 5 lin

Madagascar; liable to be confounded with *C. nilotica,* from which it differs in the form of the thorax and the elytra, especially in the ♂. I have no doubt it is the species indicated under the name of *C. owas* in the Cat. Cic. of M. de Chaudoir.

Cicindela Balucha.

C chiloleucæ (Fisch.) affinis, sed multo brevior coloreque obscuriori. Purpureo-fusca, elytris sub-ovatis versus basin angustatis, lunula humerali et apicali (hoc cornu anterior clavato) fasciaque mediana valde flexuosa, dilacerata, flavis, (lunula humerali et fascia per marginem connexis) : capite fronte grosse striato, occipite granulato, cum thorace sparsim incumbenti-grisco-pilosis; labro (♀) ut in *C. chiloleuca* rotundato-producto, medio margine recto unidentato; antennis articulis 5–11, trochanteribus et tibiis (apice exceptis) obscure rufis; pectore viridiæneo. Long 4 lin ♀.

Beloochistan.

Cicindela Swinhoei.

C. punctatissimæ (Schaum) affinis, differt colore obscuriori, thoracisque angulis utroque sexu multo magis productis. Viridi-ænea, elytris obscurioribus, his passim crebre punctulatis, margine laterali, vittula basali, fascia angusta mediana unicui vata per discum vittæ-formi continuata, lunulaque apicali, albis, interdum ♂ (an charact. sexuali?) vittula basali usque ad suturæ apicem prolongata · thorace ♂ trapeziformi, ♀ idem angulis posticis acute et valde productis : trochanteribus, tibiis tarsisque basi rufotestaceis Long. 5 lin.

Island of Formosa   Taken by the late Consul Swinhoe.

Cicindela filigera.

Parva, subcylindrica, læte cyanea, nitida, elytris violaceo-tinctis, utrinque post medium guttulis duabus a margine distantibus albis, trochanteribus palpisque (valde elongatis et tenuibus) flavis, his apice nigris, maxillarum lobis tenuissimis; labro ♂ brevi, margine antico fere recto, angulis solum dentatis; capite angustulo, striis juxta-ocularibus exceptis fere lævi, thorace angusto, lævi, fere ut in *C. elegans* (Dej.), elytris sparsim subgrosse punctatis; corpore subtus lateribus sparsim longe hirsuto. Long. 3½ lin. ♂.

Borneo.

Cicindela occulta.

Subcylindrica, fuliginosa vix cupreo-tincta, subtus cyanea, lateribus cupreis sparsim breviter hirsutis, pedibus testaceo-rufis, femoribus medio cupreis; palpis flavis apice nigris, labio ♂ semicirculari albo, antice flexuoso, medio breviter tridentato;

capite thoraceque intricato-strigosis illo juxta oculos grosse striatis; oculis modice prominulis; thorace subcylindrico, medio vix rotundato sulcis haud profundis: elytris supra paulo undulatis, sparsim punctulato-granulatis, utrinque apicem versus guttulis flavis tribus in triangulo dispositis, a margine remotis. Long. 3½ lin. ♂.

Tamatave, Madagascar.   Collected by F. Plant.

Cicindela azureocincta.

C. chloropleuræ (Chaud.) simillima.   Minor, tarsis 4 anterioribus utroque sexu sulcatis: labro viridi-æneo, medio producto valide tridentato: capite thoraceque cyaneis disco cupreo-auratis intricato-rugosis, illo vittis duabus frontalibus azureis, hoc angusto, lateribus vix rotundatis. elytris aurato-fuscis sericeoopacis, suturâ margineque laterali tridentato azureis nitidis, utrinque guttulis duabus posticis albis, margine granulatopunctulato, disco (versus basin excepto) lævi: corpore subtus violaceo, lateribus parce pilosis; trochanteribus et genubus subtus flavis; femoribus viridi-æneis tibiis et tarsis nigris obscuris   Long 4½ lin. ♂, ♀.

Bombay.

Euryoda anosignata.

Subnitida, supra medio fusco-cuprea lateribus læte æneoviridibus, subtus viridi-ænea, pedibus rufis, tarsis et tibiis anticis viridi-auratis; palpis flavis apice nigris; labro ♂ acute 5 dentato, medio subcarinato-convexo, albo; capite inter oculos eleganter strigoso, thorace angusto, convexo, transversim striguloso; elytris apice suturali acute spinosis, supra grosse confertim punctatis, prope apicem utrinque macula majori rotundata alteraque discoidali minute, flavis   Long. 6 lin. ♂.

Old Calabar.

Dromica simplex.

Supra nigra, lateribus cyaneis æneo marginatis, elytris vittula submarginali prope apicem alba; labro ♀ nigro macula mediana alba; thorace cylindrico transversim recte strigoso; elytris elongato-ovatis, humeris nullis, apice suturali valide spinoso, supra convexis discrete, confertim punctatis; corpore subtus femoribusque cyaneis.   Long. 6½ lin ♀.

Mozambique.

Belongs to the section *Cosmema*; elytra less densely punctured and much narrower and more attenuated anteriorly than in *D. citreoguttata* (Chaud.).

D D

Dromica albicinctella.

D lepidæ (Boh) similis, sed elytris discrete, haud confluenter, punctatis ; suturâ apice longe spinoso, vitta submarginali albo multo augustiori et ad basin continuata : viridi-fusco-aurata, sericeo-nitens , thorace subtiliter intricato-strigoso ; elytris discrete punctatis, punctis versus apicem rarioribus.   Long $5\frac{1}{2}$ lin ♂.

Trans-Vaal.

This is evidently the species which Baron Chaudoir (Rev. et Mag Zool Jan. 1864) mistook for *Dr. marginella* (Boh.); in which the labrum is black as Boheman truly described it.

Therates Everetti.

Th. basali (Dej.) affinis : ænescenti-niger, elytris testaceo-rufis, utrinque plaga magna oblonga post mediana nigra ; partibus oris, antennarum articulo basali, pedibusque flavis, metasterni medio abdomineque rufo-testaceis : elytris paulo ante medium tubercula discoidali, apicem truncatis, angulo suturali solum dentato, supra tantum in impressionibus basalibus sparsissime punctulatis. Long. 6 lin. ♂.

Mindanao, Philippines (Sent by Mr. Everett).

Therates punctipennis.

Th. dimidiata (Dej.) proxime affinis, ejusdem forte var geographica ; Cyaneus, elytris punctatis, apice longe spinosis, rufis fascia lata post medium (interdum fere obsoleta) ænea vel violacea ; corpore subtus, tarsis anticis posterioribusque apice, nigris ; partibus oris, antennarum articulo basali, coxis posticis intus abdomine et pedibus rufo-testaceis   Long. $5\frac{1}{2}$ lin. ♂, ♀.

N. W. Borneo ; many examples.

Therates versicolor.

Th acutipenni (Vanderl) similis, sed major, femoribus toto rufo-testaceis.   Major, violaceo- et viridi-æneo versicolor ; partibus oris, antennarum articulo basali, coxis posticis intus, abdomine et femoribus rufo-testaceis ; elytris disco lævibus, impressionibus basi punctatis, apice longe spinosis, macula humerali angusta (versus scutellum extensa) rufa. Long. $7\frac{1}{2}$ lin. ♂.

N. W. Borneo.

Therates Chennelli.

Parvus, angustus, nigro-nitidus, capite thoraceque subcyaneis, elytris vitta lata suturali in fasciam rectam medianam terminata, altera obliqua a humero fere usque ad suturam ducta, apiceque late flavo-testaceis; palpis antennarum articulo basali et pedibus albotestaceis, metasterni medio et abdomine pallidis; labio ♂ angusto, elongato, flavo nigro-marginato, margine antico dentibus acutis 6 lateribus utrinque 1 majori: elytris umbone basali excepto vix inæqualibus, grossissime sparsim punctatis, apice usque ad suturam rotundatis nec sinuatis. Long. 3½ lin. ♂.

Naga Hills, 2,000 feet. Taken by Mr. A. W. Chennell.

Therates princeps.

Th. spectabili (Schaum) affinis. Nigro-æneus, politissimus, purpureo-tinctus, elytris macula magna humerali, altera apicali, fascia lata obliqua mediana, abdomine et pedibus aurantiaco-fulvis, labro palpis femoribusque flavis; elytris apice productis et spina utrinque longissima armatis, supra valde inæqualibus, basi acute sparsim granulatis. Long 7 lin. ♂, ♀.

N.W. Borneo.

Collyris Andamana.

C. crassicorni (Dej) affinis, sed major antennarumque articulo 5 longiori et graciliori. Saturate cærulea vel violacea, femoribus testaceo-rufis thorace quam in *C. crassicorni* postice minus incrassato, magis conico, antice abrupte angustato, supra fortius transversim strigoso · elytris cylindricis, grosse subconfluenter punctatis, punctis apicem versus elongatis Palporum labialium stipite medio testaceo-rufo. Long 9 lin. ♀.

Andaman Islands. Two ♀.

Collyris rhodopus

C. saphyrinæ affinis, antennarum formâ simili. Supra æneo-purpurea, subtus violacea, pedibus (tarsis apice nigris exceptis) rufis purpureo-tinctis; antennis fulvo-rufis apice infuscatis, articulis duobus basalibus cyaneis; palpis rufis, apice cyaneis; capite inter oculos concavo, sulcis vage haud profunde incisis; pone oculos modice rotundato-inflato; thorace postice elongato-conico, prope basim vix strangulato, supra forte strigoso; elytris postice gradatim dilatatis, apice versus suturam late sinuatis, passim discrete punctatis, punctis medio parum transversim confluentibus ibique fascia indistincta rufescenti. Long. 9½ lin. ♀.

North Borneo.

Collyris rubens.

C *Sarawakensi* (Thoms.) affinis et similis. Castaneo-rufa, antennis, capite, pectore, tibiis et tarsis æneo-nigris · capite inter oculos late excavato, sulcis frontalibus curtis vix incisis, interstitio anguste convexo; thorace postice conico, strigoso, ante medium constricto, deinde ante apicem convexo, tumido ; elytris basi et apice sparsim grosse punctatis, medio grossissime transversim rugosis, ibique cyaneo-tinctis. Long. 8½ lin.

♂ Tibiis posticis apice et tarsis fulvis.

Assam, plains. Taken by Mr. A. W. Chennell.

On various genera of the Homopterous family MEMBRACIDÆ, *with
descriptions of new species, and a new genus in the collection
of the British Museum*; by ARTHUR GARDINER BUTLER,
F.L.S., F.Z.S., &c.

In this, my second paper on the *Membracidæ*, I have given an
enumeration of the species referable to the following genera of
*Darninæ—Darnis, Ochrolomia, Stictopelta, Leptosticta, Hebetica
Cryptoptera, Dectonura, Alcmeone, Hyphinoe, Aconophora,
Eumela, Combophora, Omolon, Nassunia, Rhexia, Heteronotus,*
and *Heniconotus*; and, with the exception of *Eumela, Combophora, and Nassunia,* have given references to the original
descriptions and figures of the species.

As usual, I have been very careful to examine into the
synonymy of each species for myself, and I have been astonished
at the number of careless blunders which one author has copied
from another down to the present time.

Family MEMBRACIDÆ.

Sub-Family DARNINÆ (Darnida, *Stal*).

DARNIS, *Fabricius.*

1. *Darnis lateralis.*

Darnis lateralis, Fabr., Syst. Rhyng. p. 27, 6 (1803).
Brazil. Brit. Mus.

2. *Darnis trifasciata.*

Darnis trifasciata, Fabr., Syst. Rhyng. p. 28, 7 (1803).
Darnis bifasciata, Amyot and Serville, Hist. Hemipt. p. 545,
2; pl. 11, fig. 7 (1843).
Darnis capistrata, Burm., Silb. Revue Ent. iv, p. 171, 7
(1836).
Tapajos (Bates). Brit. Mus.

3. *Darnis disrupta.*

Darnis disrupta, Walker, Ins. Saund. p. 74 (1858).
Amazons. Type Brit. Mus.

4. *Darnis partita.*

Darnis partita, Walker, Ins. Saund. p. 75 (1858).
Amazons. Type Brit. Mus.

5. *Darnis prasina.*

Darnis prasina, Fairm., Ann. Ent. Sér. 2, iv, p. 482, 14
(1846).
Darnis infixa, Walker, List Homopt. Suppl. p. 149 (1858).
Venezuela (Birschell). Type Brit. Mus.

OCHROLOMIA, *Stal.*

1. *Ochrolomia suturalis.*

Darnis suturalis, Germar, Silb. Revue Ent. iii, p. 250, 2
(1835).
Darnis trifasciata, Burm., Silb. Revue Ent. iv, p. 171, 5
(1836).
Brazil. Brit. Mus.

2. *Ochrolomia tricincta.*

Darnis tricincta, Burm., Silb. Revue Ent. iv, p. 172, 6
(1836).
Brazil.

3. *Ochrolomia incerta.*

Darnis incerta, Walker, List Homopt. Suppl. p. 149 (1858).
Mexico (Sallé). Type Brit. Mus.

4. *Ochrolomia virescens,* n. sp. Pl. VII, f. 3.

Closely allied to *O. incerta,* but greenish testaceous, the pronotum more depressed, terminally much more acuminate, with
its lateral or inferior margins much straighter (less convex); the
punctuation slightly deeper and denser; anterior margin of the
head much less convex. Length 8, width at humeral angles 4,
expanse of tegmina 16 mm.

Rio Janeiro (A. Fry). Type Brit. Mus.

5. *Ochrolomia zonifera*, n. sp   Pl VII, f. 2.

Form of *O. incerta*, but brownish olivaceous, the and head the anterior portion of the pronotum reddish castaneous , lateral margins almost to the apex, a broad triangular or pyramidal sinuated patch on each side, the two almost uniting in the centre of the dorsum so as to form an interrupted belt, and a broad V shaped zone across the posterior portion, creamy-yellowish bordered with black ; punctuation considerably finer than in the two preceding species.   Length 7½, width at humeral angles, 4 mm.

Mexico (ex Coll. Saunders).   Type Brit Mus

Darnis elegantula, Perty (not quoted by Walker), seems to be referable to this genus

6. *Ochrolomia elegantula*.

Darnis elegantula, Perty, Delect. Anim. pl. 35, fig. 11 (1830–34).
Brazil.

STICTOPELTA, *Stal.*

1. *Stictopelta affinis*

Darnis affinis, Guérin, Icon. Règne Anim. texte p. 364, Ins. pl. 59, fig. 2 (1829–44).
Darnis transversalis, Walker, List Homopt. Suppl. p. 148 (1858).
Mexico (Sallé).   Walker's type, Brit. Mus

2. *Stictopelta polita*, n. sp.   Pl. VII, f. 1.

Shining black ; head fulvous, with two central triangular spots surrounding the posterior ocelli, a spot on each side close to the eyes, and a slender bisinuated marginal line at the back, black ; humeral margin of the pronotum and a broad lateral marginal fusiform patch yellow; tegmina red-brown ; under surface of body black ; coxæ black, femora black with a round spot below and the knees fulvous; tibiæ and tarsi mahogany red. Length 9, width at humeral angles 5 mm.

Ega (Bates)   Type Brit. Mus.

Allied to the preceding species but larger, much more shining, more finely punctured, the pronotum black instead of piceous, not spotted in front, the head spotted with black, the legs altogether differently coloured

3. *Stictopelta bipunctata.*

Darnis bipunctata, Burm , Silb Revue Ent. iv, p. 171, 4 (1836).
Mexico (ex Coll. Saunders). Brit. Mus.

4. *Stictopelta adusta.*

Darnis adusta, Burm., Silb. Revue Ent. iv, p. 170, 2 (1836).
Mexico, Oaxaca (Sallé). Brit. Mus.

5. *Stictopelta strigifrons.*

Darnis strigifrons, Fairm., Ann. Ent Sér. 2, iv, p. 481, 8 (1846).
Mexico.

6. *Stictopelta ? cruenta*

Darnis cruenta, Burm., Silb Revue Ent iv, p. 173, 8 (1836).
Brazil.

7. *Stictopelta præcox.*

Darnis præcox, Burm , Silb Revue Ent. iv, p. 173, 9 (1836).
Peru (ex Coll. Saunders). Brit. Mus

8. *Stictopelta indeterminata.*

Darnis indeterminata, Walker, List. Homopt Suppl. p. 148 (1858)
Santarem (Bates). Type Brit. Mus.

9. *Stictopelta fraterna,* n. sp.

Bright reddish fulvous, gradually changing into greenish-yellow at the back and sides of the pronotum, the lateral margins bright sulphur-yellow : in form as well as in colour much like the preceding species, but differing in its somewhat less prominent humeral angles, the pronotum even more finely granulose punctate, much more abruptly acuminate at the tip, which is black, not speckled with whitish ; and not clothed with hair, as in *D. indeterminata*; the legs not banded with piceous. Length 9, width at humeral angles 4 mm.

Mexico, Oaxaca (Sallé), Peru (ex Coll. Saunders). Type Brit. Mus

The Peruvian example only differs from the Mexican one in being slightly brighter in colour.

10. *Stictopelta squarus.*

Darnis squarus, Fairm. Ann. Ent. Sér. 2, iv, p. 482, 15 (1846).
Darnis robusta, Walker, List Homopt. ii, p. 579, n. 25 (1851).
Pará (Wallace)   Walker's Type, Brit Mus.

LEPTOSTICTA, *Stal.*

1. *Leptosticta flaviceps.*

Darnis flaviceps, Burm., Silb. Revue Ent. iv, p. 169, 1 (1836).
var. *Darnis limbata,* Burm. l c. p. 173, 10 (1836)
Constancia and Tejuca (H Clark).   Brit Mus.

2 *Leptosticta latilinea*

Darnis latilinea, Walker, List Homopt Suppl. p. 147 (1858).
Constancia (H. Clark)   Type Brit Mus

Although similar in general coloration to *Stictopelta affinis* this species seems to me to be structurally closer to the preceding.

3. *Leptosticta? cyclops.*

Darnis cyclops, Fairm., Ann. Ent. Ser. 2, iv, p. 479, 1 (1846).
Columbia.

HEBETICA, *Stal*

1. *Hebetica convoluta.*

Membracis convoluta, Fabr., Ent. Syst. iv, p. 15, 28 (1794)
Membracis flavicincta, Germar, Mag Ent. iv, p 12, 2 (1821).
Membracis atrmaria, Germar, l c. 3 (1821).
Constancia and Tejuca (H Clark)   Brit. Mus.

The type is still in the Banksian Cabinet in the British Museum.

2. *Hebetica cuneata,* n. sp.   Pl VII, f. 4.

Coloration of the preceding, but without the lateral yellow border to the pronotum ; punctuation much coarser, humeral angles decidedly more acute; pronotum longer, more tapering, with the apex usually slightly curved upwards. Length 17, width at humeral angles 6 mm

Constancia (H. Clark)   Type Brit. Mus

We have three examples of this species, one of which has the apex of the pronotum straight.

3   *Hebetica apicalis.*

Darnis apicalis, Fairm., Ann, Ent. Sér. 2, iv, p 483, 23 (1846).

Brazil.

4. *Hebetica limacodes.*

Darnis limacodes, Burm., Silb. Revue iv, p. 175, 12, pl. 36, figs. 13–16 (1836).

Tejuca (H. Clark).   Brit. Mus

CRYPTOPTERA, *Stal.*

1. *Cryptoptera olivacea.*

Darnis olivacea, Fabr., Syst. Rhyn. p. 28, 8 (1803).
Constancia (H. Clark).   Brit. Mus.

2. *Cryptoptera acutula.*

Darnis acutula, Fairm., Ann. Ent. Sér. 2, iv, p. 481, 13 (1846).
Brazil.   Brit. Mus.

3 *Cryptoptera brevis.*

Darnis brevis, Fairm., Ann Ent. Sér. 2, iv, p 483, 18 (1846).
Mexico (Sallé).

The groups adopted above were characterized as sub-genera of *Darnis*, but since Stal has given good distinctive structural characters I prefer to regard them as genera.

DECTONURA, n. gen.

Pronotum, when viewed laterally, similar to *Hebetica*; but, seen from above, with a central longitudinal carina gradually increasing in distinctness from the middle to the apex, the latter broad, truncated, depressed, terminally bisinuate-tridentate. Type *D latcauda*.

Dectonura laticauda. Pl. VII, f. 21.

Darnis laticauda, Fairm., Ann. Ent Sér 2, iv, p. 483, 22 (1846).
Constancia (H. Clark) Brit. Mus.

The *Darnis lineola*, of Walker, appears to be a new genus allied to *Tomogonia*, of Stal ; *D. bistriga*, a species of *Rhexia*; *D. tripartita* and *D. stupida*, so far as I can judge from Fairmaire's figure of *H ursus*, are referable to *Hyphcus* of Stal.

The old genus *Hemiptycha* has been split up by Stal as follows:—1.*Proterpia*, type *H. rotundicornis*, Fairm.; 2.*Enalthe*, type *H. lævigata*, F. ; 3. *Bubalopa*, type *H. furcata*, F.; 4. *Hemiptycha*, typical; 5.*Pyranthe*, type *II. flava*, F.; 6.*Alcmeone** type *II. centrotoides*; 7.*Hyphinoe*, type *II cuneata*, Germ.; I shall enumerate here the species referable to the two last groups in which the Collection of the British Museum is rich.

ALCMEONE, *Stal.*

1. *Alcmeone lata.*

Hemiptycha lata, Walker, List Homopt. ii, p. 571, 18. (1851).
Hab. —? Type Brit Mus

2. *Alcmeone picea.*

Hemiptycha picea, Fairm., Ann Ent. Sér. 2, iv, p. 316, 13 (1846).
Brazil. Brit Mus.

Erroneously referred to *Pyranthe* by Dr. Stal , it is nearly allied to *A centrotoides*

---

* *Nassunia*, Stal, is more nearly allied to this genus than to typical *Hemiptycha*

3. *Alcmeone centrotoides.*

Hemiptycha centrotoides, Fairm., Ann. Ent , Sér. 2, iv, p. 317, 14 (1846).

Hab. —? Brit. Mus.

4. *Alcmeone brevis.*

Hemiptycha brevis, Walker, List Homopt. ii, p. 571, 19 (1851).

Hab. —? Type Brit. Mus

5. *Alcmeone curvicornis.*

Alcmeone curvicornis, Stal, Ofv. Vetensk. Akad. Foih. 1869, p. 256, n. 2.

Cayenne.

In colouring this species seems only to differ from *A. centrotoides* in the pale lateral margins of the posterior process

6. *Alcmeone caseoscalpris,* n. sp

Form of *A brevis,* but larger, the humeral horns longer, the centre of the pronotum less swollen with a more gradual transition into the terminal process ; bright mahogany red, the head and front of thorax spotted with yellow, pronotum with a broad lateral submarginal streak ; tips of humeral horns and terminal process black ; tegmina pale horn yellow, the veins and an apical spot slightly darker.   Length of pronotum 11, width at humeral horns 10 ; length of single tegmen 11 mm

Hab. —? Type Brit. Mus

This is the *Hemiptycha centrotoides* of Walker's List ; but it differs from that species not only in colour but in structure, the front margin of the pronotum being regularly convex and the humeral horns perfectly continuous with it, so that; instead of being slightly inclined upwards, they take a downward curve.

HYPHINOE, *Stal*

1. *Hyphinoë camelus.*

Darnis camelus, Gray in Griff. Anim. Kingd., Ins. ii, p. 260 ; pl. 109, 3 (1832).

♂*Hemiptycha camelus*, Fairm., Ann. Ent. Sér 2, ıv, p. 319, 21 ; pl. 6, fig. 21 (1846).
♂*Hemiptycha sagata*, Germar, Sılb Revue 3, p. 245, 2 (1835).
♂*Triquetra valıda*, Walker, Lıst Homopt. 2, p. 524, 16 (1851).
Thelıa oblıqua, Walker, Ins. Saunders p. 73 (1858).
Mexico. Walker's types, Bıit. Mus.

2. ♂*Hyphınoe vıridissıma.*

♀ *Hemiptycha vıridissıma*, Walker, List Homopt. 2, p. 572, 21 (1851).
Mexico (Glennie, &c.) Type Bıit. Mus.

Dr. Stal has sunk this as a synonym of the preceding on the authorıty of Walker (List Homopt. Suppl. p. 146), but, as I think, wrongly ; we have three examples of each form and *II. vırıdissıma* not only differs in size and colour, being much larger and greener than *II. camelus,* but it has considerably longer tegmına, ıs far more coarsely punctured, has the front margin of the pronotum bracket-shaped (⌒⌒), the humeral horns prominent, and the posterior process longer.

3 ♂*Hyphinoe globiceps.*

♂ *Hemiptycha globıceps*, Fairm., Ann Ent. Sér. 2, iv, p. 319, 21 ; pl. 6, fig 19 (1846).
♀ ♂*Hemiptyᴄha cuneata*, Fairm , l c , 23; pl. 6, fig. 26 (1846)
Mexıco (Sallé) Brıt Mus.

The females of this species are more like that sex of *II. camelus* than are examples of the precedıng spocies.

4. ♂*Hyphinoe placıda.*

♂*Hemiptycha placida*, Germar, Silb. Revue 3, p. 246, 4 (1835).
Rıo Janeıro (A. Fry). Bıit. Mus.

Erroneously referred by Dr. Stal to hıs genus ♂*Pyranthe.*

5. ♂*Hyphınoe bıgutta.*

♂ *Hemiptycha bıgutta*, Walker, List Homopt. Suppl p. 142 (1858).
Guatemala (Scherzer). Type Brit. Mus.

6. *Hyphinoe diabolica,* n. sp.

♀ Piceous, with slightly paler tegmina ; the head, humeral horns, a slender longitudinal dash just below the sub-dorsal impression of the pronotum, and the apex of the terminal process quite black ; densely and coarsely punctured, the anterior margin of the pronotum somewhat bracket shaped (less distinctly so than in *H. viridissima*); humeral horns rather prominent. Length of pronotum 13, width at humeral horns 9, length of tegmina 12 mm.

Hab. —? Type Brit. Mus.

In form this species is intermediate between *H. globiceps* and *H. viridissima.*

7. *Hyphinoe morio.*

Hyphinoe morio, Stäl, Ofv. Vetensk. Akad. Förh. 1869, p 257, 4.

Pacho, New Granada (Janson). Brit. Mus.

8. *Hyphinoe asphaltina.*

Hemiptycha asphaltina, Fairm., Ann. Ent. Sér. 2, iv, pl 6, fig. 20 (1846).

♂ *Hemiptycha apriformis,* Walker, List Homopt. Suppl. p 144 (1858).

♀ *Hemiptycha pubescens,* Walker, l.c. (1858)

Mexico (Sallé). Walker's types Brit. Mus.

This species differs from *H. morio,* just as *H. camelus* does from *H. viridissima.*

ACONOPHORA,* *Fairm.*

1. *Aconophora flavipes.*

Aconophora flavipes, Fairm., Ann. Ent. Sér. 2, iv, p. 294, 1 (1846).

Brazil (Children) Brit. Mus.

---

* Dr Stäl in his enumeration of the species of *Aconophora,* omits more than half the described forms

2. *Aconophora laminata.*

Aconophora laminata, Fairm., Ann. Ent Sér. 2, iv, p 295, 2 (1846).

Mexico, Oaxaca (Sallé) Brit Mus.

3. *Aconophora stabilis.*

Aconophora stabilis, Walker, List Homopt Suppl p. 135 (1858).

Mexico (Glennie). Type Brit. Mus.

4. *Aconophora mexicana.*

Aconophora mexicana, Stal, Stett. Ent. Zeit. 1864, p. 70, 427 ; Kongl. Svenska Vetensk. Akad. Handl. 8, 1, p. 35 (1869).

Mexico (ex Coll. Saunders), Guatemala (Salvin). Brit. Mus.

I think it very doubtful whether this is more than a variety of the preceding species.

5. *Aconophora spathata,* n. sp. Pl. VII, f. 16.

Colouring of *A. stabilis,* dull chocolate brown sprinkled with testaceous pubescence, but the thoracic horn blackish, more robust at the base and gradually decreasing in width to the apex, slightly more decumbent, anterior margin behind the head slightly concave and undulated, tegmina semi-transparent beyond the middle, reddish testaceous, clothed to the middle with testaceous pubescence, legs reddish-yellow, the tibiæ and tarsi clothed with pubescence, tibiæ with black marginal denticles; pronotum granuloso-punctate Length with tegmina 10, with horn, thorax and tegmina 14 ; width at humeral angles 4 mm

Brazil. Type Brit. Mus.

Most nearly allied to the succeeding species.

6. *Aconophora pubescens.*

Aconophora pubescens, Walker, Ins. Saund p 70 (1858). South America (ex Coll. Saunders). Type Brit. Mus.

7. *Aconophora cultellata.*

Aconophora cultellata, Walker, Ins. Saund. p. 70 (1858). Amazons (ex Coll. Saunders). Type Brit. Mus.

ɒ

8. *Aconophora marginata.*

Aconophora marginata, Walker, List Homopt ii, p 540, 16 (1851).
Aconophora gracilicornis, Stal, Kongl. Svenska Vetensk. Akad. Handl. 8, 1, p. 35 (1869).
Mexico (Argent, Glennie).   Type Brit. Mus.

9. *Aconophora æneosparsa,* n. sp.   Pl. VII, f. 14.

Structure of the preceding, excepting that the front of the head is slightly narrower, and that the whole exposed portion of the body, pronotum and tegmina is covered with brilliant brassy pubescence ; legs reddish-yellow, smooth, the tibiæ with black marginal denticles ; pronotum and head olivaceous, thoracic horn red-brown, tegmina testaceous hyaline, with two piceous spots near the middle of the inner margin   Length with tegmina 9 ; with horn, thorax and tegmina 12 ; width at humeral angles 3½ mm

Mexico, Volcano of Orizaba (Sallé).   Type Brit. Mus.

10. *Aconophora pugnax.*

Smilia pugnax, Germar, Silb. Revue 3, p. 239, 19 (1835).
Brazil.

11. *Aconophora gilvipes.*

Aconophora gilvipes, Stal, Kongl. Svenska, Vetensk. Akad. Handl. 8, 1, p. 35 (1869).
Rio Janeiro.   Sp ead? Mexico (ex Coll. Saunders).   Brit. Mus.

This was identified by Walker, with the preceding species, but it differs in colouring and probably in the direction of the thoracic horn.

12. *Aconophora imbellis.*

Aconophora imbellis, Fairm., Ann. Ent. Sér. 2, iv, p. 295, 4 (1846).
Aconophora surgens, Walker, Ins. Saund p. 69 (1858).
South America (ex Coll. Saunders).   Walker's type, Brit. Mus.

13. *Aconophora pugionata.*

Membracis pugionata, Germar, Mag. Ent. iv, p. 20, 17 (1821).
Pará (Wallace).   Brit. Mus.

14. *Aconophora xiphias.*

Membracis xiphias, Fabr., Syst. Rhyng. p. 12, 29 (1803).
South America.

15 *Aconophora teligera.*

Smilia teligera, Germar, Mag Ent. iv, p 21, 18 (1821).
Brazil.

16 *Aconophora curvata.*

Membracis curvata, Fabr., Syst. Rhyng p 13, 31 (1803)
South America.

17 *Aconophora concolor.*

Aconophora concolor, Walker, List Homopt ii, p 540, 17
(1851)
Aconophora nigra, Stal, Kongl. Svenska Vetensk. Akad.
Handl 8, 1, p. 35 (1869).
Mexico (Coffin, &c.). Type Brit. Mus.

18. *Aconophora laticorne.*

Aconophora laticorne, Walker, List Homopt. Suppl. p. 131
(1858).
Aconophora hastata, Stal (nec Fabr.), Kongl. Svenska Vetensk.
Akad. Handl. 8, 1, p 35 (1869)
Mexico (Sallé and Glennie). Type Brit. Mus.

19 *Aconophora caliginosa.*

Aconophora caliginosa, Walker, List Homopt. Suppl. p. 135
(1858).
Guatemala (Deby) Type Brit. Mus.

20. *Aconophora hadina*, n sp   Pl. VII, f 18.

Allied to the preceding species but much smaller, and with
differently coloured legs; black, becoming piceous at the
shoulders, the head, front of pronotum, compressed borders of
thoracic horn, dorsal region of pronotum, inner border and
central area of tegmina clothed with golden pubescence , tegmina
piceous with a costal spot, and the internal third testaceous-
hyaline; legs reddish, posterior pair with the basal three-fourths

of the femora piceous   form of *A. flavipes,* pronotum rather
coarsely punctured   Length with tegmina 8 ; with horn, thorax
and tegmina 10 ; width at humeral angles 3 mm.

Brazil (Miers). Type Brit. Mus.

Erroneously referred by Mr Walker to *A. incumbens.*

21. *Aconophora primitia,* n. sp.   Pl. VII, f. 19.

Dull laky-red with the thoracic horn purplish, apical third of
tegmina semihyaline pale brown ; pronotum rather finely punctured, the thoracic horn moderately long, rather slender, scarcely
ascending above the dorsal line, rounded at the apex, bordered
by a tolerably wide keel ; head black with laky-red border, its
posterior margin straight in the centre but deeply sinuate on
each side, corium pubescent ; tibiæ, particularly of the posterior
pair of legs, coarsely pubescent. Length with tegmina $6\frac{1}{2}$; with
horn, thorax and tegmina $1\frac{1}{2}$; width at humeral angles $2\frac{1}{2}$ mm.

Mexico, Oaxaca (Sallé) ; Peru (ex Coll. Saunders).   Type
Brit. Mus.

We have four examples of this very distinct little species.

Aconophora incumbens has been separated by Dr. Stal to form
his genus *Argante.*

22. *Aconophora obtusa.*

Aconophora obtusa, Walker, List Homopt ii, p. 542, 20
(1851).

Brazil. Type Brit. Mus.

23. *Aconophora conifera,* n sp. Pl VII, f. 17.

Chocolate-brown, tegmina paler with yellowish hyaline internal
angles ; legs ferruginous , front of pronotum and head pubescent ; thoracic horn porrect, obtusely conical, laterally compressed
at the borders, acutely conical when viewed from above, occupying nearly half the pronotum ; terminal process acute, spine-like
with a well defined dorsal carina   Length with tegmina 9 ;
with horn, thorax and tegmina 12 , width at humeral angles
$3\frac{1}{2}$ mm.

Mexico (ex Coll. Saunders)   Type Brit Mus.

The dorsal line of the pronotum (including the horn) is
oblique, with a scarcely perceptible angle at the base of the horn,
but with the terminal process horizontal and slightly convex,

24. *Aconophora compressa.*

Aconophora compressa, Walker, List Homopt. ii, p. 511, 18 (1851)
Mexico (Coffin).

25. *Aconophora subinermis.*

Aconophora subinermis, Stal, Kongl Svenska Vetensk Akad. Handl. 2, 7, p. 28, 2 (1862).
Rio Janeiro.

26 *Aconophora gladiata*

Aconophora gladiata, Stal, Kongl. Svenska Vetensk Akad. Handl. 8, 1, p 35 (1869).
Mexico, Vera Cruz (Sallé).

27. *Aconophora femoralis*

Aconophora femoralis, Stal, Kongl. Svenska Vetensk. Akad. Handl 8, 1, p. 35 (1869).
Mexico (Sallé).

28. *Aconophora quadrivittata*

Membracis quadrivittata, Say, Journ. Acad. Nat. Sci. Phil. vi, p 300, 9 (1831).
Thelia? quadrivittata, Walker, List Homopt. iv, p. 1143, 44 (1852).
Aconophora rubrivittata, Walker, l.c. ii, p 537, 11 (1851).
Aconophora porrecta, Walker, l.c p. 538, 12 (1851)
United States   Walker's types, Brit. Mus.

This is the most variable species known to me ; the following may be a form of it.

29. *Aconophora viridescens*

Aconophora viridescens, Walker, Lis Homopt. ii, p 538, 13 (1851).
Aconophora guttifera, Walker, l.c p. 539, 15 (1851).
East Florida (Doubleday); Mexico (ex Coll Saunders)   Type Brit. Mus.

30. *Aconophora lineosa.*

Aconophora lineosa, Walker, List Homopt. Suppl. p. 134 (1858)

North America   Type Brit Mus.

31 *Aconophora gigantea*, n. sp   Pl VII, f. 15.

Pronotum dull mustard-yellow, multicostate with double irregular series of coarse punctures between the costæ, dorsally carinate; thoracic horn black with two scarlet carinæ, which converge and unite before reaching the apex, oblique, decreasing in width towards the obtusely rounded apex, laterally compressed and coarsely punctured, almost linear when viewed from above, terminal spine extremely long, acute, depressed at the apex, extending to just beyond the tegmina; humeral angles rather prominent, front of thorax with a central longitudinal carina, head considerably wider than long, it, the legs and body testaceous; tegmina testaceous hyaline, with blackish terminal border. Length exclusive of horn $11\frac{1}{2}$, including horn 15 mm.

Ega (Bates).   Type Brit Mus.

32. *Aconophora lata*

Aconophora lata, Walker, Ins. Saund. p. 69 (1858).
Thelia gladiator, Walker (nec *gladiata*, Stal), List Homopt. 2, p. 567, 38 (1851)

Pará (Wallace).   Types Brit. Mus.

Although, by rights, this species should perhaps bear the name of *A. gladiator*, and Stal's insect should be renamed, I prefer for the present (as I do not know the latter), to retain Walker's later name for *A. gladiator*, and thus avoid the possibility of adding to the synomymy by giving a fresh designation to what may be identical with one of Walker's species; the fact that Stal steadily ignored the greater part of Walker's work renders this far from unlikely.

33. *Aconophora hastata.*

Membracis hastata, Fabr. Syst. Rhyn. p. 12, 29 (1803).
? *Aconophora nigrivittata*, Walker, List Homopt. ii, p. 539, 14 (1851).

Hab. — ?   Walker's type, Brit. Mus.

34. *Aconophora brasiliensis.*

Aconophora brasiliensis, Stål, Kongl. Svenska Vetensk. Akad
Handl. 8, 1, p. 34 (1869).
Rio Janeiro.

35. *Aconophora grisescens.*

Smilia grisescens, Germar, Silb. Revue iii, p 238, 17 (1835)
Aconophora interna, Walker, List Homopt. ii, p 541, 19
(1851)
Brazil. Walker's type Brit. Mus.

36. *Aconophora tenuicornis.*

Aconophora tenuicorne, (sic) Walker, Ins Saund p 70 (1858).
Amazons (ex Coll Saunders) Type Brit. Mus

37. *Aconophora pallescens.*

Aconophora pallescens, Stål, Kongl. Svenska Vetensk. Akad
Handl. 8, 1, p. 35 (1869).
Mexico.

I here add the description of a small species of *Thelia*, which
I found associated with *Aconophora* by Mr. Walker.

Thelia costigera, n. sp.   Pl VII, f. 20.

Clay-coloured, thoracic horn streaked with black ; pronotum
very convex, the dorsal line forming an arch from the back of
the horn to the posterior extremity ; dorsal keel very distinct
and continued from the anterior margin of the thorax over the
thoracic horn and thence down the centre of the dorsum ;
tegmina more than half concealed by the pronotum, the exposed
portion similar in structure, sides of the pronotum multicostate,
with three irregular series of coarse punctures between the
costæ ; thoracic horn laterally compressed with four costæ on
each side. Extreme length including horn 8 mm
British Guiana (Schomburgk) Type Brit. Mus.

EUMELLA, *Stål*

To this genus Dr. Stål refers *Smilia semiacuta* St , *Membracis
fornicata*, Germ , and *Smilia sellata*, Germ , three species
unknown to me. So far as I can comprehend the structure of

these insects from description, without seeing figures or types, I should consider them to be similar in form to *Thelia angulata* and *T. tacta*, of Walker, and therefore would add the latter to the genus.

DARNOIDES, Fairm.

To this genus I would add *Horiola semivitta* of **Walker**

COMBOPHORA, *Germ.*

The following species are referable to this genus—*C. Beskii*, Germ., *Membracis inanis*, Fabr., *C. consentanea*, Fairm. (= *C. maculata*, Guérin), and *C minor*, Fairm (= *C. discontinua*, Walker)

COMOLON, *Walker* (*Heliodore*, Stal)

1. *Omolon laportei*

Combophora laportei, Germar, Silb Revue Ent iii, p. 253, 2 (1835).
Combophora carinata, Guérin, Icon Règne Anim. p 366 (1829–44).
Brazil. Brit. Mus

2. *Omolon incongrua.*

Combophora incongrua, Walker, List Homopt. Suppl. p 340 (1858).
Tunantins (Bates). Type Brit Mus

3 *Omolon tridens*

Omolon tridens, Walker, Journ. Entom. i, p. 316, pl. xv, fig. 1 (1862)

Head yellow, with two longitudinal black stripes; pronotum coarsely and regularly reticulate-punctate, sulphur yellow, with a strongly marked rugulose black-edged castaneous dorsal carina; on either side, parallel to the latter and proceeding from the anterior margin, two black convergent stripes, which unite and taper to a point just below the centre of the dorsal arch, a trigonate clay-coloured spot, bordered by a forked and then semicircular black stripe, the outer extremity of which runs along the upper margin of the posterior lateral spines, an oblique black bordered clay-coloured patch at the inferior extremity of

the pronotum ; the area enclosed between the spines dull castanc-
ous 'bordered with black ; the spines black, excepting in the
centre at the base ; terminal process castaneous, with black base,
separated from the lateral spines by a stripe of yellow ; tegmina
hyaline with diffused yellow terminal border, the veins black ;
body and legs bright mustard-yellow. Length including the
closed tegmina 7, width between lateral spines $3\frac{1}{2}$ mm.

St. Paulo (Bates). Brit. Mus.

4. *Omolon varius.*

Omolon varius, Walker, Journ. Entom. i, p. 316 (1862).
Pará.

It is difficult to comprehend how either Walker could have
failed to recognize his two new species as being congeneric with
Combophora laportei, or Stal to recognize the identity of his new
genus with the genus figured by Walker.

NASSUNIA, *Stal.*

The following species are referable to this genus—*Smilio-
rachis bipunctata, binotata* and *bispina* of Fairm., *Nassunia
bistillata.* and *dalmanni* of Stal, *Centrotus costalis* and *Cerasa
fortis* of Walker.

RHEXIA *Stal.*

1. *Rhexia flavicans.*

Scaphula flavicans. Fairm , Ann. Ent. Sér. 2, iv, p. 294, 2
(1846).
Cayenne.

2. *Rhexia pallescens.*

Darnis pallescens, Fabr., Syst. Rhyng. p. 28, 9 (1803).
Scaphula alutacea, Fairm., Ann. Ent. Sér. 2, iv, p. 495, 4
(1846).
Santarem. Brit. Mus.

3. *Rhexia centromaculata.*

Scaphula centromaculata, Fairm., Ann. Ent. Sér. 2, iv, p.
495, 3 (1846).
Cayenne.

4. *Rhexia bistriga*

Darnis bistriga, Walker, Ins Saund. p 74 (1858).
Amazons (ex Coll Saunders). Type Brit. Mus.

5 *Rhexia varicosa*, n. sp   Pl. VII, f. 5.

Chocolate-brown, front of head carmine, with a black marginal line on each side; back of head with a central yellow spot; a submarginal semicircular sulcus round the front and sides; pronotum coarsely punctured; the humeral angles, a central spot between them, and an abbreviated transverse angulated bar formed by the confluence of two spots beyond the middle, yellow; tegmina shining, the basal two-thirds chocolate-brown, crossed by an oblique yellow belt, the veins carmine; apical third whitish hyaline with yellow veins, and with a black abbreviated marginal line at the apex within the veinless border; body and legs pale testaceous, abdomen with carmine margins to the segments. Length including tegmina 6⅓, width at humeral angles 4 mm.

Ega (Bates). Type Brit. Mus.

6. *Rhexia bifasciata*, n. sp.   Pl. VII, f. 6.

Saffron-yellow, front of head with a black marginal dash on each side in front of the eyes; a submarginal semicircular sulcus round the front and sides; pronotum rather coarsely punctured, a black belt just behind the shoulders, expanding in front into a broad semicircular patch; a black apical belt; apex carinate, depressed, pale yellow; tegmina with a basal black belt, and a second across the third fourth, the interspace between them saffron-yellow crossed by red veins; apical area hyaline white, with a black marginal line within the veinless border; body and legs pale sandy yellowish, abdomen with black margins to the segments   Length including tegmina 6½, width at humeral angles 3½ mm.

St. Paulo (Bates)   Type Brit. Mus.

HETERONOTUS, *Laporte.*

1. *Heteronotus quadrinodosus.*

Heteronotus quadrinodosus, Fairm., Ann. Ent. Sér. 2, iv, p. 499, 1; pl. 5, fig 27 (1846).
b *Heteronotus quinquenodosus*, Stål, Stett Ent. Zeit. 1864, p. 70, 125
Mexico, Volcano of Orizaba (Sallé)   Brit. Mus.

Dr Stal has mistaken the succeeding species (as did Walker), for the insect described by Fairmaire, but it is clear from the original description that the main body of the pronotum was not regarded as a node by the French author ; *H. quadrinodosus* is described as shining brown-black, with the first two nodes nearly equal and the strong ventral spine emitted from the third smaller node, whereas the *quadrinodosus* of Walker is black, with only three true nodes and the spines emitted from the third or largest and terminal node

2. *Heteronotus trinodosus.* n. sp   Pl. VII, f. 8.

Heteronotus quadrinodosus, Walker, (nec Fairm.) List Homopt. ii, p 592, 1 (1851)

Black, shining, hairy, strongly punctured ; pronotum trinodose, the anterior portion or main body of the pronotum armed with two central horizontal transverse blackish spines, with castaneous undersurface ; a central longitudinal carina, partly coloured with pale yellow ; margins pale yellow ; nodes with a central carina, the first compressed in front, and with an abbreviated transverse yellow line on each side, the second node orbicular, smaller than the first, the third oval, largest of the three, with a pale yellow line on each side in front ; two small terminal conical castaneous denticles, a strong oblique hairy castaneous spine emitted from the base of the node below ; tegmina pale yellowish-testaceous hyaline with castaneous veins ; legs castaneous ; body whity-brown.   Length 12 mm.

Mexico (Schuckard).   Type Brit. Mus

3. *Heteronotus bicornis.*

Ranatra bicornis, Lesson, Ill. Zool. pl 57, fig. 1 (1832).

Combophora vulnerans, Burm , Silb Revue Ent. 1, p. 228, 2 (1833).

Heteronotus stipatus, Walker, List Homopt. Suppl. p. 155 (1858)

Brazil (Miers) , Constancia (H. Clark, &c.).   Walker's type Brit. Mus.

4. *Heteronotus abbreviatus.*

Heteronotus abbreviatus, Fairm., Ann Ent. Sér. 2, iv, p. 500, 5 ; pl. 7, fig 26 (1846).

Brazil.   Brit. Mus.

5. *Heteronotus nodosus.*

Membracis nodosa, Germ. Mag Ent. iv, p 30, 41; pl. 1, fig. 2 (1821).
Combophora nodosa, Burm, Silb. Revue Ent i, p. 229, 6 (1833).

Brazil ; Constancia (II. Clark).   Brit. Mus.

6. *Heteronotus glanduliger.*

Ranatra glanduligera, Lesson, Ill. Zool. pl. 57, fig 2 (1832).
Heteronotus nigricans, De Laporte, Ann. Ent. i, p. 96, 2 , pl 3, fig 8.

Brazil (Miers); Rio Janeiro (II. Clark).   Brit. Mus.

7 *Heteronotus inermis*

Heteronotus inermis, De Laporte, Ann. Ent i, p. 97, 4; pl. 3, fig. 10 (1852)
Centrotus furcatus, Gray in Griff. Anim. Kingd, Ins. ii, p. 261 ; pl. 108, fig. 1 (1832).
? *Combophora reticulata,* Burm , Silb Revue Ent i, p. 227, 1 (1833).

Brazil ; Rio Janeiro (A. Fry).   Brit. Mus.

One of our examples is probably the type of Mr. Gray's description, but there is no label to identify it by.

8. *Heteronotus flavolineatus.*

Heteronotus flavolineatus, De Laporte, Ann. Ent. i, p. 96, 3 ; pl. 3, fig. 9 (1832).
Combophora signata, Burm., Silb Revue Ent i, p. 228, 3 (1833).
Brazil   Brit. Mus.

9. *Heteronotus delineatus.*   Pl. VII, f. 9.

Heteronotus delineatus, Walker, List Homopt. Suppl. p. 154 (1858).
Ega (Bates).   Type Brit Mus.

This is one of the most singular species in the genus.

HENICONOTUS, *Stal.*

1. *Heniconotus horridus.*

Membracis horrida, Fabr, Ent. Syst. iv, p. 12, 18 (1794).
Heteronotus fuscus, De Laporte, Ann. Ent. i, p. 98, 6 (1832).
Combophora bullifera, Burm, Silb. Revue Ent. i, p. 229, 4 (1833).
Heteronotus excisus, Walker, List Homopt. ii, p. 593, 5 (1851).
Pará (Wallace)   Walker's Type, Brit. Mus.

2 *Heniconotus æthiops,* n. sp.   Pl VII, f 7.

Blackish piceous, shining; head with the anterior margins and a central stripe yellow, anterior portion of the pronotum armed with two long slender oblique divergent spines, each surrounded at the base by a yellow annulus, the margins, and a U shaped line in front yellow; a yellow trigonate lateral spot on each side of the constriction in front of the first node, the latter obtusely obconical and quite black; second and terminal node obtusely conical trispinose, the lateral spines being long, slender and tipped with yellow, the third spine emitted from below (in a curved oblique position slanting outwards), still longer than the lateral spines and also tipped with yellow; tegmina pale yellowish hyaline, with the apical area burnt-sienna brown, base black, veins piceous; legs piceous, the hind femora tipped with yellow; abdomen yellow, with the exception of the sexual organs, venter grey, spotted with yellow. Length including tegmina 12½ mm.
Ecuador (Buckley).   Type Brit. Mus.

Readily distinguished from the preceding by the proximity of the nodes to each other, the small size of the terminal one and the great length of its spines.

3 *Heniconotus belliger,* r. sp   Pl VII, f 13

Testaceous; pronotum black, becoming piceous in front, the anterior portion armed with two long slender divergent curved spines, lateral borders and two arched stripes, which unite in front, yellow, first node only separable by a slight depression and its more intensely black hue from the anterior portion; terminal node separated by peduncle from the first, extremely small but armed with three unusually long slender yellow-tipped spines, the two upper ones projecting upwards and outwards at an oblique angle, the inferior spine one-third longer, dark piceous rather than black, extending obliquely downwards and backwards almost to the end of the tegmina ; tegmina pale yellowish hyaline with the apical area slightly deeper in tint, the outer border brownish, the veins yellow, excepting along the anterior margin which is brown.   Length including tegmina 12 mm.

St. Paulo (Bates).   Type Brit Mus.

4 Heniconotus xanthomelas.

Heteronotus xanthomelas, Walker, List Homopt. Suppl p 339 (1858).

Tunantins (Bates)   Type Brit. Mus.

5. Heniconotus tridens

Combophora tridens, Burm., Silb. Revue Ent i, p. 229, 5 (1833).

Pará (Wallace).   Brit Mus.

6. Heniconotus leucotelus.

Heteronotus leucotelus, Walker, List Homopt. Suppl. p. 155 (1858).

Ega (Bates).   Type Brit Mus.

Quite distinct from the species subsequently described from Ega under the same name and in the same volume.

7. Heniconotus spinosus.

Heteronotus spinosus, De Laporte, Ann. Ent. i, p. 96, 1 ; pl. 3, fig. 7 (1832).
Heteronotus flavolineatus, Amyot et Serville (nec De Laporte), Hist Nat Hemipt p. 549; pl 9, fig 6 (1843)

Tunantins (Bates).   Brit. Mus.

Local form.—*Heniconotus confusus,* Butler.   Pl. VII, f 10.

Heteronotus nodosus, Walker (nec Burm.), List Homopt. Suppl. p. 154 (1858).

Santarem and Tapajos (Bates).   Type Brit. Mus.

Much more slenderly made than *H. spinosus* (typical), the thoracic spines less curved, the terminal node smaller, with longer spines and a longer pedicle connecting it with the first node.

This species can be readily distinguished from the following, by the protuberance on the back of the main body of the pronotum, which, when viewed laterally, gives the pronotum a trinodose appearance.

8. *Heniconotus armatus.*

Heteronotus armatus, De Laporte, Ann. Ent. i, p. 97, 5 (1832)

Heteronotus abcisus, Walker, List Homopt. ii, p. 505, 16 (1851)

Pará (Wallace). Walker's type, Brit Mus.

Local form—*Membracis clavata*, Perty, Delect. Anim. pl. 35, fig 7 (1830–34).

"Province of Bahia." Brazil. Brit. Mus.

9. *Heniconotus strigosus*, n. sp. Pl. VII, f 11.

Nearly allied to *H. spinosus*, but rather more slenderly made, the head narrower, the main body of the pronotum black, with the sides, an irregular longitudinal central stripe, two small dashes on either side of the anterior margin, and an obtuse V shaped stripe, yellow ; markings of the nodes as in *H. spinosus*, but blacker ; posterior node with parallel sides, much longer than in *H. spinosus*, and crossed by a distinct yellow stripe, spines much shorter. Length including tegmina 12 mm.

St. Paulo (Bates). Type Brit. Mus.

10. *Heniconotus divisus.*

Heteronotus divisus, Walker, List Homopt. Suppl. p. 156 (1858).

Pará (Bates) Type Brit Mus.

11. *Heniconotus parvinodis*, n. sp Pl. VII, f. 12.

Heteronotus leucotelus, Walker, List Homopt. Suppl. p. 339 (nec p. 155), (1858).

Ega (Bates) ; var. St. Paulo (Bates). Type Brit. Mus

This species is remarkable for the very small nodes of the pronotum, the St. Paulo form differs from the type in having the sutural lines black.

Contributions to a knowledge of the COLEOPTERA of Madagascar ;
by CHAS. O. WATERHOUSE

The British Museum has recently acquired a small but most
interesting collection of Coleoptera from Madagascar The
specimens were collected in the neighbourhood of Fianarantsoa,
the capital of the Betsileo country, directly south of Antananarivo, by the Rev. W Deans Cowan Besides several new
species of *Cetoniidæ*, an account of which has already appeared
(Ent. Mo. Mag. September, 1878), the collection contained
several examples of *Arrhythmus* and *Logisticus*, remarkable
new genera of Longicorns described by myself in a paper read
before the Entomological Society at a recent meeting There
are also very numerous specimens of *Artelida (Toxotus) sericeus*, Guérin, showing great variation in size (7 to 11½ lines);
many of the examples have brownish elytra

CARABIDÆ.

Drypta iris, Castln , Hist. Nat. i, p. 34

This species is only known to me from description, and I am
in doubt as to whether the specimen sent by Mr. Cowan is the
same. It differs in coloration , the head and thorax very
strongly, irregularly and rather thickly punctured ; the thorax
is two-thirds longer than broad, subparallel in front, gently
constricted behind, there is an extremely fine median line. The
elytra are very strongly striate, and the striæ are very strongly
punctured, the interstices are moderately convex (subcostiform
towards the sides) microscopically transversely coriaceous, with
a stray puncture here and there , the apex of each is obliquely
truncate, the external angle of the truncature is a distinct tooth.
The underside and the legs are æneous The head and thorax
are coppery, the elytra uniform purple

A very distinct species, not only on account of the colour,
but the almost impunctate interstices readily separate it from
its allies.

MELOLONTHIDÆ.

Enthora polita, n. sp.

Ovalis, nigra, nitidissima ; capite thorace scutelloque nigro-cyaneis, vel æneis, cum elytris subtilissime sat crebre punctulatis. Long. 9–10½ lin

Oblong oval, very convex and shining All the upper surface moderately thickly and extremely finely punctured, the punctures having in the middle a minute whitish scale, only visible with a strong magnifying power The abdomen is sparingly punctured in the middle, closely at the sides.

The antennæ have the club composed of seven lamellæ in both sexes, but they are much shorter in the female than in the male, and are of unequal length. The anterior tibiæ are much narrower in the male than the female , the tarsi in the female are very short

This species differs from that which I have determined to be E chlorodera, Blanch., in being a little longer, with much finer punctuation, and in having the elytra much more distinctly angular at the sides when viewed laterally, and the abdomen is much less punctured.

A considerable number of examples of both sexes.

Pachycolus clypeatus, n sp.

Elongatus, sat convexus, nitidus, piceus; clypeo plicâ arcuatâ transeunti, post plicam evidenter punctato, fronte discrete subtiliter punctulatâ; thorace longitudine ¼ latiori, nigro-piceo, sat crebre subtilissime punctulato, angulis anticis obtusis, posticis rotundatis, lateribus arcuatis longe ciliatis ; scutello elongato triangulari, lævi, nigro-piceo , elytris thorace parum latioribus, at 2½ longioribus, sat crebre distincte punctatis, suturâ lævi , pygidio crebre fortiter punctato , metasterno medio leviter impresso, lævi Long. 2⅔ lin , lat. 1⅓ lin

This species much resembles P. madagascariensis, but is much narrower, and the form of the clypeus and claws present almost generic differences. The forehead is quite simple, without any transverse ridge behind , the line separating the clypeus from the head is well marked, nearly straight; between this line and the anterior margin there is a distinct plait or thickening, the space between this plait and the anterior margin is deeply hollowed, the margins are thickened and reflexed. The antennæ have the third joint elongate, the fourth strongly transverse, a little produced, the fifth to tenth forming an oblong club. The tarsi are long and slender, the claw joint is suddenly bent beyond the middle, the basal part furnished below with a blade similar to that seen in *Achelyna*.

In *Pachycolus* the club of the antennæ is five jointed, and the claws are strongly bifid.

TENEBRIONIDÆ.

(NYCTEROPINÆ).

Dolichoderus dimidiatus, n. sp.

Capite thoraceque supra nigris opacis; elytris læte cupreo-æneis nitidissimis fere lævibus, apice ipso cyaneo; corpore subtus nigro-æneo nitido; antennis pedibusque cupreo-piceis. Long. 8½ lin.

Head and thorax dull black, the thick and extremely fine punctuation only seen with great difficulty; head rather broad quadrate, the anterior angles of the epistoma shining blackish-æneous. Thorax one-fourth longer than broad, scarcely narrowed anteriorly, subparallel sided, the anterior angles not prominent, the fine anterior margin and the thickened posterior margin shining blackish-æneous. Elytra at the base a trifle narrower than the base of the thorax, acuminate at the apex, convex, impressed at the suture, coppery-æneous; a powerful magnifying glass reveals some very close and excessively fine punctuation; the extreme apex is not produced.

(CNODALONINÆ).

Camaria violaceipennis, n. sp.

Niger; capite thoraceque opacis, planiusculis, elytris convexis, basi thorace paulo latioribus postice paulo ampliatis, violaceis vel purpureis fortiter striatis, interstitiis bene convexis subtiliter creberrime punctulatis; corpore subtus pedibusque nitidis, tibiis piceis. Long. 15 lin.

Head and thorax dull black, very closely and extremely finely punctured; the latter about one-third broader than long, slightly narrower in front, straight at the sides, the anterior angles very little prominent, blunt, the base gently bisinuate. Elytra convex, purple, (with violet reflections), a little broader than the thorax, more ample behind, narrowed at the apex, the shoulders rounded.

In this species (and in *C. chalcoptera*, Klug) the mesosternum has the excavation in the form of a V not a short U as the American species appear to have, the first and second abdominal segments are relatively longer and flatter and the intercoxal projection is broader

CURCULIONIDÆ.

(CYPHINÆ)

Stigmatiachelus alternans, n sp

Piceo-niger, dense pallide fulvo-squamosus; fronte medio foveolatâ, rostro carinâ longitudinali nitidâ, oculis prominentibus; thorace lineis tribus nitidis, medianâ canaliculatâ; elytris basi thorace vix duplo latioribus triplo longioribus, convexis, fossato-striatis, fasciâ ante medium interstitiisque alternatis ante apicem denudatis nitidis, guttis oblongis pallidioribus in interstitiis alternatis post medium possitis. Long. 5 lin.

This species belongs to the group with prominent eyes, and compared with its allies has them small. The rostrum has a well marked shining carina, continued on the forehead by a deep shining fovea Thorax one-fourth broader than long, obliquely narrowed in front of the middle, with three longitudinal shining black lines, the middle one longitudinally channelled. Elytra convex, with the shoulders angular but not much prominent, somewhat parallel sided, a trifle broader at the posterior two-thirds, very deeply punctate striate, the punctures very large, the first and third interstices are a little elevated; there is an irregular transverse fascia a little before the middle denuded of scales (the second and fourth interstices are also denuded at the base), immediately below this fascia there is a transverse fascia of nearly white oblong spots on the alternate interstices, the first, third, fifth and seventh interstices are also without scales below the above mentioned whitish spots.

Stigmatiachelus humeralis, n. sp.

Dense brunneo-griseo squamosus, opacus; elytris basi thorace duplo latioribus postice paulo ampliatis, maculâ basali fasciâque undulatâ post medium fusco-brunneis obscure flavo cinctis, humeris prominentibus acutis. Long. $5\frac{1}{2}$ lin., lat. $2\frac{1}{2}$ lin.

This is a very broad species, nearly the form of *S. ornatus*, with very prominent acute shoulders. Dull grey-brown, with a spot in the middle of the base of each elytron, and an undulating fascia a little behind the middle chocolate-brown, the spot and the fascia both narrowly bordered with dull yellow, the apex of the elytra is also of this obscure yellow colour. Eyes very slightly prominent; forehead with a narrow mesial channel. Thorax rather narrow, one-fifth broader than long, a little more narrowed in front than behind, with a fine mesial shining ridge on the disc, and two shining punctures on each side. Scutellum shining brown. Elytra at least twice as broad as the thorax, one-fourth longer than broad, very convex posteriorly, punctate striate.

Madagascar (Crossley).

CERAMBYCIDÆ

Sagridola flavicollis, n. sp.

Picea, griseo-pilosa, opaca, antennis brevibus tenuibus; thorace scutello pygidioque dense flavo-tomentosis; elytris basi thorace $\frac{2}{5}$ latioribus, et $2\frac{3}{4}$ longioribus, brunneis, singulis postice bene angustatis, paulo divergentibus, ad apicem truncatis, suturâ flavo-marginatâ; femoribus basi apiceque brunneis. Long. $6\frac{1}{2}$ lin.

Antennæ slender, about as long as the elytra. Eyes elongate ovate, entire, widely separated. Thorax scarcely longer than broad, convex, densely clothed with yellow tomentum, constricted at the anterior margin, slightly compressed laterally, subparallel behind. Scutellum narrow triangular. Elytra light brown, separately very much attenuated at the apex which is truncate; the sides obliquely deflexed, the suture is bordered with yellow for the posterior two-thirds. The basal segment of the abdomen and the pygidium are yellow. The femora are dentate below, near the apex.

MASTODODERA.

I am unaware with whom it originated, but it seems to be a generally received notion, followed even by Thomson and Lacordaire, that *M lateralis*, Guérin, with fulvous elytra and black sutural stripe, is only the male of *M. nodicollis*, Klug, with fulvous elytra and black base. The two species are quite distinct, and the sexes of both are in the British Museum. The males have the eleventh antennal joint elongate and constricted befoi e the apex, indicating a twelfth joint; the female has this same joint shorter and simple. The male organ is oblong, bioad and flat. The female ovipositor is elongate, acuminate at the apex.

LAMIIDÆ.

Leucogi aphus * *variegatue,* n. sp.

Crassus, ater, velutinus, sabuloso-variegatus : elytris tuber-culis obtusis duobus juxta scutellum humerisque nitidis. Long. 8–10½ lin,

Build somewhat that of *Eumimetes,* but broader and more robust. Head black, with a fine sandy hue between the autennæ, and an oblique one behind each eye. Thorax with a moderately strong tubercle at the side, a small one on each side of the disc, black, with a sandy stripe in the middle and a broader one on each side of the disc, there aie also a few irregu-lar spots. Elytra two-fifths bioader than the thorax, gently narrowed posteriorly, slightly flattened on the back, obtuse at the apex, with two approximate tubercles close to the scutellum, slightly elevated at the shoulders, densely clothed with sandy tomentum, irregularly dotted with black, with an irregulai black patch on each side behind the middle (dotted with sandy), a flexuous black band beyond this, and a black spot just before the apex. Antennæ and legs sandy-white, the apices of the third to eleventh joints of the antennæ, the inside of the femora, the apex of the tibiæ, the apex of the second and fourth joints of the tarsi and the entire third joint black. Body beneath black, dotted at the sides with sandy-white.

I place this species provisionally in the genus *Leucogi aphus,* but I would point out that the antennæ differ in being simple, not fiinged at the apex, the joints gradually diminishing towaids the apex

The male has the fifth segment of the abdomen truncate at the apex. The female has this segment rathei deeply impressed at the apex.

---

* Waterhouse, Cistula Entomologica, ii, p 295 (June, 1878).

Descriptions of the PHYTOPHAGOUS COLEOPTERA *collected by the late Dr. F. Stoliczka during Forsyth's Expedition to Kashgar in 1873-74* ; by JOSEPH S. BALY, F.L.S.

The Phytophagous Coleoptera collected by Dr. Stoliczka, although few in number, and containing no striking novelties, are extremely interesting in relation to geographical distribution. The 25 species contained in the collection belong to no less than 21 genera, out of which *Nodostoma, Enneamera, Chæræa, Macrima, Mimastra, Merista* and *Leptarthra* (one-third of the whole) are exclusively Asiatic ; *Paria* has its metropolis in America, but is sparingly represented in Japan, China, and Eastern Siberia ; *Luperodes,* is largely spread throughout the Asiatic continent, and is also found (according to v. Harold, whose accuracy cannot be doubted) in South America and Abyssinia ; of the twelve others five are cosmopolitan, and the rest occur abundantly in Europe. Out of the 25 species, one only, *Plagiodera versicolora,* Laich. (*armoracie,* Auct), is found in Europe ; seven, *Lema coromandeliana, Clytra palliata, Enneamera variabilis, Galleruco indica, Gallerucella placida, Merista interrupta,* and *Leptarthra collaris,* occur in various parts of British India ; two, *Haltica cærulescens* and *H. viridi-cyanea,* have been described by myself from Japan, and one, *Chrysomela angelica,* Reiche, is not uncommon in Syria, the fourteen others have not as yet been found in any other locality, and seventeen species are described for the first time in the present paper.

List of Genera and Species.

Lema coromandeliana, Fabr. var.
Clytra palliata, Fabr.
Coptocephala dubia, n. sp.
       ,,   *dimidiatipennis,* n. sp.
Cryptocephalus interjectus, n sp.

Nodostoma concinnicolle, n. sp.

" *plagiosum,* n. sp.

Paria cuprescens, n. sp

Plagiodera versicolora, Laich.

Chrysomela angelica, Reiche.

Phratora abdominalis, n. sp.

Haltica cærulescens, Baly.

" *viridicyanea,* Baly

Enneamera variabilis, Baly.

Charæa (N.G. Gall.) *flaviventre,* n. sp.

Macrima (N.G. Gall) *armata,* n. sp.

Mimastra gracilis, n. sp.

Agelastica orientalis, n. sp.

Malacosoma flaviventre, n. sp.

Luperodes erythrocephala, n. sp.

Galleruca vittatipennis, n. sp.

" *indica,* n. sp.

Gallerucella placida, n. sp.

Merista interrupta, Redt

Leptarthra collaris, n. sp.

1. *Lema coromandeliana,* Fabr. (var. *præusta*).

Crioceris præusta, Fabr , Ent. Syst. i, 2, p 8 ; *Lema præusta,*
Lac , Mon. Phyt. i, p 340.

Hab. Jhelam Valley. A single specimen.

2. *Clytra palliata.*

Clythra palliata, Fabr. Syst El ii, p 30.

Hab. Jhelam Valley ; also various parts of India.

3. *Coptocephala dubia,* n. sp.

Subelongata, subcylindrica, nitida, subtus nigra, argenteo
sericea, prothorace pedibusque fulvis ; supra fulva, capitis
vertice nigro ; thorace lævi ; scutello piceo ; elytris tenuiter
punctatis, fasciâ communi baseos, extrorsum abbreviatâ, alterâque vix pone medium nigris. Long. $2\frac{1}{3}$ lin.

Hab. Murree.

Vertex black, impunctate, lower face fulvous, a ray of the
same colour extending upwards on the vertex ; front deeply

excavated between the eyes, irregularly punctured; anterior
margin of clypeus concave-emarginate. Thorax rather more
than twice as broad as long; sides rounded, converging from
behind the middle to the apex, the anterior angles obtuse, the
hinder ones rounded; disc transversely convex, shining, impunctate, excavated on either side near the lateral margin. Scutellum
trigonate, piceous. Elytra scarcely broader than the thorax,
parallel, very finely punctured, the black markings on their
surface extend from the base nearly to the middle of the disc,
and again from the middle itself nearly to the apex, leaving
only an irregular flavous transverse band across the middle,
which sends a narrow ramus along the suture nearly to the base.

4. *Coptocephala dimidiatipennis*, n sp.

Subelongata, subcylindrica, flava, nitida, corpore inferiori,
capite elytrorumque limbo inflexo, fulvo hirsutis, thorace lævi ;
elytris tenuiter punctatis, nigris, a basi ad paulo ante medium
flavis.   Long. 3–3½ lin.

Hab Jhelam Valley ; also India, my collection.

Head clothed with long erect hairs, minutely punctured;
clypeus not separated from the face, its anterior margin angulate-
emarginate ; apex of jaws black ; antennæ equal in length to
the head and thorax, the basal joint thickened, pyriform, the
second also thickened, short, nodose, the third small, not longer
than the second, the fourth trigonate, scarcely longer than the
third, the rest to the apex dilated, the fifth to the ninth transversely trigonate, the tenth and eleventh ovate ; eyes large,
oval, notched on the inner margin. Thorax nearly three times
as broad as long ; sides obtusely rounded, slightly converging in
front, the hinder angles rounded, the anterior ones very obtuse ;
basal margin sinuate on either side the median lobe, the latter
slightly reflexed, very obtusely rounded, upper surface transversely convex, remotely and very minutely punctured, a concave
transverse space on and immediately in front of the basal lobe,
coarsely and closely punctured. Scutellum longer than broad,
subtrigonate, its apex obtuse. Elytra scarcely broader than the
thorax at the base, slightly dilated posteriorly, convex, rather
distantly and finely punctured   Body beneath and legs clothed
with long erect fulvous hairs.

I possess two specimens of this species, both labelled India, but
without precise locality, in one of them the head is more coarsely
punctured and subrugose, in all other respects it agrees with
the type.

5. *Cryptocephalus interjectus*, n. sp.

Elongato-oblongus ♂, oblongus ♀, convexus, nitidus, subtus niger, pedibus nigro-piceis; supra flavus, capite hic illic parce fortiter punctato, fronte sulco longitudinali impresso; vertice, maculis duabus inter oculos, labro, antennisque nigris, his basi, sulco longitudinali mandibulisque piceis; thorace lævi, limbo angusto et utrinque maculâ subrotundatâ nigris; scutello sub-cordato, nigro; elytris fortiter punctato-striatis, punctis piceis, apicem versus minus fortiter impressis; interspatiis convexis, transversim rugulosis; utrisque limbo angusto, externo ante medium excepto, maculisque quinque 2, 2, 1 dispositis nigris. Long. 2½ lin.

Var A. Pygidio corporeque subtus flavis, illo maculâ cunei-formi, pectore abdominisque disco nigris.

Var. B. Corpore nigro, antennarum basi, clypeo, faci signaturis thoracisque lineâ longitudinali sordide flavis.

Hab Murree

Head rather coarsely but not closely punctured, the punc-turing varying in degree in different individuals; front impressed with a distinct longitudinal groove; clypeus broader than long, trigonate; antennæ three-fourths the length of the body in the ♀, rather longer in the ♂, the three lower joints pale piceous, the rest black. Thorax rather more than twice as broad as long at the base; sides moderately rounded and obliquely con-verging from base to apex; basal margin concave-emarginate on either side, the outer angles produced backwards, acute; above convex, minutely but not closely punctured. Elytra slightly broader than the thorax, oblong-quadrate, convex, rather strongly punctate-striate, the punctures piceous, finer and less strongly impressed towards the apex; interspaces faintly but distinctly convex, transversely wrinkled; each elytron with the extreme outer limb (interrupted on the lateral margin before its middle) and five large patches black; these spots are arranged as follows: two transversely below the base, the outer one oblong, covering the humeral callus and attached to the basal margin, the inner one subrotundate, placed on the inner disc; two just below the middle also placed transversely, both subrotundate, the outer one usually attached to the lateral margin; and lastly one apical, transversely oblong either free or attached to the apical border; these patches are often more or less confluent, and occasionally, as in var. B, cover the entire surface of the elytron. Pygidium and body beneath clothed with griseous hairs.

Apical margin of prosternum obliquely produced, deflexed, slightly emarginate, the hinder margin concave, armed on either side with a deflexed, obtuse tooth; mesosternum transverse, its apical border angulate-emarginate. Apical segment of abdomen in the ♂ impressed with a shallow fovea; the same segment in the ♀ deeply excavated, the fovea large, rotundate Basal joint of the four anterior tarsi in the ♂ dilated, elongate-ovate, longer than the following two united.

The form of the prosternum will separate this species from any nearly allied species

6. *Nodostoma concinnicolle*, n. sp.

Oblongo-ovatum, convexum, pallide piceum, nitidum, pedibus antennisque fulvis; thorace transverso, lateribus ante basin acute angulatis, disco crebre foveolato-punctato; elytris nigris, fortiter punctato-striatis, interspatiis planis. Long 2 lin.

Var. A. Elytris piceo-fulvis, punctis piceis
Hab. Jhelam Valley.

Head coarsely and deeply punctured, the punctures on the extreme vertex crowded, clypeus not distinctly separated from the face; antennæ slender, filiform, the second joint ovate, three-fourths the length of the third, the latter two-thirds the length of the fourth. Thorax more than twice as broad as long; sides abruptly diverging and acutely angled just in front of the base, thence obliquely converging to the apex, just before reaching the latter abruptly incurved, the apical angle obtuse, the hinder one armed with a lateral tooth; disc closely covered with large round, deeply impressed punctures; on either side are a few short sub-erect griseous hairs Scutellum longer than broad, cuneiform, its apex obtusely angulate Elytra convex, transversely depressed below the basilar space, strongly punctate-striate; on the transverse depression, and also below the shoulder, the puncturing is confused; interspaces plane, irregularly wrinkled on the sub-basilar depression. All the thighs armed beneath with an acute tooth

7. *Nodostoma plagiosum*, n sp.

Oblongo-ovatum, piceum, nitidum, pedibus antennisque piceo-fulvis, his extrorsum piceis; thorace profunde et crebre punc-tato, lateribus pone medium obtuse angulatis; elytris fortiter punctato-striatis, striis apicem versus fere deletis; sordide fulvis, limbo angusto, striarum punctis et utrinque plagâ irregulari magnâ, a basi ad paulo pone medium extensâ, ad marginem lateralem adfixâ, piceis. Long 1⅘ lin.

Hab. Muriee, a single specimen, also India, without precise locality, my collection.

Vertex and front sub-remotely punctured; clypeus coarsely and irregularly punctured, not distinctly separated from the upper face, its anterior border deeply excavate-emarginate, the emargination produced and forming two sub-acute teeth, labrum fulvous; antennæ slender, filiform, the second and third joints nearly equal in length, the fourth very slightly longer than the third; four or five lower joints obscure fulvous, the rest piceous. Thorax nearly twice as broad as long; sides diverging at the base, obtusely angled behind the middle, thence obliquely converging and very slightly rounded to the apex; disc transversely convex, very coarsely and deeply punctured. Elytra oblong, sub-acutely rounded at the apex, convex, strongly punctate-striate, the punctures near the apex much finer and nearly obsolete, interspaces plane, impunctate; the irregularly piceous patch on each elytron covers the outer disc (the humeral callus excepted) and extends from the base to just below the middle of the disc. All the thighs armed beneath with a small tooth.

8. *Paria cuprescens*, n. sp.

Anguste ovata, subtus cum capite picea, pedibus antennarumque basi pallidis; supra cuprea, thorace sub-conico, vage punctato; elytris regulariter punctato-striatis, interspatiis planis, impunctatis. Long. 1¼ lin.

Hab. Jhelam Valley.

Vertex swollen, shining, impunctate; clypeus transverse, its anterior border emarginate; antennæ rather more than half the length of the body, piceous, the two lower joints paler. Thorax broader than long at the base; sides straight and obliquely converging from base to apex, the hinder angles very acute; basal margin oblique on either side, the median lobe obtusely rounded; disc sub-cylindrical, impressed, but not closely, with very shallow punctures. Elytra ovate, attenuated at the apex, regularly punctate-striate, the interspaces plane, each impressed with an irregular row of minute punctures; humeral callus thickened.

9. *Plagiodera versicolora.*

Chrysomela versicolora, Laicharting, Verz. Tyrol. Ins. 1, p. 148 (1781).
Chrysomela armoraciæ, Fabr.
- Hab. Jhelam Valley.

10. *Chrysomela angelica.*

Chrysomela angelica, Reiche, Ann. Soc Ent. France, 1858, p. 33, tab. i, fig. 8; Fairm., l c. 1865, p. 80
Hab. Sind Valley; also Syria.

.I do not detect the slightest difference between specimens brought from Syria and those contained in the present collection.

11. *Phratora abdominalis*, n. sp.

Elongata, parallela, nigro-ænea aut nigro-cyanea, nitida, pedibus abdomineque nigro-piceis, hujus segmentis ultimis duobus piceo-fulvis, thorace transverso, sat fortiter irregulariter punctato, utrinque leviter rugoso; elytris thorace latioribus, parallelis, sat fortiter punctatis, punctis· subseriatim dispositis, interspatiis planis, subremote, tenuiter punctatis, infra callum humerale transversim rugulosis. Long. 2¾–3 lin.
Hab. Murree.

Head short, transverse; vertex impressed, but not very closely, with large deep punctures, lower face more closely but less coarsely punctured than the vertex, subrugulose; in the middle between the encarpæ is a short longitudinal sulcation, which extends upwards from the apex of the clypeus; the latter depressed, broader than long, its upper margin obtusely angulate, its surface closely punctured, subrugose; antennæ scarcely more than half the length of the body, filiform, slightly thickened towards the apex, the basal joint thickened, the second slender, equal in length to the first and also to the fourth joints, but slightly shorter than the third, two lower joints fulvous, stained above with piceous, the third to the sixth obscure piceous, the five others slightly thickened, black Thorax nearly one half broader than long; sides nearly straight and parallel from the base to the middle, thence obliquely converging to the apex, the hinder angles produced laterally into a large acute tooth, the anterior ones sub-acute, apical margin concave; upper surface irregularly punctured, the interspaces smooth and shining on the middle disc, finely rugulose on the sides. Elytra broader than the thorax, parallel, rather strongly punctured, the punctures arranged irregularly in ill defined longitudinal rows, which, on the inner disc below the middle, approximate in pairs; interspaces plane, sparingly and very minutely punctured on the anterior disc, rugulose on the outer one below the humeral callus. Basal joint of anterior tarsus dilated, subcordate.

12. *Haltica cærulescens.*

Haltica cærulescens, Baly, Trans Ent. Soc. 1874, p. 190.
Hab. Muricc; also China and Japan.

13. *Haltica viridicyanea.*

Haltica viridicyanea, Baly, Trans Ent. Soc. 1874, p. 191.
Hab Sind Valley, apparently common; I possess this species from Japan, it is probably found in the intermediate localities.

14. *Enneamera variabilis.*

Nonarthra variabilis, Baly, Journ. of Entom. i, p. 456, tab. 21. fig. 1.
Hab Murree; this species is also found in Northern India.

CHARÆA, n. gen.

Corpus elongato-ovatum. *Caput* exscitum, *facie* perpendiculari; *oculis* rotundatis, integris, prominentibus; *encarpis* transversis, contiguis, *carinâ* oblongo-elongatâ, apice acutâ; *antennis* filiformibus. *Thorax* transversus, dorso modice convexus. *Elytra* thorace latiora, confuse punctata, limbo inflexo fere ad apicem extenso. *Pedes*; *femoribus* posticis non incrassatis, *tibiis* simplicibus, apice spinâ acutâ armatis; *tarsis* posticis articulo basali sequentibus tribus longitudine fere æquanti, *unguiculis* appendiculatis. *Prosternum* angustum, *coxis* fere æquialtum; *acetabulis* anticis apertis.

This genus at first sight bears in its facies a strong resemblance to *Aphthora*, but the slender hinder thighs at once separate it and place it amongst the *Gallerucinæ*.

15. *Charæa flaviventre*, n. sp.

Elongato-ovata, convexa, subtus picea, æneo tincta, abdomine flavo, supra viridi-cyanea, antennis nigris; thorace lateribus

rotundatis, disco lævi, modice convexo; elytris tenuiter confuse
punctatis   Long. 1¼ lin.

Hab. Murree.

Vertex and front shining, impunctate; encarpæ transverse,
contiguous; antennæ half the length of the body, second and
third joints equal, the fourth nearly twice the length of the
third, three lower joints nigro-piceous, stained with æneous, the
rest black.   Thorax broader than long; sides converging from
the middle towards the base, the anterior angles slightly produced, obtuse, the hinder ones rounded, armed with a very small
acute tooth; disc moderately convex, very minutely punctured,
the punctures only visible under a very strong lens   Scutellum
trigonate.   Elytra broader than the thorax, parallel, finely but
not closely punctured, the interspaces obsoletely wrinkled.

MACRIMA, n. gen.

Corpus anguste oblongum, convexum.   *Caput* exsertum;
antennis filiformibus, articulo primo duobus sequentibus conjunctis æquali, his brevibus, longitudine fere æqualibus, *oculis*
sub-rotundatis, prominentibus: *encarpis* medio contiguis; *carinâ*
obsoletâ; *palpis* maxillaribus articulis duobus ultimis conjunctim
anguste ovatis, ultimo apice acuto   *Thorax* transversus, disco
leviter excavatus.   *Scutellum* trigonatum   *Elytra* thorace latiora,
oblonga, confuse punctata, limbo inflexo fere integro, concavo
Pedes mediocres, *coxis* anticis elevatis, obtrigonatis, contiguis;
tibiis apice mucronatis; *tarsis* posticis articulo primo ad tres
sequentes fere æquilongo; *unguiculis* appendiculatis   *Prosternum*
medio angustissimum; *acetabulis* anticis integris; *episternis*
posticis a basi ad apicem angustatis.   Type *Macrima armata.*

Macrima may be separated from *Aulacophora*, which genus
it strongly resembles in outer form, by the closed anterior
acetabula and by the appendiculated claws.

16. *Macrima armata*, n. sp.

Anguste oblonga, convexa, pallide flava, subnitida, pectore,
abdominis segmentis anticis tribus basi, scutelloque nigris;
thorace tenuiter punctato, utrinque leviter excavato; elytris
distincte subcrebre punctatis, punctis pallide fuscis; utrisque
super marginem basalem nigro maculatis.   Long 3½ lin.

♂ Facie tridentatâ, dente intermedio compresso, nigro, apice
deflexo; clypeo utrinque ad apicem foveolato.

♀ Facie tridentatâ, dente intermedio non compresso, apice acuto

Hab. Jhelam Valley.

Head exserted; vertex smooth, impunctate; face excavated between the eyes, clothed with hairs, tridentate, the middle tooth compressed and deflexed in the ♂, conical in the ♀; clypeus transverse, impressed at the apex on either side in the ♂ with a deep fovea; apex of jaws nigro-piceous; antennæ slender, clothed with coarse suberect hairs, second and third joints nearly equal in the ♂, the third one-half longer than the second in the ♀. Thorax about three times as broad as long; sides parallel and slightly sinuate behind the middle, obliquely converging from the middle to the apex, the anterior angles slightly produced, obtuse, the hinder ones obtusely angulate; upper surface moderately convex, the lateral margin rather broadly reflexed, disc irregularly excavated; finely but not very closely punctured, interspaces minutely granulose-strigose. Scutellum trigonate, shining black. Elytra broader than the thorax, oblong, moderately convex, faintly excavated below the basilar space, more strongly punctured than the thorax, the punctures pale fuscous.

17. *Mimastra gracilis*, n. sp.

Elongata, attenuata, pallide flava, nitida, antennis basi exceptis, fuscis, oculis nigris, genubus tarsisque piceis; thorace transverso, basi emarginato, disco irregulariter excavato, lateribus late marginatis, ante medium angulatis, elytris parallelis, tenuiter punctatis. Long 3 lin.

Hab Muriee.

. Head strongly exserted; encarpæ and clypeus thickened, the former bounded above by a transverse groove, trigonate, contiguous for their whole length; antennæ very slender, filiform, nearly equal to the body in length, second joint about half the length of the basal one, nearly a third shorter than the third, three basal joints pale flavous, the rest pale fuscous. Thorax transverse; sides broadly margined, nearly parallel, distinctly angled just beyond the middle, thence obliquely converging to the apex; disc broadly and irregularly excavated, impunctate. Scutellum trigonate. Elytra broader than the thorax, parallel, elongate; disc very minutely punctured, very faintly wrinkled. Outer edge of knees, together with the tarsi pale piceous.

18. *Agelastica orientalis*, n. sp.

Elongato-ovato, convexa, metallico-cærulea, nitida, antennis nigris; thorace elytrisque crebre punctatis, illo lateribus rotundatis Long. 3½-4 lin

Hab. neighbourhood of Sanju, apparently common.

Encarpæ and clypeus thickened, the former pyriform, contiguous, separated from the front by a deep transverse groove; antennæ filiform, half the length of the body, the second joint short, the third one-half longer than the second, more than half the length of the fourth. Thorax nearly three times as broad as long; sides rounded, slightly converging in front, the hinder angles rounded, the anterior ones obtuse; disc closely punctured. Scutellum trigonate, shining, impunctate. Elytra rather broader than the thorax, oblong, closely punctured.

Closely allied to *A. cærulea*, it may be known from that insect by the relative lengths of the second and third joints of the antennæ.

19. *Malacosoma flaviventre*, n. sp.

Elongatum, convexum, obscure viridi-æneum, nitidum, abdomine flavo, antennis (basi exceptis) nigris, thorace transverso, minute, subremote punctato; elytris oblongis, infra basin transversim excavatis, tenuiter punctatis. Long. 4 lin.

Hab. Murree.

Head trigonate; vertex and front smooth, impunctate, the latter separated from the encarpæ by a deep groove; encarpæ transverse, contiguous above, separated below by the narrow wedge-shaped carina, the surface of which is coarsely punctured; antennæ more than half the length of the body, moderately robust, filiform, the second joint short, the third twice the length of the second, the fourth about one-third longer than the preceding one. Thorax about one-half as broad again as long; sides moderately rounded, the anterior angles armed with an obtuse tubercle, the hinder ones acute; disc moderately convex, finely but rather distantly punctured; lateral margin reflexed. Scutellum smooth, impunctate. Elytra much broader than the thorax, oblong, convex, transversely excavated below the basilar space, the latter slightly elevated; surface finely but not very closely punctured, very sparingly clothed with short hairs; on the apical half of each elytron are a number of broad, ill-defined, longitudinal sulcations. Abdomen flavous, the apex of the terminal segment emarginate.

20. *Luperodes erythrocephala*, n. sp.

Auguste oblongo-ovata, convexa, nigra, nitida, capite rufo-testaceo, ore, antennis pedibusque piceis; thorace crebro punctato, disco utrinque leviter transversim excavato; elytris sat crebre punctatis. Long. 2 lin.

Hab. Murree.

Head exserted, vertex and front shining, impunctate; encarpæ transverse, contiguous; labrum piceous; jaws and palpi rufo-piceous; antennæ filiform, three-fourths the length of the body, second and third joints short, conjointly about equal in length to the first. Thorax twice as broad as long: sides rounded, slightly converging at the base, all the angles distinct, the anterior thickened, sub-tuberculate; disc closely punctured, distinctly excavated on either side. Elytra oblong, less closely punctured than the thorax.

21. *Galleruca vittatipennis*, n. sp.

Elongato-oblonga, convexa, nigro-picea aut nigra, nitida, vertice rufo-piceo, abdominis segmentorum margine apicali pallide rufo-piceo; thorace excavato, rude foveolato; elytris abdomine multo brevioribus, fortiter substriatim punctatis, sordide fulvis, utrisque lineâ suturali elevatâ, vittisque elevatis quatuor, utrinque abbreviatis, 1mâ et 4tâ, 2dâ et 3tiâ apice per paria conjunctis, nigro-piceis instructis. Long. 4½ lin.

Hab. On the road across the Pamir, from Sirikol to Panga.

Head sub-rotundate, vertex and front deeply and coarsely foveolate-punctate, impressed in the middle with a deep longitudinal groove, which extends downwards between the encarpæ as far as the apex of the clypeus, where it terminates in a triangular fovea; encarpæ thickened, trigonate, smooth, impunctate; clypeus very short, thickened and forming a transverse ridge, its anterior border narrowly edged with rufous; antennæ robust, the second joint ovate, rather more than half the length of the third, the third and fourth joints equal. Thorax rather more than twice as broad as long; sides sinuate and parallel from the base to beyond the middle, thence obliquely converging to the apex, the anterior angles slightly produced, somewhat recurved, obtuse; disc excavated on either side, the middle disc impressed with a broad longitudinal sulcation which extends from base to apex; the whole surface covered with large, deep, round foveæ. Scutellum semi-rotundate, piceous, impunctate.

22. *Galleruca indica*, n. sp.

Ovata, postice paulo ampliata, modice convexa, nigra, subtus nitida, griseo sericea, supra opaca ; capite thoraceque rude rugoso-punctatis, hoc transverso, utrinque foveolato, medio longitudinaliter sulcato, lateribus reflexis, ante medium obsolete angulatis; elytris vage rufo-piceo limbatis, rugoso-punctatis, utrisque vittis elevatis quatuor, duabus intermediis interruptis, interdum fere totidem obsoletis, instructis. Long. 5 lin.

Hab. Murree ; also Northern India, my collection.

Head very coarsely rugose-punctate. Thorax nearly twice as broad as long ; sides parallel, slightly sinuate, obtusely angled just before the middle, thence obliquely converging to the apex, the anterior angle moderately produced, its apex rounded ; disc very coarsely rugose-punctate, the middle portion with a longitudinal sulcation which extends from base to apex, either side impressed with a large fovea. Scutellum coarsely rugose-punctate. Elytra broader than the thorax, ovate, slightly dilated towards the apex, moderately convex, rugose-punctate, but less coarsely so than the head and thorax ; black, sometimes tinged with piceous, the outer margin obscure rufo-piceous ; each elytron with four raised vittæ, the two intermediate ones interrupted and sometimes almost entirely obsolete ; the suture also thickened.

23. *Galerucella** placida*, n. sp.

Anguste oblonga, griseo hirsuta, subtus picea, nitida, prothorace fulvo ; supra sordide fulva, subnitida, antennis, verticis plaga, thoracis maculis tribus transversim positis scutelloque basi piceis, thorace transverso, lateribus ante basin dente subacuto armatis, ante dentem concavis, ante medium ampliatis, disco rude rugoso, bifoveolato ; elytris profunde confuse punctatis, interspatiis granulosis. Long. 2 lin.

Hab. Jhelam Valley, one specimen ; I also possess this insect from India.

Vertex and front finely rugose-punctate, clothed with adpressed griseous hairs, the middle with a large ill defined piceous patch ; encarpæ thickened, contiguous, pyriform, antennæ moderately robust, filiform, the second joint nearly equal in length to the first, about two-thirds the length of the third.

---

* *Galerucella*, Crotch, Proc Acad Philad 1873, p. 55.

Thorax more than half as broad again as long; sides diverging at the base, and armed at the apex of the diverging portion with a subacute, setiferous tooth, immediately in front of which, before the middle, they are deeply sinuate, in front they are broadly dilated, the anterior angle armed with a subacute tooth; disc coarsely rugose-punctate, broadly excavated on either side, and again more deeply, but to a less extent, on the anterior half of the middle disc; the piceous patches, placed transversely on the disc, are large but ill defined, and cover nearly the whole of the surface.   Scutellum narrowed from its base towards the apex, the latter obtusely truncate.   Elytra oblong, nearly parallel, deeply and coarsely punctured, densely clothed with short suberect griseous hairs.

24. *Merista interrupta.*

Galleruca interrupta, L. Redtb. in Hugel's Kaschmir, iv, p. 553, tab. xxvii, fig. 4 (1844)

Hab Murree, a single specimen.

The transverse black patch differs greatly in extent in different individuals, in some being entirely obsolete; in the specimen before me it is reduced to two small fuscous points placed transversely on the middle disc.

In this species, of which I possess many specimens from various parts of India, the second and third joints of the antennæ vary in relative length in the sexes; in the ♂ these joints are very short and nearly equal; in the ♀ the third joint, though short, is distinctly longer than the second.

25 *Leptartha collaris*, n sp.

Ovata, postice ampliata, nigra, nitida; thorace transverso, fulvo; elytra fortiter sat crebre punctatis, castaneis, punctis piceis, utrisque maculâ basali juxta suturam nigro-æneâ notatis. Long. 4½–5 lin.

Hab. Murree; in my own collection from Northern India.

Vertex shining, impunctate; encarpæ thickened, contiguous, semi-lunate: antennæ nearly equal to the body in length, filiform, tapering towards the apex, second and third joints very short, equal. Thorax transverse, sides constricted behind the middle, dilated in front, the anterior angles produced, their apices obtuse; apical border concave-emarginate; disc smooth, impunctate, thickened on either side near the anterior angle, impressed on each side the middle with a faint transverse groove. Scutellum trigonate. Elytra broader than the thorax, dilated behind the middle, moderately convex, deeply punctured, the punctures piceous, arranged without order over the general surface, placed in ill-defined longitudinal striæ near the base of the suture; on the anterior disc are several short ill-defined obsoletely raised vittæ; at the base of each elytron, close to the suture, is a small nigro-æneous patch. Last two segments of abdomen bordered with fulvous

In the specimen from Murree the sides of the thorax are less dilated anteriorly, the anterior angles being less produced and at the same time more acute; the transverse depressions on the middle disc are also obsolete; in this specimen the antennæ are unfortunately broken, but the fourth and fifth joints (which remain) are slightly compressed, and are rather more robust than in the insect from Northern India; it is probably the other sex.

Remarks on the Synonymy of Vanessa C-aureum, *Linn.;* by
W. F. Kirby.

In the last number of the " Cistula Entomologica," Mr. O. E.
Janson states that he cannot see any reason for considering
Angelica, Cram., identical with *C-aureum*, Linn., alleging that
the description "though almost useless for the purpose of identification," agrees quite well with the *C-aureum*, of Fabricius,
Cramer, and Hubner. He sets aside the locality of the Linnean
insect as unworthy of consideration, and reflects upon me for
having placed Hubner's figures of *C-aureum*, and Cramer's
figure of *Angelica* together. I have just received Mr. Strecker's
"Butterflies and Moths of North America," and at p. 128, I find
a long discussion on the subject, decidedly identifying *C-aureum*,
of Linn., with the Asiatic *Angelica*, Cram , and not with the
North American *Interrogationis*, Fabr The Linnean description runs—" *Papilio C-aureum*, alis angulatis fulvis nigro-macu-
latis; posticis subtus C aureo notatis. Habitat in Asia. Simill-
mus *P. C-albo*, sed duplo major, subtus magis luteo-nebulosus, et
C. aureo minori notatis." Mr. Strecker remarks " This is plain
enough ; neither *Interrogationis* nor var. *Umbrosa* are cloudy
yellow beneath, but *C-aureum* most undoubtedly is " To which
I will add that the silver mark on the underside of *Angelica* is
always much smaller than that of *C-album*, while that of *Interrogationis* is always much larger. As regards the Linnean
localities, an error is of rare occurrence, as any one may see for
himself, who will take the trouble to compare them; always,
of course, remembering that the phrase " In Indus," must be
left out of account, as it meant no more with Linné than "an
exotic species, of which I do not know the locality." With

respect to the implied assertion that I compared Cramer's figure of *Angelica* with Hubner's *C-aureum*, and considered them identical, I will only say that Hubner's Sammlung did not then exist in any Dublin library, and that having a memorandum that Hubner had figured *C-aureum*, I quoted the figures as referring to *C-aureum*, Linn., which Godart and Doubleday correctly consider identical with *Angelica*, and having no opportunity of examining Hubner's figures, could not suspect that he had copied Cramer's error in referring the name to *Interrogationis*, Fabr.

Notices of new or little known CETONIIDÆ ; by OLIVER E. JANSON. No. 5.

Discopeltis aberrans, n sp

D. elongata, capite nigro, nitido ; thorace nigro, opaco, lateribus late sordide rufo marginato ; clytris obsolete striato-punctatis, sordide rufis, maculâ basali trigonâ nigrâ notatis ; pygidio medio rufo ; subtus nigra, nitida. Long. 13½. lat. 6½ mm.

Head with coarse confluent punctures at the base and sides, the clypeus finely punctured, a feeble central longitudinal ridge on the forehead, and an oblique one on each side united at the base smooth ; clypeus depressed at the sides, the apex rounded and emarginate in the centre , black, slightly shining ; antennæ black, the apex reddish.

Thorax convex, the sides slightly prominent in the middle, the base produced into an obtuse point over the scutellum, rather finely and obsoletely punctured : dull black, the sides broadly margined with dull red.

Scutellum partly concealed, the apex strongly produced and very acute ; dull black.

Elytra half as long again as broad, depressed, parallel-sided, the suture posteriorly and two carinæ, united at the apical callosity, feebly elevated and smooth, the interstices and sides with indistinct punctate striæ, the apex with scattered shallow punctures ; dull rusty red, with an elongate triangular dull black patch at the base, extending along the suture beyond the middle ; epimera shining black and coarsely punctured above

Pygidium dull black on each side, the centre broadly dull red.

Beneath coarsely punctured and strigose, shining black, the prothorax and posterior coxæ margined with red ; mesosternal process short and broad, the apex straight and not dilated ; abdomen with a transverse row of punctures on each segment, the apical segment closely punctured and red in the centre, the sides with sparse golden pubescence ; legs shining black, coarsely punctured, the femora with a sparse fringe of golden hairs, anterior tibiæ with two acute lateral teeth, the others with a strong tooth about the middle.

Angola.

Appears to be allied to *D. lateralis*, Gerst.

Glycyphana incongrua, n. sp.

G. subquadrata, supra obscure viridis, opaca, thorace lateribus albo-marginato; elytris bicostatis, profundius punctatis, lateribus postice, maculis quatuor, fasciaque apicali albis; pygidio albo quadri-maculato; subtus viridi-nigra, nitida.   Long. $10\frac{1}{2}$, lat. 6 mm.

Head very closely and finely punctured, the punctures confluent at the sides of the clypeus, sparsely pubescent, margins of the clypeus slightly elevated, the apex emarginate and the sides strongly rounded, black, slightly shining, the base greenish; antennæ pitchy.

Thorax strongly rounded at the sides, the basal margin slightly sinuous, rather coarsely and deeply punctured, with sparse short golden pubescence, a small space before the scutellum smooth; dark green, opaque, the sides narrowly margined with white.

Scutellum large, triangular, with a few coarse punctures at the base; dark opaque green.

Elytra subquadrate, the suture and two discal carinæ on each distinctly elevated and smooth, the interspaces and sides with rows of coarse deep setiferous punctures; dark green, opaque, the apex black, a small spot just behind the shoulder, one on the inner carina about the middle, another nearer the apex and close to the lateral margin, a larger one near the suture about one fourth from the apex, a narrow lateral marginal line on the posterior half, and a large angulated transverse fascia close to the apex white.

Pygidium coarsely strigose and pubescent; shining black, with a transverse row of four white spots.

Beneath greenish black, shining, strigose and pubescent; mesosternal process broad and rounded, with a transverse impressed line fringed with golden hairs; abdomen with rows of coarse semicircular impressions, legs greenish black, shining, punctured and pubescent, anterior tibiæ with three acute lateral teeth.

Formosa.

On a collection of Lepidoptera from Madagascar; by Arthur
G. Butler, F.L.S., F.Z.S.

I have recently had the pleasure of examining a collection
forwarded to us by the Rev. R. Toy, and collected by his son at
Antananarivo.

The following interesting species were amongst those selected :—

Rhopalocera.

Pseudonympha tamatavæ, Boisd.

Both sexes. of this species appear to be common at Antananarivo.

Pseudonympha ankova (Mycalesis ankova, Ward).

Pseudonympha ibitina (Mycalesis ibitina, Ward).

In a recent paper in the "Annals and Magazine of Natural
History," I have noted this species as coming from Fianarantsoa;
I am, however, now convinced that the insect there indicated
is a distinct species, although it agrees almost as well with
Mr. Ward's description as that just received; I therefore append
·descriptions of both.

Pseudonympha ibitina.

Dark fuliginous brown, with darker submarginal line parallel
to the outer margin, the margin itself blackish; primaries with a
large subapical black ocellus, with two blue pupils and a rather
broad deep orange iris; secondaries with two smaller rounded
black ocelli, with single bluish-white pupils and narrow deep
orange irides, upon the median interspaces; wings below with
the basal three-fifths fuliginous brown, its outer edge oblique
and slightly sinuous upon the primaries, triundulate upon the
secondaries; disc greyish, with numerous brown striations,
outer border of primaries more densely striated than the disc;

H H

ocellus as above; secondaries with a large patch of fuliginous
brown, with darker striations at centre of external border;
ocelli very small, that upon the second median interspace barely
visible, a third very small subapical ocellus   Expanse of wings
$1\frac{1}{2}$ inches
    Hab. Antananarivo.

We have two examples of this species.

Pseudonympha Wardii, n. sp.

♀ Paler than the preceding, ocellus of primaries with narrower iris and whiter pupils, an additional small blind ocellus
upon the first median interspace, submarginal line more distinct;
secondaries with the outer margin slightly undulated, the ocelli
paler ; a small additional subapical ocellus, submarginal line
more distinct ; primaries below much paler ; secondaries fuliginous brown, the basal, abdominal and apical areas densely striated
with grey ; a spot before the middle of the costa, a large patch
across the centre of costal area, and a spot near the end of the
cell creamy-whitish, striated with dark brown ; anal area broadly
testaceous, striated with olive-brown ; the ocelli upon the median
interspaces feebly indicated and very small.   Expanse of wings
1 inch 9 lines.
    Hab Fianarantsoa.

Allowing for the generally adopted method of measuring from
tip to tip, this insect would be only two lines wider in expanse
than *P. ibitina*, and this would be accounted for by its sex.
The coloration of the undersurface of the secondaries scarcely
agrees with Mr. Ward's description, but the latter was only
intended to be provisional ; however, now that we have a species'
of the exact size and the general coloration indicated in the
description—"Hind wing with numerous waved markings of
darker brown mingled with lighter brown, and the ocelli faintly
showing, " it is evident that I allowed too wide a margin for the
provisional nature of that description

In my opinion, all diagnoses not accompanied by figures ought
to be sufficiently precise to enable the student to decide, without
hesitation, whether or not he has the species in his cabinet , otherwise they become rather a hindrance than a help to science,
benefiting only their author, if indeed there is any personal
profit in attaching one's name to that of a butterfly, which I for
one do not admit,

P. Wardii, though it agrees in structure with *Pseudonympha* (excepting in the outline of the wing), has more nearly the aspect of the New World genus *Stibomorpha* than of anything else.

Ypthima batesii, Felder (? = *Y. vinsoni*, Guénée).

The description in Vinson's "Voyage à Madagascar" does not quite suit Felder's species, but nevertheless comes so near that I can hardly believe the two forms to be distinct species.

Mycalesis fraterna, Butler

Both sexes are common in Madagascar, and differ constantly from the Mauritian form with which my species is associated in Kirby's catalogue.

Charaxes andara, Ward.

A fine male of this handsome species was in the collection; unfortunately it only has one antenna, but scientifically this is quite sufficient.

Junonia epiclelia, Boisd.

Almost too closely allied to the African form to be regarded as distinct.

Eurytela narinda, Ward.

Much like *E. dryope* on the upper surface.

Lycæna atrigemmata, Butler.

This little species will probably prove to be as common as the allied *L. Knysna* of Trimen, it is a distinct and pretty little butterfly.

Belenois coniata, n sp.

Wings above white, with a tint of sulphur-yellow, primaries with the basal two-thirds of discoidal area salmon coloured; apex and four confluent triangular spots forming the external border, black; costal border grey, becoming blackish towards apex; secondaries with six decreasing squamose black spots terminating the veins; body grey; wings below pearly-white;

primaries with the costal border at base sulphur-yellow; basal two-thirds of discoidal area bright orange; secondaries with yellow costal margin, becoming bright orange towards the base; body white. Expanse of wings 2 inches 5 lines.

Allied to *B. thysa.*

Teracolus evanthe, Boisd.

Quite like African examples.

Proteides ramanatek, Boisd.

This barbarously named species has been referred erroneously to the genus *Ismene* (*Hesperia,* Fabr.), it, however, agrees both in structure and general pattern with *Proteides.*

Tagiades ophion, Boisd.

This belongs to the African group of the genus.

Hesperia margarita, n. sp.

Allied to *H. forestan,* with which it has been confounded, but readily distinguishable by the emerald green patch at the base of the primaries, and the coloration of the secondaries, in which the whole of the ochraceous area, excepting the anal border and fringe (which, however, are rather orange than ochreous) replaced by white, tinted with green. Expanse of wings 2 inches 3 lines.

Hesperia pansa, Hewits (= *ernesti,* Grand).

This is a beautiful species, allied, though not very closely, to the preceding.

Heterocera.

Macroglossa milius, Boisd

Either the figure of this species is incorrect or the examples which I have seen are referable to a distinct species; Dr. Boisduval represents his species as having the secondaries orange, with a broad ferruginous border and four of the abdominal segments orange at the sides, the common *Macroglossa* of Madagascar has the outer border of secondaries dark brown, with ferruginous inner edge, and only three of the abdominal segments are *tawny* at the sides; the anal tuft also has a ferruginous border; about half of the specimens seen by me have a transverse bar of snow-white scales along the anterior margin of the last segment.

Deilephila biguttata, Walker.

The collection contained a good series of this handsome moth; hitherto we have only possessed the type, a damaged ♂ example

Nephile charoba, Kirby.

A very variable species, the wings being of all sorts of shades between rust-red and dark smoky-brown.

Triptogon meander, Boisd.

A male of this very rare species, unfortunately somewhat damaged; the form of the primaries is somewhat aberrant for a *Triptogon*, so that eventually a genus may have to be erected for its reception.

Bizone amatura, Walker.

B hova of Guénée is identical with this species.

Sozuza marginata, Guérin.

This is one of the prettiest of the Mascarene *Lithosiids*.

Borocera madagascariensis, Boisd.

There cannot be a question but that *B. Cajani* is the same species; Boisduval's figure is indeed rough, but it is just recognisable.

Cyligramma conturbans, Walker.

C. raboudou of Lucas is happily identical with this species, so that the latter name may be expunged.

Ophiodes hottentota, Guénée.

This agrees with S. African examples.

Hypochroma Grandidieri, n. sp.

Nearly allied to *H. nyctemerata* (*ruginaria*, Guénée), but the basal area sordid, the subbasal black line sharply defined, simply angulated instead of crinkled, the discocellulars black; the outer black line, limiting the dark area, much straighter; secondaries with the white patch upon the outer border reduced to a small spot. Expanse of wings 2 inches.

This is one of the not uncommon instances in which species from Madagascar nearly resemble those from Southern India and Ceylon.

Macaria deerraria (= *Tephria deerraria*, Walker).

Quite like African examples

Comibæna stibolepida, n. sp.

Wings snow-white, densely mottled with dull bluish-green; a slightly arched testaceous stripe across the basal area, and an undulated discal stripe of the same colour; body whitish testaceous; wings below white, primaries with testaceous costal border; body white, legs red-brown above. Expanse of wings 11 lines.

Allied to *C. pieridoides*.

Sindris aganzini, Boisd.

This pretty little moth is not well represented by Boisduval; the abdomen is much more slender than in his figure, and has a much more fully developed anal tuft. M. Guénée refers it to his family *Scirpophagidæ* and places it amongst the *Tineites*.

New Genera and Species of CALLICHROMINÆ (Coleoptera Longi-
cornia) ; by H. W. BATES, F.L S.

Colobus fulvus.

Fulvus, ventris segmentis dimidio basali nigro-fuscis : capitis
vertice, thorace, elytris et pectore subaureis dense velutinis :
thorace basi tantum sulcato-constricto . antennis ♀ corpore
multo brevioribus, articulis basali et 2–10 apice extus acute
productis · elytris singulis triangularibus, metathoracem paululum
superantibus ; femoribus gradatim incrassatis, tibiis posticis mox
a basi modice dilatato-compressis, tarsis articulo 1 cæteribus
longitudine æquali. Long. 17 lin. ♀ .

Sylhet. From Mr. W. W. Saunders' collection ; probably the
C. velutinus, Saund. in litt., Munich Cat. p. 2,901.

AMPHIONTHE, n. gen.

Gen. Polyschisis (Serv.) affinis; differt antennis ♂ valde elongatis, 11 articulatis. Corpus elongatum postice vix angustatum,
supra planatum. Mandibulæ modicæ elongatæ Epistomate a
fronte sutura arcuata diviso. Palpi longitudine subæquales,
maxillarum lobo haud elongato. Thorax latus, transversus,
tuberculo laterali antice curvato. Scutellum lanceolatum.
Elytra apice truncata. Prosternum processu marginato, apice verticali . mesosterno medio subtuberculato Abdomen ♂ segmentis
5 ventralibus, quinto lato apice truncato Antennæ ♂ corpore
fere duplo longiores, velutinæ, opacæ, scapo gradatim clavato
simplici, articulo 4to quam 3io vel 5to paulo breviori ; 3–11
carinatis, 5–7 apice extus acute spinosis. Pedes modice elongati :
breviter pilosi femora gradatim paulo incrassata : tibiæ posticæ
a basi usque ad apicem recte modice compresso-dilatatæ longius
et densius pilosis.

A remarkable genus, allied to Polyschisis in the form of the
maxillæ and palpi, the arched suture separating the epistome
from the forehead and the hairy hind tibiæ In the antennæ it
is totally different ; the length of these organs and the style of
coloration, giving the insect the facies of Callichroma.

Amphionthe Doris

Viridi-aurata, thorace disco elytrisque vittis duabus (altera lata discoidali altera angustiori submarginali) nigro-velutinis; antennis pedibusque nigris: capite minute punctato: thorace antice et postice sulcato-constricto, dorso postice et in sulco lævi, lateribus et prosterno confertim punctatis · elytiis confertissime subalveolato-punctatis, pilis brevibus erectis nigris vestitis, vittis nigris opacis. Long. 12 lin. ♂.

New Granada, from Mr. W. W. Saunders' collection. Taken I believe by Mr. Chesterton.

Pachyteria Javana.

Subgracilis, postice gradatim fortiter angustata; chalybea, subtus grisco-sericea, elytris dimidio basali badiis nitidis, antennis articulis 3–6 et 7 basi badio-flavis, cæteribus nigris; thorace parvo, nitido, basi et apice sulcato-constricto, disco grosse subsparsim punctato: elytris post medium juxta suturam et apud discum longitudinaliter excavato-depressis velutinis, cæteris partibus glabris discrete punctatis. Long. 13 lin. ♂.

Java (From Dr. Monicke's collection).

Phyllocnema semifulva.

Ph. mirificæ (Pasc.) affinis. Minor, capite thoraceque nigro-obscuris opacis; elytris dimidio basali chalybeo-violaceis, dimidio apicali, antennis pedibusque rufo-fulvis, tibiis posticis mox pone basin valde dilatato-compressis, parte dilatata basi excepta chalybea: corpore subtus chalybeo · thorace convexo, æquali, alveolato-punctato: elytris subtilissime rugulosis, opacis, costula discoidali sublævi fere apicem attingenti. Long. 6 lin. ♂.

The fulvous colouring of the elytra occupies rather less than the apical half and graduates into the blue of the basal half. The foliaceous expansion of the hind tibiæ is of the same form as in *Ph. mirifica*, i.e., it extends on both sides of the axis, but more so on the outer side.

Angola (collected by J. J. Monteiro).

Mecaspis fuscoænea.

Valde elongata, cupreo-vel æneo-fusca, interdum purpurascens; fere glabra, thorace et elytris discrete (illo sparsissime hoc lateribus subtilius) punctatis; antennis pedibusque nigris tarsis argenteo-pilosis: capite punctulato: thorace disco elevato utrinque punctulato plagâque tenui velutina medio lævi, interdum fere omnino lævi · elytris gradatim attenuatis, nitidis, lateribus et medio basi subtiliter punctulatis et tenuiter sparsim velutinis, interdum toto glabris et punctis majoribus sparsim conspersis. corpore subtus fere glabro, lateribus tenuiter argenteo-sericeo, abdomine plerumque violaceo. Long. 14–17 lin. ♂, ♀.

Distinguished from its nearest ally *M plutina* by the relatively longer elytra and the colour, which is dark brassy (slightly golden) or coppery brown, sometimes inclined to purple. The majority of examples compared also differ in the more glabrous surface, both of thorax and elytra; the parts clothed with thin pile and minutely punctured are here of much smaller area, and the elytra are sometimes entirely naked and tolerably strongly punctured throughout, the thorax in the same examples being nearly impunctate The posterior corners of the disk of the latter are sometimes strongly wrinkled.

Mt. Cameroons (G. Thomson).

Mecaspis chrysina.

Aurato-viridis politissima, antennis et pedibus nigris, femoribus (basi exceptis) rufis, tarsis posticis argenteo-pilosis. thorace omnino (tuberculis anterioribus 2 exceptis) transversim ·rugosis, interstitiis punctatis · elytris passim punctatis, versus humeros solum pilis nonnullis nigris Long. 14 lin. ♂.

M. læta, Hope, Ann & Mag. Nat. Hist. vol. xi, 1843, p 368 partim ?

Distinguished by its transversely wrinkled thorax. The rugæ are slightly waved and extend (with interruptions in the lateral and anterior depressions and on the dorsal tubercle) to the fore and hind margins and the lateral spines. The elytra are pretty evenly and not closely punctured throughout The colour is a splendid golden-green, more brassy on the under surface.

Sierra Leone.

Mecaspis plutina.

Viridi-ænea subaurata interdum subcyanea, nitida, thoracis disco elytrorumque basi et lateribus subvelutinis; antennis pedibusque nigris, tarsis argenteo-pilosis capite subtiliter punctulato thorace disco elevato subtilissime punctulato et breviter nigro-velutino : elytris gradatim attenuatis subtilissime alutaceis linea lata utrinque longitudinali glabriori sparsim punctulata; corpore subtus tenuiter argenteo-sericeo. Long. 14 lin ♀.

M. læta, Hope, Ann, & Mag. Nat. Hist. vol. xi, 1843, p. 368 partim?

The colour varies between bright brassy-green, sometimes verging towards golden, especially at the apex of the elytra, and greenish-blue. The neighbourhood of the suture is slightly depressed. There are always traces of short black velvety pile, chiefly on the disc of the thorax, at the middle of the base, and along the sides and suture of the elytra; but it is never dense enough to obscure the bright metallic colour of the integument; the latter is more strongly punctured, even along the glabrous central longitudinal line, where a few sparse points are visible, the rest of the surface, like the disc of the thorax, being excessively minutely punctulate-rugulose. The transverse ridge which bounds posteriorly the elevated disc of the thorax, is vertical (as in the foregoing species), but depressed in the middle. The fifth ventral segment ♂ is normal in size and shape, i e., not notably narrowed and elongated, and the apex is very slightly sinuated in the middle.

Cameroons River.

Mecaspis chrysogaster.

Viridi-ænea, elytris vittis saturatioribus duabus velutinis, altera a medio basi usque ad apicem suturalem extensa, altera breviori sublaterali, reliquis lineis longitudinalibus nitidis punctato-rugulosis: abdomine igneo-aureo resplendenti: antennis pedibusque nigris, tarsis pectoreque argenteo-sericeis. Long. 13 lin. ♀.

The head is thickly punctured in front and golden-green. The thorax is transverse as in the other species, strongly sulcate-constricted in front and behind, with the middle part elevated and nearly plane, this part has a scarcely perceptible pile and is throughout finely alutaceous and moderately shining.

Cameroons.

Mecaspis subvestita.

Saturate cærulea vel viridi-cyanea, supra plagis nigro-velutinis exceptis glabra, antennis pedibusque nigris, tarsis argenteo-pilosis, pectore abdominisque lateribus subtiliter argenteo-sericeis· capite punctulato. thorace antice et postice sulcato-constricto, lævi, disco elevato subplano: elytris a basi usque ad apicem attenuatis, subtiliter alutaceis, regione suturali per totam longitudinem late depressa. Long. 12 lin ♂, ♀.

The variation in colour of this species extends from rich dark-blue to greenish-blue, and the black velvety pile in fresh specimens is visible chiefly in slight depressions on the elevated disc of the thorax, at the base of the elytra, in the sutural depression, and on the sides. In some individuals there is a sparse and fine punctuation along the shining and slightly elevated central line of the elytra, from the shoulders to the apex. The scutellum varies in length and in the number of transverse wrinkles; in some examples the latter being replaced near the base by a finer granulation. The sexes do not differ except in the usual character of the number of ventral segments, the ♂ having six and the ♀ five only. The antennæ differ very slightly in length, being in both sexes a little shorter than the body.

Cameroons, also Angola

Mecaspis crœsus.

Splendide aurata, subviridis · antennis et pedibus nigris, illis scapo castaneo-rufo, his femoribus (basi et apice exceptis) sanguineis, tarsis argenteo-pilosis : capite fere lævi · thorace disco elevato sparsim punctato vix ruguloso, sulcis anticis et posticis lævibus : elytris passim haud crebre punctulatis, plagis subhumerali et sublaterali tenuiter velutinis · margine laterali mox ab humero usque paulo ante apicem explanato-reflexo : prosterno (ante pedes) utrinque vitta griseo-pilosa.

♀ Antennæ breves, dimidio corpori æquales. Segmentum 5 ventrale apice classi-marginatum vix sinuatum. Long. 20 lin ♀.

Agrees with the following species in the reflexed-explanate lateral margins of the elytra, and in the pilose vitta on each side of the anterior part of the prosternum; but differs in the bright golden colour, shorter antennæ, punctured thorax, and form of last ventral segment. There is but a very slight trace of velvety vitta on the disc of the elytra.

Gaboon.

Mecaspis explanata.

Saturate viridi-cyanea, elytris plaga basali vittisque suturali et sublaterali cæruleo-violaceo-velutinis. antennis pedibusque nigris, tarsis argenteo-pilosis, femoribus interdum medio rufis capite subtiliter punctulato : thorace lævi, disco elevato utrinque violaceo-velutino : elytris amplis, margine laterali explanato-reflexo, supra politis sparsim punctulatis, vittis violaceo-velutinis opacis : propectore utrinque griseo-piloso.

♀ Segmentum 5 ventrale, apice fortiter emarginato.

♂ Segmenta 5 et 6 apice fortiter arcuata; hoc medio sulcato. Long. 15–18 lin. ♂, ♀.

Distinguished by the amplitude of the elytra, and the dark brassy-green or greenish-blue colour, and the rich violet hue of its velutine patches and stripes. The antennæ in both sexes are nearly three-fourths the length of the body. In one ♀ example the scutellum is much shorter than in the others, the narrow apical prolongation being wanting The single ♂ example has the central part of all the femora red.

Cameroons River

SYNAPTOLA, n. gen.

Gen. *Philematio* affinis: differt antennis ♂ corpore brevioribus, thoracisque lateribus tumidis, haud acute spinosis. Femora omnia subtus acute dentata, 4 antica pedunculata. Scutellum haud elongatum plerumque transverse rugulatum. Prosternum apice tumidum interdum tuberculatum Mandibulæ elongatæ aut subrectæ aut apice subiter incurvæ.

Synaptola brevicornis .

Saturate viridi-cyanea, nitida; antennis pedibusque nigris, tarsis argenteo-pilosis mandibulæ elongatæ, apice incurvo excepto rectæ, sinistra intus flexuosa nec dentata: thorace quam in *Mecaspis* angustiori, antice et postice sulcato-constricto, lateribus tuberculo valido, conico, obtuso: dorso elevato, sparsim transverse strigoso (linea dorsali abbreviata lævi) disco utrinque tenuiter nigro-velutino . scutello apice obtuso, transversim ruguloso· elytris passim subtiliter subcrebre punctatis: prosterno apice valide tuberculato· antennis ♀ dimidio corporis vix longioribus, articulo 3 valde elongato 4–10 serratis. Long. 13 lin. ♀.

♀ Segmentum 5 ventrale apice emarginatum.

Approaches nearer to *Mecaspis* than the rest of its congeners, in the tuberculation of the prosternum and the transverse rugæ of the scutellum It has, however, an acute tooth on the underside of the hind femora.

Sierra Leone.

Synaptola armipes.

Violacea, antennis et pedibus nigris, femoribus 4 anticis medio rufis, tarsis argenteo-pilosis: thorace antice (haud profunde) et

postice sulcato-constricto lateribus tuberculo lævi obtusissimo;
dorso haud strigoso, utrinque sparsim velutino : scutello triangulari, transversim ruguloso, medio lævi : elytris confertissime
punctulatis, brevissime pilosis : prosterno apice convexo nec
tuberculato · femoribus omnibus apicem versus acute dentatis ·
tibiis posticis versus apicem compresso-dilatatis · antennis ♂
corpore quinta parte brevioribus articulo 3 quam 4 et 5 conjunctis longiori. Long. 9½ lin. ♂.

Angola (collected by J. J. Monteiro).

Synaptola rugulosa.

Angusta, saturate viridi-ænea pilis brevibus nigris vestita,
subtus lætius viridi-ænea, griseo-sericea et erecte griseo-pilosa ·
mandibulis elongatis apice modice incurvis, sinistra ante apicem
dente lata armata. thorace utrinque latere medio producto,
rotundato, antice et postice sulcato-constricto, dorso subtilissime
punctato : scutello fere lævi. elytris passim subtilissime transversim rugulosis· antennis pedibusque nigris femoribus 4 anticis
medio rufis, tarsis argenteo-pilosis. prosterno apice tumido.
Long. 8 lin. ♂.

Cameroons.

Synaptola chlorina.

Subangusta, æneo-viridis læte subsericeo-nitens, pilis decum-
bentibus tenuiter vestita; subtus tenuiter argenteo-sericea;
mandibulis brevibus et latis, apice citius angustatis et falcatis.
thorace antice et postice sulcato-constricto, lateribus medio
obtuse tuberosis, dorso utrinque subtilissime punctulato · elytris
passim confertissime et subtiliter punctulatis antennis pedibusque nigris; femoribus omnibus medio rufis, tarsis albo-pilosis:
scapo apice extus nullomodo producto Long. 9 lin. ♂.

Cameroons.

Synaptola obtusa.

Modice elongata, postice valde attenuata, æneo-viridis, elytris
paulo saturatioribus vel subcæruleis, sericeo-nitens, tenuissime
decumbenti-pilosa, subtus griseo-sericea, antennis pedibusque
nigris, femoribus 4 anticis medio rufis, tarsis argenteo-pilosis.
mandibulis elongatis apice vix hamatis thorace lateribus fortiter
rotundatis, antice haud profunde, postice magis, constricto, disco
æquali subtiliter punctulato-velutino. scutello æneo nitido apice
paululum producto · elytris quam maxime subtiliter transversim

rugulosis, et longitudinaliter vage superficialiter flexuoso-
undulatis.   Antennis ♀ corpore paulo brevioribus; scapo apice
extus spinoso.   Long. 10 lin. ♀.

Differs from the other species of the genus in the spinose apex .
of the scape, and the feebleness of the tooth on the undersurface
of the hindmost femora.   The length of the antennæ in the ♂ is
unknown.

Gaboon.

Philematium natalense

Ph. albitarse, (Fabr.), Fahræus, Ofv. Vetensk. Akad. Foih.
1872, 1, 59.

Viridi-auratum, subtus aureum, antennis pedibusque nigris,
femoribus (basi et apice exceptis) rufis, tarsis argenteo-pilosis:
thorace supra passim strigoso, strigis mediis antice usque ad
sulcum anteriorem curvatis, inter strigas punctato : elytris confertissime et subtilissime punctatis et undulato-strigosis · femorum
dentibus brevibus vix acutis.   Long. 12–14 lin. ♂, ♀.

An apparently common Natal species erroneously determined
in some collections as *Call. hottentota*, Buq., with the description
of which it does not at all agree.   *Call. hottentota* is in fact a
true *Callichroma*, strikingly distinguished by its red metathoracic
episterna, as mentioned by Buquet.

The present species is closely allied to *Ph. Sansibaricum*,
Gerst., and *Ph. Curroni*, White.

Callichroma sapphira.

Saturate cærulea tenuiter velutina ; femoribus (basi et apice
exceptis) abdomineque rufis ; antennis, tibiis et tarsis nigris:
capite grosse punctato ; antennarum scapo grosse rugoso, sub-
punctato · thorace omnino transversim ruguloso . elytris apice
attenuatis subacutis, supra confertissime et subtilissime punctulato-rugulosis . pectore viridi-cyaneo.   Long. 17 lin. ♀.

Mexico.   Received from M. Sallé under the inappropriate
name of *C. smaragdinum*, Chevr., M.S.   The colour makes no
approach to " emerald green."

Callichroma chiriquina.

C. holochlora (Bates) proxime affinis vel ejusdem var. geographica.   Supra violacea, chalybea vel viridi-cyanea, elytris

interdum saturate viridibus, nigro-velutinis; antennis pedibusque nigris, femoribus 4 anticis (basi et apice exceptis) 2 posticis dimidio basali, rufis: thorace subtilissime transversim ruguloso, sparsim velutino: elytris apice subito rotundatis vel obtuse truncatis. corpore subtus nitido. Tibiis posticis fortiter dilatato-compressis, supra arcuatis subtus flexuosis. Long. 15–17 lin. ♂, ♀.

Chiriqui.

Callichroma euthalia.

C. holochloræ (Bates) affinis. Viridi-ænea, elytris cyancis vel subviolaceis, densius velutinis linea suturali nuda viridi-ænea. thorace confertim subtiliter transverso strigoso, disco velutino linea dorsali sulcoque basali viridi-æneis nitidis: elytris apice latius rotundatis: antennis pedibusque nigris, femoribus 4 anticis (basi et apice exceptis), 2 posticis dimidio basali castaneo-rufis. Tibis posticis ut in *C. holochlora* compresso-dilatatis, supra paulo minus arcuatis. Long. 17 lin. ♂, ♀.

Venezuela.

Callichroma trilineata.

Subtus viridi-metallica, tenuiter argenteo-sericea, supra atro-velutina, thorace linea dorsali, elytris utrinque linea angusta suturali alteraque discoidali, vittaque sublaterali minus definita viridi-æneis: thorace linea dorsali lævi vel parce transversim rugato: scutello velutino, linea centrali impressa lævi: elytris lineis viridibus subtilissime rugulosis: antennis pedibusque nigris; femoribus 4 anticis omnino, 2 posticis dimidio basali rufis. Long. 13 lin. ♀.

Var. Elytrorum linea discoidali obsoleta, vitta submarginali latiori et distinctiori.

The black velvety pile is almost as dense as in *C. suturalis,* F., but on the thorax there is a well defined metallic green dorsal line, the flanks and lateral tubercles being also glabrous; and the longitudinal vittæ of the elytra are narrow, linear and well defined; the submarginal vitta is tolerably narrow and well defined from the base to the middle, but it then becomes diffused, and blends with the general faint green or violaceous tinge of the apical portion of the elytra.

The type form is from Minas Geraes, Brazil. The var. is from "S. Brazil," exact locality unknown.

Callichroma viridipes.

C. cosmicæ (White) affinis. Læte metallico-viridis, thoracis disco utrinque elytris vitta lata subsuturali alteraque laterali minus distincta, nigro-velutinis; femoribus quatuor anticis splendido-viridibus, duobus posticis chalybeo-nigris, tibiis et tarsis omnibus antennisque nigris. thorace antice et postice sulcato-constricto, sulco posteriori linea acuta elevata transversa diviso; disco linea longitudinali lævi-nitida: elytris sutura viridi transversim rugulosa, cæteris subtilissime vix conspicue sculpturatis: corpore subtus metallico-viridi, albo-sericeo. Tibiæ posticæ ut in *C. cosmica* paulo dilatatis Long. 12 lin. ♂.

New Granada.

Callichroma chloropus.

Subtus læte cyanea, thorace et elytris atro-cyaneo-velutinis, illo linea dorsali, tuberculo laterali, et sulco posterior, elytris utrinque vittis angustis duabus (altera suturali altera discoidali) scutelloque, cyaneis: capite viridi-cyaneo nitido; femoribus quatuor anticis læte cyaneis, duobus posticis violaceis, tibiis tarsis et antennis nigris. Long. 11 lin. ♀.

Venezuela (Caraccas).

Callichroma gracilipes.

Supra planata, elytris vix angustatis apice late rotundatis Viridi-sericea, subtus viridi-cyanea, splendida vix sericea: thorace relative parvo, tuberculo laterali valido, conico, apice antrorsum curvato; dorso subtiliter punctulato-ruguloso: elytris indistincte obscuro-viridi-lineatis, sutura postice subaineo-viridi: pedibus gracilibus, præcipue femoribus posticis fere linearibus, nigris, femoribus rufis, posticis triente apicali chalybeis Long. 11 lin. ♀.

Province of Paraná, Brazil.

Callichroma Buckleyi.

C. phyllopo (Buq.) affinis Elongatum parallelopipedum, supra planatum, cæruleum, vix nitidum, thorace brevi, lato, violaceo-atro velutino, tibiis posticis ut in *C. phyllopo* dilatato-foliaceis. elytris nudis, omnino intricato-rugulosis et punctulatis, costulis utrinque duabus vix elevatis, interiori multo abbreviata: corpore subtus chalybeo vel æneo nitido, prosterno apice tuberoso. Long. 19 lin ♀.

Very closely allied to *C. phyllopus*, but certainly distinct, the elytra being of a fine dark blue colour, and destitute of velvety pile, and the thorax being much broader, including the lateral spines, as broad as the elytra.

R. Macas, Equador (C. Buckley)

Callichroma piliventris.

C. afro (Fab. Drury) et *C. obscuricorni* (Chevr) affinis et similis; differt corpore subtus haud velutino-aurato, sed erecte breviter griseo-piloso; tibiis antennisque autem nigris. Viridis, velutinis, sutura aurata, antennis nigris, pedibus rufis, tibiis nigro-piceis, tarsis posticis albo-pubescentibus: thorace sub-velutino, alutaceo haud strigoso, supra fere æquali, spina laterali latâ conicâ. Long. 8–10 lin. ♂, ♀.

Gaboon (collected by R. B. N. Walker).

Callichroma chrysaspis.

Angusta, modice elongata elytris postice attenuatis, supra glabra subtus viridi-ænea auro-sericea: capite thoraceque purpureo-cupreis, hoc elongato, antice nullomodo postice modice sulcato-constricto, utrinque breviter spinoso, dorso tantum recte transversim strigoso reliquo spatio hastiformi mediano glaber-rimo, pleuris glabris, igneo-splendidis, propectore subtiliter strigoso: scutello lætissime aureo, nudo, punctato· elytris vix nitidis, confertissime punctulatis, viridibus, vitta laterali apiceque violaceis subtilius punctatis: antennis (♂) corpore multo longi-oribus: scapo apice extus producto: articulo 4 quam 3 vel 5 vix breviori. pedibus violaceis.   Long. 9½ lin ♂

The proportions of the antennal joints in this species are the same as in *Chloridolum* (Thoms.), comprising the Indo-Malayan series of *Callichromæ*, the chief distinctive character of which is the relative elongation of the fourth joint.

Gaboon (R B N Walker).

Callichroma lamprodera.

Valde elongata et angustata . capite et thorace viridi-auratis, hoc disco ignicolori, elytris subtiliter velutinis, opacis, violaceis, vitta angusta suturali apice haud attingenti viridi corpore subtus viridi-æneo, subtiliter argenteo-velutino: pedibus omnino cyaneo-violaceis: thorace elongato, antice et postice

I I

sulcato-constricto, dorso transversim (medio subinterrupte) strigoso, dimidio antico sparsim punctulato, margine antico pluri-strigoso. lateribus fortiter spinosis et antea angulatis: elytris subtilissime punctulato-rugosis: antennis gracillimis; scapo scabroso. Long. 13 lin. ♂.

Lagos (Ussher).

Callichroma discoidalis.

Elongato-angusta, ferc cylindrica postice paullo attenuata· capite, thoraceque violaceis, politis, hoc elongato, antice et postice fortiter sulcato-constricto, utrinque plica anteriori et spina valida mediana, dorso transversim ruguloso, dimidio anteriori et spatio lato dorsali lævissimis: scutello lævi, viridi-æneo elytris confertissime punctulato-rugulosis, absque costis, disco communi viridi, lateribus et apice late violaceis, subtilius rugulosis: antennis gracilibus nigris, scapo cyaneo, punctato, apice extus producto; articulo 4 quam 3 vel 5 paulo breviori. corpore subtus læte viridi-æneo, tenuiter argenteo-velutino pedibus elongatis chalybeis, tibiis posticis flexuosis, compressis vix dilatatis, tarsis albo-pilosis. Long. 12 lin ♂.

Loango

Callichroma prolixa.

Valde elongata et angustata, postice paulo attenuata· capite thoraceque cyaneis nitidis, hoc elongato, antice et postice sulcato-constricto, lateribus utrinque medio valde spinoso, antea angulato, dorso transversim uninterrupte strigoso, dimidio antico (margine antico strigoso excepto) lævissimo. scutello viridi-æneo, punctulato elytris viridibus, confertissime punctato-rugulosis, margine laterali angusto, apiceque late, violaceis et subtilius rugosis: corpore subtus viridi-æneo vel aurato, subtilissime argenteo-velutino. antennis pedibusque (tarsis posticis inclusis) violaceis, scapo scabroso, articulis 3–11 fortiter carinatis. Long. 13 lin ♀.

The fourth antennal joint in this species is much shorter than the third or the fifth.

Angola (J. J. Monteiro.)

Callichroma longissima.

Maxime elongata, angustata, supra planata viridi-ænea; elytris disco communi subtiliter æneo-velutino, lateribus late saturatius viridibus, apice violaceis: thorace elongato, nudo, antice et postice sulcato-constricto lateribus utrinque medio valde spinoso, antea angulato, dorso transversim uninterrupte strigoso, dimidio antico (margine antico strigoso excepto) lævissimo. scutello viridi-æneo punctulato: elytris opacis subtilissime argenteo-velutino· pedibus valde elongatis, cyaneo-nigris, femoribus posticis gradatim et paullo incrassatis : antennis gracillimis nigris, scapo, scabroso, cyaneo ; articulis 3–11 fortiter carinatis. Long. 15 lin. ♂.

This and the preceding species belong to a group of African *Callichrominæ*, distinguished by their greatly elongated narrow form, and the long hind legs, of which the femora are but slightly thickened. · The middle femora are also less clavate and pedunculate than in the rest of the genus These characters, however, shade off by insensible gradations (*C. discoidalis, chrysaspis*) into the typical forms.

Cameroons.

EULITOPUS, n. gen.

Corpus maxime elongatum, fere cylindricum, postice vix angustatum. Caput antice prolongatum, lateribus parallelis Mandibulæ falcatæ : maxillæ lobo haud exserto, palpis gracilibus; labialibus multo majoribus apice securiformibus.   Thorax inermis; antice et postice constrictus, parte mediana subgloboso, lævi, nitido. Pedes graciles; posticis maxime elongatis: femoribus 4 anticis subito clavatis, 2 posticis elongatis vix incrassatis.

A genus formed for the reception of *Litopus glabricollis* (Murray), a species nearest allied to the *longissima* group of African *Callichrominæ* and having no near affinity to the genus *Litopus*.

Eu glabricollis, A Murray, List Coleop. Old Calabar, p. 174. Murray's specimens came from Old Calabar; I have received it also from Loango

Chloridolum vittigerum.

Modice elongatum, supra purpureo-velutinum; capite, thoracis lateribus corporeque subtus viridi-æneis, pedibus cyaneis, femoribus basi rufis; elytris utrinque vitta tomentosa cinerea thorace antice et postice transversim pluri-striato, disco utrinque sublævi, velutino : elytris velutino-opacis : corpore subtus tenuiter argenteo-sericeo. Long. 9 lin. ♂.

Cambodia.

I I 2

Chloridolum Everetti.

Gracile, subviridi-auratum, vix velutinum, antennis rufis, articulis basalibus apice apicalibusque omnino atro-fuscis; pedibus rufis tibiis posticis tarsisque omnibus fuscis : thorace læte striato, striis versus discum anticum convergentibus, plagaque hastiformi centrali lævi : elytris coriaceis : corpore subtus aureo-sericeo. Long. 8½ lin. ♂, ♀.

Cebu, Phillipines (Mr. Everett).

Leontium robustum

Robustum, convexum, viridi-æneum, submitidum, antennis, maculis duabus thoracis pedibusque cyaneis, corpore subtus aurato, griseo-sericeo· fronte profunde retuso. thorace antice et postice sulcato-constricto, dorso aspere crebre punctato, linea dorsali sublævi. elytris modice attenuatis, apice rotundatis, subtiliter punctulato-rugulosis (sutura nitida), disco tenuissime pubescentibus: antennis (♂, ♀) corpore haud longioribus: scapo crebre punctulato, articulis 3–10 apice extus productis 5–10 spinosis: tarsis posticis robustis modice elongatis. Long. 13–16 lin. ♂, ♀.

♂ Segmentum ventrale sextum apice rotundatum, integrum. Darjeeling and N.W. India.

Belongs to Thomson's genus *Chelidonium*, which Lacordaire treated as a section only of *Leontium*, at the same time giving a confused and erroneous summary of its characters (Genera tom. ix, p 20 note) conf Thomson, Syst. Ceramb p. 175. Thomson on the other hand named several species under *Chelidonium* which do not offer the characters of the group. *C. gibbicolle* (White) is certainly a *Leontium*.

Leontium subtruncatum.

L argentato (Dalm) *prima facie* similis, at differt antennis simplicibus, elytrisque apice obtuse truncatis Cylindricum, saturate viridi-æneum supra fere opacum subtus lætius viridi-æneo, argenteo sericeo, antennis pedibusque chalybeis· capite antice (cum mandibulis) elongato, fronte grosse rugoso-punctato: thorace elongato, basi sulcato-constricto, tuberculo laterali conico mediano, dorso confertissime et tenuissime punctulato, linea dorsali sublævi impressa· elytris confertissime et minutissime rugulosis, apice subtruncatis angulo suturali producto, dorso carinis duabus obsoletis: tarsis posticis paulo magis quam in *L. argentato* elongatis et compressis· antennis (♀) corpore vix brevioribus, scapo apice haud producto, articulis 4–7 fere æqua libus apice haud productis, 8–11 paulo abbreviatis. Long. 10½ lin. ♀.

Hong Kong.

From its resemblance to *L.* (*Chelidonium*) *argentatum* this species cannot well be removed from the genus, but its simple antennæ do not fit with the generic character. In structure it fits better with *Polyzonus*, but the absence of yellow bands or spots would render it incongruous there

Leontium optimum.

Supra subplanum, viridi-æneum, tenuiter velutinum, elytris macula communi, antemediana, suturali, fasciaque postmediana, flavis, disco saturatius viridi: thorace dorso scabrose marginibus rugulose punctato, lateribus medio obtuse et grosse tuberculatis, dorso maculis duabus atro-velutinis. antennis (♀) corpore triente brevioribus haud incrassatis, chalybeis, scapo apice extus acute producto, articulis 4–10 apice extus modice productis: femoribus posticis versus apicem incrassatis, tibiis omnibus violaceis, posticis valde flexuosis. Long. 14 lin. ♀

Laos (Mouhot).

Forms a distinct section in the genus, from its obtuse thorax, thickened hind thighs, style of coloration, &c.

AMBLYONTIUM, n. gen.

Gen. *Leontio* affine. Corpus angustum elongatum, supra planatum. Caput antice modice elongatum. Mandibulæ subrectæ, juxta apicem abrupte incurvæ, intus late dentatæ. Antennæ (♂) corpore multo breviores, articulo 1 apice extus paulo producto, 3 cæteris distincte longiori, 3–10 apice extus breviter subspinosis, 5–11 lateraliter carinatæ Thorax subovatus lateraliter inermis, supra planus, juxta basin haud profunde sulcato-constrictus Elytra apice obtuse rotundata Femora 4 antica incrassata, basi subpedunculata, 2 postica elytrorum apicem attingentia, gradatim incrassata tibiæ gradatim compresso-dilatatæ. tarsi subgraciles. Prosternum apice tuberculatum: mesosternum planum angustatum. Venter segmentis sex, 5 apice arcuato, 6 fortiter emarginato, a pygidio elongato tecto.

Amblyontium inerme.

Viridi-æneum subauratum, antennis pedibusque cyaneis: thorace antice linea transversa impressa, juxta basin sulcato-constricto, supra confluenter irregulariter punctato linea dorsali sublævi et utrinque velutino-plagiato: elytris confluenter (juxta suturam grossissime) punctulatis, vitta lata discoidali et lateribus saturatius viridibus: subtus argenteo sericeo. Long. 10 lin.. ♂

Sarawak, Borneo.

OXYPROSOPUS, Thomson.

According to the descriptions the two species following will range under this genus:—

1. *O. Fabricii*, Schönh. Synon. Ins. App. p. 152, Sierra Leone.
2. *O. speciosus*, Dalm.   id.   p. 153, Sierra Leone.

The latter is evidently closely allied to *O. cæruleus* (Oliv.)= *jucundus*, Guér. The following are new:—

Oxyprosopus chloreus.

Viridi-æneus, palpis, antennis pedibusque fulvo-rufis (antennis, basi excepto, tibiisque posticis interdum nigris) labio fusco testaceo-marginato, fronte subarmata, crebre punctata: thorace angustiori medio rotundato-dilatato haud tuberculato, creberrime et subtilissime confluenter punctulato elytris subtilissime rugu-loso-punctatis, tenuiter atro-pubescentibus plaga communi trans-versa post scutellum glabra parce punctata: corpore subtus griseo-pubescenti. tibiis posticis dilatato-compressis, margine superiori regulariter curvato. Long. 12–15 lin. ♂, ♀.

♂ Segmenta 5 et 6 ventralia curta, arcuato-truncata.

One ♂ (red antennæ and legs) Sierra Leone, one ♀ (black antennæ and posterior tibiæ) Guinea.

Oxyprosopus cylindricus.

Elongatus, subcylindricus, subcyaneo-viridis, pedibus chalybeis, tarsis posticis argenteo-pilosis, antennis nigris: palpis nigris: labro fusco, testaceo-marginato; fronte viridi-ænea, dense punc-tata: thorace longiori, medio modice angulatim dilatato, utrinque subtuberculato, supra subtilissime punctato-ruguloso, velutino, linea angusta dorsali sublævi: elytris minutissime creberrime punctulatis, haud vittatim velutinis, sed plagis pubescentibus transversis communibus duabus, altera basali altera post-scutel-lari, interjacenti plaga nitida glabra parce punctata: tibiis posticis gradatim compresso-dilatatis, vix flexuosis. Long. 10½ lin. ♀.

Cameroons.

Oxyprosopus angulicollis.

Viridi-æneus vel cyaneus: palpis nigris, maxillaribus medio rufis. antennis pedibusque nigris vel chalybeis, femoribus omni-bus medio rufis, tarsis posticis argenteo-pilosis; tibiis anticis triquetris: labro et fronte viridi-æneis crebre punctatis· thorace medio fortiter angulatim dilatato, transverso. elytris subtilissime rugulosis atro-velutinis, vitta lata densius pubescenti; macula magna triangulari subglabra grossius rugosa: corpore subtus argenteo-sericeo· tibiis posticis compresso-dilatatis, margine superiori flexuoso. Long. 12 lin. ♀.

Cameroons.

Oxyprosopus comis.

Elongatus, subcylindricus, læte viridi-æneus, nitidus, labio et fronte metallicis punctatis. thorace lateribus obtuse tuberoso, dorso utrinque juxta constricturam basalem tuberculato, supra confluenter punctulato tenuissime velutino: scutello atro-cyaneo dense velutino: elytris quam maxime subtiliter rugulosis, versus scutellum et suturam anticam grossius et parcius punctatis, læte æneis vitta utrinque obsoleta saturatiori et subvelutina: antennis et pedibus violaceis, femoribus (posticis apice exceptis) rufis, tarsis argenteo-pilosis· corpore subtus tenuiter argenteo-sericeo. Long. 10½ lin. ♂.

Cameroons.

Oxyprosopus protractus.

Elongatus, linearis, viridi-æneus, antennis pedibusque nigris, femoribus medio rufis, tarsis posticis pallide testaceis, pedibus posticis elongatis, femoribus corporis apicem attingentibus. capite antice parce punctato thorace post medium rotundato-dilatato, antice gradatim angustato, basi subito constricto, supra paulo inæquali distincte passim punctulato. elytris longissimis, parallelis passim crebre punctulatis: corpore subtus lateribus tenuiter pubescenti· antennis ♂ apicem versus haud incrassatis, corpore multo brevioribus. Long. 10 lin. ♂.

♂ Segmentum ventrale 5um late emarginatum, 6um magnum supra excavatum hirsutum.

Mozambique

Anubis dissitus.

A. clavicorni (F.) affinis; at differt colore chalybeo fasciaque clytrorum secunda in maculas tres divisa, scilicet unam communam suturalem alteras angustas utrinque marginales. Linearis, chalybeus, capite thoraceque grosse subconfluenter punctatis: clytris subtilius confluenter punctatis, obsolete bicostatis, fasciis tribus flavis, prima et tertia latis integris, secunda utrinque medio interrupta: pygidio lato apice vix angustato integro, margine reflexo   Long. 8 lin. ♂, ♀.

Caffraria.

The three allied species *A clavicornis* (= *sexmaculatus*, White), *dissitus* and *scalaris*, Pasc , are distinguishable from each other by the form of the pygidium. In *clavicornis* it is sinuated or notched at the apex, in *scalaris* abruptly narrowed and subacute, in *dissitus* rounded.

Anubis rostratus

A. bifasciato (Newm) coloribus simillimus; differt capite antice valde elongato et angustato.   Cylindricus, subæneo-cyaneus, clytris saturatioribus et medio opacis, his fasciis duabus fulvis, apice obtuse rotundatis vix ciliatis: thorace antice gradatim angustato, confertim subrugose punctato, linea brevi dorsali lævi: corpore subtus subaurato-sericeo.   Long. 9 lin. ♂.

♂ Segmentum sextum ventrale valde elongatum (4–5 con-. junctim longius)· antennæ corpore haud longiores.

Saigon

Anubis fimbriatus.

Linearis, subaurato-viridis, antennis pedibusque nigris, elytris fasciis duabus fulvis violaceo-fimbriatis ad suturam interruptis: capite lato, antice brevissimo: thorace medio rotundato, basi sulcato-constricto, dorso transversim punctulato-ruguloso, lateribus lævibus politis: elytris subtilissime punctulatis, apice late rotundatis· corpore subtus argenteo-sericeo.   Long. 8 lin. ♂.

♂ Segmentum sextum ventrale breve, dense hirsutum.
Cochin China.

Anubis unifasciatus.

Linearis, gracilis, violaceus (capite thoraceque interdum cyaneis). capite antice elongato, frontis lateribus elevato-marginatis· thorace fere cylindrico, basi paulo constricto, dorso discrete punctato, linea dorsali sublævi: elytris omnino discrete sed crebre punctulatis, post medium fascia angusta flava: corpore subtus argenteo-sericeo. Long 7–8 lin. ♀.

Cochin China and Saigon

Distinguished from the closely allied *A. bipustulatus* (Thoms.) by the much more conspicuous and larger punctuation, besides the margined muzzle and nearly continuous fascia of the elytra.

Polyzonus meridionalis.

P. bicincto (Oliv.) multo major et robustior: obscure cyaneus, opacus, elytris fasciis duabus latis rectis flavis: capite scabroso-punctato: thorace grosse confluenter punctato: elytris pube tenui decumbenti vestitis, fundo subtiliter punctulatis, utrinque obsolete bicostatis, fasciis flavis quàm fascia cyanea interjecta dimidio latioribus: corpore subtus dense griseo velutino. Long. 8–10 lin. ♂, ♀.

♂ Segmentum 5 ventrale apice arcuatim emarginatum; sextum angustum apice profunde emarginatum. pygidium valde convexum, subovatum.

Hong Kong.

Polyzonus Saigonensis.

Robustus, capite et thorace relative elongatis; atro-chalybeus, elytris fasciis duabus flavis latissimis capite punctato scabroso· thorace elongato, tuberculis lateralibus validis acute conicis, supra intricato-rugoso, basi sulcato-constricto, margine postico dorsi elevato: elytris gradatim angustatis, pube tenui griseo vestitis, subtilissime punctulatis corpore subtus pedibusque chalybeis illo argenteo-sericeo: antennis scapo difformi, antice retuso postice valde sinuato. Long 9 lin ♂.

Saigon.

Polyzonus obtusus

Robustus, atro-chalybeus, elytris fasciis duabus flavis latissimis. capite antice subtiliter rugoso opaco; thorace medio rotundato-dilatato, pleuris anticis tumidis, basi fortiter constricto, dorso longitudinaliter, margine antico transversim, elevato-strigoso, pleuris minute granulatis· scutello lævi: elytris pube tenui griseo vestitis, subtilissime punctulatis corpore subtus griseo-sericeo· antennis scapo normali, punctato, nitido. Long. 11½ lin ♂.

Saigon.

Resembles the last in colours and pubescence, but differs remarkably in the large rounded thorax with obtusely dilated sides and striated surface.

Gen. HYPOCRITES, Fahræus.

Coleop. Caffr. in Ofvers. Vetensk.-Akad Forh. 1872, No. 1, p. 62.

The type of this genus, *H. mendax*, differs from the typical *Promeces* in the ♂ having 11- instead of 12-jointed antennæ. Although in *H. mendax* ♂ these organs are filiform (as in *Promeces* ♂, but much shorter), the species cannot be generically separated from *Promeces Krausii* (White) and *Closteromerus imperialis* (White), in which the terminal joints are more or less thickened; it will be convenient, therefore, to extend the limits of *Hypocrites*, so as to include all the numerous forms of *Promeces* in which the antennæ are 11-jointed in both sexes, rarely longer than the body even in the ♂, with apical joints more or less abbreviated and thickened and the third joint distinctly longer than the fourth   The width of the head and thorax and the length of the muzzle vary considerably, and offer no reliable generic characters; some of the species being even more slender than *Promeces longipes*. A more important difference among the species lies in the form of the femora, the middle and anterior pair especially being distinctly more abruptly clavate in some than in others, but this does not correspond with other characters

Of the already described species the following belong to *Hypocrites·—*

H. mendax, Fahr., l.c.

H. ambiguus, id

> Closely allied to *H. imperialis* (White), if not a colour variety of the same.

H. Krausii, White, Cat. Long. Brit. Mus. p. 169.

H. imperialis, id p 168.

H. viridis, Pascoe, Journ Ent. ii, p. 53.

> = *claviger*, Dalm., Schonh. Syn Ins. i, 3, App. 155?
>
> = *pauper*, Fahr, l.c. p. 61 ? according to the description appears to differ only in the opaque elytra

Hypocrites porphyrio.

Robustus, supra purpureo-cupreus, subnitidus, corpore subtus antennis et pedibus violaceis· capite sparsim punctato: antennis

(♀) dimidium corporis paulo superantibus, articulo 3 quam 4 duplo longiori, 6–11 valde incrassatis, 3–11 fortiter sulcatis: thorace oblongo, lateribus paulo arcuatis, basi sulcato-constricto, dorso inæquali sparsim grosse punctato: elytris creberrime rugoso-punctatis, obsolete bicostulatis· femoribus 4 anticis sub-abrupte, 2 posticis gradatim, clavatis.   Long. 9 lin. ♀.

Zoutpansberg, R. Limpopo (collected by Karl Mauch).

Closely allied to *H. imperialis*, (*Closteromerus id*, White), but thorax not bulging in the middle, and antennæ (♀) rather shorter.

Hypocrites obtusipennis.

Linearis, supra planus, cyaneus, elytris opacis: capite punctato: antennis (♂) corpore paullulum longioribus, articulo 3 sequenti distincte longiori, 6 apice dilatato 8-11 abbreviatis et incrassatis: thorace fere ut in *Promeces longipes*, antice modice angustato, lateribus post medium tumidis, basi sulcato-constricto, marginibus antice et postice transversim strigosis, dorso parce punctato: elytris apice obtuse rotundatis, supra reticulato-punctatis: femoribus posticis corpore longioribus gradatim incrassatis: corpore subtus tenuiter argenteo-sericeo, crebre punctulato. Long 6½ lin. ♂.

♂ Segmentum ventrale sextum medio profunde excavatum
Delagoa Bay (taken by J. J. Monteiro).

Hypocrites manicatus.

Linearis, cyaneus, elytris opacis, antennis pedibusque chalybeis, femoribus 4 anticis (apice exceptis), et 2 posticis basi, rufis capite angusto, antice elongato grosse punctato. thorace medio dilatato supra crebre discrete punctato, linea dorsali lævi· elytris nigro-cyaneis opacis, sparsim pubescentibus, confertissime ruguloso-punctatis : corpore subtus griseo-pubescenti : femoribus posticis gracilibus gradatim incrassatis, 4 anticis gradatim clavatis.   Long. 6 lin. ♂, ♀.

♂ Segmentum ventrale sextum quadratum medio profunde excavatum; pygidio medio valde emarginato.
.   Natal

Apparently closely allied to *Promeces fulvipes* (Fahr.), in which the four anterior tibiæ, as well as the femora, are fulvous. The species differs from the typical *Promeces* in having 11-jointed incrassated antennæ in the ♂ as well as in the ♀.   The antennæ are nearly the same in length and thickness in the sexes, in neither being quite so long as the body, and the third joint being much longer than the fourth, with the apical ones much thickened and the 11th obtuse.

Hypocrites alveolatus.

H. viridi (Pascoe) proxime affinis, at brevior, thoraceque alveolato-punctato haud rugoso. Modice elongatus, viridi-cyaneus, vix nitidus, antennis pedibusque chalybeis vel violaceis: interdum corpore supra fere nigro: capite thoraceque crebre alveolatis vel rotunde-punctatis interstitiis reticulatis; hoc basi constricto sed nullomodo sulcato, lateribus paullum dilatatis: elytris passim confertissime confluenter punctatis · corpore subtus tenuiter sparse griseo-pubescenti Femoribus omnibus subabrupte clavatis. Long 5–6 lin. ♂.

♂ Segmentum ventrale 6 brevissimum, concavum Antennæ corpore breviores, articulo 3 sequenti dimidio longiori.

Cape of Good Hope Port Elizabeth.

The femora are more distinctly clavate than in *H. viridis* and allied species.

Hypocrites cyanellus.

Gracilis, cyaneus, subnitidus. capite scapoque antennarum sparsim punctatis. thorace elongato, post medium dilatato, supra foveolis rotundatis sparsis impressis, linea lata dorsali lævi. elytris basi sparsim, reliqua superficie confluenter, punctatis: corpore subtus maculis lateralibus argenteo-sericeis · prosterno antice grosse punctato et strigoso, ventro confertim punctulato: antennis (♀) corpore paulo brevioribus articulo 3 sequento fere duplo longiori, 6–11 incrassatis. Long 5 lin ♀

Natal (Pastor Guenzius), also Delagoa Bay (J. J. Monteiro).

Hypocrites tenuis.

Gracillima, linearis, cyaneus, subnitidus · capite scapoque antennarum grosse punctatis hoc scabroso: thorace angusto, elongato, medio vix dilatato, supra passim parce punctato, sulco basali transversim pluri-strigoso · elytris basi sparsim reliqua superficie crebrius versus suturam rugoso-punctatis, asperulis: corpore subtus maculis lateralibus argenteo-pilosis, prosterno antice grosse punctato et strigoso; ventro punctulato · antennis (♀) corpore paululum brevioribus, articulo 3 sequento fere duplo longiori 6–11 incrassatis Long. 5–5½ lin. ♀.

Natal

Narrower than *H. cyanellus*, thorax especially longer and narrower, scattered with punctures over the whole upper surface, scape of antennæ shorter and much more coarsely rugosely punctured.

MOMBASIUS, n. gen

Gen. *Promecido* (Fahr.) proxime affinis, differt epistomate a fronte suturâ impressâ transversâ separato; antennis scapo apice extus acute spinoso, sulcis ab apice articuli 4ti tantum incipientibus, articulo 4to precedenti longiori, ambobus asperatis. Femora omnia apice abrupte et fortiter clavata. Antennæ ♂ setaceæ 12-articulatæ, ♀ 11-articulatæ articulis 6–11 incrassatis sed non ut in *Hypocrite* clavam formantibus.

Mombasius frontalis

Pr. chalybeato (White) paulo brevior. Saturate cyaneus, antennis pedibusque nitidis: epistomate transversim depresso a fronte linea impressa transversa separato: thorace medio dilatato tumido, basi paulo constricto, dorso nitido, punctis vix impressis consperso, base et apice transversim plicato· elytris passim æqualiter discrete punctatis· antennis scapo rugoso apice extus spinoso corpore subtus polito, lateribus maculatim griseo-sericeo. Long. 5½–6½ lin. ♂, ♀.

Ribé, near Mombasa, E. Africa (Rev Thos. Wakefield).

Euporus liobasis.

Eu. strangulato (Serv.) similis. Viridi-cyaneus nitidus, vertice, thoracis parte anteriori, elytrisque basi et apice violaceis· thorace postice tantum grosse punctato. elytris subtilissime et creberrime strigulosis, plaga magna basali glabra: antennis pedibusque violaceis Long 9 lin

Sierra Leone and R. Ogowé.

In the Sierra Leone specimen the smooth part of the base of elytra extends across as a broad fascia; in the R. Ogowé example it is interrupted at the suture

Phrosyne poriferus.

Linearis, viridi-æneus; occipite, thoracis parte antica, antennis, femorum clavâ, tibiis et tarsis posticis, læte violaceis· antennis ♀ quam in *Ph. brevicorni* paullo gracilioribus : thorace medio parum dilatato lævi, postice foveolis dispersis rotundis peiforato: elytiis subtilissime punctulatis subopacis, sutura nitida, vitta laterali obscura violacea . femoiibus omnibus basi, tibiis 4 anticis, posticisque medio, flavis. Long. 6 lin.

Lagos, Guinea

Apparently allied to *Euporus amabilis*, (Hope)., in which, however, the femora are described as "*cyaneis*," and no mention is made of the yellow colour of the gieater pait of the length. IIis species, moreover, may be a true *Euporus*.

Prosyne tenellus.

Gracillimus, viridi-æneus, pedibus posticis antennisque chaly-beis, femoium quatuor anteiorum clavis rufis. capite antice elongato-angustato, grossissime confertim, occipite sparsim, punc-tato thorace valde elongato, fere cylindrico, antice et postice modice constricto, supra sparsissime (antice subtilius postice grossius) punctato· scutello aurato, lævi: elytris subtiliter crebei-rime punctulato basi sublævi nitido. antennis (♀) gracilibus sed corpore brevioiibus, aiticulis 7–11 tantum multo abbreviatis. Long. 5 lin. ♀

Lagos, Guinea

Ipothalia esmeralda

Satuiate viiidis, haud nitida, subtus læte aigenteo-seiicea, pedibus rufis nitidis, femoium posticoium clavis, tibiis posticis et antennis, chalybeo-violaceis: capite thoiaceque crebre sub iugoso-punctatis, hoc medio spatio sublævi, maiginibus anticis et posticis transveisim plicatis : scutello lateiibus arcuatis apice pioducto : elytiis confeitim intricato- rugulosis. Long. 8 lin. ♂ .

♂ Segmentis ventialibus sex, 6to paivo, 5to apice aicuato-subemarginato.

North West Borneo (fiom Mi. Low's collection

Closteropus argentatus

C. specioso (Klug) gracilior. Subcyaneo-viridis, metallicus, antennis chalybeis· elytris velutinis vitta utrinque viridi-aigentea; femoiibus æneis, tibiis chalybeis, tarsis aigenteo-sericeis corpore subtus argenteo-pubescenti : thoiace antice et postice acute sulcato-constiicto, dorso valde tubeiculato, partibus concavis subtiliter stiiatis. Long $6\frac{1}{2}$–$7\frac{1}{2}$ lin. ♂ .

Cordillera of Venezuela (Goring).

The genus *Closteropus* belongs but imperfectly to the *Calli-chrominæ*, connecting the group with *Cosmisoma* in the *Rhopalo-phorinæ*. The absence of the tuft of hairs on the fifth antennal joint is all that separates *C. argentatus* from *Cosmisoma martyrus* (Thoms.). *Closteropus lineatus* (Kirsch) on this view must be considered a *Cosmisoma*.

Corrections to be made in the Munich Catalogue.

Ionthodes clavipes, White, = *Promeces nitens*, F. Ol. *(Rhopal-izus*, id.) = *Rhopalizus Chevrolati*, Thoms.

Callichroma assimile, Hope, = *afrum*, L.

,,   *calcaratum*, Chevr., = *Philematium id.*

,,   *chalybeatum*, White, = *Mecaspis id.*

,,   *Currori*, White, = *Philematium id.*

,,   *Fabricii*, Schonh., = *Oxyprosopus id.*

,,   *Goryi*, White, = *speciosum*, Gory, = *Callichroma Hottentotta*, Buq.

,,   *Guenzii*, White, = *Phyllocnema id.*

,,   *lætum*, Hope, = *Mecaspis id.*

,,   *neoxenum*, White, = *Aphrodisium id.*, India.

,,   *scitalum*, Pascoe, = *rugicolle*, Guér.

,,   *speciosum*, Dalm., = *Oxyprosopus id.*

,,   *virens*, L., = *Philematium id.*, West Africa.

Philematium fragrans, Dalm , = *Callichroma id.*

,,   *hottentottum*, Buq , = *Callichroma id.*

Rhopalizus Chevrolati, Thoms., = *Promeces nitens*, F. (genus *Rhopalizus*).

Polyzonus venereus, Thoms , = *Leontium id*

Litopus glabricollis, Murray, = *Eulitopus id.*

Promeces nitens, F., = *Rhopalizus id.*

Eutactus lineatus, Fabr., = *Zosterius lætus*, Thoms.

Descriptions of new COLEOPTERA from Medellin, Colombia, recently added to the British Museum Collection; by CHAS. O. WATERHOUSE.

An interesting series of Coleoptera, selected for the British Museum from a collection made by Mr. Salmon, at Medellin in Colombia, has been found to contain numerous undescribed species. The present paper only contains descriptions of the more interesting novelties.

XANTHOLINIDÆ

Sterculia simplicicollis, n. sp.

Cærulea, nitida; capite lato, creberrime fortiter punctato; thorace capite bene angustiori, convexo, antice angustato, lateribus parce punctulatis postice haud impressis, margine posteriori haud elevato; elytris discrete subtiliter punctatis; antennarum basi pedibus abdomineque virescentibus. Long. 12 lin.

Head a little longer than broad, very strongly and densely punctured, the posterior angles and the base moderately rounded, the sides very slightly arcuate. Thorax one-third narrower than the head, one-third longer than broad, sparingly and obscurely punctured at the sides, parallel at the sides for two-thirds its length, narrowed in front, rounded at the base, at each side near the base there is a slight indication of an impression, but not an oblique impression as in most of the species of the genus, and the lateral and posterior margins are deflexed (not expanded as is very usual). The elytra are as long as broad, sparingly, finely but distinctly punctured, blue with slight green reflections. Abdomen green with blue reflections, finely and sparingly punctured. The head below has large punctures scattered over the sides and base; the longitudinal gular channel is short but well defined.

MELOLONTHIDÆ.

Faula lineata.

Bene convexa, lata, nigra, nitidissima; thorace marginibus lineâque obliquâ laterali punctatis, punctis squamiferis; elytris

K K

latitudine paulo longioribus, gibbosis, lateribus apiceque rotundatis, singulis lineis tribus marginibusque punctatis punctis squamiferis; pedibus flavo-piceis. Long. 7 lin., lat. 3¾ lin.

Although of quite a different form, this species by its coloration calls *Ancistrosoma Klugii* at once to mind. Head strongly and rather thickly punctured. Thorax about one-third broader than long, very convex, glabrous, strongly angular in the middle of the sides, the anterior angles slightly prominent, acute; the region of the anterior angles, the lateral margins, as well as an irregular oblique line at the sides are rather thickly and strongly punctured, the punctures each having an elongate narrow yellow scale Elytra at the base not broader than the base of the thorax, very convex, glabrous, the margins and three rather broad stripes on each elytron closely and distinctly punctured, each puncture bearing a narrow elongate yellow scale, the second and third lines abbreviated behind. Legs pitchy-yellow, rather short for this group; tarsi rather short and stout, claws simple.

DYNASTIDÆ.

Lycomedes Burmeisteri, n. sp. Pl. IX, f. 1.

Niger, dense sabuloso-tomentosus, fusco-variegatus.   Long. 13–17 lin.

♂ var. max.   Head with a long flat curved shining horn, narrow at the extreme base, rather broad and parallel (when seen from the front) to near the apex, the apex divided into two rather long slender diverging points. Thorax one-third broader than long, obliquely narrowed in front and behind, the disc very much raised and surmounted by an erect broad horn, which rises perpendicularly from the anterior margin ; the horn is broad (seen from the front), slightly narrowed at the apex, concave and tomentose in front, the apex is obtuse and slightly bends forward, and has a small notch in the middle, the horn behind is deeply channelled, the channel reaching nearly to the base of the thorax. Elytra rather broader than the thorax, as broad as long, impressed at the sides below the shoulders, the subapical callosity small and not prominent, there is a well marked line of punctures near the suture, the surface is mottled with sandy-grey and yellowish brown. The underside of the prothorax, the margins of the abdominal segments and the tarsi are not covered with tomentum. Long. 17 lin.

♂ var. minor.   This has the cephalic horn only 2½ lines long, bifid at the apex.   The thoracic horn is as in the larger variety, but is only one line above the level of the disc.

♀ Head without any horn, clypeus densely and - strongly punctured. Thorax gently convex; very thickly and strongly punctured, the punctures only filled with tomentum, the sides are less angular at the sides than in the male. The underside and legs are almost destitute of tomentum, but the sternum is pubescent. Pl. IX, f. 1*b.*

This species differs from *L. Reichei* in being of a shorter broader form, and the cephalic horn has no tooth above at the base, and the thoracic horn is broader and rises more directly perpendicular to the anterior margin. The canthus of the eye is much narrower and in the male especially is curved forward like a small horn.

Chauliognathus excellens, C. Waterh. Pl IX, f. 2.

C. excellens, Waterh., Trans. Ent. Soc. p. 327, Dec 1878

Niger, nitidus, thorace flavo. Long. 14½ lin.

CYPHIDÆ.

Præpodes annulonotatus, n. sp. Pl. IX, f. 3.

Statura *P. sphacelati,* niger, dense squamis pallide viridibus tectus; thorace dorsim lineis duabus viridi-albis notato; elytrorum dorso litterâ O magnâ flava-albâ notato. Long. 11 lin.

Black, more or less densely clothed with minute pale green scales which vary somewhat in tint. Rostrum with a mesial shining carina. Thorax with a pale greenish-white line on each side of the disc. Elytra very strongly striate-punctate; with a well marked circle of yellowish-white scales on the back; there is also a yellow stripe on the underside of the thorax and along the margin of the elytra.

ZYGOPIDÆ.

Copturus pulcher, n. sp.

Niger, supra dense nigro-squamosus, thorace lineis tribus, elytris maculis sat magnis novem læte ochraceis, maculâque medianâ fere albâ ornatis; corpore subtus plus minusve flavo-squamoso Long. 3½ lin , lat. 1⅔ lin

Rather elongate. Rostrum stout, shining, sparingly and very delicately punctured, rather closely and more strongly punctured

on each side of the base.   Head with an ochreous line surrounding each eye.   Thorax a little broader than long, regularly
narrowed anteriorly, scarcely constricted in front, with an
ochreous stripe in the middle, interrupted, with the whole of the
sides ochreous with a denuted spot on the flank.   Elytra at
the base distinctly broader than the thorax, one-quarter longer
than broad, regularly narrowed towards the apex, which is
obtuse, rather flat on the back, very strongly punctate-striate,
the interstices nearly flat; there is a nearly white spot on the
middle of the suture, and nine rather large ochreous spots, viz.,
one in the middle of the base of each elytron, one below the
shoulder joined to a lateral subapical one, one sublateral spot
rather behind the middle, and an apical spot at the apex common
to both elytra.   The legs and body beneath are here and there
clothed with very pale yellow scales; the posterior femora have
a strong tooth beneath, rather beyond the middle; the apical
angles of the posterior femora are rather acute.   The prosternal
channel is very deep.

Copturus brevis, n. sp.

Brevis, piceus, miniato-squamosus; thorace transverso, medio
maculâ transversâ nigrâ ˙ notato ; elytris thorace latioribus,
latitudine haud longioribus, apicem versus parum arcuatim-
angustatis, apice obtuso, suturâ basi bene impressâ, punctato-
striatis, interstitiis parum convexis, nigro-squamosis, fasciis
duabus, guttâ suturali, annulâque apicali miniato-squamosis.
Long. 3 lin., lat 1⅔ lin.

Rostrum black, shining, punctured closely at the sides of the
base.   Antennæ not very long, reddish.   Thorax considerably
broader than long, convex, thickly and strongly punctured,
moderately narrowed anteriorly, clothed above with bright red
scales, with a transverse lunate spot on the disc of black scales.
Elytra much broader than the thorax, as long as broad, slightly
narrowed towards the apex which is very obtuse; pitchy, clothed
with black scales, with a quadrate red spot on the suture behind
the middle, and on each elytron a small red spot in front of
the shoulder, an oblique stripe reaching from the scutellum
to below the shoulder, another more oblique stripe from the
suture (rather above the middle) to the margin, and a broad
ring of the same bright red surrounding the subapical callosity.
The sides of the prosternum are denuded of scales and are rather
thickly and moderately strongly punctured.   The apical angles

of the femora are somewhat spiniform; with no distinct tooth below. The prosternal channel is very deep; metasternum with a slight shallow impression in front.

The metasternum in this species is slightly different from that of typical *Copturus,* it is more perpendicular in front and slightly impressed, but the impressed part is equally clothed with red scales as the rest. The metasternum is also not quite so flat, it is slightly impressed longitudinally, but not channelled.

SIPALIDÆ.

Mesocordylus gracilicornis, n. sp.

Elongatus, ater, opacus; antennis gracilibus; thorace latitudine paulo longiore, crebre fortiter rugoso; elytris thorace paulo latioribus, obsolete striatis, guttis parvis flavo-tomentosis irregulariter dispositis. Long. 10 lin.

Somewhat the form of *M. subulatus,* but narrower, altogether of more slender make, thorax strongly rugose, elytra nearly parallel to near the apex, and at once distinguished from its allies by the slender and longer antennæ. Rostrum comparatively slender, strongly and thickly punctured, finely punctured beyond the insertion of the antennæ; head distinctly and moderately thickly punctured; antennæ a little longer than the length of the thorax, the scape slender, the second joint of the funiculus elongate, narrowed at the base, the third joint one-third shorter, the fifth and sixth scarcely as broad as long, narrowed a little at their bases, the club ovate, the apical half spongy. Thorax narrowed in front, broadest rather before the middle, a little narrowed towards the base, very strongly rugose, impressed on the disc. Elytra subparallel, narrowed at the apex, the striæ only distinct near the suture, the interstices nearly flat, with small round spots of yellowish tomentum irregularly placed at intervals.

CALANDRIDÆ.

Sphenophorus costatus, n. sp.

Niger, nitidus; rostro piceo; thorace elongato, ante medium angustato, postice parallelo, fere lævi, medio longitudinaliter impresso; scutello angusto, lævi; elytris thorace ¼ longioribus, apicem versus angustatis, striatis, interstitiis lævibus, 2 et 4 convexis costiformibus, piceo-rufo guttatis, interstitiis 1, 3, 5, 6,

et 7 hic et illic furfurosis; corpore subtus lævi; abdominis segmento ultimo pygidioque fortiter punctatis. Long. rostr. excl.
10 lin.

Rostrum about two-thirds the length of the thorax, rather
stout, with a fine mesial line·above at the base terminating
posteriorly in a deep puncture between the eyes; antennæ
inserted at the extreme base, club oblong-ovate, about as long
as the five previous joints of the funiculus.   Thorax rather less
than one-third longer than broad, narrowed in front, nearly
parallel at the sides for more than half its length, constricted
within the apex, not visibly punctured, with a broad shallow
dull longitudinal impression which extends from the base nearly
to the apex.   Scutellum very narrow.   Elytra considerably
narrowed towards the apex, striated, the striæ obscurely punctured, the suture shining, impressed at the base and pitchy, black
and slightly convex posteriorly   First interstice slightly convex
and shining at the base, flat and velvety posteriorly; second
interstice convex and shining, with a reddish spot at the base
and apex, and one a little behind the middle; third interstice
dull, flat, rather narrower, with two obscure reddish spots, one
before and one behind the middle; fourth similar to the second;
the fifth, sixth and seventh flat and velvety, the two latter
shining at the shoulder; the eighth gently convex, shining,
pitchy-red.   The whole of the underside of the body shining
and impunctate, the apical segment of the abdomen strongly
punctured, the pygidium still more strongly and more closely
punctured.   Tibiæ pitchy-red, black at the apex.

Sphenophorus tibialis, n. sp.

Robustus, convexus, obscure rufus, opacus sicut velutinus;
thorace maculis quinque nigris; elytris striatis, striis punctatis,
interstitiis vix convexis, maculis octo nigris; corpore subtus
nigro, nitido, piceo-maculato, metasterno lateribus fortiter punctatis, medio cum abdominis segmentis 1o et 2o late impressis;
pedibus plus minusve rufo-piceis, tibiis intus dimidio apicali
leviter sinuatis ciliatis, quatuor posterioribus medio intus peni-
cillatis.   Long rostr. excl 13 lin

In general form this species somewhat approaches *S. sene-
galensis*, but it is more robust and more convex.   Rostrum
stout, dull red, shining, with a deep channel above at the base,
commencing between the eyes and terminating a little beyond
the insertion of the antennæ, there are a few extremely fine
punctures on each side of the line, the antennal pit is deep, the

anterior part of its inner margin is marked by a well developed
obtuse triangular tooth.* Thorax a very little (one-seventh)
longer than broad, very slightly convex, constricted at the apex,
narrowed before the middle, gently arcuate at the sides, the
broadest part a little before the base, with a few large punctures
in the middle near the base, red, with five large black spots, one
discoidal anterior, one at each anterior angle, and a triangular
one on each side of the base. Elytra at the shoulders very little
broader than the thorax, gradually (but not much) narrowed
towards the apex, rather deeply striated, the striæ distinctly but
not very closely punctured, interstices very slightly convex, dull
red, with a black spot common to both elytra at the scutellum
and another at the apex, each elytron has also three rather large
black spots, one just within the shoulder, another in the middle
near the suture, and a third near the apex extending from the
fourth stria to the margin. There are a few rather large punctures scattered on the middle and sides of the prosternum; the
metasternum is very strongly punctured at the sides, the middle
portion as well as the middle of the first and second abdominal
segments are broadly and rather strongly impressed; the sides of
the abdomen and the apical segment are strongly punctured.
Legs smooth, the middle of the femora and tibiæ pitchy-red,
the tibiæ have the inner apical half sinuate, especially the four
posterior in which the commencement of the sinuation is marked
by a tuft of stiff hair.

HISPIDÆ.

Arescus lævicollis, n. sp.

Flavus, nitidus; capite lævi, fronte canaliculatâ, antennis
nigris, articulis tribus basalibus subtus flavis; thorace paulo
transverso, lævi, angulis anticis extus leviter sinuatis, lateribus
rectis, posticis acutis; scutello cyaneo-nigro; elytris striato-
punctatis maculâ humerali dimidioque apicali cyaneo-nigris;
tarsis tibiisque anticis nigris. Long. $5\frac{1}{2}$ lin.

Close to *A. labiatus,* which it resembles in form, but, besides a
coloration which I have not met with in any varieties of that
species, it differs in having the thorax entirely destitute of punctures, the inter-antennal production of the head is broader and
truncate at the apex. The sutural angle of the elytra has a
small oblique truncature without any tooth at the suture

---

* Something similar is seen in some other species of this genus, but
I have not seen any in which it is so pronounced

Prosopodonta costata, n. sp.

Elongata, niger; thorace postice crebre sat fortiter punctato basi foveâ impresso, lateribus post medium dente parvo instructo; elytris flavo-piceis, fortiter striato punctatis, interstitiis alternatis subcostiformibus. Long. 6 lin.

General form nearly that of *P. limbata*, Baly (Cat. Hip. p. 69, t. vi, f. 2), but the elytra are very parallel, and the thorax is very slightly constricted before the base. Thorax is little shorter than broad, considerably narrower than the elytra, arcuately narrowed in front, not very shining, smooth in the middle in front, moderately thickly and rather strongly punctured behind, with a large fovea in the middle at the base. Elytra light brown, strongly striate-punctate, very strongly towards the sides, the second, fourth, sixth and eighth interstices somewhat costiform, the second broader than the others, the fifth and seventh very narrow and lost towards the shoulders.

Prosopodonta punctata, n. sp. Pl IX, f. 4.

Elongata, depressiuscula, atra ; thorace antice angulatim angustato, dorso punctis nonnullis notato , elytris piceo-flavis, parallelis, punctis distantibus nigris subseriatim dispositis. Long. 6 lin.

Thorax a little narrower than the elytra, one-fifth broader than long, obliquely narrowed in front, angular at the sides, a little narrowed towards the base, rather dull in front, with a few punctures on each side of the disc behind. Elytra pitchy-yellow, with very distinct black rather distant punctures, which appear irregular but are in lines on the back.

EROTYLIDÆ.

Cyclomorphus glabratus, n sp. Pl. IX, f. 5.

Glabratus, per convexus, nitidissimus, niger; thorace lateribus vittâque medianâ, elytris lineis quatuor rufo-sanguineis ; corpore subtus rufo-piceo, abdominis segmentis nigro-notatis. Long. 5 lin., lat. 4 lin.

Thorax not quite twice as broad as long, gently narrowed anteriorly, deeply emarginate in front, moderately rounded at the sides, impunctate, dull red, with a longitudinal black stripe on each side of the disc, anterior angles rather obtuse, base sinuate on each side with a slight impression above each sinuation. Scutellum dull red. Elytra two-fifths broader than the thorax, as broad as long, extremely convex, almost globular, impunctate, each elytron with four dull red stripes, the first and third abbreviated, the fourth lateral. Each segment of the abdomen has a black spot on each side.

COCCINELLIDÆ

Epilachna bituberculata, n. sp.

Cyaneo-nigra, subnitida; elytris creberrime evidenter punctulatis, reflexo-marginatis, dorsim tuberculis duobus approximatis obtusis piceis instructis. Long. 3⅔ lin.

This species although presenting nothing remarkable in form when compared to *E. peltata,* Er., and its allies, is at once distinguished by its having two round obtuse pitchy tubercles on the dorsal region, one on each elytron close to the suture. Thorax very transverse, distinctly but finely and very closely punctured; the sides slightly reflexed anteriorly. Elytra densely and distinctly punctured (larger and smaller punctures intermixed), rather broad at the shoulders, arcuately acuminate towards the apex, very gibbous, broadly reflexed at the shoulders, more narrowly posteriorly.

Descriptions of new BUTTERFLIES *of the Indian Region*; by
ARTHUR G. BUTLER, F.L S, F.Z S.

Ixias insignis, n. sp. Pl. VIII, f. 1.

Pale sulphur-yellow, base of the wings broadly greenish-grey;
a very large, almost triangular, orange patch, from the centre of
the cell to the centre of the disc, crossed by black veins, limited
by the first median branch, its outer margin oblique above the
lower or true radial, and zigzag below it; apical area, outer
border, and the inner half of the interno-median area, dark
chocolate-brown; a pale centred black spot on the lower discocellular; secondaries with a rather broad and slightly sinuated
external border; wings below sulphur-yellow, irrorated with
brown; secondaries with a squamose subcostal spot and three or
four across the disc. Expanse of wings 2 inches 7 lines

Tai-wau-foo, Formosa (Rev. W. Campbell).

Nearest to *I. balice*, much larger, rather paler, and with a
considerably larger orange patch on the primaries; base of
wings darker.

Nepheronia lutescens, n. sp.

♂ Allied to *N. Valeria* but larger; above rather greener in
tint, with slightly narrower black external borders. on the under
surface the external border and apical area of primaries and the
whole ground-colour of secondaries suffused with butter-yellow;
veins dark brown as in *N. Valeria* Expanse of wings 3 inches
5 lines.

Borneo (Low).

I labelled this species with the above name some years since,
but by some oversight omitted to describe it. Mr. Moore having
found the species in a Collection which he was determining from
Tenasserim, was unable to discover that any description had been
published and called my attention to the fact. I can only
account for this by the supposition that I wrote out an isolated
description of the species, and it consequently got mislaid.

Hypolimnas charybdis, n. sp.

Nearly allied to *H. bolina*, rather larger; the white fascioles on the bright ultramarine patches of the upper surface narrower and more elongated: the white discal spots on the female reduced to dots (excepting two near the costa of primaries); the sub-marginal notched spots and the crescents close to the margin narrower and suffused with brown; below intermediate in character between *H. bolina* and *H. jacintha*, the oblique white belt beyond the cell of primaries being distinct, but broken up into spots; the belt beyond the middle of the secondaries sordid whitish, with a brownish tint in the male, and a creamy tint in the female, corresponding with the submarginal belt in colour; the latter, the undulated whitish marginal stripe and the discal series of pearly white spots quite as in *II. jacintha*. Expanse of wings ♂ 3 inches 7 lines; ♀ 4 inches 2 lines.

Bombay (Dr. Leith).

Nearest to *D. incommoda* in general appearance.

Hypolimnas Labuana, n. sp.

♀ Dark chocolate brown, the wings with the sinuations of the fringes white; a nearly marginal slender squamose series of whitish crescent-like markings; a submarginal series of more or less semicircular white spots, small at apex and anal angle of secondaries, very small towards apex of primaries; a discal series of white spots, beginning with a large trifid patch near the costa of primaries, on the secondaries decreasing in size towards the abdominal margin, primaries with the usual bluish costal spots; a broad brilliantly shot oblique ultramarine belt beyond the discoidal cell; under surface slightly paler, sericeous; the usual black-edged white discoidal spots; belts beyond the middle of all the wings narrow, squamose, sordid whitish; discal spots as above; submarginal markings whiter and broader than above. Expanse of wings 4 inches 1 line.

Labuan, Borneo (Low).

I have seen several examples of this species, it is most nearly allied to *II. philippensis*.

Descriptions of two new Eastern species of the genus Papilio;
by Oliver E. Janson.

Papilio Butleri, n. sp.   Pl. VIII, f. 3.

Primaries above deep black, velvety, two spots in the cell,
three near the apex and six longitudinal stripes between the
nervures on the outer disc deep metallic blue, there is also an
obscure spot of the same colour at the costa, just beyond the
cell, and a very small one at the anal angle; secondaries dark
brown, blackish at the base with a marginal series of darker
stripes between the nervures, the four outer ones with a small
pale blue spot, the fringe spotted with white between the nervures; beneath dark brown, both wings with a marginal row of
seven bluish white spots, those on the primaries small and round
but on secondaries large and sublunate; body black, head, underside and sides of the abdomen spotted with white   Expanse of
wings 3 inches 8 lines.
Malacca.

I have only seen a solitary male of this species, which was
recently received in a small collection of East Indian insects from
Malacca, without indication of its precise habitat, it appears to
be most nearly allied to *P. Slateri*, Hew., although more like
P. Icrosa, Butler, in some respects.

Papilio Walkeri, n. sp.   Pl. VIII, f. 2.

Above black-brown, the fringes of both wings spotted with
white between the nervures, primaries with four faint lines in
the cell at the base, and two rather indistinct longitudinal stripes
on the outer disc between each of the nervures, of rather sparse
pale ochreous scales; secondaries with a broad ill defined transverse band about the middle, deeply emarginate between the
nervures on its outer edge pale slate-blue, a submarginal series
of seven irregular spots and the usual lunule on the abdominal
margin cinerous, tails short and broad, not contracted at the

base; primaries beneath not so dark as above, the markings similar but rather more pronounced; secondaries with four ochreous spots in a transverse row about the middle on the abdominal half, broadly margined with pale blue on their outer sides (these spots are also slightly indicated on the costal half of the wing), the submarginal spots and abdominal lunule similar to those above, but larger and of a pale ochreous colour; head and body black-brown, several small spots on the former, the breast and the outer side of the legs white   Expanse of wings 4¼ inches.

S India.

This species is very unlike any with which I am acquainted, it evidently belongs to the *polytes* group, and in some respects resembles *P. Schmeltzi,* H. Sch.   I have dedicated it to the Rev. F. A. Walker, M.A., F.L.S., whose fine collection of this tribe of insects is well known to Entomologists   The male here described and figured is the only specimen I have seen.

List of the PHYTOPHAGOUS COLEOPTERA *collected in Assam by
A. W. Chennell, Esq., with notes and descriptions of the
uncharacterized Genera and Species* ; by JOSEPH S. BALY,
F.L.S.

The insects brought over by Mr. Chennell are all large or of
medium size, the smaller species having apparently been overlooked or neglected ; thus *Cryptocephalus, Hispa* proper, and the
smaller genera of *Eumolpidæ* and *Halticinæ* (known to be spread
over the whole Indian continent), are unrepresented. The
collection as it stands includes a great number of Asiatic
forms, and probably contains the great majority of the most
common and salient Assamese species. Many of the larger
kinds have been previously described from various parts of
India, by Hope, Redtenbacher and others ; amongst the most
noticeable must be mentioned the genus *Pentamesa,* recently
characterized by Von Harold, and also a specimen (unfortunately very imperfect) of the rare genus *Macrispa.*

The new forms include several striking genera and species of
Gallerucinæ, many of the latter remarkable for the peculiar
sculpture of the lower face in the ♂ sex , the occurence of the
genus *Entomoscelis* for the first time in India is also worthy of
note.

Genus SAGRA, Fab.

1. *Sagra carbunculus,* Hope.*

Hab The Upper Hills, 4,500 to 6,000 feet.

Genus LEMA, Fab.

1. *Lema russula,* Boh

Hab. The Lower Hills, 1,500 to 2,500 feet.

---

* References to the original descriptions, unless published since the
appearance of Gemminger and Von Harold's Catalogue, or for some
other special reason are omitted,

Two specimens of this species from Assam agree in every particular with one in my Cabinet from Hong Kong.

2. *Lema rufotestacea*, Clark.

Hab. The Lower Hills.

Genus CRIOCERIS, Geoff.

1. *Crioceris quadripustulata*, Fab.

Hab. The Hills.

2. *Crioceris locuples*, Clark.

Hab The Upper Hills, 4,000 to 6,000 feet.

3. *Crioceris semipunctata*, Fab.

Hab. The Lower Hills.

4. *Crioceris impressa*, Fab.

Hab. The Plains, Sibsagar, and Hills, 200 feet.

Genus DIAPROMORPHA, Lac.

1. *Diapromorpha pallens*, Oliv. (*melanopus*, Lac.).

Hab. The Hills, and Plains, 250 feet.

Diapromorpha being now characterized as a distinct genus, Olivier's name, originally given to the above species, must be restored.

2. *Diapromorpha turcica*, Fab.

The Plains.

Genus AGASIA, Hope.

1. *Agasta formosa*, Hope.

Hab. The Hills, and Plains.

Var. A.   Elytrorum maculis intermedus obsoletis.

Specimens both of the typical form and also of the variety A are in the collection.

Genus MELASOMA, Stephens.

1. *Melasoma longicollis*, Saffr.

Hab. The Lower Hills.

The specimens of this species, which is spread over Eastern Siberia and Mongolia, are more deeply punctured than the European ones, in other respects they agree with the type.

Genus PARALINA, Baly.

1. *Paralina indica*, Hope.

Hab. The Hills.

Genus EUMELA, Baly.

(Trans Ent. Soc. 1875, p 23).

1. *Eumela cyanicollis*, Hope, (*Chrysomela**).

Hab. The Hills and Plains.

Genus CHRYSOMELA, Linn.

1. *Chrysomela Grutn*, Baly.

Hab. The Plains and Lower Hills

Genus CHALCOLAMPRA, Blanchard.

1. *Chalcolampra octoguttata*, Fab.

Hab. Assam.

Genus ENTOMOSCELIS, Chevr.

1 *Entomoscelis Assamensis*, n. sp.

Anguste ovata, convexa, picea, nitida, cupreo micans, supra rufo-picea, thorace sparse tenuiter punctato; elytris tenuiter punctatis, punctis sub-striatim dispositis. Long. 3-4 lin.

Hab. Plains and Hills.

---

* Gemminger and Von Harold's Catalogue

Head shining, sparingly impressed with fine punctures; antennæ rather slender, filiform, more than three fourths the length of the body. Thorax nearly twice as broad as long, sides rounded, nearly straight and parallel behind the middle; the hinder angles acute, the anterior ones sub-acute; above convex, smooth and shining, impressed on either side near the anterior angle with a shallow fovea, disc rather sparingly impressed with minute punctures. Elytra broadly oblong-ovate, convex, impressed with very fine punctures irregularly arranged in longitudinal striæ; interstices shining impunctate.

The genus *Entomoscelis*, although containing few species, is remarkable for its wide geographical range, being found over the whole of central and southern Europe, northern Africa and Asia minor, in North America as far south as New York, in eastern Siberia, and, as the present insect shews, in northern India. The tropical and South African species placed by Dejean and Vogel in *Entomoscelis*, belong to an entirely different generic group, since characterized by myself, under the name of *Mesoplatys*.

Genus PAROPSIS, Oliv.

1. *Paropsis Chennelli*, n. sp.

Late ovata, valde convexa, sordide fulva, nitida, thorace transverso, sat crebre punctato, utrinque excavato et varioloso-punctato, elytris punctato-striatis.   Long $4\frac{1}{2}$ lin.

Hab Plains of Assam, a single specimen.

Head coarsely punctured; antennæ slender, scarcely exceeding the head and thorax in length. Thorax nearly three times as broad as long; sides straight and nearly parallel from the base to the middle, thence rounded and converging to the apex, the anterior angles acute, submucronate; apical margin deeply excavated; upper surface rather coarsely and closely punctured, broadly excavated on either side near the outer margin, surface of the excavations very coarsely and irregularly varioloso-punctate. Elytra broader than the thorax, very slightly dilated posteriorly, broadly rounded at the apex, convex, regularly punctate-striate, the interspaces minutely punctate, the fourth, sixth, eight and tenth obsoletely thickened; outer limb narrow, slightly reflexed, its surface concave, strongly and coarsely punctured.

Genus CORYNODES, Hope.

1. *Corynodes Assamensis*, n. sp.

Elongatus, subcylindricus, metallico-purpureus, nitidus, interdum viridi micans; thorace disperse sat fortiter punctato;
elytris infra basin fortiter transversim excavatis, juxta marginem
lateralem longitudinaliter sulcatis, subseriatim punctatis. Long.
4-5½ lin.

Mas. Antennis corporis dimidio multo longioribus, articulis
sex ultimis compressis, paullo dilatatis.

Fœm. Antennis brevioribus, articulis sex ultimis sat valde
dilatatis; elytris intra sulcum laterale costatis.

Hab The Hills and Plains; Dibru.

Vertex strongly but not very closely punctured; front
impressed with a longitudinal groove, which terminates just
above the apex of the clypeus in a large ill defined fovea; clypeus
rather broader than long, semi-ovate, separated from the front
on either side by a deep groove, its extreme apex transversely
depressed, surface closely punctured, clothed with fulvous
hairs; antennæ nearly three fourths the length of the body in
the ♂, the six outer joints only slightly dilated, scarcely more
than half the length of the body in the ♀, the six terminal
joints in this sex more broadly dilated. Thorax rather more
than one half broader than long; sides straight and slightly
converging from the base to the middle, thence rounded and
converging to the apex; disc convex, subcylindrical, sparingly
punctured, impressed on either side, just behind the middle,
with an ill defined fovea Elytra narrowly oblong, convex,
impressed below the basilar space with a deep transverse, slightly
curved sulcation; just within the lateral margin in both sexes is
a broad ill defined longitudinal groove, within this in the ♀ is a
narrow elevated longitudinal costa, which extends from the
humeral callus nearly to the apex of the elytra, claws appendiculated.

In habit closely resembling *C. asphodelus*, Marsh., separated
from that insect by its broader thorax, by the longitudinal costa
on the elytra in the ♀, and by the six (not five) dilated outer
joints of the antennæ.

2. *Corynodes peregrinus*, Fuessly.

Hab. Sadia; Dibru.

Genus CHRYSOLAMPRA, Baly.

1. *Chrysolampra piceipes*, n. sp.

Oblongo-ovata, viridi-metallica, nitida, labio antennisque fulvis, his apice nigro-piceis; pedibus nigro-piceis, æneo micantibus, femoribus tibiisque basi rufo-piceis; thorace tenuiter minus crebre punctato; elytris evidenter sat crebre punctatis.

Mas. Tarsorum anticorum quatuor articulo basali dilatato; femoribus anticis incrassatis, subtus angulatis. Long. 3 lin.

Hab. The Upper Hills.

Intermediate in size between *C splendens*, mihi, and *C. smaragdula*, Boheman, distinguished from either species by its piceous legs Antennæ slender, filiform, the two upper joints nigro-piceous. Thorax finely punctured, the puncturing rather coarser on the sides Elytra much more strongly punctured than the thorax, the punctures forming longitudinal striæ at the apex near the suture, the interspaces on the sides obsoletely wrinkled.

Genus COLASPOSOMA, Laporte.

1 *Colasposoma coeruleatum*, n. sp.

Late oblongum, convexum, metallico-coeruleum, labio, mandibulis antennisque extrorsum nigris, capite crebre subrugoso-punctato; thorace transverso, tenuiter punctato; elytris infra basin leviter transversim depressis, tenuiter punctatis, punctis prope suturam subseriatim dispositis apicem versus fere deletis, interspatiis infra humeros transversim rugulosis Long. 3½–5 lin.

Hab Dibru.

Head closely subrugose-punctate; anterior margin of clypeus concave-emarginate; antennæ half the length of the body, the five outer joints compressed, slightly dilated, opaque, black. Thorax nearly three times as broad as long; sides rounded and converging from base to apex, each of the angles armed with an acute tooth; disc transversely convex, deflexed near the anterior angles, faintly excavated on either side, minutely punctured, the punctures rather more strongly impressed on the sides. Scutellum scarcely longer than broad, its apex very obtuse, its disc smooth and shining. Elytra much broader than the thorax, subquadrate-oblong, broadly rounded at the apex, convex, faintly but broadly depressed below the basilar space, finely punctured, the punctures nearly obsolete below the middle, irregularly arranged in longitudinal rows near the suture; on the outer margin below the humeral callus are three or four short deeply impressed, longitudinal rows of striæ, the interspaces between which are thickened and subcostate; interspaces smooth, transversely rugulose below the humeral callus. Each of the thighs armed beneath with a minute tooth.

2. *Colasposoma pulcherrimum*, Baly.

Hab. The Hills.

Genus HALTICA, Geoff.

1. *Haltica cyanea*, Weber.

Hab. Dibru.

Genus PODONTIA, Dalm.

1. *Podontia quatuor-decimpunctata*, Linn

Hab The Hills.

2. *Podontia affinis*, Groendal.

Hab. Dibru.

3. *Podontia rufocastanea*, Baly

Hab. The Upper Hills.

Genus BLEPHARIDA, Rogers.

1. *Blepharida flavopustulata*, n. sp.

Ovata, postice paullo attenuata, convexa, pallide piceo-fulva, nitida, labro flavo; thorace transverso, irregulariter excavato, hic illic profunde punctato; elytris regulariter punctato-striatis, sparse flavo pustulatis. Long. 4½ lin

Hab. The Hills; a single specimen.

Vertex sparingly impressed with round punctures; face between the eyes impressed on either side with an ill defined, coarsely punctured, oblique groove; the basal joint of antennæ rufo-fulvous (the rest wanting); clypeus coarsely punctured; labrum pale yellow, apices of the jaws nigro-piceous Thorax thrice times as broad as long; sides straight and parallel from the base to just beyond the middle, thence obliquely rounded to the apex, anterior angles produced, thickened, slightly excurved,

obtuse, the hinder ones produced, acute; disc irregularly excavated on the sides, impressed with large deep punctures, rather
crowded at the base, forming irregular rows on the sides, the
rest of the surface finely punctured. Scutellum trigonate, its
apex rounded. Elytra much broader than the thorax, slightly
narrowed towards the apex, convex, deeply and regularly punctate-striate, the interspaces plane, distantly impressed with very
minute punctures; sparingly scattered over the surface are a
number of small irregular yellowish-white spots.

Genus SEBAETHE, Baly.

1. *Sebaethe pallidipennis*, n sp.

Late ovata, modice convexa, nigro-picea, nitida, antennis
nigris, harum basi, scutello labioque piceis, thorace tenuissime
punctato, nigro, lateribus anguste piceis; elytris tenuiter punctatis, fulvis. Long. 2 lin

Hab. Assam.

Head trigonate; vertex shining, impunctate, encarpæ well
defined, subquadrangular, contiguous, carina rather strongly
raised, narrow, linear, its apex dilated, narrowly ovate-lanceolate;
antennæ less than two-thirds the length of the body, moderately
robust, slightly attenuated towards the apex, the three basal
joints pale piceous, the rest black. Thorax three times as broad
as long; sides narrowly reflexed, edged with piceous. Scutellum
trigonate Elytra much broader than the thorax, broadly ovate,
slightly narrowed towards the apex, finely punctured; outer
limb narrowly dilated, slightly reflexed, its surface obsoletely
thickened, impunctate; inflexed limb broad, obsoletely concave.
Hinder thighs strongly thickened; outer edge of hinder tibiæ
emarginate near the apex.

Genus HYPHASIS, v. Harold.

(Deutsche Ent. Zeitschr. xxi, 1877, p. 454)

1. *Hyphasis indica*, n. sp.

Ovata, modice convexa, pallide flava, nitida, antennis extrorsum pallide piceis; thorace lævi, lateribus late marginatis, rotundatis; elytris confuse punctatis, pallide castaneis, fulvo limbatis.
Long. 3½ lin.

Hab. The Plains; a single specimen.

Head smooth, impunctate, face raised between the antennæ; carina narrow in front, dilated posteriorly, its apex lanceolate; encarpæ transverse, quadrangular, contiguous, separated from the front by a transverse groove; antennæ filiform. Thorax three times as broad as long; sides broadly margined, rounded, emarginate just in front of the hinder angle, the latter acute, the anterior angle mucronate, excurved; disc transversely convex, sparingly impressed with very minute punctures, lateral margin reflexed, its surface concave. Scutellum trigonate, its apex obtuse. Elytra broader than the thorax, moderately convex, flattened on the suture, distinctly but not very closely punctured, the outer margin moderately dilated, reflexed. Prosternum twice as broad as long, its sides parallel, its apex truncate, its disc longitudinally concave.

Genus EUPHITREA, Baly.

1. *Euphitrea Assamensis*, n. sp.

Rotundata, convexa, rufo-picea, nitida, thorace lævi, elytris piceis, æneo-micantibus, subfortiter sat crebre punctatis, limbo laterali paullo reflexo, irregulariter incrassato, fere impunctato. Long. 2½ lin.

Hab. The Plains.

Nearly allied to *E. micans*, Baly, much smaller, rather more rotundate, the elytra more strongly and closely punctured, their outer limb more distinctly reflexed. in the single specimen before me the hinder legs are unfortunately broken off.

Genus PENTAMESA, Lac.

1. *Pentamesa duodecimmaculata*, v. Harold.

Hab. The Upper Hills.

Genus OIDES, Weber.

1. *Oides indica*, n. sp.

Late rotundato-ovata, ad apicem paullo attenuata, valde convexa, flava, nitida, antennis extrorsum, oculis, metasterno, abdominisque segmentorum singulorum maculis duabus nigris. Long. 6 lin.

Hab. The Hills.

Vertex smooth, impunctate; face just above the encarpæ deeply impressed; encarpæ transverse, subclavate, separated (the extreme apex excepted) by the triangular clypeus; eyes rather small, shining black. Thorax nearly three times as broad as long; the apical margin concave, sides converging from the base towards the apex, slightly rounded, anterior angles produced, their apices obtuse, hinder angles broadly rounded; disc shining, impunctate. Scutellum trigonate Elytra much broader than the thorax, the humeral angles anteriorly produced, broadly rounded; sides rounded and diverging from the shoulders nearly to the middle, thence rounded and obliquely converging to the apex, the apex itself regularly rounded; upper surface very minutely punctured, the outer limb broadly dilated. Metasternum and a large patch on either side of each of the abdominal segments black.

2 *Oides inornata*, n. sp.

Ovata, convexa, pallide flava, nitida, antennis apice, tibiis tarsisque vix infuscatis, his unguiculis nigro-piceis; thorace remote punctato; elytris tenuiter, subcrebre punctatis, interstitiis punctis minutis impressis. Long 4 lin.

Hab. Assam; Sibsagar, Kamrup.

Head trigonate, vertex smooth, impunctate; front impressed with a longitudinal groove, encarpæ thickened, well defined, contiguous, subquadrangular; carina obsolete; clypeus thickened, trigonate, antennæ filiform, concolorous with the body, the terminal joint piceous, the two preceding ones slightly stained with fuscous Thorax three times as broad as long; sides broadly rounded at the base, thence obliquely converging towards the apex, sinuate and slightly excavated in front, the anterior angles obtuse, the hinder ones obsolete, disc sparingly punctured, the puncturing rather close on the sides. Scutellum scarcely longer than broad, trigonate Elytra broader than the thorax, convex, sinuate on the sides below the humeral callus, finely but distinctly punctured, the interspaces impressed with very minute punctures; outer limb reflexed.

3. *Oides japonica*, Hornst.

Hab. The Hills.

I have received this insect from northern China as well as Japan, I also possess it from northern India, but without precise locality.

Genus AULACOPHORA, Chevr.

1 *Aulacophora testacea*, Fab. Mant. Ius. i, p 87 (1789) =
   abdominalis, var Fab. Ent. Syst ii, p. 23 (1792).

Hab. The Hills of Assam.

This *Aulacophora*, specimens of both sexes of which are before
me, was originally described by Fabricius under the above
specific name, and was subsequently, both in the Ent. Syst. and
Syst. El, reduced to a variety of *abdominalis*; an examination of these specimens has convinced me that it must be regarded
as a distinct species—the principal points of difference between
it and *foveicollis*, Kust.* are as follows the transverse groove
on the thorax is less deeply excavated, and the abdomen is
entirely black in both sexes, the anal segment in the ♂ is as
usual trilobate, but the medial lobe instead of being longer than
the lateral ones and longitudinally concave (as in *A foveicollis*)
is plane, quadrate, and of equal length with the other lobes; the
anal segment of the ♀ also differs in form from that of the
same sex of *foveicollis*.

2. *Aulacophora cornuta*, n sp.

Oblonga postice paullo ampliata, flava, nitida, pectore abdomineque nigris, pube adpressâ argenteo-sericeâ sat dense vestitis;
thorace transverso, disco transversim impresso, fere impunctato,
lateribus distincte, subremote punctatis; elytris distincte punctatis. Long 4 lin

Mas Antennis articlo basali incrassato, subtus compresso;
clypeo utrinque infra antennas cornu lato compresso brevi, apice

---

* The name *abdominalis*, Fab as far as relates to our European species
must fall—Fabricius in the Spec Ins p 151, originally described this
insect from a specimen in Forster s Cabinet, brought from one of the
islands in the Pacific Ocean subsequently some individuals from India
and the Cape of Good Hope (regarded by him as belonging to the same
species) came under his observation, thus in his later works, he gave
those localities as Habitats for the species *A foveicollis*, Kust, ranges
over Southern Europe the north of Africa, and a considerable extent of
Continental Asia but in the Malay Archipelago, Australia, and the
South Sea Islands it is replaced by closely allied but specifically distinct
forms, one or other of which doubtless must be regarded as the true
abdominalis, which of them unfortunately. from the type being no
longer extant, it will be next to impossible to determine

oblique truncato et inter cornua laminâ compressâ nigrâ, pilis erectis numerosis fulvis circumdatis, armato.

Hab. The Plains.

Vertex and front shining, impunctate; encarpæ transverse, subtrigonate, contiguous; clypeus armed on either side with a broad, compressed short horn, the apex of which is obliquely truncate and forms a narrowly ovate flattened disc; between these horns is a short transverse black plate, which is surrounded, as well as the horns themselves, with numerous coarse erect fulvous hairs, immediately above this plate is a tuft of still coarser hairs, which curve obliquely to either side from the medial line; antennæ filiform, the basal joint thickened, compressed beneath and forming a raised longitudinal ridge; eyes large, prominent. Thorax more than twice as broad as long; sides straight and parallel from the base to beyond the middle, thence converging to the apex; basal margin sinuate in front of the scutellum, faintly bisinuate on either side; disc sparingly impressed with round punctures on the sides, its central portion impunctate, transversely sulcate just behind its middle, the sulcation rather more deeply excavated on either side. Scutellum elongate-trigonate, shining, impunctate Elytra broader than the thorax, oblong, scarcely dilated posteriorly, moderately convex, distinctly punctured. Apical abdominal segment in the ♂ deeply trilobate, the medial lobe subquadrate-oblong, its apex truncate, faintly sinuate, its disc impressed with a .large deep fovea.

I only know the ♂ of this species.

3. *Aulacophora pulchella*, n. sp.

Ovata, postice ampliata, convexa, rufo-testacea, nitida, antennis, tibiis tarsisque fuscis, oculis elytrisque nigris, his apice rufo-testaceis. Long. 3½ lin.

Hab. Assam, the Hills

Head trigonate; vertex smooth, impunctate, front impressed with a longitudinal groove, encarpæ transverse, contiguous; carina raised, narrow, linear, its apex acute; eyes very large, prominent, shining black; antennæ slender, filiform. Thorax more than twice as broad as long, sides straight and slightly converging from the base to beyond the middle, thence obliquely converging and slightly rounded to the apex, the angles obtuse; disc coarsely but closely punctured on the sides, nearly impunctate in the middle, transverse groove broad, rather more deeply

excavated on the sides than in the centre Scutellum wedge
shaped, its apex obtuse. Elytra broader than the thorax, somewhat dilated towards the apex, convex, excavated on the inner
disc below the basilar space, sinuate on the sides below the
humeral callus, distinctly punctured, the interspaces obsoletely
granulose. Apical segment of abdomen in the ♂ trilobate, the
medial lobe scarcely longer than the lateral ones, quadrate, its
disc concave.

4. *Aulacophora perplexa*, n. sp.

Ovata, postice paullo ampliata, convexa, flava, nitida, abdominis
segmentibus maculis bifariis (segmento ultimo excepto) pectoreque nigris; thorace nitido, leviter transversim sulcato; scutello
piceo; elytris sat fortiter punctatis, utrisque maculis subrotun-
datis quatuor, 2 ante, 2 pone medium oblique positis nigris
Long. 3⅔ lin.

Hab. The Hills of Assam.

Vertex shining impunctate, front impressed on either side,
just above the encarpæ, with a deep round fovea, in the middle,
continuous with the sutural line separating the encarpæ is a short
longitudinal groove; encarpæ transverse, contiguous: carina short,
thickened, its apex acute, antennæ filiform, about three-fourths
the length of the body Thorax twice as broad as long; sides
rather broadly margined, straight and converging from the base
nearly to the middle, rounded and slightly dilated in front of
the latter, the anterior angles excavated, obtuse; very sparingly
punctured above, the punctures irregularly scattered here and
there over the surface; middle disc impunctate; transverse
groove distinct on either side and extending to the lateral
margin, nearly obsolete on the medial line. Elytra broader
than the thorax, rather closely punctured, each with four rather
large subrotundate spots; two placed on the inner disc near the
suture, one just below the base, the other at some distance just
below the middle, the two others near the lateral margin, the
first below the humeral callus, the second about half-way
between the middle and the apex; these spots taken conjointly
with those on the opposite elytron form two curved fasciæ, one
before, the other behind the middle. Body beneath with the
breast and two large spots placed transversely on each of the
abdominal segments (the anal one excepted) black. Claws
appendiculated

Aulacophora perplexa differs from the other species in having
appendiculated, subbifid claws; in the absence of any other

essential character, I do not consider this peculiarity of sufficient importance to remove it from its present position.

Genus AGETOCERA, Hope.

1. *Agetocera lobicornis*, Baly.

Hab. The Hills.

One specimen, a ♀.

2. *Agetocera pulchella*, Baly.

Hab. The Upper Hills.

Genus CNEORANE, Baly.

1. *Cneorane fulvicollis*, Baly.

Mas Antennarum articulis ultimis quatuor incrassatis, subtus subcomplanatis, clavam elongatam ad apicem attenuatam sordide flavam formantibus; tibiis, basi exceptis, tarsisque infuscatis.

Hab. The Hills, Sadia

Genus MIMASTRA, Baly.

1. *Mimastra quadripartita*, n. sp.

Elongata, parallela, fulva, nitida, scutello, pectore antennisque nigris, verticis maculâ, abdominis lateribus pedibusque (femoribus subtus, tibiisque anticis quatuor basi exceptis) nigro-piceis; thorace transverso, late transversim excavato, impunctato, elytris leviter rugulosis, nigris vel nigro-piceis, utrisque limbo fasciâque vix pone medium fulvis   Long $3\frac{1}{2}$ lin.

Mas. Tarsis anticis articulo basali paullo incrassato, leviter incurvato

Var. A. Thoracis disco piceo tincto.

Hab. The Plains.

Face smooth, impunctate, clypeus large, concave on either side, its apex produced into an acute tooth, which extends upwards between the encarpæ for nearly half their length; eyes large, prominent, shining black; antennæ much longer than the body, very slender, filiform, the third joint twice the length of the second, the two conjointly scarcely equal in length to the fourth, the latter slightly curved. Thorax twice as broad as long; sides straight and parallel, the hinder angle thickened, setiferous; disc shining, impunctate, nearly covered with a broad deep transverse excavation, which does not quite extend to the lateral margin; in the medial line is a narrow longitudinal space less deeply excavated than the rest of the surface. Scutellum trigonate, shining black. Elytra broader than the thorax, obsoletely dilated towards the apex, faintly excavated below the basilar space, rugulose, rather closely punctured. Apex of the last abdominal segment deeply concave-emarginate.

2. *Mimastra limbata,* n. sp.

Elongata, angustata, parallela, nitida, nigra, femoribus anticis quatuor (vittâ dorsali exceptâ) tibiisque anticis quatuor basi, sordide fulvis; suprâ sordide fulva, antennis (basi piceâ exceptâ) nigris, capitis vertice thoracisque maculis piceis; thorace lævi, utrinque late transversim excavato, lateribus rectis, parallelis; elytris thorace latioribus, parallelis, infra basin leviter transversim depressis, fortiter et sat crebre punctatis, interspatiis, transversim rugulosis, viridi-metallicis, utrisque, apice excepto, fulvo limbatis. Long. 6 lin.

Var. A Thoracis maculis intermediis piceis obsoletis.
Hab. The hills of Assam.

Vertex impressed with very fine transverse striæ; encarpæ thickened, transverse, elongate-trigonate, contiguous, their surfaces finely granulose, carina ill defined; antennæ slender, filiform, nearly equal to the body in length, the second joint very short, the third twice its length, the fourth equal in length to the two preceding united; three basal joints obscure piceous, the rest black; clypeus granulose; apices of jaws nigro-piceous Thorax nearly one-half broader than long, sides straight and parallel, the anterior angles thickened, oblique; basal margin obliquely sinuate at either end, transversely truncate in the middle, faintly truncate just in front of the scutellum; disc shining, impunctate, broadly excavated transversely on either side, impressed just before the base with a round fovea; surface marked with five black spots, two large placed one on either side near the lateral border, two smaller situated transversely just in front of the middle, and one very small placed on the basal fovea. Scutellum trigonate, pale piceous. Elytra coarsely punctured, their whole surfaces covered with coarse irregular transverse rugæ.

3 *Mimastra Chennelli*, n. sp.

Angustata, parallela, flava, nitida, oculis, antennis extrorsum, tarsis, tibusque posticis quatuor, his basi exceptis, tibiis anticis dorso, pectore abdomineque nigris, thorace nitido, disco transversim excavato, elytris crebre punctatis. Long $3\frac{1}{2}$–$4\frac{1}{4}$ lin.

Mas. Tarsis anticis articulo basali intus curvato, articulo secundo pone apicem articuli primi inserto.

Hab. Hills of Assam.

Encarpæ raised, trigonate, contiguous; eyes large, prominent, shining black; antennæ slender, filiform, equal to the body in length, the third joint twice the length of the second, the two conjointly equal in length to the fourth, the four lower joints fulvous, the fifth piceous, the rest black. Thorax one-half broader than long; sides nearly straight and parallel, slightly sinuate behind the middle; disc shining impunctate, broadly and deeply excavated, the excavation not quite extending to the lateral margin. Scutellum trigonate, its apex acute. Elytra rather broader than the thorax, parallel, closely punctured, the interspaces subrugulose. Basal joint of the anterior tarsus in the ♂ falcate, its apex obtuse, the second joint inserted on the outer edge of the basal one, some distance behind its apex; apical segment of abdomen in the same sex trilobate, the medial lobe emarginate; its disc impressed with a smooth wedge shaped fovea.

The ♀ is rather larger, less deeply depressed on the middle of the thorax, and has the fourth and fifth joints of the antennæ piceous.

Genus CLITENA, Baly.

1. *Clitena Vigorsii*, Hope; (*igneipennis*, Baly.)

Var. A. *cærulans*, Hope, *cyanea*, Clark
Hab The Hills, Sadia.

This insect, which has been described by Hope, Clark and myself, under several distinct names, is very variable in tint, and sometimes (the antennæ excepted) entirely metallic green, the specimens from Assam belong to var. A.

Genus DORYXENA, Baly.

1. *Doryxena grossa*, Hope.

Hab. The Upper Hills,

2. *Doryxena geniculata*, n. sp

Ovata, postice ampliata, convexa, flava, nitida, scutello, genubus tarsisque nigris, thorace transverso, lateribus pone medium sinuatis, disco parce punctato, utrinque transversim excavato; elytris pallide castaneis, postice ampliatis, apice obtusis; supra convexis, sat crebre fortiter punctatis   Long. $6\frac{1}{2}$–$7\frac{1}{2}$ lin.

Var. A. Elytris flavis.
Hab. The Upper Hills.

Vertex and front with a longitudinal groove, sparingly impressed with large round punctures, encarpæ well defined, large, subpyriform, contiguous, upper half of clypeus thickened, the carina obsolete; antennæ rather more than half the length of the body, filiform, pale yellow.   Thorax rather more than twice as broad as long; sides nearly parallel, sinuate from the base to the middle, thence obliquely converging to the apex, the anterior angles produced, thickened, subacute; basal margin faintly bisinuate on either side, obtusely emarginate in front of the scutellum, the outer angle thickened, obtuse; disc transversely excavated on either side, sparingly impressed with large round punctures   Scutellum longer than broad, its sides straight and converging from the base towards the apex, the latter broadly obtuse   Elytra much broader than the thorax, broadly margined, increasing in width towards the apex, the apex itself very obtuse; upper surface convex, coarsely and rather closely punctured.

Genus GALERUCA, Geoff.

1. *Galeruca submetallescens*, n. sp.

Elongata, nigra, nitida, pube adpressâ griseâ minus dense vestita, supra æneo micans, minus nitida; thorace transverso, lateribus rotundatis, medio obsolete angulatis; disco late sed leviter transversim excavato, rude rugoso; elytris thorace latioribus, anguste oblongis, parallelis, rude rugosis.   Long. 4 lin,
Hab Assam.

Whole upper surface, the antennæ excepted, faintly tinged with æneous, and rather sparingly clothed with adpressed griseous hairs, head coarsely rugose; antennæ rather more than half the length of the body, the third joint about a third longer than the second, equal in length to the fourth.   Thorax twice as broad as long; sides rounded, obsoletely angled in the middle; disc transversely concave, only slightly depressed in the middle, rather more deeply so on either side, whole surface very coarsely

rugose-punctate. Elytra much broader than the thorax, narrowly oblong, their sides parallel, upper surface faintly depressed
below the basilar space, coarsely rugose-punctate. Apex of anal
segment of abdomen obtusely truncate, edged with piceo-fulvous.

2. *Galeruca tarsalis*, n. sp.

Subelongata, postice vix ampliata, pallide fusca, sericea, oculis,
genubus, tibiis apice, tarsorumque articulis basalibus duobus
nigris; thorace transverso, lateribus angulatis, disco transversim
excavato, crebre punctato, utrinque puncto nigro instructo;
elytris crebre punctatis. Long. 4 lin.

Hab. Sadia.

Head strongly and coarsely punctured, antennæ stained above
with piceous   Thorax twice as broad as long, disc transversely
concave, strongly and coarsely punctured, rugose on the sides.
Elytra closely but less coarsely punctured than the thorax

Genus HAPLOSONYX, Chevr.

In *Haplosonyx* proper (as distinguished from *Sphenoraia*,
Clark) the antennæ usually taper towards the apex, and the third
joint is always distinctly longer than the second ; the punctures
are as a rule arranged without order on the disc of the elytra;
the basilar space is always bounded beneath and on the outer
side by a distinct depression.

1. *Haplosonyx chalybeus*, Hope ; (*elongatus*, Baly.)

Hab. The Plains.

I am indebted to Mr. Janson for the determination of this
species, he having in this as in several other instances compared
my specimen with the Hopean type.

2 *Haplosonyx scutellatus*, n. sp.

Oblongus, convexus, fulvus, nitidus, pectoris lateribus nigro-
piceis; scutello, antennis pedibusque nigris, thorace transverso,
lateribus parallelis, bisinuatis, disco transversim excavato; elytris
fortiter confuse punctatis. Long 4–5 lin.

Var. A. Scutello femoribusque flavis.

Hab. Hills of Assam.

Vertex shining, nearly impunctate; encarpæ pyriform, contiguous; carina obsolete; eyes large, prominent; antennæ moderately robust, the third joint nearly twice the length of the second, the two conjointly shorter than the fourth. Thorax twice as broad as long; sides parallel, deeply bisinuate, the hinder angles produced, subacute, the anterior ones excurved, acute; disc transversely excavated, more deeply depressed on either side; the transverse depression, together with the apical surface on either side near the anterior angles, impressed with a few deep coarse punctures, the rest of the surface impunctate Scutellum longer than broad, trigonate. Elytra broader than the thorax, strongly and deeply punctured.

Genus SPHENORAIA, Clark.

(Ann. & Mag. Nat. Hist. October, 1865).

This generic group, unknown to Dr Chapuis, and reduced by Von Harold into a synonym of *Galerucida*, is quite distinct from that genus, and is more allied to *Haplosonyx*; from the former it may be known by the different form and sculpture of the thorax, together with the different structure of the antennæ; from the latter by the short and equal second and third joints of the antennæ, these organs themselves being usually shorter than in *Haplosonyx*, in addition, in *Sphenoraia* the transverse depression below the basilar space is either obsolete or very indistinct, the elytra are more deeply punctured, and the punctures are arranged in irregular longitudinal striæ.

1. *Sphenoraia bicolor*, Hope (*Galerucida*, Cat.).

Oblonga, sordide fulva. thorace nigro bimaculato; elytris fortiter punctatis, punctis disco interno in striis gemillatis, disco externo confuse dispositis; utrisque maculis decem 2 2.2.2.1 positis, nigris instructis.

Var. A. Elytrorum maculis nonnullis inter se confluentibus. *G. bicolor*, Hope.

Var. B. Elytris totis ingris.* *S. nigripennis*, Clark, l c., p. 297.

Var. C. Elytrorum maculis fere totis obsoletis.
Hab. Assam.

---

* *G nigrofasciata*, mihi, quoted by Von Harold under this species must be placed as a synonym of *G bifasciata*, Motsch

As may be seen by the above diagnosis, in this species the black markings on the elytra vary greatly; in the original specimen of Hope (kindly examined for me by Mr C. O. Waterhouse) the four central spots are confluent and form a large quadrate patch on the middle disc of each elytron.

2. *Sphenoraia fulgida,* Redt., Hug. Kaschm. iv, 1848, p. 554
(*Merista,* Cat.).

Var. A. Corpus metallico purpureum, antennis nigris, elytris viridi- aut cupreo-aureis.

Var. B. Corpus supra viridi-aureum

Var. C. Corpus totum (antennis exceptis) metallico-purpureum.
Hab. The Hills of Assam.

Genus LEPTARTHRA, Baly.

Whilst engaged in working out the insects of the present collection, I have had occasion to look into the distinctive characters separating Dr. Chapuis' genus *Merista,* from *Leptarthra.* The two groups agree so closely, both in habit and other essential points, that the armature of the claws, on which Dr Chapuis has alone divided them, must as in *Corynodes,* be considered of secondary importance; in any case my original definition "unguiculis unidentatis" will agree better with the species placed by Chapuis in *Merista* than with that left by him in the older genus. *Leptarthra* as thus extended forms a very natural genus, the species of which are separable as shewn below, into two good sections.

SECTION I. (*Merista,* Chapuis).

Unguiculi bifidi, dente interno breviori.

L. *trifasciata,* Hope (*Haplosonyx* v. Har. Cat.)[*]
　,,　*quadrifasciata,* Hope.
　,,　*interrupta,* Redt.
　,,　*sexmaculata,* Redt.
　,,　*fraternalis,* Baly.
　,,　*Dohrni,* Baly.

---

[*] *L. trifasciata,* Hope, is very nearly allied to *L. quadrifasciata,* Hope, it may be known by the narrower, smooth and immaculate thorax, by the more strongly produced anterior angles of the latter and by the more finely punctured elytra.

SECTION II. (*Leptarthra*, Chapuis).

Unguiculi appendiculati.

L. *abdominalis*, Baly.

1. *Leptarthra fraternalis*, n. sp.

Ovata, postice ampliata, convexa, metallico-purpurea, nitida; thorace trifoveolato; elytris sat fortiter punctatis, disco interno ante medium confuse gemellato-striatis; flavis, basi, fascia ante, alterâ longe pone medium, utrinque abbreviatis, maculâque transversâ subapicali, nigro-purpureis. Long. 6 lin.

Hab. The Plains.

Front impressed just above the encarpæ with a deep fovea; encarpæ quadrangular, contiguous; carina raised, linear; antennæ slender, attenuated towards the apex, the third joint twice the length of the second, the fourth to the ninth slightly compressed. Thorax nearly twice as broad as long; sides nearly straight and converging from base to apex, the anterior angles thickened, anteriorly produced; anterior margin concave; disc impressed transversely with three deep foveæ, the middle one rotundate, the lateral ones transverse. Scutellum wedge-shaped, its apex rounded. Elytra much broader than the thorax, dilated posteriorly, convex, slightly excavated below the basilar space, strongly punctured, the punctures irregularly arranged in double rows on the inner disc before its middle, placed without order over the rest of the surface, claws bifid.

Nearly allied to *L. sexmaculata*, Redt., less coarsely punctured, the punctures being arranged on the inner disc of the elytra in irregular double rows, the pattern of the elytra is also different.

Genus ANTIPHA, Baly.

1 *Antipha posticata*, n. sp.

Ovata, postice ampliata, convexa, flava, nitida, elytris sat crebre et sat fortiter punctatis, cyaneis, a basi fere ad medium flavis. Long 3 lin.

Hab. Assam, the Plains.

Vertex and front smooth, impunctate; clypeus thickened, transversely trigonate, its apex acute, produced upwards between the encarpæ for half their length; encarpæ well defined, contiguous; apices of jaws nigro-piceous; antennæ nearly two-thirds the length of the body, filiform, the second joint very short, the third more than twice its length, slightly longer than the fourth. Thorax nearly three times as broad as long; sides straight and parallel from the base to beyond the middle, obliquely converging in front, the anterior angles produced, slightly recurved, obtuse, hinder angles acute, disc very sparingly impressed here and there with fine punctures, the sides broadly margined, the middle disc flattened. Scutellum trigonate Elytra broader than the thorax, slightly dilated posteriorly, rather closely punctured, the puncturing denser and coarser towards the apex.

2. *Antipha flavofusciata*, n. sp.

Ovata, postice ampliata, nigra, nitida, femoribus anticis quatuor, posticis apice, capite thoraceque flavis, antennis apice infuscatis; tibiis anticis dorso, tarsis anticis quatuor, tarsisque posticis articulo penultimo piceis; elytris tenuiter sed distincte punctatis, fasciâ latâ prope medium flavâ   Long. 2¼ lin

Hab. The Plains of Assam.

Head impunctate; encarpæ transverse, separated by the apex of the triangular clypeus. Thorax nearly three times as broad as long; sides straight and parallel, converging beyond the middle, all the angles produced, acute; disc smooth, impunctate. Scutellum trigonate. Elytra broader than the thorax, dilated posteriorly, moderately convex, slightly excavated below the basilar space, finely and distinctly but not very closely punctured.

This and the preceding species have the facies and antennæ of *Monolepta*, with the structural characters of *Antipha*.

3. *Antipha histrio*, n. sp.

Anguste ovata, postice paullo ampliata, rufo-testacea, nitida, mesosterno, scutello capiteque nigris, pedibus anticis, facie inter oculos, antennis thoraceque flavis, pedibus posticis quatuor nigro-piceis, genubus, tibiis apice tarsisque sordide fulvis, elytris rufo-testaceis, fasciâ latâ vix pone medium, antice sinuatâ flavâ, basi anguste et utrisque fasciis irregularibus duabus unâ ante, alterâ pone fasciam flavam positis, nigris. Long. 2⅔ lin.

Hab. Assam.

Vertex shining, impunctate; encarpæ transverse, slightly curved, separated by the apex of the triangular clypeus; carina obsolete; eyes large, prominent; antennæ with the second joint

short, the third nearly twice the length of the second, the fourth
longer than the two preceding united; the eight lower joints
flavous (the rest broken off). Thorax three times as broad as
long; sides rounded, nearly parallel at the base, anterior angles
produced, excurved, obtuse, the hinder ones acute; disc shining
impunctate Elytra finely punctured, rufo-testaceous, a broad
common fascia scarcely below the middle, flavous; this band is
bordered both above and below by a broad somewhat irregular
black fascia, abbreviated at the extreme sutural and lateral
margins, the base of each elytron also black

Genus EUPHYMA, Baly, n. gen.

Corpus rotundato-ovatum, convexum *Caput* modice exsertum, *facie* declivi; *encarpis* magnis, transversis, apice contiguis;
carinâ distinctâ; *antennis* filiformibus, corporis dimidio longioribus, articulo primo clavato, secundo ovali, tertio illo dimidio
longiori. cæteris cylindricis, magis robustis, *oculis* rotundato-
ovatis, prominulis; *palpis* maxillaribus ovatis, articulo ultimo
acuto. *Thorax* transversus, utrinque basi sulco brevi longitudinali impressus *Elytra* convexa, substriatim punctata, limbo
inflexo fere ad apicem extenso. *Pedes: coxis* anticis transversis,
femoribus posticis non incrassatis, *tibiis* apice muticis, dorso
carinatis, *tarsis* posticis articulo basali sequentibus tribus conjunctis breviori, *unguiculis* acute appendiculatis *Prosternum*
inter coxas bene distinctum, illis fere æquialtum, apice abrupte
dilatatum: *acetabulis* anticis integris

Somewhat similar in form to *Emathea*, but separated from
that genus by the cylindrical joints of the antennæ, the ovate
palpi and the longitudinal grooves at the base of the thorax.

1 *Euphyma collaris*, n. sp.

Rotundato-ovata, convexa, nitida, subtus piceo-rufa, tibiis,
tarsis femoribusque posticis piceis, abdomine nigro; supra
obscure rufa, antennis, basi exceptis, nigris, thorace impunctato,
utrinque basi sulco brevi impresso; elytris cærulcatis, sat
fortiter substriatim punctatis Long 3 lin

Hab The Hills.

Vertex smooth, impunctate; encarpæ separated from the front
by a transverse groove, transverse, thickened, their apices contiguous, carina raised, narrowly oblong, its apex acute and
extending upwards between the encarpæ for half their length,

antennæ with the three lower joints piceo-rufous, the rest black.
Thorax twice as broad as long, the anterior margin concave;
the sides distinctly margined, rounded, nearly straight and
parallel at the base, all the angles produced, the hinder ones
acute, the anterior ones excurved, obtuse; disc transversely
convex, impunctate, impressed on either side on the basal margin
with a short perpendicular groove   Elytra much broader than
the thorax, convex, rather strongly punctured.

This insect at first sight has quite the facies of *Podagrica*.

Genus LUSTENA, Baly, n. gen

Corpus elongatum, angustatum   *Caput* exsertum; *oculis*
rotundatis, integris; *encarpis* contiguis, *carinâ* elevatâ; *antennis*
gracilibus, filiformibus, articulo secundo brevi   *Thorax* transversus, dorso non sulcatus. *Elytra* thorace latiora, parallela,
confuse punctata, limbo inflexo longe pone medium producto
Pedes elongati, gracilis, *coxis* anticis elevatis, subconicis, non
contiguis, *femoribus* simplicibus; *tibiis* inermibus; *tarsis* posticis
articulo basali sequentibus paullo longiori; *unguiculis* appendiculatis   *Prosternum* angustum, paullo elevatum, inter coxas
distinctum; *acetabulis* anticis integris.   Type *E pretiosa*.

Following the tabular arrangement of Dr. Chapuis, *Eustena*
would enter into his 22nd section, it has, however, but little
affinity in habit with the genera belonging to that group, from
either of which it is separated by its narrow elongate form.

1 *Eustena pretiosa*, n sp.

Elongata, angustata, nigra, nitida, femoribus, capite (antennis
exceptis) thoraceque obscure rufis, facie inferiori piceo-fulvâ;
thorace lævi, utrinque obsolete excavato; elytris viridi-cyaneis,
crebre punctatis.   Long. 3-3½ lin.

Mas. Abdominis segmento anali trilobato; disco longitudinaliter
sulcato, utrinque mamillosis et pube erectâ vestito.
Hab. The Hills.

Vertex smooth, impunctate; encarpæ thickened, transversely
subtrigonate, contiguous; carina narrow, linear, strongly raised;
antennæ slender, rather longer than the body in the ♂, shorter
in the ♀, the second joint short, the third nearly three times
its length, and about a third longer than the fourth, face below
the antennæ piceo-flavous, apex of jaws nigro-piceous.   Thorax

twice as broad as long; sides rounded, narrowly margined, straight and diverging from the base to the middle, all the angles produced, the hinder ones acute, the anterior ones excurved, the apex obtuse, disc smooth and shining, faintly excavated on either side near the middle. Scutellum black, trigonate. Elytra broader than the thorax, parallel, convex, not impressed below the basilar space, rather closely and somewhat strongly punctured.

Genus MONOLEPTA, Erichs.

1. *Monolepta cavipennis*, n. sp.

Elongato-ovata, convexa, flava, nitida, pectore, scutello, femoribus basi capitisque vertice nigris; thorace lævi, tenuissime punctato; elytris tenuissime punctatis, basi et apice, plagâque irregulari vix pone medium transversim positâ, nigris; utrisque disco externo foveâ magnâ cuneiformi, a callo humerali ad paullo pone medium extensâ, extus et postice ad apicem, elevato-marginatâ, impressis. Long 2⅔ lin.

Mas. Antennis corpore multo longioribus; abdominis apice trilobato.

Hab. The Hills

Vertex shining, impunctate; encarpæ separated from the front by a transverse groove, thickened, subtrigonate, their upper halves contiguous; carina raised, its apex extending upwards between the lower halves of the encarpæ; antennæ much longer than the body, filiform, the third joint one-half longer than the second, the fourth equal in length to the two preceding united. Thorax twice as broad as long, sides sinuate near the base and apex, rounded in the middle, the anterior angles produced, slightly thickened, obtuse, basal margin sinuate-emarginate just in front of the scutellum; disc convex, minutely punctured, the punctures only visible under a deep lens. Elytra broader than the thorax, narrowly oblong-ovate, convex, as finely punctured as the thorax; each elytron with a large wedge shaped excavation, which, commencing just below the shoulder and increasing in depth and width towards the apex, runs downwards on the outer disc to just below its middle, the apex, which is rounded, is surrounded by a strongly raised callosity, which forms a transverse hump extending nearly across the disc of the elytron, the outer edge of the fovea is also narrowly thickened for the lower half of its course.

The above description is drawn up from a ♂, in the ♀ the fovea and also the hump on the elytra are probably absent.

Genus OCHRALEA, Clark.

1. *Ochralea nigricornis*, Clark.

Hab. The Lower Hills.

Genus HYLASPES, Baly.

1. *Hylaspes Assamensis*, n. sp

Oblonga, convexa, pallide fulva, nitida, tibus tarsis, culis
antennisque extrorsum nigris; thorace transverso, lateribus
rectis, disco lævi, utriuque profunde transversim excavato;
elytris tenuiter punctatis, utrisque plagâ suffusâ magnâ a vix
pone medium fere ad apicem extensâ, fuscâ instructis. Long.
$4\frac{1}{2}$–5 lin.

Mas. Antennæ corpore æquilongæ

Fœm.   „   „   breviores.

Var. A. (*fœm*) elytris totis flavis.

Hab The Plains.

Vertex smooth, nearly impunctate, being only impressed on
either side with a few fine punctures; encarpæ transverse,
curved, not contiguous; carina thickened, trigonate, its apex
extending upwards between the encarpæ; eyes large, prominent,
shining black; antennæ equal in length to the body in the ♂,
rather shorter in the ♀, the second and third joints very short
and equal in the former sex, slightly longer in the latter, the
third in this sex being nearly one-half longer than the second,
the fourth to the ninth joints in both sexes compressed, very
narrowly dilated, narrowly elongate-trigonate, the upper internal
angles produced, acute, the three upper joints, together with
the apex of the preceding one, black Thorax nearly three
times as broad as long; sides straight and parallel, the anterior
angles broadly and obliquely truncate, thickened, the outer end
in the ♂ produced laterally into a small acute tooth; disc
smooth and shining, impressed on either side on the medial line
with a deep transverse groove, which extends from just without
the middle disc nearly to the lateral margin. Scutellum longer
than broad, trigonate. Elytra much broader than the thorax,
broadly oblong, their sides parallel, their apices broadly rounded;
disc convex, each elytron impressed just within the humeral
callus with a short longitudinal row of deep punctures, the rest
of the surface minutely punctured.

Genus ΓARASTETIIA, Baly, n. gen.

Corpus late oblongum, convexum. *Caput* exsertum, *oculis* magnis, rotundato-ovatis, prominentibus, integris; *encarpis* transversis, contiguis;· *antennis* quam corpore multo brevioribus, robustis, articulo primo subclavato, secundo et tertio brevioribus, cylindricis, cæteris compressis, modice dilatatis. *Thorax* transversus. *Elytra* thorace longiora, confuse striatim punctata. *Pedes* modice robusti, *coxis* anticis conicis, paullo compressis; *femoribus* simplicibus; *tibiis* posticis quatuor apice spinâ acutâ armatis; *unguiculis* appendiculatis *Prosternum* angustum, inter coxas distinctum, apice abrupte dilatatum , *acetabulis* anticis apertis *Mesosternum* occultum. *Metasternum* in spinum validum inter coxas intermedias productum. Type *P. nigricornis.*

This genus must stand very close to *Hylaspes*, it is chiefly separated from that genus by its much shorter antennæ, which scarcely exceed half the body in length.

1. *Parastetha nigricornis*, n. sp.

Late oblonga, convexa, flava, nitidᴀ, pedibus nigro-piccis, oculis antennisque (articulis basalibus tribus exceptis) nigris, abdominis segmentibus utrinque fusco maculatis, thorace transverso,· utrinque leviter sed late foveolato ; elytris distincte, substriatim punctatis. Long. 3 lin.

Hab. Assam.

Head trigonate: vertex sparingly punctured; encarpæ transverse, arcuate, contiguous; labrum deeply notched; antennæ less than two-thirds the length of the body, robust, the basal joint clavate, the second and third short, equal, obconic, the fourth and following ones compressed, moderately dilated, the fourth (which is nearly equal in length to the preceding three united) to the tenth elongate-trigonate, the eleventh ovate. Thorax nearly three times as broad as long; sides nearly parallel, slightly rounded, the posterior and anterior angles thickened, the latter produced, very obtuse; disc sparingly punctured, impressed on either side towards the lateral margin with a large ill-defined shallow fovea, hinder portion of middle disc flattened. Scutellum elongate-trigonate, its apex obtuse. Elytra much broader than the thorax, parallel, rounded at the apex, above convex, not depressed below the basilar space, distinctly punctured, the punctures indistinctly arranged on each elytron in four or five double rows, interspaces impressed with punctures, scarcely finer than those on the rows themselves, and so render- ing them still less distinct.

Genus EUSTETHA, Baly.

1. *Eustetha limbata*, n. sp.

Oblongo-ovata, convexa, nigra, nitida, cyaneo vix tincta, abdomine elytrisque flavo-fulvis, his substriatim punctatis, utrisque limbo, apice dilatato, nigro-piceo: thorace transverso, utrinque transversim sulcato, disco sparse et tenuiter, lateribus magis profunde punctatis   Long. 3–3¼ lin.

Hab. The Plains

Vertex shining, nearly impunctate; encarpæ transverse, quad- rangular, contiguous, separated by a deep longitudinal groove, which extends downwards for a short distance on the clypeus; the clypeus itself thickened, trigonate, antennæ nearly three- fourths the length of the body, the second and third joints very short, equal, the fourth and following ones compressed, not dilated, the fourth nearly equal in length to the preceding three united   Thorax three times as broad as long; sides parallel, very slightly curved, the hinder angles acute, the anterior ones thickened, obliquely truncate, produced laterally into a short . acute tooth, upper surface transversely sulcate on either side, the sulcation terminating at some distance from the lateral margin in a large deep fovea.   Scutellum slightly longer than broad, trigonate, its apex obtuse.   Elytra broader than the thorax, the sides parallel, the apex rounded; above convex, each elytron with the whole limb (dilated at the apex) nigro-piceous; on the disc of each are four ill-defined double rows of punctures, the interspaces between which are impressed with punctures rather finer than those on the rows themselves; inflexed limb shining black.

Genus ACROXENA, Baly, n. gen.

Corpus elongatum. *Caput* exsertum; *oculis* rotundatis, pro- minentibus; *antennis* robustis, ad apicem attenuatis   *Thorax* transversus, dorso non impressus   *Elytra* thorace latiora, parallela, modice convexa, infra basin non excavata, confuse punctata; limbo reflexo fere ad apicem extenso   *Pedes* modice robusti, simplices; *coxis* anticis magnis, contiguis, *tibiis* apice muticis; *unguiculis* appendiculatis   *Prosternum* medio coxis occultum, postice triangulaiitei ampliatum; *acetabulis* anticis integris; *mesosternum* cuneiforme; *metasternum* postice inter coxas posticas spinâ bifidâ armatum. Type *A. nasuta.*

This genus falls into Dr. Chapuis' 26th section, it is separated from *Platyxantha* and *Stenoplatys* by the shape of its antennæ, from *Doridea* and *Ænidea* by its elongate form.

1. *Acroxena nasuta*, n. sp.

Elongata, parallela, modice convexa, fulva, nitida, subtus pube griseâ sat dense vestita, pectore nigro-piceo, abdomine, tibiis posticis dorso antennisque lineâ dorsali nigris; thorace transverso, lævi; impunctato; elytris sat crebre punctatis, interspatiis granulosis: utrisque punctis duobus ante medium transversim positis nigris. Long 5½ lin.

Mas. Capite magno, clypeo infra antennis in cretam transversam elevato, margine antico profunde transversim excavato, medio spinâ acutâ, antrorsum productâ armato, antennarum articulo tertio curvato, ad apicem incrassato.

Hab. The Hills

♂ Head broad, clypeus transversely concave, elevated below the antennæ into a strong transverse ridge, from the middle of which the narrow lanceolate carina runs upwards to separate the encarpæ; anterior margin deeply and broadly excavated, the middle of the excavated portion armed with a long acute, flattened spine; on the disc immediately behind the base of the latter are two very short acute erect teeth, labium large, transversely quadrate, the medial disc slightly concave and furnished with a tuft of erect hairs; antennæ robust, tapering towards their extremity, the third to the fifth distinctly thickened, the third curved, clavate, the fourth and fifth each with a longitudinal ridge on the upper surface, all the joints, with the exception of the apical ones, stained above with nigro-piceous; encarpæ transverse, separated from the front by a transverse groove. Thorax before the middle nearly twice as broad as long; sides straight and diverging from the base nearly to the apex, thence suddenly rounded and converging to the apex, hinder angles produced, acute, the anterior ones also produced, obsoletely excurved, obtuse, disc shining, impunctate, the sides narrowly margined Scutellum not longer than broad, its apex emarginate. Elytra broader than the thorax, subelongate, parallel, moderately convex, rather coarsely and somewhat closely punctured, the interspaces granulose

Genus ÆNIDEA, Baly.

1. *Ænidea barbata*, n. sp.

Subelongata, flava, nitida, pectore elytrisque nigris; his vage, tenuissime punctatis; thorace transverso, utrinque sat profunde foveolato. Long. 3¾ lin

Mas. Capite lato, valde exserto, clypeo transversim excavato, utrinque profunde foveolato, margine antico laminis duabus curvatis suberectis armato, disco infra antennis, fasciâ transversâ tripartitâ pilis erectis nigro-griseis formatâ, instructo; labro tumido

Hab. Hills of Assam.

Head broad, strongly exserted; vertex shining, impunctate; encarpæ transverse, separated by a deep fovea; interocular spaces swollen, clypeus very deeply transversely depressed, excavated at either end into a very large deep fovea; on the middle portion, just below the insertion of the antennæ, is a tripartite transverse band, formed of erect nigro-griseous hairs, which spring from a black trilobate base; anterior margin armed with two narrow, slightly curved, suberect, concave processes, at the inner base of each of which is a small acute tooth; labium swollen, its under margin notched, its anterior edge concealing from above the mandibles; upper joints of maxillary palpi swollen, obovate, the terminal one very short, obtuse, and nearly buried in the preceding one, antennæ slender, nearly equal to the body in length, the basal joint curved, abruptly thickened at its apex. Thorax twice as broad as long, sides straight and diverging from the base to beyond the middle, then obliquely converging to the apex, all the angles thickened, obtuse, surface sparingly impressed with very minute punctures, only visible under a strong lens, on either side the middle disc is a large fovea, the space between them depressed Elytra broader than the thorax, oblong, convex, excavated below and on the outer border of the basilar space, shining black, impressed with minute punctures, quite as fine as those on the thorax. Apical segment of abdomen trilobate, the medial lobe truncate.

The above description is that of a male.

2. *Ænidea eximia*, n. sp

Anguste oblonga, fulva, nitida, antennis flavis, oculis nigris: thorace parce tenuiter punctato, disco transversim sulcato, sulco utrinque magis fortiter impresso; elytris infra basin distincte depressis, tenuiter punctatis. Long. 4 lin.

Mas Antennis corpore longioribus; facie infra antennis cretâ transversâ elevatâ, medio leviter emarginatâ instructo; clypeo antice profunde inciso, disco profunde excavato, utrinque fasciâ e pilis longis instructo; palpis articulo penultimo incrassato, compresso, ultimo brevi conico, apice obtuso.

Hab. The Plains of Assam.

Head large, vertex smooth, impunctate; encarpæ transverse, pyriform, separated by a broad groove; on the face just below the antennæ is a broad obliquely elevated lamina, its apex sinuate on either side, its middle angularly notched, a longitudinal groove running downwards from this notch to its base, clypeus very deeply excavated, its anterior margin very deeply incised, the incision extending upwards nearly to the base of the transverse ridge, and dividing the anterior portion of the clypeus into two large lobes, each of which is armed within with a short recurved tooth; disc on either side furnished with a transverse band of very long fulvous hairs, the apices of which curl spirally outwards; labrum very large, its apex obtuse. Thorax nearly twice as broad as long, sides straight and very slightly diverging from the base nearly to the apex, sinuate just behind the latter, the anterior angles thickened, obtuse. Scutellum semiovate, Elytra oblong, convex, excavated below the basilar space, finely punctured.

A single specimen only, a ♂, is known to me.

Genus MACRISPA, Baly.

1. *Macrispa Saundersi*, Baly.

Hab The Plains

A single individual, unfortunately much broken, fixes the habitat of this rare insect; the unique specimen (now in my cabinet), on which the original diagnosis was made, being without a locality ticket.

Genus ANISODERA, Baly.

1. *Anisodera Guerini*, Baly.

Hab The Plains.

2. *Anisodera excavata*, Baly

Hab, The Plains

Characters of the new genera and species of HETEROMERA *col-lected by Dr. Stoliczka during the Forsyth Expedition to Kashgar in 1873–4*; by FRED. BATES.

SYACHIS, n. gen. (*Teutyrinæ*)

Intermediate between *Ascelosodis* and *Capnisa*. From the former at once distinguished by the outer apical angle of the anterior tibiæ not dentiform. From *Capnisa* by the antennary orbits more convex and more rounded in front; the prothorax wider and more deeply emarginate in front, the sides rounded and decidedly contracted behind; the elytra shining black and distinctly punctured, the epipleuræ sometimes minicately punctured: the prosternal process horizontal and pointed behind and the mesosternal declivous and concave in front.

Syachis Himalaicus, n. sp.

Black, shining, underside and legs reddish-brown, antennæ and palpi paler: labrum entire in front, head wrinkled above the eyes and along the base epistoma strongly separated from antennary orbits, sides slightly emarginate, truncated at apex, shoulders of elytra rounded; epipleuræ rather strongly muricately punctured, the fold more feebly so Length 3½ to 4 lines.
Dias, Kargil and Leh.

Syachis picicornis, n sp.

Black, a little shining, underside of body black; legs and antennæ piceous labrum a little emarginate in front, head not wrinkled above the eyes nor along the base, epistoma feebly separated from antennary orbits, being almost continuous with them, broadly rounded in front, shoulders of elytra distinct, not rounded; epipleuræ not muricately punctured, the fold smooth. Length 3½ to 4 lines
Dias, Kargil and Leh.

ASCELOSODIS, Redtenb. Reise Novara, p. 117.

Prothorax and elytra more or less ciliate at the sides

 Base of prothorax not lobed in the middle

  Elytra densely rugose punctate

   Head and prothorax with mixed punctures *i e*, there are minute punctures scattered between the regular punctuation

    Antennary orbits feebly separated from sides of epistoma punctuation on back of elytra not muricate - - - *assimilis*, n sp

    Antennary orbits strongly separated from sides of epistoma punctuation of back of elytra muricate - - - *ciliatus*, n sp

   Head and prothorax simply punctured - *serripes*, Redt

   Elytra thinly and feebly rugose punctate.

    Sides of epistoma well separated from antennary orbits - - - - - - *concinnus*, n sp

   .. Sides of epistoma nearly continuous with antennary orbits - - - - - - *Haagi*, n sp

  Base of prothorax distinctly broadly lobed in middle - - - - - - - - - - - *grandis*, n sp.

Prothorax and elytra not ciliate at the sides - *intermedius*, n sp

Ascelosodis assimilis, n. sp.

Very close to *A. serripes*, Redt , differs in having head distinctly wrinkled above the eyes, the punctuation on the head and prothorax composed of larger punctures with minute ones on the interspaces, hind angles of prothorax and humeral angles of elytra distinct Length $2\frac{3}{4}$ to $3\frac{1}{2}$ lines.

 Dras, Kargil and Leh.

Ascelosodis ciliatus, n. sp.

Very near the preceding and perhaps only an extreme variety of it: differs by its larger size, epistoma more prominent and strongly separated from antennary orbits; the elytra entirely muricately punctured; and the hairs that fringe the sides of prothorax and elytra much longer and fuller. Length 4 lines.

 Dras, Kargil and Leh.

Ascelosodis concinnus, n. sp

Dark brown, shining, underside reddish-brown, legs, antennæ, palpi, labrum, and front half of epistoma, red: head feebly wrinkled above the eyes, prothorax strongly transverse, front angles prominent, sides gradually expanding from apex to behind the middle, thence rounded to the base almost obliterating hind angles; elytra not closely and scarcely rugosely punctured; epipleuræ muricately punctured.   Length 3 to $3\frac{1}{4}$ lines

Pamir, between Sırıkol and Panga.

Ascelosodis grandis, n. sp.

Broadly ovate, convex, black and nitid, underside black, legs piceous, tarsı and antennæ paler· head strongly wrinkled above the eyes, sides of prothorax gradually curvedly expanded to near the base, hınd angles obtuse, base broadly lobed ın the middle; elytra closely and slightly rugosely punctured, humeral angle distınct. epipleuræ strongly muricately punctured.   Length $5\frac{1}{2}$ lınes

Dras,·Kargıl and Leh.

Ascelosodis intei medius, n sp.

Ovate, black, a little nitid, legs pitchy-brown, antennæ and palpi rufescent: labrum notched ın front; head rugosely punctured above the eyes; prothorax rounded at the sıdes, more contracted ın front than behınd, base feebly sınuate, finely but not closely punctured, a little rugulose at the sides: elytra broadest behınd the mıddle, not closely nor deeply punctured and but faintly rugulose. sides not cılıate.   Length 4 lınes.

Dras, Kargıl and Leh

I avail myself of this opportunity to descrıbe an allied species not contaıned ın Dr Stolıczka's collection

Ascelosodis Haagi.

Oblong, ıeddısh-brown, legs, antennæ and palpı, red: epıstoma very short, bıoadly rounded dırect from the antennary orbits, densely punctured: head sparsely punctured, not wrınkled above the eyes· pıothorax strongly transverse, sides strongly rounded behind, hınd angles obsolete, finely and sparsely punctured on the middle, the punctuıes larger and denser at the sides elytra oblong, subparallel, humeral angle dıstınct and somewhat promınent; sides cılıated, very finely, ındıstınctly, and somewhat

N N

muricately punctured, more distinctly so at the sides, and much more strongly so on the epipleuræ : flanks of prothorax rugose, and, together with the sterna, &c., minutely sparsely tuberculate: abdomen rather uniformly but not closely punctured. Length $3\frac{1}{3}$ lines.

Ladakh (Schlagintwait).

In Dr. Haag's collection.

Anatolica montivaga, n. sp.

Habit of *Colospcelis*. Head and prothorax finely punctured : epistoma prominent, hollowed out at the sides, broadly truncated in front ; mandibles without superior tooth: prothorax as long as broad, widest in front, rather strongly but gradually contracted behind, base subangularly rounded, front angles rounded; elytra more or less elongate, depressed down by the suture, minutely and not closely punctulate, base strongly emarginate; the basal fold entire, humeral angle strongly produced ; prosternum strongly thickened at each side between the coxæ, and, together with the flanks of prothorax, finely and not closely punctured: base of metasternum and of first abdominal segment somewhat coarsely but not closely punctured. Length $4\frac{1}{2}$–$5\frac{3}{4}$ lines.

Yangi Hissar and Kogyar.

Microdera laticollis. n. sp.

Approaching *gracilis*, Esch in habit but more robust. Head moderately, prothorax closely, elytra sparsely and minutely punctured: prothorax transverse, widest before the middle, sides well rounded, strongly narrowed behind, base broadly margined, rounded, front angles rounded, depressed· elytra elongate oval; epipleural fold continued round the shoulders, parapleuræ and sides of the sterna and abdomen coarsely, closely and confluently punctured. Length $5\frac{1}{2}$ lines.

Kashgar, Yangi Hissar and Kogyar.

Microdera parvicollis, n. sp.

Approaching *conexa*, Tausch., in habit, but prothorax more rounded anteriorly, broadest before the middle, thence gradually narrowed to the base, which is strongly margined. Head, prothorax and elytra minutely and sparsely punctulate: prothorax nearly as long as broad, the basal margin strongly convex; all the angles depressed and obtuse: elytra oval; epipleural fold continuous round the shoulders: inner side of flanks of prothorax, and prosternum rugosely punctured ; sides of metasternum, and of the two first joints of abdomen with a few coarse punctures. Length 4⅔ lines.

Kogyar.

Cyphogenia plana, n. sp.

Narrow, elongate, flat, black, more or less obscure· epistoma widely and subtriangularly notched in front, the angles acute; head behind the eyes prominent and coarsely rugosely punctured: prothorax quadrate, apex wider than base, front angles produced, subacute, sides sometimes a little angular, and with a narrow flattened margin, base truncated; disc irregularly foveate, finely sparsely punctured: elytra faintly minutely muricately punctured; keeled from behind the shoulders to the apex: epipleuræ strongly inflexed   Length 7-9½ lines.

Dras, Kargil, Leh and Pankong Valley

Cyphogenia humeralis, n. sp.

Habit of *aurita*, Pall, but having a short carina at the shoulders. Head and prothorax very finely dispersedly punctured; epistoma widely emarginate in front in ♂, more strongly and subangularly so in ♀, the front angles broadly rounded: prothorax transverse, disc convex, transversely impressed near the base; front angles not produced but slightly acute; hind angles acute and outwardly directed , sides well rounded anteriorly, rather broadly margined, a little reflexed, and finely transversely rugulose   elytra depressed, widest behind the middle, obsoletely punctured, the shoulders alone showing a short keel.   The ♂ is smaller than ♀ and has the abdomen more distinctly punctured.   Length 10-12 lines.

Yangi Hissar.

Blaps Stoliczkana, n. sp

Approaching *mortisaga*, Linn., in habit: head more or less coarsely punctured; epistoma widely and feebly emarginate in front: prothorax slightly transverse, sides rounded anteriorly and gradually contracted posteriorly; base wider than apex, front angles rounded, hind angles obtuse, more or less coarsely punctured, somewhat confluently so at the sides, with minute

punctures scattered between; sides feebly guttered: elytra depressed, attenuated behind, sides feebly rounded, apex briefly mucronate; confusedly and more or less densely rugose granulose.
Length 8½–10 lines.

Pamir, between Suikol and Panga.

Blaps Indicola, n. sp

Habit of ♀ *montisaga*, Lin., dull black, underside and legs shining black: head and prothorax very finely and not closely punctured; the latter subquadrate, feebly but regularly convex, widest before the middle, strongly contracted in front, more gradually behind, sides slightly sinuous near the base, narrowly channelled, front angles narrowly rounded the hind rectangular: elytra not wider at base than base of prothorax, sides very slightly widest behind the middle, apex gradually produced into a distinct but short mucro; uniformly minutely granulose punctate, a little stronger on the epipleuræ and at the base. Length 12 lines.

Sind Valley.

Blaps perlonga, n sp.

Elongate, slender, acuminate behind, obscure black: head and prothorax finely punctured; the latter gently convex, scarcely wider than long, sides gently evenly rounded and finely margined, base but little wider than apex, both truncated, front angles rounded, hind rectangular. elytra elongate, widest behind the middle. attenuate behind, distinctly but not elongately mucronate at apex, a short costa down the middle of apex; finely, uniformly and not closely muricate punctate and transversely rugulose: legs long and slender. Length 10 lines.

Tanktze to Chagra, Pankong Valley.

Blaps Ladakensis, n. sp.

Black, elytra a little shining, oblong ovate: head rather closely punctured: prothorax decidedly broader at base than at apex, transverse, sides well rounded anteriorly, a little sinuously contracted posteriorly; but little convex, finely and not densely punctured; front angles rounded, hind obtuse: elytra depressed at the suture, not wider at base than base of prothorax, somewhat rapidly declivous behind, apex not mucronate; disc irregularly finely muricate punctate and intricately rugulose; apex and epipleuræ imbricately tuberculose, the tubercles flattened and pointed behind: legs and antennæ rather short and robust. Length 7½–8¼ lines.

Tanktze to Chagia, Pankong Valley.

Blaps Kashgarensis, n. sp.

Elongate, black, elytra more or less nitid. head and prothorax finely remotely punctured, sometimes obsoletely so on the latter: prothorax regularly convex, sides well rounded in front, but little contracted behind, base decidedly wider than apex, hind angles obtuse, front angles well rounded; median line faintly impressed. elytra more or less elongate-ovate, somewhat rapidly declivous behind, apex terminating, in the ♂, in a distinct, moderately elongate mucro; convex, slightly depressed at the suture; very finely, sometimes almost obsoletely, seriate-punctate, the punctures simple, intervals finely punctured, and more or less feebly convex. legs rather long. first ventral segment in ♂ emarginate at each side and with a villose tuft of rufous hairs, more or less strongly transversely rugose, and with traces of a callosity on the middle. Length 9–13 lines.

Kashgar, Yangi Hissar.

Prosodes trisulcata, n sp.

♂ Elongate, parallel, pitchy-brown, prothorax, legs and antennæ approaching castaneous: head and prothorax finely sparsely punctate, a little stronger on the sides of the latter: prothorax gently convex, uneven at the sides, a fovea near the hind angle, and several faint depressions on the disc: lateral margins finely rugulose; sides slightly rounded anteriorly, but little narrowed posteriorly, widest before the middle; front angles depressed and narrowly rounded, hind angles rectangular. elytra not wider at base than base of prothorax, depressed on the back, gradually attenuated and gently declivous behind, margins reflexed at apex; trisulcate, the sulci broad and shallow and somewhat densely irregularly granulous; intervals subcosti-form, nearly smooth; both sulci and costæ effaced at the base: epipleuræ very broad, vertical, smooth, shining, the fold also smooth and broad, obliquely and sinuously narrowing from humeral angle to apex: underside piceous, nitid, abdomen feebly wrinkled at the sides legs rather slender, hind tibiæ feebly flexuous.

♀ Larger, more robust, punctuation, &c., stronger, sides of prothorax slightly sinuate before the basal angle; hind tarsi shorter. Length ♂ 8½ lines, ♀ 10 lines; width of elytra across the middle ♂ 2¾ lines, ♀ 4 lines.

Dras, Kargil and Leh.

Prosodes vicina, n. sp.

Differs from preceding as follows:—form broader, prothorax, underside, legs, &c., shining black: sides of prothorax more contracted in front, the front angles more broadly rounded: elytra still more gradually declivous behind, dorsal costæ more elevated, narrower, and rugose punctate: epipleuræ rugulose; antennæ and legs stouter, middle joints of the former submoniliform. Length ♂ 10 lines, ♀ 11 lines; width of elytra across middle ♂ 3½ lines, ♀ 4⅔ lines.

Sind Valley.

COELOCNEMODES, n. gen. (*Blaptides*).

Habit of *Coelocnemis*, Mann. Differs from all the genera of the group except *Dila*, by its toothed anterior femora: and from *Dila* by its totally different habit, granulose surface, &c. Last joint of maxillary palpi feebly securiform: antennæ nearly as in *Blaps mortisaga*, Linn.; joint 3 elongate, 4–7 equal, obconic, 8–11 perfoliate, setose, and clothed with a fine silky-yellowish pubescence, 8–10 moniliform, 11 larger, acuminate: 1–7 coarsely punctured: head subquadrate, not prolonged behind the eyes; antennary orbits subangularly prominent, epistoma short, gradually narrowed to the front; labrum strongly transverse, pilose, nearly entirely visible, angles rounded: eyes very narrow, flat, obsoletely facetted, anterior margin entire: prothorax moderately convex; sides well rounded, abruptly narrowed behind, narrowly channelled: front angles rounded, hind angles distinct but not prominent, and reposing on the shoulders of the elytra: elytra oblong ovate, not wider at base than base of prothorax, rapidly declivous behind, apex produced but not mucronate: shoulders depressed, sides a little sinuous near the base: epipleuræ broad, the fold extending from the humeral angle to the apex, gradually narrowed behind: legs moderate; four hind femora a little compressed; all the tibiæ rounded, the anterior not denticulate at outer edge, and with a curved excision on the inner edge near the base; first joint of hind tarsi shorter than the last.

Coelocnemodes Stoliczkanus, n. sp.

Obscure brownish-black; head uneven, coarsely but not deeply punctured, with smaller punctures between, labrum and palpi rufescent, the former lightly punctate; prothorax with a transverse impression near the base, and 2 or 3 foveate depressions on the disc, granulose, the sides confluently granulose punctate; elytra rather closely subseriately punctured, and faintly transversely rugulose and granulose. Length 10 lines.

Murree.

Trigonoscelis setosa, n. sp

Black, more or less broadly oblong-ovate head remotely punctured, setose; epistoma and labium more strongly and closely punctured: prothorax transverse, quadrate, more or less gently convex, sometimes depressed on the disc, front angles prominent, acute; base scarcely wider than apex, strongly sinuate in the middle, hind angles a little outwardly directed; sides a little rounded before the middle: granulose, setose; scutellum small, petiolate · elytra more or less depressed above, more or less broadly oval; base wider than base of prothorax, shoulders more or less strongly advanced; granulose, setose, the granules more or less seriate, near the sides is a row of more distinct and closely placed granules; margin closely subseriately granulose. a flexuous elevated more or less granulose line running obliquely down the epipleuræ: underside and legs moderately closely granulose and clothed with fine ashy pubescence. four hind tibiæ hispid and fringed outwardly with long fuscous hairs; front tibiæ spinose down outer edge · four hind tarsi fringed with long hairs. Length 7–9½ lines, width of elytra across middle 3½–4½ lines.

Kashgar to Kogyar.

Trigonoscelis lacerta, n sp.

Ovoid, black, thinly tomentose: head feebly remotely punctured: prothorax transverse, quadrate, depressed on disc and down median line, front angles a little prominent and acute; sides moderately rounded in front, sinuately narrowed behind; base not wider than apex, moderately sinuate at the middle; hind angles slightly outwardly directed; irregularly covered with largish flattened tubercles, with a few small pointed tubercles between · elytra oval, regularly convex, on each elytron five irregular rows of from seven to nine rather large rounded and flattened tubercles, with minute granules scattered between, apex more closely tubercled; the margin closely set with smallish, oblique, pointed, setiferous, tubercles, the carina which traverses the epipleuræ tubercled at base and apex, minutely denticulate between· four hind tibiæ not fringed with long hairs· hind tarsi not compressed, and with a few longish hairs outwardly. Length 7½ lines.

Yangi Hissar.

The following four species of *Pterocoma* form a distinct group in the genus, distinguished by the third joint of antennæ much elongated; prosternum strongly protuberant in front, its process being enormously produced· the elytra having each three (except *semicarinata*) costæ, besides the marginal; and the third unites with the marginal just behind the shoulder.

Pterocoma tibialis, n. sp.

Black, somewhat nitid, four hind tibiæ distinctly rufescent: antennæ and legs slender: labrum notched in middle of front margin: head feebly punctured and pilose: prothorax convex, front angles acute and prominent: base strongly sinuate, the angles small and outwardly directed: sides feebly rounded; finely sparsely (especially on disc) tuberculate, the tubercles erect, pointed, setiferous: elytra with a depression behind the scutellum; first costa continued along the base to scutellum· intervals minutely remotely granulose, and with a few long decumbent hairs: epipleuræ finely rugose granulate, the hairs shorter and denser: marginal costa closely set with long pointed teeth: prosternal process coarsely corrugated. Length 4¾–6⅓ lines.

Neighbourhood of Sanju.

Pterocoma serrimargo, n. sp.

Smaller, dull brownish-black: four hind tibiæ not distinctly rufescent; labium entire in front· elytra not depressed behind scutellum, first costa not continued along the base; intervals from near the base clothed with cinereous pubescence, prosternal process sparsely granulose. Length 5¼ lines.

Kogyar.

Pterocoma convexa, n. sp.

More narrowly ovate and convex; black, a little nitid: thinly clothed with fine cinereous pubescence, and setose: labrum entire in front: head and prothorax at bottom minutely, densely and rugosely punctulate, and with scattered small setiferous tubercles. intervals of elytra with scattered small punctures, mixed with minute setiferous tubercles; first costa strongly continued along the base· prosternal process rugosely tuberculate. Length 5 lines.

No locality given; probably Kogyar.

Pterocoma semicarinata, n. sp.

Very broadly ovate, elytra almost rotundate: black, a little shining: labrum emarginate in front head sparsely punctured, and with small setiferous tubercles clustered above the eyes: prothorax with a few flattened tubercles on the disc, which are distinctly umbilicate; on each elytron a single costa composed of flattened tubercles, placed half way between the suture and shoulders, and not extending more than half down the elytra from the base; between this and the side are indications of two other costæ, the outer one most distinct, these are composed of very small distant setiferous tubercles, the marginal carina is composed of a double row of closely set bluntish tubercles; no trace of pubescence on the intervals, but they have a few very minute setiferous tubercles near the base; prosternum coarsely, deeply and confluently punctured, the process smooth and polished. Length 6 lines.

Yangi Hissar.

Ocnera sublævigata, n. sp.

Habit of *O. imbricata*, Fisch Black, more or less obscure, legs fuscous, antennæ and tarsi rufescent and clothed with ferruginous hairs, palpi and labrum reddish: head minutely sparsely muricate punctate, with minute simple punctures mixed with them: prothorax quadrate, front angles slightly prominent, sparsely furnished with small round flattened umbilicate granules, and with minute punctures scattered between: elytra regularly oval and convex, on each three distinct rows of small tubercles, with four others placed between, these latter more or less obscure; intervals plane and with scattered small granules, the marginal costa is finely serrate prosternal process horizontal, triangulate behind: hind tibiæ feebly sinuous. Length 9-10 lines.

Kashgar, Yangi Hissar.

BIORAMIX, n. gen. (*Platyscelides*).

Head strongly transverse: epistoma very short, broadly rounded, or truncated, in front; prothorax variable, always transverse, more or less convex, sometimes a little flattened at the lateral margins, front angles generally depressed, subacute, or rounded, hind angles variable, sides usually rounded in front and subparallel behind: scutellum rather large, transversely triangular: elytra variable, usually elongate oval, regularly convex; diffusedly, or seriately punctured; more or less hispid (generally only at the apex), epipleuræ usually continuous with the sides, the fold generally broad, always attaining the humeral angle and gradually curvedly narrowed from the base to near the apex· legs robust; front and middle tibiæ more or less expanded outwardly, the outer apical angle of the front pair not dentiform; the hind straight, or feebly curved. The mouth organs and the tarsi do not materially differ from *Platyscelis*. The ♀ have all the tarsi simple; and are generally more robust and convex; and elytra more rounded at the sides.

Bioramix Pamirensis, n. sp.

Elliptic oval, black, a little nitid, underside and legs dark brown. head finely punctured, closely so, and pubescent behind: prothorax finely uniformly punctured, gently convex direct from the side margins, not closely applied to base of elytra, sides contracted in front, subparallel behind, hind angles rectangular: shoulders of elytra broadly rounded, sides feebly rounded, gently declivous behind, moderately, but distinctly, punctured, with traces of a longitudinal seriate arrangement, faintly irregularly rugulose and alutaceous, thinly hispid at sides and apex; epipleural fold punctured: underside finely corrugated and appearing granulous, front tibiæ moderately expanded outwardly, and trigonal, outer edge sharp and sinuous   Length 5 lines.

Pamir, from Sirikol to Panga.

Bioramix ovalis, n. sp.

Oval, less elongate and relatively broader than preceding; head more closely and slightly rugosely punctate, not pubescent behind: prothorax more transverse, less convex, sides more rounded, more contracted behind, slightly depressed at the margins, foveolate at each side the middle, punctuation less clean, the angles distinctly more obtuse: elytra more convex, more rounded at the sides, punctuation finer and less regular: front tibiæ more compressed, not sinuate at outer edge. Length $4\frac{1}{3}$–$4\frac{1}{2}$ lines.

Dras, Kargil and Leh.

Bioramix puncticeps, n. sp.

Differs from preceding in having the epistoma distinctly and squarely truncated in front: prothorax still more strongly transverse, front angles more obtuse, sides strongly rounded behind effacing the hind angles: elytra much more faintly punctate, shoulders more strongly rounded : epipleural fold not visibly punctured: front tibiæ more compressed, more triangular, the outer apical angle a little produced ; intermediate tarsi distinctly narrower and more pilose. Length 4–$4\frac{1}{2}$ lines.

Dras, Kargil and Leh.

Bioramix asidioides, n. sp.

Very distinct from the three preceding by its larger size, broader and more depressed form, distinctly seriately punctured elytra, &c Oblong oval, black: head subangular in front, coarsely punctured, more finely and closely, and pubescent, behind; front angles of epistoma distinct, almost rectangular· third joint of antennæ as long as 4 and 5 united: prothorax transverse, scarcely convex, closely applied to base of elytra, moderately and setiferously punctured, apex arcuately emarginate, base much wider than apex, sinuate, hind angles subacute, a little outwardly directed, reposing on shoulders of elytra; sides gradually expanded from apex to the middle, thence slightly and sinuately contracted to base ; the margins irregularly depressed and transversely rugose: elytra a little depressed, shoulders slightly rounded, sides gradually feebly rounded to the middle, thence gradually narrowed behind ; on each elytron eight rows of punctures, intervals finely punctured, transversely rugulose, the alternate ones convex, except at base and apex ; lateral margins costiform ; epipleuræ distinct, the fold faintly rugulose punctate: hind tibiæ a little curved. intercoxal process truncated in front. Length 6 lines

Sind Valley.

CHIANALUS, n. gen. (*Platyscelides*).

Near *Bioramix*. Head longer and narrower ; epistoma distinctly larger: elytra strongly costate and densely hispid: anterior tibiæ finely denticulate at outer edge, the outer apical angle strongly dentiform: intermediate tarsi feebly dilated, the joints longer than broad: epipleural fold continued to the apex of elytra.

Chianalus costipennis, n. sp.

♂ Oblong-ovate. dark brown; head rather strongly and closely punctured; prothorax transverse, feebly convex, wider at base than apex, sides well rounded, a little uneven, margins narrowly depressed; finely punctured. foveate at each side of the disc, and a depression at each side at the base; the angles obtuse: elytra oval, suture costiform, and on each elytron four stout costæ, 2–3 united before the apex and continued as but one; the intervals also each with a fainter costa; finely granulose-punctate, rugulose and hispid.

♀ All the costæ on elytra subequal   Length ♂ $5\frac{1}{4}$ lines; ♀ $5\frac{1}{2}$–6 lines
Dras, Kargil and Leh.

MYATIS, n. gen. (*Platyscelides*).

Head very short and transverse, epistoma truncated nearly level with base of antennæ: prothorax variable, usually curvedly narrowed in front, subparallel behind; front angles obtuse, hind angles acute. elytra oblong, gently convex, shoulders more or less oblique, humeral angle prominent, sometimes dentiform; sides feebly rounded, narrowed and gently declivous behind; a little hispid at the apex and sides· intermediate tarsi scarcely at all dilated: intermediate tibiæ in ♂ thickened behind and, as well as the hind tibiæ, densely fringed within with silky golden yellow hairs, the pro- and meso-sterna are not nearly so convex, or bulged out, as in the other genera of the group: the epipleural fold does not reach the apex of elytra.

Myatis humeralis, n. sp.

Oblong, pitchy-brown, head and prothorax nitid: head finely punctured, pubescent at sides and behind epistoma squarely truncated in front and ciliated: prothorax gently convex, nearly as long as broad, finely uniformly punctured, narrowed in front, slightly incurved behind, hind angles prominent, subacute, outwardly directed: elytra a little expanded to behind the middle, minutely and not closely granulose punctate, with distinct indications of striæ, intervals very faintly rugulose and delicately subreticulately alutaceous, not perceptibly hispid; humeral angle dentiform. Length $4\frac{1}{4}$–$4\frac{1}{2}$ lines.

No locality given

Myatis quadraticollis, n sp

Of a paler brown than preceding, head more strongly punctured, distinctly foveolated between the eyes prothorax dull reddish castaneous clouded with dark brown, less evenly convex, foveolately depressed at each side near the margins, sides more contracted behind, hind angles not produced, punctuation distinctly coarser at the sides elytra a little less cleanly and distinctly punctate, distinctly hispid at sides and apex, humeral angle prominent but not dentiform. Length $4\frac{1}{4}$ lines.

Between Leh and Yarkand.

Myatis variabilis, n. sp.

Varying from light reddish to very dark brown· prothorax distinctly less transverse than preceding, more uniformly brown, punctuation stronger, median line distinctly smooth, more regularly and evenly convex, more rounded at sides, hind angles rectangular, or a little outwardly produced, elytra more parallel, humeral angle distinct but never prominent, punctuation, &c., a little closer and stronger, more distinctly and uniformly hispid. Length $3\frac{1}{2}$–$4\frac{1}{2}$ lines

Between Yangi Hissar and Sirikol, and Sirikol to Panga.

These three forms may probably constitute but one very variable species

Opatrum Kashgarense, n. sp.

Belongs to the *rusticum*, Oliv., group of species. Oblong, brown: head broadly and sinuately rounded in front; epistoma not sharply angularly notched in the middle of fore margin; studded with small black granules which emit a short scale-like hair of a golden yellow colour. prothorax gently convex, deeply emarginate in front, front angles subacute: sides gently regularly rounded, margins a little reflexed, base a little wider than apex, hind angles produced, acute, directed behind; the surface more distinctly and regularly granulose &c., than the head: scutellum semicircular, finely granulose and pubescent : elytra oblong, slightly widest behind the middle, shoulders distinct, very finely transversely rugulose, punctate-striate, intervals slightly convex, finely granulose, each granule emitting a short scale-like hair as on head and prothorax. Length 4¼ lines.

Kashgar.

Penthicus (Loboderus) gracilis, n. sp.

Near *rufescens*, Muls: larger, sides of prothorax subangular in the middle, front angles more pointed; finely closely and uniformly punctured on a minutely granulose ground; uneven at each side the disc : elytra more gradually narrowed behind; faintly sulcated, the intervals sparsely minutely granulose, and showing a line of minute punctures · abdomen thinly minutely granulose, somewhat transversely arranged: joints 3–7 of antennæ more elongate. Length 4½ lines

Kogyar.

Length of *rufescens* 2¾–3¾ lines.

Allecula (Dietopsis) costipennis, n sp.

Elongate, narrow, chocolate-brown, head and prothorax a little deeper in colour: underside rufescent and shining: head closely and finely punctured and pubescent; epistoma long, convex, expanding outwardly, apex truncated; labrum entire in front, the angles rounded: last joint of maxillary palpi broadly cultriform: antennæ subfiliform, joints 3–11 subequal, obconic, 11th narrowly rounded at tip: prothorax convex, transverse, sides parallel, narrowed in front, the angles broadly rounded, hind angles obtuse; finely uniformly punctured, a foveate depression each side median line elytra crenate-striate, intervals convex, minutely punctulate, each puncture carrying a fine minute pale decumbent hair: sterna finely densely punctured and rugulose, flanks with close well marked rounded punctures, abdomen and legs finely uniformly punctured and pubescent. Length 5 lines.

Murree.

HYPOCISTELA, n. gen. (*Ctenopides*)

Near *Ctenopus*, but joint 3 of antennæ much shorter than 4, 3–6 obliquely truncated at apex ; palpi slender, last joint of all elongate-oval; eyes larger, more approximate beneath, more coarsely facetted: prothorax narrower at base than base of elytra, and not curvedly narrowed in front.

Hypocistela tenuipes, n. sp.

Pale testaceous, legs yellow, antennæ palish brown, eyes and tips of mandibles black, head fuscous behind. Entirely above uniformly and very minutely punctulate and rugulose, and finely pubescent: elytra delicately striated; flanks of prothorax, breasts, and abdomen clouded with fuscous. Length $3\frac{1}{2}$ lines.

Kogyar.

Lagria Indicola, n. sp.

Form, size and color of *glabrata,* Oliv. Eyes silvery-grey, with a fuscous spot above : antennæ filiform, last joint elongate and straight· prothorax broader at base than at apex, somewhat shining, piceous, front and hind margins reddish, feebly punctate, and, as well as the head, clothed with a longish fuscous pile: elytra delicately striated, distinctly uniformly punctured, irregularly transversely wrinkled : underside, femora and antennæ pitchy-brown, tibiæ and tarsi paler. Length $4\frac{1}{6}$ lines.

Murree.

Meloe servulus, n sp

Small, black, a faint bluish tinge on elytra : antennæ shining black, compact, a little thickened outwardly, joints obconic, 5–7 shorter than 3–4 or 8–10 ; 10 a little cylindric, 11 elongate, tapering· head large, convex, rather uniformly punctured· prothorax small, quadrate, transverse, all the angles rounded, base arcuately emarginate, punctured like the head, and with a foveate impression at each side the disc· elytra faintly reticulately rugulose, somewhat scrobiculate on the epipleuræ; dehiscent from one-third their length, base emarginate at each side, shoulders rounded. Length $3\frac{3}{4}$ lines.

No locality; probably between Leh and Yarkand.

Epicauta Haagi, n. sp.

♂ Head dull red, a blood red callosity at base of each antenna, strongly, closely punctured, a short fine elevated line running down middle of crown, scantily furnished with fine black hairs at sides and behind: epistoma broadly truncate in front, black in the middle, labrum black, sinuate in front: antennæ with two basal joints red above, the rest black, strongly depressed, the joints longitudinally excavated on their inner side, joint 3 long, triangular, 4–6 much shorter, gradually narrower, 3–7 more or less strongly obliquely emarginate at apex, the inner angle produced, 8–9 nearly equal in length, but gradually narrower, truncated at apex, 11 longer and narrower than 10, cylindric, and rounded at tip: prothorax black, convex, depressed in middle of base, strongly contracted in front, feebly so behind; closely and deeply punctured and pilose; sides, apex and median line usually covered with a dull whitish pubescence: elytra dull black, strongly divaricate, finely densely granulose and pubescent, transversely rugulose, margins, and sometimes a dorsal stripe, clothed with a dull whitish pubescence: underside black, and clothed with dull whitish decumbent hairs: front tibiæ emarginate in the middle within: tarsi simple.

♀ Smaller, antennæ shorter, narrower, 3–7 not emarginate at apex.   Length ♂ 9–10 lines, ♀ 7½ lines.

Muree.

Sitaris (Criolis) pectoralis, n sp

Shining testaceous, tips of mandibles, eyes, scutellum, meso- and meta-sterna and their flanks, black, middle and hind coxæ shining black   antennæ filiform, last seven joints fuscous black, last joint elongate, tapering. head convex, smooth, faintly punctate; labrum notched in front· prothorax convex, transverse, widest in the middle, more abruptly narrowed in front than behind, faintly punctured   elytra pale cinnamon-brown, tapering gradually behind, thinly clothed with a fine silky-greyish pubescence, and with two or three slightly flexuous costæ· upper division of the tarsal claws finely pectinated.   Length 4¾ lines.

Kogyar.

Note sur un Elatéride *de Madagascar, du groupe des* Allotriites ; par le Dr. E. Candèze.

Morostoma, n gen.

Frons leviter convexa immarginata ; labrum productum, inclinatum ; palporum quatuor articulus ultimus maximus, antennis longior.

Antennæ breves, filiformes, undecim articulatæ.

Prosterni suturæ laterales rectæ, haud canaliculatæ.

Mesosterni fossula triangularis, marginibus declivibus.

Coxarum posticarum laminæ parum dilatatæ, extus sensim attenuatæ.

Pedes normales ; tarsorum articuli 2–4 subtus dilatati, quarto lobato.

En faisant connaitre, l'an dernier, le genre *Parallotrius* je disais: " Jusqu'ici le groupe des *Allotriites* n'était représenté que par des espèces de l'Inde. L'espèce suivante (*P pallipes*), qui est américaine, vient ainsi combler une lacune."

Aujourdhui, c'est Madagascar qui nous présente un type du même groupe, que l'on peut, à bon droit, considérer comme le plus extraordinaire de la famille entière des Elatérides.

L'espèce sur laquelle est établi le genre actuel se distingue, en effet, par une particularité qui pourrait être prise pour une monstruosité individuelle, si elle n'avait été constatée chez plusieurs individus

Cette particularité consiste dans le développement extraordinaire du quatrième article des quatre palpes, qui dépasse les antennes en longueur et en épaisseur, est cylindrique, arqué, noir brillant (Pl X, f. 1). Elle suffit à elle seule pour caractériser le genre, à l'exclusion de tout autre.

Voici les caractères de l'espèce.

o o

Morostoma palpale, n. sp.

Nigrum, nitidum, glabrum. Antennis palpisque basi rufis ; prothorace subquadrato, parum convexo, crebre punctato, angulis posticis brevibus, divaricatis, haud carinatis ; elytris striis profundis fortiter punctatis ; pedibus rufis. Long. 13 mill., lat. 3 mill.

D'un noir assez profond et brillant, dépourvu de pubescence. Palpes longs de trois millimètres, leurs articles basilaires courts, rouges. Antennes un peu moins longues que les palpes, à articles grenus, les deux premiers rouges, tous un peu pubescents. Front légèrement convexe, arrondi et non rebordé en avant, très ponctué. Prothorax carré, médiocrement convexe, densément ponctué, marqué d'un fin sillon longitudinal au milieu, ses angles postérieurs petits, divergents, aigus, sans carène. Ecusson triangulaire. Elytres un peu plus larges que le prothorax, parallèles, profondément sillonnées avec les intervalles convexes, les sillons marqués de gros points Dessous brunâtre, pubescent ; pattes rouges.

Madagascar

Je ne puis préciser la localité exacte d'où provient cet Elatéride. Tout ce que je sais, à cet égard, c'est qu'il est des mêmes lieux que *l'Hexodon unicolor.*

J'en ai vu autrefois plusieurs exemplaires au Musée de Berlin· je n'ai pu le décrire alors. Je l'ai retrouvé récemment à Londres. Le type détaillé ci-dessus fait partie de la collection de M. E Janson.

On a small Collection of Heterocerous Lepidoptera, *from New Zealand*; by Arthur G. Butler, F.L.S., F.Z.S., &c.

The series of Moths recorded in the present Paper, has been sent to me for identification, by Professor Hutton, of the Otago Museum, Dunedin; it is a singularly interesting little consignment, not only from the comparatively large number of novelties which it contains, but also from the assistance which it has rendered in correcting the synonymy of the known species, and the light which it has shed upon the sexual differences of the species of the genus *Pseudocoremia*.

ARCTIIDÆ.

1. *Phaos Huttoni*, n. sp (No. 1).

Nearly allied to *P. interfixa* of Tasmania; primaries pale ochraceous, with the borders and veins rather broadly black, a submarginal transverse black line or stripe, or these wings might perhaps better be described as black, with an abbreviated basal dash, a cuneiform discoidal dash, an interno-median longitudinal streak, five subconfluent longitudinal discal dashes, and a submarginal series of small conical spots pale ochraceous; a basal subcostal carmine streak, secondaries bright ochreous, greyish on interno-median area; an oblique black spot on the discocellulars; outer border, to beyond the first median branch, broadly black, uniting with a large subanal marginal black spot, and intersected by an interrupted macular ochreous line close to the margin; fringe ochreous; body black, with sordid whitish fringes to the tegulæ, abdomen with ochraceous borders; wings below ochreous with black discocellular spots; outer borders black, intersected by a series of ochreous dots; costal borders dark orange, the primaries with an ill-defined subcostal carmine streak; body black, pectus fringed with pale sericeous hair; tibiæ and tarsi of legs ochreous; anterior femora carmine in front; venter bordered and banded with ochreous. Expanse of wings 1 inch 3 lines.

Queenstown (two examples).

The Tasmanian species is larger, with more elongated primaries, the latter best described as creamy-white clouded at the end of the cell with ochreous; the veins, borders and *three* transverse lines black; a basi-costal scarlet streak; the secondaries are dark ochreous, with a broad external black border interrupted by two marginal ochreous dots; the interno-median area blackish; the body with whitish margins to collar and tegulæ, the abdomen *scarlet* at the sides; indications of the same colour appearing also on the margins of the segments; a lateral series of black and whitish spots; there are, therefore, plenty of well-defined characters whereby to distinguish the New Zealand form.

IIEPIALIDÆ.

2. *Porina fuliginea*, n. sp (No. 79).

Allied to *P. cervinata*; smoky brown; primaries with slightly greyish outer border, limited by an interrupted blackish line; a marginal series of small whitish-edged black spots between the veins; an interrupted greyish-edged blackish discal line, also two or three transverse black spots nearer to the end of the cell, and crossing the subcostal interspaces; discoidal cell and base varied with unequal black-edged white spots; secondaries with the basal area broadly clothed with paler hair; abdomen with pale hair at the base; under surface immaculate. Expanse of wings 1 inch 5 lines

Otago.

LEUCANIIDÆ.

3. *Leucania atristriga* (No. 5).

Xylina atristriga, Walker, Lep Het. Supp. iii, p. 756 (1865).
Bityla atristriga, Butler, Proc Zool. Soc. 1877, p. 387, n 37.
Otago.

This species is evidently allied to *L. propria* and *L. dislocata*; I was therefore in error when I referred it to *Bityla*

XYLOPHASIIDÆ.

4. *Xylophasia stipata*.

Xylina stipata, Walker, Lep. Het. Suppl. iii, p. 753, (1865).
Otago.

5. *Xylophasia rubescens*, n. sp. (No. 18).

.Allied to *X. lithoxylea* and *X. lignicolora.* Primaries sandy pale brown, with the ordinary markings (including the cuneiform external patch, and a diffused patch at external angle) ferruginous ; reniform spot enclosing a blackish J-shaped marking, and bounded externally by two black dots ; orbicular represented by a black dot, below which is an oblique ferruginous dash ; a discal arched series of minute black dots on the veins ; secondaries smoky-brown, with rosy-cupreous reflections, fringe and margin sandy-brown ; body pale sandy-brown ; thorax somewhat ferruginous down the centre ; abdomen whitish at the base, with four brown-banded dorsal tufts ; under surface uniform pale shining sandy-brown, with faint rosy reflections ; discocellulars blackish. Expanse of wings 1 inch 7 lines.

Otago.

Most like the North American *X. lignicolora,* but the primaries decidedly paler, and the secondaries darker.

NOCTUIDÆ.

6. *Agrotis? moderata* (No. 15).

Agrotis? moderata, Walker, Lep. Het. Suppl. ii, p 705 (1865)

Mamestra griseipennis, Felder, Reise der Nov. Lep. iv, pl. cix, fig. 22

Wairarapa.

This species would perhaps be better placed in the genus *Hapalia*

7. *Agrotis mitis,* var.? (No. 13).

Agrotis mitis, Butler, Proc. Zool. Soc. 1877, p 383, n. 19, pl. xlii, fig. 5.

Otago.

More heavily marked and of a much less bluish tint than the type, still I believe it to be conspecific with it.

8. *Chera virescens*, n. sp. (No. 7).

Primaries above greyish-green, with black costal spots indicating the origin of the usual lines ; all the lines and spots black or blackish, margined either outwardly or inwardly with pale ochraceous; the discoidal spots and a spot below the orbicular indicated in outline ; an oblique zigzag line from the reniform to the inner margin, followed by a subangulated series of lunate markings from costa to inner margin, an extradiscal series of ill-formed hastate subconfluent black spots parallel to the outer margin; fringe blackish towards the apex ; secondaries sericeous grey with a feeble lilacine tint ; a broad deep brownish grey external border , fringe yellowish at base, tipped with white and intersected by a grey line ; thorax greyish-green, abdomen sordid whitish, sericeous ; anus yellowish; under surface of wings silvery-greyish, the primaries with the costal and external borders finely white-speckled but not distinctly ; an ochraceous tuft close to the base covering a bare and swollen space at the base of the costal vein ; a slightly arched grey discal line ; internal area white at base ; secondaries paler than primaries, the fringe yellowish at base ; an arched grey discal line ; disco-cellulars greyish : body below sordid white.   Expanse of wings 1 inch 10 lines.

Otago.

This species is evidently nearly allied to the smaller and greyer species which I have hitherto considered to be Guénée's *Xylocampa ? cucullina.*

9. *Chersotis sericea*, n. sp. (No. 16).

♂ Shining grey; primaries tinted with brown, with indications of the discoidal spots, and of a third spot near the base of interno-median area, they being slightly paler than the ground-colour, and outlined in black ; fringe tipped with white ; secondaries with white fringe; abdomen pale stramineous, clothed at the base with pale grey hair ; under surface pale silvery-grey. Expanse of wings 1 inch 4 lines

Wairarapa.

Excepting in the structure of its antennæ this species has more nearly the aspect of a *Spælotis* than of a *Chersotis.*

10. *Graphiphora purpurea*, n. sp. (No 6).

Primaries above rich chocolate-brown shot with purple; the central area limited by two undulated squamose lines of white and fulvous scales, a third similar but less distinct line across the base, a semicircular blackish spot edged with whitish near the end of the cell, its outer edge, together with a portion of the outer undulated line, indicating the reniform spot, its inner edge united at the extremity to an oblique black-edged whitish dash which replaces the orbicular spot; an indistinct series of black marginal dots; secondaries chocolate-brown becoming pale brown towards the base; fringe pale brown intersected by a darker line; head, collar, and centre of thorax rich chocolate-brown edged with fulvous scales; first joint of palpi tipped with fulvous; tegulæ dark brown with a sericeous slaty-grey lustre; abdomen chocolate-brown with pale basal tufts; under surface pale sericeous red-brown with darker margins and fringe; primaries with whitish interno-basal area; secondaries with a lunule at the end of the cell and a bisinuated discal series of spots black; body below darker than the wings, chocolate-brown. Expanse of wings 1 inch 7 lines.

Otago.

More nearly allied to *G. tartarea* than to any other described species; the figure of *G. tartarea* is badly coloured, the black spots being wholly omitted.

HADENIDÆ.

11. *Hadena plena* (No 9).

Erana plena, Walker, Lep. Het. Suppl. iii, p. 744 (1865).
Otago, in July.

This species differs entirely from *Erana* in the structure of the primaries.

12. *Hadena debilis* (No. 11).

Hadena debilis, Butler, Proc. Zool. Soc. 1877, p. 385, n. 26, pl. xlii, fig. 6.
Otago.

13. *Hadena mutans* (No. 12).

Hadena mutans, Walker, Lep. Het. xi, p 602 (1857).
Xylina spurcata, Walker, Lep. Het. xi, p 631 (1857).
Mamestra angusta, Felder, Reise der Nov. Lep. iv, pl. cix, fig. 19.
Wairarapa.

It is possible, though scarcely probable, that *H. mutans, insignis, debilis, lignifusca,* and *vexata* may be all modifications of one extremely variable species.

14. *Hadena insignis* (No. 14).

Euplexia insignis (part) Walker, Lep Het. Suppl. iii, p. 724 (1865).
Mamestra acceptrix, Felder, Reise der Nov. Lep. iv, pl. cix, fig. 19.
Otago.

15. *Erana graminosa* (No. 97).

Erana graminosa, Walker, Lep. Het. xi, p. 605 (1857).
Erana vigens, Walker, Lep. Het. Suppl. iii, p. 743 (1865).
Otago.

Walker says that his *E. vigens* is "nearly allied to *E. graminosa* but the abdomen is not crested," it would have been more strictly correct to say "but the dorsal tufts have been rubbed off."

XYLINIDÆ.

16. *Xylina ustistriga* (Nos. 10 & 80).

Xylina ustistriga, Walker, Lep. Het. xi, p. 630, (1857).
Otago.

This species varies considerably in tint and in the distinctness of the markings on the under surface; we however possess all gradations between the extreme forms.

HERMINIIDÆ.

17. *Rhapsa scotinalis* (Nos. 19 & 81).

Rhapsa scotinalis, Walker, Lep. Het. Suppl. iv, p. 1150 (1865).
Herminia lilacina, Butler, Proc. Zool. Soc. 1877, p. 388, n. 43; pl. xlii, fig. 11.
Otago.

This species varies a little in size and tint, some examples being very pale and without the lilacine reflection typical of the variety named by me.

BOTIDIDÆ.

18. *Adena hybreasalis* (No. 99).

Scopula? *hybreasalis*, Walker, Lep. Het. xviii, p. 797, n. 51 (1859).

Adena xanthialis, Walker, Lep. Het. xxvii, p. 198, n. 1 (1863).

Otago.

Differs in colour from Walker's types, the primaries being ochraceous instead of brick-red; I have no doubt, however, that it is a mere variety.

19. *Scopula flavidalis* (Nos. 21 & 22).

Margaritia flavidalis, Doubleday, Dieff, New Zeal. 1, p. 287. n. 125.

♂, ♀, Otago

The female example is slightly larger and darker than usual.

20. *Scopula notata*. n. sp. (No. 20).

Primaries reddish clay-colour, slightly sericeous; discoidal area dusky; a black-edged white rhomboidal spot at the end of the cell; a grey discal line, arched beyond the cell, zigzag from first median branch to inner margin; fringe grey; secondaries pale creamy ochreous, speckled at apex and on interno-basal area with grey scales; two black spots placed obliquely at the end of the cell, a marginal series of black dots; thorax red-brown; abdomen greyish, white at base; primaries below blackish as far as the discal line; costa and external area sordid sandy-brown, tinted with a feeble rosy gloss; white spot as above; fringe grey, a marginal row of black dots; secondaries silvery-white, slightly yellowish; black discocellular spots and marginal dots as above; a discal irregular series of grey spots; body below whitish, legs reddish Expanse of wings 11 lines.

Otago.

21. *Scoparia conifera*, n sp. (No. 92)

Primaries clay-coloured, speckled all over with snow-white scales, and with a few black scales towards the inner margin; a blackish-brown band across the base; a zigzag (almost M-shaped) fascia, dark brown edged with white, from near the base to beyond the end of the discoidal cell, its superior angles extending to the costal margin; a broad external brown border edged internally by a pale angular line, a marginal series of blackish dots; secondaries sericeous brassy-brown, very pale with diffused dusky apical border; fringe silvery-white; body silvery-whitish, the thorax longitudinally streaked with brown;

under surface pale sericeous brassy-brown, with dusky disco-celhulars; fringe white; body below white. Expanse of wings 10 lines.

Otago.

The pale-edged triangular area in the centre of the M-shaped marking is the first thing which catches the eye when examining this species.

ENNOMMIDÆ.

22   *Gargaphia haastiaria*, (Nos. 98 & 82)

Zanclopteryx ? haastiaria, Felder, Reise der Nov. Lep. iv, pl. cxxiii, fig. 32.

. Otago.

In one example the wings are uniform rust-red without the broad dark belt, this is doubtless nothing but variation.

G. muniferata (= *Panagra ephyraria*) is probably the species figured by Felder, under the name of *Zanclopteryx? cookaria.* The genus *Gargaphia* seems most nearly allied to *Drepanodes.*

23.   *Sestra flexata* (No. 71).

Cidaria flexata, Walker, Lep. Het. xxv, p. 1421, n. 93 (1862).
Sestra fusiplagiata, Walker, l. c. p. 1751.
Wairarapa.

24.   *Sestra humeraria* (Nos. 23 & 106).

Macaria ? humeraria, Walker, Lep. Het. xxiii, p. 940 (1861).
Lozogramma obtusaria, Walker, l. c p. 985.
Cidaria? obtruncata, Walker, Lep. Het. xxv, p. 1421 (1862).
Wairarapa.

I have now no hesitation in uniting the above synonymes, but at present I have not sufficient evidence to prove *S. flexata* con-clusively to be conspecific.

25.   *Hyperythra panagrata*

Scotosia panagrata, Walker, Lep. Het. xxv, p. 1360, n. 36 (1862).

♀   Otago.

The female example sent approaches most nearly to the typical form of the species, it is, however, paler and has a greyish lilacine tint, thus forming a more extreme contrast to the orange-spotted form ; the *Angerona menanaria* of Walker (which certainly belongs to *Hyperythra*) may be a still more modified variety of the latter type.

26. *Hyperythra desiccata* n. sp. (Nos 29 & 31).

♂ Allied to the preceding species, the lines crossing the wings of the same form ; primaries sandy-ochraceous, with the base, costa and external border laky-brown irrorated with grey; two widely-separated parallel transverse lines inarched towards the costa, a discocellular spot and the inner margin of the external border indistinctly grey; the outer or discal transverse line dotted with black upon the veins, a marginal series of blackish dots; secondaries paler than the primaries, sandy-yellowish irrorated with grey, and crossed by two parallel undulated dotted discal grey lines; a marginal series of blackish dots; thorax laky-brown ; abdomen sandy-yellowish ; under surface much paler, the whole surface irrorated with grey, the transverse lines indistinct ; discocellular blackish spots on all the wings, a marginal series of black dots. Expanse of wings 1 inch 7 lines.

♀ Duller and greyer than the male, otherwise similar, excepting that the external area below is limited by a dusky streak, and the primaries exhibit a whitish apical patch. Expanse of wings 1 inch 8 lines.

Otago.

27. *Hyperythra arenacea,* n. sp. (No. 28).

♀ Primaries above sandy-ochraceous speckled with black, and with feebly indicated rusty lines as in the preceding species ; an additional line or stripe (usually present in *H. panagrata*) immediately beyond the cell ; a blackish discocellular spot ; secondaries much paler, whitish on basi-costal area, irrorated with black points ; a discal series of black dots ; a grey spot at the end of the cell, from which indications of a grey line extend to the abdominal margin ; body pale sandy-yellowish ; under surface considerably paler, irrorated with black and grey atoms ; all the wings with well-defined black discocellular spots ; a feebly indicated grey discal streak, and a diffused rusty-brownish submarginal stripe, primaries with a clearly defined pale yellow apical patch. Expanse of wings 2 inches.

Otago.

28. *Lyrcea alectoraria* (No. 24).

Lyrcea alectoraria, Walker, Lep. Het. xx, p. 259 (1860).
Otago.

29 *Lyrcea varians*, n sp. (Nos. 25 & 26).

Olive-brown speckled with black, with more or less defined cupreous reflections; primaries crossed by two widely divergent dusky stripes, and a number of short dusky striations; two white dots on the lower discoidal interspace; interno-median area, and an abbreviated fascia, bounding the outer dusky stripe towards apex, golden-yellow mottled with laky-purplish; a black discocellular dot; secondaries varied here and there with fiery cupreous; two parallel grey discal lines, body testaceous; under surface altogether greyer, the transverse lines obsolete; black discocellular dots; primaries with yellow apical fascia nearly as above, and white dots on lower discoidal interspace; body below sandy ochraceous.   Expanse of wings 1 inch 7 lines.

Wairarapa.

A dull variety occurs, in which the purplish-mottled yellow areas are wanting   This species is allied to *"Amilapis?"* *achroiana*, of Felder, but the genus *Lyrrea* has nothing in common with *Amilaps*, being much more nearly related to *Azelina*.

30. *Polygonia fortinata* (No. not indicated).

Polygonia fortinata, Guénée, Ent. Month   Mag. v, p. 41 (1868).
Otago.

BOARMIIDÆ.

31. *Boarmia dejectaria* (No. 27).

Boarmia dejectaria, Walker, Lep Het. xxi, p. 394 (1860).
Otago.

PSEUDOCOREMIA, *Butler.*

32. *Pseudocoremia lupinata* (Nos 65 & 66).

♂ *Cidaria lupinata*, Felder, Reise der Nov. Lep. v, pl. cxxxi, fig. 19.

♀ Primaries white, greyish towards apex; costa grey; outer border broadly grey bounded internally by a blackish-edged zig-zag white line; the inner edge widening into three blackish spots corresponding in position with the prominent markings of the male; a sinuous grey central belt, wide upon the costa, where it is bounded on both sides with black, tapering towards the external angle, spotted internally with dark red-brown hastate spots, limited externally by a whitish and a blackish line; a sub-basal interrupted line formed of black spots; a black **G**-shaped marking and a black dot at base; a longitudinal red-brown streak through the interno-median area; secondaries creamy yellowish becoming brownish at outer border, which is limited internally by a dusky line; body white with black tegulæ; under surface greyish, the markings ill-defined. Expanse of wings 1 inch 6 lines

Otago

33. *Pseudocoremia suavis*, n. sp.

♂ Primaries grey, base brownish; two subangulated parallel subbasal black-speckled brown lines; a nearly central sinuous blackish line; two black-speckled parallel sigmoidal discal lines just beyond the cell; discocellulars blackish, external border limited internally by a dentate sinuate white line margined with brown and black on both sides; a marginal series of black dots; secondaries pale sericeous straw-colour, the external border irrorated with brown; thorax brown; abdomen testaceous; under surface stramineous, the primaries clouded with grey and with grey indications of the lines of the upper surface; a marginal series of black dots, secondaries as above; tibiæ and tarsi banded with black. Expanse of wings 1 inch 8 lines.

♀ Altogether paler than the male, the ground-colour of the primaries white. Expanse of wings 1 inch 8 lines.

Canterbury.

Somewhat allied to *Selidosema pungata* of Felder, but altogether paler and less prominently marked, the lines across the primaries more sinuous and less parallel.

34. *Pseudocoremia productata* (No. 85).

♀ *Larentia productata*, Walker, Lep Het. xxiv, p. 1197, n. 69 (1862).

♂ Much like *P. indistincta*, but the ground-colour uniformly creamy whitish, the markings of the primaries much more defined, the external border being bounded internally by a complete series of blackish spots. Expanse of wings 1 inch 3 lines

Otago.

35. *Pseudocorema indistincta* (No. 60).

♂ *Pseudocoremia indistincta*, Butler, Proc. Zool. Soc. 1877, p. 394, n. 78 , pl. xliii, fig. 8.

Otago.

I have little doubt but that the *Larentia productata* of my last List (P. Z. S. 1877, p. 394) is the ♀ of this species, it differs from Walker's type much in the same way as the two males from each other.

ZYLOBARA, n. gen.

Allied to *Pseudocoremia* and *Bylazora*, but differing from both in the outline of the secondaries, the margin being distinctly sub-angulated, owing to the prominence of the area enclosed by the second and third median branches; abdomen much elongated; head large ; antennæ similar to those of *Tephrosia* and allies. Type *Z. fenerata*.

36. *Zylobara fenerata*.

Rhyparia fenerata, Felder, Reise der Nov. Lep. v, pl cxxxi, 7. Wairarapa.

Felder's figure fails to show the projecting character of the secondaries, it was probably taken from an injured specimen.

ACIDALIIDÆ.

37. *Asthena ondinata* (No. 32).

Asthena ondinata, Guénée, Phal. i, p. 438, n 724; pl. 19, fig. 4.

Otago.

38. *Asthena subpurpureata* (No. 33).

Asthena subpurpureata, Walker, Lep. Het. xxvi, p. 1588 (1862).

Otago

39. *Acidalia schistaria* (No. 35).

Acidalia schistaria, Walker, Lep Het xxiv, p. 782 (1861).

Otago.

40. *Acidalia rubraria* (No. 36).

Acidalia ? rubraria, Doubleday, Dieff., N. Zeal. App. p. 286 (1843)

Otago

41. *Acidalia undosata* (No. 51).

Cidaria undosata, Felder, Reise der Nov. Lep. v, pl. cxxviii, fig. 2.
Otago

FIDONIIDÆ.

42. *Samana falcatella* (No 34).

Samana falcatella, Walker, Lep. Het. xxvii, p 197, n. 1, (1863).
Otago.

The genus *Samana* is very closely allied to *Panagra*, but has the aspect of *Sterrha*; M. Guénée's *Panagra scissaria* may be referred to it.

43. *Selidosema ægrota*, n. sp. (Nos. 39 & 54).

Whity-brown, wings with a marginal series of small blackish spots in pairs; fringe white, spotted with blackish and intersected by a dark grey line ; basal two-thirds of the primaries crossed by about seven parallel dusky lines commencing upon the costal margin in black dots ; discocellulars black ; under surface of primaries greyish-brown with pale grey borders, the costal border crossed by four or five white-edged blackish dashes ; marginal spots as above ; secondaries white, crossed by about eight strongly arched parallel brown lines which become very indistinct upon the costal area ; disc from the radial to the abdominal margin clouded with brown ; marginal spots as above ; body white Expanse of wings 1 inch 2 lines.
Wairarapa.

44 *Fidonia catocalaria* (No. 37).

Larentia catocalaria, Guénée, Ent. Month. Mag v, p. 26 (1868).
Otago

LIGIIDÆ.

45. *Declana floccosa* (No 3).

Declana floccosa, Walker, Lep. Het. xv, p. 1649 (1858).
Wairarapa.

46. *Declana nigrosparsa*, n. sp. (No. 2).

Wings snow-white, the primaries slightly greyish upon the borders, a black-mottled subquadrate grey patch on the basal half from the median vein to the inner margin; an indication of a belt just beyond the middle, represented by a diffused bisinuated grey streak, and a series of ferruginous discal spots parallel to it, a black marginal line; fringe traversed by a grey line; secondaries crossed from the origin of subcostal branches to the abdominal margin by two-subconfluent conical grey spots, a darker lunule on upper discocellular; a grey marginal line; body greyish, mottled with black and white, tegulæ testaceous in the middle; abdomen with a longitudinal dorsal series of small clay-coloured projecting-spots; tibiæ and tarsi white, banded with black; antennæ white with clay-coloured internal surface; under surface snow-white; wings with slender brown marginal line; the primaries with transverse conical grey spots as in the secondaries; a bisinuated grey discal line, body greyish. Expanse of wings 1 inch 6 lines.

Otago.

Nearest to *D floccosa*, but with all the markings considerably less pronounced and with white secondaries

47. *Declana scabra* (No 4)

Argua scabra, Walker, Lep Het. xxviii, p. 448, n. 1 (1863).
Wairarapa

48. *Declana niveata*, n. sp (No. 8).

Snow white, the primaries covered all over with embossed mottling; costal and outer borders faintly speckled with grey, an irregularly undulated band of which, limited internally by a blackish line, runs across the disc; external border limited internally by a very irregular interrupted line; traces of a blackish oblique line across the basal third of the wing; costal margin dotted with black; secondaries immaculate; body with slightly greyish tegulæ; antennæ clay-coloured internally; sides of palpi and a tuft on each side of the pectus behind the eyes, blackish; under surface of wings and body snow-white, immaculate   Expanse of wings 1 inch 3½ lines.

Otago

Readily separable from all the other species by the much more closely approximated lines which cross the primaries and the immaculate white secondaries.

49. *Pachycnemia usitata,* n. sp (No. 67).

Very similar to *P. hippocastanaria,* of Europe, the same colours; primaries grey with a slight lilacine gloss, crossed by one or two ill-defined dusky subbasal lines, two slightly divergent and nearly central lines, the outer one sigmoidal; a pale zigzag line edged on both sides with blackish, limiting the external border which is dusky, discocellulars dusky, secondaries sericeous whity-brown irrorated with grey on external border, body grey; under surface sericeous grey. Expanse of wings 1 inch 3 lines

Otago

LARENTIIDÆ.

50. *Larentia? punctilineata* (No. 40).

Larentia punctilineata, Walker, Lep. Het. xxiv, p. 1202, n. 79 (1862).

Otago.

51. *Larentia? falcata,* n. sp. (No. 87)

Allied to *L. punctilineata* (which it much resembles in colour and markings), but larger and with distinctly falcate primaries, primaries reddish-brown, with the base and a broad central belt dark brown traversed by blackish lines and margined by white dots; a black discocellular dot, external border blackish, diffused; two or three whitish subapical dots, secondaries silvery-grey with a darker waved central belt formed of parallel dark grey lines, dotted with black upon the abdominal margin, white bordered; a submarginal series of white-bordered grey spots; a marginal series of blackish dots in pairs, fringe pale reddish-brown; abdomen with dorsal pairs of black dashes on each segment, primaries below grey with darker white-bordered central belt; costa cream-coloured between the markings; a zigzag white-bordered subapical dusky stria; secondaries whitish with a broad irregular central belt formed by two blackish limiting lines and two grey intermediate lines, the outer black line distinctly undulated; a very ill-defined blackish speckled submarginal band; body below testaceous. Expanse of wings 1 inch 3 lines

Otago.

This and the other forms with falcate primaries referred to *Larentia, Corema, Camptogramma* and *Cidaria* will probably prove, upon careful examination, to be congeneric, and referable to a distinct and hitherto uncharacterized genus ; at present I cannot spare time to look into the matter critically, but I am satisfied that there is some confusion in the above-mentioned genera.

52. *Larentia ? rufescens*, n. sp. (Nos. 52, 56 & 101).

Intermediate between the preceding species and *L. megaspilata*. primaries pale lakey-brown, crossed by numerous undulated brownish lines, with indications of a broad central belt, cuneiform blackish subapical patch and black discocellular dot, all as in *L. megaspilata* ; secondaries pale sericeous testaceous, crossed in the middle by four parallel sinuous undulated grey lines in pairs ; three similarly undulated grey lines upon the external area and the commencement of a fourth between these and the central ones ; external border pale lakey-brown, with a marginal series of black dots in pairs ; fringe traversed by a grey line, a black discocellular dot ; head and thorax pale lakey-brown speckled with blackish, abdomen pale testaceous banded with blackish ; primaries below grey, costa pale ochraceous, a whitey-brown discal band immediately following the limiting lines of the central band, otherwise nearly as above, but the central lines rather darker ; secondaries altogether darker than above, the ground-colour sandy, the central lines blackish, the lines on external border ill-defined, body below pale lakey-brown. Expanse of wings 1 inch 1 line.

Otago (four examples).

53. *Larentia ? megaspilata* (No. 38).

Larentia megaspilata, Walker, Lep. Het. xxiv, p 1198 (1862).
Cidaria assata, Felder, Reise der Nov. Lep. v, pl. cxxxi, fig 4.
Otago.

In my former paper I followed Dr. Felder, in referring this species to *Cidaria*, because of its apparent affinity to the *C. congregata* group, it agrees with this latter in neuration and coloration, but differs in its longer palpi, so that until *Larentia* is broken up into several genera it will have to be retained, with its allies, in that genus.

54. *Larentia? nehata* (No. 49).

Cidaria nehata, Felder, Reise der Nov. Lep. v, pl. cxxxi, fig. 6.
Otago.

Allied to the preceding species, but smaller; the primaries
much darker/ and more uniform in colouring, the secondaries
ochraceous.

55. *Larentia? inverata* (No. 58).

Larentia inverata, Walker, Lep. Het. xxiv. p. 1199, n. 73
(1862).
Larentia inoperata, Walker, l.c., p. 1201, n. 77 (1862).
Otago.

The smallest species of this group.

56. *Larentia? heliacaria* (No 88).

Coremia heliacaria, Guénée, Phal. ii, p. 420, n. 1583 (1857).
Otago.

This species seems to be far more nearly allied to the six preceding forms than to any section of the genus *Coremia*; it is
new to the New Zealand fauna, being hitherto known only from
Australia and Tasmania; the example now sent differs slightly
from the typical form in the width and angulation of the belt
on the primaries, but as this belt is not identical in any two
specimens of the species, it is probable that this is nothing more
than variation

57 *Melastia indicataria* (No. 41).

Eupithecia indicataria, Walker, Lep. Het xxvi, p. 1708
(1862).
Otago.

58 *Helastia charybdis,* n. sp (No. 44).

Allied to the preceding; primaries above smoky-grey, crossed
by about eight zigzag blackish lines in pairs, forming indications
of four bands which are most strongly defined upon the costa,
a whitish-edged black lunule between the last two bands; the
last band partially filled in with sandy-whitish and brown;
fringe whitish flesh-coloured intersected by a grey line and

interrupted at the terminations of the veins by blackish spots; secondaries pale smoky-grey, the veins black spotted with whitish; extreme outer margin black; fringe as in the primaries; body brownish-grey, head yellowish; antennæ smoky-grey. strongly pectinated; under surface sericeous grey; markings of upper surface ill-defined; discocellulars black; primaries with pale reddish cupreous costal area; secondaries with a series of short black dashes beyond the cell, fringe paler than the rest of the wings, spotted with dark grey. Expanse of wings $10\frac{1}{2}$ lines.

Otago.

59. *Helastia calida*, n. sp. (No. 43).

Primaries above pale reddish-brown; base chocolate-brown, crossed and margined by blackish lines; a subangulated undulated black-edged chocolate-brown band across the basal two-fifths, indications of a whitish-edged black discal line represented above the third median branch by a strongly defined lunule and a blackish costal spot; an undulated chocolate-brown submarginal band edged externally with a white line which is zigzag from the second median branch to the costal margin; a black marginal line slightly interrupted at the extremity of the veins; fringe whitish, intersected by a grey line and heavily spotted with blackish; secondaries grey, veins banded with black, margin and fringe as in primaries; body reddish-brown, abdomen with pale dorsal tufts, head ochreous; under surface sericeous grey; disco-cellulars black; primaries with a faint reddish tint on costal area; the bands of the upper surface indicated upon costal half by darker grey with whitish interspaces; secondaries paler than primaries, almost white; an angulated series of black dots beyond the cell, also three dusky costal dots between the latter and the base. Expanse of wings $11\frac{1}{2}$ lines.

Otago.

In this species the primaries are more elongated in appearance than in the two preceding forms; in this respect it approaches *H. inexpata.*

60. *Tatosoma transitaria* (No. 68).

Cidaria transitaria, Walker, Lep. Het. xxv, p. 1419, n. 90 (1862).

Wairarapa.

The genus *Tatosoma* should be placed near to *Lobophora*; it was confounded with *Sauris* by Dr. Felder, but may be readily distinguished from that genus by the position of the lobate excrescence from the male secondaries.

61. *Melanthia arida*, n. sp. (No. 57).

Primaries whity-brown, crossed by gravel-reddish irregularly zigzag parallel lines; basal, apical and external angles broadly black-brown, bordered and varied with red-brown; discocellular dot and several abbreviated costal lines indicating the commencement of the zigzag reddish lines black; secondaries sordid sericeous white, with the outer border and two or three very indistinct lines across the abdominal area greyish, head and thorax blackish, abdomen whity-brown, transversely barred with black, basal segment above black with two pale spots; under surface pale sericeous pinky-brown, the markings of the upper surface very feebly represented. Expanse of wings 1 inch 1 line.

Otago.

This species is referable to the *M. albicillata* group of the genus.

62 *Coremia rosearia* (No. 47).

Cidaria rosearia, Doubleday, Dieff. N Zeal. App. p. 285 (1843).

Otago

Under this species Walker placed examples of *C. cymaria*, *relictata* and *acutata*.

63. *Coremia squalida*, n. sp. (No. 48).

Silvery greyish-brown; primaries above with the usual irregular central belt very broad, its central area dark grey, its borders broadly yellowish olivaceous, edged on both sides and intersected with undulated black lines; a silvery-white line on each side of the central belt; base olivaceous, traversed by blackish lines and limited externally by a white line, a subbasal yellowish belt occupying the space between the base and the central belt; disc crossed immediately beyond the central belt by two yellowish-brown lines on a white ground, and followed by a

white-edged band of the same colour; outer border yellowish
olivaceous; a blackish marginal line; fringe whitish, traversed
by two dark brown parallel lines; secondaries with a black
undulated marginal line, fringe traversed by a slender dusky
line; under surface greyish-brown; basal three-fourths of the
wing, limited externally by a very irregular dark brown line,
followed by a white line; discocellulars dark brown; apical
borders irrorated with white; fringe whitish, spotted with
brown   Expanse of wings 1 inch 2 lines

Otago.

Nearer to *C. ferrugata* than to any other species known to
me: its general aspect is pale greyish or silvery-brown, with
darker white-edged belt across the primaries.

64. *Phibalapteryx gobiata* (No 85).

Cidaria (Phibalapteryx) gobiata, Felder, Reise der Nov. Lep.
v, pl cxxxi, fig. 2.

Otago.

The present example agrees closely with Felder's figure, which
was by no means the case with those in the collections formed
by Dr Hector and Mr. Enys, the latter probably represent a
distinct species, but the example retained for the Museum is
hardly sufficiently perfect to enable me to form a very decided
opinion respecting it.

65 *Phibalapteryx simulans*, n. sp. (No. 86).

Closely allied to the preceding species, but the two lines
nearest to the base of primaries more arched and not duplicated;
the discal angulated line more oblique and distinctly more
sinuated towards the apex; secondaries with the outermost discal
blackish line distinctly zigzag and nearer to the outer margin,
the four lines between the latter and the base equidistant and
parallel; veins upon the disc alternately black and white; marginal line black; primaries below more lakey in tint than
P. gobiata; discocellular dots black.   Expanse of wings 1 inch
4 lines.

Otago.

66. *Phibalapteryx undulifera*, n. sp. (No. 83).

Also allied to *P. gobiata*, but larger, of a more sandy tint;
the primaries with a strongly defined black discocellular dot;

the interno-median area crossed by *three* convergent dark brown
lines between the extrabasilar and the widely sinuated oblique
discal line; disc crossed by five or six indistinct undulated
parallel greyish lines; fringe reddish brown, secondaries crossed
by nine or ten undulated parallel lines, the second, fourth and
seventh distinct, the last mentioned black with white external
edge; veins on the disc white dotted with black; a slender
undulated black marginal line; fringe reddish-brown; collar and
several interrupted lines across the abdomen black, primaries
below distinctly darker and more lakey in tint than *P. gobiata*;
secondaries whiter, all the wings with strongly defined black
discocellular dot.   Expanse of wings 1 inch 5 lines.

Otago.

67. *Phibalapteryx anguligera* n sp. (No 84)

♀ More sandy in coloration than *P gobiata*, with a distinct
oblique olivaceous brown central belt, limited by the discal
blackish line, which is widely zigzag, but diverging from this
line above the lower radial, whence it runs transversely but
irregularly to the costal margin; a large dusky discocellular
spot; veins on the disc white dotted with black as usual; secondaries with the margin rather more strongly dentated than in
P gobiata, the inner blackish line represented by a grey band,
outer border limited by a dusky line; a slender black marginal
line; primaries below with a lakey tint; the discocellular dot
black, a transverse irregular discal line answering to that of
the upper surface, secondaries pale sandy-whitish, the basal
half crossed by five dusky lines, disc crossed by a darker
sandy nebula.   Expanse of wings 1 inch 4 lines

Otago.

Phibalapteryx anguligera ♂ ? (No 100)   In this form, which
I take to be the male of the preceding, the markings of the
primaries are well-defined but do not form a belt as in the
female, the under surface of these wings is dull rose-red;
the secondaries are smaller and more strongly dentated than in
the female, and on the under surface are marked with a discal
series of black dots, this species bears considerable resemblance
to the European *P. tersata* upon the upper surface, but differs
in its dentated secondaries.

68. *Phibalapteryx rivularis*, n. sp. (Nos. 45 & 50).

Allied to *P. verriculata* of Felder, but smaller, more sandy n tint, with the lines of primaries transverse, instead of oblique and undulated, secondaries with all the lines undulated, as well as the margin; discal veins of all the wings white, dotted with black; discocellular spots black, more or less developed. Expanse of wings 1 inch 3 lines.

Otago

69. *Cidaria? inclarata* (No. 53).

Cidaria inclarata, Walker, Lep Het. xxv, p 1411, (1862).
Otago

The specimen now sent shows none of the white irroration common to the primaries of this species.

70. *Cidaria? aggregata* (No. 46)

Cidaria aggregata, Walker, Lep. Het. xxv, p 1415 (1862).
Cidaria mopnata, Felder, Reise der Nov Lep v, pl. cxxxii, fig 3.
Otago.

The example now sent is a female, and agrees in all respects with Felder's figure.

71. *Cidaria beata* (No. 55).

Cidaria beata, Butler, Proc. Zool. Soc. 1877, p. 397, pl. xliii, fig. 6
Otago

The specimens in the present collection are larger and rather more distinctly marked than those obtained by Mr. Enys

72. *Cidaria similata* (Nos. 61 & 91)

Cidaria similata, Walker, Lep. Het. xxv, p. 1413 (1862).
Cidaria timenata, Felder, Reise der Nov. Lep v, pl. cxxxii, fig. 19.
Otago.

73. *Cidaria muscosata* (Nos. 69 & 89).

Eupithecia muscosata, Walker, Lep. Het. xxiv, p. 1246 (1862).
Helastia muscosata, Butler, Proc. Zool Soc 1877, p. 395.
Cidaria sphœrnata? Felder, Reise der Nov. Lep. v, pl. cxxxi, fig 14.
Otago.

The ♀ is very similar to Felder's figure of *C aquosata*.

74. *Cidaria callichlora*, n. sp. (Nos. 59, 70 & 90).

Nearly allied to the European *C. miata*, from which it differs
as follows primaries above more densely green ; basal patch
smaller and darker, not so angular , central belt wider, its inner
edge not so sharply defined, its outer edge widely zigzag from
above the second median branch ; the white submarginal spots
replaced by a pale greenish festooned line , the double marginal
black dots replaced by ⟨-shaped markings ; secondaries crossed
by two widely separated indistinct dentate-sinuate grey discal
lines; no discocellular dot , abdomen pale brown with white
dorsal dots on each side of which are black dots ; below there
are similar differences, but here all the wings exhibit black
discocellular dots   Expanse of wings 1 inch 3 lines.
Wairarapa.

In one example (No. 90) the primaries above and the whole
under surface are more dusky than in the two others, giving it
a very different aspect

75. *Elvia glaucata* (No. 42).

Elvia glaucata, Walker, Lep. Het. xxv, p. 1431 (1862).
Otago.

CRAMBIDÆ.

76. *Crambus flexuosellus* (No. 73).

Crambus flexuosellus, Doubleday, Dieff., New Zeal. App.
p 289 (1843).
Otago

77. *Crambus sabulosellus* (No 102).

Crambus sabulosellus, Walker, Lep. Het xxvii, p. 178, n. 139
(1863).
Otago.

78. *Chilo leucanialis* (No. 72).

Chilo leucanialis, Butler, Proc. Zool. Soc. 1877, p. 401, n. 112.
Otago.

TORTRICIDÆ.

79 *Heterognomon biguttanum* (No. 95)

Teras biguttana, Walker, Lep. Het. xxviii, p. 305, n. 76 (1863).
Otago.

- 80. *Heterognomon excessanum* (Nos. 74, 93 & 94).

Teras excessana, Walker, Lep. Het. xxviii, p 303, n. 71 (1863).
Otago.

The female is larger than the male, and of a redder colour.

81. *Heterognomon cuneiferanum* (No. 75).

Teras cuneiferana, Walker, Lep. Het. Suppl. v, p. 1780 (1866).
Otago.

82. *Cacoecia herana?* (No. 96).

Tortrix herana, Felder, Reise der Nov. Lep v, pl. cxxxvii,
fig. 52
Otago.

83 *Pædisca luciplagana* (No. 103).

Pædisca luciplagana, Walker, Lep Het xxviii, p. 381, n. 83
(1863).
Otago.

Allied to " *Conchylis* " *plagiatana,* of Walker.

TINEIDÆ.

84. *Tinea terranea* n. sp (No. 105).

Aspect of the genus *Safra*, sericeous earthy brown, the primaries reticulated with greyish-brown, two spots in the cell, a
semicircular subconfluent series beyond the cell and a series
round the costal and outer margins black ; secondaries tinted
with violet ; head testaceous ; wings below shining sepia-brown
with paler fringes ; body pale testaceous.   Expanse of wings
1 inch
Otago.

Resembles the genus *Safra* in coloration.

GELECHIIDÆ.

85. *Œcophora peroneanella* (No. 77).

Gelechia peroneanella, Walker, Lep. Het. xxix, p. 638, n. 384
(1864).
Otago.

86. *Œcophora Huttonii,* n sp. (No. 76)

Allied to *Œ picarella*; primaries above greyish-white; a short bifurcate black line lying along the base of costal margin, a ⋈-shaped black marking at base of median vein, and beyond it an oblong spot, above the latter a zigzag line running to the costal margin; an irregularly zigzag black line from the centre of costal margin to the first median branch; a ?-shaped black character on the disc, and a series of black spots round the margin of the wings, from the costa just behind the middle to the inner margin near external angle; secondaries shining-grey, with darker subconfluent marginal spots; apical half of fringe sordid white, intersected by a grey line, body white; wings below shining brown, with whitish margins and white fringes; body below white, the venter with black lateral patches; legs white externally with the tarsi black-banded, anterior pair black internally with white joints. Expanse of wings 1 inch 1 line.

Otago.

A very distinct and pretty species.

87. *Tingena bifaciella* (No. 104).

Tingena bifaciella, Walker, Lep. Het. xxix, p. 810, n. 1 (1864)

Otago.

This species greatly resembles *Œcophora parca* and *Œ. apertella,* but differs in the form of the secondaries and the dark coloration of the under surface of the wings

88. *Cryptolechia galactina* (No. 78)

Cryptolechia galactina, Felder, Reise der Nov. Lep. v. pl. cxi. fig 31

Otago

On Phytophagous Coleoptera *collected by Mr Thamm at Chanchamayo, Peru;* by Martin Jacoby.

Mr Thamm, who recently visited London, collected during a great number of years in Peru; the Phytophaga in his collection are mostly those which have been already described by Erichson, in his Fauna Peruana, the new species are, with a few exceptions, described in this paper, and I have added a few species which I had previously obtained from Peru.

CRIOCERIDÆ.

Lema peruana, n sp.

Elongate, parallel, black; thorax, margin of the elytra and apex of abdomen flavous. Length 3½ lines.

Head black, impunctate, shining, not constricted behind the eyes, the lateral grooves very deep; antennæ, second joint short, third twice the length, the rest elongate, black, pubescent, the first joint swollen, entirely rufous. Thorax quadrate, deeply constricted in the middle, surface smooth, with an obsolete transverse depression, impunctate, shining, flavous Elytra much broader than the thorax, convex, punctate-striate, the punctures almost disappearing towards the apex, with a short obsolete transverse depression below the scutellum, where the punctuation is more deeply impressed; the suture towards the apex and the lateral margins through their entire length distinctly raised and thickened; surface metallic aeneous, the margins and apex, the latter more broadly, flavous Underside and legs black, sides of the abdominal segments and the last two entirely flavous or ferruginous

Differs from *Lema flavo-marginata,* Clark, by the colour of the head, of the underside and legs.

EUMOLPIDÆ

Chalcoplacis rufiventris, Erich.

The specimen before me differs from Erichson's description in having only the sides of the abdominal segments red, and in being larger (measuring three lines), but as Erichson says nothing about the punctuation I can only consider it a variety.

Colaspis Haroldi, n. sp.

Ovate, convex, cupreous; antennæ testaceous, joints 6–7 and 10–11 fuscous; thorax 3-dentate, coarsely rugose; elytra with five or six rows of interrupted costæ, the interstices transversely reticulate. Length 2 lines.

Head coarsely wrinkled; palpi testaceous, their apex fuscous; antennæ with the third joint longer than the fourth, and more slender than the rest of the joints. Thorax transverse, widened in the middle, angles acute, surface coarsely rugose and irregularly wrinkled, sides obtusely 3-dentate, of a dark æneous or copper colour intermixed with spaces, and a longitudinal central line of brassy-green Scutellum with a metallic tint, rounded. Elytra slightly depressed below the base and widened posteriorly, very convex and rounded, each elytron with about six elevated rows of costæ, which are frequently interrupted, the interstices transversely reticulate, of the same colour as the thorax, mixed with a brassy tint, but rather opaque. Underside and legs æneous with greenish reflections.

Although this insect bears some resemblance to a species of the genus Leprorota, the angulated sides of the thorax and the colour of the antennæ show it to be a true species of Colaspis, which ought to follow close to the C interrupta, described by von Harold in the Coleopt Hefte.

Chalcophana gigas, n. sp.

Oblong ovate, fulvous; antennæ, the first three joints excepted, tibiæ and tarsi black. Length 5 lines.

Head and clypeus distinctly punctate, the former impressed with an oblong fovea; antennæ more than half the length of the body, the three basal joints fulvous, the rest black with a bluish gloss. Thorax short, the anterior angles produced into a distinct tooth, surface sparingly punctate, more distinctly on the disc than at the sides Elytra convex, broader than the thorax, deeply punctate-striate, the striæ arranged irregularly in three rows of punctures each, closely approached and interrupted by three short raised costæ, of which the middle one only is distinct, and commencing from the shoulder extends to a little below the middle of the elytra; another distinct costa runs near the lateral margin, from below the middle to the apex, the space below the base in front of the costæ is depressed by a short transverse fovea on each elytron. Underside and thighs fulvous, tibiæ and tarsi shining black.

Hab Chanchamayo, Peru.

This fine species bears a close resemblance to *C dimidiata,* Baly, but cannot be a mere variety of that species on account of the different sculpture of its elytra, its uniform coloration and its black tibiæ.

The elytral striæ in *dimidiata* are geminate, whereas in the present species three parallel lines are placed together, the elytra are unicolorous and the abdomen is fulvous

Chalcophana unifasciata, n. sp.

Oblong ovate, rufous; last seven joints of the antennæ and the abdomen black, elytra punctate-striate, subcostate laterally, metallic-green, the lateral margin anteriorly, a transverse fascia in the middle and the extreme apex rufous. Length 4 lines

Head elongate, finely punctured and grooved longitudinally, labium testaceous, apex of mandibles black ; antennæ with the first five joints shining, flavous, the rest opaque, black. Thorax much wider at the base than at the apex, transversely convex, surface with a few very minute punctures, shining rufous. Scutellum black. Elytra without basal depression, deeply geminate punctate-striate from base to the middle, thence to the apex very finely punctate, the intervals, near the lateral margin, raised into short costæ commencing below the shoulder and extending nearly to the apex Underside and the legs rufous, abdomen black with a violet tint.

Hab. Peru

Easily distinguished from *C. cincta,* Harold, by its large size and the colour of the underside.

*Otilea * tarsalis,* n sp.

Elongate, glabrous, greenish æneous , antennæ and tarsi testaceous ; thorax sparsely punctate, elytra geminate punctate-striate, apex deeply sulcate. Length 3½ lines.

---

*Lefèvre, Ann Soc Ent France, 1877

Head deeply longitudinally sulcate in middle, widely but deeply punctate, lower part of clypeus smooth, labrum fulvous; antennæ two-thirds the length of the body, filiform, second joint short, the others elongate of nearly equal length, uniformly testaceous. Thorax transverse, anterior angles acutely produced, sides distinctly angulate in middle, thence to the base straight, surface deeply punctate, the disc with only a few punctures, the the sides a little more closely punctured. Scutellum smooth. Elytra much wider than the thorax, much narrowed towards the apex, deeply impressed below the base, shoulders very prominent and obliquely truncate, produced outwards in the form of an elongate tubercle ; distinctly geminate punctate, the interstices near the lateral margin and at the apex raised into longitudinal costæ, very shining, greenish æneous. Underside of the same colour, tibiæ piceous, tarsi testaceous, the anterior dilated. Prosternum deeply bilobed

CHRYSOMELIDÆ

Doryphora opacicollis, n sp

Ovate, convex, greenish-black; thorax opaque, elytra violaceous-blue, or greenish, shining, deeply geminate punctate-striate, interstices aciculate. Length 6 lines.

Head minutely granulate, distinctly but not closely punctate; labrum fulvous, stained with fuscous, the first five joints of the antennæ violaceous-blue, their tips fulvous, shining, the rest opaque Thorax with the sides anteriorly rounded, surface punctured like the head, greenish-black, opaque and also finely granulate. Scutellum smooth. Elytra a little wider at the base than the thorax, convex and evenly rounded, conspicuously deeply geminate punctate, interstices aciculate. Underside and legs black, shining; mesosternal process long, slightly curved.

Doryphora fulvicollis, n. sp.

Ovate, very convex, fulvous; elytra confusedly punctate, black, extreme apex fulvous. Length 5½-6 lines.

Head finely punctured, fulvous, with a short longitudinal groove at the base, labium testaceous; apex of mandibles black; antennæ robust, the last joints much flattened, as broad as long, black, with a bluish gloss, the basal joint fulvous beneath. Thorax rather deeply sinuate behind the eyes, the sides nearly parallel, anterior angles acutely produced ; upper surface very

widely punctured, the punctures more strongly impressed near
the sides and intermixed with minute punctures, of a bright
fulvous colour and very shining.   Scutellum large, fulvous.
Elytra scarcely broader at the base than the thorax, very convex
and slightly widened posteriorly, covered with irregularly
arranged distinct punctures, the intervals aciculate and very
finely alutaceous, of a uniform black colour, with the extreme
apex narrowly fulvous.   Underside and legs of the latter
colour, mesosternal process stout and straight.

Doryphora transversofasciata, n. sp.

Broadly ovate, very convex, flavo-testaceous ; four spots on
the head, four transversely placed spots on the thorax, and two
deeply dentate bands across the disc, together with two spots
near the apex of elytra piceous.   Length 6 lines.

Face obsoletely depressed in the middle, rather closely and
deeply punctate, two transverse spots each side at the base, a
triangular shaped one in the middle and another on the clypeus
piceous; antennæ flavo-testaceous, the last four joints black.
Thorax of the usual shape, broadly depressed near each side,
surface closely covered with large and smaller punctures, the
.base at each side and four spots across the disc piceous or fulvous.
Scutellum fulvous   Elytra wider than the thorax, very convex,
deeply but not regularly punctate-striate, the intervals minutely
punctured, testaceous, an oblique fascia from the shoulder to the
suture below the scutellum, consisting of four elongated connected
spots, another band behind the middle deeply dentate anteriorly
and posteriorly, extending from the margin to the suture, and
two quadrate spots near the apex piceous.   Underside and legs
flavous, femora with an obsolete æneous spot in the middle ;
mesosternal process short and stout.

Hab Peru.

Doryphora elegantula, n. sp.

Oblong ovate, very convex, greenish æneous, elytra punctate-
striate, testaceous, suture and lateral margin dark green sub-
metallic.   Length 4 lines.

Head broad, impressed with distinct punctures, which are
more strongly marked near the base, although nowhere crowded;
labrum fulvous, stained transversely with fuscous ; antennæ a
little longer than the head and thorax, shining, dark green, the
apical joints opaque   Thorax transversely convex, the sides

nearly straight at the base, thence rounded to the apex ; surface irregularly and rather widely covered with minute and larger punctures, dark metallic-green. Scutellum of the same colour, smooth, shining. Elytra widened behind the middle, very regularly punctate-striate, each elytron having ten rows of punctures, of which the first is abbreviated, interstices impunctate, a common sutural stripe from base to apex, widened anteriorly and limited by the third stria, and the lateral margin joined at the apex with the sutural stripe, dark green, shining Underside and inflexed limb of the elytra greenish æneous; claws dark fulvous; mesosternal process stout and slightly curved.

Doryphora glabrata, n. sp.

Ovate, convex, black, thorax glabrous ; elytra obsoletely punctate-striate, a subsutural and submarginal vitta joined at the apex, flavous Length 4 lines

Head black, semiopaque, almost impunctate, antennæ longer than the thorax, black, the first two joints flavous beneath. Thorax narrowed at the base, thence to the apex much widened and rounded, narrowly margined laterally, surface convex, black, entirely impunctate. Scutellum black. Elytra slightly narrower at the base than the thorax, widened towards the middle, very obsoletely punctate, the punctures near the suture arranged · in rows and widely apart, black, opaque, a narrow stripe near the suture from base to apex joined to another submarginal stripe, dark flavous; margin and entire underside black; mesosternal process short and stout.

The almost entire absence of any punctuation (no punctures being visible even under a strong lens), and the small size will distinguish this species from others similarly coloured.

Doryphora euchalca, Stal.

One specimen of a uniform metallic-green agrees in general form with the above species, but the elytra are more minutely punctate, and the intervals are throughout aciculate or scratched ; it may possibly prove to be a different species.

Doryphora amabilis, Baly.

The single specimen before me agrees in every respect with the descriptions given by Baly and Stal, but differs in the underside being marked with fuscous, which colour prevails along the sides of the metathorax, the inner side of the tibiæ, and the margins of the abdominal segments   The surface of the elytra is also finely punctate in semi-striate rows and the intervals are aciculate; but as I have only a single specimen and have not compared it with the type I am scarcely justified in describing it as new.

Doryphora fulvonotata, n. sp.

Rotundate, subdepressed; above opaque, dark bluish-green; elytra punctate, the punctures arranged in geminate rows on the disc, confused externally, with four narrow transverse irregular bands, and a spot below the base, fulvous.   Length 6 lines.

Head minutely punctate, plane, labrum piceous, anterior margin testaceous; antennæ not reaching farther than the base of the thorax, the first five joints shining blackish-green, the rest opaque black; thorax narrow, sides nearly straight at the base, much rounded towards the apex, the anterior angles acute and slightly produced, surface more strongly punctured than the head, but the punctures very irregularly distributed, a distinctly raised central line extending from the base nearly to the apex; scutellum impunctate. elytra very much rounded, very deflexed from the middle towards the sides and only slightly convex at the base, deeply geminate punctate-striate near the suture, the rest of the surface less deeply confusedly punctate, dark bluish-green, without gloss, each elytron with two small spots near the scutellum and four very narrow tranverse zigzag bands on the disc (not extending to the suture), fulvous, the last band emitting more or less distinct vittæ to the apex   Underside rather shining.

This curiously shaped *Doryphora* is remarkable from its general resemblance to some of the *Cassidulæ*, for one of which I at first mistook it

Stilodes fulvipennis, n. sp.

Oblong ovate, beneath piceous; thorax black; elytra reddish-brown, the suture and the extreme lateral margin narrowly æneous or black.   Length 3 lines

Head distinctly but not closely punctate, black, antennæ a little longer than the thorax, piceous, the four basal joints flavous, shining   Thorax transverse, sides evenly rounded, anterior angles distinct but not produced, surface not very closely punctate, the punctures deeper near the sides than on the disc, the intervals covered with minute punctures. Scutellum triangular, smooth. Elytra moderately convex, punctate-striate, the first stria abbreviated, intervals minutely punctured, shining, fulvous, suture narrowly, more broadly anteriorly, extreme lateral margin, and base more or less nigro-æneous. Underside and legs, with the exception of the coxæ, which are fulvous, black, shining.

HALTICIDÆ.

Rhoicus trifasciatus, n. sp.

Elongate, parallel, flavous, shining; thorax broadly angulate before the middle; elytra punctate-striate, with three transverse piceous bands, one at the base, one at the middle, and the third at the apex. Length 4 lines.

Head rather coarsely punctate on the vertex, with two highly raised elongate tubercles above the insertion of the antennæ, prolonged anteriorly into a short longitudinal ridge; antennæ reaching to about one-third of the length of the elytra, entirely flavous, the third joint as long as the first, the second short, the rest shorter than the third. Thorax as long as broad, glabrous, sides before the middle produced into a broad rounded angle, surface with three transverse depressions near the base, depressed also along the anterior margin, thus giving the disc an elevated appearance, the entire surface is covered with distinct punctures, but rather irregularly distributed, of a uniform flavous colour. Scutellum triangular, flavous. Elytra much wider than the thorax, about four times as long, deeply punctate-striate, the intervals here and there impressed with single deep punctures, and slightly raised on the disc, of a paler flavous tint than the thorax, a band at the base narrowed at the shoulders, a broad fascia across the middle with its posterior margin sinuate, and another at the apex, convex at its anterior margin, piceous. Underside flavous, thighs a little darker. Claws appendiculate.

The elongate palpi, broadly angulated thorax, 1-spined tibiæ, and glabrous elytra agree very well with Clark's definition of his genus *Rhoicus* The present species may be easily distinguished from that described by Clark, by its large size, and its deeply punctate and three banded elytra.

Hapalotrius flavofasciata, n. sp.

Broadly ovate, finely pubescent, black ; thorax, an almost circular band on the elytra, the four anterior thighs, and the three last joints of the antennæ flavous. Length 2½ lines.

Head black, coarsely rugose, punctate on the vertex, the space between the antennæ impunctate and deeply foveolate immediately above it ; antennæ filiform, the third joint distinctly longer than the first, the following joints gradually decreasing in length, black, the last three joints flavous ; maxillary palpi much thickened towards the apex, the apical joint not acute. Thorax subquadrate, a little broader than long, sides nearly parallel, not angulate, posterior margin distinctly sinuate at each side, surface entirely covered with fine silky pubescence, flavous, the anterior angles slightly stained with fuscous. Scutellum triangular, flavous. Elytra much wider at the base than the thorax, widened behind the middle, punctate-striate, interstices distinctly costate and extremely finely pubescent, black, with an almost circular flavous band, which, commencing at the shoulder, extends to below the middle, and is common to both elytra, this band is slightly narrower at the shoulder, increasing in width posteriorly. Abdomen and all the tibiæ stained with fuscous; posterior thighs black, the rest of the underside and legs flavous or testaceous; claws appendiculate; posterior tibiæ with two spurs.

Hab. Peru.

The shape of the thorax and other characters coinciding with Clark's genus *Apalotrius* (subsequently altered to *Hapalotrius*), have induced me to refer this species to his genus; while its coloration is very similar to that of *Allochroma lunatum*, the generic differences and the pubescence of the elytra will at once distinguish it.

Omototus rufolimbatus, n. sp.

Elongate, robust, black ; thorax ferruginous, clothed with yellow pubescence, elytra shining, violaceous-blue or green, lateral margin and apex ferruginous, pubescent; abdomen ferruginous.

Var. The blue colour of the elytra divided by a broad ferruginous band across the disc.

Length 3 lines.

Head short, black, pubescent, with two indistinctly raised tubercles above the insertion of the antennæ of a flavous colour, lower part of face fuscous; antennæ black, closely covered with hairs, the first and fourth joints of equal length, the third the longest. Thorax narrow, transverse, the sides slightly widened before the middle, ferruginous, closely and thickly covered with golden pubescence. Scutellum black. Elytra subdepressed, antemedially transversely depressed, finely punctate-striate, dark violaceous-blue or green, nearly glabrous, a narrow marginal vitta, greatly increasing in width at the apex, of a ferruginous colour and closely yellowish pubescent. Underside and legs black, pubescent, apex of abdomen ferruginous. Posterior tibiæ with one spur, maxillary palpi incrassate.

In the variety, a broad ferruginous band extends across the middle of the disc, and is also covered like the lateral vitta with yellow pubescence, but agrees in all other respects with the typical specimens.

Omototus rubripennis, n. sp.

Elongate, robust, flavous, antennæ, apex of femora and tibiæ black; elytra darkish red with a violet tint, very closely pubescent, obsoletely punctate-striate. Length 3 lines.

Head deeply punctate on the vertex, antennæ rather closely approximate, second joint short, third joint longer than the first, fourth and following joints decreasing in length, entirely black, the apical joints pubescent, the others beset at their apex with bristle-like hairs; maxillary palpi incrassated. · Thorax broader than long, the sides widened and rounded in the middle, depressed at each side near the base, closely rugose punctate, dark reddish, slightly pubescent. Elytra very little widened posteriorly, punctate-striate, thickly covered with short yellowish pubescence and single stiff long hairs, rendering the punctuation rather obscure, of a uniform opaque reddish colour with a purplish or violet hue in certain lights. Underside flavous, pubescent, femora darker, their apex and the four anterior tibiæ black, posterior tibiæ piceous or dark brown, with a single spur.

Asphæra octopunctata, n. sp.

Oblong ovate, beneath piceous; head, thorax, elytra and abdomen flavo-testaceous, each elytron with two spots near the base and two behind the middle violaceous or green. Length 2½ lines.

Head smooth, with only a few punctures near the eyes, shining, flavous or fulvous, with a deep transverse groove; antennæ fuscous, the two basal joints shining flavous. Thorax transverse, the sides rounded, anterior angles produced into a short tubercle, surface impunctate, shining, testaceous Elytra convex, narrowly margined, disc smooth, without punctures, of the same colour as the thorax, each elytron with two oblong spots, of which one is placed on the humeral callus, the other near the scutellum, and two placed transversely behind the middle, not touching either the margin or the suture, violaceous, more or less tinted with green. Underside piceous, tibiæ lighter, abdomen testaceous. Claws swollen.

Three specimens in my collection agree in every respect. This species may be distinguished from *limitata,* Harold, by the swollen (not simple) claw joint and the impunctate elytra

Asphæra maculipennis, n. sp.

Ovate, convex, black; thorax and elytra pale fuscous, the latter covered with numerous irregularly shaped testaceous spots. Length 4 lines.

Head shining, black, smooth on the vertex, with some punctures near the eyes, the space between the latter deeply foveolate, with two distinct elongated tubercles in front; antennæ as long as half the body, entirely black, the basal joint obscure fulvous beneath. Thorax with the posterior margin straight, the anterior semicircular, anterior angles produced into a distinct tooth, surface impunctate, obscure fuscous or dark flavous Scutellum black. Elytra widened behind the middle, convex at their posterior half, fuscous, extremely finely punctured and covered with numerous irregular small spots, of a light testaceous colour, distributed over the entire surface. Underside and legs black, basal joint of metatarsus as long as the two following joints united, claws not swollen.

GALERUCIDÆ.

Diabrotica dorsalis, n. sp.

Elongate, flavous, the first seven joints of the antennæ, two submarginal stripes on the thorax, and the knees and tibiæ black; elytra rugose punctate, violaceous, the lateral margin and a dorsal vitta flavous. Long. $2\frac{1}{2}$ lin.

Head obsolctely punctured, with a medial fovea, flavous, labrum piceous; antennæ with the first seven joints black, the rest flavous. Thorax transverse, obliquely depressed on the disc at either side, surface minutely punctate, flavous, a longitudinal black stripe near the lateral margins, dilated anteriorly. Scutellum flavous. Elytra dilated posteriorly, closely rugose punctate, of a dark violaceous-blue, the lateral margin and apex, and a sutural stripe extending from the base to behind the middle, slightly narrowed posteriorly, flavous. Underside testaceous, knees, tibiæ and tarsi black.

Diabrotica undecimpunctata, n. sp.

Pale green; head, middle joints of the antennæ and tibiæ black; thorax dark green, shining; elytra olive-green, with a broad longitudinal orange-coloured vitta, and 11 small black spots. Length 3 lines.

Head with a cruciform impression in the middle, black, shining, antennæ with the first joint olive-green, the second and third of almost equal length, fuscous, 4 to 8 black, 9 and 10 flavous, and the terminal black. Thorax rather convex, shining, bright green, minutely punctured, deeply bifoveolate on the disc. Scutellum black. Elytra convex, broadly margined, and closely punctured, olive-green, with a broad orange-coloured vitta, extending from immediately below the shoulder to a little distance before the apex, each elytron with a longitudinal stripe at the shoulder, and a short sutural one from the base to the end of the scutellum, two transversely placed small spots in the middle and two others behind the middle, black. Underside and legs pale green, breast, tibiæ and tarsi black.

Diabrotica sanguinicollis, n. sp.

Elongate, widened behind; black, abdomen flavous; thorax bifoveolate, dark red, shining, elytra finely punctate, black, the lateral margin and the apex fulvous. Length 3½ lines.

Head black, impunctate; antennæ flavous or fulvous, the fifth to the eighth joint black. Thorax transversely subquadrate, surface rather convex near the sides, with two deep foveæ on the disc, the latter impunctate, very shining, dark red. Scutellum black. Elytra gradually increasing in width from base to apex, closely but not coarsely punctured, the intervals slightly wrinkled here and there, with an obsolete costa from below the shoulder to the middle, black, shining, the lateral margin narrowly and the apex broadly flavous. Underside flavous, breast and legs black, claws and tarsi more or less piceous.

Diabrotica terminalis, n. sp.

Elongate ovate, olive-green, underside, head, a spot on each shoulder, and a broad band near the apex of the elytra black. Length 4 lines.

Head sparingly punctate between the eyes, with a short fovea and a tubercular elevation between the antennæ; lower part of face olive-green; palpi black; antennæ flavous, the apical joints darker. Thorax transversely subquadrate, the sides margined and slightly rounded, surface very minutely punctured, shining, olive-green. Scutellum black. Elytra subdepressed, widened posteriorly, very finely punctured, olive-green, with a slight flavous tint, a spot on each shoulder, the suture near the base and around the scutellum, and a large transverse band close to the apex, the anterior margin of which is convex, the posterior concave, of a black colour. Underside black, the upper part of the breast and the legs light green, tarsi dark piceous.

Diabrotica abdominalis, n. sp.

Elongate, much widened behind, convex, thorax deeply longitudinally and transversely sulcate, elytra finely punctate, posterior half and abdomen black. Length 4 lines.

Head elongate, testaceous, with an elevated longitudinal ridge from between the antennæ to the clypeus, impunctate, antennæ rather robust, flavous. Thorax transverse, sides margined, all the angles acute, surface very convex, divided longitudinally and transversely into two halves, the transverse depression only extending across half the disc, irregularly and rather obsoletely punctured, flavous. Elytra slightly depressed below the base, ventricose, the anterior portion distinctly, the posterior one scarcely punctured, flavous, divided by deep black from the middle to the apex. Underside and legs flavous, abdomen black.

Allied to *D. Saundersi,* Baly, but distinguished by the shining (not opaque) elytra and the flavous legs and antennæ.

Diabrotica Balyi, n. sp

Elongate, black; abdomen, legs, antennæ, margin and apex of the elytra flavous, the latter elevate strigose, rugosely punctate. Length 3 lines.

Head impunctate, with a fovea in the middle, black ; palpi flavous ; antennæ pale flavous, basal joints rather darker, the last two fuscous. Thorax broader than long, constricted near the base, sides margined, deeply bifoveolate, scarcely punctate, black. Elytra sculptured precisely as in *D. viridipennis*, black, outer limb and apex, the latter dilated, flavous, the male has the same excavation near the sutural angle as *viridipennis*. Breast black, abdomen and legs flavous.

This species is closely allied to *D. puncticollis*, Baly, but differs in the almost smooth thorax and head, and the colour of the antennæ.

Diabrotica viridipennis, n sp.

Elongate, beneath flavous, head and middle joints of antennæ black; thorax bifoveolate; elytra transversely rugose punctate, with several elevated vittæ, light green, lateral margin and apex flavous. Length 3 lines.

Mas. Lower part of face testaceous; elytra with a hollow protuberance near the apex

Head impunctate, with a fovea in the middle, black; palpi flavous; antennæ more than half the length of the body black, the first two and the last four joints light flavous, extreme apex fuscous. Thorax transverse, very narrow, constricted near the base, deeply excavated on each side, impunctate, flavo-testaceous. Scutellum black. Elytra widened posteriorly, with four or five more or less distinct elevated vittæ, the intervals coarsely rugose punctate and transversely wrinkled, lighter or darker green, subnitidous, lateral margins and apex flavous. Underside and legs flavous, the femora with an indistinct longitudinal fuscous streak.

In the male the lower part of the face is of a testaceous colour, and near the apex of the elytra, close to the suture, is a smooth longitudinal elevation, hollowed out near the sutural margin.

Diabrotica minuta, n. sp.

Elongate, subovate, pale green, base of the head and the antennæ black; thorax bifoveolate; elytra obsoletely bicostate, finely punctured, green, the suture, a longitudinal stripe from the shoulder to the middle, and a round spot near the apex fuscous. Length 2 lines

Head transversely impressed between the eyes, vertex smooth, black, lower part of face testaceous, mouth piceous; antennæ nearly as long as the body, the second and third joints short, of equal length, the first three joints flavous, the rest black, closely pubescent. Thorax subquadrate, bifoveolate, impunctate, pale green. Scutellum piceous. Elytra closely punctured, with an obsolete short costa from the shoulder towards the suture, and another longer one near the lateral margin; pale green, with an irregular shaped longitudinal streak much widened posteriorly, and hollowed out at its interior margin, and another large round spot near the apex, fuscous, these two spots are obsoletely connected at their outer margin; the suture is also narrowly fuscous, slightly extending in width towards the apex. Underside very pale green, tibiæ and tarsi piceous.

New species of CLERIDÆ *and other Coleoptera from Madagascar*;
by CHAS. O. WATERHOUSE.

The species described in this paper have recently been received
by the British Museum from Antananarivo, and were collected
by Mr. Kingdon, with the exception of *Lissaulicus lævis*, which
is from Fianarantsoa, and was brought by Mr. Shaw.

PARNIDÆ.

Potamophilus abdominalis.

Elongatus, parallelus, opacus, nigrescens; thorace trapezoidali,
subtiliter confertim punctato, antice lineâ impressâ, angulis
posticis acutis, elytris sat fortiter punctato-striatis, ad apicem
arcuatim angustatis, apice ipso oblique truncato, pedibus basi
tarsisque plus minusve piceis, abdomine late concavo, segmentis
piceo-marginatis,   Long 4⅓ lin.

An elongate, narrow species, with very long legs, closely allied
to *P. africanus*, Bohem. The thorax is relatively less transverse
than in that species, about one-third broader than long, obliquely
narrowed in front, gently convex, the anterior impressed line is
more angular in the middle than in *P. africanus*, and there is
a cuneiform impression posteriorly, the anterior angles are a
little greater than right angles, the posterior angles are acute,
but do not diverge as in *africanus*. The elytra are very long,
a little narrower in the middle than at the base, rather strongly
punctate-striate, the intervals moderately convex, irregularly and
extremely finely punctured, the apex of each elytron is obliquely
truncate, the angles not dentiform

CLERIDÆ

Cladiscus rugosus.

Niger, nitidus, rugosus, parce pilosus; elytris thorace fere
duplo latioribus, abdomine piceo. Long. 4⅓ lin.

Head broad, with a transverse impression between the eyes,
the forehead raised in the middle, the neck with some small

tubercles, eyes prominent. Antennæ about three-quarters the length of the elytra, pilose, the third to tenth joints each with two long slender branches springing from the base below. Thorax not so broad as the head with the eyes, one-third longer than broad, subcylindrical, angularly widened in the middle, moderately constricted between the middle and the base, the surface tuberculoso-rugose. Elytra parallel, nearly twice as broad as the thorax, densely tuberculoso-rugose, the tubercles having a tendency to form lines.

Pallenis bipenicillatus.

Elongatus, cylindricus, niger, nitidus; elytris basi bipenicillatus, medio fasciâ angustâ albâ ornatis. Long. 4 lin.

Convex, cylindrical; shining, except the base of the elytra which is somewhat dull. Head gently convex in front, not very thickly and extremely delicately punctured and pubescent, the eyes rather large. Antennæ about the length of the elytra, filiform, the joints elongate, the apical one one-half longer than the preceding, the basal joint pitchy below. Thorax very convex, enveloping the head in front, constricted at the base, thickly and finely punctured and pilose. Elytra parallel, with a narrow white band across the middle; each elytron with a long fine pointed pencil of hair in the middle of the base, resembling a spine, directed forwards, with seven lines of deep elongate punctures which terminate just beyond the white band, the apex coriaceous. The metasternum with an oblique white stripe on each side. The legs with a fine white line in front and behind. The palpi piceous.

The eyes in this species are proportionately large, and the antennal pit is close to them.

This species, has a somewhat striking resemblance to the Longicorn *Ancylistes bicuspis*, Chev., received in the same collection, and is not unlikely to be parasitic upon that insect, the spine on the base of the elytra in *Ancylistes* being represented by a pencil of hair.

ACHLAMYS, n. gen.

Head (with the eyes) broader than the thorax, the eyes prominent, coarsely granular, scarcely emarginate in front. Antennæ with the first joint thick, ovate, the second joint small, the third elongate, subcylindrical, the fourth, fifth and sixth becoming gradually stouter and shorter, the seventh as broad as long, the eighth, ninth, tenth and eleventh forming a distinct club. Apical joint of the maxillary palpi elongate, a little narrowed before the apex; the apical joint of the labial palpi securiform. Prothorax convex, strongly constricted before the base. Elytra parallel, convex, obtuse at the apex. Tarsi with five distinct joints, the claws with a single tooth at the base.

Closely allied to *Pallenis*, but with prominent eyes and distinct club to the antennæ.

Achlamys uniformis.

Cylindricus, nitidus, ferrugineo-rufus, lævis; antennarum clava, tibiis tarsisque nigris, elytris striato-punctatis, apice lævi. Long. 3 lin.

Head broader than the thorax, finely and moderately thickly punctured, the eyes prominent. The apical joint of the palpi blackish Antennæ as long as the head and thorax taken together, the club black. Thorax very convex, one-third longer than broad, very slightly constricted before the front margin, strongly constricted before the base, delicately and not very thickly punctured. Elytra parallel, a little broader than the thorax, each with seven lines of deep oblong punctures which do not extend quite to the apex.

Stenocylidrus frontalis.

Elongatus, cylindricus, niger, griseo-pubescens; fronte ochraceâ, thorace crebre punctato, scutello albo, elytris basi striato-punctatis, apice crebre punctatis, singulis guttis tribus albis, femorum basi flavo   Long. 3 lin.

Antennæ with the basal and the two apical joints yellow; the front of the head and the apex of the abdomen are also yellow. Thorax densely and distinctly punctured. Elytra striate-punctate, the apical third finely and densely punctured, the apex clothed with grey pubescence. Each elytron has three white spots, one below the shoulder, one near the suture before the middle, the third lateral, slightly elongate and oblique, at one-third from the apex

This species closely resembles *C. azureus*, but is smaller and nearly black, only the front of the head, and only the base of the femora are yellow, and the thorax is a trifle more finely punctured,

LISSAULICUS, n. gen.

Tarsi with only four joints visible above. Eyes emarginate in front, widely separated. Eyes finely granular. Antennæ with a large club formed of three transverse joints. The apical joints of all the palpi strongly securiform Mesosternum horizontal. Claws of the tarsi simple. Anterior coxæ approximate. Thorax nearly as broad as long semicircularly rounded posteriorly before the basal constriction, with no anterior constriction. Elytra arcuately narrowed at the apex.

This genus appears to be closely allied to *Aulicus,* from which it differs in not having any impressed lines on the thorax, in having smooth elytra, in the large short-oblong club to the antennæ, and in the strongly securiform labial palpi.

Lissaulicus lævis.

Leviter convexus, rufo-piceus, nitidus, lævis; antennarum clavâ, femorum et tibiarum apice tarsisque nigris, elytris basi punctis nonnullis juxta scutellum, suturâ ad apicem albo-sericeâ. Long. 3½ lin.

Head smooth, with a few extremely fine indistinct punctures on the vertex; the mandibles and part of the apical joint of the palpi nearly black; antennæ as long as the head and thorax together, the third joint and the abrupt large club black. Thorax gently convex and smooth, with a slight impression above the anterior angles, very slightly narrowed in front, rounded at the sides and posteriorly before the posterior constriction. Elytra smooth, a little broader than the thorax and not quite three times as long, arcuately narrowed towards the apex, slightly impressed at the suture, with a few punctures near the scutellum, the suture towards the apex is margined with white pubescence. A spot at the apex of the femora, the apex of the tibiæ and the tarsi are black, all beset with long hairs. There are some long hairs on the head and thorax, and a few on the elytra.

Hab. Fianarantsoa (Mr. Shaw).

Eburifera tuberculicollis.

Parallela, angusta, depressa, obscure cyanea, nitida; capite thoraceque crebre asperato-punctatis, elytris tuberculis minutis numerosis, guttisque quatuor pallide flavis ornatis, antennis pedibusque ferrugineo-testaceis. Long. 3¼ lin.

Head thickly and rather strongly punctured, the eyes moderately prominent. Thorax somewhat flattened above, subparallel for the anterior two-thirds, then strongly constricted within the base, closely beset with small obtuse tubercles, with the extreme anterior and posterior margins smooth. Scutellum yellow. Elytra parallel, depressed, studded with minute obtuse tubercles; each elytron with two round, raised, smooth whitish spots, one before and the other behind the middle, the latter is near the margin.

Var. The base of the elytra pale pitchy, the pitchy colour extending at the suture and at the sides as far as the second yellow spot.

Eburifera lœvicollis.

Parallela, angusta, depressa, cœrulea, nitida, pallide hirsutâ; thorace parce punctulato, elytris crebre rugoso-punctatis, guttis quatuor albis notatis, antennis pedibusque flavis. Long. 2⅔ lin.

Of a brighter blue than *E. tuberculicollis*, but nearly of the same form. The head and thorax have some small punctures scattered over the surface, the latter has the sides more oblique. Scutellum white. Elytra thickly and strongly punctured, the punctures forming lines at the base, at the apex the punctures are replaced by small obtuse tubercles. Legs yellow; the hairs on the posterior tibiæ are very long.

Two examples received with the above are a little larger (3 lin.) and have not spots on the elytra, but they are evidently conspecific.

Eburifera inclita.

Latior, picea, nitida, longe pubescens; thorace guttis duabus, elytris regione scutellari plagâque subapicali nigris, his singulis guttis duabus flavis ornatis, antennarum clavâ pedibusque nigris, femoribus basi piceis. Long. 4⅓ lin.

A somewhat broad depressed species. Head with minute obtuse tubercles moderately thickly placed in front Antennæ with the three apical joints slightly enlarged, pitchy-black. Thorax as broad as long, nearly straight in front, semicircularly rounded posteriorly before the basal constriction, with some minute tubercles scattered over the surface, and with four black spots, two large round ones on the disc and two small ones before the posterior constriction. Elytra scarcely broader than the thorax, with seven or eight lines of deep strong punctures, the first and second extend to one-third the length of the elytra, the third, fourth and fifth are shorter, the sixth extends to the posterior yellow line, the punctures on the sides are somewhat confused; each elytron has an abbreviated black stripe near the scutellum close to the suture, a small round yellow raised spot at one-third from the base (with a small brown mark above it), an oblique, curved, raised yellow streak rather behind the middle, not reaching the suture, the region beyond this is chiefly occupied by an ovate blackish patch, and is sparingly punctured. Abdomen pitchy-black.

HYPERIDÆ.

Chloropholus bioculatus.

Niger ; capite, genubus, abdominis maculis nonnullis squamis aureo-viridibus tectis, thorace et elytris squamis cupreo-rufis densi tectis, illo maculâ medianâ nigrâ viridi-cinctâ, singulo elytro maculâ discoidali rotundatâ guttisque lateralibus nigris viridi-cinctis. Long. 4½–5 lin.

Closely resembles *C. rubrovittatus* in form, but the thorax is relatively narrower Thorax and elytra densely clothed with coppery-red scales, the former with a cordiform black mesial spot, which is surrounded by green scales and connect it with the anterior margin. Each elytron has a round black discoidal spot on the third and fourth interstices surrounded by green scales; on the margin there are three black spots, which are partly surrounded and connected to each other by green scales, on the fifth interstice posteriorly there are two very small black dots. The sides of the metasternum are clothed with coppery scales. The knees, the tarsi and eight spots on the abdomen are covered with green scales.

TRAGOSOMINÆ.

TERETICUS, n. gen.

Palpi short, stout, the apical joint a little swollen at its base. Mandibles very short, vertical. Head as in *Microplophorus*; the eyes a little more separated above. Antennæ nearly half the length of the elytra, stout, the first joint obconic, emarginate-truncate at the apex, the second joint small and transverse, the third to tenth joints short, with the lower anterior angle produced into a long stout branch. Thorax transverse, with the lateral ridge only traceable near the posterior angles, the anterior angles effaced, with no lateral spines. Elytra scarcely covering the abdomen, slightly dehiscent posteriorly, broader than the thorax at the shoulders. Legs short, the posterior femora reaching a little beyond the second segment of the abdomen, unarmed at the apex. The third joint of the tarsi not so strongly bilobed as in *Microplophorus*. The metathoracic episterna very broad at their base acuminate posteriorly. Head, thorax, and body beneath pilose.

The species upon which I propose founding this new genus has somewhat the appearance of a small *Polyarthron*, with short antennæ and short legs; its position, however, is evidently close to *Microplophorus*.

Tereticus pectinicornis.

Obscure piceus; capite thoraceque crebre fortiter punctatis, fulvo pilosis, elytris brunneis apicem versus angustatis, confertim punctatis, tricostulatis, antennis pedibusque nigro-piceis. ♂. Long 9 lin.

Antennæ as long as the head, thorax and scutellum taken together, strongly punctured above, the third to tenth joints each with the anterior lower angle produced into a thick rather broad branch, which is about three times as long as the joint itself Head densely punctured, pilose, slightly concave in front, with a fine channel between the eyes. Thorax thickly punctured, nearly twice as broad as long, obliquely narrowed in front, very declivous at the sides, especially at the anterior angles, the posterior angles distinct but obtuse, the base arcuate. Scutellum strongly punctured. Elytra at their base one-third broader than the thorax, narrowed towards the apex, pale pitchy-brown, very densely and rather strongly punctured, each elytron with three obtuse costæ, the first distinct only in the middle, the second extending from the shoulder to the apex, the third lateral. Legs thickly punctured. The thorax and sterna with long fulvous pubescence.

Notices of new or little known CETONIIDÆ; by OLIVER E. JANSON. No. 6.

Gymnetis Buckleyi, n. sp.

G. robusta, convexa, atra, supra opaca; capite vittâ utrinque, thorace lateribus (maculis duabus nigris includente), elytris vittis humeralibus, maculis quatuor marginalibus, punctisque nonnullis minutis coccineis, subtus nitida, metasterno abdomine-que marginibus rufo-maculatis. Long. 25 mm.

Head coarsely but sparingly punctured on the disc, the punctures much closer and confluent at the sides and apex of the clypeus, the latter narrowed in front with the margins elevated; black, the clypeus shining, the base dull with a short linear spot on each side between the eyes red.

Thorax convex, the posterior lobe broad and obtusely rounded, the sides slightly prominent about one-third from the base and obsoletely punctured, the disc smooth; deep velvety black, with a broad red lateral band on each side slightly branched inwardly at its base and apex, and enclosing two black spots.

Elytra convex, slightly narrowed behind the middle, the apical sutural angles not produced, the disc faintly punctured in rows behind; deep velvety black, several very small spots on the disc, a curved lateral stripe at the shoulder, two spots on the lateral margin, two on the apical margin, and a smaller one just within the apical callosity red; epimera large, shining black, rather coarsely punctured with a smooth tubercle.

Pygidium coarsely and closely strigose; shining black, with dense short black hairs

Beneath shining black, with two large spots on the metasternum and four spots on each side of the abdomen red; very coarsely strigose and punctured at the sides and at the apex of the abdomen; mesosternal process strong, bent downwards and rounded at the apex, keeled in front; legs coarsely punctured, anterior tibiæ with three strong lateral teeth.

Ecuador.

The only specimen I have seen of this fine species (recently sent home by Mr. C. Buckley, after whom I have named it) has been communicated to me for description by Mr. Higgins; it belongs to Burmeister's sect. 10, and although resembling several species in general characters, its coloration is conspicuously distinct and beautiful.

Cetonia impavida, n. sp.

C. late ovata, convexa, cæruleo-nigra, nitida; elytris albo-maculatis, arcuato-striatis.   Long. 19, lat. 11 mm.

Blue-black, shining.

Head short, rather closely and coarsely punctured, clypeus transverse, the anterior angles rounded, sides slightly elevated and closely punctured, anterior margin elevated and slightly sinuous; apex of antennæ reddish.

Thorax convex, basal margin strongly rounded and scarcely emarginate above the scutellum, the disc very finely and sparsely punctured, the punctures becoming coarser and confluent at the sides, the base with two indistinct shallow depressions before the scutellum.

Scutellum short, apex rounded, impunctate, with an indistinct impression in the centre.

Elytra rather convex and very finely and sparsely punctured in the region of the scutellum, the sides and apical half with rows of semicircular striæ, each of which contains a small puncture, the suture rather strongly elevated posteriorly, but not produced at the apical angle, the disc with an indistinct longitudinal ridge behind the middle; each elytron with about twelve small white spots, of which six or seven are on the margin, two very small near the base, two placed obliquely about the middle, and a transverse linear one close to the suture, about one-fourth from the apex.

Pygidium finely irregularly strigose, with sparse golden pubescence.

Beneath strigose and pubescent at the sides; mesosternal process short, apex dilated and rounded; abdomen with some fine punctures at the base of the segments, the apical segment very closely punctured; legs coarsely punctured, strigose and slightly pubescent, anterior tibiæ with three small acute lateral teeth, intermediate and posterior tibiæ with an acute tooth about the middle and an indistinct one just above it, all the knees marked with a white spot.

India.

A very distinct and apparently undescribed species; I have seen several specimens but have not been able to ascertain its precise habitat.

Cetonia famelica, n. sp

C. subangustata, cupreo-brunnea, albo-variegata, nitida, clypeo antice tarsisque viridis, grosse profundeque punctata. Long. 17–18 mm.

Coppery-brown, tinged with green, shining, apex of clypeus, knees, apex of tibiæ and tarsi bright green, elytra with irregular white marks and spots.

Head short and broad, very closely and coarsely punctured, the punctures confluent and forming striæ at the sides, the centre scarcely elevated; clypeus broadest at the apex, transversely impressed in front, the sides elevated, apical margin strongly elevated and emarginate, forming two small obtuse points.

Thorax rather convex, regularly rounded at the sides, posterior angles strongly rounded, the basal margin only slightly emarginate above the scutellum, very closely and coarsely punctured, a longitudinal central line smooth, sides coarsely strigose, the disc with three distinct impressions on each side, usually marked with a white spot.

Scutellum triangular, apex obtuse, impunctate.

Elytra rather flat with the usual depression behind, commencing rather abruptly before the middle, very closely covered with semicircular striæ, most of which contain a fine puncture, at the sides and apex they become closer and more confused, forming irregular wavy striæ intermixed with punctures, in the region of the scutellum they are more sparse and assume the form of coarse irregular punctures, the suture elevated posteriorly but not produced at the apex.

Pygidium convex, finely transversely strigose, with several indistinct whitish spots

Beneath sparsely pubescent and closely strigose; mesosternal process short, strongly dilated, apex truncate; abdomen with semicircular striæ at the sides and scattered punctures in the middle; legs coarsely strigose, the anterior tibiæ with three obtuse teeth

The female is rather more coarsely sculptured, with the apical segment of the abdomen very closely punctured, and a much stronger tooth on the intermediate and posterior tibiæ.

Shantung, N. China.

Allied to *C. intricata*, Saund., *submarmorea*, Burm., and *confuciusana*, Thoms,

On the larva of EUSCHEMA MILITARIS, Linn.; by OLIVER E. JANSON

Professor J. Wood-Mason, of the Calcutta Museum, recently placed in my hands for publication, the accompanying figures of the larva and pupa of *Euschema militaris*, drawn from nature by Mr. S. E. Peal, who has succeeded in rearing this moth through its earlier stages, thereby setting at rest the long disputed question as to its location amongst the *Bombycina* or *Geometrina*, to both of which groups it has been assigned. The majority of authors have referred it to the former group with which (from a study of the imago alone) it appears to offer most characters in common. M. Guenée, however (Spec. Gen. Lep. x, p. 188), argues in favour of its affinity with the latter group (placing it between the *Fidonidæ* and *Zerenidæ*), but at the same time remarking that it is impossible to decide the question until the larva is known. Mr. Peal's discovery of its "Looper" caterpillar at once confirms the views of M. Guenée as to its pertaining to the *Geometrina*.

The drawings are not coloured, and Mr. Peal merely describes the larva as being yellow; the pupa cases sent are pale brown speckled with black, the black spots at the sides and the eye-like spots on the head are encircled with pale yellow, the latter are very conspicuous.

Explanation of the figures:

PLATE X.

Fig 2 larva of *Euschema militaris*.
  „ 3, 4 & 5 pupa of   *ditto*

On a collection of Lepidoptera Heterocera from Marlborough Province, New Zealand; by Arthur G. Butler, F.L.S., F.Z S.

The series of Lepidoptera enumerated here, represents the greater part of a collection forwarded to me last year by Mr William Skellon, of Blenheim; unfortunately one of the boxes, containing many of the smaller and some novelties of the larger moths, was literally smashed into strips during transit; whilst the other box, although whole, had evidently been very roughly handled; so that the identification of several of the species has been quite impossible, whereas in some instances nothing but the bare pins remained to show that the numbers had represented something.

Notwithstanding the condition of many of the species the collection is a very interesting one, the novelties which it contains are sufficient evidence that there is still much to be done before we can pretend to anything like a complete knowledge of the Lepidopterous resources of New Zealand

HEPIALIDÆ.

1. Porina fuliginea (No. 35).

Porina fuliginea, Butler, Cist. Ent. ii, p. 488, n. 2 (1879).

One specimen, in good condition; taken "in the bush at dusk."

2. Porina umbraculata (Nos. 33 & 34).

Pielus umbraculatus, Guenée, Ent. Month Mag. v, p. 1 (1868).

"Common in the Phormium swamps at dusk." Two examples, in good condition, differing slightly in tint.

Respecting the Noctuites, Mr. Skellon writes—"the Noctuæ for the most part have been taken on sugar; Nos. 10, 14, 15,

S S

20, 21, 25, 26, 28 and 32 in January, February and March (the best time for sugaring here) are rather rare, and I have not been able to get many specimens of them."

LEUCANIIDÆ.

Mr Skellon has sent no less than nine species of this family, four of which (all probably new to science) are so much broken as to be unfit for description; of these, Nos. 25, 38 and 58 are typical *Leucaniæ*, and No. 62 apparently an *Ipana*, but too much injured for satisfactory identification.

3. *Leucania atristriga* (No. 30).

Xylina atristriga, Walker, Lep. Het. Suppl. iii, p. 756 (1865).

This seems to be a common species.

4. *Leucania propria* (No. 15).

Leucania propria, Walker, Lep. Het. ix. p. 111 (1856).

Also a common species

5. *Leucania dentigera*, n sp. (No. 4).

Primaries above greyish-white, the centre of the wing occupied by a gradually expanding diffused brownish longitudinal streak which, towards the base, encloses a slender curved blackish line; slender brown longitudinal lines near the base of the median interspaces, and black dots between them upon the veins, so as almost to form a continuous zigzag line; external border formed of two triangular brown patches with dentated inner edges, the two together having a Σ-shaped inner margin; base of costal border white, bounded on each side by a short slender blackish line; discoidal spots linear, brownish with white borders, the orbicular modified into an elongated ᴐ-shaped marking and transfixing the reniform, which is lunate; a series of black marginal dots; fringes brown, intersected by white lines at the extremities of the veins; secondaries greyish-brown with bronzy reflections, the external border and a discocellular lunule rather darker: fringe white; body pale sandy-brown, thorax white behind, abdomen sericeous; under surface sericeous white; wings with minute black marginal dots; primaries with dusky discoidal area; secondaries with a blackish discocellular dot; a feebly indicated dusky discal belt. Expanse of wings 1 inch 4 lines.

Two specimens, one in good condition, the other slightly broken; it resembles "*Mamestra maori*" of Felder in pattern.

6. *Leucania extranea*, var.? (No. 39).

Leucania extranea, Guenée, Noct i, p. 77, n 104 (1852).

One singularly red example, with the basal half of the secondaries unusually transparent; otherwise differing in no respect from Indian examples referred to this species

7. *Leucania unica* (No 5).

Leucania unica, Walker, Lep Het. ix, p. 112 (1856)

Two nearly perfect specimens.

XYLOPHASIIDÆ.

8. *Xylophasia stipata* (No. 61).

Xylina stipata, Walker, Lep. Het. Suppl. iii, p. 753 (1865).

A fragment of this well-marked species arrived.

9. *Xylophasia morosa*, n. sp. (No. 26).

Allied to *X lignana*, and referable to the *X. rurea* group, smoky-brown, primaries with the internal area and disc paler; ordinary spots greyish with black-edged white borders, the reniform extending over the base of the second median interspace and streaked with blackish, a line of which colour runs backwards from it along the median vein, a black-edged white spot close to the base of the interno-median area and three at equal distances on the costal margin; three white costal dots beyond the cell; ordinary lines obsolete; a discal series of black and white dots on the veins followed by a series of externally-yellowish-edged ferruginous lunules between the veins; two dusky, somewhat triangular, patches on outer border, with black spots upon them at the extremities of the veins; fringe black spotted and traversed by a central black line, secondaries shining smoky-brown; fringe with a grey-edged yellow basal line; externally silvery-white; head and thorax brown, traversed by bisinuated darker lines; abdomen shining greyish-brown; anal segment blackish at the base, with lateral reddish-brown fringe: body below pinky-whitish, front of pectus pale purplish-brown; knees black, posterior tibiæ striped at the end with black; venter with lateral black spots; primaries below shining grey, with cupreous reflections, border whitish; costal borders crossed towards the apex by grey lines; a marginal series of black dots; fringe rather paler than above; secondaries whitish, with cupreous reflections; a grey discocellular dot; a brown discal line; a marginal series of black dots. Expanse of wings 1 inch 6 lines.

One specimen without antennæ.

APAMIIDÆ.

10. *Apamea vitiosa* (No. 14)

Apamea vitiosa, Butler, Proc. Zool. Soc. 1877, p. 384, pl xlii, fig. 3.

Two specimens, but without antennæ, January to March, on sugar.

11. *Agrotis admirationis* (Nos. 18 & 27).

Agrotis admirationis, Guenée, Ent. Month. Mag. v, p. 38 (1868).

The two specimens sent by Mr. Skellon show considerable variation from one another in tint, and in the distinctness of the ordinary dark lines on the primaries, still I believe them to be conspecific; M Guenée describes his species as having whitish fringes, but states at the same time that he has only seen one specimen in poor condition, the fringe of the primaries is pale sandy-yellow traversed by a greyish band, immediately followed by a line of the same colour, that of the secondaries is creamy-white traversed by a grey line   If, as I believe, I have rightly identified M. Guenée's species, it should come near *A. simplonia* of Europe

12. *Spœlotis cœrulea*.

Agrotis (Spœlotis) cœrulea, Guenée, Ent. Month. Mag. v, p. 38 (1868).

Two specimens have come in a somewhat shattered condition
and the collector's No has been lost; but the species is easily
recognizable from its peculiar coloration; the thorax and p-im-
aries being bluish-grey with whitish markings, and the secondaries pale sandy-yellowish with ill-defined greyish border and
whitish fringe; the abdomen has the general tint of the secondaries, and the entire under surface is of a pale sandy-yellow
colour with the upper discocellular veinlet of the primaries black
and the anterior legs ashy-grey above

13 *Spælotis inconstans*, n sp (No 23)

Primaries above greenish-grey, indistinctly speckled with
black; the ordinary lines ill-defined, formed by series of pale
hastate or lunate markings edged internally with black, and
connected here and there; the innermost line replaced by three
oblique independent zigzag lines, the outermost of which is
interrupted by the "orbicular" spot, the latter being bounded
internally by the central of the three lines; the discoidal spots
large, whitish, separated from one another and from the postmedian line by black-edged dusky intervening spots, a marginal
series of black dots; fringe sordid white, traversed by two slightly
undulated greyish-brown lines, secondaries shining fuliginous
brown with faint pinky reflections and diffused dusky border,
fringe sordid white with very indistinct grey intersecting line;
thorax grey, abdomen greyish-brown, under surface greyish-
white, speckled with grey scales towards the costal margins and
apices of the wings; the latter are also sericeous with blackish
discocellular >-shaped markings and indistinct traces of two
nearly parallel greyish discal lines; primaries with the discoidal
area slightly dusky; tarsi brown. Expanse of wings 1 inch
5 lines.

Var Primaries above pale smoky-grey, with scarcely a trace
of the dusky intervening spots between the discoidal spots and
postmedian line, otherwise similar to the type.

Excepting in the loss of their antennae these specimens have
sustained no injury.

14 *Chersotis inconspicua*, n sp (No. 31).

Primaries above greyish-brown speckled with grey; the ordinary lines blackish, but ill-defined, with the exception of the
submarginal one which is black, internally diffused, dentated in

the middle; costal margin black-spotted, discoidal and interno-median spots relieved by black margins, the interval between the 'orbicular" and "reniform" spots black, the former pyriform with grey centre, the latter of the typical shape enclosing an outline grey crescent; interno-median spot elliptical; basal third of fringe sandy whitish, remainder grey, traversed by two closely approximated pale lines; secondaries pale fuliginous brown, sericeous with cupreous reflections; fringe white traversed by two slender grey lines, thorax grey with one or two transverse slightly angulated dusky lines on the collar; front margin of head white; abdomen whitish slightly tinted with brown and speckled with grey; under surface of wings pale sericeous grey with dusky discocellular spots, basi-costal areas whitish; body below white, legs and sides of venter grey-speckled. Expanse of wings 1 inch 5 lines

One fairly perfect specimen; it is most nearly allied to *C. rect-angula*, of Europe.

15. *Mamestra griseipennis?* (No. 60).

Mamestra griseipennis, Felder, Reise der Nov. Lep. 4, pl. cix, fig. 22.

The specimen sent by Mr. Skellon agrees in pattern with Felder's figure, but in colour more nearly resembles *M. brassicæ*, whereas Felder's colouring is rather what one would expect to find in *Spælotis* than in *Mamestra*.

NOCTUIDÆ.

16. *Nitocris plusiata* (No. 24).

Hadena plusiata, Walker, Lep. Het. Suppl. iii, p 742 (1865).

Although, in accordance with my previous lists, I here adopt M Guenée's generic name, I much doubt the distinctness of his genus from *Graphiphora*; the three examples sent are in good condition, and represent the extreme varieties of the species.

ORTHOSIIDÆ.

17 *Dasycampa innocua* (No 28).

Cerastis innocua, Walker, Lep. Het. 15, p. 1710 (1858).

Orthosia communicata, Walker, Lep. Het. Suppl. iii, p 716, (1865).

One specimen.

HADENIDÆ

18. *Dianthæcia viridis,* n. sp. (No 32).

Primaries above sap-green spotted with brown, markings almost as in *D. carpophaga,* but all the lines white with black borders, the submarginal line broadly bordered externally with black, and not preceded by three hastate black spots as in *D. carpophaga* ; a marginal series of white-edged black dots; the reniform spot almost wholly white; secondaries smoky-brown, shining, purplish in certain lights; fringe sandy-yellowish at base, with grey central line and white tips; thorax sap-green varied with black; abdomen pale brown, whitish at base; under surface whitish, wings sericeous, grey-speckled with blackish discocellular and marginal dots; secondaries with an abbreviated blackish discal line, pectus reddish-brown in front; tarsi black-banded, brown below. Expanse of wings 1 inch 3 lines

Two specimens in good condition.

19. *Euplexia insignis*

Euplexia insignis, Walker, Lep. Het. Suppl. iii, p. 724 (1865).

· One specimen, imperfect, no No. attached.

20. *Euplexia mutans* (No. 7).

Hadena mutans, Walker, Lep. Het. vi, p 692 (1857).

A specimen without antennæ.

21. *Euplexia debilis* (No. 56).

Hadena debilis, Butler, Proc Zool Soc. 1877, p. 385. pl. xlii, fig 6.

A fragment.

22. *Hadena Skelloni,* n. sp (No. 65).

Primaries above laky-brown; a broad longitudinal internal sap-green streak, through which the submedian vein passes, and which is interrupted near the base by an oblique *B*-shaped black patch; an oblique abbreviated black dash near the base of interno-median area; discoidal and submedian spots bordered with pale green edged with black; discoidal area dark brown, "orbicular" spot of the same colour, slightly oblique and almost reniform, "reniform" spot pale laky-brown with a curved blackish internal stripe; submedian spot obtusely hexagonal, laky-brown; the two central lines slender, black, opposed, dentate-sinuate, not distinctly traceable above the median vein; submedian line black, with white inner border bounded within by sap-green and dark brown spots or. patches, irregularly dentated as in *H pisi*; the usual costal markings; secondaries pinky-brown, with diffused dusky border, enclosing an ill-defined abbreviated sinuated whitish streak; abdominal border broadly fringed with pinky-whitish, fringe of outer margin narrow, yellowish, tipped with dark brown, body rufous-brown, varied with pale greenish and whity-brown scales; collar with the usual bisinuated blackish line, wings below pale sericeous pinky-brown, with blackish discocellular spots and a brown discal line; primaries with a pale submarginal line; secondaries with an indistinct greyish submarginal streak; body below dull laky-brown, pectus slightly greyish venter with a lateral black line. Expanse of wings 1 inch 6 lines.

One example, slightly injured.

23. *Meterana pictula.*

Dianthæcia pictula, White, in Taylor's New Zealand, pl. 1, fig 3 (1855).

The only specimen of this beautiful green and rose-coloured *Noctua* was much broken and the No knocked off the pin.

XYLINIDÆ.

24 *Xylina inceptua* (No. 11).

Xylina inceptua, Walker, Lep. Het. xv, p. 1736 (1858).

Two specimens, representing the extremes of variation.

25 *Xylina ustistriga* (No. 3).

Xylina ustistriga, Walker, Lep. Het. xi, p 630 (1857).

A pair, in fairly good condition.

26 *Xylina?* sp. (No. 2).

The only specimen is too much damaged for certain identification, it may perhaps be a new species.

HELIOTHIDÆ.

27. *Heliothis conferta* (Nos. 36 and 37).

Heliothis conferta, Walker, Lep. Het. xi, p. 690 (1857).

Two specimens showing the extremes of colour, like most of the other *Noctuæ* they have lost their antennæ but are otherwise in good condition.

ERIOPIDÆ.

28. *Cosmodes elegans* (No. 61)

Phalæna elegans, Donovan, Ins New. Holl., pl 36, fig. 5 (1805).

One damaged specimen.

PLUSIIDÆ.

29. *Plusia verticillata* (No 9)

Plusia verticillata, Guenée, Noct. ii, p 344 (1862).

Two specimens.

AMPHIPYRIDÆ.

30. *Bityla thoracica* (No 22)

Bityla thoracica, Walker, Lep. Het. Suppl iii, p 869 (1865).

One fairly good specimen.

TOXOCAMPIDÆ.

31. *Toxocampa? fortis,* n sp. (No. 20).

Greyish-brown; primaries with a slightly irregular L-shaped black marking at the base; two widely separated black costal dots commencing the ordinary lines, which are slender, black and very irregularly angulated, external border pale, limited

internally by an ill-defined irregular black line; a marginal series
of little slender black lines; secondaries much darker than the
primaries and more decidedly sericeous, fringe white-spotted;
collar crossed by a bisinuated black stripe; abdomen dark grey
with brownish fringes and anal tuft; under surface pale brown;
wings sericeous, speckled with blackish, and with blackish discal
stripe; primaries greyish excepting at the borders; secondaries
with a large black discocellular lunule; legs above dusky,
banded with whitish.   Expanse of wings 1 inch 2 lines

One specimen.   I cannot be certain that it is a true *Toco-
campa*, as its palpi are broken.

OMMOTOPHORIDÆ

32. *Dasypodia selenophora* (No. 1).

Dasypodia selenophora, Guenée, Sp Gen. Lep. Noct. iii, p
175 (1852)

One fine specimen.   Mr Skellon says of it "Comes to sugar
in summer, also occasionally to light, and is very scarce some
summers; although I got four or five specimens last summer.
I think it comes from the Phormium swamps, as I have not seen
it in the bush "

ENNOMIDÆ.

33 *Sestra humeraria* (No 87).

Macaria humeraria, Walker, Lep. Het. xxiii, p 940 (1861).

One specimen somewhat injured.   Taken in the bush.

BOARMIIDÆ.

34. *Boarmia dejectaria* (No. 29).

Boarmia dejectaria, Walker, Lep. Het xxi, p. 391 (1860).

One damaged example.

35. *Pseudocoremia suavis*, ♂ .

Pseudocoremia suavis, Butler, Cist Ent. ii, p. 497, n. 33
(1879).

A good example, but unfortunately without its No.

36. *Pseudocoremia indistincta* ♂ (No 85).

Pseudocoremia indistincta, Butler, Proc. Zool. Soc. 1877, p. 394, n. 78; pl. xliii, fig. 8.

One example without antennæ.

37. *Pseudocoremia productata*, n. sp

♂ *Pseudocoremia productata* ♂ , Butler, Cist. Ent. ii, p. 497, (1879).

♀ Only differs from the male in the greyer and less defined markings of the upper surface of the primaries; in the latter character it more nearly resembles dull examples of the female of *P productata*. Expanse of wings 1 inch 4 lines.

One specimen without antennæ, unnumbered ; possibly mistaken for the female of the preceding species, which its male much resembles; indeed the species of this genus either run very close to each other, or else are subject to strange and unusual variations of pattern. *P. productata* proves to be the female of *P. fragosata* of Felder.

38. *Pseudocoremia productata* (No. 86)

♀ *Larentia productata*, Walker, Lep. Het. xxiv, p. 1197, n. 69 (1862).
♂ *Selidosema? fragosata*, Felder, Reise der Nov. Lep. v, pl. cxxxi, fig. 20.

One female example, a good deal injured.

ACIDALIIDÆ.

39. *Asthena subpurpureata* (No. 89).

Asthena subpurpureata, Walker, Lep. Het. xxvi, p. 1588 (1862).

Three specimens, all more or less damaged.

40. *Asthena risata* (No. 83).

Asthena risata, Guenée, Phal i, p. 438, n. 725.

One perfect and two broken specimens; this species is new to New Zealand.

41. *Acidalia undosata* (No 45)

Cidaria undosata, Felder, Reise der Nov. Lep 5, pl cxxviii, fig. 2.

Two specimens, slightly broken. It is " common in the bush "

42. *Acidalia rubraria* (No. 82)

Ptychopoda? rubraria, Doubleday, Dieff. New Zeal. App. p. 286, n. 12 (1843)

Three specimens, all more or less damaged

FIDONIIDÆ

43. *Selidosema ægrota* (No. 84)

Selidosema ægrota, Butler, Cist. Ent. ii, p. 499, n. 43 (1879)

Two specimens.

LARENTIIDÆ.

44. *Larentia? heliacaria* (No 81).

Coremia heliacaria, Guenée, Phal. ii, p. 420, n. 1583 (1857).

Two broken examples

45. *Larentia subductata* (No. 88).

Larentia subductata, Walker, Lep. Het xxiv, p. 1198, n. 71 (1862).

Two fragments of specimens

46 *Larentia inverata* (No. 64).

Larentia inverata, Walker, Lep Het. xxiv, p 1199, n. 73 (1862).

Part of a specimen   " Rare, at sugar."

47. *Larentia punctilineata?* ♀ (No. 12).

Larentia punctilineata, Walker, Lep. Het. xxiv, p. 1202, n. 79 (1862)

One specimen, somewhat rubbed.

48. Laientia megaspilata (No 69).

Laientia *megaspilata*, Walker, Lep. Het. xxiv, p. 1198, n. 70 (1862).

Two specimens without antennæ.

49. Laientia nehata.

Culaiia *nehata*, Felder, Reise der Nov. Lep. v, pl. cxxxi, fig. 6.

A fragment, without a No.; probably taken for a vaiiety of the preceding species.

50. Helastia charybdis (No. 53).

Helastia charybdis, Butler, Cist. Ent. ii, p. 503, n 58 (1879).

Two fragments of specimens. It occurs " in Manuka scrub (*Leptospeimum scoparium*)."

51. Coiemia rosearia (No. 72).

Cidaria *iosearia*, Doubleday, Dieff. New Zeal. App, p. 285, n. 119 (1843).

Two broken specimens.

52. Coiemia sp. (No 75).

Probably an undescribed species, but in too bad condition for satisfactory recognition " Caught in the bush."

53. Coremia squalida (No. 94).

Coremia *squalida*, Butler, Cist. Ent. ii, p. 505, n. 63 (1879).

One fairly good example.

54. Coremia casta, n. sp. (No. 90).

Allied to the preceding species, but in the pattern of the primaiies reminding one of *Laientia* (*L. parallelaiia*); wings above white, slightly yellowish on the veins; primaries with

three narrow basal bands, a broad central belt and two narrow
external bands, all with more or less undulated margins, dark
brown traversed by pale undulated lines ; a slender brown line
on each side of the central belt ; a black discocellular stigma ;
a marginal series of linear black dots in pairs; secondaries grey,
crossed in the middle by four externally white bordered dusky
lines in pairs, the third line dentate-sinuate and dotted with
black ; a submarginal dentate-sinuate white line, body greyish-
brown, banded with white; under surface whity-brown, with
slightly yellowish veins ; the markings of the upper surface
dimly visible and uniform on all the wings, so that the whole
basal area to the centre of the disc is greyish, and a band of
the same colour crosses the wings half-way between the latter
and the outer margin ; discocellular and marginal dots black.
Expanse of wings 1 inch 1 line

One specimen in recognizable condition, and a second much
shattered.

55. *Camptogramma subochraria* (Nos. 44 and 84).

Aspilates ? subochraria, Doubleday, Dieff. New Zeal. App.,
p. 285, n. 114 (1843).

Three fair specimens Common in the bush.

56. *Phibalapteryx verriculata* (No. 55).

Cidaria verriculata, Felder, Reise der Nov. Lep. v, pl. cxxxi,
fig. 20.

Two fragments. " In the bush at dusk."

57. *Phibalapteryx undulifera*.

Phibalapteryx undulifera, Butler, Cist. Ent. ii, p 506, n. 66
(1879).

One fair example. not numbered.

58. *Phibalapteryx gobiata* (No. 42).

Cidaria (Phibalapteryx) gobiata, Felder, Reise der Nov. Lep.
v, pl. cxxxi, fig 2

Two specimens.

59. *Cidaria beata* (No. 47).

Cidaria beata, Butler, Proc. Zool. Soc 1877. p. 397; pl. xliii, fig. 6.

A fragment only of this beautiful species arrived.

60. *Cidaria? inclarata* (No. 46).

Cidaria inclarata, Walker, Lep Het. xxv, p. 1411, n. 75 (1862).

Three good specimens. "Common in the bush," *W.S.*

61. *Elvia glaucata* (No. 52)

Elvia glaucata, Walker, Lep. Het. xxv, p 1431, n 1 (1862).

Three examples, but all more or less injured. "In Manuka scrub," *W.S.*

The remaining *Geometrites* are all too much broken for certain identification.

HYPENIDÆ.

62. *Rhapsa scotosialis* (No. 21).

Rhapsa scotosialis, Walker, Lep. Het. Suppl. iv, p. 1150, (1850).

Two specimens, one of which is much damaged.

PYRALIDÆ

63. *Pyralis farinalis* (No. 121).

Phalæna-Pyralis farinalis, Linneus, Syst Nat. p. 880, n 327.

One fair specimen of this widely distributed European species M Skellon says of it "No. 121 I think must be an English naturalized one, it is caught in houses."

64 *Deana paronalis* (No. 49).

Scopula? paronalis, Walker, Lep Het. xviii, p 797, n 52 (1859).

One example, slightly injured. "Common in the bush," *W.S.*

ASOPIIDÆ.

65. *Isopteryx nitidalis* (No. 44).

Isopteryx nitidalis, Walker, Lep. Het. Suppl. iv, p. 1317 (1865).

One damaged example; it was previously only recorded from Australia. "In the bush at dusk," *W.S.*

STENIIDÆ.

66. *Diasemia grammalis* (No. 9).

Diasemia grammalis, Doubleday, Dieff. New Zeal. App., p. 287, n. 124 (1843).

Two examples. "Came to light one sultry night in December," *W S.*

HYDROCAMPIDÆ.

67. *Paraponyx nitens*, n. sp. (No. 40).

Primaries above shining, bronzy-brown; a basal transverse stripe, a broad belt before the middle, not reaching the costal margin, a spot beyond the cell; an irregular elbowed discal stripe, an irregular marginal line and a central line through the fringe silvery-white; fringe tipped with greyish-white; second-aries snowy-white; a streak on the median vein, the extremities of the subcostal and median branches, a curved submarginal stripe and a slender marginal line bronzy-brown; body fuliginous brown banded with white; under surface white, a feeble indication of the brown markings of the primaries. Expanse of wings 8 lines

Two specimens, slightly broken. "Common in the bush," *W S*, No 124, probably belongs to the *Hydrocampidæ*, but the two specimens are too much rubbed for certain definition.

BOTYDIDÆ.

68. *Scopula flavidalis* (No. 123).

Margaritia flavidalis, Doubleday, Dieff. New Zeal App., p. 288, n. 125 (1843).

One poor specimen,

69. *Scopula quadralis* (No. 48).

Margaritia quadralis, Doubleday, Dieff. New Zeal. App., p. 288, n. 126 (1843).

One broken example. "Common in the bush," *W.S.*

70. *Mecyna deprivalis* (Nos. 71 and 80).

Mecyna deprivalis, Walker, Lep. Het. xix, p. 806, n. 7 (1859)
Mecyna ornithopteralis, var., Walker, l.c., p. 807, n. 8 (1859).

Three injured examples, each differing from the other and from the specimens noted by Walker in tint, but all agreeing in their main characters with the Indian species, and differing but little from the European *M. polygonalis.*

·SCOPARIIDÆ.

71. *Scoparia diptheralis* (No. 106).

Scoparia diptheralis, Walker, Lep. Het Suppl. iv, p. 1501 (1865).

Two damaged specimens.

There is a fragment of a species which looks like my *S. altivolans,* and numbered (136), but I cannot be sure of its identification, it may perhaps not even belong to the family.

72. *Scoparia minusculalis* (No 108)

Scoparia minusculalis, Walker, Lep. Het. Suppl. iv, p. 1503 (1865).

Two fragments. I much regret the condition of these specimens as the species appears to be rare, we have much need of specimens in good condition.

73. *Scoparia indistinctalis* (No. 120).

Hypochalcia indistinctalis, Walker, Lep. Het. xxvii, p. 48, n. 23 (1863).

Two specimens. This species is the *S. epuncula* of Knaggs

PHYCIDÆ.

74. *Nephopteryx subditella* (No. 130).

Nephopteryx subditella, Walker, Lep. Het. Suppl. v, p. 1720 (1866).

A fragment.

75. *Gadira acerella* (No. 84).

Gadira acerella, Walker, Lep. Het. Suppl. v, p. 1742 (1866).

A fragment.

CRAMBIDÆ.

76 *Crambus flexuosellus* (No. 105).

Crambus flexuosellus, Doubleday, Dieff. New Zeal. App., p. 289 (1843).

One broken specimen.

77. *Crambus vulgaris* (No. 103).

Crambus vulgaris, Butler, Proc. Zool. Soc. 1877, p. 400, n. 110; pl. xliii, fig. 7.

Two broken specimens

78. *Crambus trivirgatus* (No. 8).

Crambus trivirgatus, Felder, Reise der Nov Lep. v, pl. cxxxvii, fig 29.

One fairly good and one much injured specimen. "Came to light on a sultry night in December," *W.S.*

79. *Chilo simplex* (No 102).

Chilo simplex, Butler, Proc. Zool. Soc., 1877, p. 400, n. 111; pl. xliii, fig. 12.

One fairly good and two broken specimens

80. *Eromene lepidella* (No. 41).

Eromene lepidella, Walker, Lep. Het Suppl. v, p. 1761 (1868).

Two broken specimens. "Common in the bush," *W.S.*, but rare in European collections.

81. *Eromene auriscriptella,* (No. 109).

Eromene auriscriptella, Walker, Lep. Het. xxx, p. 976 (1864).

One broken specimen. "Caught in the bush," *W.S.*

TORTRICIDÆ.

82. *Pædisca excessana* (No. 125).

Teras excessana, Walker, Lep. Het. xxviii, p. 303, n. 71 (1863).

Two fragments.

83. *Pædisca biguttana* (No. 118).

Teras biguttana, Walker, Lep. Het. xxviii, p. 305, n. 76 (1863).

Two fairly good specimens.

84. *Teras cuneigera,* n. sp. (No. 16).

Primaries above whitish ash-colour, with a large cuneiform costal patch occupying about a third of the wing, and extending from basal third to apex, blackish, speckled upon the costal margin with black, and indistinctly spotted with rust-brown; external area slightly dusky and indistinctly striated with blackish dots; all the margins dotted with black, a subbasal angulated grey line; secondaries pale sericeous brown spotted with grey, fringe whitish; head and thorax grey, abdomen pale brown; primaries below pale sericeous greyish-brown, with slight bronzy reflections, costal border dotted with black; secondaries whitish with slight bronzy reflections, mottled with greyish-brown; body below whitish. Expanse of wings 10 lines.

One fair specimen and a fragment of a second.

85. *Cacæcia vilis.*

Cacæcia vilis, Butler, Proc. Zool Soc. 1877, p. 402, n. 119; pl. xlii, fig. 15.

One fairly good example, but without its No.

TINEIDÆ.

86. *Tinea rectella* (No. 134).

Tinea rectella, Walker, Lep. Het. xxviii, p. 482 (1863).

Two specimens, of which one is broken.

GELECHIIDÆ.

87. *Gelechia conspicuella*.

Gelechia conspicuella, Walker, Lep. Het. xxix, p. 651 (1864).

One specimen, but without its No.

88. *Gelechia seduta*.

Primaries above pale brown, mottled with blackish; a whitish bordered blackish stigma; a series of black dots along the outer margin; secondaries grey, changing in certain lights to silver, fringes golden-brown; body pale sericeous brown; legs and under surface of body whity-brown with silver reflections; wings below greyish, silvery in certain lights and with golden-brown fringes.   Expanse of wings $7\frac{1}{2}$ lines.

One specimen without a No.

There are two fragments of what Lord Walsingham kindly determined for me to be either an *Ypsolophus* or a *Nothris;* it seems nearer to the former, but as even the better example has lost both palpi and antennæ it is impossible to identify it with any certainty.

89. *Œcophora flavidella* (No. 101).

Gelechia flavidella, Walker, Lep. Het. xxix, p. 655, n. 377 (1864).

One specimen and a fragment.   "In the bush," *W.S.*

90. *Œcophora limbata*, n. sp. (No. 111).

Fuliginous brown, wings with pale golden-brown fringes; primaries with bright crocus-yellow costal border; head, collar and tegulæ crocus-yellow; under surface sericeous; primaries brown, greyish towards the inner margin, costal margin stramineous, fringe grey in certain lights; secondaries creamy-white, slightly greyish towards the base; fringe white; body below silvery, anterior tibiæ yellow. Expanse of wings 8 lines.

Two specimens, one nearly perfect.

91. *Æcophora picarella* (No. 13).

Æcophora picarella, Walker, Lep. Het. xxix, p. 699 (1864).

One example and a fragment of a second.

92. *Tingena bifaciella* (No. 93).

Tingena bifaciella, Walker, Lep. Het. xxix, p. 810 (1864).

One specimen and a fragment of another.

GLYPHIPTERYGIDÆ.

93. *Glyphipteryx bifaciella* (No. 97).

Gelechia bifaciella, Walker, Lep. Het. xxix, p 657 (1864).

Two specimens.

GRACILARIIDÆ.

94. *Gracilaria rutilans*, n. sp (No. 92).

Primaries above with the costal two-thirds metallic brassyellow, slightly greenish in certain lights, internal or dorsal third, a spot at basal third and the outer margin fiery cupreous, spotted with deep ultramarine blue, these spots are partially confluent along the internal border so as to produce a longitudinal irregular streak; fringe rosy on outer margin, rest of fringe and secondaries greyish brown; frons and base of palpi opaline white, remainder of palpi fiery cupreous internally but with the terminal joint blue-black externally; top of head and thorax cupreous flecked with purple; abdomen grey, with pale golden metallic hair at the base; primaries below pale cupreous mottled with gold, which becomes dull brown in certain lights; apex minutely tipped with blackish; fringe of outer margin rosy, changing towards the apex to orange, remainder of fringe greyish-brown; costal margin cream coloured; secondaries greyish-brown; pectus white, legs partly ferruginous, venter silvery Expanse of wings 6½ lines.

One specimen of this beautiful little species has escaped with only the loss of part of an antenna, and a slight abrasion towards the base of the secondaries   " Caught in the Bush," *W.S.*

BOOCARA, n. gen.

Allied to *Gracilaria*, wings of the same form and character; head considerably broader, shorter, smooth and shining; palpi unusually long, smooth, arched and standing on each side of the head like the horns of an ox, their length is nearly twice that of the depth of the head.   Type *B. Skelloni.*

95. *Boocara Skelloni*, n. sp. (No. 98).

Primaries above ochreous, fringe slightly greyish, costal margin slightly tinted with shining pink; secondaries silvery whitish, with pale greyish-brown fringes; head, collar and thorax pearly white, indistinctly banded with gold, abdomen silvery-white, banded with gold; primaries below shining golden-brown, minutely speckled with grey, fringe as above; secondaries silvery, slightly golden towards the apex; fringes pale greyish-brown; body below wholly pearly-white.   Expanse of wings $7\frac{1}{2}$ lines.

One example nearly perfect and two much broken; this species, in general coloration, somewhat reminds one of *Parasia.*

ELACHISTIDÆ.

96. *Laverna phragmitella* (No 126).

Laverna phragmitella, Stainton, Cat Suppl. iv, 1 B, p. 238.

Two broken examples.

I have to thank Lord Walsingham for assistance in the location of some of the *Tineina* and *Tortrices* in this paper.

Descriptions of new Coleoptera belonging to the families
PSEPHENIDÆ *and* CYPHONIDÆ; by CHAS. O. WATERHOUSE.

Recently I have met with a new species of the genus
Psephenus, below described; and as the question of the relationship between the *Parnidæ* and *Cyphonidæ* through *Psephenus*
and *Eubria* is very interesting, I take the opportunity of
describing three new genera, which I consider undoubtedly
belong the *Eubriinæ*, but which have much in common
with *Tychepsephus*, placed by myself in the *Psephenidæ*.
These three new genera, as well as most of the species of *Scirtes*
here described, were received by the British Museum from
Mr. Bowring.

Psephenus Darwinii, n. sp.

Fuscus, sat nitidus, subtilissime pilosus; thoracis angulis
posticis acutis, pedibus sordide testaceis   Long. 2½ lin.

Closely resembles *P. Lecontei*, but is at once distinguished by
the thorax being broadest at the posterior angles, which are
moreover very acute.   The apical joint of the maxillary palpi
much smaller than in *P. Lecontei*   Thorax gently convex, very
finely and very closely punctured, bisinuate at the base.   Elytra
densely and finely punctured, with traces of three or four obtuse
costæ on each.
Hab. Rio Janeiro.

A single example taken by Mr. Charles Darwin in May,
1832, during the voyage of H.M.S. Beagle; it has the following
note respecting it, "habits the same as *Elmis*, living under
stones in running water."

SCHINOSTETHUS, n. gen.

General form of *Eubria*   Lobes of the maxillæ slender,
acuminate, the outer one twice as long as the inner; the
inner lobe more penicillate; maxillary palpi rather large,
penultimate joint cylindrical, one-third longer than broad; the

apical joint not quite twice as long as the previous joint, triangular, emarginate at the apex, the outer angle rather more
prominent than the inner one. Apical joint of the labial palpi
subparallel, truncate, or *very* slightly emarginate at the apex.
Basal joint of the antennæ* obconic, the second round, the
third elongate, the fourth joint one-third shorter than the third,
broader at its apex, the following joints of about the same
length as the fourth, but with the internal angle much more
angularly produced. Prosternum produced posteriorly between
the coxæ, gradually acuminate. Mesosternum horizontal, a
little longer than broad, with an impression in front for the
reception of the prosternal process. Abdomen with five segments, the margins of the first four segments straight, the
apical segment semicircular. Legs slender; tarsi long and
slender, the second, third and fourth joints subequal, about
half the length of the first, the fifth joint as long as the three
basal joints together; claws a little dilated at their base. Body
below finely pilose.

Very close to *Eubria*, but without impressed lines on the
elytra, with more simple palpi, &c.

Schinostethus nigricornis, n. sp.

Ferrugineus, supra rufo-ferrugineus, opacus, convexus; antennis nigris, thorace basi subtiliter serrato-marginata. Long.
2 lin

Very convex, rusty yellowish-red. Antennæ black, except
the two basal joints. Forehead with a slight longitudinal impressed line. Thorax very convex, semicircular in outline,
truncate in front, when seen from above, twice as broad at the
base as in front; arcuate at the sides, with a blunt oblique impression at the base, on each side of the middle; the base is
nearly straight, only very slightly sinuate on each side; the
angles are nearly right angles, the whole basal margin is very
finely crenulate, and there is similar crenulation along the base
of the elytra and scutellum. The scutellum is nearly an equilateral triangle. Elytra broadest rather behind the middle,
together obtusely rounded at the apex, the lateral margins near
the shoulder a little impressed above. The metathoracic episterna are rather strongly and moderately thickly punctured.
All the underside of the insect is exceedingly finely pilose.

---

* The specimens in the Museum may be females.

The upper surface of the thorax, scutellum and elytra is clothed with a dull film, somewhat of the nature of that which clothes the species of *Livus,* and to which the term *furfuosus* is usually applied.

Hab N. China (J. C Bowring, Esq.).

HOMŒOGENUS, n. gen.

Apical joint of the maxillary palpi elongate, subparallel, flattened towards the apex, which is truncate or very slightly arcuate. The apical joint of the labial palpi is rather longer than broad, obliquly arcuate at the apex Prosternum produced between the coxæ, very acute at the apex. Mesosternum sloping down, almost hollowed out between the coxæ Tarsi slender, the fourth joint much smaller than the preceding joint. Second and third segments of the abdomen very slightly sinuous at the sides.

Very close to *Schinostethus,* from which I have separated it, on account of the apex of the apical joint of the maxillary palpi being arcuate instead of emarginate; the mesosternum is sloping and the fourth joint of the tarsi very small. The specimen is possibly a· female.

Homœogenus punctatum, n. sp

Nigrum, convexum, nitidum, subtillissime pilosum; antennarum basi, femoribusque plus minusve flavo-testaceis, thorace elytrisque sat fortiter punctatis Long. 1½ lin

General form of *Eubria palustris,* the antennæ nearly the same, but with the joints a little more elongate; the two basal joints pale Thorax as in that species, but strongly and rather thickly punctured, less thickly on the disc; there is an impression on each side of the middle of the base, and the anterior angles, which are yellow, are also impressed above; the posterior angles are more rounded than in *E. palustris*, all the basal margin has the same fine crenulate appearance as in *Schinostethus,* but not so distinctly visible Scutellum subequilateral, moderately thickly punctured Elytra strongly and thickly punctured Anterior border of the prosternum, the coxæ and femora pale yellow; the posterior femora dusky yellow; tarsi fuscous

Hab. China (J. C. Bowring, Esq.).

COPHÆSTHETUS, n. gen.

General form of *Eubria* but a little more oblong. ♂ Antennæ with the fifth to tenth joints with the inner apical angle produced into a long thick branch; the eleventh joint very long, having the form of the branch of the tenth. Apical joint of the maxillary palpi elongate, subparalled, the apex flattened, very slightly arcuate, almost truncate. The apical joint of the labial palpi is similar, but less elongate. Prosternal process a little enlarged at its apex, obtuse. Mesosternum horizontal, emarginate in front to receive the prosternal process. The rest as in *Schinostethus*.

The form of the apical joint of the palpi, and the blunt prosternal process are the characters upon which I separate this from *Schinostethus;* the difference in the structure of the antennæ may be only sexual.

Cophæthetus opacus, n. sp.

Oblongus, convexus, opacus, fuscus; thoracis lateribus ferrugineis, prosterno pedibusque flavo-ferrugineis. Long. 1½ lin.

Antennæ with the two basal joints pitchy. All the upper surface of the insect opaque, with very short close pubescence, only visible with a high magnifying power. Thorax nearly as in *Eubria palustris*, but with the sides rather more arcuate, and more semicircularly emarginate in front; there is a slight impression on each side of the middle of the base; the posterior angles are a trifle less than right angles; the basal margin has the same serrate appearance as in *Schinostethus* but in a less marked manner. Scutellum nearly an equilateral triangle. Elytra dark fuscous, the fine pubescence rather paler; the surface posteriorly is finely vermiculate, the pubescence shows itself particularly in two narrow curved lines on the back, arising in the middle of the base, and turning towards the suture of the elytra.

Hab. Java (J. C. Bowring, Esq).

A single example only, not in perfect condition. I have, however, described it on account of its great interest, as having the antennæ branched as in some *Cyphonidæ*, but undoubtedly closely allied to *Schinostethus*, which closely approaches *Tychepsephus*, placed by me in the *Psephenidæ*. I cannot, however, alter my opinion as to the position of *Tychepsephus*, which has the prosternum produced anteriorly, so as partly to cover the lower part of the head as in *Parnus*,—a character wanting in *Schinostethus*.

Scirtes nigricans, n. sp.

Fusco-niger, breviter ovalis, convexus, griseo-pubescens, creberrime punctulatus, tibiis fuscis. Long 1⅓ lin.

This is very close to *S. hemisphæricus.* It is the same blackish colour, and is nearly the same form. It is, however, smaller and shorter, and has the longer spur to the posterior tibia about two-thirds the length of the basal joint of the tarsus The punctuation appears the same throughout The antennæ are sordid testaceous, and the apex of the femora and the tibiæ are the same colour or pale fuscous.

Hab. China (J. C. Bowring, Esq.).

A specimen marked "Java" has the legs nearly the same colour as the rest of the insect

Scirtes elegans, n sp.

Flavo-testaceus, flavo-pilosus; capite piceo, elytris basi maculisque sex piceo-nigris. Long. 1 lin.

Var. Fuscus; elytrorum disco sordide flavo.

Much flatter and rather narrower than *S. hemisphæricus.* Antennæ dusky towards the apex. Thorax pale yellow, shining, not quite so convex as in *hemisphæricus*, rather more transverse, the base regularly arcuate and not bowed out in the middle; the punctuation as on the disc of *hemisphæricus*, equally distributed throughout. The elytra are very finely, regularly and delicately punctured; the punctures are perhaps not less numerous than in *hemisphænicus*, but being finer they appear a little less close; there is a fuscous band at the base; a trapezoidal spot on the margin, about the middle, whence the margin is fuscous to the apex, where it dilates, the fuscous colour then ascends the suture for a short distance and forms a triangular spot, from the outer angle of which a fine line is emitted to join with the original lateral spot, the suture itself is pale Abdomen pitchy.

Hab. Penang (J. C Bowring, Esq.).

Var. With the two specimens above described is a third, which at first sight appeared to be a distinct species, but which I nevertheless believe only to be a variety. It differs in having the whole upper surface dark fuscous, with the exception of a sordid yellow patch on the disc of the elytra.

Scirtes maculatus, n. sp.

Piccus, nitidus; elytris ochraceis, singulis maculis quinque piceo-nigris   Long. 1½ lin.

Form of *S hemisphæricus*, but a trifle broader across the middle   Thorax the same as in that species, with not very close but distinct punctuation. Elytra yellow, the punctuation like that in *hemisphæricus* but not quite so close   Each elytron has five rather large blackish-brown spots: one near the middle of the base ; an oblong one close to the suture, attached by one angle to the basal spot, and united at its apical angle with a large round spot on the margin ; there is an ovate spot close to the apex, more or less joined to a transverse spot at the apical margin.

Hab. India.

Scirtes quadrimaculatus, n. sp.

Oblongo-ovalis, nitidus, piceus, fulvo-flavo-pilosus ; elytris rufo-piceis, maculis quatuor nigris notatis.   Long 2½ lin.

Regularly oblong-ovate, moderately convex, dark pitchy. Antennæ black, a little pitchy at the base.   Thorax not quite so transverse as in *S. hemisphæricus*, the anterior angles a little more directed forwards; the punctuation very close, but not crowded, and although fine is very distinct when the pubescence is removed   The elytra are pitchy-red, clothed with yellowish fawn-coloured pubescence; the punctuation is like that on the thorax, but rather stronger; rather behind the middle there is a large quadrangular black spot, touching the margin, but not reaching the suture; and at the apex there is another spot, more rounded, also touching the margin but not the suture   The hind femora are dark pitchy, the impressions above at the apex are rather deep, and there is a deep incision near the apex at the posterior margin ; the longer spur to the tibia is about two-thirds the length of the basal joint of the tarsus.

Hab Burmah (J. C. Bowring, Esq.).

Scirtes costulatus, n. sp.

Oblongo-ovalis, pallide piceus, griso-flavo-pubescens; antennis nigris, elytris singulis costis tribus obtusis.   Long 2¾ lin.

This species has somewhat the appearance of *Cyphon coarctatus*, but is rather flatter and relatively a trifle broader.   The antennæ are black with the three basal joints ferruginous.   The thorax is as in *S. hemisphæricus*, but rather less convex, very thickly and moderately strongly punctured. The elytra are very thickly and moderately strongly punctured towards the base; towards the apex the punctuation is finer; and the subapical region near the suture is highly polished and very sparingly punctured; each elytron has four very obtuse, only slightly raised ridges; the first terminates in the subapical smooth part; the second and third are continued nearly to the apex, the space between them slightly concave, the fourth, not very distinct near the shoulder, becomes much stronger posteriorly, and again diminishes at the apex.

Hab Penang (J. C. Bowring, Esq.).

Scirtes æqualis, n. sp.

Pallide piceus; antennis nigris, elytris sordide flavis, creberrime punctatis. Long. 2⅔ lin.

This species resembles the last; the elytra, however, are paler yellow, and the costæ can scarcely be traced, the punctuation is very close and rather strong, and is nearly equal all over. The antennæ are black, with the three basal joints pale The larger spur to the hind tibia is strong, about two-thirds the length of the first tarsal joint, curved at its apex

Hab. Borneo (Wallace).

Scirtes uniformis, n sp.

Ovalis, nitidus, flavus, subtiliter pubescens. Long. 2¼ lin.

Very shining, uniform sordid yellow Relatively narrower than *S. æqualis*, and more narrowed posteriorly. The thorax is a little narrower, convex; the punctuation is moderately strong, moderately thick, but not at all crowded, much less thick than in *æqualis*. The elytra are decidedly more attenuated posteriorly, evenly convex, not costate; moderately strongly and thickly punctured, the punctures not so crowded as in *æqualis*. The longer spur to the hind tibia is more slender than in that species.

Hab. Borneo (Wallace).

Scirtes irregularis, n. sp.

Sat depressus, flavus, nitidus, brevissime pilosus, guttis numerosis piceis adspersus. Long. 1½ lin., lat. 1¼.

This species is of peculiar form. It is broadest behind the middle of the elytra, narrowed anteriorly; somewhat depressed, but the elytra are rather more convex behind the middle. Head with two pale brown spots between the eyes. Thorax very transverse, not much convex, not nearly so much deflexed at the sides and anterior angles as in *S. hemisphæricus*; with some dusky marks and spots, the punctuation is very fine and extremely close; the sides are almost rectilinear, or only in the slightest degree arcuate; the base is nearly straight at the scutellum, slightly oblique on each side of it The scutellum is punctured in the same way as the thorax.   Elytra each with about five lines of small, round, brown dots; the surface is rather uneven, the scutellar region is impressed, and about the middle of each elytron may be traced two short obscure costæ; the punctuation is irregular, rather strong and moderately close, but the punctures are uneven in form; the margin seen from the side, is rather unusually sinuous about the middle, as if to give freedom of action to the hind femora.   The longer spur to the hind tibia is about half the length of the basal joint of the tarsi.

Hab. Java (J. C. Bowring, Esq.).   •

Scutes sericeus, n. sp.

Elliptico-ovalis, leviter convexus, pallide piceus, flavo-pubescens. capite thoraceque piceis, elytris æqualibus, creberrime punctatis Long. 2 lin.

Rather narrow and regularly elliptical ovate.   Thorax as in *S. hemispæricus*, and the punctuation is similar except that it is much stronger.   The scutellum is thickly and finely punctured. Elytra long, attenuated very gradually towards the apex, evenly convex, the punctuation is even, very close (but not crowded), and moderately strong   The head and thorax are pitchy; the elytra are pale pitchy-brown, becoming yellowish towards the apex   The longer spur of the hind tibia is about two-thirds the length of the basal joint of the tarsi.

Hab. Siam (J. C. Bowring, Esq.).·

This species is allied most nearly to *S. æqualis*, but is much more elliptical in form and narrower.

Scutes marginatus, n sp. ·

Elliptico-ovalis, depressus, nitidus, piceus, pubescens; elytrorum disco, corpore subtus pedibusque sordide flavis.   Long. 1¾ lin.

Most nearly resembles *S. serceus* in form, but is more depressed and has the elytra more attenuated towards the apex. Antennæ blackish, with the three basal joints yellow. Head and thorax pitchy; the latter paler at the lateral margins, rather distinctly lobed in the middle of the base; anterior angles deflexed, not at all prominent, rather obtuse; the punctuation on the disc is half as close again as in *S. hemisphæricus*, and distinctly stronger; but towards the sides it is much more delicate. The elytra are pale pitchy-yellow, with a broad margin of dark brown; the punctuation is very close but not crowded, moderately fine, and not well defined; as compared with that in *hemisphæricus*, the punctuation is a little less close and distinctly less strong.

Hab. India.

Scirtes elongatus, n. sp

Elongatus, fusco-piceus, nitidus, creberrime punctulatus, corpore subtus pedibusque pallide piceis   Long. 1¾ lin.

More elongate, and more parallel at the sides than any other species known to me, except the following new species. It is perhaps most nearly allied to *S serceus*, but is narrower and straighter at the sides. The punctuation of the thorax is very similar to that of the *elytra* in *S. hemisphæricus*, but is a trifle less strong, and a little more clearly defined. The punctuation of the elytra is a little stronger than that of the thorax, and the punctures are not quite so close together. The pubescence is grey

Hab. Hong Kong (J. C. Bowring, Esq.)

Scirtes difficilis, n. sp.

Elongatus, flavescens, nitidus, creberrime punctulatus, elytrorum apice infuscato.   Long. 1½ lin.

This species closely resembles *S. elongatus* in form. It differs in being pale pitchy-yellow, with the apex of the elytra fuscous; in having the anterior angles of the thorax acute and less turned down, the sides rather less strongly punctured, and the base less distinctly lobed in the middle. The punctuation of the elytra is the same. The antennæ are dusky except at the extreme base.

Hab Penang (J. C. Bowring, Esq.).

Scirtes pallidus, n. sp.

Pallide picco-flavus, nitidus, griseo-pubescens, subtiliter crebre punctulatus. Long. 1⅓ lin.

Somewhat the form of *S. hemisphæricus*, but with less prominent shoulders, and with the elytra more attenuated towards the apex. Pale pitchy-yellow, with fine yellowish-grey pubescence. The anterior angles of the thorax are not so much deflexed and are not at all prominent, and the base is more regularly arcuate; the punctuation is fine and very delicate, and distinctly closer. The punctuation of the elytra is the same as that of the thorax.

Hab. Penang (J. C. Bowring, Esq.).

This species has much the appearance of *Rhizobius litura*.

There is a specimen from Siam which differs from the Penang example above described, in being relatively a little shorter, more rounded at the sides, and more obtuse at the apex of the elytra. The punctuation of the elytra appears a little stronger. This may prove to be distinct from *S. pallidus*, but I consider it better to regard it as a variety until I have more specimens for examination.

Scirtes pellucidus, n. sp.

Flavo-testaceus, nitida, pallide pubescens. Long. 1⅘ lin.

Very close to *S pallidus*, but a little longer, and a little more elongate. The punctuation of the thorax is like that on the disc of the thorax of *S. hemisphæricus*, (less distinct towards the sides), not so fine as in *pallidus*. The punctuation of the elytra is closer and much stronger than in *pallidus*; it is less strong and rather closer than in *hemisphæricus*, but resembles it in character.

Hab. Java (J. C. Bowring, Esq).

Scirtes lutescens, n. sp.

Flavo-testaceus, pallide pubescens. Long. 1 lin.

Very pale yellow, depressed, rather broad elliptical-ovate; the head, underside of the body, and posterior femora very pale pitchy. The thorax is the same form as in *S pellucidus*, but the punctuation is much closer (rather irregular), and much stronger, close but not crowded, except here and there, and the punctures' are as if made with a blunt point. The elytra are rather broad, but arcuately attenuated towards the apex; the punctuation (not forgetting the different sizes of the insects) is relatively the same as in *S. hemisphæricus.*

Hab. Java (J. C. Bowring, Esq.).

Scirtes exoletus, n. sp.

Oblongo-ovalis, depressus, nitidus piceo-flavus; thorace maculis duabus basalibus piceis, scutello flavo. Long 2½ lin.

Rather depressed, sordid yellow. Head densely punctured, forehead with a shallow oblique impression on each side between the eyes, the vertex marked with pitchy. Thorax densely and rather strongly punctured, with a triangular pitchy spot on each side of the middle of the base, in front of each of which a small shallow fovea is seen; anterior angles rounded, the posterior angles also rounded but in a less degree. Elytra rather strongly and very thickly punctured, but the punctures are not crowded; two fine obtuse costæ may be traced on each elytron, and the sutural margin is also slightly raised.

Hab. W. Australia (Du Boulay).

Descriptions of new American CETONIIDÆ; by OLIVER E.
JANSON.

Cotinis malinus, n. sp.

♂ Pale green, opaque, head, pygidium, underside and legs
shining green, lateral margins of the thorax behind and the
elytra, except in the region of the scutellum and the suture,
pale luteous, tinged with green.   Head finely and sparsely
punctured, with whitish pubescence, the outer margins of the
clypeus strigose, its sides strongly elevated, the frontal horn
curved inwardly and dilated towards the apex where it is
truncate, the apical horn slightly narrowed towards the apex.
Thorax impunctate, sides slightly prominent in the middle,
posterior lobe large and obtusely rounded.   Elytra impunctate,
separately rounded at the apex, the sutural angles slightly produced.   Pygidium finely and closely strigose.   Beneath punctate
and strigose at the sides and apex, with long whitish pubescence,
mesosternal process broad, rounded at the apex, centre of
abdomen with a broad shallow depression; anterior tibiæ with
one small tooth near the apex and an almost obsolete one above
it, the outer apical spine very long and acute.   Length 25 mm.
Mexico.

Allied to *C. nitida*, L , but rather larger, the sides of the
thorax more prominent in the middle and the posterior lobe
much broader, the horn on the forehead more depressed and
widened towards the apex, the colour is also much paler than
in that species.

Cotinis senex, n. sp.

♂ Blue-black, with a greenish tinge, underside and legs with
black pubescence.   Head very finely and sparsely punctured,
with a short, strongly elevated longitudinal ridge between the
eyes; clypeus dilated in front, the sides and apex strongly
elevated, the latter slightly rounded.   Thorax narrow, the sides
slightly prominent in the middle, the posterior lobe short and
pointed, finely and sparsely punctured on the disc, with scattered

coarser punctures at the sides and several large shallow impressions. Scutellum almost concealed by the thoracic lobe, its apex very acute. Elytra slightly transversely wrinkled and finely punctured in longitudinal rows on the disc, the punctures coarser and irregular at the sides and apex. Pygidium convex, very finely strigose. Beneath punctured at the sides, mesosternal process very short, broad and rounded, abdomen depressed; anterior tibiæ with an obsolete tooth before the apex, the intermediate and posterior tibiæ with a strong tooth in the middle. Length 16–19 mm.

Mexico.

Most nearly allied to *C. smaragdina*, G.P., but of a narrower and more convex form, different colour, shorter head, the clypeus wider in front, with the central ridge shorter and more elevated, the thoracic lobe pointed, and the pygidium more swollen.

Gymnetis spurca, n. sp.

Above dull dusky, cinereous thorax dull pitchy black, the sides broadly cinereous, elytra clouded with dusky black in the region of the scutellum and suture, the humeral callosity, two small spots placed obliquely in the middle, and a V-shaped mark behind dusky black, underside and legs shining black, irrorated with cinereous. Head coarsely punctured, clypeus rounded in front, the apex slightly elevated and sinuous. Thorax much narrower than the elytra at the base, with sparse coarse punctures on the disc, which become closer and crescent shaped at the sides. Elytra with the inner carina smooth and well marked, the outer one obsolete, the disc with close rows of coarse crescent shaped punctures, becoming confused and confluent at the apex, the suture elevated and acutely produced at the apex. Pygidium coarsely and closely strigose. Beneath smooth in the middle, the sides with coarse crescent shaped punctures, mesosternal process broad and obtusely rounded at the apex; anterior tibiæ with a small obtuse tooth before the apex. Length 17 mm.

Ecuador (Buckley).

Allied to *G. liturata*, Oliv., but easily distinguished by its broader and more robust form and very coarse sculpture.

Gymnetis fumata, n. sp.

Above dull smoky cinereous, elytra with a small rather ill-defined pale luteous spot on the outer carina at about one-third from the apex, the apical callosity obscure reddish-brown; underside and legs shining reddish-brown, irrorated with cinereous. Head rather closely punctured, clypeus slightly rounded at the sides, the apex strongly elevated and sinuous. Thorax sparsely and finely punctured on the disc, the punctures coarser and closer at the sides and confluent at the anterior angles, the posterior lobe smooth. Elytra with two well marked carinæ, the disc with rows of crescent shaped punctures which become confused at the apex, the sides with rows of very fine punctures, suture strongly elevated and acutely produced at the apex. Pygidium closely strigose and sparsely pubescent. Beneath coarsely strigose and with sparse brown pubescence at the sides, mesosternal process obtuse and rounded, not divergent; anterior tibiæ with two teeth and the apical spine rather obtuse. Length 20 mm.

Sarayaco, Ecuador (Buckley).

Allied to *G. margineguttata*, G.P.

Gymnetis fabaria, n. sp.

Brownish luteous, opaque, with four very small red-brown marginal spots on the elytra, apex of mesosternal process and tarsi pitchy black, shining Head very finely and obsoletely punctured, clypeus slightly narrowed in front, not rounded, apical margin slightly elevated and sinuous. Thorax impunctate, the posterior angles acute. Elytra narrowed behind, impunctate, the disc slightly wrinkled, the carinæ almost obsolete, suture scarcely elevated, the apical angles obtuse; epimera large with a rather acute shining tubercle. Pygidium strigose. Beneath very coarsely punctured on the mesosternum, with sparse pubescence, sides and apex of the abdomen more finely punctured, mesosternal process large, bent down and obtuse; legs punctured, and fringed with brownish hairs, anterior tibiæ without teeth. Length 15 mm.

Balzar Mountains, Ecuador (Illingworth).

Apparently belonging to section 8 of Burmeister, but with the apical angles of elytra not produced. It resembles *G. cinerea*, G.P., in colour, but in other respects is very distinct from any species with which I am acquainted.

Gymnetis scapularis, n. sp.

Above obscure greenish cinereous, thorax and elytra with numerous irregular obscure black spots and marks, apex of clypeus, pygidium, underside and legs shining black, the breast and a small spot on each side of the abdominal segments greenish cinereous   Head convex in the centre, finely and closely punctured, the base more sparsely punctured, clypeus slightly dilated and rounded at the sides, the apical margin slightly elevated. Thorax punctured at the sides, the posterior angles rather acute. Elytra with several indistinct rows of fine punctures on the disc, the costæ distinct behind, the suture strongly produced at the apical angles into an obtuse point, epimera large, sparsely punctured with a prominent shining tubercle.   Pygidium closely and finely strigose, with a slightly raised longitudinal line.   Beneath coarsely punctured and strigose at the sides and apex, mesosternal process obtuse, with an acute point in front; legs coarsely punctured, anterior tibiæ with two small teeth, the apical spine rather blunt.   Length 19 mm.

Sarayaco, Ecuador (Buckley)

Allied to *G. schistacea*, Burm , but smaller, narrower, more convex, of a different colour and with the elytra less punctured.

Gymnetis cupriventris, n. sp.

Above reddish-brown, opaque, with numerous ill-defined confluent black marks on the thorax and elytra, the latter pale luteous at the apex, with a small brown spot at the sutural angle, the lateral margins behind the middle black, with several luteous spots, beneath shining coppery, irrorated with brown, the abdominal segments with a small brown spot on each side, legs opaque brown, the inner sides, tarsi and punctures coppery. Head convex, with sparse fine punctures, apex of the clypeus slightly elevated and sinuous.   Thorax with a few scattered fine punctures at the sides, posterior angles rather acute, the lobe broad and obtusely rounded.   Elytra impunctate, rounded at the apex, the suture feebly elevated behind, the apical angles not produced; epimera almost impunctate, with a conspicuous shining tubercle   Pygidium coarsely but not very closely strigose.   Beneath coarsely strigose, centre of the mesosternum smooth, with a deeply impressed line, the process obtuse at the apex, with a prominent obtuse point in front, abdomen coarsely punctured at the sides and apex; anterior coxæ with long brown hairs, anterior tibiæ with two small teeth, and the apical spine obtuse   Length 21 mm.

Peru

Allied to *G. pardalis*, G.P., but in colour more like *chontalensis*, O. Jans.

Gymnetis dispersa, n. sp.

Dull fuscous black, head cinereous brown, apex of clypeus coppery, thorax with obscure fuscous marks, elytra obscure pitchy-red towards the sides, with irregular undulating confluent marks, a large patch before the apex, and several small spots at the sides and next the suture luteous, underside and legs with a coppery tinge and slightly shining. Head closely punctured, clypeus slightly rounded at the sides, the apex elevated and sinuous. Thorax rather sparsely punctured at the sides, the posterior angles prominent and acute. Elytra sparsely and finely punctured at the apex, the inner carina well marked and the apical callosity prominent, the suture only slightly elevated at the apex; epimera punctured, with a distinct tubercle Pygidium very closely and finely strigose, with short pubescence Beneath with very coarse confluent punctures, centre of mesosternum smooth, with a deeply impressed line, the process obliquely bent down, obtusely pointed at the apex and keeled in front, sides and apex of the abdomen and the legs coarsely punctured; anterior tibiæ with two teeth and the apical spine rather obtuse. Length 23 mm.

Jima, Ecuador (Buckley).

Allied to *G. hebraica*, Drap., but broader, less punctured above and differently coloured.

Gymnetis discolor, n. sp.

♂ Dull fuscous cinereous, thorax and elytra with obscure fuscous black spots and marks, lateral margins of the elytra pitchy black, with small luteous spots, the apex luteous with fuscous spots, a transverse spot in the centre of the abdominal segments, mesosternal process and the tarsi shining black. Head finely punctured, apex of the clypeus elevated and rounded. Thorax punctured at the sides, the posterior angles acute, the lobe short and broad. Elytra sparsely punctured at the apex and between the carinæ, the suture obtusely produced at the apex; epimera sparsely punctured, with an obtuse tubercle. Pygidium strigose, the striæ sparse and broken towards the apex, the centre with a slightly elevated longitudinal line. Beneath punctured and strigose at the sides, mesosternum with a deep central line, the process obliquely bent down and obtuse; legs punctured, anterior tibiæ without teeth Length 18–20 mm.

The female has the dark markings on the upper side better defined, the clypeus, underside and legs shining black, irrorated with cinereous, is more strongly punctured beneath and has two teeth on the anterior tibiæ.

Balzar Mountains, Ecuador (Illingworth).

Allied to *G. hebraica*, Drap., smaller, broader and less convex, less punctured above and differently marked.

Gymnetis balzarica, n. sp

♂ Deep black, opaque, elytra with the external margins and numerous irregular, confluent, transverse marks pale yellow. Head sparsely and finely punctured, clypeus quadrate, the apex elevated and sinuous. Thorax with scattered fine punctures at the sides, the posterior angles acute. Elytra with obsolete rows of punctures on the disc, the suture elevated behind and slightly produced at the apex ; epimera large, with a shining tubercle. Pygidium finely strigose with sparse short pubescence. Beneath sparsely punctured at the sides, mesosternal process large, bent down, obtuse at the apex and slightly prominent in front; anterior coxæ with brown hairs, the tibiæ with two small teeth. Length 21–24 mm.

The female is shorter and broader, more strongly punctured, with the clypeus, underside and legs shining and the teeth on the anterior tibiæ larger.

Balzar Mountains, Ecuador (Illingworth).

This fine species belongs to the *holosericea* group, and varies considerably in the extent of the yellow markings on the elytra, which in some specimens are so extended as to leave only the suture and a few small spots of the ground colour, the thorax is often marked with several small obscure yellow spots.

Descriptions of new American CETONIIDÆ; by OLIVER E. JANSON.
Part II.

Gymnetis suilla, n sp.

Above obscure smoky-black, the sides of the thorax and the
elytra obscure smoky cinereous, the latter clouded with black,
and with an ill-defined spot in the middle, a J-shaped mark
behind and the punctures black; apex of the scutellum covered
with pale yellow pubescence; underside and legs shining black,
sparsely pubescent. Head sparsely but rather coarsely punctured, apex of the clypeus slightly elevated and impressed in the
centre. Thorax with a central elevation in front, the sides
rounded, sparsely and finely punctured on the disc, with some
scattered coarser punctures at the sides. Elytra with irregular
rows of very coarse punctures on the disc, and rows of fine
punctures at the sides, the apex strigose, the suture and inner
carina moderately elevated, apical angles acutely produced.
Pygidium and underside coarsely strigose; mesosternal process
rather short, rounded and slightly divergent. Length 12–14 mm.

Venezuela (Coll. A. Fry).

Allied to G liturata, Oliv., but differs in its narrower form,
more coarsely punctured elytra, dark colour, and in having the
thorax elevated in front.

Gymnetis ravida, n. sp.

Above fulvous-brown, opaque, slightly clouded with fuscous,
the punctuation, pygidium, underside and legs pitchy-black,
elytra with two small black spots near the lateral margin, the
first in the middle and the other about one-fourth from the
apex, pygidium, sides of the body and legs speckled with
fulvous. Head and thorax sparsely punctured, the lobe of
the latter smooth at the apex, apex of the clypeus slightly
emarginate. Elytra with irregular rows of semicircular punctures on the disc, a confluent mass of similar punctures at the
apex, and some fine punctures at the sides, the suture and the
inner carina slightly elevated and smooth, the apical angles

W W

strongly produced.   Pygidium, underside and legs coarsely strigose, mesosternal process short, obtuse and somewhat oblique, anterior tibiæ with a prominent angle before the middle. Length 14 mm

Venezuela (Coll. A. Fry.)

Allied to *G. liturata*, Oliv, but of a narrower and more parallel form, different colour and with the mesosternal process oblique.

Euphoria acerba, n. sp.

♂ Above dark green, opaque; head, underside and legs shining green, with long brown pubescence, antennæ and tarsi pitchy-black, elytra reddish at the sides, and marked with small white spots.   Head coarsely punctured, a small impression on each side between the eyes, clypeus rounded at the sides and narrowed in front, with the apex elevated and emarginate. Thorax sparsely pubescent, coarsely punctured at the sides, the punctures finer on the disc, smooth in front of the scutellum. Scutellum elongate, acute at the apex, impunctate.   Elytra with somewhat obsolete rows of punctures on the disc, the sides coarsely punctured and sparsely pubescent, the apex strigose, outer carina distinct, the inner one almost obsolete.   Pygidium closely and finely strigose and pubescent. Beneath strigose, mesosternal process short, twice as broad as long, abdomen deeply impressed in the centre, anterior tibiæ with two strong lateral teeth, posterior tibiæ slightly curved.

The female is larger and more robust, with the punctuation coarser, the sides of the thorax polished, the club of the antennæ shorter, and the centre of the abdomen with only a slight longitudinal line.   Length 17–19 mm.

Quito, Ecuador (Coll. A. Fry).

Allied to *E. Lesueuri*, G.P., but readily distinguished by its shorter and broadly rounded clypeus, more obliquely narrowed thorax, its short, broad mesosternal process, etc ; the colour varies to reddish-olivaceous, and the number of white spots is also variable as in that species.

Euphoria morosa, n. sp.

♂ Above dull greenish-black; head, underside and legs shining greenish-black and sparsely pubescent, elytra sparsely and irregularly spotted with yellow, pygidium and the antennæ piceous red. Head closely punctured at the base, with a small, slightly elevated space in the centre smooth, the clypeus somewhat more coarsely punctured, convex in the centre, the sides rounded and the apex strongly elevated and rounded; lamellæ of the antennæ nearly as long as the head. Thorax obliquely narrowed from the base, only slightly prominent in the middle, very closely punctured at the sides, more sparsely so on the disc. Scutellum impunctate, the apex acute. Elytra slightly narrowed behind, the suture and both the carinæ strongly elevated and smooth, the interstices with rows of fine punctures, the sides coarsely punctured and the apex strigose. Pygidium very finely and closely strigose. Beneath strigose at the sides, abdomen with coarse punctures at the sides and scattered fine punctures in the middle, mesosternal process short, broad and punctured, anterior tibiæ with one lateral tooth and the apex very obtuse. Length 15 mm.

Quito, Ecuador (Coll. A. Fry).

Allied to *E. abreona*, O. Jans., but of a broader and more quadrate form, less pubescent, with the thorax more obliquely narrowed, the costæ of the elytra more strongly elevated and the colour and markings quite different.

Euphoria precaria, n. sp.

♂ Above dark olive green, opaque, with sparse, short pubescence; head, underside and legs brassy-green and covered with long pubescence, a fine median line on the thorax, and some small obscure spots on the elytra yellow, pygidium with a small chalky spot on each side. Head closely punctured, a narrow longitudinal ridge at the base, clypeus slightly rounded at the sides, the apex elevated and slightly emarginate, lamellæ of the antennæ about half as long as the head. Thorax sparsely punctured on the disc, the sides closely and more coarsely punctured. Scutellum impunctate. Elytra scarcely narrowed behind, the apex somewhat truncate, the suture and carinæ slightly elevated, the interstices with rows of indistinct punctures, the sides sparsely punctured and the apex strigose. Pygidium finely strigose. Beneath coarsely strigose at the sides, abdomen with sparse coarse punctures in the middle, mesosternal process short and broad, punctured and pubescent, anterior tibiæ with one lateral tooth and the apical spine short but acute. Length 17 mm.

New Granada (Wallis).

Allied to *E. morosa*, O. Jans., but larger, more convex, less punctured, more pubescent, with the antennæ shorter, the legs more robust and the colour different. Given to me by the late Ed. Steinheil, with the MS. name of *Jansoni*.

Euphoria punicea, n. sp.

♂ Dull red, varying to olivaceous, opaque and sparsely pubescent, elytra with small irregular white spots, head, pygidium, underside and legs shining, with long whitish hairs. Head coarsely punctured, with a slight transverse ridge between the eyes, clypeus rounded at the sides, narrowed in front, the apex strongly elevated and emarginate. Thorax coarsely but not very closely punctured, the punctures confluent near the anterior angles, smooth and emarginate in front of the scutellum. Elytra sparsely punctured in rows, the sides and apex strigose, the discal carinæ and suture moderately elevated and smooth, the apical angles slightly produced. Pygidium convex, coarsely strigose   Beneath strigose, mesosternal process short, very broad and slightly rounded at the apex, abdomen with three impressions on each side, deeply and broadly impressed in the centre, anterior tibiæ with two large teeth before the apex. Length 16–17 mm.

The female is broader, more coarsely sculptured, has the thorax more rounded at the sides, the legs stouter and the abdomen convex in the centre.

Balzar Mountains, Ecuador (Illingworth).

Allied to *E Steinheili*, O Jans., but narrower and more convex, with the pygidium larger, the underside more pubescent, the mesosternal process broader, and the colour different.

Euphoria avita, n. sp.

♀ Dull greenish-black, sparsely pubescent, elytra with irregular yellowish undulating marks and spots, a central line, the margins and a small spot on each side of the thorax, the clypeus and base of the scutellum obscure red, beneath shining, sides of the breast and legs pitchy-red.   Head closely punctured, clypeus elongate, the sides straight, the apex slightly elevated and sinuous   Thorax coarsely punctured, the punctures confluent at the sides, with a slightly raised median line, the base shallowly emarginate before the scutellum. Scutellum acute at the apex, a few punctures at the base. Elytra with rows of coarse shallow punctures, the sides and apex strigose, the carinæ rather strongly elevated. Pygidium finely strigose. Beneath punctate and strigose at the sides, abdominal segments with a transverse row of fine punctures, mesosternal process short, transverse, anterior tibiæ with two strong obtuse teeth before the apex. Length 12 mm.

Guatemala (from the collection of the late A Murray).

Allied to *E. vestita*, G.P.

Euphoria limatula, n. sp.

♂ Blackish blue, shining, tinged with green, a narrow marginal line at the sides of the thorax, irregular transverse impressed spots on the elytra, and some spots on the pygidium silvery-white, underside and legs with sparse pale pubescence, the second to fourth abdominal segments with a transverse white spot on each side. Head with coarse confluent punctures, clypeus rounded at the sides, the margins slightly elevated, the apex sinuous. Thorax convex, rather coarsely punctured, with a smooth central line, the base strongly emarginate before the scutellum. Scutellum with a few punctures disposed in the form of a V. Elytra with irregular coarse punctures on the disc, the sides strigose, the carinæ and suture moderately elevated and smooth. Pygidium convex and strigose. Beneath strigose at the sides, sparsely punctured in the centre, mesosternal process short, transverse, anterior tibiæ with two teeth and the apical spine acute. Length 13–14 mm.

Guatemala.

Allied to *E. melancholica*, G.P., but shorter, broader, and more convex, with the punctuation more sparse, and the clypeus broader and less elevated at the apex.

Descriptions of CURCULIONIDÆ; by FRANCIS P. PASCOE, F.L.S., &c. Part I.

The *Curculionidæ* described in the following pages are selected from a large number of unnamed species in my collection. There are so many forms differentiated by characters so slight and indefinite, that it is a matter of exceeding difficulty to determine, in some cases, even the genera to which they respectively belong, and, in other cases, to decide how far they may lie within the range of individual variation. There are, however, a sufficient number of fairly well-marked forms to render their publication desirable. Tropical America—so rich in species—is excluded from these pages, as it furnishes the material of a series of papers I am now publishing in the Annals and Magazine of Natural History.

The following is a list of the species and their subfamilies described in the present part.

BRACHYDERINÆ.
Enaptorhinus granulatus.
Astycus flavovittatus.
Eupholus cyphoides.
OTIORHYNCHINÆ.
Elytrurus rusticus.
subvittatus.
APIROCALUS, n gen.
cornutus.
Isomerinthus asper.
gramineus.
decipiens.
scaposus.
Apocyrtus castaneus.
nigrans.
Sitentes graniger
cœruleatus.

DIETHICUS, n. gen.
tumens.
tenuicornis.
PIOTYPUS, n. gen.
gravidus.
ATTELABINÆ.
Apoderus tenuissimus.
verrucosus.
Auletes major.
CRYPTORHYNCHINÆ.
IDASTES, n. gen.
elevatus.
Poropterus python.
lemur.
PANTOXYSTUS, n. gen., for
Cleogonus rubricollis, Bo.s.
ZYGOPINÆ
Chirozetes insignis.

Enaptorhinus granulatus.

E. elongatus, niger, subnitidus; elytris striatis, interstitiis granulatis; funiculo articulo ultimo obconico. Long. 4½–5 lin.

Hab. North China.

Elongate, black, glossy, with mostly fine, hair-like scales, a line on the prothorax, two basal lines on the elytra, their sides, a short band at the apex, and the apex itself more or less covered with whitish scales; rostrum stout, with two raised lines above; head coarsely punctured; last three joints of the funicle obconic; prothorax closely granulate, each granule tipped with a minute bristle; scutellum small, triangular; elytra not wider than the prothorax at the base, striate, the interstices with a close-set row of setiferous granules; body beneath covered with approximate whitish scales, mixed with long hairs; legs, especially the posterior tibiæ, also with long hairs.

This species differs from *E. Sinensis*, Waterh., Senr, in the sculpture of the prothorax and elytra, the form of the funicular joints, and other characters.

Astycus flavovittatus.

A. oblongo-ovatus, aureo-viridi-squamosus; prothorace confertim granulato; elytris vittis duabus flavo-aureis ornatis. Long. 8 lin.

Hab. India.

ʼ Oblong-ovate, covered with small golden-green approximate scales, on the elytra two golden-yellow stripes, united at the base and near the apex; antennæ slender, clothed with a delicate glaucous pubescence; prothorax transverse, closely granulate, the sides with a yellow patch anteriorly; elytra punctate-striate, the interstices convex, apices acuminate; scales beneath a paler green.

The other prominent characters are those of the type, *A. chrysochlorus*, Wied., which is nearly uniform in colour, except the head and legs

Eupholus cyphoides.

E. niger, omnino albido-squamosus; rostro modice robusto, carinato, lateribus parallelis; prothorace supra planato; elytris breviusculis. Long. 11 lin. (rostr. incl).

Hab Aneiteum

Black, densely covered with white scales, with a slight tinge of rose, especially beneath; rostrum moderately robust, the sides parallel, a well-marked ridge in the middle above, and a linear impressed line on each side in front of the eye; antennæ slender, joints of the funicle obconic; prothorax transverse, distinctly flattened on the disc; scutellum small, subcordiform; elytra short and convex, with distinct punctures in scarcely impressed lines; basal joint of the tarsi not transverse.

In form this species does not differ from the ordinary *Eupholi*, except that the elytra is a little shorter and more convex.

Elytrurus rusticus.

E subellipticus, fuscus, sparse griseo-squamulosus; rostro sat elongato, late canaliculato; elytris in medio latioribus, ad latera postice serrulatis. Long. 8 lin.

Hab. Fiji.

Subelliptic, dark brown, with small grey scattered scales; head sparingly and finely punctured; rostrum rather long, somewhat deeply canaliculate, with a nearly obsolete line in the middle; second joint of the funicle twice the length of the first; prothorax punctured anteriorly, granulate behind; scutellum minute, triangular; elytra broadest at above the middle; apparently striated, the interstices minutely granulate; abdomen glossy black, the first two segments punctured; legs normal, femora more or less granulate.

The nearest ally appears to be *E. serrulatus*, C. Waterh., but, *inter alia*, the elytra are much more attenuated behind, the rostrum longer and canaliculate. The apparent striæ are due to certain rows of punctures bearing each a greyish scale.

Elytrurus subvittatus.

E. subellipticus, niger, sparse griseo-squamosus; rostro in medio carinato; elytris ante medium latioribus, singulis vittis duabus approximatis inconspicuis, ornatis Long. 6 lin.

Hab Fiji.

Subelliptic, shorter in proportion, dull black, with two inconspicuous greyish approximating stripes on each elytron; rostrum rather short, a raised line in the middle; prothorax finely granulate; scutellum very small, triangular; elytra broadest at above the basal third, lineated with minute granules, the interstices with obscure whitish scales—only seen through a strong lens—apices slightly produced; abdomen glossy black; legs with whitish scales mixed with bristles; femora granulate.

Shorter than any other species, except *E. cinctus*, and further characterized by the two pale approximate stripes on the elytra.

APIROCALUS.

Rostrum a capite separatum, robustum, apice modice declivum. *Antennæ* breviusculæ, *scapus* incrassatus. *Elytra* ad latera haud angulata, apice integra. *Coxæ* anticæ haud contiguæ; *femora* incrassata; *tibiæ* arcuatæ. *Abdomen* segmentis duobus basalibus ampliatis.

This genus differs from *Elythurus* in the elytra not forming an angle at the sides, and not inflected at the apex so as to form a cavernous, more or less elongate, process. The dilatation of the elytra on each side posteriorly is found, although in not so remarkable degree, in *E. alatus* and *E. expansus*, and cannot be considered a generic character. In *Elytrogonus* the rostrum is not separated from the head by a grooved line, it has also a well-marked naked triangular clypeus, and contiguous anterior coxæ.

Apirocalus cornutus.

A. triangularis, niger, griseo-squamosus; elytris gradatim latioribus, apicem versus truncatis, lateribus postice bicornutis. Long. 5 lin.

Hab. Fiji.

Triangular, black, densely covered with pale grey scales; rostrum with a well-marked ridge above, scaly to the base of the mandibles; scrobes triangular, not quite reaching the eye; funicle with the first and third joints equal, the second longest; prothorax narrowed anteriorly, rounded at the sides; scutellum very small, transversely triangular, black, scaleless; elytra not broader than the prothorax at the base; gradually expanding posteriorly and produced into a stout horizontal, slightly diverging and somewhat compressed process tipped with a short fascicle of hairs, the elytra between the two processes abruptly declivous, as if truncated, the apex itself rounded; third and fourth abdominal segments very short .

Isomerinthus asper.

I. oblongo-ovatus, niger, supra granulatus, indumento fusco parce vestitus; rostro basi carinato. Long. 4½ lin.

Hab. Tondano.

Oblong-ovate, black, granulate above and clothed with a brownish tomentum; rostrum raised between the insertion of the antennæ, the base with a well-marked carina; between the eyes a sharp impressed line, continuous with a similar one on the rostrum; antennæ with the first and third joints of the funicle subequal; prothorax longer than broad, rather closely granulate; elytra shortly ovate, with several large scattered granules, the intervals minutely granulate and clothed with a brownish tomentum; body beneath sparsely scaly; legs somewhat slender.

The uniform colour and the granular surface will at once distinguish this species.

Isomerinthus gramineus.

I. oblongus, niger, squamulis viridi-cæruleis fere omnino tectus; rostro supra rotundato, haud carinato; elytris utrinque ante apicem nodoso; tibiis anticis denticulatis.   Long. 3 lin.

Hab. Tondano.

Oblong, black, almost everywhere covered with approximate greenish-blue scales; rostrum rounded above, scrobes oblong foveiform; funicle brown, second and third joints longest; prothorax with scattered punctures, each bearing a pale bristle-shaped scale; elytra rather shortly ovate, lineately punctured, each with a gibbosity, tipped with a fascicle of pale brownish hairs, posteriorly; abdomen with the first and second segments with a black central spot, the other segments entirely black; legs with scattered bluish scales; anterior tibiæ with six or seven denticles on the inner margin.

Dr. Kirsch has described another species from Jobi with apparent similar gibbous elytra (*I. bituberculatus*) which, *inter alia*, is clothed with whitish, very minute, scales.

Isomerinthus decipiens.

I. oblongo-ovatus, minus convexus, niger, parce viridi-squamosus; elytris subdepressis, apice constrictis, supra irregulariter granulatis; tibiis anticis subdenticulatis.   Long. 6 lin.

Hab. Tondano.

Oblong-ovate, less convex above, black, partially clothed with greenish scales, and speckled with black granules; rostrum short, stout; scrobe large, extending nearly to the eye; antennæ moderate; third joint of the funicle a little longer than the others, which are subequal in length; prothorax above equal in length and breadth, punctured, the intervals granulate; elytra rather depressed, broadest at the middle, suddenly compressed towards the apex, irregularly granulate, each above the compressed portion with an area of fewer granules—hence a pale spot, which, in certain lights, has the appearance of a callosity; beneath and base of the femora closely covered with glaucous green scales, anterior tibiæ slightly denticulated.

Allied to *I. scabratus,* from which, *inter alia,* the depressed and irregularly granulate elytra will readily distinguish it.

Isomerinthus scaposus.

I oblongo-ovatus, niger, albo-lineatus; prothorace rotundato; scapo antennarum compresso, basi subito truncato.   Long. $2\frac{1}{2}$–$3\frac{1}{2}$ lin.

Hab Dorey (New Guinea).

Oblong-ovate, black, varied with lines of snow-white scales; rostrum somewhat slender, white; scape of the antennæ compressed, suddenly contracted at the base; joints of the funicle subequal; prothorax somewhat globose, coarsely granulate, four stripes at the base and anterior border, white; elytra lineately punctured, the intervals finely granulate, two stripes on each elytron, connected by a transverse band behind, and a stripe at the apex, white; body beneath and legs with scattered white scales.

The peculiar character of the scape will at once distinguish this species; it is allied to *I. albolineatus* (Guér.).

Apocyrtus castaneus.

A. oblongo-ovatus, glaber, castaneus, geniculis tarsisque infuscatis; prothorace subcylindrico, subtilissime punctato; elytris ampliatis, depressis, lateribus equaliter rotundatis.   Long. $8\frac{1}{2}$ lin.

Hab. Philippine Islands.

Oblong-ovate, smooth, chesnut-coloured and slightly glossy; rostrum flattish above, a lightly impressed line extending to the

front; funicle with the first and second joints—first longest—
equal in length to the rest together; prothorax subcylindrical,
moderately convex, minutely punctured; elytra broad, depressed,
equally rounded at the sides from the base to the apex, finely
seriate-punctate, the suture smooth and glossy; beneath dark
brown; legs chesnut, the knees and tarsi dark brown; tibiæ,
particularly the hind pair, denticulate.

A slight approach to this species is made by *A. conicus*, Boh ,
but it is very slight indeed.

Apocyrtus nigrans.

A. oblongo-ovatus, glaber, niger, pedibus concoloribus; prothorace punctis minutis, in medio plus minusve confluentibus,
munito; elytris depressis, medium versus latioribus. Long. 7 lin.
Hab. Philippine Islands.

Oblong-ovate, smooth, black, slightly glossy; rostrum flattish
above, with a median and a short lateral impressed lines, funicle
with the two basal joints equal, shorter than the rest together;
prothorax subcylindrical, minutely punctured, punctures in the
middle more or less confluent; elytra depressed, broadest and
somewhat angular at above the middle, finely seriate-punctate,
suture smooth and glossy; beneath black, the first three abdominal segments fused together; fore tibiæ only denticulate.

Differentiated from the former, *inter alia*, by the punctuation
of the thorax, the form of the elytra, &c.; they are both very
distinct species, and but for *A. conicus*, and its allies, might
form a genus apart.

Siteutes graniger.

S. late subovatus; prothorace confertim granulato; elytris
granulatis, squamulis albidis adspersis. Long 5½–6½ lin.
Hab. Yule Island.

Broadly ovate, slightly convex above, black, the prothorax
occasionally tinged with chesnut, everywhere studded with small
white scales; head slightly punctate, a Λ-shaped impression
between the eye; rostrum with a fine impressed line at the base;
antennæ stout, the club not thicker than the funicle; prothorax
scarcely longer than broad, closely granulate; elytra a little
longer than the breadth at the middle, closely and finely granulate; body beneath and legs with scattered bristle-shaped scales.

Differs from *S. lugubris* in its broader outline, finer granulations, and the prothorax granulate, not punctate.

Siteutes cæruleatus.

S late subovatus; prothorace lævi, nitide rufo-testaceo; elytris subtiliter granulatis, cæruleo-squamulosis. Long. 5--6 lin.

Hab Yule Island

Broadly ovate, head, rostrum, and antennæ as in the last, the latter sprinkled with small blue scales; prothorax very smooth and glossy, chesnut-red; elytra short, rather depressed, studded with small granules, the intervals covered with small blue scales; body beneath black; legs dark chesnut, with scattered bristle-shaped scales.

Only traces of the blue scales sometimes remain; the highly polished prothorax is distinctive. *Siteutes* was founded by Schonherr on an African form unknown to Lacordaire, who took his description of the gēnus from *S. lugubris*—a Philippine insect; it is possible that the two are not congeneric. My *S. glabratus*, from its concave and somewhat bilobed mesosternum, should probably represent a genus of its own.

DIETHICUS.

Rostrum capite paulo angustius, haud compressum, supra utrinque elevatum, a capite separatum; *scrobes* superiores, profundæ, foveiformes *Antennæ* elongatæ; *scapus* curvatus, apice haud incrassata, elytrorum basi superans; *funiculus* tenuior, articulo secundo primo vel tertio duplo longiore, cæteris subcylindricis; *clava* parvula. *Prothorax* brevis, haud lobatus. *Scutellum* nullum. *Elytra* ampla, exhumerata. *Pedes* breviusculi; *ungues* basi connati *Abdomen* segmento secundo duobus sequentibus longiori.

Allied to *Ellimenistes*, Schon, but differs in form of the rostrum, which is broader, and not compressed, the longer antennæ; and the scape not enlarged, or only at the extreme point, at the apex.

Diethicus tumens.

D, dense cervino-squamulosus, maculatim fusco-variegatus;

rostro supra modice excavato; scapo crassiusculo, apice haud crassiore.   Long. 2⅔ lin.

Hab. Delagoa Bay.

Closely covered with fawn-coloured scales, varied with dark spots, which on the elytra appear as two ill-defined bands; rostrum with a shallow groove above; antennæ reaching to the apex of the elytra, the scape stout, not enlarged at the apex, attaining to the base of the elytra; prothorax short, nearly twice as broad as long, with few punctures, and a slightly raised line in the middle; elytra a little longer than broad, very convex, striate, the striæ limited to very narrow lines which do not appear to be punctured, the interstices rather broad and convex; legs with numerous setiferous scales; two basal joints of the tarsi rather narrow.

Diethicus, tenuicornis.

D. dense cervino-squamulosus, fusco maculatim subvariegatus; rostro supra magis sulcato, scapo tenuato, apice sat subito incrassato.   Long. 2½ lin.

Hab. Natal.

Closely resembling the preceding, but with more indefinite and paler spots, the rostrum narrower, the ridge on each side more marked, and inclosing a longer and deeper groove between them; the scape of the antennæ very much more attenuated with the ordinary dilatation of the apex confined to the extreme point, and the prothorax more nearly equal in length and breadth.

PIOTYPUS.

Caput et rostrum lata, hoc breve, a fronte separatum, margine externa angulatum; *scrobes* laterales, arcuatæ.   *Oculi* prominuli. *Antennæ* breviusculæ; *scapus* curvatus, apicem versus dilatatus, extus dente parvulo instructus; *funiculus* tenuatus; *clava* ovata acuminata   *Prothorax* brevis, haud lobatus.   *Scutellum* nullum.   *Elytra* ampla, exhumerata.   *Pedes* breves, *tarsi* lati, *ungues* basi connati.   *Abdomen* segmentis tribus intermediis longitudine æqualibus.

This genus belongs to Lacordaire's "groupe iii *Oosomides*" of the *Otiorhynchinæ.*   From the many genera of that group it is differentiated by its remarkable scape. In outline it resembles *Sphrigodes*, Gerst., which has a normal scape, and the second abominal segment as long as the two next together.

Piotypus gravidus.

P. omnino griseo-squamulosus, funiculo piceo; elytris tenuiter seriatim punctatis, interstitiis alternis basi pallidioribus. Long. 2 lin.

Hab. Grahamstown.

Everywhere covered with small greyish or silver-grey scales; head slightly convex above, with a well-marked prominence over the eye; rostrum narrower towards the apex, a longitudinal impression in the middle; first two joints of the funicle as long as the rest together; prothorax nearly twice as broad as long, rugulose; elytra a little longer than broad, truncated at the shoulders, finely seriate-punctate; legs with scattered setiform scales; tibiæ stout, the inner margin flexuous, apex of posterior pair, externally, with two spines.

Apoderus tenuissimus.

A. (♂) nigro-castaneus, nitidus; collo tenuissimo, recto, quam corpore multo longiore; femoribus infra dentatis; apice antennarum mutico. Long. 5 lin. (corpore solo 1¾ lin.).

Hab. Philippine Islands.

Dark or blackish-brown, shining; rostrum very short, constricted in the middle, where the antennæ are inserted, the latter, except the basal joint, pale ferruginous, terminal joint of the funicle obconic, club pubescent, not hooked at the tip; head prolonged behind in a very long rugulose neck, tapering gradually posteriorly and much longer than the thorax and elytra together; prothorax scarcely longer than broad, irregularly impressed, slightly prolonged anteriorly; scutellum transverse, bilobed behind, elytra subquadrate, broader behind, punctate-substriate, the interstices flattish, the punctures subfoveiform; legs smooth; femora with a small distinct tooth beneath.

A remarkable species on account of its very long perfectly straight neck, to which the prothorax, not as in other long-necked species, contributes nothing It does not fit into any of M. Jekel's genera and manipuli!

Apoderus verrucosus.

A. (♀) rufo-brunneus; elytris tuberculis nitide flavidis numerosis ornatis; femoribus muticis. Long. 3¼ lin.

Hab. Laos.

Reddish-brown, the elytra with numerous smooth yellowish or
amber-coloured tubercles; rostrum very short, broad; antennæ
short, inserted nearer the base than the apex, rather widely
apart, the terminal joints of the funicle transverse, club stout,
pubescent, nearly obsoletely jointed; head sharply constricted
behind, but not prolonged; prothorax conical, broader than
long, strongly grooved both at the apex and base, the disc convex and having a deep longitudinal groove; elytra subquadrate,
coarsely punctate-striate, the interstices strongly raised and
more or less spotted with yellow lines and tubercles, the intervals between the punctures granuliform; legs smooth; spurs of
the tibiæ and claws black.

For the tubercles on the elytra this species may be approximated to *A. flavotuberosus*, Jek., but they are more numerous
and differently placed; in form it is allied to *A. Tranquebaricus*.

Auletes major.

A. omnino rufo-castaneus, pilis tenuissimis griseis adspersus;
rostro elongato; clava antennarum laxe articulata. Long. 5-5½
lin. (rostr. incl.).

Hab. Andaman Islands.

Reddish-chesnut with numerous very slender grey hairs;
rostrum as long as the elytra, finely punctured, grooved at the
base behind the insertion of the antennæ, the latter extending
to the apex of the rostrum, the club very loose, of three joints,
the first two obconic, the third ovate; prothorax rather longer
than broad, rounded at the sides, irregularly punctured, the
intervals slightly corrugated; scutellum small, triangular; elytra
a little depressed, punctate-substriate, tibiæ slender, straight;
abdomen with the second segment longer than the first.

Except that the rostrum is nearly as long in proportion in
A. filicornis, this very distinct species is not to be compared to
any of its congeners.

IDASTES.

Rostrum vix elongatum, gracile, rotundatum; *scrobes* sub-
apicales. *Antennæ* graciles; *scapus* oculo attingens; *funiculus*
articulis tribus basalibus elongatis, sed secundo longiori, cæteris
gradatim brevioribus; *clava* distincte articulata, ovata, pubescens.
Prothorax brevissimus, conicus, lobis ocularibus ciliatis. *Scutellum*
rotundatum. *Elytra* cuneiformia, compressa, humeris angulatis.
Rima pectoralis mesosterno terminata, apice fornicata. *Pedes*
tenuatæ; *femora* sublinearia, infra dente valida armata; *tibiæ*
flexuosæ, unguiculatæ, angulo anteriore fasciculato; *tarsi* normales.

This genus belongs to Lacordaire's third "groupe *Mecistosty-
lides*" of his "subtribu *Cryptorhynchides* vrais"; it includes a
number of isolated forms confined to Australia and the neigh-
bouring islands. The specimen here described is probably a
female; the genus appears to have the nearest affinity to
Protopalus, although strikingly different in habit. The genera
of the group may be tabulated thus.—

Rostrum rounded
    Scape longer than the body - - - - - - - *Mecomastix.*
    Scape shorter than the body
        With a scutellum
            Elytra not broader than the prothorax at
               the base - - - - - - - - - - *Hemideres*
            Elytra broader
               Last five joints of the funicle transverse
                  Club of the antennæ distinctly jointed   *Aporolaxus.*
                  Club of the antennæ unjointed.
                    Rostrum slender
                       Sides of the prothorax straight at
                         the base - - - - - - - - *Paranomocerus*
                       Sides of the prothorax expanded
                         Pectoral canal open behind - - *Mecistostylus*
                         Pectoral canal wanted behind - *Blepiarda.*
                    Rostrum stout
                    Last five joints of the funicle gradually
                    shorter - - - - - - - - - - - *Amalthus*
                  Tibiæ straight - - - - - - - - *Protopalus.*
                  Tibiæ flexuous - - - - - - - - *Idastes*
            Without a scutellum - - - - - - - *Anomocerus.*
    Rostrum depressed - - - - - - - - - - *Amydala.*

Idastes elevatus.

I. compressus, fuscus, squamulis pallidioribus adspersis; prothorace basi quam longitudine duplo latiore. Long. 5 lin.
Hab. New Hebrides.

Compressed—the elytra especially—dark brown, with paler
scattered scales, much smaller and less numerous (perhaps
partially abraded) on the elytia; head convex in fiont; eyes
rather widely apart; rostrum black, with scales only at the base;
antennæ glossy ferruginous, the first and third joints of the
funicle of equal length, the second nearly twice as long, club
somewhat short, of four distinct joints; prothorax rounded
above, gradually broader towards the base, which is about twice
broader than long; scutellum rounded, velvety; elytra much
broader than the prothorax at the base, gradually narrowing
to the rounded apex, much compressed and raised into a sort of
crest at the middle portion of the suture; three intermediate
segments of the abdomen nearly equal in length; anterior tibiæ
more flexuous than the others; penultimate joint of the tarsi
strongly bilobed; claws simple.

Poropterus python.

H. ellipticus, subdepressus, niger, opacus, parce pallide fusco-
squamosus; prothorace apice producto, bilobo; elytris remote
foveato-impressis, apice rotundatis. Long. 5½–6 lin.
Hab. Port Bowen.

Elliptic, subdepressed, black, opaque, partially clothed with
pale brownish scales, which are more scattered on the middle
of the prothorax and elytra; rostrum rather broad, remotely
punctured; antennæ ferruginous, the club with a blackish
pubescence—pale in certain lights—second joint of the funicle
much longer than the first; prothorax about equal in length and
breadth, impunctate, the sides anteriorly a little incurved, the
apex projecting and bilobed; elytra half as long again as broad,
the shoulders with a projecting lobe directed forwards, the apex
rounded, above with a few irregular foveate impressions; femora
scarcely thickened, tibiæ at the apex black and without scales.

In outline this species resembles *P. rubetra*, Boh., a smaller
and shorter species, and, *inter alia*, the shoulders not tuber-
culiferous.

Poropterus lemur.

P. ellipticus, niger, opacus, supra leviter granulatus, inter-stitiis squamulis pallidis instructis; prothorace apice producto, integro; elytris postice abrupte declivis, bigibbosis, apice seipso rotundato. Long. $4\frac{3}{4}$ lin.

Hab. Port Bowen

Elliptic, black, opaque, finely granulated above, the intervals with minute brownish dispersed scales; rostrum moderately long, coarsely punctured, punctures crowded at the tip; antennæ ferruginous, second joint of the funicle a little longer than the first; prothorax about equal in length and breadth, incurved anteriorly at the sides, the apex projecting, entire, impunctate, granules flattish on the disc, smaller and more numerous at the sides, many of them with a small glossy spot in the centre; elytra half as long again as broad, not prominent at the shoulders, abruptly declivous behind, each elytron with a stout compressed gibbosity behind; two basal abdominal segments very large, the third and fourth very short.

This species is somewhat like *P. foveipennis*, which, *inter alia*, has a smooth punctured prothorax and non-gibbous elytra.

PANTOXYSTUS

Rostrum sat robustum, cylindricum. *Antennæ* normales. *Oculi* rotundati, infra remoti. *Prothorax* conicus, lobis ocularibus nullis *Elytra* subcordata, prothorace latiora, humeris rotundatis. *Rima* pectoralis obsoleta *Coxæ* anticæ subapproximatæ *Femora* infra dentata, haud canaliculata; *tibiæ* unguiculatæ; *ungues* appendiculati. *Abdomen* segmentis duobus basalibus ampliatis.

The type of this genus is *Cleogonus rubricollis*, Bois, a New Guinea species. The ordinary Brazilian forms of *Cleogonus* have oblong-ovate eyes nearly contiguous beneath, the prothorax with ocular lobes, a deep pectoral canal, femora channeled beneath, and the tibiæ with a short mucro only; these characters are all opposed to those given above

Chirozetes insignis.

C. (♂) fuscus, interrupte fulvo-squamosus; pedibus, præsertim anticis, elongatis; tarsis anticis articulo primo quam cæteris

simul sumptis fere triplo longiore ; cornubus pectoralibus acutis.
Long 8 lin.

Hab Labuan.

Derm brown, with patches and spots of fulvous scales; rostrum
finely punctured, two indistinct lines on each side, the lower
boundary of the scrobe with four or five tubercles; first and
second joints of the funicle longer than the next four together;
prothorax equal in length and breadth, punctures shallow and
somewhat remote, four lines of scales—the two middle united at
the extremities—on the disc, the sides speckled; elytra punctate-
striate, the alternate interstices more elevated, each having a
line of punctures, behind the middle a brown sutural spot, and
another at the apex externally, rest of the elytra speckled;
pectoral cavity small, pectoral spines—or horns—tapering gradually to a point; legs long, the anterior pair nearly twice the
length of the intermediate; basal joint of the anterior tarsi nearly
three times as long as the rest together, all, except the last
joint, fringed beneath.

In colour and general outline like *C. sphærops*, Wied., but
larger, with proportionally longer anterior legs, prothorax less
closely and elytra more strongly punctured, the smaller pectoral
cavity and the tapering breast-spines. The female is unknown
to me.

Some of the more remarkable species here described will be
figured in Mr. C. O. Waterhouse's " Aid to the identification of
insects."

Notices of new or little known C<small>ETONIID</small>.<small>F</small>; by O<small>LIVER</small> E. J<small>ANSON</small>. No. 7.

Hæmatonotus lugens, n. sp.

♂ Dull black; head, underside and legs pitchy-black, shining; lateral margins of the thorax, the epimera above, some spots on the metasternum and sides of the abdomen chalky-white; pygidium pitchy-red and shining in the centre, with a large white spot on each side. Head coarsely punctured, with long brownish pubescence at the base, clypeus widened in front, the apical margin strongly reflexed, rounded and scarcely emarginate Thorax strongly and regularly rounded at the sides, the base slightly produced, anterior margin with an elevated point in the centre, somewhat coarsely punctured and with short erect brownish hairs. Scutellum large, punctured at the base. Elytra deeply and rather coarsely punctured, the punctures very close at the sides, the suture and two curved carinæ slightly elevated and smooth. Pygidium finely strigose. Beneath sparsely punctured and pubescent, mesosternal process short and broad, abdomen strongly and broadly impressed in the centre, anterior tibiæ with a large apical spine and an obtuse lateral angle. Length 17 mm.

Lake Nyassa (Cotterell)

Differs from *H. Fritschi*, Kraatz, which I have also received in the same collection, in coloration, its more strongly reflexed clypeus and deeply impressed abdomen.

Clinteria decora, n. sp.

♂ Above dull black; head, pygidium, underside and legs shining black ; thorax with two elongate almost confluent spots on the lateral margins, and a transverse spot on each side at the base near the posterior angles red ; elytra with five red spots on each, the first in the centre and close to the base, the second near the suture just behind the middle, two on the lateral margin, also behind the middle, and one close to the apical angle; epimera with a red spot above; an ochreous spot on each

side of the pygidium; beneath with ochreous spots and marks at
the sides.   Head closely punctured, clypeus slightly impressed at
the sides the apex rather strongly notched.   Thorax sparsely and
finely punctured, the apical lobe large and obtuse.   Elytra with
rows of coarse punctures which become almost obsolete in the
region of the scutellum and a strong sutural stria, the apex
and the pygidium strigose.   Beneath strigose and with sparse
cinereous hairs at the sides, mesosternal process obtuse, abdomen
lightly impressed in the middle, anterior tibiæ bi-dentate, the
lower tooth and the apical spine very long and acute.   Length
11 mm.

India.

This pretty species is apparently most nearly allied to *G.
sexpustulata*, G.P., but is smaller and flatter, has the thorax
narrower behind, the head closely punctured and the markings
quite different.

Macronota nigricollis, n. sp.

Head coppery-black ; deeply and closely punctured, with an
elevated central longitudinal ridge between the eyes; clypeus
broad, rounded at the sides, the apex deeply end broadly emarginate   Thorax dull black, coppery at the anterior angles, with
fine short brown pubescence; closely punctured at the sides, the
disc more sparsely punctured, slightly narrowed from the middle
to the base; the lobe broadly rounded.   Scutellum dull black,
margined with cinereous at the apex, the base punctured and
shining.   Elytra obscure yellowish-red with a greenish reflection,
an oblique line and a linear spot on the basal half and the apex
dull black, a common somewhat V-shaped mark about the
middle continued narrowly along the suture to the base
cinereous; depressed at the suture and sides, and with rows
of rather obsolete punctures.   Pygidium dull black, finely
strigose.   Beneath shining black, coppery in the centre, broadly
cinereous and pubescent at the sides, abdomen with four
cinereous marginal stripes at the sides , mesosternal process
short and round; legs coppery, pubescent, anterior tibiæ with
two acute lateral teeth   Length 17 mm.

Assam.

Allied to *M. malabariensis*, G.P.   The specimen described is
from the late A Murray's collection and is said to have come
from Capt. Blackwood at Cherrapoongee.

Pyrrhopoda beryllina, n. sp.

♂ Bright golden-green, with sparse long cinereous pubescence; elytra bluish-green on the disc; median line of the thorax, scutellum and shoulders golden-red; apex of the clypeus, antènnæ and legs pitchy-red. Head rather closely punctured, somewhat impressed and more closely punctured between the eyes; clypeus widened in front and impressed on each side, the apex slightly elevated and emarginate. Thorax broadest in the middle, thence obliquely narrowed to the base, slightly emarginate before the scutellum; coarsely punctured, the punctures close and confluent on each side of the median line which is broadly elevated and smooth. Scutellum smooth and convex, the apex acute. Elytra prominent at the shoulders, rounded at the apex, each with five deep, punctured striæ, the third and fourth being very close together, the interstices and the suture convex. Pygidium coarsely and sparsely punctured. Beneath sparsely punctured; mesosternal process broad and rounded; abdomen with a broad central impression; anterior tibiæ with two lateral teeth, the lower one and the apex acute. Length 9 mm

Madagascar.

A pretty little species allied to *P hirsuta*, Waterh,, but of a more elongate form and different colour, with the shoulders more prominent, the thorax narrowed behind and with a smooth elevated central line, the elytra differently sculptured, etc

Platedelosis pinguis, n. sp.   Pl. XI, f. 2.

Above dull brick-red; base of the head, thorax, base of the scutellum, three spots on each of the elytra and the pygidium dull black; the latter with a large central yellow spot, thorax with a triangular spot in front, the posterior angles and two spots before the scutellum brick-red; beneath shining black; abdomen pitchy-red; mesosternal process, the epimera above, legs and antennæ shining red. Head sparsely punctured, clypeus more coarsely punctured in front, the sides nearly straight and slightly elevated, the apex deeply emarginate; maxillæ (fig 2a) with the inner lobe simple, mentum (fig. 2b) broad and deeply emarginate in front. Thorax obsoletely punctured, the base strongly trisinuous. Scutellum large, impunctate. Elytra obliquely narrowed behind, leaving the sides and apex of the abdomen exposed, with regular rows of coarse shallow punctures and a strong sutural stria, apical angles slightly

produced.   Pygidium transversely convex, sparsely strigose.
Beneath coarsely punctured at the sides, abdomen with two
deep foveæ on each side; mesosternal process short, broad and
rounded.   Length 19 mm.

New Guinea.

This interesting insect was recently received, together with
several other fine *Cetoniidæ*, from Goldie River, about 30 miles
inland from Port Moresby; it agrees in all the principal
characters with *Platedelosis*, a genus lately established by Kraatz
for the *Diaphonia Bassi*, White.

Celidota parvula, n. sp.

♂ Pale yellow, shining; base of head pitchy; two small spots
at the apex of the clypeus, two large triangular spots on the
disc of the thorax, and a central spot on the scutellum dark
green; elytra with irregular, ill-defined, transverse greenish-
brown marks, the suture and base narrowly margined with
green; centre of the metasternum greenish-black; margins of
the abdominal segments, knees, apex of the tibiæ, tarsi and
antennæ pitchy-black.   Head coarsely punctured, with long
brownish pubescence; clypeus rounded and slightly elevated at
the sides, widened in front, the apex strongly elevated and
entire.   Thorax punctured and pubescent at the sides, the
median line smooth, the base rounded and emarginate before
the scutellum   Scutellum triangular, sparsely punctured, with
an impressed central line behind.   Elytra uneven and with large
irregular punctures.   Pygidium convex, sparsely strigose at the
sides.   Beneath punctured and sparsely pubescent; metasternum
with a central impression in front, mesosternal process flat,
dilated and rounded at the apex; abdomen with a slight longitudinal impression at the base; anterior tibiæ with a sharp
lateral angle, the apex strongly produced   Length 8–9 mm.

Madagascar.

Smaller and much narrower than *C. Stephensi*, G.P., also
differs in colour, its coarser sculpture, pubescent head and
thorax, broader clypeus, etc.

Glycyphana pexata, n. sp.

Above dull black; head, underside and legs shining black;
basal half of the lateral margins of the thorax dull red; elytra

with a marginal line extending inwardly from the shoulders to
the apex of the scutellum, a transverse ovate lateral spot behind
the middle, and a small round one between it and the suture, two
transverse marks at the base of the pygidium, the outer edge of
the posterior coxæ, a spot at the side of the metasternum, one
on the epimera and three outer and two inner spots on each side
of the abdomen ochreous-white. Head finely punctured, apex
of the clypeus slightly notched. Thorax nearly half as broad
again as long, slightly emarginate before the scutellum, sparsely
punctured in front. Elytra with five discal striæ, the second
from the suture and the outer one short, the interstices and sides
with scattered coarse punctures. Beneath coarsely strigose,
abdomen with transverse rows of coarse punctures, median line
of the metasternum deeply impressed, anterior tibiæ with two
obtuse teeth. Length 17 mm.

Leyte, Philippine Islands.

Apparently most nearly allied to *G rubromarginata*, Mohn.

Glycyphana subcincta, n. sp

Above dull velvety-black; clypeus, underside and legs shining
black; basal half of the thorax with a broad dull red margin
slightly interrupted before the scutellum; elytra with a large
chrome-yellow lateral spot just behind the middle; scutellum
with a fine white line at the sides. Head sparsely punctured,
clypeus rather closely punctured, the apex deeply impressed and
narrowly emarginate in the centre, the margins not elevated.
Thorax transverse, strongly rounded at the sides and base, the
latter rather strongly emarginate before the scutellum, anterior
margin elevated and slightly produced over the head. Scutellum
elongate, the apex obtuse, impunctate. Elytra with five discal
striæ, the inner two abbreviated anteriorly, the outer one almost
obsolete behind the middle, the sides and apex and the pygidium
sparingly punctured. Beneath coarsely strigose, the abdomen
with coarse semicircular punctures at the sides, mesosternal
process short and dilated, anterior tibiæ with a strong subapical
tooth and an almost obsolete one before the middle Length
15–16 mm.

Andaman Islands.

Allied to *G. torquata*, Fab., but has the thorax more strongly
rounded and emarginate at the base, the clypeus more deeply
notched and impressed at the apex, the pygidium entirely black,
the spots on the elytra larger and of a different colour, the
thorax only partly margined with red, etc.

Glycyphana forticula, n. sp.

Above light green opaque; head, lateral margins of the thorax and the epimera shining green ; a narrow lateral border and two small spots on the disc of the thorax white; elytra with a small spot on the inner carina about the middle, two transverse lateral spots on the apical half, one near the suture about one-fourth from the apex and one on the outer margin near the sutural angle white; pygidium shining black, with brownish pubescence and four small white spots; underside and ·legs shining green, with a reddish tinge and long pubescence, tarsi greenish-pitchy. Length 16 mm.

Japan.

Allied to *G. albosetosa*, Mots, but broader and more convex, with the clypeus finely punctured, narrow in front and more deeply emarginate, the scutellum shorter and broader and the colour and markings different.

Glycyphana rutilans, n. sp.

Above light green, opaque; head, lateral margins of the thorax, epimera, pygidium, underside and legs coppery-red, with sparse pale pubescence, tarsi green, elytra with a narrow transverse lateral spot, about two-thirds from the base, another at the outer apical angle, and one next the suture about one-fourth from the apex white.   Length 15–18 mm

India.

Allied to *G. albosetosa*, Mots., but much more coarsely punctured, with the thorax broader at the base and more deeply emarginate before the scutellum, the scutellum longer and the markings different.

Glycyphana illusa, n. sp.

Euryomia rufovittata, Wallace, Trans Ent. Soc. Lond. iv, p. 573 (1868) (nec Guérin).

Above dull green.   Head reddish-green, shining; closely punctured, clypeus impressed and emarginate at the apex Thorax with the anterior margin and a transverse, curved, discal band, more or less interrupted in the middle and dilated at the sides dull red ; rather coarsely and deeply punctured, the base rounded and emarginate. . Scutellum impunctate, obtusely rounded at the apex. Elytra with a broad obscure reddish discal stripe extending from the base to the apical callosity, the sides and apex pitchy black, the former marked with two small transverse white lines; punctured in regular rows on the disc and with two striæ near the suture behind, the sides and apex sparsely punctured and hirsute, the discal carinæ evident. Pygidium dull piceous, with an angulated white mark on each side; strigose and hirsute. Beneath reddish-green, shining, thorax, margins of the metasternum, posterior coxæ and four transverse stripes at the sides of the abdomen white; mesosternal process short and strongly dilated with an impressed hirsute line; legs greenish-red. Length 11 mm.

Borneo

Very distinct from *G. rufovittata*, Guér., more nearly allied to *Bowringi*, Wall.

Protætia nox, n. sp., Pl. XI, f. 3.

♂ Above dull black; thorax with a fine interrupted marginal line in front and a basal marginal line interrupted in the middle and on each side white; elytra with two large transverse spots on the disc and two small marginal ones white; pygidium with two large longitudinal white marks; underside and legs shining black with some large patches at the sides and the whole of the abdomen, except the apex and several lateral spots, white. Head smooth; clypeus subquadrate, with sparse punctures at the sides, the apex elevated and emarginate in the centre. Thorax impunctate, the base trisinuous, Scutellum large, obtuse at the apex. Elytra with the suture and lateral carina strongly elevated, the apical angles acutely produced. Beneath sparsely strigose; mesosternal process dilated and rounded. Length 26 mm.

Dinagat, Philippine Islands.

Allied to *P. bifenestrata*, Chev.

GOLIATHOPSIS, n. gen.

Body depressed, densely squamulose and finely hirsute. Head rounded in front, the male with a strong erect furcate horn on each side above the eyes, in the female with a small elevated point; maxillæ (fig. 4b, c) with the inner lobe bidentate on one side and with one tooth on the other, the galea long and obtuse; mentum (fig. 4d) broad and slightly rounded in front. Thorax almost hexagonal. Elytra prominent at the shoulders, rounded at the apex. Pygidium slightly impressed on each side, prominent at the apex. Abdomen somewhat compressed, the apical lateral tubercles small. Legs moderately long, anterior tibæ with one tooth near the apex.

A remarkable new genus of the subfamily *Cremastocheilides*, allied to *Pilinurgus*, but resembling the *Goliathides* in the extraordinary armature of the head.

Goliathopsis cervus, n sp   Pl. XI, f. 4 ♂, 5 ♀.

Above tawny-brown ; head, median line of the thorax, scutel- and some small spots on the elytra paler; underside and legs tawny-grey, with a pearly lustre; margin of the clypeus, underside of the horns, penultimate and apical segments of the abdomen, apex of the pygidium, upper side of the femora and · tibiæ, the tarsi and antennæ shining black, the entire surface of the body and the legs covered with fine hirsute punctures; mesosternal process depressed and only slightly produced between the coxæ. Length 11 mm.

The female is of a darker pitchy colour, with the clypeus and the centre of the abdomen shining black.

Siam.

The male of this interesting insect has the appearance of a small *Dicranocephalus*, the female appears to scarcely differ from a specimen which stands in the national collection as "*Pilinurgus despectus*, Westw. (type)," but as the present species differs so conspicuously (especially in the head and maxillæ) from Mr. Westwood's figures, which were evidently not taken from that specimen, I have not hesitated to regard them as distinct. The male and female now described and figured are from the collection of the late Andrew Murray.

PARATRICHIUS, n gen.

Body elongate, moderately convex, sparsely pubescent beneath Head broad ; clypeus small, concave, the apex rounded and strongly reflexed; antennæ very large, the lamellæ one third longer than the head. Thorax transverse, slightly narrowed behind, the posterior angles rounded. Scutellum almost semicircular. Elytra strongly rounded behind. Pygidium large, convex. Abdomen compressed. Legs long, anterior tibiæ with one small tooth close to the apex.

Allied to *Trichius* and *Trigonopeltastes*.

Paratrichius longicornis, n. sp.   Pl. XI, f. 1.

Head, thorax and disc of the elytra dull black; clypeus, scutellum and the margins of the elytra testaceous-yellow; a triangular spot in the centre and a small spot on each side of the forehead, a fine marginal line, median line and two discal sinuous lines on the thorax pale sulphur-yellow; the elytra with a short transverse discal line before the middle, a longer curved one behind the middle and a fine sutural line in front ochreous-white; pygidium and underside pale sulphur-yellow; the anterior coxæ, the margins of all the segments, the centre of the meta-sternum and the apex of the abdomen shining black; legs and and antennæ testaceous-yellow, shining; the inner side of the femora, the posterior tibiæ and tarsi and the apical joint of the anterior and intermediate tarsi pitchy-black.   Head and thorax sparsely punctured; the former with the margin elevated in front of the eyes, clypeus narrow, rounded and strongly turned up at the apex   Elytra with regular rows of fine punctures.   Pygidium sparsely and finely punctured and pubescent. Beneath with sparse brownish pubescence, finely punctured, centre of the metasternum closely punctured, apex of the abdomen with two small impressed spots.   Length 16 mm.

Jesso, N Japan.

EXPLANATION OF PLATE XI.

Fig. 1. *Paratrichius longicornis*, O. Janson

,, 2. *Platedelosis pinguis*, O. Janson.

,, 3. *Protœtia nox*, O. Janson.

,, 4. *Goliathopsis cervus*, O. Janson, ♂ .

,, 5.   ,,   ,,   ,,   ♀ .

INDEX.

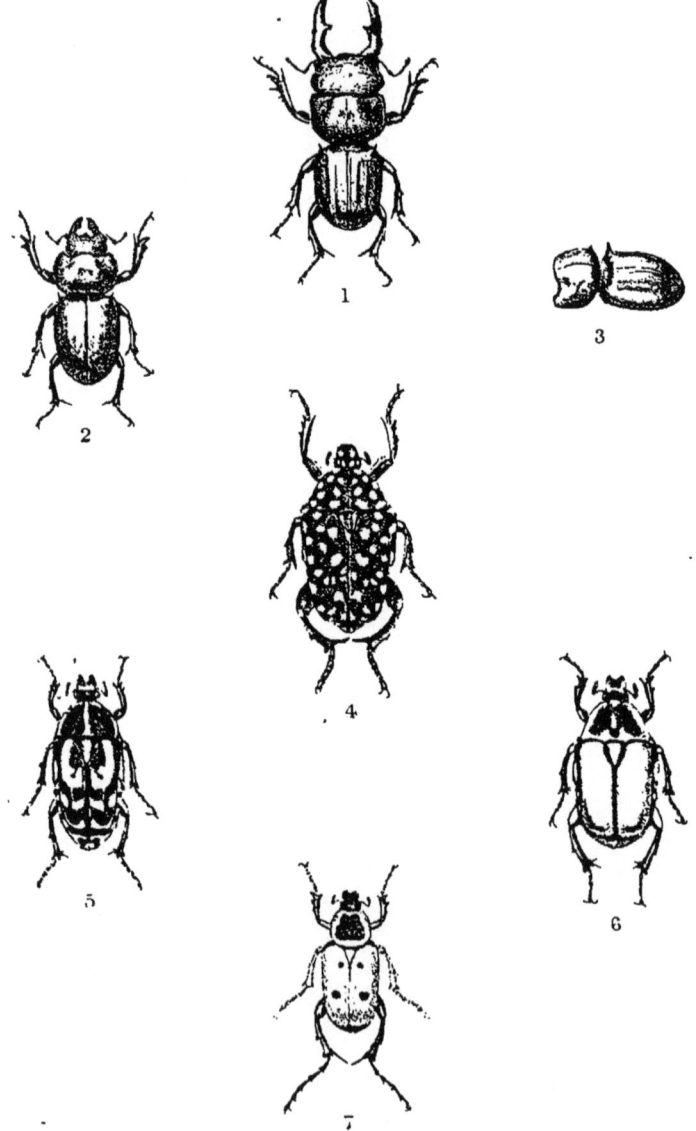

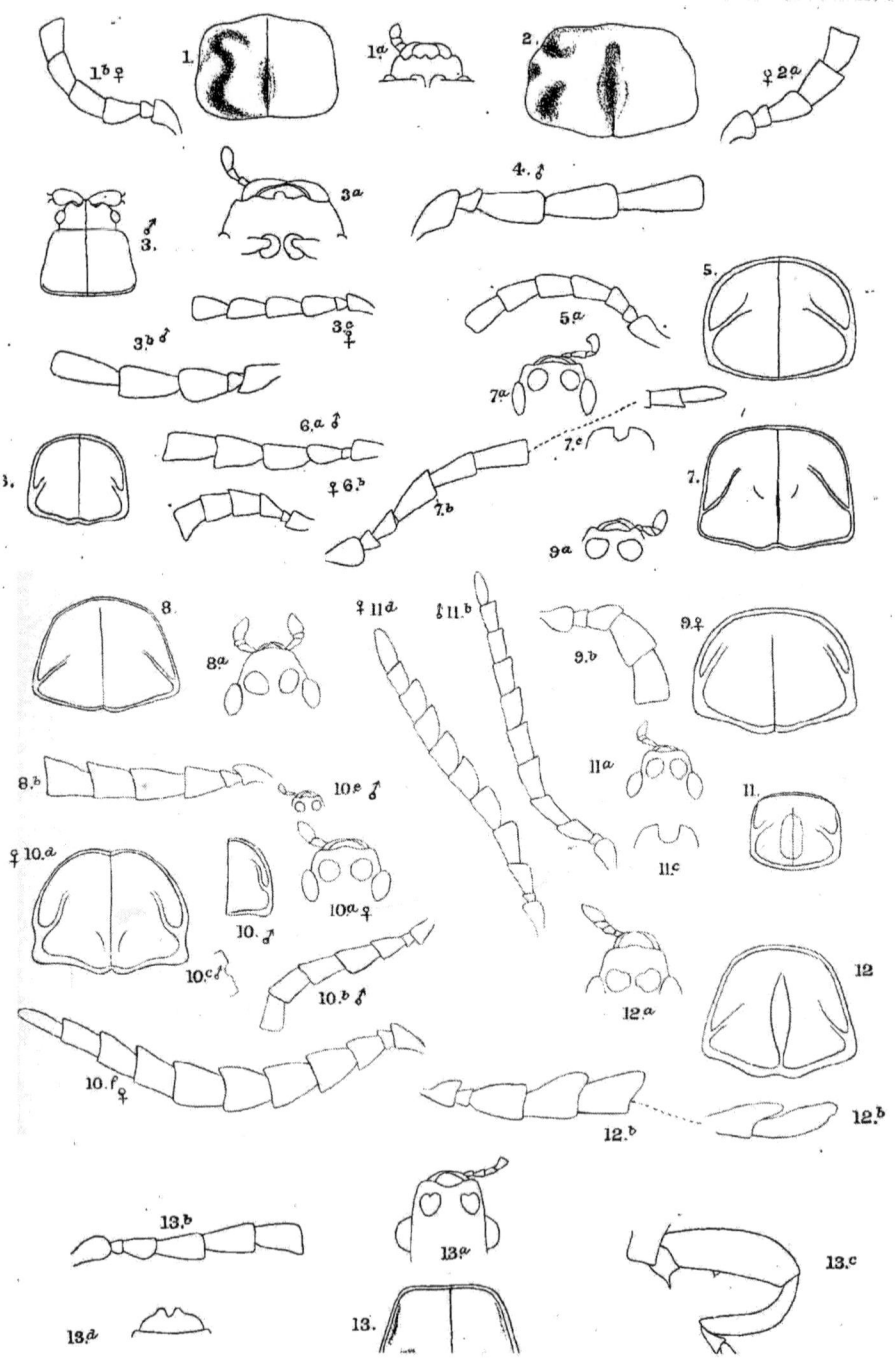

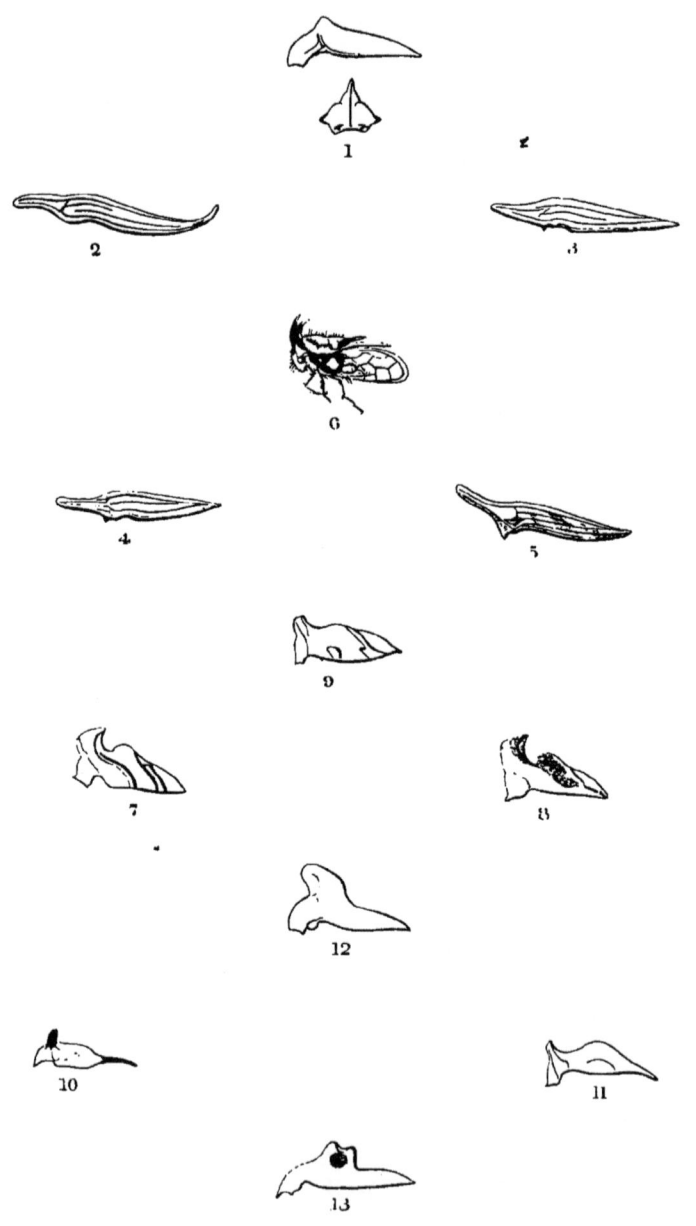

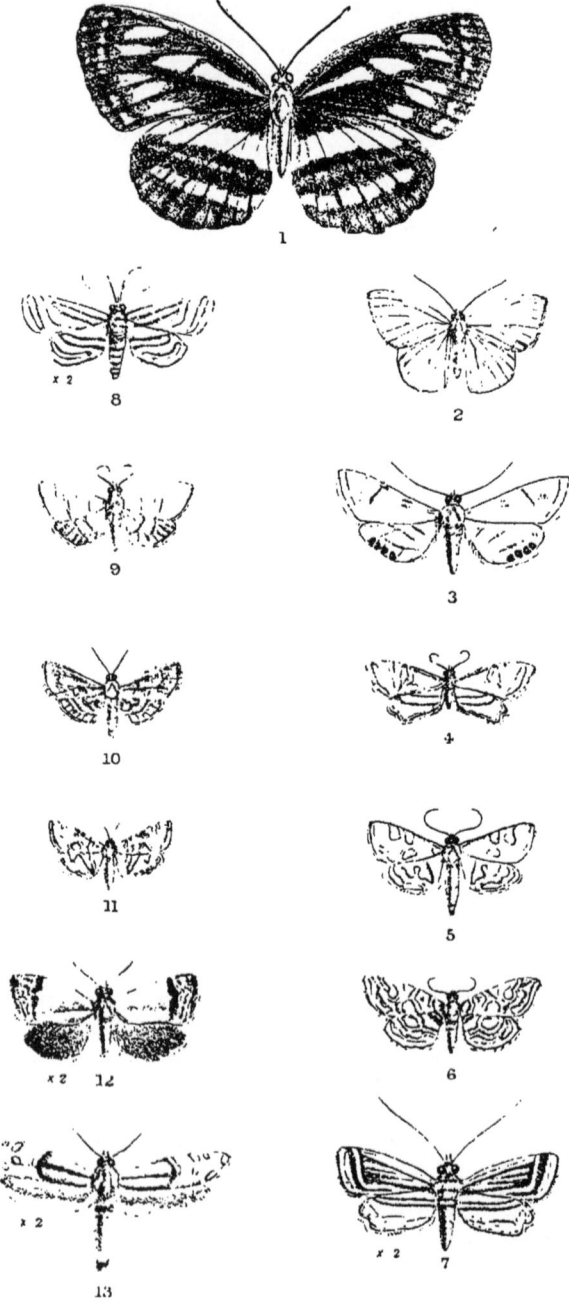

Mintern Bros imp

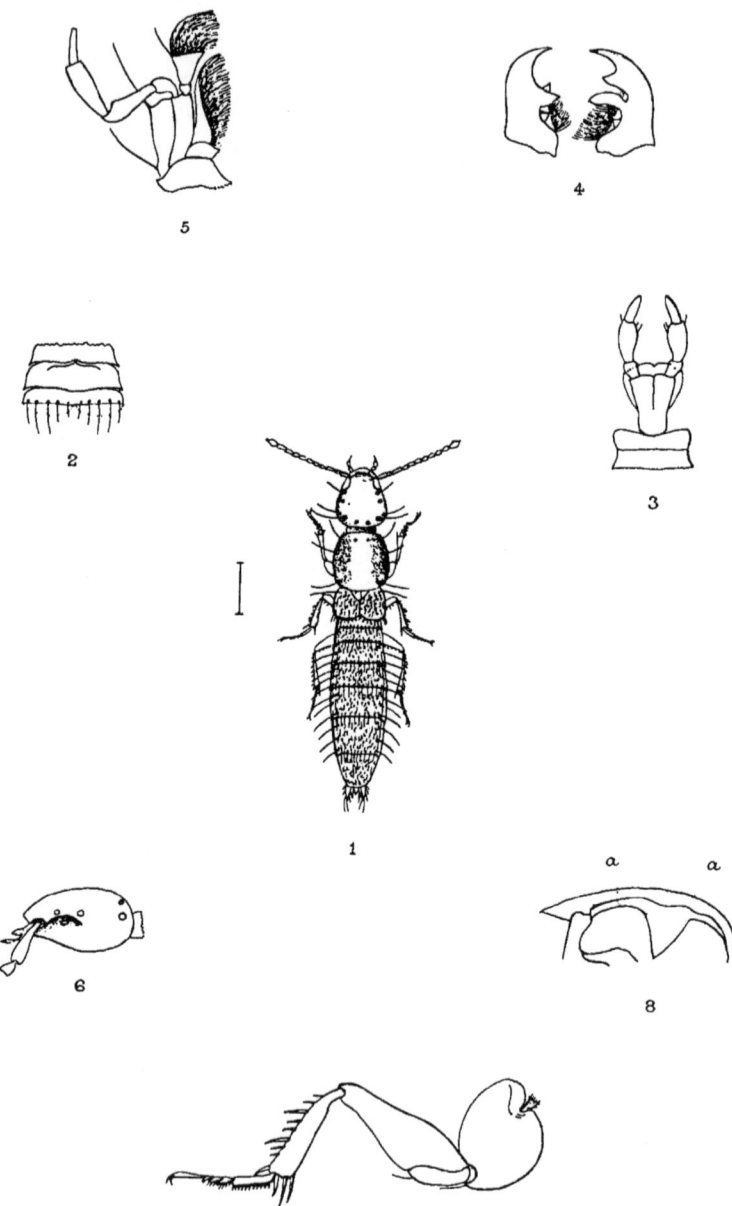

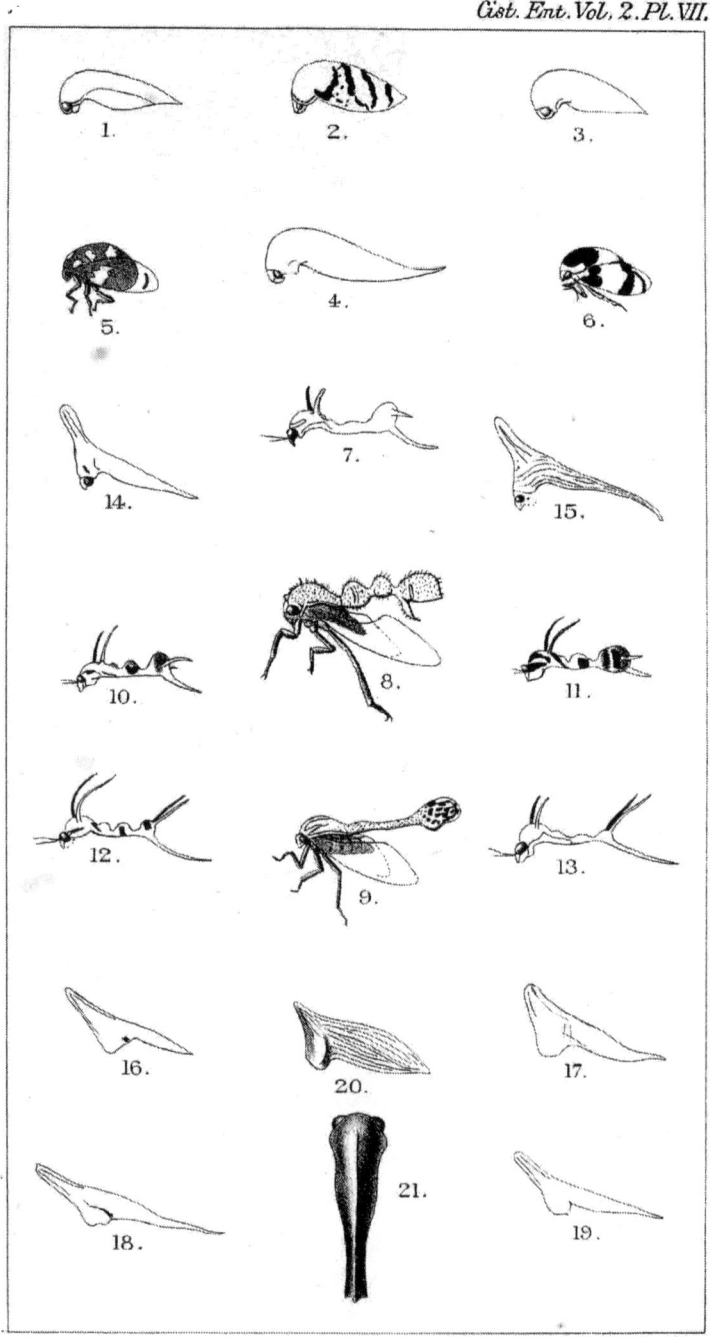

A.G. Butler. del.

Mintern Bros imp.

. NEW OR RARE MEMBRACIDÆ.

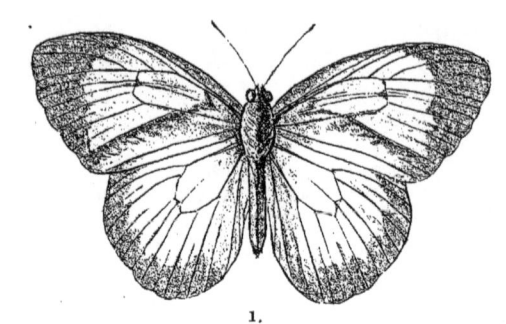

1.

2.

3.

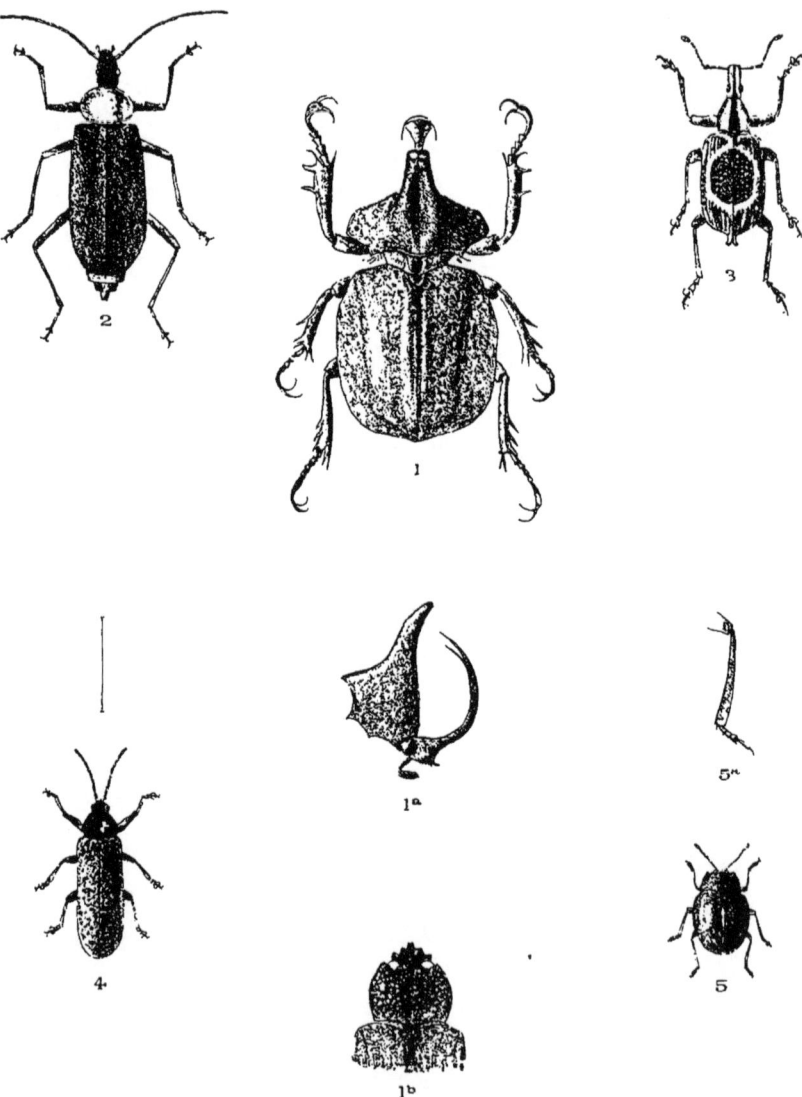

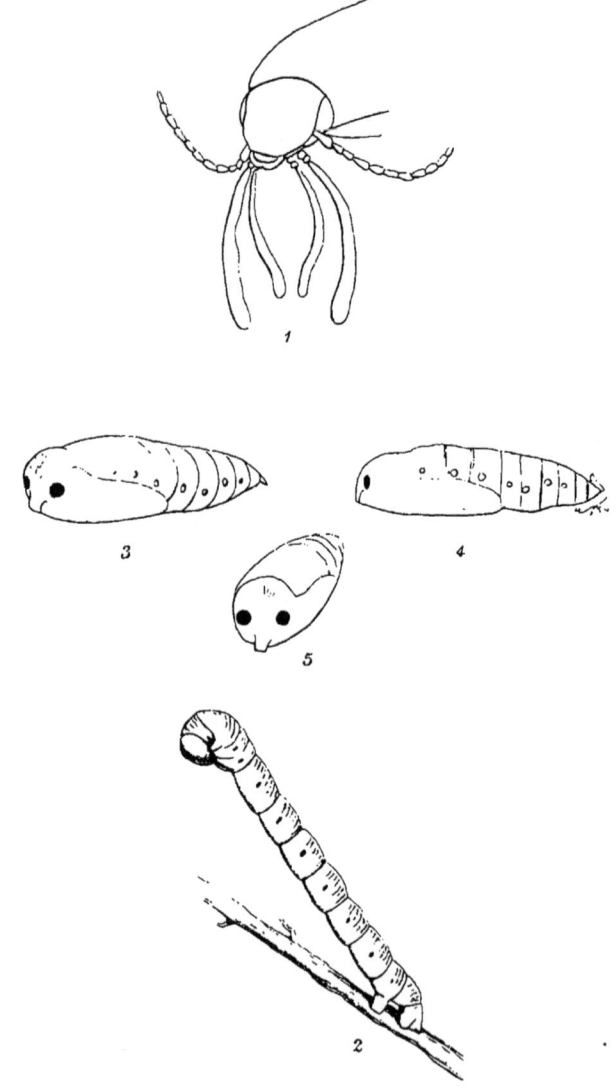

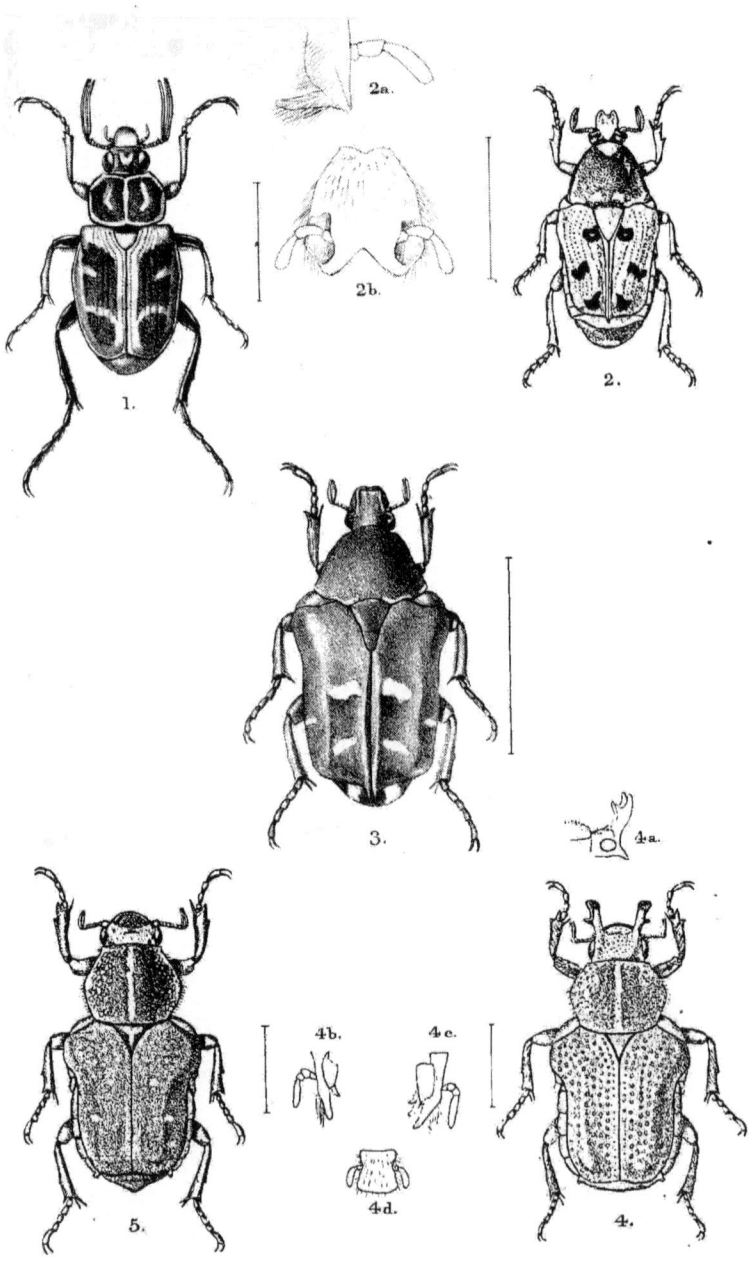

Edwin Wilson del. et lith.

Mintern Bros. imp.

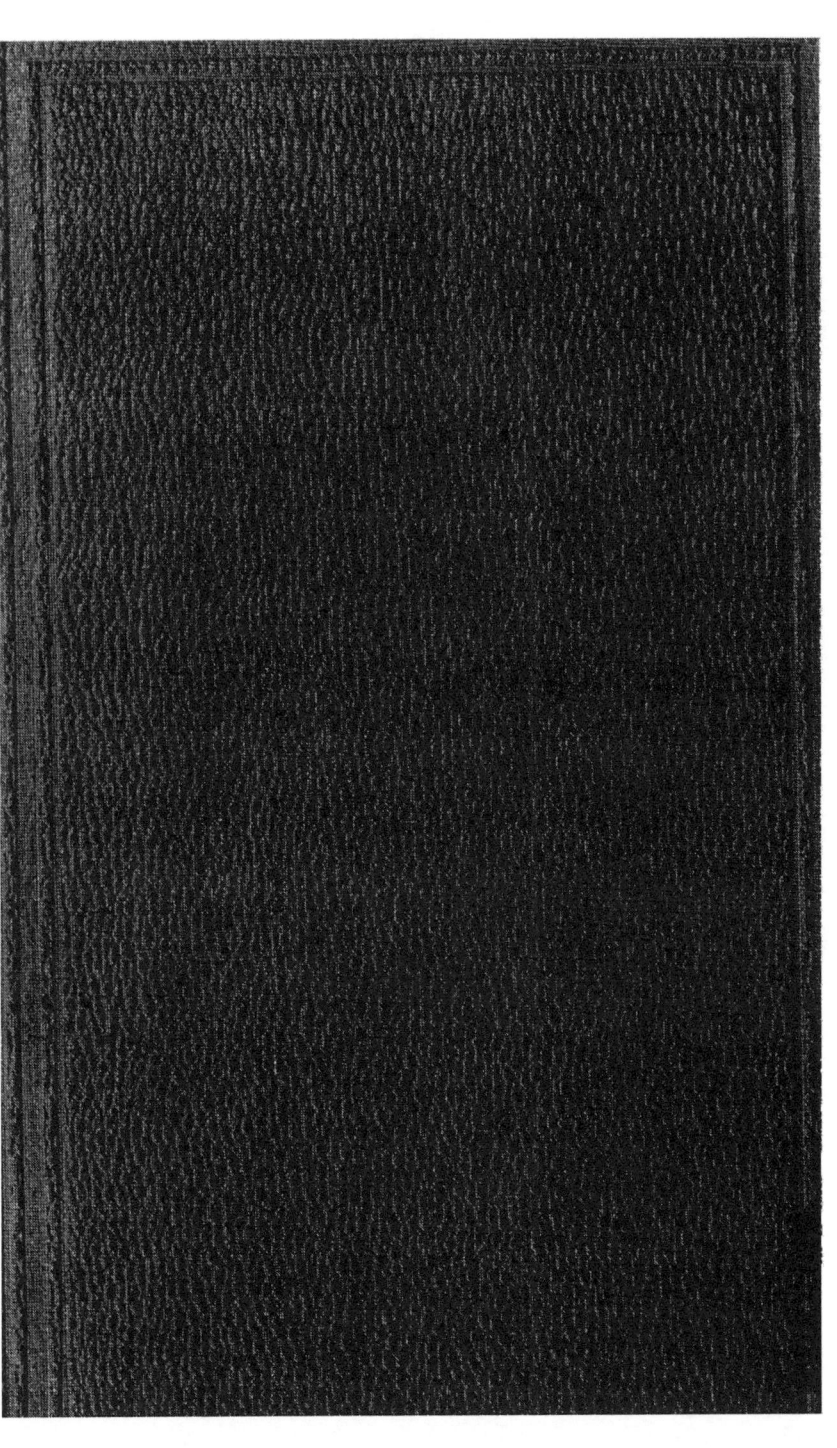

Lightning Source UK Ltd.
Milton Keynes UK
UKHW020708220321
380773UK00007B/712